The SABBATH
in the
Old Testament
and the
Intertestamental Period

Biblical Research Institute Studies on the Biblical Sabbath
Vol. 1

General Editor
Ekkehardt Mueller

Editors
Daniel Bediako, Ekkehardt Mueller

Consulting Editor
Elias Brasil de Souza

Managing Editor
Marly Timm

Biblical Research Institute Staff

Elias Brasil de Souza   Ekkehardt Mueller
Kwabena Donkor   Clinton Wahlen
Frank M. Hasel

Biblical Research Institute Committee (BRICOM)
Members 2015-2020

Adolfo Suarez	Elie Henry	Jo Ann Davidson	Michael Sokupa
Alain G. Coralie	Elias Brasil de Souza	John K. McVay	Myron Iseminger
Alberto Timm	Ella S. Simmons	John Reeve	Ricardo A. Gonzalez
Angel M. Rodriguez	Eugene Zaitsev	Jon Paulien	Richard A. Sabuin
Anthony R. Kent	Frank M. Hasel	Juan R.	Richard Davidson
Artur Stele	Gerald Klingbeil	Prestol-Puesan	Richard Rice
Barna Magyarosi	Gerard Damsteegt	Kim Sung-Ik	Roy Gane
Bill Knott	Gordon E. Christo	Kwabena Donkor	Sampson Nwaomah
Clinton Wahlen	Graeme J. Humble	Kyoshin Ahn	Ted N.C. Wilson
Daniel Bediako	Gregory King	Lael Caesar	Teresa Reeve
Denis Fortin	GT Ng	Laszlo Gallusz	Thomas Shepherd
Edward Zinke	Hensley Moorooven	Leslie Pollard	Vanderlei Dorneles
Efrain Velazquez	James Gibson	Merlin Burt	Wagner Kuhn
Ekkehardt Mueller	Jiri Moskala	Michael Hasel	

Copy Editor
Schuyler Kline

Inside Layout
Nancy Reinhardt

Cover Design
Trent Truman

The SABBATH

in the

Old Testament

and the

Intertestamental Period

Implications for Christians in the Twenty-First Century

DANIEL K. BEDIAKO & EKKEHARDT MUELLER
Editors

Biblical Research Institute

Silver Spring, MD 20904
2021

Copyright © 2021, by Biblical Research Institute
General Conference of Seventh-day Adventists
Silver Spring, MD 20904
adventistbiblicalresearch.org

Scripture quotations marked ESV are from The Holy Bible, English Standard Version, copyright © 2001 by Crossway Bibles, a division of Good News Publishers. All rights reserved. Used by permission.

Scriptures marked KJV are taken from the KING JAMES VERSION (KJV): KING JAMES VERSION, public domain.

Scripture [marked NASB are] taken from the NEW AMERICAN STANDARD BIBLE®, Copyright © 1960, 1962, 1963, 1971, 1972, 1973, 1975, 1977, 1995 by The Lockman Foundation. Used by permission.

Scriptures quoted as NCB are from The Holy Bible: New Century Version®. Copyright © 2005 by Thomas Nelson, Inc. Used by permission.

Scripture quotations [marked NEB are] taken from the New English Bible, copyright © Cambridge University Press and Oxford University Press 1961, 1970. All rights reserved.

Scripture quoted by permission. Quotations designated (NET) are from The NET Bible® Copyright © 2005 by Biblical Studies Press, L.L.C. www.netbible.com All rights reserved.

Scripture quotations taken from The Holy Bible, New International Version® NIV® Copyright © 1973, 1978, 1984, 2011 by Biblica, Inc.™ Used by permission. All rights reserved worldwide.

Texts credited to New Jerusalem are from The New Jerusalem Bible, copyright © 1985 by Darton, Longman & Todd, Ltd., and Doubleday & Company, Inc. Used by permission.

Texts credited to NKJV are from the New King James Version. Copyright © 1979, 1980, 1982 by Thomas Nelson, Inc. All rights reserved. Used by permission.

Scripture quotations marked (NLT) are taken from the Holy Bible, New Living Translation, copyright © 1996, 2004, 2015 by Tyndale House Foundation. Used by permission of Tyndale House Publishers, Carol Stream, Illinois 60188, USA. All rights reserved.

[Scripture quotations marked NRSV are from the] New Revised Standard Version Bible, copyright © 1989 National Council of the Churches of Christ in the United States of America. Used by permission. All rights reserved worldwide.

Scripture quotations [marked RSV] are from the Revised Standard Version Bible, copyright © 1946, 1952 and 1971 the Division of Christian Education of the National Council of the Churches of Christ in the United States of America. Used by permission. All rights reserved.

The Sabbath in the Old Testament and the Intertestamental Period Implications for Christians in the Twenty-First Century – Vol. 1 /
 [edited by] Daniel Bediako and Ekkehardt Mueller
 1. Sabbath - Biblical Teaching 2. Sabbath - History 3. Judaism – History - Post Exilic Period
BS680.Sa11 2020

ISBN 978-0-925675-33-0

Contents

About the Authors and Editors	vii
Abbreviations	xi
Introduction	1

Exegetical Perspectives

Chapter 1
 The Sabbath in the Pentateuch — 5
  —*Mathilde Frey*

Chapter 2
 The Sabbath in the Decalogue: Creation and Liberation as a Paradigm for Community — 43
  —*Gerald A. Klingbeil*

Chapter 3
 "Bread of the Presence" and Sabbath as Culminating Expressions of Covenant Holiness — 71
  —*Roy Gane*

Chapter 4
 The Punishment of the Sabbath Breaker in Numbers 15:32–36 — 93
  —*Daniel K. Bediako*

Chapter 5
 The Sabbath in the Psalms and Wisdom Literature — 119
  —*Richard M. Davidson*

Chapter 6
 The Sabbath in the Prophets — 149
  —*Laurentiu G. Ionescu and Gerhard Pfandl*

Thematic Perspectives

Chapter 7
   The Origin of the Sabbath   167
     —Martin Pröbstle

Chapter 8
   The Sabbath at Creation: Character and Theology   213
     —Lael O. Caesar

Chapter 9
   The Sabbath and the New Covenant   249
     —Roy Gane

Chapter 10
   The Sabbath in the Old Testament: Day of Rest or Day of Worship?   277
     —Elias Brasil de Souza

Chapter 11
   Israelite Festivals, Sabbath Year, Jubilee, and the Sabbath for Christians   303
     —Michael Sokupa

Chapter 12
   Torah's Seven Vibrant Dimensions of Sabbath Rest   325
     —Richard M. Davidson

Intertestamental Literature

Chapter 13
   The Sabbath at Qumran   353
     —Teresa Reeve and Roy Gane

Chapter 14
   The Sabbath in the Apocrypha and the Pseudepigrapha   377
     —Daegeuk Nam

Epilogue   397
Scripture Index   401
Index of Extrabiblical Writings   415

About the Authors and Editors

Daniel K. Bediako, PhD, is professor of Old Testament language and exegesis at Valley View University (Accra, Ghana). He holds a PhD in religion from the Adventist International Institute of Advanced Studies (Silang, Philippines), and has authored a number of articles in peer-reviewed journals and several books, including *Genesis 1:1–2:3: A Textlinguistic Analysis*. He is an associate editor of the forthcoming *Andrews Bible Commentary* and has edited several other works. He currently serves as president and vice chancellor of Valley View University.

Lael O. Caesar, PhD, has been a pastor and university chaplain, college and university professor, and, most recently, an associate editor at Adventist Review Ministries, with special responsibilities for the magazine *Adventist Review*. His principal scholarly focus has been the book of Job. But more than any other practical consideration, it was his concern for issues such as the judgment and the Sabbath that impelled him toward engagement in Old Testament scholarship.

Richard M. Davidson, PhD, is professor of Old Testament interpretation at the Seventh-day Adventist Theological Seminary at Andrews University (Berrien Springs, MI, USA). He has a PhD in religion from Andrews University. He is the author of numerous articles in theological journals and other publications, having published many books, including *Typology in Scripture: A Study of Hermeneutical τύπος Structures*, *Hermeneuticã biblicã*, *In the Footsteps of Joshua*, and his magisterial work *Flame of Yahweh: Sexuality in the Old Testament*.

Elias Brasil de Souza, PhD, is director of the Biblical Research Institute at the General Conference of Seventh-day Adventists, world headquarters of the Seventh-day Adventist Church. He previously served as a church pastor in the Southern Brazil Union. He was dean of the Theological Seminary at

Northeast Brazil College in Bahia, and also taught in the seminary as a professor of biblical studies. He holds a BA and MA in theology from the Latin American Adventist Theological Seminary at Brazil Adventist University in Engenheiro Coelho, Sao Paulo, and a PhD in Old Testament exegesis and theology from Andrews University in Berrien Springs, Michigan. His main areas of interest are the sanctuary and biblical theology. He has authored, co-authored, and published several academic publications in English, Spanish, and Portuguese.

Mathilde Frey, PhD, is professor of Hebrew Bible/Old Testament at Walla Walla University (College Place, WA, USA). Frey has taught at the Adventist International Institute of Advanced Studies, where she also served as chair of the MA in theology program and editor of the *Journal of Asia Adventist Seminary*. She has authored articles and book chapters on the topic of the Sabbath, including a commentary on the book of Deuteronomy in the forthcoming *Andrews Bible Commentary*, and a commentary on the book of Judges for the forthcoming *Seventh-day Adventist International Bible Commentary*. Frey is the president (2020) of the Adventist Society for Religious Studies.

Roy Gane, PhD, is professor of Hebrew Bible and ancient Near Eastern languages at the Seventh-day Adventist Theological Seminary at Andrews University. He has a PhD in biblical Hebrew language and literature from the University of California, Berkeley. He has published numerous scholarly journal articles and book chapters, and was the primary translator for the Leviticus portion of the *Common English Bible*. He has published nine books, including *Leviticus, Numbers* (NIV Application Commentary); *Cult and Character: Purification Offerings, Day of Atonement, and Theodicy*; and *Old Testament Law for Christians: Original Context and Enduring Application*.

Laurentiu G. Ionescu, PhD, is an Old Testament scholar who has taught at for several years at Adventus University (Cernica, Romania), and at Universidad Adventista del Plata (Libertador San Martín, Argentina), and is currently pastoring in Spain. He was editor of *Theorhema*, a theological journal, and has published a number of articles. Among other publications, he authored a Hebrew-Romanian dictionary. He is a member of the Biblical Research Committee of the Inter-European Division of Seventh-day Adventists.

Gerald A. Klingbeil, DLitt, is research professor of Old Testament and ancient Near Eastern studies at Andrews University, and also serves as associate editor of Adventist Review Ministries at the General Conference of Seventh-day Adventists. He holds a DLitt from Stellenbosch University (Stellenbosch, South Africa), and has authored or edited twelve books, including *A Comparative Study of the Ritual of Ordination as Found in Leviticus 8 and Emar 369* and *Entender la Palabra: Hermenéutica Adventista para el Nuevo Siglo*. He has contributed dozens of chapters in academic monographs and entries to dictionaries and encyclopedias published by Oxford University Press, Baker Academic, among others, and has published more than fifty peer-reviewed articles.

Ekkehardt Mueller, ThD, DMin, is associate director of the Biblical Research Institute of the General Conference of Seventh-day Adventists. He holds a ThD in biblical exegesis and theology from Andrews University. He has written numerous articles for scholarly books, journals, and magazines, as well as several books in English and German, such as *The Letters of John* and *Der Erste und der Letzte: Studien zum Buch der Offenbarung* ("The First and the Last: Studies on the Book of Revelation"). A number of these have been translated into various languages.

Daegeuk Nam, ThD, is professor emeritus at Sahmyook University (Seoul, Korea). He holds a ThD in Old Testament from Andrews University, and has authored a number of books and professional articles in the area of biblical and theological studies. He served as the president of Sahmyook University for five years. He contributed articles in the *Handbook of Seventh-day Adventist Theology* and the forthcoming *Andrews Bible Commentary*. He currently serves as an assistant editor of the *Seventh-day Adventist International Biblical-Theological Dictionary*.

Gerhard Pfandl, PhD, retired associate director of the Biblical Research Institute, is a native of Austria and holds an MA and PhD in Old Testament from Andrews University. He has worked as a church pastor in Austria and in the Southern California Conference. From 1977–1989 he was professor of religion at Bogenhofen Seminary (St. Peter am Hart, Austria). Prior to joining the Biblical Research Institute in 1999, he served for seven years as field secretary of the South Pacific Division in Sydney. He has published many articles for scholarly and popular journals in German and English, and is the author or editor of several books and study guides, such as *Daniel: The Seer of Babylon*, *The Gift of Prophecy*, *Interpreting Scripture*, and *The Great Controversy and the End of Evil*.

Martin Pröbstle, PhD, is professor of Old Testament and dean of the Theological Department at Seminar Schloss Bogenhofen. He has a PhD in religion from Andrews University and an MA in ancient Near Eastern studies from the University of Stellenbosch. He has published numerous articles and several books, including *Where God and I Meet: The Sanctuary, Himmel auf Erden: Gott begegnet uns im Heiligtum* ("Heaven on Earth: God Meets Us in the Sanctuary"), and is a contributor to the *Andrews Bible Commentary* and the *Seventh-day Adventist International Bible Commentary*.

Teresa Reeve, PhD, is a New Testament scholar who currently serves as associate professor of New Testament contexts and associate dean of the Seventh-day Adventist Theological Seminary of Andrews University. Her PhD is from the University of Notre Dame (South Bend, IN, USA). She is a long-term member of the Biblical Research Institute Committee. She has contributed peer-reviewed chapters to several anthologies and serves on the executive committee for the *Seventh-day Adventist International Bible Commentary*, contributing and evaluating commentaries.

Michael Sokupa, PhD, DTh, is an associate director of the Ellen G. White Estate. His doctoral degrees are from Adventist International Institute of Advanced Studies and Stellenbosch University. He has written a number of scholarly articles and book chapters. He served as a member of the Biblical Research Committee of the Seventh-day Adventist Church and chair of New Testament Society of Southern Africa for a number of years.

Abbreviations

AB	*Anchor Bible*
ABD	*Anchor Bible Dictionary*
ABR	*Australian Biblical Review*
AHw	*Akkadisches Handwörterbuch*
AJSL	*American Journal of Semitic Languages and Literature*
Ant	*Jewish Antiquities*
AOTC	*Apollos Old Testament Commentary*
AsTJ	*Asbury Theological Journal*
AUSS	*Andrews University Seminary Studies*
BAR	*Biblical Archaeology Review*
BBR	*Bulletin for Biblical Research*
BDB	*Brown, F., S. R. Driver, and C. A. Briggs. A Hebrew and English Lexicon of the Old Testament.*
Bib	*Biblica*
BibInt	*Biblical Interpretation*
BiOr	*Biblica et orientalia*
BJRL	*Bulletin of the John Rylands University Library of Manchester*
BN	*Biblische Notizen*
BZ	*Biblische Zeitschrift*
CBQ	*Catholic Biblical Review*
CTJ	*Calvin Theological Journal*
CurBS	*Currents in Research: Biblical Studies*
CurTM	*Currents in Theology and Mission*
DCH	*Dictionary of Classical Hebrew*
DSD	*Dead Sea Discoveries*
EBC	*Expositors Bible Commentary*
EstBib	*Estudios bíblicos*
ETR	*Etudes théologiques et religieuses*
GKC	*Gesenius' Hebrew Grammar*
HALOT	*Hebrew and Aramaic Lexicon of the Old Testament*
HBT	*Horizons in Biblical Theology*
HCOT	*Historical Commentary of the Old Testament*

HTKAT	Herders theologicher Kommentar zum Alten Testament
HTR	Harvard Theological Review
HUCA	Hebrew Union College Annual
ICC	International Critical Commentary
JAAS	Journal of Asia Adventist Seminary
JANESCU	Journal of the Ancient Near Eastern Society of Columbia University
JAOS	Journal of American Oriental Studies
JATS	Journal of Adventist Theological Society
JBL	Journal of Biblical Literature
JBQ	Jewish Bible Quarterly
JBT	Jahrbuch für Biblische Theologie
JET	Jahrbuch für Evangelische Theologie
JETS	Journal of Evangelical Theological Society
JHS	Journal of Hebrew Scriptures
JPSTC	JPS Torah Commentary
JQR	Jewish Quarterly Review
JRAS	Journal of the Royal Asiatic Society
JSJ	Journal for the Study of Judaism
JSNT	Journal for the Study of the New Testament
JSOT	Journal for the Study of the Old Testament
JSOTSup	Journal for the Study of the Old Testament Supplement Series
JSP	Journal for the Study of the Pseudepigrapha
JW	Jewish Wars
MTZ	Münchener theologische Zeitschrift
NAC	New American Commentary
NIBC	New International Bible Commentary
NICOT	The New International Commentary on the Old Testament
NIDOTTE	New International Dictionary of Old Testament Theology and Exegesis
NIVAC	NIV Application Commentary
NTS	New Testament Studies
OTE	Old Testament Essays
OTL	Old Testament Library
OTS	Old Testament Studies
PEQ	Palestine Exploration Quarterly
PSBA	Proceedings of the Society of Biblical Archaeology
RelSRev	Religious Studies Review
RevQ	Revue de Qumran
SBJT	Southern Baptist Journal of Theology
ScEs	Science et esprit
SDABC	Seventh-day Adventist Bible Commentary
SJOT	Scandinavian Journal of the Old Testament

SJT	*Scottish Journal of Theology*
TDOT	*Theological Dictionary of the Old Testament*
ThQ	*Theologische Quartalschrift*
ThZ	*Theologische Zeitschrift*
TLOT	*Theological Lexicon of the Old Testament*
TWOT	*Theological Wordbook of the Old Testament*
TynBul	*Tyndale Bulletin*
TZ	*Theologische Zeitschrift*
UF	*Ugarit-Forschungen*
VT	*Vetum Testamentum*
VTSup	*Vetum Testamentum Supplement Series*
WBC	*Word Biblical Commentary*
WUB	*Welt und Umwelt der Bibel*
WW	*Word and World*
ZABR	*Zeitschrift für altorientalische und biblische Rechtgeschichte*
ZAH	*Zeitschrift für Althebräistik*
ZAW	*Zeitschrift für die alttestamentliche Wissenschaft*
ZDMG	*Zeitschrift der deutschen morgenländischen Gesellschaft*
ZTK	*Zeitschrift für Theologie und Kirche*

General Abbreviations

A.D.	*anno domini* (in the year of our Lord)
ANE	Ancient Near East
b.	Babylonian Talmud
B.C.	Before Christ
BHS	*Biblia Hebraica Stuttgartensia*
c.	*circa* (about)
cf.	compare
ed.	edited by
e.g.	for example
ET	English Translation
et al.	and others (Lat. *et alii*)
Ibid.	in the same place (Lat. *ibidem*)
Idem	the same (author)
i.e.	in other words (Lat. *id est*)
LXX	Septuagint
m.	Mishnah
MT	Masoretic Text
MS, MSS	Manuscript(s)
par.	paragraph
NT	New Testament
OT	Old Testament

Bible Versions

ESV	English Standard Version
KJV	King James Version
NASB	New American Standard Bible
NCB	New Century Bible
NEB	New English Bible
NET	New English Translation
NIV	New International Version
NJB	New Jerusalem Bible
NKJV	New King James Version
NLT	New Living Translation
NRSV	New Revised Standard Version
RSV	Revised Standard Version

Tg(s). Targum(s)
v., vs. Verse(s)
y. Jerusalem Talmud

Hebrew Alphabet

Consonants

א = ʾ
ב = b; v (spirant)
ג = g; gh (spirant)
ד = d; dh (spirant)
ה = h
ו = w
ז = z
ח = kh
ט = t
י = y
כ = k; kh (spirant)
ל = l
מ = m
נ = n
ס = s
ע = ʿ
פ = p; f (spirant)
צ = ts
ק = q
ר = r
שׁ = sh
שׂ = s
ת = t; th (spirant)

Masoretic Vowel Pointings

ָ ַ ָה = a; ah (final qamets he)
ֵ ֶ ְ ֱ ֲ ֳ ֵי = e
ִ ִי = i
ֹ ָ ֳ וֹ = o
ֻ וּ = u
יו = ayw

Introduction

Over the past three decades, scholars have shown a renewed interest in the biblical Sabbath, as demonstrated by many studies from both Christian and Jewish perspectives. These studies have dealt with historical, exegetical, conceptual, and theological aspects of the Sabbath. Some of these studies have questioned the biblical origins of the Sabbath, others have answered the question of whether Christians need to observe the seventh-day Sabbath, and still others have focused on the importance of Sabbath rest for humanity. Studies emphasizing the need for Sabbath rest have emerged within Seventh-day Adventist circles and especially among non-Adventist theologians, highlighting the joy and blessing of the Sabbath and discovering in it a paradigm for vibrant Christian spirituality.

The last major scholarly study of the Sabbath by Adventist scholars was published in 1982 and had been in the works for approximately a decade prior to its publication. Probably influenced by the interests and expertise of the editor, the contributions in that volume—*The Sabbath in Scripture and History*[1]—bear a significant historical focus, as opposed to an exegetical and theological one. For example, the Sabbath in the Old Testament is treated only in two chapters, constituting less than ten percent of the volume. Also, a significant number of studies have since appeared either challenging or enriching the Adventist perspective. Therefore, further study of the biblical Sabbath is warranted.

The present work is a project organized and guided by the Biblical Research Institute of the General Conference of Seventh-day Adventists in response to the need for a further study, both to react to publications challenging the Adventist perspective and to harness those studies that have further enriched the Adventist perspective since the appearance of *The Sabbath in Scripture and History*. This project restudies the relevant

---

[1] Kenneth A. Strand, ed., *The Sabbath in Scripture and History* (Washington: Review and Herald Publishing Association, 1982).

biblical, historical, theological, and practical aspects of the Sabbath, while meaningfully interacting with other scholars and theologians. The studies are presented in two volumes.

In both the OT and the NT, the Sabbath features prominently as a time of rest, fellowship for believers, and particularly worship. It reminds humanity of God's work of creation and redemption, and speaks to other important themes of Scripture. This two-volume set not only serves to emphasize the permanence, universality, and relevance of the seventh-day Sabbath, but also seeks to highlight the experiential joy and blessing that accompany Sabbath celebration for the contemporary Christian. Authors from around the world have contributed to each volume, adding diversity of perspective to the central Sabbath theme.

Volume 1 comprises three sections. In the first section, contributors present the exegesis of key Old Testament passages related to the Sabbath. The second section comprises thematic perspectives, including the theology and character of the creation Sabbath, Sabbath and the covenant, Sabbath as a day of worship, Sabbath and Israelite festivals, and Sabbath and rest that goes beyond law. The last section studies the concept of the Sabbath in Jewish literature of the intertestamental period (Second Temple period), particularly Sabbath at Qumran and in the Apocrypha and Pseudepigrapha. Together, these essays deepen our understanding of the Sabbath and strengthen the Adventist perspective on the subject. Rather than being restrictive and limiting, the Sabbath is a gift and a blessing in the relationship between God and humanity.

It is our hope that you will find this volume useful as you continue to experience and share with others Jesus Christ, the "Lord of the Sabbath" (Mark 2:23, NKJV), recognizing His creatorship and lordship through Sabbath observance.

Daniel K. Bediako
Editor

Exegetical Perspectives

CHAPTER 1

THE SABBATH IN THE PENTATEUCH

Mathilde Frey

Introduction

The Sabbath is a unique day with a revolutionary idea both in the ancient world and in contemporary society. As an integral element of the Pentateuch, the Sabbath speaks to ever-present theological questions about God, and about the human being in relation to God and to the created world. Each of the five books of Moses contains texts, written in different literary forms, with fascinating insights into the significance, rationale, and meaning of the Sabbath. The book of Genesis sets the tone for the Sabbath, with the story of creation as the most unique text ever written in the ancient world (Gen 1:1–2:4).[1] Biblical scholars and literature

---

[1] Many biblical scholars recognize that the creation account in Genesis 1:1–2:4 is a text unparalleled in the ancient world and identify its literary form as *sui generis*. John H. Stek, "What Says Scripture?" in *Portraits of Creation: Biblical and Scientific Perspectives on the World's Formation*, ed. Howard J. van Till, Robert E. Snow, John H. Stek, and Davis A. Young (Grand Rapids, MI: Eerdmans, 1990), 241, suggests that the "literary type [of the creation account], as far as present knowledge goes, is without strict parallel; it is *sui generis*." Cf. Gerhard F. Hasel, "The 'Days' of Creation in Genesis 1: Literal 'Days' or Figurative 'Periods/Epochs' of Time?" *Origins* 21 (1994): 5–38, who concluded that, compared with other biblical genre, the creation account is not a hymn, parable, poem, cultic liturgy, metaphor, story, or allegory. Walter C. Kaiser, "The Literary Form of Genesis 1–11," in *New Perspectives on the Old Testament*, ed. J. Barton Payne (Waco, TX: Word, 1970), 61, notes that here "we are dealing with the genre of historical narrative-prose, interspersed with some lists, sources, sayings, and poetical lines." Jacques B. Doukhan, *The Genesis Creation Story: Its Literary Structure* (Berrien Springs, MI: Andrews University Press, 1978), 182, identifies the creation account as "prose-genealogy" because of the term "generations" (*toledhoth*) (Gen 2:4), an expression which introduces twelve other genealogies in Genesis. From a textlinguistic perspective, Daniel Bediako, "Genesis 1:1–2:3 as Historical Narrative Text Type," *Valley View University Journal of Theology* 1 (2011): 19–36, has concluded that this text is a historical narrative in its own right.

experts call Genesis 1:1–2:4 *sui generis* ("of its own kind/genus; in a class by itself; unique") and acknowledge the unique characteristics of language and style in presenting the Sabbath as a day of divine origin, all-encompassing scope, and crowning quality at the end of God's work week (Gen 2:1–3).

The book of Exodus contains a complex narration on the Sabbath and the gift of manna (Exod 16:1–36), followed by legal speech that places the Sabbath in the center of Israel's covenant relationship with Yahweh (Exod 20:8–11; 23:12; 31:12–17; 34:21; 35:2–3). The Sabbath texts in the book of Leviticus are part of an elegant literary structure on the sanctuary with its time-oriented services and implications for people who live on holy grounds (Lev 19:3, 30; 23:3; 24:5–9). The book of Numbers tells a story about a man gathering wood on Sabbath as an example of legal enforcement in Israel's covenant community (Num 15:32–36). In Deuteronomy's discourses the Sabbath commandment is reiterated for the generation of Israelites at the borders of the promised land. The context is the exodus from Egypt, and the exhortation is formulated in terms of covenant making/renewal ceremonies (Deut 5:12–15).

Over the past two centuries, the Sabbath has received much attention in academic circles, mainly from investigations of the biblical text in comparison with other ancient texts with the purpose of understanding "the world behind the text."[2] While critical studies have advanced our understanding of ancient life and customs in Israel and other Near Eastern cultures, they have not been able to prove that the biblical Sabbath has roots in cultures outside of Israel;[3] neither have they helped towards a meaningful discussion on the biblical Sabbath.[4]

---

[2] Richard N. Soulen and Kendall R. Soulen, *Handbook of Biblical Criticism* (Louisville, KY: Westminster, 2001), 78.

[3] At the end of the nineteenth century, biblical scholars started to recognize the importance of the seventh-day Sabbath, but ignoring its literary contexts they searched for the origin of the biblical Sabbath outside of the biblical text. Even though the studies carried out then contributed to the understanding of ANE life and culture in relation to feast days including the Babylonian *shappatu*, which some associate with the Israelite Sabbath, the discussion on the origin of the biblical Sabbath has remained unfruitful. Other exegetical studies dealt with the Sabbath texts of the Hebrew Bible based upon the presuppositions of hypothetically reconstructed texts or sources (J, E, D, P) for the canonical text. See Wilhelm Lotz, *Questiones de historia Sabbati libri duo* (Leipzig: Hinrichs'sche Buchhandlung, 1883), 57–58, 106; Abraham Kuenen, *The Religion of Israel* (London: Williams and Norgate, 1874), 276; Johannes Helm, *Siebenzahl und Sabbat bei den Babyloniern und im Alten Testament* (Leipzig: Hinrichs'sche Buchhandlung, 1904), 58–62, 112–114; Ernst Jenni, *Die Theologische Begründung des Sabbatgebotes im Alten Testament* (Zürich: Evangelischer Verlag, 1956), 12–13; and Gnana Robinson, *The Origin and Development of the Old Testament Sabbath: A Comprehensive Exegetical Approach* (Bern: Peter Lang, 1988), 171–185.

[4] Critical studies are conditioned by the discovery of ancient Babylonian texts and by the search

The present study values the Sabbath texts of the Pentateuch in their present form and does not accept dissecting methods that ascribe the biblical text to disparate sources.[5] Rather, the study favors a canonical reading with appreciation of the individual artistry, conceptual links, and theological implications of the Sabbath texts in the Pentateuch.

Sabbath in Creation

The uniqueness of the Sabbath is about God's intimate presence in time and in the world He created. Karl Barth speaks of Sabbath rest as God's way of attaching Himself to His creation.[6] A close reading of the creation text with its elevated language, style, and structural arrangement will give insight into the exquisite nature of the Sabbath.

At first, one notices that the seven days of creation are one unit of time divinely designed in relation with a perfectly created world.[7] While the Sabbath is part of the creation week as a unit of time, it is different in its content. The contrastive aspect of the Sabbath to the weekdays is first recognized in the divine work–rest juxtaposition. This distinction is reflected in the literary arrangement of the text where the creation acts of the six days place the Sabbath outside of the paralleling structure with thematic correspondence (see table below). In this way, the seventh day

---

for the origin of the biblical Sabbath outside the Hebrew Bible. Divergent theories such as the Babylonian hypothesis, the Kenite hypothesis, the Arabic hypothesis, the Ugaritic hypothesis, and the sociological hypothesis have proven to be unsuccessful. Such studies did not contribute much to the meaning of the Sabbath texts in the Bible, but led to a hypothetically reconstructed history of the Sabbath in Israelite culture and history of religion. See Baruch J. Schwartz, "The Sabbath in the Torah Sources," http://www.biblicallaw.net/2007/schwartz.pdf (accessed December 6, 2007).

[5] Although critics identified a style and language in Genesis 2:1–3 different from the rest of Genesis 1:1–2:4, they came to acknowledge that in the final form of the text these verses present a literary unit. See Johannes G. Eichhorn and Johann Ph. Gabler, *Urgeschichte I* (Altdorf-Nürnberg, 1790), 144; Werner H. Schmidt, *Die Schöpfungsgeschichte der Priesterschrift* (Neukirchen-Vluyn: Neukirchener, 1961), 9, 155; Odil H. Steck, *Der Schöpfungsbericht der Priesterschrift* (Göttingen: Vandenhoeck & Ruprecht, 1975), 178; and Claus Westermann, *Genesis* (Neukirchen-Vluyn: Neukirchener, 1974), 230–231.

[6] By "resting on the seventh day, He [God] does not separate Himself from the world but binds Himself the more closely to it." Karl Barth, *Church Dogmatics*, vol. 3, part 1: *The Doctrine of Creation*, ed. G. W. Bromiley and T. F. Torrance (Edinburgh: T&T Clark, 1958; repr. 2004), 223.

[7] The seventh day stands as the climax, not as an appendix to the six weekdays. The clause "God created" marks the beginning and the end of the creation week, and, like an envelope, encloses God's acts of the seven days (Gen 1:1; 2:3). In the Hebrew, the grammatical aspect of the verb "created" (*bara'*) connotes a completed creation.

(1) stands in contrast to the weekdays, (2) complements the six days, and (3) brings closure and completeness to the creation week.

Unordered becomes ordered	Uninhabited becomes inhabited
Day 1: light	Day 4: lights
Day 2: air / water	Day 5: birds / fish
Day 3: land / vegetation	Day 6: animals / humans
Day 7: Sabbath	

The distinction–completion scheme is not something that belongs only to the literary arrangement of the days in the text. Throughout the six weekdays God created by separating contrastive elements and then placing them into a relationship to each other in order to bring about something new that is whole or complete. This is best observed on the first, second, and sixth days of creation: On the first day, God separated light from darkness and initiated the rhythm of time (Gen 1:5). On the second day, He separated earth from sea to set up the environment for life (Gen 1:10). On the sixth day, God made a distinction between Himself and the human being, establishing the divine-human relationship (Gen 1:27). He also distinguished between male and female and established the horizontal relationship between humans for the sake of unity between husband and wife (Gen 1:27; 2:24). Finally, God differentiated between human beings and the surrounding world so that humans would rule and enjoy the benefits of the earth. In so doing, God initiated what we recognize as the principle of wholeness in a perfectly created world. At the end of the creation week stands the Sabbath, the epitome of wholeness.

Another structural feature of the creation Sabbath may be observed only in the original language of the text (Gen 2:1–3). Words, carefully chosen and counted, are placed into rhythmic clauses. Other clauses and formulas used for the six weekdays are omitted.[8] The exclusive selection of thirty-five Hebrew words—of which twenty-one are arranged in three

---

[8] The formulas in the account of the six weekdays include "and God said" (Gen 1:3, 6, 9, 14, 20, 24), "and there was evening and there was morning, day . . ." (Gen 1:5, 8, 13, 19, 23, 31); "and it was so" (Gen 1:8, 9, 12, 15, 24, 30); and "that it was good" (Gen 1:4, 11, 13, 18, 21, 25) followed by "behold, it was very good" (Gen 1:31) as the summary statement of the six weekdays. These formulaic expressions tie the six weekdays together as an organized structure. The seventh day breaks with the formulaic patterns established for the six weekdays. These formulas are missing in the account of the seventh day.

parallel lines, with each line composed of seven words—marks the Sabbath as the pinnacle of the *sui generis* creation account.

While the descriptions and divine speeches, including the formulas of the six weekdays, stimulate the reader's imagination about a world coming alive, Genesis 2:1–3 does not have any descriptive word, imagery, dialogue, or direct speech. It has a different rhetorical style: The four verbs "He completed," "He ceased," "He blessed," and "He sanctified" at the beginning of four sentences are arranged according to their increasing importance. The climax is with "He blessed and sanctified" as the most intense point in the text. The chiastic structure of Genesis 2:2–3 demonstrates this aspect well:

> A On the seventh day God completed His work, which He had made,
> > B and He ceased on the seventh day from all His work, which He had made.
> > > X God blessed the seventh day and sanctified it,
> > B¹ because on it He ceased from all His work,
> A¹ which God had created by making.

Furthermore, the Sabbath text creates echoes in the mind of the reader/hearer with its repetitious outline. The threefold "on the seventh day" occurring in the middle of successive sentences (that is, mesodiplosis) and the thrice-repeated relative clause about God resting from "His work, which He had done/created" at the end of successive sentences (that is, epistrophe) place highest importance upon these clauses and their connotations.

Some interpreters wonder about the lack of the formulaic expression "there was evening and morning, day . . ." on the seventh day. Some have argued that because of the lack of a closing formula, the seventh day is not meant to be understood as a day composed of nighttime and daytime. This argumentation has led some to interpret the seventh day as unending spiritual rest that may be related to the eschatological day of the Lord in the OT and to the rest found in Jesus Christ.[9]

However, a sequential reading of the entire creation account shows that the formula "there was evening and there was morning" is not to be taken only as a closing formula, but also as a literary device that points to what comes next within a series of sections. The formula functions as a transition from one section/day to another and moves the text forward throughout the six sections/weekdays with the intention to arrive at the end, which is the

---

[9] Richard H. Lowery, *Sabbath and Jubilee* (St. Louis, MO: Chalice, 2000), 90; C. John Collins, "Reading Genesis 1:1–2:3 as an Act of Communication: Discourse Analysis and Literal Interpretation," in *Did God Create in Six Days?* ed. Joseph Pipa Jr. and David Hall (Taylors, SC: Southern Presbyterian Press, 1999), 137.

seventh section/day.[10] Once the final section/day has arrived, the text highlights its identity by stating it three times ("seventh day") and so has no more need for the evening-morning formula because there will not be an eighth day of creation. Creation has come to an end. Therefore, the omission of the closing formula does not suggest a difference in the nature or length of time of the seventh day, nor speak of eschatological dimensions; rather, it simply signifies the seventh day as the last one in the sequence.

The creation Sabbath contains at least one more unique feature. A unique cause-and-effect logic authenticates the seventh day as presented in the causal clause of Genesis 2:3: "He blessed and sanctified it because He ceased/rested in it."[11] Such reasoning, constructed with divine actions that do not have any logical relation to each other—sanctification of the day because of cessation from work—and seem incomprehensible to the human mind, will not be found anywhere else in Scripture.[12] The cause-and-effect principle of the link between ceasing and sanctifying seems to work according to a kind of logic that belongs solely to God's sphere on Sabbath. The seventh-day Sabbath is sanctified by purpose. The verbs have a direct relationship to each other that is intended in the biblical text and is reserved for the Sabbath.

The most significant theological theme that may be developed from the text of the creation Sabbath is holiness. The *sui generis* style and language of the text contribute to the exceptional theological import of the creation Sabbath for the human being. God's cessation from all work becomes His signature of the seventh day and the prerequisite for blessing and holiness.

The Sabbath reveals God as Creator of the world. In the holiness of the Sabbath God discloses His divine being. During the weekdays, as God spoke, attention was directed to the creation and arrangements of elements of life. On the Sabbath, the divine words cease, His works are complete, and God makes Himself known solely by His presence. The human being, however, in order to grasp the sacred event of God's disclosure in the event of the

---

[10] Schmidt, *Die Schöpfungsgeschichte*, 69, also points out that the numbering of the days does not have meaning in itself, but it prepares the reader for the arrival of the seventh day in Genesis 2:2–3.

[11] Author's translation. All biblical quotations are from the NKJV, unless otherwise indicated.

[12] Of interest is that throughout the six weekdays the Hebrew causal particle "because, that" (*ki*) occurs six times in the formula "and God saw that/because it was good" (Gen 1:4, 10, 12, 18, 21, 25). At the end of the sixth day, the formula occurs twice; however, at the second time, the particle *ki* is replaced by the deictic expression, "see, behold," so we read, "and God saw . . . and behold it was very good" (Gen 1:31). By exchanging the word "because, that" with "behold" the text not only stresses a high point at the end of the six weekdays, but reserves the seventh occurrence of "because" (*ki*) for the seventh day.

Sabbath, looks at the Creator's works, for these acts and works reveal His passion for life on earth. Turning toward God's creation causes the psalmist to admire, to marvel, and to burst into praise songs (Ps 19). An academic discourse is inadequate to reflect what the mind's eye might capture in the moment of divine revelation. When God, the Creator of life, *sabbathed*, He, the Fullness of Life, was surrounded by a world bursting with life.

The Sabbath's theology of wholeness connects to God's revelation in creation. Genesis 1 presents creation as the great book of the Creator who intends a relationship with the human being. God's words are heard over the course of six days and His acts are seen in nature. However, it is when God's work is complete and His words unheard that His presence is perceived in the sacredness of the seventh day.

Furthermore, the holistic presentation of humankind in Genesis 1 speaks of an image of God that is equally designed for male and female. Its intention is for an *I-Thou* relationship between the human beings and God. That such wholeness was indeed achieved in the Garden of Eden is described in the narrative of Genesis 2, when the man and woman experience intimate relationship within sacred time.[13] On that first Sabbath, God would have brought humans into communion with Himself.

The wholeness of creation needs to be understood in light of the arrangement made on the sixth day when God placed man and woman into a direct relationship to nature and all earth. This interrelatedness in creation became one of the Sabbath's major concerns in the world after the fall into sin when poor humans, animals, and the land were to have rest in Israel's seventh year and in the Jubilee.[14] Sabbath rest continues to speak to environmental and ecological issues in today's world.

"Holiness... makes its entrance into the world through the Sabbath."[15] Sabbath as sacred cessation is based upon the distinct combination of the verbs "cease" and "sanctify" in a causal clause (Gen 2:3). The argument of the causal clause reflects the Sabbath's exclusive character as a day existing on terms of divine reason. Nowhere else in Scripture is there an explicit cause provided for God's declarative act of sanctification. In Scripture, holiness is presented as an attribute of God and His character.[16] Holiness

---

[13] Richard M. Davidson, *Flame of Yahweh: Sexuality in the Old Testament* (Peabody, MA: Hendrickson, 2007), 53.

[14] Howard N. Wallace, "Rest for the Earth? Another Look at Genesis 2:1–3," in *The Earth Story in Genesis*, ed. Norman C. Habel and Shirley Wurst (Sheffield: Sheffield Academic Press, 2000), 52.

[15] David S. Shapiro, "The Meaning of Holiness in Judaism," *Tradition* 7 (1964–1965): 51.

[16] Exodus 15:11; Leviticus 21:8.

is then required of the human being who lives in a covenantal relationship with God,[17] and of places and objects related to God's dwelling place.[18] In these cases, holiness is recognized as an implication or consequence of God's presence. But in no case in Scripture is there a specific act of God, such as His ceasing from work, which provides a cause for sanctification, except for the sanctification of the seventh-day Sabbath.

The Hebrew word for "sanctify, make holy" is usually explained in terms of the aspect of separation. The book of Leviticus makes it clear that a holy element must be separated from what is regarded as unclean. In view of the Sabbath, OT scholars often refer to the whole reality of ancient Israel as divided into two categories, the holy and the common, with the Sabbath as God's holy day.[19] One scholar translates this aspect into human reality: "The sanctification of the Sabbath constitutes an order for humankind according to which time is divided into time and holy time, time to work and time to rest."[20] Sabbath holiness as separation is for the sake of God's relationship with the human being. As another scholar notes, "holiness means not only 'separation from' but 'separation to'. It is a positive concept, an inspiration and a goal associated with God's nature and his desire for man."[21]

Sabbath holiness becomes the platform for holiness in space, such as when God's presence filled the place surrounding the burning bush (Exod 3:5), Mount Sinai (Exod 19:11–20:17), the wilderness sanctuary (Exod 40:34–38), Solomon's magnificent temple (1 Kgs 8:10–11), Ezekiel's visionary temple (Ezek 48:35), and Haggai's prophetic temple (Hag 2:7, 9). The Sabbath holiness established in the realm of the perfect world at creation is not discontinued when sin enters the world. The rhythmic recurrence of the Sabbath in time assures that holiness, once established, remains even when the world changes into an imperfect and corrupt place.[22] Sabbath holiness will be the mark of humans who enter God's sanctuary to receive forgiveness of sin (Exod 31:12–17).

---

[17] Exodus 19:10, 14, 22; 22:31; 28:36; 29:44; see esp. Leviticus 11:44.

[18] Exodus 28:2; 29:29, 37; 30:27, 35, 37; 31:10; 40:10; Leviticus 21:22; Numbers 5:9; 1 Kings 8:4.

[19] Schwartz, "The Sabbath in the Torah Sources," 10.

[20] Claus Westermann, *Genesis 1–11: A Commentary* (Minneapolis, MN: Augsburg, 1984), 171.

[21] Jacob Milgrom, *Leviticus 1–16*, AB (New York: Doubleday, 1991), 731.

[22] Sigve K. Tonstad, *The Lost Meaning of the Seventh Day* (Berrien Springs, MI: Andrews University Press, 2009), 118–123.

God places Himself into the Sabbath day[23] by sanctifying it for the sake of open access between Him and humans. God makes Himself available and so guarantees life on earth in relationship to Himself as the Creator. One scholar captures the divine-human relationship as follows: "The meaning is that mankind is created so that something can happen between God and man: mankind is created to stand face to face with God."[24]

The Creator's sanctifying affirmation of the Sabbath stands out as a remarkable sign of His constant presence in the world. From now on, divine life will overflow into the world's days, weeks, and times and will assure the gift of life, embedded in the context of the divine-human relationship for all future to come. It has been observed that "the Sabbath was designed to become the place of encounter between God the creator and man the creature, the occasion for the vertical relationship."[25] Jesus expresses the relational character of the Sabbath with the remarkable words, "The Sabbath was made for man, and not man for the Sabbath" (Mark 2:27).

Sabbath Narratives

The Pentateuch contains two narratives about the Sabbath: Exodus 16:1–36 and Numbers 15:32–36. In Exodus 16, the people who disobey and go out to gather manna on Sabbath are admonished, but in Numbers 15 the man gathering wood on Sabbath is executed by stoning.[26] The contexts of

---

[23] Fernando Canale develops a model for theological reason based on biblical exegesis and theology regarding God's temporal eternity and His acting within time versus classical and modern theologies that ground themselves in Plato's philosophical system on the timelessness of God. See Fernando Canale, *A Criticism of Theological Reason: Time and Timelessness as Primordial Presuppositions* (Berrien Springs, MI: Andrews University Press, 1987); idem, *The Cognitive Principle of Christian Theology* (Berrien Springs, MI: Andrews University Lithotech, 2005), 248. See also Jacques B. Doukhan, *Hebrew for Theologians: A Textbook for the Study of Biblical Hebrew in Relation to Hebrew Thinking* (Lanham, MD: University Press of America, 1993), 213–214.

[24] Claus Westermann, *Creation* (Neukirchen-Vluyn: Neukirchener, 1974), 56. The German text in Claus Westermann, *Schöpfung* (Stuttgart: Kreuz-Verlag, 1971), 82, reads, "Von der Menschheit wird gesagt, dass sie geschaffen ist, damit etwas geschehe zwischen Gott und Mensch: die Menschheit ist zu Gottes Gegenüber geschaffen."

[25] Doukhan, *Genesis Creation Story*, 222.

[26] For the vast majority of scholars and commentators, both texts, Exodus 16 and Numbers 15:32–36, present difficulties with respect to authorship, sources, traditions, and redactions. In Exodus 16, scholars see repetitions in the text and arrangements that appear out of chronological sequence. For example, it is argued that (1) although the Sabbath commandment is not yet proclaimed, the Sabbath and its prohibitions are spoken of as matters that are already known; (2) Exodus 16:34 contains the expression "before the Testimony," although the sanctuary is not yet in existence; and (3) Moses announces in Exodus 16:8 something that he was told by the Lord

the two narratives help in understanding the contrast. Exodus 16 occupies the middle part of a section of three stories dealing with the people's grumbling against their leaders and God before they arrive at Mount Sinai where they agree to the covenant stipulations declared by God (Exod 15:22–27; 16:1–36; 17:1–7). According to the Sabbath narrative of Exodus 16:1–36, God does not punish the people for their rebellious attitude, but responds with provisions of water and food and with the gift of the Sabbath. Numbers 15:32–36 is also placed between two narratives that report Israel's rebellion in the wilderness (Num 14:1–45; 16:1–50). However, its thematic connection with the preceding law section about unintentional and deliberate sin (Num 15:1–31) indicates that the wood gatherer's behavior on Sabbath is considered deliberate and thus inexpiable (Num 15:30–31).[27]

Exodus 16:1–36

After the magnificent story of creation with its awe-inspiring insights about the Sabbath, the reader of the Pentateuch must read through many chapters before finding another story about the Sabbath.[28] And then, when the Sabbath occurs again, it is placed into such an ordinary context

---

only subsequently in Exodus 16:11–12. See Umberto Cassuto, *A Commentary on the Book of Exodus* (Jerusalem: Magnes, 1967), 186. About Numbers 15:32–36, it is widely accepted that this text is a late element placed into the priestly material of the book of Numbers. See the discussion in Philip J. Budd, *Numbers*, WBC (Waco, TX: Word, 1984), 175. A recent study ascribes its redaction to the exilic period, particularly to the Holiness Code. See Tzvi Novick, "Law and Loss: Response to Catastrophe in Numbers 15," *HTR* 101 (2008): 1–14.

[27] Commentators link the story of the man gathering wood on Sabbath to the prohibition of gathering manna on Sabbath. While there are elements connecting the two narratives of Exodus 16 and Numbers 15:32–36, there are also differences with regard to linguistic, structural, and thematic features that make each of these narratives and their messages unique. See Roy Gane, *Leviticus, Numbers*, NIVAC (Grand Rapids, MI: Zondervan, 2004), 622. See also Thomas B. Dozeman, "The Book of Numbers," *New Interpreter's Bible* (Nashville, TN: Abingdon, 1998), 2:128.

[28] Some scholars recognize Sabbath awareness or Sabbath-keeping allusions during the patriarchal period (Gen 6–8; Gen 26:5). See Martin Buber, *Moses: The Revelation and the Covenant* (New York: Harper, 1958), 80; Brevard S. Childs, *The Book of Exodus* (Philadelphia, PA: Westminster, 1974), 290; Gerhard F. Hasel, "The Sabbath in the Pentateuch," in *The Sabbath in Scripture and History*, ed. Kenneth A. Strand (Washington, D.: Review & Herald, 1982), 26–27; James K. Hoffmeier, *Ancient Israel in Sinai* (New York: Oxford University Press, 2005), 173; Gordon J. Wenham, *Genesis 1–15*, WBC (Waco, TX: Word, 1987), 180–181; idem, "The Coherence of the Flood Narrative," *VT* 28 (1978): 345; and idem, *Story as Torah: Reading the Old Testament Ethically* (Edinburgh: T&T Clark, 2000), 27. A more direct indication to the Sabbath seems to occur in the story of Exodus 5 where Moses and Aaron appear before Pharaoh and make the request to let the people go out into the wilderness to worship God. Pharaoh rejected the request, and in his response uses the word "cease" or "rest" (*shavath*) from labor (Exod 5:5), which may point to Sabbath rest. See Mathilde Frey, "Sabbath in Egypt? An Examination of Exodus 5," *JSOT* 39.3 (2015): 249–263.

of everyday human life that it almost seems irreverent to comprehend. One may wonder how the presence of God and sacredness of the Sabbath (Gen 2:1–3; Exod 20:8–11; cf. Isa 58:13–14) made compatible with humanity's mundane need and routine of securing and consuming food (Exod 16).

However, the textual interrelatedness between the creation Sabbath and the Sabbath in Exodus 16 becomes visible in several features. There is the evening-morning motif in Exodus 16:5–6. Here is the literal translation of these verses: "So Moses and Aaron said to all the sons of Israel: 'Evening, and you will know that the Lord has brought you out from the land of Egypt; and morning, and you will see the glory of the YHWH'" (cf. Gen 1:5, 8, 13, 19, 23, 31). Another link is the 6 + 1 pattern in Exodus 16 (see vs. 4–5, 22, 26–27, 29), which directly alludes to the creation week (Gen 1:1–2:3). Further, the work-free aspect of the Sabbath (Exod 16:23, 25–26, 27, 29–30) directly relates to the seventh day of creation when God had finished all His work (Gen 2:1–3). Most importantly, both texts contain the identifying verb for the Sabbath, "cease, rest" (*shavath*) from work (Gen 2:2–3; Exod 16:30), which then introduces for the first time in the biblical text the derivative noun "the Sabbath" (*ha-shabbath*) (Exod 16:23, 25–26, 29).

The narrative of the Sabbath and the manna presents a complex sequence of events happening over the course of one week in a deserted place to a multitude of hungry people. Emotionally laden dialogues occur between Moses, Aaron, the elders, and the people. Dramatic scenes depict the people's behavior and reactions to Moses' instructions, the appearance of the glory of the Lord, and the description of the manna.[29] The narrative describes the appearance of the bread and the people's bewildered reaction to something that is completely unknown to them ("What is it?" [*man hu*'] in Exod 16:15). As they follow Moses' instructions for gathering the mysterious bread, the people are surprised again by the fact that everyone is

---

[29] Scholars see problems in the way this narrative is composed. To literary critics the plot of the narrative does not move along smoothly. Some details are emphasized; others seem to be missing. The way in which the text is arranged makes it difficult to retrace a train of thought and thus gives the impression of a text of little literary value. See the discussions in Niels-Erik A. Andreasen, *The Old Testament Sabbath: A Tradition-Historical Investigation* (Atlanta, GA: Scholars Press, 1972), 67; David Frankel, *The Murmuring Stories of the Priestly School* (Leiden: Brill, 2002), 63–117; Stephen A. Geller, "Manna and Sabbath: A Literary-Theological Reading of Exodus 16," *Interpretation* 59 (2005): 5–16; Martin J. Noth, *Exodus* (Philadelphia, PA: Westminster, 1962), 131; William H. C. Propp, *Exodus 1–18*, Anchor Yale Bible Commentaries (New York: Doubleday, 1998), 589–590; Ludwig Schmidt, "Die Priesterschrift in Exodus 16," *ZAW* 119 (2007): 483–498; and Paul Maiberger, *Das Manna: Eine Literarische, Etymologische und Naturkundliche Untersuchung* (Wiesbaden: Otto Harrassowitz, 1983).

served according to one's need, and not according to the amount of manna gathered (Exod 16:18). Yet, when some people do not consume the entire amount, the leftovers become rotten and foul overnight. In addition, the manna that has been left on the ground melts in the sun.

Starting in Exodus 16:22, the narrative introduces the Sabbath as the seventh day when the people will eat the second portion of manna they have gathered and prepared on the sixth day. The miracle of the Sabbath manna is that it does not become foul when left overnight but remains fresh and edible. The speeches in verses 23–29 are structured, highly poetic, and resonate with much passion. Out of fourteen imperative verbs used in the chapter, the section on the Sabbath has seven imperatives. Three verbs instruct the people about their preparation of the manna for the Sabbath: "bake," "boil," and "put to rest" (Exod 16:23); and three other imperative verbs teach about the Sabbath: "see/understand," "remain," and "let not go out" (Exod 16:29). In the center is the Sabbath command itself: "eat!" (Exod 16:25). The speech about the Sabbath in verse 25, with its three imperative verbs, has three rhythmic sentences that mark the presence of the Sabbath by the threefold word "today." In the Hebrew, the first sentence has two words with "today" as the second word; the second sentence has three expressions with "today" in the middle position; and the third sentence has four words with "today" in the first place.[30] "Today" identifies the Sabbath as the day when the people are to enjoy food. "Today" is the day of YHWH. "Today" is when the fields remain empty and bread is truly a miracle of the Lord.

Furthermore, the Lord's response with regard to those who had gone out to look for manna on the seventh day speaks of His commandments (*mitswoth*) and instructions (*toroth*) that these people refused to keep. Moses turns to the people and makes a case in pointing out that they need to understand that the Lord "has given" (*nathan*) the Sabbath to them (note the perfect form of the Hebrew verb *nathan* conveying a completed action in the past). The following reasoning is noteworthy: "Therefore, He gives [*nothen*; Heb. participle, conveying an ongoing, repeated, or continuous action] to you bread for two days on the sixth day" (Exod 16:29). The Sabbath's observance as a commandment of the Lord, and the statement that it is a divine gift of the past, tell of its existence not only for the present and future generations of Israel but also for their ancestors.[31] For the

---

[30] Brevard Childs, *The Book of Exodus*, 290, understands the threefold "today" as carrying "a festive ring."

[31] The Hebrew verb *nathan* indicating a completed action in the past helps to invalidate the theory that the Sabbath was only given to the Israelites when they received the Ten Commandments on Mount Sinai.

people in the wilderness, the Sabbath was guaranteed by the ongoing and repeated double gift of the manna on the sixth day until they arrived in the promised land (Exod 16:35; cf. Josh 5:12). In Exodus 16:30, the narrative simply concludes that the people "rested" on the seventh day. Here, the link to the creation Sabbath is unambiguous, with the verb "rest" (*shavath*) identifying the seventh day (cf. Gen 2:2–3) as the Sabbath to the Lord (Exod 16:25).

The intricate features of the narrative in Exodus 16 may be interpreted as reflecting on the complications of Israel's life in the wilderness. Yet, God who once entered into a perfect world on the Sabbath day, again, on the Sabbath, comes into the lives of distressed people with His gifts and glory. In this sense, the rhythmic recurrence of the Sabbath stands as assurance for divine presence and benefaction in a hostile and life-threatening world.

Sabbath and food have been intertwined since creation. God's intimate relationship with the first human couple was established over food (Gen 1:29). The Sabbath followed, endowed with blessings and sacredness for all creation—and especially for the sake of human beings. In the transition from the sixth day of that perfect world described in Genesis 2 into the fallen world of Genesis 3, one may observe that food is the decisive element that incurs loss of God's perfect world. From here on, Genesis is silent about the Sabbath and only tacitly refers to the recurrence of the seventh day until God enters the wilderness with the miraculous gift of food and the Sabbath.

In Exodus 16, Sabbath and food are closely linked by the divine gift of the manna. The narrative shows the difference between the manna provided for the six weekdays and the manna given for the seventh day. Each morning during the weekdays, the people witnessed God's glory in the wilderness with fields abounding with bread. On the Sabbath, the people were to remain at rest. During the weekdays, the manna kept overnight became rotten. On the Sabbath, the manna kept overnight was fresh. Death and decay, so easily growing overnight during the weeknights, surrendered to the Creator God during Sabbath night. On Sabbath, no toxic smell filled the tents. The Sabbath miracle in Exodus 16 tells of the commitment of the Creator God, who, over the course of forty years, miraculously sustained the lives of His people in a life-threatening environment. Further, the testing of Israel in relation to the Sabbath and manna (Exod 16:4–5) shows that the Sabbath regulation would epitomize God's law: Israel was so tested to demonstrate "whether or not they will walk in my instruction" (Exod 16:4, NASB).

Numbers 15:32–36

The Pentateuch tells the incident of an unnamed man gathering wood on Sabbath in the wilderness. The man is caught and brought before Moses, Aaron, and the whole congregation. The narrative briefly records this event, with the only speech coming directly from the Lord, who declares: "The man must surely be put to death; all the congregation shall stone him with stones outside the camp" (Num 15:35), followed by the response of the congregation (Num 15:36).

The narrative of the wood gatherer seems to be used as an example of defiant sin in the context of the cultic legislation about offerings for expiation of inadvertent versus defiant sin that precedes the narrative about the wood-gatherer (Num 15:22–31). Some commentators conclude that the narrative serves to impress upon the hearer/reader the severity of religious prohibitions, especially the severity of the Sabbath commandment.[32] However, the narrative context, which deals with Israel's leadership crisis in the desert (Num 14; 16), adds more information and shows that the focal subject in the wood-gatherer's case is (1) the binding agreement that was established between the Lord and the individual Israelite within his/her community, and (2) the significance of the Sabbath as a sign of freedom from slavery.

Numbers 15:22–36 emphasizes the concept of Israel as the Lord's covenant community by displaying a chiastic structure based on the expression "all the congregation" and shows how unintentional or defiant sin of the people or of one individual affected the entire community of Israel.

    A   Law on unintentional sin of all the people: "all the congregation" (*kol-ha'edhah*) brings an offering to YHWH (Num 15:22–24)
        B   Priest makes atonement for "all the congregation" (*kol-ha'edhah*) (Num 15:25)
            Divine verdict: "all the congregation" (*kol-ha'edhah*) will be forgiven (Num 15:26)
            X   Law on unintentional sin of one person: forgiveness (Num 15:27–29)
            X¹   Law on intentional sin of one person: cut off (Num 15:30–31)
        B¹   Investigation of the wood-gatherer's sin: man is brought before "all the congregation" (*kol-ha'edhah*) (Num 15:32–34)
            Divine verdict: "all the congregation" (*kol-ha'edhah*) shall stone him to death (Num 15:35)
    A¹   Law on intentional sin executed: "all the congregation" (*kol-ha'edhah*) stoned him (Num 15:36).

---

[32] Baruch A. Levine, *Numbers 1–20*, AB (New York: Doubleday, 1993), 386.

The center of the chiasm (X and X¹) focuses on the distinction between unintentional versus defiant sin, and even emphasizes that the same law is to be applied for the native and for the alien who lives within the covenant community. The parallel sections A and A¹ speak of the entire congregation's participation in the offering (Num 15:22–24) and in the execution of the wood-gatherer (Num 15:36). The sections B and B¹ each emphasize the charge given to "all the congregation" and the verdict for "all the congregation."

The wood-gatherer's sin is attached to the law dealing with intentional sin as an actual example of an individual who deliberately acted against the covenant stipulations of the community of Israel. The man's rebellious act affected and disturbed the life of the whole community. The fact that deliberate sin is marked with the example of Sabbath breaking and not with any other violation of law shows that the Sabbath commandment was regarded as the ultimate sign of the covenant relationship between the Lord and Israel (cf. Exod 31:12–17).

In a study on defiant or "high-handed" sins versus inadvertent sins, one scholar concludes that even "wrongs that are open, bold, and shameless . . . may be undetectable by human beings,"[33] however, before God these sins cannot be covered up (cf. Josh 7). In the case of the wood-gatherer, the context shows that he committed openly defiant sin that could not be expiated through animal sacrifice because of the rebellious attitude and affront against the authority of YHWH. The expression "high-handed" (Num 15:30) signifies "the physical gesture of the raised hand, with or without a weapon in it, which indicates that one is triumphantly determined to fight and to win."[34]

The Sabbath shows another aspect in the narrative of the wood-gatherer: The text uses a specific verb when it tells of the man "gathering" (*qashash*) wood on Sabbath. This verb occurs only four times in the Pentateuch—twice when describing the toil and oppression of the Israelites in Egypt (Exod 5:7, 12), and twice in the present story of the wood-gatherer (Num 15:32–33) who has been delivered from Egyptian slavery. The link between the two stories is highly telling in the sense that a free man acted in defiance against

---

[33] Roy Gane, "Numbers 15:22–31 and the Spectrum of Moral Faults," in *Inicios, Paradigmas y Fundamentos: Estudios teologicos y exegeticos en el Pentateuco*, ed. Gerald Klingbeil (Libertador San Martin: Editorial Universidad Adventista del Plata, 2004), 155.

[34] Caspar J. Labuschagne, "The Meaning of *beyad rama* in the Old Testament," in *Von Kanaan bis Kerala: Festschrift for J. P. M. van der Ploeg*, ed. W. C. Delsman et al. (Neukirchen-Vluyn: Neukirchener, 1982), 146.

the supreme law of freedom expressed in the Sabbath commandment and thereby placed himself back into the position of a slave.[35] To "gather" wood like an Egyptian slave on the day that celebrated freedom from slavery (Deut 5:15) was considered a treacherous act and in the ancient covenant community received the penalty of death.

A further insight into the importance of the Sabbath in the wood-gatherer's story is when the man was "put to rest" (*nuakh*) until the Lord spoke the verdict. The verb "rest" (*nuakh*) is unquestionable in the context of the Sabbath (Exod 16:23–24, 33–34; 20:11; 23:12; Deut 5:14) when the Lord God "rested" (*nuakh*) on the seventh day of creation week (Exod 20:11). Sadly, the man could have enjoyed this rest in celebrating the day of rest and freedom, but like a slave he now was "put to rest" in forced confinement.

The narrative of Numbers 15:32–36 portrays two contrastive systems—slavery versus freedom. While a slavery system has fixed structures, which may lead one to believe there is security within prison walls, the Creator God never intended such a system for His creatures. Human beings were to be the "image of God" living in His presence and fulfilling their own responsibilities on planet earth. Israel's slavery narratives become extremely graphic in portraying the exploitative Egyptian system that turned humans into robotic characters without dignity. The Sabbath stands at the critical juncture inviting human beings into freedom of fellowship with their Creator God.

The wood-gatherer stands as a microcosm of the whole Israelite congregation in the wilderness when they rebelled against God and preferred slavery in Egypt to leadership by God under Moses and Aaron. He acted out his personal decision to openly renounce the freedom gained by his liberation from slavery and demonstrated his choice to turn back to Egypt. Breaking the Sabbath law demonstrated his determination to break out of the covenant relationship with the Lord. By requiring the whole congregation to stone this man, God appealed to the Israelites to reject the rebellious attitude that in a larger sense they all shared.

Sabbath Laws

The legal texts of the Pentateuch place the Sabbath into the center of the covenantal context between God and Israel. The Sabbath commandment occurs at the heart of the Decalogue in both the Exodus text and in the Deuteronomy version. Formal language is used to clearly communicate

---

[35] See Novick, "Law and Loss," 5, who briefly alludes to this aspect of the verb "gather."

God's will. The Sabbath commandment explicitly states (1) the authority of the lawgiver: God, the Creator of heaven and earth; (2) the reason and motivation for Sabbath-keeping: God rested on the seventh day (Exod 20:11) and God brought Israel out of slavery (Deut 5:15); (3) the goal for Sabbath-keeping: "to keep it holy" (Exod 20:8; Deut 5:12); (4) the benefactor: the Israelite householder as Sabbath-keeper; and (5) the beneficiaries of Sabbath rest: "you or your son or your daughter, your male or your female servant or your cattle or your sojourner who stays with you" (Exod 20:10, NASB). Legal language is used to express the covenant relationship between God and Israel and the non-discriminating, non-selective, and equalizing aspects of the Sabbath. When the Sabbath becomes a legal institution, it benefits each individual of society, even foreigners and animals.

In apodictic and casuistic laws addressing various aspects of life (Exod 21–23), Sabbath legislation is linked to the motif of God hearing the cry of the oppressed and acting as their Redeemer. God is heavily involved in the lives of widows, orphans, and strangers, and on the Sabbath He comes closest to the least appreciated members of society and takes care of hard working animals (Exod 23:12).

With respect to the legal emphasis within the covenant at Sinai, Christianity in general has perceived the Decalogue and the laws of the Pentateuch "to function as a principle of salvation by works."[36] However, as one theologian notes, this aspect fails to recognize that "Israel assembled at Sinai only because God had redeemed them from Egypt."[37] The covenantal relationship between God and Israel formed the basis for their redemption and for the revelation of the law. The law, including the Sabbath commandment, was conveyed as God's gift for life within the covenantal relationship, and not as a requirement to be fulfilled in order to enter the relationship.

There is more to the Decalogue and the covenant when it is read in the narrative context of Exodus 19. One scholar points out that it is precisely this context that sets the Decalogue apart from other ancient Near Eastern treaty patterns and imparts meaning and special significance to the covenant.[38] Israel's God is portrayed as an eagle carrying its young on its back to the destination identified by the emphatic statement, "I brought you to me" (Exod 19:4). This expression demonstrates that the essence of the covenant

---

[36] O. Palmer Robertson, *The Christ of the Covenants* (Phillipsburg, NJ: Presbyterian and Reformed, 1980), 174.

[37] Ibid.

[38] Nahum M. Sarna, *Exodus: The Traditional Hebrew Text with the New JPS Translation*, JPSTC (Philadelphia, PA: Jewish Publication Society, 1991), 201.

is captured in the unique relationship between God and Israel, and not in legal obligations and responsibilities.[39]

Exodus 20:8–11

Two characteristics distinguish the Sabbath commandment from all other commandments in Exodus 20. First, the Sabbath commandment is the longest commandment in the Decalogue, with fifty-five words in the Hebrew Bible. It is preceded by three commandments that focus on God and is followed by six commandments that focus on humanity.[40] This double focus creates an alternating thematic movement in the Decalogue, in which the Sabbath commandment occupies a strategic position:

Commandments 1–3:	God (Exod 20:3–7)
Sabbath Commandment:	Humanity (Exod 20:8–10)
	God (Exod 20:11)
Commandments 5–10:	Humanity (Exod 20:12–17)

Second, the Sabbath commandment has an atypical word at the beginning. In the Hebrew language, this is an infinitive absolute verb, *zakhor* ("remember"),[41] only paralleled by the imperative "honor" in the fifth commandment, which grammatically could also be an infinitive absolute. The rest of the commandments are negatively formulated (Exod 20:3, 4, 5, 7, 13, 14, 15, 16, 17). Most grammarians recognize the infinitive absolute form of the Sabbath commandment as denoting an emphatic imperative.[42]

---

[39] Abraham J. Heschel, *The Prophets* (New York: Harper & Row, 2001) describes the covenantal relationship between God and Israel in terms of the divine pathos. He observes that God's involvement in human history is never impersonal. God is not a spectator watching the events of history from afar, He is "personally and emotionally involved in the life of man" (ibid., 29). Heschel further holds that while the covenant may be understood as a juridical commitment between the parties, it is God's emotional engagement and His constant concern and involvement that maintain the covenant. This engagement, then, is the divine pathos, not passion, arbitrary attitude, or unreasoned emotion. It is a divine act "rooted in decision" and "the real basis of the relation between God and man, of the correlation of Creator and creation, of the dialogue between the Holy One of Israel and His people" (ibid., 298).

[40] Jacques B. Doukhan, "Loving the Sabbath as a Christian," in *The Sabbath in Jewish and Christian Traditions*, ed. Tamara C. Eskenazi, Daniel J. Harrington, and William H. Shea (New York: Crossroads, 1991), 159.

[41] The Samaritan Pentateuch uses the verb "keep" (*shamar*) (cf. Deut. 5:12), instead of "remember" (*zakhar*) likely in an attempt to harmonize Exodus 20:8 with Deuteronomy 5:12.

[42] The infinitive absolute form *zakhor* functioning as an emphatic imperative also occurs in Exodus 13:3; Deuteronomy 7:18; 24:9; 25:17; Joshua 1:13. Cf. Wilhelm Gesenius, *Gesenius' Hebrew Grammar* (New York: Appleton & Company, 1851), 245–246. Bruce K. Waltke and Michael O'Connor, *An Introduction to Biblical Hebrew Syntax* (Winona Lake, IN: Eisenbrauns,

When read in the context of the other commandments characterized by imperfect verb forms, the infinitive absolute "remember" may have a nuance of an intensifying promise (cf. 2 Kgs 4:43).[43]

The verb "remember" (*zakhar*) occurs eight times in the book of Exodus, each in the context of God's covenant with Israel (Exod 2:24; 3:15; 6:5; 13:3; 20:8, 24; 23:13; 32:13). Close examination of these occurrences shows that the focus of "remember" is on two specific days established as memorial days—the day of the exodus (Exod 13:3) and the Sabbath (Exod 20:8). Interestingly, only these two memorial days are marked by the atypical infinitive absolute form *zakhor* ("remember").[44]

While there are similarities between the two memorial days (both involve a seven-day cycle, remembrance of God's redemptive act, and rest, and both benefit native and alien alike), there are significant differences between them. The first differentiation consists of the infinitive absolute "remember" linked to what could be termed the aim of the Sabbath (that is, "to keep it holy"), but is not the aim of the day of the exodus. To remember the Sabbath in connection with holiness suggests that the purpose of remembering is directed toward the definite action of separating the Sabbath from the rest of the weekdays.[45] Indeed, the theme of holiness functions so prominently in the Sabbath commandment that Exodus 20:8–11 is framed by the verb "holy" in an *inclusio* consisting of similar phraseology at the beginning and at the end of the commandment: "Remember the Sabbath day to keep it holy" (Exod 20:8) and "Therefore the Lord blessed the Sabbath day and kept it holy" (Exod 20:11).[46] Second, the link between Sabbath and holiness shows that unlike the Passover, where the people

---

1990), 593–594, point out that the usage of absolute infinitives as command forms is extremely old and can be detected in other Semitic languages. Cf. Reuven Yaron, "Stylistic Conceits II: The Absolute Infinitive in Biblical Law," in *Pomegranates and Golden Bells: Studies in Biblical, Jewish, and Near Eastern Ritual, Law, and Literature in Honor of Jacob Milgrom*, ed. David P. Wright, David N. Freedman, and Avi Hurwitz (Winona Lake, IN: Eisenbrauns, 1995), 449–460.

[43] Wilhelm Gesenius, E. Kautzsch, and A. E. Cowley, *Gesenius' Hebrew Grammar* (New York: Dover, 2006), 346.

[44] Benno Jacob, *The Second Book of the Bible: Exodus* (Hoboken: KTAV, 1992), 582; Propp, *Exodus 19–40*, 112. Even though Jacob and Propp notice the infinitive absolute forms in the two texts (Exod 13:3 and 20:8), they do not explore their impact and meaning, but focus instead on diachronic issues of the words "remember" in Exodus 20:8 and "observe" in Deuteronomy 5:12. Other biblical scholars and interpreters do not deal at all with the literary structure that the Hebrew root *zkr* displays in the book of Exodus.

[45] Hasel, "The Sabbath in the Pentateuch," 30.

[46] Ekkehardt Mueller, "The Sabbath Commandment in Deuteronomy 5:12–15," *JATS* 14 (2002): 144.

are reminded of their experience of servitude and of the bitterness of their life in Egypt, the Sabbath aims back at creation time, a dimension of life that the Israelites of the exodus never experienced in the reality of life. Sabbath holiness has its beginnings long before oppression, sin, and death. Third, unlike Passover, the Sabbath reveals the essential relationship between God and humanity, a relationship that exists on the basis of God's will for the human being as "image of God." In Exodus 31:13, this concept is directly connected to Sabbath observance as a "sign that you may know that I am the Lord, your Sanctifier." While the account of the creation Sabbath (Gen 2:1–3) focuses on God and His sanctifying presence and not on the human being, it is through compliance with the Sabbath commandment that the human being lives within the realm of the sanctifying presence of God. Finally, the Sabbath commandment prohibits "all work," and is in this regard different from the Passover commandment that declares, "No work at all shall be done, except what must be eaten by every person" (Exod 12:16, NASB).

The structure of Exodus 20:8–11 reveals a careful arrangement by paralleling human activity with divine activity (see A and A¹).

    A "Remember the Sabbath day, to keep it holy.
        B Six days you shall labor and do all your work, but the seventh day is a Sabbath of YHWH your God; you shall not do any work,
            X you or your son or your daughter, your male servant or your female servant or your cattle or your sojourner who stays with you.
        B¹ For in six days YHWH made the heavens and the earth, the sea and all that is in them, and rested on the seventh day;
    A¹ therefore YHWH blessed the Sabbath day and made it holy."[47]

The contrast is about work during the weekdays and refraining and resting from work on the Sabbath (B and B¹). Different from Genesis 2:2–3, where the text states that God "ceased [*shavath*] from His work," God's resting is now identified with the Hebrew verb *nuakh*, which carries a sense of tranquility and quietness.[48] Note that the Sabbath keeper is instructed to "not do work," which equals God's ceasing from work at creation, but is not commanded to "rest" in the sense of *nuakh*. God is the subject of *nuakh* rest. Further record of this kind of rest shows that it does not originate with the human being, but God causes the human being to experience

---

[47] Doukhan, "Loving the Sabbath as a Christian," 159.

[48] H. D. Preuss, "מנחה ,נוח *nuakh, menukhah*," *TDOT* 9:297.

such rest.⁴⁹ The *nuakh* rest is the gift of God; He grants *nuakh* and makes it available for the Sabbath keeper, but does not order it.

By linking the Sabbath of the Decalogue to the creation Sabbath, universal aspects become evident. In this regard, one scholar notes,

> It is humanity in general and not any people in particular that is created. Israel is not primordial. It emerges in history, twenty generations after the creation of human species in the image of God (or the gods, 1:26–27). . . . It is neither descended from the gods nor divine itself. All people are created equally in the divine image.⁵⁰

In the center of the Sabbath commandment is a full household portrayed by a list of seven members.⁵¹ These seven beneficiaries, covering every category of humans and animals, also highlight the universal nature of the Sabbath.⁵²

The covenantal context of the Sabbath law focuses on matters of identity and relationship. God is identified as the one who liberated the Israelites from Egyptian oppression and as the personal God of the Sabbath observer (Exod 20:2, 9). The Sabbath observer receives identity on the basis of his relationship with God and his household, and in direct relation to his work. The Creator God as a personal and relational being entered the world at creation, initiated human history in the sacredness of the Sabbath, liberated the Israelites from bondage, and established them as a holy nation (Exod 19:3–5). He takes part in the lives of people living in a desolate and barren world and offers Himself as the supreme example for weekday work

---

⁴⁹ The verb *nuakh* occurs eight times in the Qal form and twenth-five times in the Hiphil form. The Qal form is used with the following subjects: God (Exod 20:11), the Spirit of God (Num 11:25–26), human beings (Deut 5:14), the ark (Gen 8:4), the locusts (Exod 10:14), and animals such as the ox and the donkey (Exod 23:12). The references just mentioned show different nuances of the verb: God "rested" on the seventh day; the Spirit "rested" upon the prophets; the ark "settled down" on the mountains; the locusts "settled" in a territory; and the ox, the donkey, the male servant, the female servant, and the Sabbath observer are dependent upon the Sabbath observer's ceasing (Exod 23:12) or not doing any work (Deut 5:14) in order that they may "rest" (Exod 23:12; Deut 5:14).

⁵⁰ Jon D. Levenson, "The Universal Horizon of Biblical Particularism," in *Ethnicity and the Bible*, ed. Mark G. Brett (Boston, MA: Brill, 1996), 147.

⁵¹ The household includes "your sojourner who stays in your gates" (Exod 20:10). This places a further difference from the Passover festival, which is to be observed by native Israelites only and aliens who were circumcised in order to be considered as natives (Exod 12:48). The Sabbath commandment does not require of the alien to be circumcised in order to participate in Sabbath observance and enjoy the Sabbath as a work-free day.

⁵² Doukhan, "Loving the Sabbath as a Christian," 159.

and Sabbath life. He is concerned with each member of the household, regardless of social status—including the animals.

Furthermore, the use of the word "remember" in Exodus shows that the covenant theme underscores and highlights the two commandments that are at the basis of the covenant with Israel—the day of the exodus and the day of the Sabbath. The exodus constitutes the historical event of deliverance that marks Israel's history. The Sabbath constitutes the recurring commemoration of the covenant relationship established at creation.

Within the history of Israel, the exodus deliverance calls for the Sabbath, and Sabbath keeping necessitates the exodus. One without the other is simply incomplete. The enslaved people needed to be liberated before they received the commandment to keep the Sabbath. This observation seems important, for it shows that God issues laws such as the Decalogue only to liberated people who entered into a personal covenant relationship with Him. The Sabbath commandment is given to and observed by freed people, not slaves.

Exodus 23:12

The Sabbath commandment in Exodus 23:12 states, "Six days you are to do your work, but on the seventh day you shall cease from labor so that your ox and your donkey may rest, and the son of your female slave, as well as your stranger, may refresh themselves" (NASB). The rarely used verb "breathe, refresh" (*nafash*) sets this Sabbath commandment apart from the Decalogue versions in Exodus 20:8–11 and Deuteronomy 5:12–15. When this verb occurs again (Exod 31:17; 2 Sam 16:14) it designates the catching of one's breath during rest.[53] In 2 Samuel 16:14, the verb speaks of David and his people recovering from fatigue during their flight from Absalom. In Exodus 31:17, God is being refreshed after the work of creation. Scholars suggest that the anthropomorphic language employed for God's refreshment on the seventh day is used as an example for human Sabbath rest and refreshment.[54]

The context of Exodus 23:12 provides a particular aspect to understanding the verb *nafash* ("breathe") in relation to the Sabbath. In Exodus 23:9, we read, "You shall not oppress a stranger, since you yourselves know the feelings [*nefesh*] of the stranger, for you were strangers in the land of Egypt" (NASB). The verb *nafash* relates to the cognate noun *nefesh*, which is often translated as "soul" but denotes the whole being or the life of a person.

---

[53] Daniel C. Fredericks, "נפשׁ *nafash*," *NIDOTTE* 3:133. The Akkadian *napasu* has a similar meaning, i.e., "to blow, breathe (freely), to become wide." Cf. *HALOT* 1:711.

[54] Cassuto, *A Commentary on the Book of Exodus*, 245, 404; John H. Sailhammer, *The Pentateuch as Narrative* (Grand Rapids, MI: Zondervan, 1992), 309.

The resonance between the verb and the noun highlights the experience of the Israelite Sabbath keeper who had been a stranger in Egypt and knew of weariness and depletion, and therefore would give an opportunity for the slave and stranger in his house to breathe and experience refreshment.

Another aspect of the context of Exodus 23:12 shows that Israel's concern for the oppressed is taken as the human analogue of God's compassionate listening to the cry of suffering people. The laws that precede this Sabbath commandment (Exod 22:21–27; 23:6–11) speak about the protection of those whose social or legal statuses made them victims of injustice: the poor, the widow, the orphan, the resident alien, and the slave. The Sabbath commandment speaks to this context and must be seen as part of the preceding social legislation.[55] The cry and compassion motif is fundamental to the entire book of Exodus, even appearing as a trigger for the exodus event in Exodus 3:7: "The Lord said, 'I have surely seen the affliction of my people who are in Egypt, and have given heed to their cry'" (NASB). From this perspective, all the laws of the Covenant Code, and especially the Sabbath law, must be understood as prescription by the same God who was moved by the outcry of the slave in Egypt and brought redemption to Israel.

Furthermore, Exodus 23:12 defines who will catch his breath when the Israelite householder keeps Sabbath rest—namely, "the son of your female servant." This slave is not mentioned in the Sabbath commandment of the Decalogue (Exod 20:10; Deut 5:14); only the male and female servants are.[56] Besides the Sabbath commandment in Exodus 23:12, the only other reference to the son of the female servant in the Pentateuch is in the story of Hagar and Ishmael's expulsion from the household of Abraham and Sarah, in which Ishmael is twice called the "son of the female servant" (Gen 21:10, 13). Mention is also made of "the stranger" (Exod 23:12) as one who will benefit from Sabbath rest. While the Sabbath commandments in Exodus 20:11 and Deuteronomy 5:14 mention "your stranger" (*gerkha*), Exodus 23:12 uses "the stranger" (*hagher*). The audience and the reader of the text may recognize a pun on *hagher*, which may reinforce the link to Hagar. The allusion to Hagar and Ishmael opens the concept of the Sabbath in particular toward people

---

[55] Paul Hanson, "The Theological Significance of Contradiction within the Book of the Covenant," in *Canon and Authority: Essays in Old Testament Religion and Theology*, ed. George W. Coats and Burke O. Long (Philadelphia, PA: Fortress, 1977), 110–131; Eduard Nielsen, *The Ten Commandments in New Perspective* (London: SCM, 1967), 113–114; Felix Mathys, "Sabbatruhe und Sabbatfest: Überlegungen zur Entstehung und Bedeutung des Sabbat im AT," *TZ* 28 (1972): 246.

[56] The Samaritan Pentateuch reads "your male servant and your female servant" in Exodus 23:12.

who are usually excluded from family and society. In the Israelite household, the responsibility for an inclusionist Sabbath observance rested with the Sabbath keeper. When he/she allowed the servant and the stranger time to breathe, to rest, to live,[57] he recognized himself as "a stranger and a sojourner among you" (cf. Gen 23:4). The Sabbath keeper would bring good news to the afflicted mother, bind up her broken heart, and provide time and space for regeneration to her and the dying child (cf. Isa 61:1; Luke 4:18).

The Sabbath commandment of the Covenant Code is clearly put in the context of the theological motif of God's compassionate listening to the cry of the oppressed. The Sabbath keeper's role is not fulfilled by worshipping God or by relating only to family members. The Sabbath calls for the care of hardworking animals and for the marginalized and outcast in order to experience a time to "breathe," to live. In Exodus 23:12, the ox and the donkey are even placed before the humans, truly signifying the caring perspective of the Sabbath. God Himself expresses self-identification with the marginalized and the most burdened members of society.

Exodus 31:12–17

The Sabbath is directly related to the sanctuary in a number of legal portions of the Pentateuch (Exod 31:12–17; 35:1–3; Lev 19:3, 30; 23:3; 24:5–9; 26:2; Num 28:9–10). The most elaborate of these Sabbath texts is the seventh speech of YHWH's sanctuary building instructions (Exod 31:12–17).[58] While the preceding six speeches (Exod 25:1; 30:11, 17, 22, 34; 31:1) contain information about how to make, assemble, use, and operate the sanctuary building and its services, the seventh speech turns the focus from the sanctuary to the Sabbath.

There is consensus among biblical scholars on the conceptual relationship between the Sabbath and the sanctuary in Exodus 25–31,[59] also based

---

[57] See Hans Walter Wolf, *Anthropology of the Old Testament* (Philadelphia, PA: Fortress, 1974), 139: "These are people who are particularly without redress against any orders given to them. Though a master might not dare to exact work on the sabbath from his adult woman slave, he was much more easily able to exert pressure on her son, or on the foreign worker, who was all too easily viewed as being outside the sphere of liberty set by Yahweh's commandment. This version of the sabbath commandment therefore picks up the borderline case: the sabbath has been instituted for the sake of all those who are especially hard-driven and especially dependent."

[58] Peter J. Kearney, "Creation and Liturgy: The P Redaction of Ex 25–40," *ZAW* 89 (1977): 375–386; Moshe Weinfeld, "Sabbath, Temple and the Enthronement of the Lord: The Problem of the 'Sitz im Leben' of Genesis 1:1–2:3," in *Melanges bibliques et orientaux en l'honneur de M. Henri Cazelles*, eds. A. Caquot and M. Delcor (Neukirchen-Vluyn: Neukirchener, 1981), 501–512.

[59] See, e.g., Shimon Bakon, "Creation, Tabernacle and Sabbath," *JBQ* 25 (1997): 79–85; Samuel E.

on parallels to ancient Near Eastern temple-building texts.[60] However, the rationale and meaning of the biblical Sabbath-sanctuary link is still open to debate. William Propp asks precisely this question: "What exactly is the connection between the Sabbath and the Tabernacle?"[61] He suggests the idea that if the Sabbath is a kind of Sanctuary in time, as Abraham Heschel eloquently put it,[62] "no less is the Tabernacle a Sabbath in space."[63] However, Propp argues for the Sabbath and the sanctuary as symbols of the

---

Balentine, *The Torah's Vision of Worship* (Minneapolis, MN: Fortress, 1999), 67–68, 138–141; G. K. Beale, "Eden, the Temple, and the Church's Mission in the New Creation," *JETS* 48 (2005): 15–19; idem, *The Temple and the Church's Mission: A Biblical Theology of the Dwelling Place of God* (Downers Grove, IL: InterVarsity, 2004), 60–61; Joseph Blenkinsop, "The Structure of P," *CBQ* 38 (1976): 275–292; Martin Buber, "People Today and the Jewish Bible: From a Lecture Series," in *Scripture and Translation*, ed. Martin Buber and Franz Rosenzweig (Bloomington, IN: Indiana University Press, 1994), 18–19; Cassuto, *Commentary on the Book of Exodus*, 404, 476–477; Davidson, *Flame of Yahweh*, 47; idem, "Cosmic Metanarrative for the Coming Millennium," *JATS* 11 (2000): 108–111; Rachel Elior, *The Three Temples: On the Emergence of Jewish Mysticism* (Oxford: The Littman Library of Jewish Civilization, 2004), 37, 70–71, 190–191; Eric E. Elnes, "Creation and Tabernacle: The Priestly Writer's 'Environmentalism,'" *Horizons in Biblical Theology* 16 (1994): 144–155; Michael Fishbane, *Text and Texture: Close Reading of Biblical Texts* (New York: Schocken, 1979), 11–13; Crispin H. T. Fletcher-Louis, *All the Glory of Adam: Liturgical Anthropology in the Dead Sea Scrolls* (Leiden: Brill, 2002), 61–66; idem, "The Cosmology of P and Theological Anthropology in the Wisdom of Ben Sira," in *Of Scribes and Sages: Early Jewish Interpretation and Transmission of Scripture*, vol. 1, *Ancient Versions and Traditions* (London: T&T Clark, 2004), 77–79; idem, "God's Image, His Cosmic Temple and the High Priest: Towards an Historical and Theological Account of the Incarnation," in *Heaven on Earth: The Temple in Biblical Theology*, ed. T. Desmond Alexander and Simon J. Gathercole (Carlisle: Paternoster, 2004), 81–99; Arthur Green, "Sabbath as Temple: Some Thoughts on Space and Time in Judaism," in *Go and Study: Essays and Studies in Honor of Alfred Jospe*, ed. Raphael Jospe and Samuel Z. Fishman (Washington, DC: Hillel Foundations, 1980), 294–298; C. T. R. Hayward, *The Jewish Temple: A Non-Biblical Sourcebook* (London: Routledge, 1996); and Weinfeld, "Sabbath, Temple and the Enthronement," 506.

[60] See, e.g., Beale, *The Temple and the Church's Mission*, 50–60; Victor Hurowitz, *I Have Built You an Exalted House: Temple Building in the Bible in Light of Mesopotamian and North-Western Semitic Writings* (Sheffield: Sheffield Academic Press, 2009); idem, "The Priestly Account of Building the Tabernacle," *Journal of the American Oriental Society* 105 (1985): 21–30; idem, "YHWH's Exalted House—Aspects of the Design and Symbolism of Solomon's Temple," in *Temple and Worship in Israel*, ed. John Day (London: T&T Clark, 2005), 79–82; Bernd Janowski, *Gottes Gegenwart in Israel: Beiträge zur Theologie des Alten Testaments* (Neukirchen-Vluyn: Neukirchener, 1993), 214–223; idem, "Der Temple als Kosmos—Zur Kosmologischen Bedeutung des Temples in der Umwelt Israels," in *Egypt—Temple of the Whole World: Studies in Honor of Jan Assmann*, ed. Sybille Meyer (Leiden: Brill, 2003), 163–186; and Stefan Paas, *Creation and Judgement: Creation Texts in Some Eighth Century Prophets* (Leiden: Brill, 2003), 88–94.

[61] Propp, *Exodus 19–40*, 692.

[62] Heschel, *The Sabbath*, 29.

[63] Propp, *Exodus 19–40*, 692.

divine "rest" (*menukhah*), which in his understanding is primordial inertia in a timeless realm. Ultimately, humanity's goal is to enter such a Sabbath-sanctuary rest that is timeless and spaceless in order to be godlike.[64]

In addition, scholars have recognized parallels between Genesis 1–3 and Exodus 25–40 that portray creation and the garden of Eden as a sanctuary, with the creation Sabbath playing a center role.[65] Both creation and the instructions for the sanctuary in Exodus 25–40 occur in seven stages and both end with the expression "finished the work" (Gen 2:2; Exod 40:33).[66] Richard Davidson points out intertextual links supporting the idea that the pre-fall garden of Eden is presented as the original sanctuary on Earth in parallel to the wilderness sanctuary and the Solomonic temple.[67] John Walton proposes that Sabbath rest in creation is intimately related to the "cosmic temple," which he identifies with the created world in Genesis 1.[68] The sanctuary in Exodus 25–40 and Solomon's temple (1 Kgs 8) are understood as a model of the cosmos or the cosmic temple.[69] The seven days of creation are seen as the period of inauguration of the cosmic temple,[70] and the Sabbath functions as the climactic day when God enters the temple, takes up His residence, and exercises His divine authority over the cosmos.[71]

The scholarly propositions show that the relationship between the Sabbath as holy time and the sanctuary as holy space is indeed complex.

---

[64] Propp, *Exodus 19–40*, 694.

[65] For a detailed discussion, see Eric Bolger, "The Compositional Role of the Eden Narrative in the Pentateuch" (PhD diss., Trinity Evangelical Divinity School, 1993); William J. Dumbrell, *The End of the Beginning* (Homebush: Lancer Books, 1985), 35–76; Fishbane, *Text and Texture*, 12–13; Jon D. Levenson, *Sinai and Zion: An Entry into the Jewish Bible* (Minneapolis, MN: Winston, 1985), 142–145; Daniel C. Timmer, *Creation, Tabernacle, and Sabbath: The Sabbath Frame in Exodus 31:12–17; 35:1–3 in Exegetical and Theological Perspective* (Göttingen: Vandenhoeck & Ruprecht, 2009); Gordon J. Wenham, "Sanctuary Symbolism in the Garden of Eden Story," *Proceedings of the World Congress of Jewish Studies* 9 (1986): 19–25.

[66] Jacques B. Doukhan, *Secrets of Daniel* (Hagerstown, MD: Review and Herald, 2000), 129, observes that the same parallelism exists in the text regarding the construction of Solomon's Temple: the construction takes place in seven stages and ends with the same expression, "finished the work" (1 Kgs 7:40).

[67] Davidson, "Cosmic Metanarrative for the Coming Millennium," 108–111; idem, *Flame of Yahweh*, 47, 57.

[68] John H. Walton, *The Lost World of Genesis One* (Downers Grove, IL: InterVarsity, 2009), 72–92.

[69] John H. Walton, *Ancient Near Eastern Thought and the Old Testament: Introducing the Conceptual World of the Hebrew Bible* (Grand Rapids, MI: Baker, 2006), 127.

[70] Walton, *The Lost World of Genesis One*, 92.

[71] Ibid., 146.

The reason for this complexity is not just because of the distinct nature of the two entities—non-physical versus physical—but also because of the interrelated meaning that the pentateuchal text ascribes to both institutions. Both the Sabbath and the sanctuary are exclusively under YHWH's authority and connected, as shown by the words, "You shall keep my Sabbaths and revere my sanctuary; I am YHWH" (Lev 19:30; cf. 26:2).

The Sabbath commandment in Exodus 31:12-17 reflects reasoning, passion, effect, substance, motivation, caring, and mentoring. This passage communicates basic information about Sabbath keeping, but overtones of potential character transformation engage the Sabbath observer in the covenantal meaning of the holy day. Several themes appear in the text that set this Sabbath commandment apart from others: (1) the Sabbath concludes the instructions given to Moses for the building of the sanctuary, (2) the Sabbath is called a sign of the Sabbath observer's sanctification by the Lord (Exod 31:13), (3) the Sabbath marks the enduring covenant relationship between the Lord and the Sabbath observer (Exod 31:13, 16-17), and (4) the one who infringes the Sabbath is placed under the penalty of death and will be cut off from the community of the people of Israel (Exod 31:14-15).

A careful analysis of the sanctuary pericope (Exod 25-40) discloses the interconnectedness between the Sabbath and the sanctuary in the form of a chiastic structure. The building instructions for the sanctuary and the report of its construction are divided into two main sections in the book of Exodus. The building instructions are found in Exodus 25:1-31:17 and consist of seven speeches of YHWH with the Sabbath commandment in the seventh speech (Exod 31:12-17). The construction report is in Exodus 35:1-40:38 and begins with the Sabbath commandment in Exodus 35:1-3. Thus, Propp is right in recognizing that the two Sabbath commandments (Exod 31:12-17; 35:1-3) constitute the hinge of the whole sanctuary pericope in the book of Exodus.[72]

    A Sanctuary building instructions (Exod 25:1-31:11)
        B Sabbath commandment (Exod 31:12-17)
        B¹ Sabbath commandment (Exod 35:1-3)
    A¹ Sanctuary building constructions (Exod 35:4-40:38)

In order to understand the connection between the Sabbath and the sanctuary, it is important to find the reason for the need of the sanctuary, since the Sabbath had already existed since creation. In Exodus 25-31, the Lord reveals to Moses not only the divine pattern and model for the building and its services, but also, most importantly, its purpose: "that I may dwell

---

[72] Propp, *Exodus 19-40*, 692.

among them" (Exod 25:8). In addition, the sanctuary will be a meeting place for God with human beings (Exod 25:22). The aspect of meeting is foreign to other ancient temple buildings where humans were to build temples as relaxation and resting places for the gods but not as meeting places.

A closer look into the text gives details on the aspect of meeting that will occur between the Lord and humans. There will take place a specific meeting between the Lord and Moses in front of the Ark of the Testimony (Exod 25:22; 30:6). Another meeting will then take place between the Lord and the people of Israel in front of the bronze altar in the outer court of the sanctuary (Exod 29:42–43). Linguistic parallels between Exodus 25:22 and 30:6 are striking and suggest that the reference to the individual meeting in the beginning and at the end of the first speech needs to be seen in terms of a parallel structuring of this section in the sanctuary pericope.

In support of a parallel structuring of the individual meeting is the placement of the meeting with the whole congregation. The reference about the congregational meeting occurs in between the two references to the individual meeting, which frame and highlight the congregational meeting.

   A Individual meeting in front of the ark of the testimony:
      "There I will meet with you [singular]" (Exod 25:22)
     X Congregational meeting in front of the bronze altar:
        "I will meet with you [plural] there" (Exod 29:42–43)
   A¹ Individual meeting in front of the ark of the testimony:
      "Where I will meet with you [singular]" (Exod 30:6)

In light of the two different meetings where God speaks to Moses and gives him commandments to deliver to Israel, the link between the Sabbath and the sanctuary is supported by several intertextual aspects. First, except for the call to raise funds for the building of the sanctuary (Exod 25:1), it is only in the seventh speech where Moses has the explicit task of speaking to the people of Israel (Exod 31:13). Thus, the first and seventh speeches correspond to each other in Moses' task to directly speak to the people about the building of the sanctuary (Exod 25:1) and about the Sabbath (Exod 31:12–13). Second, in the individual meeting between the Lord and Moses, the task to speak to the people is made clear with reference to what Moses is to transmit—namely, the Lord's commandments for Israel. Third, the seventh speech in Exodus 31:12–17 stresses its importance by the unusual use of the adverbial particle "indeed, surely" that introduces the Sabbath commandment: "indeed, my Sabbaths you shall keep" (Exod 31:13). Fourth, after the Israelites have recuperated from the crisis with the golden calf, Moses gathers the congregation, and the first word he speaks is not about the sanctuary but about the Sabbath (Exod 35:1–3).

In light of the literary and conceptual aspects, it can be concluded that the Sabbath in Exodus 31:12–17 is the goal towards which the sanctuary will be built, similar to the creation Sabbath, which stands as the ultimate goal of the six creation days. The Sabbath linked to the sanctuary calls for observance of the holy day of rest under the aspect of the sanctifying act of the Lord in the life of the Sabbath observer. This act suggests a transformation from within, a transformation of the heart that occurs within the sphere of a personal encounter with God.

The text about the building of the sanctuary in the wilderness is divided into two sections: instructions to build the sanctuary (Exod 25–31) and construction reports of the sanctuary (Exod 35–40). In between these two sections occurs the record about the golden calf crisis (Exod 32–34). However, what deserves one's full attention in reading these chapters is the fact that Israel's most rebellious moment in the wilderness is framed by God's most sacred moment in time, the "Sabbath of Sabbaths holy to the Lord" (Exod 31:12–17; 35:1–3). The significance of the Sabbath in this context concerning God's desire to dwell in the midst of human depravity is incomparable in the Hebrew Bible.

Holiness is the very essence of both the Sabbath (Gen 2:3; Exod 31:13–14) and the sanctuary (Exod 29:44), not merely in terms of an abstract idea of a day or an edifice in space, but in the sense of a restored creation. The holiness of the Sabbath and of the sanctuary originates in the Creator God, who sanctified both the Sabbath (Gen 2:3) and the sanctuary (Exod 29:44; 40:34), with the purpose to enter and live within a personal relationship with human beings. Holiness within the divine-human relationship may be described as God's "absolute selflessness" in order to "give everything of Himself."[73] It speaks of God who ceased all His work in order to dedicate all of Himself to the world that He had created, to be present, dwell, and live in the world, and to make Himself available and accessible. The human being, then, is called to observe the Sabbath and revere the sanctuary (Lev 19:30; 26:2).

The Sabbath observer's sanctification is bound up with the word "know" (Exod 31:13). To know the Lord denotes the basic concept of an intimate divine-human relationship between God and the Sabbath observer.[74] This relationship is based upon the saving act of the Lord (Exod 20:2)

---

[73] Shapiro, "The Meaning of Holiness," 58.

[74] See, among a wealth of references, Exodus 33:12, 17; Deuteronomy 13:3[4]; Psalm 139:23;

and calls for a response on the part of the human being in direct relation to the Sabbath (Exod 31:16): The Sabbath observer, who "knows" the Lord as his or her Sanctifier, responds by "making" the Sabbath an everlasting covenantal bond.

Leviticus 19:3, 30; 23:3; 24:1–9

In Leviticus 19, under the mandate of holiness, religious life intersects with proper social behavior, which, according to one scholar, are "two dimensions of life that were never meant to be regarded as separate."[75] Sabbath keeping is linked to the command to respect one's parents: "Every one of you shall fear/revere/respect his mother and his father, and you shall keep my Sabbaths; I am YHWH your God" (Lev 19:3). The Sabbath commandment appears again in the chapter, but is now related to the sanctuary: "You shall keep my Sabbaths and revere my sanctuary; I am YHWH" (Lev 19:30; cf. 26:2). Leviticus 19:3 reverses the order set up in the Decalogue by placing reverence toward the parents before the command of Sabbath keeping. While this creates an intertextual chiasm between the two books, Exodus and Leviticus,[76] the chiastic relationship in Leviticus 19 between verses 3 and 30 is significant in terms of the Sabbath's central position between the human and the divine realms:

    A Revere (*yare'*) mother and father (Lev 19:3)
       B Keep (*shamar*) YHWH's Sabbath (Lev 19:3)
       B¹ Keep (*shamar*) YHWH's Sabbath (Lev 19:30)
    A¹ Revere (*yare'*) YHWH's sanctuary (Lev 19:30)

Leviticus 23, the chapter that records the annual festival calendar, places the Sabbath commandment in a prominent and distinct position. The Sabbath is framed by two calls to proclaim the "appointed times of YHWH" and the "holy convocations," "assemblies,"[77] or "proclamations of holiness" (*miqra' qodhesh*)[78] for the people of Israel. The first call in verse 2 may be understood to introduce the entire festival year, with the weekly Sabbath

---

Nahum 1:7, which show the biblical understanding of divine-human relationship. Cf. G. J. Botterweck, "ידע *yada'*," *TDOT* 5:468–470.

[75] Baruch E. Levine, *Leviticus: The Traditional Hebrew Text with the New JPS Translation*, JPSTC (Philadelphia, PA: Jewish Publication Society, 1989), xv.

[76] Gane, *Leviticus, Numbers*, 335.

[77] *HALOT* 1:629.

[78] Jacob Milgrom, *Numbers: The Traditional Hebrew Text with the New JPS Translation*, JPSTC (Philadelphia, PA: Jewish Publication Society, 1990), 63–64.

as the source and basis for the festivals. The second call in verse 4 then introduces the six annual festivals.[79] The distinguished place of the Sabbath comes also with the language used in the original text about ceasing from the work of the weekdays, connecting the Sabbath to God's ceasing from the work on the creation Sabbath (Gen 2:2–3).

There may be three reasons for the prominence and inclusion of the Sabbath in the festival calendar: (1) the people's faithful observance of the Sabbath would establish the pattern for their faithful observance of the festivals, (2) the Sabbath plays a role in determining the time for the celebration of the feasts of weeks (Lev 23:15–16), and (3) the laws on Sabbath observance carry over to special solemn days during the feasts.[80] Here, the Day of Atonement is of high significance, because it is the only day of the cultic festivals that requires cessation from all work, like the weekly Sabbath. In addition to that, the Day of Atonement is a "Sabbath of Sabbaths" or "Sabbath of solemn rest" (*shabbath shabbathon*) (Lev 16:31; 23:32) like the weekly Sabbath (Exod 31:15; 35:2; Lev 23:3).

Leviticus 24:1–9 follows the record of the annual festival cycle with the details for lighting the lampstand (Lev 24:1–4) and the weekly Sabbath provision of bread for the golden table in the outer sanctum of the sanctuary (Lev 24:5–9). These rites provided Israel with powerful symbols about God's dwelling in their midst. The combination of the daily lighting of the lampstand and the bread constantly on the table associated with the burning of incense impresses the fact that the Lord had truly taken up residence in the tabernacle. "If there is a lamp burning, incense burning and bread on the table, then someone is 'home.'"[81] Roy Gane further develops the idea of the Creator-in-residence in relation to the bread of the Presence.[82] The regular changing of the bread once a week on the Sabbath day limits the anthropomorphism of God usually involved in the idea of divine residence. While the Babylonian god received daily meals in the temple accompanied by libations, the Israelite priest performed the ritual of bread-laying only once a week on the specific day of the Sabbath (Exod 25:30; Lev 24:8) without any libation rituals.[83]

---

[79] See Gane's structure of Leviticus 23 in *Leviticus, Numbers*, 387.

[80] John E. Hartley, *Leviticus*, WBC (Dallas, TX: Word, 1992), 372.

[81] Richard E. Averbeck, "Tabernacle," *Dictionary of the Old Testament: Pentateuch*, ed. David W. Baker and T. Desmond Alexander (Downers Grove, IL: InterVarsity, 2003), 815.

[82] Roy Gane, "'Bread of the Presence' and Creator-in-Residence," *VT* 42 (1992): 179–203.

[83] Ibid., 202.

Furthermore, the bread of the Presence is a covenant similar to the Sabbath (Exod 31:16) and pointed to the "eternal covenant" (Exod 31:8) between God and Israel (cf. Ps 105:10).[84] Jacob Milgrom observes that the change of the bread of the Presence every Sabbath corresponded to the change of the priestly courses and temple guards, which also took place on the Sabbath (2 Kgs 11:4–9; 2 Chr 23:4–6).[85] The old bread loaves were eaten partly by the priests who came into the temple and started their service and partly by the priests who went out of the temple when they had finished their service.[86] In Milgrom's perspective, Sabbath is both a sign and a covenant and by implication the bread loaves changed every Sabbath are a sign and a covenant. The twelve bread loaves show that they are a "pledge of the covenant between the twelve tribes and the Lord."[87]

The book of Numbers mentions one more ritual connection between the Sabbath and the sanctuary. In addition to the daily morning and evening burnt offerings, on the Sabbath two more male lambs were to be sacrificed as burnt offerings (Num 28:9–10). The sacrificial calendar in Numbers 28–29 largely parallels the annual festival calendar in Leviticus 23, but also fills in specifications for additional sacrifices on some of the feast days.[88] Gane observes that the number seven is prominent in the listing of the offerings and suggests that the festival days of the Israelite calendar "are, in a sense, extensions of the weekly Sabbath."[89]

The theological implications of the Sabbath-sanctuary link flow from the two regulations—the bread of the Presence and the additional sacrifices for the Sabbath. These two regulations show that the Pentateuch

---

[84] Gordon J. Wenham, *The Book of Leviticus*, NICOT (Grand Rapids, MI: Eerdmans, 1979), 310.

[85] Milgrom, *Leviticus 23–27*, 2094 (cf. *m. Ta'an.* 4:2; *b. Ta'an.* 27a–b).

[86] Milgrom, *Leviticus 23–27*, 2098 (cf. *b. Suk.* 56a; *Sipra* Emor 18:8; *m. Menah.* 11:7; 11QT 8:11).

[87] Roland de Vaux, *Ancient Israel: Its Life and Institutions* (New York: McGraw-Hill, 1961), 422; cf. Milgrom, *Leviticus 23–27*, 2094. The intricate structuring of Sabbath commandments in the book of Leviticus relating to sanctuary rituals that include food presents a perspective on the Sabbath-sanctuary link that in the past has received little consideration by biblical scholars: Sabbath and sanctuary are connected over food. The identical wording in Leviticus 19:30 and 26:2, "You shall keep my Sabbaths and revere my sanctuary; I am YHWH," frames a section in the book of Leviticus that to a large extent deals with matters of food. The regulations in Leviticus 21–22 identify holiness of the priesthood in relation to the holy food offerings of God at the sanctuary (Lev 21:6, 8, 17, 21–22; 22:25). The same laws regulate food consumption of the priests and a layman's unintentional eating of the food reserved for the priests (Lev 21:22; 22:4, 6–8, 10–14, 16, 30).

[88] Milgrom, *Leviticus 23–27*, 750–754.

[89] Ibid., 754.

establishes the Sabbath not only as a "household observance,"[90] but also as a day of worship for the entire community within the cultic system of the sanctuary. However, it is interesting to note that the cultic regulations for the Sabbath in the sanctuary are scanty when compared with the festivals of the Israelite calendar with its substantial and diverse rituals.[91]

The laying of the bread of the Presence acknowledges that God is Israel's gracious host who generously provides food for the people and cares in a special way for the needy: the poor, the stranger, the slave, and the animal. Sabbath receives the character of a hospitable institution. Everybody is invited to rest and be refreshed. Food is a gift for all, because God, the host of the feast, freely imparts it.

Furthermore, the Sabbath's festive banquet table endorses the "everlasting covenant" concept between God and Israel that Exodus 31:16 proclaims. Milgrom puts it this way: "Israel's everlasting obligation to supply the grain for the bread becomes a ritual demonstration that it eternally pledges itself anew to uphold the covenant."[92] On the other hand there is God, the host of the covenant meal, who provides the food and so every Sabbath pledges Himself anew to uphold the covenant. This divine-human relationship, first established in creation times by the divine gift of food on the sixth day of creation (Gen 1:29), is complemented at the table of God inside the sanctuary. The relationship is renewed and maintained every Sabbath. God dines with people on the Sabbath.

Deuteronomy 5:12–15

Biblical scholars have recognized the sermonic and hortatory character of Deuteronomy 5:1–33[93] and speak of the oral nature of this text, which interacts with other legal texts in order to speak in relevant terms to the new generation of Israel in the plains of Moab. The oral character of the Decalogue in Deuteronomy 5:6–21 may help in understanding the changed formulations and additions that occur specifically in the Sabbath commandment, such as "observe," "as the Lord your God has commanded you," "your ox," "your donkey," and "all your livestock" (Deut 5:12–14) and

---

[90] Lowery, *Sabbath and Jubilee*, 115.

[91] Matitiahu Tsevat, "The Basic Meaning of the Biblical Sabbath," *ZAW* 84.4 (1972): 456.

[92] Milgrom, *Leviticus 23–27*, 2100.

[93] J. W. Marshall, "Decalogue," *Dictionary of the Old Testament: Pentateuch*, ed. David W. Baker and T. Desmond Alexander (Downers Grove, IL: InterVarsity, 2003), 172; and Stephen K. Sherwood, *Leviticus, Numbers, Deuteronomy*, Berit Olam: Studies in Narrative & Poetry (Collegeville, PA: Liturgical, 2002), 202.

may be understood as a form of contextualization, rather than contradictions to Exodus 20:8-11.[94]

The greatest difference between Exodus 20:8-11 and Deuteronomy 5:12-15 concerns the part that is regarded as the motivation clause for Sabbath observance. The Sabbath commandment in Deuteronomy seems to replace the focus on creation and God's rest on the seventh day (Exod 20:11) with Israel's deliverance from Egypt (Deut 5:15).

Already in the introduction to the Decalogue in Deuteronomy, Moses focused on the applicability of the covenant and the covenant law for the new generation: "not with our fathers, . . . but with us, with all those alive here today" (Deut 5:3). In addition, the deliverance motivation suggests that Israel is urged to observe the Sabbath because of their liberation from Egypt, which implies letting others rest on this day. As has already been pointed out, the deliverance motivation for the Sabbath features prominently in the Sabbath commandment of the Covenant Code (Exod 23:12), a text that contains the motif of God's compassionate interest in the liberation of the oppressed. Furthermore, the Sabbath commandment in Exodus 20:8-11 has at its basis a direct connection with the exodus (the infinitive absolute *zakhor*, "remember," introduces both the Sabbath and the Passover; Exod 13:3) and with God as the "Lord who brought you out of the land of Egypt, out of the house of slavery" (Exod 20:2). Therefore, the deliverance motivation clause in Deuteronomy 5:15 is not a new aspect or contradictory to the creation motif in Exodus 20:11, but applies creation themes such as rest, freedom, and equality into the actual life situation of the new generation of Israel.[95]

The Sabbath commandment in Deuteronomy 5:12-15 addresses the Israelite as a human being delivered from slavery in Egypt and calls everyone to remember his or her personal deliverance and therefore observe

---

[94] The term "legal innovation" has been used for terminological changes such as the ones in Deuteronomy 5:626. See Bernard M. Levinson, "'Du sollst nichts hinzufügen und nichts wegnehmen' (Dtn 13,1): Rechtsreform und Hermeneutic in der Hebräischen Bibel," *ZTK* 103 (2006): 157-183; idem, "'You Must Not Add Anything to What I Command You': Paradoxes of Canon and Authorship in Ancient Israel," *Numen* 53 (2003): 1-53; idem, *Deuteronomy and the Hermeneutics of Legal Innovation* (New York: Oxford University Press, 1997); cf. Gerald A. Klingbeil, "Looking over the Shoulders of Ancient Translators: Contextualization and Ancient Translation Techniques," in *Misión y contextualización, Llevar el mensaje bíblico a un mundo multicultural*, ed. Gerald A. Klingbeil (Libertador San Martin: Editorial Universidad Adventista del Plata, 2005), 3-21.

[95] Moshe Weinfeld, *Deuteronomy 1-11*, AB (New York: Doubleday, 1991), 309, draws the attention to what he labels the humanistic tendency in the book of Deuteronomy that may be recognized in texts such as Deuteronomy 15:15; 16:12; 24:18, 22. See also Moshe Weinfeld, *Deuteronomy and the Deuteronomic School* (Oxford: Clarendon, 1983), 282-297.

the Sabbath to keep it holy. The individual Israelite delivered from slavery experienced a new beginning marked by the gift of freedom and Sabbath rest. He or she is in a way a new creation similar to the first created human being in Genesis 1:26–29.

The liberation of Israel out of the land of Egypt is the starting point of a new creation similar to the creation of the human race (Gen 1–2). Israel, as a liberated people, is God's new creation. This concept occurs frequently in the prophets and is often associated with the new creation after the exile (e.g., Isa 40:26; 42:5; 43:1, 7, 15; Mal 2:10). This new creation is rooted in God's election of Abraham and his family (Gen 12:1–3). In this sense, the Sabbath links the cosmic creation of the world to the establishment of a people who are to reflect the image and holiness of God (Exod 19:6).

The Sabbath commandment addresses the individual Israelite with the appeal of the law that has its place in the heart and calls to love the Lord "with all your heart and with all your soul and with all your might" (Deut 6:5). It is this same law of the heart that reminds of, and asks obedience to, all of God's commands, including Sabbath observance aiming for Sabbath holiness. In following the law out of love for the Creator, the new created human being will receive the gift of Sabbath rest and Sabbath holiness and imitate the Creator's Sabbath observance, which testifies to the holiness of this day and to the sanctifying power of the God of the Sabbath.

The Sabbath's significance is emphasized by Deuteronomy's Sabbath commandment, which is a reiteration by Moses after the establishment of the Levitical priesthood. The Sabbath commandment in Deuteronomy 5:12–15 contains a more detailed list than that of Exodus 20:8–11 in that it distinguishes nine individuals ("you, your son, your daughter, your male servant, your female servant, your ox, your donkey, all your cattle, and your stranger") and places emphasis on the clause "your male servant and your female servant may rest as well as you" by repeating it (Deut 5:14). Furthermore, the importance of this list lies in the act of remembering that Israel is a nation saved from slavery. The bonds of a world of dominance and hierarchical power are broken, and Israel is called to witness to this event by its weekly Sabbath celebrations with the message of equality and inclusion to all human beings and animals living in the surroundings of the Sabbath keeper. The Sabbath tells the Israelite man and woman that each is set free from the bonds of any kind of slavery. He or she exists as a human being in direct relation to God, and each individual is placed into relational bonds with others with the same privileges, rights, status, and opportunities.

Finally, the Sabbath commandment reminds us that the day, in the sense of created time, belongs to the Creator God. The sentence "but the seventh day is the Sabbath of the Lord, your God" (Exod 20:10a; Deut 5:14a) is a reminder of lordship and ownership and again points back to creation. This insight has much to say in today's contemporary culture where time is too often identified with accomplishments, and the individual is measured by his or her achievements. God has a different way of computing, measuring, and categorizing time. His creation laws are recognized in a rhythm of time that is distinct from our own perception and life in a modern or postmodern world.

Summary and Conclusion

To portray the majestic entrance of God into the new, perfect, and beautiful planet earth, the writer of the creation account in Genesis 1:1–2:3 utilizes stylistic balance and coherent symmetry. Although the divine introduction of the Sabbath in Genesis 2:1–3 omits the usual reference to "evening and morning" that appears with each of the preceding weekdays, the Sabbath is clearly identified as the seventh day of the creation week. Without adding divine action or approval, this Sabbath text expresses completion of all creation activity. God's cessation from all work becomes the signature of the seventh day and the prerequisite for blessing and holiness. The Creator's sanctifying affirmation of the cyclical Sabbath stands out as a remarkable sign of God's constant presence in the world. From now on, divine life will overflow into the world's days, weeks, and times and will assure the gift of life, embedded in the context of the divine-human relationship for all future to come.

Recounting divine engagement with a disordered and desolate world, Exodus 16 tells of Israel's struggle for existence in a seemingly disordered and unbalanced narrative. When God intervenes in the wilderness, jars are filled with food to sustain life on the Sabbath, even though open country remains empty (Exod 16:31, 35; Ps 78:24–25). In addition, the miracle of the Sabbath manna testifies to the Creator God, who stops decay of this food only on Sabbath. While the manna, the sweet-tasting "bread," remains a mystery and a miracle throughout the forty years of the people's wanderings, the Sabbath establishes the rhythm of their lives and becomes a testing marker in God's formula $6 + 1 =$ life (Exod 16:26, 29–30). Thus, to a people struggling for existence in a chaotic and barren world, God offers the rhythmic order of time identified by the Sabbath as the means for the divine gift of life.

For divine holiness to be present in Israelite homes and become part of familial bonds and work-related connections, the Pentateuch promotes a body of Sabbath laws within the formal stipulations of the divine-human covenant relationship (Exod 20:8–11; 23:12; Deut 5:12–15). The Sabbath becomes a sign/marker of this covenant with the nation of Israel, which is based on the patriarchal covenant. The covenant, then, builds the foundation for Sabbath laws in the Pentateuch. Rather than regulating the course of the seventh day or prescribing formal procedures or rites regarding its observance, the Sabbath laws simply call for rest to promote the well-being of the Sabbath observer within the relational bonds of the household, which include all members, regardless of their status in society, and even animals. In addition, the Sabbath laws establish the link to the creation Sabbath and promote its universal and inclusive nature on the basis of the creation week.

The Sabbath laws in Exodus (20:8–11; 23:12) and Deuteronomy (5:12–15) imply that when God's people follow His instructions to allow everyone to rest on the Sabbath, this egalitarian Sabbath rest preserves identity and relationships, and the Sabbath observer's work emulates the Creator's work. The Sabbath attests the sacredness of human beings, without a trace of favoritism, equally touching the lives of the Sabbath observer and his dependents, regardless of their gender, rank, and position. The Sabbath becomes God's personal pledge of identity to the Sabbath observer, who is identified in direct relation to "YHWH your God" (Exod 20:2, 10; Deut 5:6, 12, 14–15). The Sabbath is God's guarantee of particular concern for the most oppressed and exploited in society (Exod 23:12), and His declaration of active involvement in human and animal rights (Exod 23:12; 31:17).

The fact that the Sabbath laws employ anthropomorphic and anthropopathic terms when referring to God's experience, such as God "rested on the seventh day" (Exod 20:10) and "was refreshed" (Exod 31:17), conveys personal relationship and deep affinity that connects God as the Creator and Redeemer with humanity and all creation. This implies an ecological dimension: as a sign that celebrates God's work of creation, it promotes covenantal responsibility toward the environment. It calls for a holistic world that recognizes the Creator's concern for its well-being, including justice and peace for all creatures. Opposing exploitation, the Sabbath calls for compassion and responsibility toward others, especially the disadvantaged.

Although God's earthly dwelling was constructed in an infertile and desolate place, the biblical text describes it with language that evokes the perfectly created world. Studies on Exodus 25–40 have demonstrated the link between the creation Sabbath and the building of the sanctuary. This link shows that the creation Sabbath inspires, motivates, and sets the framework for YHWH's house in the wilderness so that life will be ensured in a desolate world marked by death. The contextual arrangement of the passages dealing with the building of the sanctuary implies that the Sabbath deeply affects the Israelites' attitude toward the construction of the sanctuary (Exod 35:20–29).

The magnificent design of the sanctuary is fit for YHWH, who fills its precincts with His glory (Exod 40:34–38). His rationale for the building of the sanctuary is to meet with human beings and communicate His will to them (Exod 25:22). From the details of the text in Exodus 25–31, this study has demonstrated that the Sabbath in Exodus 31:12–17 is the subject matter between YHWH and the human being. The relational aspect of the Sabbath within this context emerges from two aspects of the Sabbath: (1) a sign of sanctification provided by YHWH ("I am YHWH your sanctifier" [Exod 31:13]), and (2) a sign of the everlasting covenant ("it [the Sabbath as an everlasting covenant] is a sign between me and you" [Exod 31:16]). The Sabbath observer becomes aware of the meaning of the Sabbath inside YHWH's sacred dwelling: divine presence in the world, empathy with mortal human beings, and the transformation of sanctification.

The main theological aspect of the Sabbath in the Pentateuch may be summarized as follows: The Sabbath encapsulates and reveals God's presence in the world, regardless of its nature and condition. The Sabbath was introduced by divine cessation from work in order for holiness to enter the world for the benefit of all humanity. Holiness is the essence of the divine-human relationship, which enables human beings to fully become what they were created to be: the image of the Creator. In its rhythmic recurrence, the Sabbath signifies the Creator's constant presence in the world and His care for it. Since the fall into sin, the Sabbath has liberated people from oppressive regimes of man-made gods; it places them in proper relationships with each other; it relieves their attitude toward work in a society exhausted and stressed by hard labor; and it testifies to the sacred design in time and space whereby they can recognize and emulate the Maker of all. Thus, the Sabbath is an important part of God's program for restoring *imago Dei* in fallen human beings.

CHAPTER 2

The Sabbath in the Decalogue: Creation and Liberation as a Paradigm for Community

Gerald A. Klingbeil

Introduction

In 2007, during a congress of European Seventh-day Adventist professors of religion and theology,[1] my wife Chantal and I were walking through the town center of Wittenberg and came across a prominent and fascinating sticker on the side window of a parked vehicle. It read, "Without Sunday there would only be work-days."[2] The sticker was sponsored by the German Lutheran Church and highlighted the increasing importance of Sabbath (or rather Sunday) rest in contemporary (Protestant and Catholic) theology, often associated with issues of creation, ethics, stewardship, ecological responsibility, or community and fellowship, and rooted in texts found in the Hebrew Bible.[3] Over the past

---

[1] The congress was held from March 29–April 1, 2007 at Theologische Hochschule Friedensau, Germany under the theme "Finding the 'World' in Theology: Empirical Dimensions in the Study of Faith."

[2] In German: "Ohne Sonntag gibt's nur noch Werktage."

[3] For some examples, see Josef Scharbert, "Biblischer Sabbat und modernes Wochenende," in *Die alttestamentliche Botschaft als Wegweisung: Festschrift für Heinz Reinelt*, ed. Josef Zmijewski (Stuttgart: Verlag Katholisches Bibelwerk, 1990), 285–306; Stanley L. Jaki, "The Sabbath-Rest of the Maker of All," *AsTJ* 50 (1995): 37–49; Stanley J. Grenz, "Burnout: The Cause and the Cure for a Christian Malady," *CurTM* 26 (1999): 425–430; Dorothy C. Bass, "Rediscovering the Sabbath," *Christianity Today* 41 (1997): 39–43; idem, "Receiving the Day the Lord Has Made," *Christianity Today* 44.3 (2000): 63–67; William P. Brown, "'Whatever Your Hand Finds to Do': Qoheleth's Work Ethic," *Interpretation* 55.3 (2001): 271–284; Belden C. Lane, "Holy Silence," *Christian Century*

two decades there have appeared an increasing number of important studies dealing with distinct aspects of the biblical Sabbath, authored by Christian and Jewish scholars, suggesting a renewed interest in relevant exegetical, historical, and, above all, conceptual and theological aspects of the biblical Sabbath.[4] In

---

118.29 (2001): 24–27; and Friedhelm Hartenstein, "Der Sabbat als Zeichen und heilige Zeit: Zur Theologie des Ruhetages im Alten Testament," *JBT* 18 (2003): 103–131. Most of these studies seem to perform a mental leap by considering the content and practice of Sabbath worship in the OT and infusing these into the Christian Sunday.

[4] Some of these include (chronologically) Jacques Briend, "Le sabbat en Jr 17, 19–27," in *Mélanges bibliques et orientaux en l'honneur de M. Mathias Delcor*, ed. André Caquot, S. Légasse and M. Tardieu (Neukirchen-Vluyn: Neukirchener, 1985), 23–35; Samuele Bacchiocchi, "Sabbatical Typologies of Messianic Redemption," *JSJ* 17 (1987): 153–176; Israel Knohl, "The Priestly Torah Versus the Holiness School: Sabbath and the Festivals," *HUCA* 58 (1987): 65–117; Gerhard F. Hasel, "'New Moon and Sabbath' in Eighth Century Israelite Prophetic Writings (Isa 1:13; Hos 2:13; Amos 8:5)," in *'Wünscht Jerusalem Frieden': Collected Communications to the XVth Congress of the International Organization for the Study of the Old Testament, Jerusalem 1986*, ed. M. Augustin and K. D. Schunck (Frankfurt: Peter Lang, 1988), 37–64; Tamara C. Eshkenazi, Daniel J. Harrington, and William H. Shea, eds., *The Sabbath in Jewish and Christian Traditions* (New York: Crossroads, 1991); Duane L. Christensen, "Jonah and the Sabbath Rest in the Pentateuch," in *Biblische Theologie und gesellschaftlicher Wandel: Für Norbert Lohfink*, ed. Georg Braulik, Walter Groß, and Sean E. McEvenue (Freiburg: Herder, 1993), 48–60; Heather A. McKay, *Sabbath and Synagogue: The Question of Sabbath Worship in Ancient Judaism* (Leiden: Brill, 1994); William H. Shea, "Sargon's Azekah Inscription: The Earliest Extrabiblical Reference to the Sabbath?" *AUSS* 32 (1994): 247–251; Bernard Gosse, "Les rédactions liées à la mention du sabbat dans le Deutéronome et dans le livre d'Ésaïe," *ETR* 70 (1995): 581–585; Guy L. Robbins, Jr., *"And in the Seventh Day"* (New York: Peter Lang, 1995); Yong-Eui Yang, *Jesus and the Sabbath in Matthew's Gospel* (Sheffield: Sheffield Academic Press, 1997); Lutz Doering, *Schabbat: Sabbathalacha und -praxis im antiken Judentum und Urchristentum* (Tübingen: Mohr Siebeck, 1999); Roy Gane, "Sabbath and the New Covenant," *JATS* 10.1–2 (1999): 311–332; Niels-Erik Andreasen, "Sabbath and Synagogue: Postexilic Israelite Religion," in *Creation, Life, and Hope, Essays in Honor of Jacques B. Doukhan*, ed. Jiří Moskala (Berrien Springs, MI: Theological Seminary, Andrews University, 2000), 233–250; James Hilton, "From Sabbath to Lord's Day: Examining the Ethics of Sunday," *Faith and Mission* 17.3 (2000): 65–78; H. R. Cole, "The Sabbath and the Alien," *AUSS* 38 (2000): 223–229; Klaas A. D. Smelik, "The Creation of the Sabbath (Gen 1:1–2:3)," in *Unless Some One Guide Me: Festschrift for Karel A. Deurloo*, ed. Janet W. Dyk et al. (Maastricht: Shaker, 2001), 9–11; Leszek Ruszkowski, "Der Sabbat bei Tritojesaja," in *Prophetie und Psalmen: Festschrift für Klaus Seybold zum 65 Geburtstag*, ed. Beat Huwyler, Hans-Peter Mathys, and Beat Weber (Münster: Ugarit-Verlag, 2001), 61–74; Gerard Rouwhorst, "The Reception of the Jewish Sabbath in Early Christianity," in *Christian Feast and Festival: The Dynamics of Western Liturgy and Culture*, ed. Paul Post et al. (Leuven: Peeters, 2001), 223–266; Rüdiger Bartelmus, "Sabbat und Arbeitsruhe im Alten Testament," in *Auf der Suche nach dem archimedischen Punkt der Textinterpretation: Studien zu einer philologisch-linguistisch fundierten Exegese alttestamentlicher Texte*, ed. Rüdiger Bartelmus (Zürich: Pano, 2002), 159–200; Bruce Chilton, *Redeeming Time: The Wisdom of Ancient Jewish and Christian Festal Calendars* (Peabody, MA: Hendrickson, 2002); Pinchas Kahn, "The Expanding Perspectives of the Sabbath," *JBQ* 32 (2004): 239–244; Shubert Spero, "Shabbat: Three Stages in Israel's Experience," *JBQ* 32 (2004): 167–170; Henry Sturcke, *Encountering the Rest of God: How Jesus Came to Personify the Sabbath* (Zürich: Theologischer Verlag Zürich, 2005); Markus Bockmuehl, "'Keeping It Holy': Old Testament Commandment

Seventh-day Adventist scholarship the last major scholarly study of the Sabbath dates back to 1982 and had been in the works for many years prior to its publication. Due to the particular interests and expertise of the editor, one notes a significant historical focus of the contributions. The discussion of the Sabbath in the Hebrew Bible was divided into two distinct chapters ("The Sabbath in the Pentateuch" and "The Sabbath in the Prophetic and Historical Literature of the Old Testament") and covered only thirty-five pages.[5] Considering the increase in publications about different aspects of the biblical Sabbath and the quarter century of research and publications that passed since the publication of this work on the Sabbath, it is high time to revisit the issue of the biblical Sabbath.[6]

This study is rather limited and focuses on the Sabbath in the Decalogue (Exod 20:8–11; Deut 5:12–15). First a concise introduction to the locus (textual, structural, historical, and theological) of the Sabbath command in the Decalogue is attempted. This is followed by some reflections and considerations as to the differences between the two forms of the Decalogue in Exodus and Deuteronomy. The next section deals in more detail with Exodus 20:8–11 and seeks to establish intertextual links to creation. Furthermore, this study pays attention to the ritual elements and holiness language associated with the biblical Sabbath command. The following section focuses

---

and New Testament Faith," in *I Am the Lord Your God: Christian Reflections on the Ten Commandments*, ed. Carl E. Braaten and Christopher R. Seitz (Grand Rapids, MI: Eerdmans, 2005), 95–124; Asher Eder, "The Sabbath: To Remember, to Observe, to Make," *JBQ* 34 (2006): 104–109; and Mathilde Frey, "The Sabbath Commandment in the Book of the Covenant: Ethics on Behalf of the Outcast," *JAAS* 9 (2006): 3–11.

[5] The relevant chapters are Gerhard F. Hasel, "The Sabbath in the Pentateuch," in *The Sabbath in Scripture and History*, ed. Kenneth A. Strand (Washington, DC: Review & Herald, 1982), 21–43; and Gerhard F. Hasel and W. G. C. Murdoch, "The Sabbath in the Prophetic and Historical Literature of the Old Testament," in *The Sabbath in Scripture and History*, ed. Kenneth A. Strand (Washington, DC: Review & Herald, 1982), 44–56.

[6] The present study is part and parcel of a larger research project, organized and guided by the Biblical Research Institute of the General Conference of Seventh-day Adventists, that aims at interacting and restudying, on an academic level, relevant biblical, theological, historical, and practical aspects of the biblical Sabbath. A number of doctoral dissertations, relevant to the study of different aspects of the biblical Sabbath, have been written at Seventh-day Adventist institutions of higher learning, including Bernabe M. Atiteo, "The Sabbath as a Sign of Liberation" (MTh diss., Adventist International Institute of Advanced Studies, 1989); H. Ross Cole, "The Sacred Times Prescribed in the Pentateuch: Old Testament Indicators of the Extent of Their Applicability" (PhD diss., Andrews University, 1996); Merlin D. Burt, "The Historical Background, Interconnected Development, and Integration of the Doctrines of the Sanctuary, the Sabbath, and Ellen G. White's Role in Sabbatarian Adventism from 1844 to 1849" (PhD diss., Andrews University, 2003); and Mathilde Frey, "The Sabbath in the Pentateuch: An Exegetical and Theological Study" (PhD diss., Andrews University, 2011).

on the additional arguments for Sabbath observance that are presented in Deuteronomy 5:12–15. Finally, the main elements and arguments for Sabbath observance in the Decalogue are brought together, focusing on key theological components such as creation, liberation, community, and holiness. Due to space limitations, this study does not attempt to interact with all the available literature on the subject. Rather, it limits most scholarly interaction to the copious footnotes and focuses primarily on the data in the biblical texts themselves.

Form, Function, and Structure of the Decalogue

The narrative structure of the book of Exodus[7] employs two key elements of textual design (i.e., space and time)[8] in order to form a coherent unit.[9] The narrative begins with a flashback to Genesis and a list (involving

---

[7] The term "book" is used here very loosely. One should not forget that the Torah seems to be an integrated text. The emphasis on sources, layers of redaction, and editorial work of traditional historical criticism seems to miss this important literary, structural, and theological integration. Furthermore, in antiquity "books" did not come into existence until the invention of the codex. See the comments of William W. Hallo, *The Book of the People* (Atlanta, GA: Scholars Press, 1991), 13–16; Alan Millard, "Authors, Books, and Readers in the Ancient World," in *The Oxford Handbook of Biblical Studies*, ed. John W. Rogerson and Judith M. Lieu (Oxford: Oxford University Press, 2006), 544–564; and William M. Schniedewind, *How the Bible Became a Book: The Textualization of Ancient Israel* (Cambridge: Cambridge University Press, 2004). Concerning the literary structure and unity of the Pentateuch, see Caspar J. Labuschagne, "The Pattern of the Divine Speech Formulas in the Pentateuch," *VT* 32 (1982): 268–296 (heavily criticized in Philip R. Davies and David M. Gunn, "Pentateuchal Patterns: An Examination of C. J. Labuschagne's Theory," *VT* 34 [1984]: 399–406); Thomas W. Mann, *The Book of the Torah: The Narrative Integrity of the Pentateuch* (Atlanta, GA: John Knox, 1988); John H. Sailhamer, *The Pentateuch as Narrative: A Biblical-Theological Commentary* (Grand Rapids, MI: Zondervan, 1992), 1–3, 24, 77–78; Hendrik Koorevaar, "The Torah as One, Three or Five Books: An Introduction to the Macro-Structural Problem of the Pentateuch," *Hiphil* 3 (2006): 1–19.

[8] The author of this study argues elsewhere for the importance of movement and space in biblical narrative. See Gerald A. Klingbeil, "'Up, Down, In, Out, Through and Back': Space and Movement in Old Testament Narrative, Ritual and Legal Texts and their Application for the Study of Mark 1:1–3:12," *EstBib* 60 (2002): 283–309. Other relevant studies discussing the link between space and time in texts include Dalene Heyns, "Space and Time in Amos 7: Reconsidering the Third Vision," *OTE* 10 (1997): 27–38; Frank H. Gorman, Jr., "Priestly Rituals of Founding: Time, Space, and Status," in *History and Interpretation: Essays in Honour of John H. Hayes*, ed. M. Patrick Graham, William P. Brown, and Jeffrey K. Kuan (Sheffield: Sheffield Academic Press, 1993), 47–64; and Shimon Bar-Efrat, *Narrative Art in the Bible* (Sheffield: Sheffield Academic Press, 1989).

[9] Cf. here the comments in Arie C. Leder, "The Coherence of Exodus: Narrative Unity and Meaning," *CTJ* 36 (2001): 251–269; and earlier John I. Durham, *Exodus*, WBC (Waco, TX: Word, 1987), xx–xxiv, who laments the unfortunate tendency of the historical-critical method

significant interpretation and interaction with the stories of Genesis) of the members of the family of Jacob that came to Egypt (Exod 1:1–7).[10] Geographically, these first seven verses remind the reader of Abraham's descendants' move from Canaan to Egypt. Beginning in Exodus 1:8, the narrative zooms in and focuses on Egypt, only to refocus on Midian, northeast of Egypt, when Moses has to flee from Pharaoh after murdering the Egyptian overseer (Exod 2:11–15). The sojourn of Moses in Midian is also marked by important movement involving a well, the compound of Reuel/Jethro, and the desert where Moses hears the divine voice from the burning bush (Exod 3). Interestingly, Egypt never really disappears from the radar of the biblical storyteller, a fact easily seen in the brief references to the increased suffering of Israel in Egypt (Exod 2:23–25) and the manifold references to Egypt in the dialogue between Moses and YHWH. Once Moses has accepted the divine call and returned to Egypt, there is little movement besides the appearances before Pharaoh.

The narrative gears up for further movement once the Passover ritual is introduced (Exod 12). It is noteworthy that it is also at this crucial point that specific time is linked to location and movement to form an important literary device.[11] The moment of liberation begins at midnight (Exod 12:29) and during the night the order to leave Egypt is promulgated (Exod 12:31–36). According to Exodus 13:17–22, Israel left Egypt following a specific route (again, movement is important and getting increasingly specific).[12] After crossing the sea of reeds (Exod 14) and a number of way

---

to draw one's attention away from the "finished product" (which we have) to the ingredients (we can guess at, but do not have) and suggests a look at the larger picture and organization of Exodus.

[10] Cf. the insightful study of Andrew E. Steinmann, "Jacob's Family Goes to Egypt: Varying Portraits of Unity and Disunity in the Textual Traditions of Exodus 1:1–5," *Journal Biblical Textual Criticism* 2 (1997), http://rosetta.reltech.org/TC/vol02/ Steinmann1997.html (accessed September 10, 2007).

[11] Prior to Exodus 12:2–3 (referring to "this month" as being the first month of the year, with further explanation in v. 3 ["the tenth of this month"]), the references to time are generic. In chapter 1, an unspecified amount of time passes as Jacob's descendants' situation changes drastically. In Exodus 2, no specific time for the flight of Moses is given; verse 23 mentions "in those many days," which is not specific and absolute but relative time, describing the increased suffering of Israel. There is no specific time reference when YHWH calls Moses in Exodus 3 and, similarly, no absolute dates are mentioned for Moses' return trip to Egypt or the ten signs (= plagues).

[12] Discussion of this route can be found in Charles R. Krahmalkov, "Exodus Itinerary Confirmed by Egyptian Evidence," *BAR* 20.5 (1994): 55–62, 79; Benjamin Edidin Scolnic, "A New Working Hypothesis for the Identification of Migdol," in *The Future of Biblical Archaeology: Reassessing Methodologies and Assumptions*, ed. James K. Hoffmeier and Alan Millard (Grand Rapids, MI:

stations along the way,[13] they finally reach the desert of Sinai (Exod 19:1) and camp at the foot of the mountain. The mountain becomes an important organizing factor for the remainder of the book of Exodus, with upward and downward movements recorded repeatedly[14] and emphasizes the important theological motif of divine and human interaction that is also visible in the structure of the ten words (Ten Commandments) and the construction of the tabernacle.[15] Interestingly, it is also at the arrival at the foot of the mountain that the last specific time reference of the book of Exodus can be found ("in the third month of the coming out of the sons of Israel from Egypt, on this [very] day, they came to the desert of Sinai," Exod 19:1),[16] except for the reference marking the completion of the construction of the tabernacle in the final chapter of the book ("in the first month of the second year, on the first of the month," Exod 40:17). This suggests a time span of at least nine months at the foot of the mountain of God.

As has been observed by many commentators, a clear literary and structural unity of Exodus 19–24 exists, also including the "Book of the

---

Eerdmans, 2004), 91–120; and James K. Hoffmeier, *Ancient Israel in Sinai: The Evidence for the Authenticity of the Wilderness Tradition* (New York: Oxford University Press, 2005). William Johnstone, "From the Sea to the Mountain, Exodus 15:22–19:2: A Case Study in Editorial Techniques," in *Studies in the Book of Exodus: Redaction—Reception—Interpretation*, ed. Marc Vervenne (Leuven: Leuven University Press, 1996), 245–263, argues that the space references, particularly "sea" and "mountain," should be interpreted in terms of ancient cosmology and theology and not necessarily as references to real locations. However, the author of the present study does not see textual markers that suggest a cosmological interpretation, particularly if one does not adopt an allegorical interpretation of the text.

[13] According to the biblical text, these included the desert of Shur (Exod 15:22), Marah (Exod 15:23), Elim (Exod 15:27), the desert of Sin (Exod 16:1), Rephidim (Exod 17:1; to be called Massah and Meribah), and finally the desert of Sinai (Exod 19:1). Israel is said to camp "in front of the mountain," already hinting at the importance of *the* mountain.

[14] Cf. R. W. L. Moberly, *At the Mountain of God: Story and Theology in Exodus 32–34* (Sheffield: JSOT Press, 1983); Thomas B. Dozeman, *God on the Mountain: A Study of Redaction, Theology and Canon in Exodus 19–24* (Atlanta, GA: Scholars Press, 1989); Edward G. Newing, "Up and Down—In and Out: Moses on Mount Sinai: The Literary Unity of Exodus 32–34," *ABR* 41 (1993): 18–34; Martin Ravndal Hauge, *The Descent from the Mountain: Narrative Patterns in Exodus 19–40* (Sheffield: Sheffield Academic Press, 2001); and Gerald A. Klingbeil, "Quebrar la ley: algunas notas exegéticas acerca de Éxodo 32:19," *DavarLogos* 1 (2002): 73–80.

[15] Everett Fox, *The Five Books of Moses: A New Translation with Introductions, Commentary, and Notes*, The Schocken Bible (Dallas, TX: Word, 1995), 359, notes that "the mountain naturally functions as a bridge between heaven and earth."

[16] All translations are the author's, unless otherwise noted.

Covenant" (Exod 20:22–23:33).[17] The key word "covenant" (*berith*) can be found four times in the larger unit (Exod 19:5; 23:32; 24:7–8) and, interestingly, appears in parallelism with "divine speech" in Exodus 19:5: "And now, if you truly listen to my voice [*qol*] and [if] you keep my covenant [*berith*]" already introduces the important divine speech motif with which Exodus 20:1 opens and suggests a link between divine speech and divine covenant (and by extension, commandments). The remainder of Exodus 19 includes specific divine commands that Moses communicates to the people and that involve ritual activity[18] by the people and movement by God and Moses. Following this, God begins to speak in "ten words" (Exod 34:28; also Deut 4:14; 10:4), which are closely associated with "the tables of the words of the covenant" (Exod 34:28).

Generally, scholars have distinguished between apodictic and casuistic law—the former referring to categorical and unconditional law that often deals with the interaction between the human and the divine realm, and the latter usually dealing with specific cases and representing a legal tradition well known from other ANE texts and cultures.[19] Exodus 20:1–17 (together with the added narrative section in Exod 20:18–21) clearly represents apodictic law, and the formulation of each law is not uniform and one can note structural imbalance. Some of the laws are

---

[17] See, for example, Joe M. Sprinkle, *The Book of the Covenant: A Literary Approach* (Sheffield: Sheffield Academic Press, 1994); T. Desmond Alexander, "Book of the Covenant," in *Dictionary of the Old Testament: Pentateuch*, ed. David W. Baker and T. Desmond Alexander (Downers Grove, IL: InterVarsity, 2003), 94–101; and Yitzhak Avishur, "The Narrative of the Revelation at Sinai (Ex 19–24)," in *Studies in Historical Geography and Biblical Historiography Presented to Zecharia Kallai*, ed. Gershon Galil and Moshe Weinfeld (Leiden: Brill, 2000), 197–214. Donald E. Gowan, *Theology in Exodus: Biblical Theology in the Form of a Commentary* (Louisville, KY: John Knox, 1994), 173–178, argues that the unifying element of Exodus 19–24 is concerned with worship in a liturgical and not a historical context. Cf. Raymond Westbrook, "What is the Covenant Code?" in *Theory and Method in Biblical and Cuneiform Law: Revision, Interpolation and Development*, ed. Bernard M. Levinson (Sheffield: Sheffield Academic Press, 1994), 36, who, based on comparative data, argues strongly for the unity of the *Bundesbuch*. For a similar argument, see also David P. Wright, "The Laws of Hammurabi as a Source for the Covenant Collection (Exodus 20:23–23:19)," *Maarav* 10 (2003): 11–87. These studies suggest a basic unity of the section.

[18] E.g., consecration rites, involving washing and sexual abstinence (Exod 19:10, 14–15). Furthermore, the people are to observe specific ritual time (Exod 19:11), space (Exod 19:12–13, 17), and movement (Exod 19:3–7, 18–25). See Gerald A. Klingbeil, *Bridging the Gap: Ritual and Ritual Texts in the Bible* (Winona Lake, IN: Eisenbrauns, 2007).

[19] Cf. here Samuel Greengus, "Law (Biblical and ANE Law)," *ABD*, 4:245. Cf. earlier Gerhard Liedke, *Gestalt und Bezeichnung alttestamentlicher Rechtssätze: Eine formgeschichtliche-terminologische Studie* (Neukirchen-Vlyn: Neukirchener, 1971); and John Bright, "The Apodictic Prohibition: Some Observations," *JBL* 92 (1973): 195–204; Westbrook, "What is the Covenant Code?" 28–32.

broadly formulated while others are brief and to the point.[20] The biblical data concerning the Decalogue suggests that it was written on both sides of two tablets of stone (Exod 24:12; 31:18; 32:15–16; 34:1, 28; Deut 4:13; 5:22; 9:9; 10:4). Seeing that these laws represented the essence of the covenant between YHWH and His people, the second set of tablets[21] was deposited in the Ark of the Covenant (Exod 25:16, 21; 40:20), thus highlighting the foundational nature of this covenant agreement.

When dealing with the Decalogue (the ten words/commandments), one of the *crux interpretum* has been the numbering of the laws.[22] Generally, Jewish readers have understood the prologue (Exod 20:2) as the first commandment, followed by the second commandment in Exodus 20:3–6.[23] Based on a division that dates to Clement of Alexandria and Augustine, the Catholic Church regarded Exodus 20:3–6 as the first commandment and split Exodus 20:17 into two commandments. Luther followed this enumeration while the Reformed churches (Zwingli and Calvin) and the Anglican Church viewed Exodus 20:3 as the first commandment, followed by Exodus 20:4–6 as the second commandment. Exodus 20:17 is treated as a single commandment. This study follows the traditional Reformed tradition (not to be mixed up with Luther's position), understanding Exodus 20:2–3 as the first commandment, Exodus 20:4–6 as the second

---

[20] Cf. the detailed observations found in Cornelis Houtman, *Exodus*, vol. 3, HCOT (Leuven: Peeters, 2000), 6.

[21] Moses smashed the first set to pieces when he came down from the mountain of God and saw the people worshipping the golden calf. Moses' reaction in Exodus 32:15–19 should not be interpreted as a rash, thoughtless reaction to a great evil, but rather as a deliberate, ritual reaction, involving the demolition of the legal basis of the covenant and the destruction of the object of idolatry, which was then burned, ground to powder, mixed with water, and given to the people to drink. See Klingbeil, "Quebrar la ley," 73–80.

[22] See also J. W. Marshall, "Decalogue," in *Dictionary of the Old Testament: Pentateuch*, ed. David W. Baker and T. Desmond Alexander (Downers Grove, IL: InterVarsity, 2003), 172. Cf. William H. C. Propp, *Exodus 19–40*, AB (New York: Doubleday, 2006), 302–304.

[23] See Houtman, *Exodus*, 3. Jewish delimitation of the Decalogue actually involves two distinct systems of lower and upper cantillation, which are to be understood as alternative systems. For a detailed discussion of these two systems see Mordechai Breuer, "Dividing the Decalogue into Verses and Commandments," in *The Ten Commandments in History and Tradition*, ed. Ben-Zion Segal and Gershon Levi (Jerusalem: Magnes, 1985), 291–330. A helpful review of the interpretation and understanding of the Decalogue throughout the past millennia can be found in Paul Grimley Kuntz, *The Ten Commandments in History: Mosaic Paradigms for a Well-Ordered Society* (Grand Rapids, MI: Eerdmans, 2004). Cf. also Aron Pinker, "Decalogue or Dodecalogue?" *JBQ* 28.4 (2000): 233–244, who, based on the assumption of three categories (God, family, and society), suggests that originally the Decalogue contained twelve commandments, with each tablet including six. His argumentation is speculative.

commandment, Exodus 20:7 as the third commandment, and Exodus 20:8–11 as the fourth commandment. Interestingly, the masoretic delimitation system (*setumah* and *petuhah*) follows the traditional division (Exod 20:17 being one commandment), but does not distinguish between the first and second commandment.[24]

Having understood the position of the ten words of YHWH in the larger context of Exodus 19–24 and the structure and delimitation of these words, the next section seeks to understand the interaction between two occurrences of the Decalogue in Exodus 20 and Deuteronomy 5, paying particular attention to the Sabbath commandment where one notices the most significant differences.

Contextualization and the Decalogue: Exodus 20:8–11 and Deuteronomy 5:12–15

The two "versions" of the Decalogue as found in Exodus 20 and Deuteronomy 5 have long caused critical scholarship to suggest a complex and convoluted textual history.[25] It is interesting to note that in one text from Qumran (4QDeut^n), an attempt at harmonizing both sections was made, resulting in a composite text,[26] which at least suggests that ancient

---

[24] A *setumah* follows Exodus 20:2–6.

[25] A good example of this can be found in the 2006 commentary by Propp on Exodus, which appears in the Anchor Bible series. Propp spends a considerable amount of space discussing the source-critical and redaction-critical analysis of the biblical data. It is laudable of Propp to mark a substantial part of this section as "speculation," thus highlighting the hypothetical nature of this enterprise. See Propp, *Exodus 19–40*, 141–154. Niels-Erik A. Andreasen, *The Old Testament Sabbath: A Tradition-Historical Investigation* (Atlanta, GA: Scholars Press, 1972), 83, speaks of two "recensions." Andreasen seems to suggest that the differences of the Sabbath commandment between Exodus 20 and Deuteronomy 5 are due to later expansions of an "Ur-command," some "kind of midrash" (ibid., 89).

[26] See Sidnie White Crawford, "Reading Deuteronomy in the Second Temple Period," in *Reading the Present in the Qumran Library: The Perception of the Contemporary by Means of Scriptural Interpretations*, ed. Kristin De Troyer and Armin Lange (Atlanta, GA: Society of Biblical Literature, 2005), 129–130. The critical edition of 4QDeut^n was also published by White Crawford. Cf. Sidnie White Crawford, "41. 4QDeut^n," in *Qumran Cave 4.IX: Deuteronomy, Joshua, Judges, Kings*, ed. Eugene Ulrich et al. (Oxford: Clarendon, 1995), 124–125. The translation of the text is as follows and comes from Crawford, "Reading Deuteronomy," 129–130: "Observe the sabbath day to sanctify it, according as the Lord your God commanded you. Six days you shall labor and do all your work, but the seventh day is a sabbath to the Lord your God. You shall not do in it any work; you, your son, your daughter, your male slave or your female slave, your ox or your ass or your beast, your sojourner who is within your gates, in order that your male slave and your female slave may rest like you. And remember that you were a slave in the land of Egypt, and

interpreters were aware of the problem and often sought to harmonize both versions. Even though many critical scholars would concede that a textual reconstruction of the evolution of the Decalogue in the Pentateuch is at best hypothetical or speculative,[27] the textual and redaction history are still important sections in many recent commentaries of the Pentateuch or individual books of the Pentateuch. However, a change from what may be termed a "text-oriented" approach towards a "meaning-oriented" approach in Pentateuchal research can be noted,[28] which is most likely due to the growing realization that hypothetical sources make for bad data in redaction history.[29] Many literary approaches working with the final text of the Hebrew Bible have replaced earlier historical-critical methods which were often more concerned with the (imaginary) pre-history or history of

---

the Lord your God brought you out from there with a mighty hand and an outstretched arm; therefore the Lord your God commanded you to observe the sabbath day to sanctify it. For six days the Lord made the heavens and the earth, the sea and everything which is in them, and he rested on the seventh day; therefore the Lord blessed the seventh day to sanctify it."

[27] Crawford, "Reading Deuteronomy," 129–130. Cf. the quick review in Hasel, "The Sabbath in the Pentateuch," 28.

[28] Cf. Klingbeil, *Bridging the Gap*, 50–51. Martin Pröbstle, "Truth and Terror: A Text-Oriented Analysis of Daniel 8:9–14" (PhD diss., Andrews University, 2005), 1–3, has observed a similar development in Hebrew Bible research, even though he called it "text-oriented."

[29] A good review of the history of Pentateuchal criticism can be found in Bill T. Arnold, "Pentateuchal Criticism, History of," in *Dictionary of the Old Testament: Pentateuch*, ed. T. Desmond Alexander and David W. Baker (Downers Grove, IL: InterVarsity, 2003), 622–631. The common underlying theme of current discussions of the state of the art in Pentateuchal criticism seems to be the realization that, due to a wide variety of distinct data, including comparative material, literary theory, archaeological and historical evidence, etc., the old models just will not do anymore. See, for example, Mart-Jan Paul, "Der archimedische Punkt der Pentateuchkritik— zur josianischen Datierung des Deuteronomiums," *JET* 20 (2006): 115–137; Raúl Kerbs, "La crítica del Pentateuco y sus presuposiciones filosóficas," in *Inicios, fundamentos y paradigmas: estudios teológicos y exegéticos en el Pentateuco*, ed. Gerald A. Klingbeil (Libertador San Martín: Editorial Universidad Adventista del Plata, 2004), 3–45; Georg Fischer, "Zur Lage der Pentateuchforschung," *ZAW* 115 (2003): 608–616; Hans-Winfried Jüngling, "Das Buch Levitikus in der Forschung seit Karl Elligers Kommentar aus dem Jahre 1966," in *Levitikus als Buch*, ed. Heinz-Josef Fabry and Hans-Winfried Jüngling (Berlin: Philo, 1999), 1–45; Gordon J. Wenham, "Pondering the Pentateuch: The Search for a New Paradigm," in *The Face of Old Testament Studies: A Survey of Contemporary Approaches*, ed. David W. Baker and Bill T. Arnold (Grand Rapids, MI: Baker, 1999), 116–144; Rolf Rendtorff, "Directions in Pentateuchal Studies," *CurBS* 5 (1997): 43–65; David M. Carr, "Controversy and Convergence in Recent Studies of the Formation of the Pentateuch," *RelSRev* 23.1 (1997): 22–31; Rolf Rendtorff, "The Paradigm is Changing: Hopes— and Fears," *BibInt* 1 (1993): 34–53; and Gordon J. Wenham, "Method in Pentateuchal Source Criticism," *VT* 41 (1991): 84–109.

a given text than the text itself.[30] Intertextuality, or inner-biblical exegesis,[31] is one of those helpful approaches (even though it is not "new" as the work of Michael Fishbane on inner-biblical exegesis has shown)[32] that may also be useful when considering the two "versions" of the Decalogue.

Following a synchronic strategy of reading the text of the Pentateuch (and disregarding the supposed sources and their hypothetical editions and revisions),[33] both in location in the larger body of the Pentateuch as well as narrative time, Deuteronomy 5 picks up on an earlier text, given soon after the exodus event, at the foot of the mountain of God. This perspective is also clearly visible in the introductory section of Deuteronomy 5:1–5. There is reference to the "covenant" (*berith*) that YHWH made with the

---

[30] Linguistics, pragmatics, narrative, structural, or (new literary) methods are only some of the approaches that scholars have used to better understand the text of the Hebrew Bible. Unfortunately, co-text and historical context have often suffered because of this emphasis. It seems as if the pendulum were swinging from one extreme to the other.

[31] It should be noted that inner-biblical exegesis and intertextuality are not necessarily identical terms. A good discussion of the distinct methodological presuppositions of these two methods can be found in Segundo Teófilo Correa, "Intertextualidad y exégesis intra-bíblica: ¿dos caras de la misma moneda? Breve analisis de las presuposiciones metodológicas," *DavarLogos* 5.1 (2006): 1–13. Helpful introductions (in chronological order), including further bibliographical references, can be found in Pröbstle, "Truth and Terror," 565–574; William M. Schniedewind, "Innerbiblical Exegesis," in *Dictionary of the Old Testament: Historical Books*, ed. Bill T. Arnold and H. G. M. Williamson (Downers Grove, IL: InterVarsity, 2005), 502–509; Craig C. Broyles, "Traditions, Intertextuality, and Canon," in *Interpreting the Old Testament: A Guide for Exegesis*, ed. Craig C. Broyles (Grand Rapids, MI: Baker, 2001), 157–175; Kirsten Nielson, "Intertexuality and Hebrew Bible," in *Congress Volume Oslo 1998*, ed. André Lemaire and M. Sæbø (Leiden: Brill, 2000), 17–31; Patricia Tull, "Intertextuality and the Hebrew Scriptures," *CurBS* 8 (2000): 59–90; idem, *Remember the Former Things: The Recollection of Previous Texts in Second Isaiah* (Atlanta, GA: Scholars Press, 1997), 57–84.

[32] Cf. the important work of Michael Fishbane, *Biblical Interpretation in Ancient Israel* (Oxford: Clarendon, 1985); see also idem, "Inner-Biblical Exegesis," in *Hebrew Bible/Old Testament: The History of Its Interpretation*, vol. 1: From the Beginnings to the Middle Ages (Until 1300), Part 1: Antiquity, ed. Magne Sæbø (Göttingen: Vandenhoeck & Ruprecht, 1996), 33–48; and idem, "Use, Authority and Interpretation of Mikra at Qumran," in *MIKRA: Text, Translation, Reading & Interpretation of the Hebrew Bible in Ancient Judaism & Early Christianity*, ed. Martin J. Mulder (Peabody, MA: Hendrickson, 2004), 339–377.

[33] A good example of a standard diachronic interpretation of the relationship between Exodus 20 and Deuteronomy 5 can be found in E. W. Nicholson, "The Decalogue as the Direct Address of God," *VT* 27 (1977): 422–433, who argues that Exodus 20 is a secondary insertion into the Sinai narrative that was placed there for theological reasons. Recently, John van Seters, *The Edited Bible: The Curious History of the 'Editor' in Biblical Criticism* (Winona Lake, IN: Eisenbrauns, 2006), has challenged the notion of an editor (which is a fairly modern concept) as being useful for explaining the literary development of the Pentateuch. While the author of the present study does not agree with van Seters' solution to the problem, he finds Seters' observations highly relevant in the larger discussion of Pentateuchal criticism.

people ("us") at Horeb.³⁴ This is a clear reference to a past event and the Masoretic Text uses here a suffix conjugation form (*karath*), which in the overall context of the five-verse paragraph appears to be background or off-line information.³⁵ Deuteronomy 5:3 continues with the off-line information in the first section and then links it to the current living generation: "not with our fathers made YHWH this covenant, but with us." The background information is continued in verse 4 (referring to YHWH talking to the people from the mountain), and again a suffix conjugation form is used (*dibber*, "he spoke"), followed by two similar forms in verse 5 that describe the fear of the people (*yere 'them*, "they feared"), which—in consequence—resulted in the people remaining at the foot of the mountain (*lo '-'alithem*, "they did not go up"). After this background information is given, the ten words of YHWH are recounted at the end of verse 5.

Many scholars have recognized the sermonic and exhortative quality of Deuteronomy.³⁶ It is important to keep in mind this oral nature, without diminishing the clear structural links to ANE covenant and treaty literature.³⁷ After an involuntary forty-year sojourn Israel finds itself again at the

---

³⁴ Many different explanations have been suggested for the use of the different place names "Horeb" and "Sinai," chief among them being the standard historical-critical hypothesis that they may be correlated to different sources, even though it is admitted that the use of Horeb and Sinai is not always parallel to the seams of the supposed sources (thus creating more confusion). A less complicated and more probable solution to this issue suggests that Horeb refers to the larger area and that Sinai belongs to Horeb. Cf. Cornelis Houtman, *Exodus*, vol. 1, HCOT (Kampen: KOK Publishing, 1993), 117. See also Marshall, "Decalogue," 172. Graham I. Davies, "The Significance of Deuteronomy 1:2 for the Location of Mount Horeb," *PEQ* 111 (1979): 87–101, argues that the geographical indications of Deuteronomy 1:2 suggests that Mount Horeb should be located in the southern part of the Sinai peninsula, possibly Jebel Musa, which is also the traditional site of Mount Sinai.

³⁵ Stephen K. Sherwood, *Leviticus, Numbers, Deuteronomy*, Berit Olam: Studies in Narrative & Poetry (Collegeville, PA: Liturgical Press, 2002), 223–224, provides a useful list of YHWH's past action, referred to in the book of Deuteronomy. The establishment of the covenant and His salvific acts for His people features prominently here. Cf. also Jason S. DeRouchie, "A Call to Covenant Love: Text Grammar and Literary Structure in Deuteronomy 5–11" (PhD diss., Southern Baptist Theological Seminary, 2005), 124.

³⁶ This phrase has been taken from Marshall, "Decalogue," 172. Cf. also the comments found in Sherwood, *Leviticus, Numbers, Deuteronomy*, 202: "At another level Deuteronomy is well known for its power as 'preached law.' Much of the language is elevated and poetic, spoken in person-to-person address, appealing to the reader through its intradiegetic listeners to take the instruction to heart 'so that you may live in the land that the Lord swore to give to your ancestors, to Abraham, to Isaac, and to Jacob' (30:20)."

³⁷ See Eugene H. Merrill, *Deuteronomy: An Exegetical and Theological Exposition of Holy Scripture*, NAC (Nashville, TN: Broadman & Holman, 1994), 27–32. Cf. Delbert R. Hillers, *Covenant: The History of a Biblical Idea* (Baltimore, MD: Johns Hopkins University Press, 1969), for a (still)

border of the Promised Land. Many things have changed since the covenant ritual described in Exodus 19, which was followed by the promulgation of the basic principles (the ten basic words) of this covenant between YHWH and His people: Moses is an old man now; the previous generation that rebelled against YHWH has passed away (Num 14:33–35; 32:13); the people are just about to enter the Promised Land, which is, however, not empty and requires military action if Israel is to conquer it. At this crucial time and as part of a covenant renewal ceremony, Moses recounts the principles of covenant living, namely the ten words of YHWH.

The applicability of the covenant and its terms to the new generation is argued right from the beginning: "not with our fathers . . . *but* with *us*" (Deut 5:3). This statement and the ones following underline an important rhetorical strategy of the author of Deuteronomy: while standing on the shoulders of an earlier generation and previous revelation, God is speaking directly to the present generation, or, in other words, God's talking is relevant and applicable even though most of the original participants of the covenant ritual have perished. This may lead to changed formulations in both sets of the Decalogue and should be understood as a form of contextualization.[38] A reader of the Pentateuch would return to

---

helpful review of the development of the covenant concept. Thomas Edward McComiskey, *The Covenants of Promise: A Theology of the Old Testament Covenants* (Grand Rapids, MI: Baker, 1985), presents a helpful discussion of the theological dimensions of covenant in the Hebrew Bible. There is sufficient comparative data to establish clear structural links between covenants and treaties of the ANE and the Hebrew Bible. See, for example, Frank H. Polak, "The Covenant at Mount Sinai in the Light of Texts from Mari," in *Sefer Moshe: The Moshe Weinfeld Jubilee Volume, Studies in the Bible and the Ancient Near East, Qumran, and Post-Biblical Judaism*, ed. Chaim Cohen, Avi Hurvitz, and Shalom M. Paul (Winona Lake, IN: Eisenbrauns, 2004), 119–134.

[38] Bernard M. Levinson, "'Du sollst nichts hinzufügen und nichts wegnehmen' (Dtn 13,1): Rechtsreform und Hermeneutik in der Hebräischen Bibel," *ZTK* 103 (2006): 157–183, takes up the issue of innovation (or contextualization) of legal texts and notes an important problem: How is it possible to innovate on a text that is divinely inspired? His answer, suggesting a complex canonical process that involves critique, rejection, and replacement of previous legal texts, will not be shared by all studying these phenomena, especially considering distinct models of revelation and inspiration. The author is grateful to Prof. Levinson for his study and for their friendly dialogue. Cf. also Bernard M. Levinson, "You Must Not Add Anything to What I Command You: Paradoxes of Canon and Authorship in Ancient Israel," *Numen* 53 (2003): 1–51; and idem, *Deuteronomy and the Hermeneutics of Legal Innovation* (New York: Oxford University Press, 1997). However, contextualization is not an issue that concerns biblical interpreters exclusively, involving inner-biblical quotes or the intertextual use of earlier material. Bible translators have faced similar issues and important relevant principles of contextualization can be gleaned by looking at how ancient translators worked and reworked the biblical text. See Gerald A. Klingbeil, "Looking over the Shoulders of Ancient Translators: Contextualization and Ancient Translation Techniques," in *Misión y contextualización, Llevar el mensaje bíblico a un mundo multicultural,*

a particular legal (or narrative) construct several times (as can be seen in the many references and additional explicatory statements concerning Sabbath observance) and would not necessarily understand these as contradictory, but rather as additional explanations of the same basic concept.[39] Considering the fact that Israel stood on the brink of changing from a nomadic lifestyle to a more sedentary lifestyle, one may understand additions to the command such as "your ox," "your donkey," and the addition of "all" in "all your livestock" in Deuteronomy 5:14.

Comparing the Decalogue in Exodus 20 and Deuteronomy 5, one immediately notes the significant changes in language use, argumentation, and even quantity between the two, particularly considering the Sabbath commandment. While the Sabbath command in Exodus 20:8–11 is made up of fifty-five words, the later re-telling of it in Deuteronomy 5:12–15 consists of sixty-four words. The expansion involves some additions in Deuteronomy 5:12 and 5:14, involving the list of all those affected by the Sabbath commandment. At the end of Deuteronomy 5:12, one can also note a very well-known formula that in other contexts refers to previous divine commands or declarations: "as YHWH, your God, had commanded." This formula occurs frequently in the Pentateuch and has been identified by critical scholars as a trademark of P that provides structure and indicates the execution of a command given directly or indirectly by YHWH.[40] In the present context, however, the phrase that supposedly marks P appears at a crucial point in Deuteronomy (which, according to critical scholarship, was shaped by a different source/editor at a different time), appearing three times (Deut 5:12, 15 [with slight variation], and 16), and highlighting the previous proclamation of YHWH's ten words.[41]

---

ed. Gerald A. Klingbeil (Libertador San Martín: Editorial Universidad Adventista del Plata, 2005), 3–21, for examples and further relevant bibliography. Obviously, the ramifications of this issue for missiology and interpretation are huge and cannot be dealt with here conclusively.

[39] Cf. Christoph Dohmen, *Exodus 19–40*, HTKAT (Freiburg: Herder, 2004), 90, who unfortunately keeps in line with current Decalogue scholarship and argues for the priority of Deuteronomy 5 over Exodus 20, following scholars such as Hossfeld and Perlitt.

[40] Cf. the study of Joseph Blenkinsopp, "The Structure of P," *CBQ* 38 (1976): 275–292.

[41] Similar also Jeffries M. Hamilton, *Social Justice and Deuteronomy: The Case of Deuteronomy 15* (Atlanta, GA: Scholars Press, 1992), 111–112. The phrase often functions as a structural marker and the author of the present study suggests that its sevenfold use in Leviticus 8 is a good marker for a septenary chiastic structure. Cf. Gerald A. Klingbeil, *A Comparative Study of the Ritual of Ordination as Found in Leviticus 8 and Emar 369* (Lewiston, NY: Edwin Mellen, 1998), 111–114. The formula appears also seven times in Exodus 39:1, 5, 7, 21, 26, 29, 31 (detailing the construction of the tabernacle and the making of the priestly garments) and Exodus 40:19, 21, 23, 25, 27,

However, the greatest difference between Exodus 20 and Deuteronomy 5 concerns the final motivation clause of the Sabbath commandment (Exod 20:11; Deut 5:15). The texts simply use two distinct motivations for the keeping of the Sabbath. While Exodus 20:11 focuses on creation and God's rest as a paradigm for humanity's rest, Deuteronomy 5:15 highlights YHWH's mighty deliverance of Israel from Egypt, and thus emphasizes liberation. As already suggested, this is most likely due to the changed historical situation, roughly forty years after the first proclamation of YHWH's ten words. When considering this changed situation, it must be noted that the different motivation clauses are not contradictory, but seem to complement each other. In other words, Deuteronomy 5:15 makes something explicit that is already present in Exodus 20, and appears in another Sabbath commandment in the Book of the Covenant (Exod 23:12), which highlights God's compassion for the oppressed and His interest in liberation, which is in turn rooted in creation.[42] In this view, creation is the underlying basis for liberation, including also the foreigner, because *all* humanity has been created in the image of God. The universal aspect of creation (as referred to in Exod 20:11) is now illustrated specifically in God's liberation of His covenant people from Egypt (Deut 5:15).

However, one should remember that creation terminology is also present in Deuteronomy 5:14 and should not be overlooked. The phrase "so that your male servant and your female servant may rest [*nuakh*] as you" is a clear link to the "rest" (*nuakh*) of God mentioned in Exodus 20:11, 31:17, and Genesis 2:2, even though the latter two verses employ the verb *shavath* instead of the verb *nuakh*.[43] We will return to these issues in the following sections that deal with the specifics of the Sabbath commandments of Exodus 20:8–11 and Deuteronomy 5:12–15 and their theological implications.

The Sabbath in Exodus 20:8–11: Creation and Holiness

In the context of the Decalogue in Exodus 20, the fourth commandment is marked by a structure that is distinct from all other commandments. First, it is the longest commandment, with fifty-five words in the Masoretic Text (over

---

29, 32 (in the context of the setting up and furnishing of the tabernacle). Cf. here also Peter J. Kearney, "Creation and Liturgy: The P Redaction of Ex. 25–40," *ZAW* 89 (1977): 375–386.

[42] See here Frey, "The Sabbath Commandment," 3–11, who ably demonstrates the linguistic and intertextual links of the Sabbath commandment in Exodus 23:12 with the story of the exclusion of Ishmael and Hagar from the household of Abraham, as well as the clear reference to creation.

[43] Hasel, "Sabbath in the Pentateuch," 32.

against forty-four for the second commandment in Exod 20:4–6). Second, it employs a distinct syntactic structure that does not involve the more familiar "*lo* ' + prefix" conjugation form (or imperfect) that is used in Exodus 20: verse 3 (first commandment), verses 4–5 (second commandment), verse 7 (third commandment), verse 13 (sixth commandment), verse 14 (seventh commandment), verse 15 (eighth commandment), verse 16 (ninth commandment), and verse 17 (tenth commandment). As can be easily seen from this list, only the fourth and fifth commandments do not follow the structure of an absolute negative command ("You shall not . . ."). Since the source-critical work of Wellhausen and later followed with different nuances and emphases by form-critical scholars such as Gunkel and Mowinckel, the Decalogue in Exodus 20 has been dated to the eighth century BC and was considered to belong to the Elohist source, followed later by a Deuteronomic revision (as in Deut 5). More recent critical scholarship has moved away from some of the basic premises of the Wellhausen school and some scholars suggest an exilic or postexilic *Sitz im Leben* of the Decalogue, which would then not reflect realistic historical realities, but rather an important piece of literature.[44] A mainstay of this search for the historical context of the Decalogue has been the idea of a short "Ur-Decalogue" which—according to most practitioners of the historical-critical method—would be shorter and, of course, hypothetical.[45]

---

[44] Frank-Lothar Hossfeld, "Der Dekalog als Grundgesetz—eine Problemanzeige," in *Liebe und Gebot: Studien zum Deuteronomium*, ed. Reinhard G. Kratz and Hermann Spieckermann (Göttingen: Vandenhoeck & Ruprecht, 2000), 46–59; William Johnstone, "The Revision of Festivals in Exodus 1–24 in the Persian Period and the Preservation of Jewish Identity in the Diaspora," in *Yahwism after the Exile: Perspectives on Israelite Religion in the Persian Period*, ed. Rainer Albertz and Bob Becking (Assen: Van Gorcum, 2003), 99–114. For more information see the helpful summary of old and recent trends in the study of the Decalogue in Eckart Otto, "Alte und neue Perspektiven in der Dekalogforschung," in *Kontinuum und Proprium: Studien zur Sozial-und Rechtsgeschichte des Alten Orients und des Alten Testaments*, ed. Eckart Otto (Wiesbaden: Harrassowitz Verlag, 1996), 285–292. Otto himself feels that the Decalogue provides a helpful insight into the development of Israelite law. See Otto, "Der Dekalog als Brennspiegel israelitischer Rechtsgeschichte," in *Kontinuum und Proprium: Studien zur Sozial- und Rechtsgeschichte des Alten Orients und des Alten Testaments*, ed. Eckart Otto (Wiesbaden: Harrassowitz Verlag, 1996), 303: "Die Überlieferungsgeschichte der Dekaloggebote öffnet einen Blick auf die israelitische Rechtsgeschichte, die sich parallel zum Dekalog auch im 'Bundesbuch' und den deuteronomistischen Rechtsüberlieferungen und Redaktionen des Deuteronomiums niedergeschlagen hat."

[45] Cf. Durham, *Exodus*, 288–289. See also Propp, *Exodus 19–40*, 146, for speculative suggestions about a possible original prior to both the writing of Exodus 20 and Deuteronomy 5. Obviously, this concept is based on the existence of sources and editorial processes per se, a concept not shared by every reader of the Pentateuch.

The fourth commandment commences with the atypical and asyndetic *zakhor* ("remember"), which is a Qal infinitive absolute form.[46] As has been argued elsewhere, the use of an absolute infinitive in the sense of an imperative is not uncommon in Hebrew grammar.[47] "Remember" presupposes earlier information or practice[48] and is linked in Exodus 20:8 with *leqaddesho* ("to keep it holy"), an infinitive construct form that suggests purpose. In this introductory clause of the fourth commandment, the link between remembrance and holiness should not be overlooked. As a matter of fact, following Gerhard Hasel's structure for Exodus 20:8–11,[49] the reference to holiness in both the introduction and conclusion of the commandment seems to function as some type of *inclusio* of a carefully structured section:

Table 1: Content Structure of Exodus 20:8–11

A Introduction	"Remember the Sabbath day, to keep it holy" (20:8)
B¹ Command	"Six days you shall labor and do all your work" (20:9)
C¹ Motivation	"But the seventh day *is* the Sabbath of the Lord your God" (20:10a)
B² Command	"*In it* you shall do no work: you, nor your son, nor your daughter, nor your male servant, nor your female servant, nor your cattle, nor your stranger who *is* within your gates" (20:10b)

---

[46] It should be noted that the later Samaritan Pentateuch has here—most likely in an attempt to harmonize Exodus 20:8–11 with Deuteronomy 5:12–15—the Hebrew *shamor* ("keep") which also appears in Deuteronomy 5:12. On the other hand, the LXX reads here *mnestheti* ("remember") (aorist imperative), which suggests that this is not a text-critical issue but rather a conscious decision on the part of the editor/compiler of the Samaritan Pentateuch text.

[47] See Bruce K. Waltke and M. O'Connor, *An Introduction to Biblical Hebrew Syntax* (Winona Lake, IN: Eisenbrauns, 1990), 593–594, who suggest that the usage of infinite absolute forms as command forms is extremely old and can be seen in other Semitic languages. J. D. W. Watts, "Infinitive Absolute as Imperative and the Interpretation of Exodus 20:8," *ZAW* 74 (1962): 141–147, argues that the infinitive absolute only serves as a command form if it is adjacent to an imperative, which is not the case in Exodus 20:8. Cf. also Reuven Yaron, "Stylistic Conceits II: The Absolute Infinitive in Biblical Law," in *Pomegranates and Golden Bells: Studies in Biblical, Jewish, and Near Eastern Ritual, Law, and Literature in Honor of Jacob Milgrom*, ed. David P. Wright, David N. Freedman, and Avi Hurwitz (Winona Lake, IN: Eisenbrauns, 1995), 449–460, who has studied the use of infinitive absolute forms in the book of the covenant and suggests that its use in legal texts reflects common use in Hebrew grammar.

[48] This is one of the arguments used by critical scholars to support the priority of Deuteronomy 5 over against Exodus 20. Cf. Dohmen, *Exodus 19–40*, 119.

[49] See Hasel, "The Sabbath in the Pentateuch," 29.

C² Motivation	"For *in* six days the Lord made the heavens and the earth, the sea, and all that *is* in them, and rested the seventh day" (20:11a)
D Conclusion	"Therefore the Lord blessed the Sabbath day and hallowed it" (20:11b)

Following the programmatic statement of the introduction ("Remember the Sabbath day in order to keep it holy"), Exodus 20:9 provides the first specifics of the Sabbath commandment: "Six days you shall labor and do all your work." Even without the extensive motivation clause in Exodus 20:11, the reference to six days is telling and suggests a link to creation. First, it links to the six days of creation, especially considering the reference to the seventh day in verse 10a, which seems to be a verbatim quote from Genesis 2:2–3. The seventh day as part of a central weekly cycle is also important in the festival ordinances (e.g., Exod 12:16 [Passover]; 13:6 [feast of unleavened bread]) and together with the six-day unit has already appeared in the mannah provisions found in Exodus 16:26, 29. The unit of seven days is significant in biblical narrative and ritual texts, and more often than not (though not exclusively) refers to crucial moments of transition (as, for example, in the case of ritual acts such as mourning rites [Gen 50:10; 1 Sam 31:13], ordination rites [Exod 29:35–37; Lev 8:33–35], purification rites [Lev 12:2; 14:8, 38; 15:13, 19, 24, 28; etc.]).[50] Based on the important unit of creation time, transitional periods require similar time periods in order to achieve transition, which in turn are often associated with holiness and purity concerns.[51]

Second, the holiness concerns of the fourth commandment need to be seen against the backdrop of creation holiness. After the completion of a perfect creation (Gen 2:3), God blesses (*wayevarekh*) the seventh day

---

[50] For more details, cf. Gerald A. Klingbeil, "Ritual Time in Leviticus 8 with Special Reference to the Seven-Day Period in the Old Testament," *ZAW* 109 (1997): 500–513. Herbert Chanan Brichto, *The Names of God: Poetic Readings to Biblical Beginnings* (New York: Oxford University Press, 1998), 401–407, discusses what he has termed the "septets of social morality," involving septets such as the seventh-year release of a slave (Exod 23:10–12), the seventh-year remission of debt (Deut 15:1–3), and the Jubilee year (Lev 25:8–26:2) at the end of 7 × 7 years.

[51] This is also noted by Samuel A. Meier, "The Sabbath and Purification Cycles," in *The Sabbath in Jewish and Christian Traditions*, ed. Tamara C. Eshkenazi, Daniel J. Harrington, and William H. Shea (New York: Crossroads, 1991), 7–8, who suggests that "in all of these rites of purification, the passage of seven days is an essential part of the restoration of the unclean and a means of achieving holiness."

and makes it holy (*wayeqaddesh*)—that is, sets it apart. This link between Sabbath and holiness is actually a link between God Himself and His creation. A study dealing with the fourth commandment but focusing nearly exclusively upon the often-forgotten issue of holiness notes, "Holiness pertains first of all to God, and by derivation to his entourage in heaven and to the people, places, times, and objects associated with him on earth."[52] This holiness claim is often forgotten in modern western Christianity and finds an important expression in the Sabbath commandment of the Decalogue. As a matter of fact, holiness language is *used only in the fourth commandment* in the Decalogue. In view of the obvious question of Sabbath observance in Protestant Christianity, one scholar's interesting solution argues that sacred time (= Sabbath, creation) and the emphasis upon the holiness and otherness of God's name (third commandment) can be united in the practice of prayer, which is

> the hallowing of time, whether it happens to be externally placid or overwhelming. Perhaps that is why in Matthew and Luke he prefaces his teaching on the subject with the words "*Whenever you pray....*" Such hallowing of our time is not erratic but habitual, as it were the punctuation of a life with God.[53]

This suggestion does connect with the holiness concerns of the Sabbath, but seems to fail to take seriously the important creation time aspect.

This creation link seems to be highly relevant and was important to the author of Exodus 20:8–11 and thus cannot (and should not) be set aside. In the Hebrew Bible, creation is one of the foundational concepts and always associated with YHWH Himself.[54] Creation is effected by God's speaking, a concept that reappears in the use of the *memra* in intertestamental Judaism[55] and is also repeated and further developed in

---

[52] Bockmuehl, "'Keeping It Holy,'" 103.

[53] Ibid., 119. Emphasis original.

[54] Important discussions of creation theology in the Hebrew Bible can be found (in chronological order) in Bernard F. Batto, "Creation Theology in Genesis," in *Creation in the Biblical Traditions*, ed. Richard J. Clifford and John J. Collins (Washington, DC: Catholic Biblical Association, 1992), 16–38; Ronald A. Simkins, *Creator and Creation: Nature in the Worldview of Ancient Israel* (Peabody, MA: Hendrickson, 1994); Gnanamuthu S. Wilson, "A Descriptive Analysis of Creation Concepts and Themes in the Book of Psalms" (PhD diss., Andrews University, 1996); Paul R. House, "Creation in Old Testament Theology," *SBJT* 5.3 (2001): 4–17; and John Goldingay, *Old Testament Theology*, vol. 1: Israel's Gospel (Downers Grove, IL: InterVarsity, 2003), 42–130.

[55] Cf. here James H. Charlesworth, "The Jewish Roots of Christology: The Discovery of the Hypostatic Voice," *SJT* 39 (1986): 19–41. See also the more recent discussion on the use of *memra*

John 1. Creation is not associated with a particular people or nation, but results in the forming of "humanity," thus emphasizing a universal perspective beyond the realms of ethnic or national borders. This perspective is also expressed by the use of the term ʾadham as a reference to "humanity" (Gen 1:26), a usage that has been questioned,[56] but which cannot be ignored in view of the many references to the unity of mankind as found in biblical theology (both Hebrew Bible and New Testament).[57] Note one author's observation:

> It is humanity in general and not any people in particular that is created. Israel is not primordial. It emerges in history, twenty generations after the creation of human species in the image of God (or the gods, 1:26–27). . . . It is neither descended from the gods nor divine itself. All people are created equally in the divine image.[58]

By invoking creation language and creation imagery, the biblical author of Exodus 20:8–11 invokes and highlights the universal nature of the Sabbath. This comes even more to the forefront when one considers the command in Exodus 20:9 with its reference to "your works" (melaʾkhtekha), which clearly suggests an intertextual link to "his work" (melaʾkhto) in Genesis 2:2–3. The command is very clear and the use of the pronominal suffix ("your") puts the six days (used for humanity's work) in contrast with the seventh day, which is "the Sabbath of YHWH, your God" (Exod 20:10a). Note here the contrastive use of the conjunction waw (weyom hasheviʿi, "but the seventh day"): "During six days you can do *your* work, *but* the seventh day is the Sabbath of YHWH your God."

This important contrast is followed by a more detailed command in Exodus 20:10b, which provides further insight into what it means not to

---

in the Targumim in Martin McNamara, "Interpretation of Scripture in the Targumim," in *A History of Biblical Interpretation*, vol. 1: The Ancient Period, ed. Alan J. Hauser and Duane F. Watson (Grand Rapids, MI: Eerdmans, 2003), 167–197.

[56] James Barr, "Adam: Single Man, or All Humanity?" in *Hesed Ve-Emet: Studies in Honor of Ernest S. Frerichs*, ed. Jodi Magness and Seymour Gitin (Atlanta, GA: Scholars Press, 1998), 3–12.

[57] Cf. Moshe Greenberg, "Mankind, Israel, and the Nations in the Hebraic Heritage," in *Studies in the Bible and Jewish Thought*, ed. Moshe Greenberg (Philadelphia, PA: Jewish Publication Society, 1995), 369–393; and Stephen C. Barton, "The Unity of Humankind as a Theme in Biblical Theology," in *Out of Egypt: Biblical Theology and Biblical Interpretation*, ed. Craig G. Bartholomew et al. (Grand Rapids, MI: Zondervan, 2004), 233–258.

[58] Jon D. Levenson, "The Universal Horizon of Biblical Particularism," in *Ethnicity and the Bible*, ed. Mark G. Brett (Boston, MA: Brill, 1996), 147.

do one's own work. The list of those who should not work is extensive and includes the individual Israelite ("you" [*'attah*], a reference to the household head), his son, his daughter, his male servant, his female servant, his domestic animals, as well as the stranger within his sphere of influence. Scholars have wondered why the wife is not detailed in that list, especially considering the fact that sons and daughters and so on are mentioned. However, the embeddedness of husband and wife often resulted in their perception as being one, which is, no doubt, based in creation order: "and they will be one flesh" (Gen 2:24).[59] Creation order again can be seen in the close association between animals and human beings.[60] Sons and daughters, male and female servants, and the domestic animals summarize the important relations in a household. However, the reference to the "stranger, foreigner" (*ger*) again underlines the universal nature of the Sabbath commandment.[61] While the covenant is made with Israel, the larger community, including the stranger, is envisioned, especially when the stranger is within the zone of influence of the involved party. One scholar argues the shift between exclusivism and inclusivism in the citizen motif in the Pentateuch and later texts.[62] Exodus 20:10 would be a definite text for inclusivism, which again points at the universality of the commandment.[63]

The final clause of Exodus 20:11 describes the motivation of the Sabbath commandment. It refers to the divine creative activity described in Genesis 1–2.

---

[59] See Gerald A. Klingbeil, "'Not so Happily Ever After...': Cross-Cultural Marriages in the Time of Ezra–Nehemiah," *Maarav* 14 (2007): 39–75. The embeddedness of Israelite society as a whole has also been noted by K. C. Hanson, "Sin, Purification, and Group Process," in *Problems in Biblical Theology: Essays in Honor of Rolf Knierim*, ed. Henry T. C. Sun et al. (Grand Rapids, MI: Eerdmans, 1997), 171, who states that "every individual is perceived as embedded in some other, in a sequence of embeddedness so to say."

[60] See Gerald A. Klingbeil, "Agriculture and Animal Husbandry," in *Dictionary of the Old Testament: Historical Books*, ed. Bill T. Arnold and H. G. M. Williamson (Downers Grove, IL: InterVarsity, 2005), 8; Simkins, *Creator and Creation*," 15–40; Peter Riede, *Im Spiegel der Tiere: Studien zum Verhältnis von Mensch und Tier im alten Israel* (Göttingen: Vandenhoeck & Ruprecht, 2002); Hermann-Josef Stipp, "'Alles Fleisch hatte seinen Wandel auf der Erde verdorben' (Gen 6,12): Die Mitverantwortung der Tierwelt an der Sintflut nach der Priesterschrift," *ZAW* 111 (1999): 167–186.

[61] For a discussion of the relationship between God, Israel, and the stranger, see Bernadeth Carmen Caero Bustillos, "Liebt Gott den נכרי?" *BN* 111 (2002): 48–65, and also Rolf Rendtorff, "The *ger* in the Priestly Laws of the Pentateuch," in *Ethnicity and the Bible*, ed. Mark G. Brett (Boston, MA: Brill, 1996), 77–87; and C. van Houten, *The Alien in Israelite Law* (Sheffield: JSOT Press, 1991).

[62] Martin G. Klingbeil, "Exclusivism versus Inclusivism: Citizenship in the Pentateuch and Its Metaphorical Usage in Ephesians," *JAAS* 9 (2006): 129–144.

[63] Cf. also Cole, "The Sabbath and the Alien," 223–229.

Similar to Genesis 2:2, the commandment language uses the more general verb "do" (*'asah*) over against the more specialized verb "create" (*bara'*). Interestingly, Exodus 20:8 employs the Tetragrammaton *YHWH*, whereas Genesis 1–2 uses "God" (*'elohim*). Apparently, the biblical authors did not always distinguish between different divine names, making them a rather precarious tool in determining sources.[64] Heaven, land, sea, and all that is within them summarize comprehensively the divine creation, which is followed by a reference to the rest of YHWH and His blessing and sanctifying activities. As already indicated, the use of the verb "keep holy" (*qadhash*) forms an important marker of the internal structure of the fourth commandment and represents a significant theological element of a Sabbath theology based upon the Decalogue. The following section attempts a close reading of the Sabbath commandment in Deuteronomy 5:12–15, paying particular attention to the similarities to Exodus 20:8–11.

The Sabbath in Deuteronomy 5:12–15: A People Created for Freedom

Up to this point this study, considering the two manifestations of the Decalogue, has focused upon the differences. However, while these distinctions exist (and have already been discussed), there are clear similarities that should not be overlooked. First, the overall context and location of the commandment is the same. Second, the general structure also reflects the same interaction between command and motivation for the command as already noted in Exodus 20:8–11. The structure of Deuteronomy 5:12–15 is outlined as follows:[65]

Table 2: Content Structure of Deuteronomy 5:12–15

A Introduction	"Observe the Sabbath day, to keep it holy, as the Lord your God commanded you" (5:12)
B¹ Command	"Six days you shall labor and do all your work" (5:13)

---

[64] See discussion in Gerald A. Klingbeil, "Historical Criticism," in *Dictionary of the Old Testament: Pentateuch*, ed. T. Desmond Alexander and David W. Baker (Downers Grove, IL: InterVarsity, 2003), 406–407. Comparative data (both textual and iconographical) provides a useful source of information as to how ancient writers employed names and epithets and how interchangeable divine names were in the ANE.

[65] Hasel, "The Sabbath in the Pentateuch," 31. Translation is based on NKJV.

C¹ Motivation	"But the seventh day *is* the Sabbath of the Lord your God" (5:14a)
B² Command	"*In it* you shall do no work: you, nor your son, nor your daughter, nor your male servant, nor your female servant, nor your ox, nor your donkey, nor any of your cattle, nor your stranger who *is* within your gates" (5:14b)
C² Motivation	"That your male servant and your female servant may rest as well as you. And remember that you were a slave in the land of Egypt, and the Lord your God brought you out from there by a mighty hand and by an outstretched arm" (5:14c–15a)
D Conclusion	"Therefore the Lord your God commanded you to keep the Sabbath day" (5:15b)

As already noted, some of the differences between Exodus 20:8–11 and Deuteronomy 5:12–15 were most likely due to the oral nature of the communication in Deuteronomy.[66] However, another important strategy can also be observed: elements or concepts implicit in Exodus 20 are made explicit in Deuteronomy 5. A good example for this concept can be seen in the second motivation clause, which is completely distinct in Deuteronomy 5 from the one found in Exodus 20. As creation suggests equality, the liberation of inequality would be implicit.[67] By adding the phrase, "So that your male servant and your female servant shall rest [*nuakh*] as well as you" as an introduction to the second motivation clause in Deuteronomy 5:14c, a clear link to creation is presupposed: the rest (*nuakh*) motif links Exodus 20:11 with Deuteronomy 5:14 and is also present in the important reiteration of

---

[66] It is interesting to note that the book of Deuteronomy was very popular in intertestamental Judaism as can be easily seen from the number of copies found at Qumran, whose top three spots are taken by the Psalms (39), Deuteronomy (32), and Isaiah (21–24). See C. D. Elledge, *The Bible and the Dead Sea Scrolls* (Atlanta, GA: Society of Biblical Literature, 2005), 87. Cf. the more detailed discussion in Eugene Ulrich, "The Bible in the Making: The Scriptures Found at Qumran," in *The Bible at Qumran: Text, Shape, and Interpretation*, ed. Peter W. Flint (Grand Rapids, MI: Eerdmans, 2001), 53–54, who has slightly different numbers, i.e., Psalms (37), Deuteronomy (32), and Isaiah (22). Crawford, "Reading Deuteronomy," 140, suggests that the popularity of Deuteronomy in the Second Temple period was due to its authoritative nature, and its use for legal and liturgical issues which shaped the exegetical strategies of Jewish texts of that period.

[67] One of the key arguments for the notion of equality in creation is the fact that both man and woman are created in God's image (Gen 1:27). As has been argued by Goldingay, *Old Testament Theology*, 104, "creating humanity male and female speaks of relationship, and associating this with God's image presupposes that God is also a relational being. Humanity's Godlikeness lies in the relational capacity."

the Sabbath command in Exodus 23:12.[68] As already pointed out, this link between creation and liberation did not appear to be opposites in the mind of the ancient readers of the law, a fact that can be seen in the conscious effort of bringing the two motivation clauses together as seen in 4QDeut^n.

Liberation theology as a theological system has received mostly negative feedback in Seventh-day Adventist scholarship. This is due to the underlying hermeneutical perspective of practitioners of liberation theology of an *extra*-biblical hermeneutical stance (in the true sense of the word), elevating political liberation as the litmus test of biblical interpretation and ignoring traditional hermeneutical categories and procedures.[69] However, liberation and justice are foundational biblical motifs that should not be ignored just because a particular theological system is unacceptable on many different levels.[70] In Deuteronomy 5:12-15, liberation is the key motif in the Sabbath command, as is clearly visible in the second motivation clause and the addition in 5:14c, involving the rest of the male and the female servants that should reflect (or echo) the rest of the Sabbath keeper. This addition is justified by a reference to the exodus experience. Israel is reminded that the Sabbath is a sign of liberation that should not be forgotten. It is interesting to note that while Deuteronomy 5:12 does not commence the Sabbath commandment with the verb "remember" (*zakhar*) as found in Exodus 20:8, the act of remembering is highly significant and the verbal stem does appear in the second motivation clause in Deuteronomy 5:15: "and remember [*wezakharta*] that you have been a slave in the land of Egypt."[71] There seems to be a sequence of remembering

---

[68] See Frey, "The Sabbath Commandment," 3-11.

[69] A critique of a particular element of liberation theology from a Seventh-day Adventist perspective can be found in Atilio Rene Dupertuis, "Liberation Theology's Use of the Exodus as a Soteriological Model" (PhD diss., Andrews University, 1982). Núñez argues the vitality of liberation theology in the twenty-first century and its changed (and continuously changing) focal points. See Miguel Ángel Núñez, "Relevancia y pertinencia actual de la Teología de la Liberación," *DavarLogos* 4.1 (2005): 49-63.

[70] The MTh thesis of Atiteo, "The Sabbath as a Sign of Liberation," provides a unique discussion of the important aspect of liberation in the Sabbath commandment and has sought to contextualize it in a Filipino cultural context.

[71] The exodus motif has been recognized as an important theological motif in the Hebrew Bible. See Friedbert Ninow, "Indicators of Typology within the Old Testament: The Exodus Motif" (PhD diss., Andrews University, 2001) and Ronald Hendel, "The Exodus in Biblical Memory," *JBL* 120 (2001): 601-622. The activity of remembering is very significant in the Hebrew Bible. See, for example, the helpful observations in Heinz-Josef Fabry, "'Gedenken' im Alten Testament," in *Freude am Gottesdienst: Aspekte ursprünglicher Liturgie*, ed. Josef Schreiner (Stuttgart: Verlag Katholisches Bibelwerk, 1983), 177-187.

when comparing both passages: the Sabbath is to be remembered because it is based on creation (Exod 20:8–11); this remembering is shifted to the more recent divine act of liberation from oppression as experienced during the exodus (Deut 5:15). Biblical remembrance is not a sentimental or even intellectual activity, but rather seems to happen on the level of an active response.[72]

The latter half of the second motivation clause involves divine activity, which is parallel to the (seemingly paradoxical) divine activity of rest during the creation week: "because the Lord your God brought you out from there with a strong hand and an outstretched arm" (Deut 5:15). The instrumental use of the preposition "with" (Heb. *be*) focuses the attention of the reader on the "strong hand" and the "outstretched arm" of the Lord. It is not only the bringing out, but also the way this was achieved, which (in a sense) fits the present circumstances of the Israelites standing for a second time at the border of the Promised Land, some forty years after the first generation failed so miserably. They need this God who acts with a "strong hand" and an "outstretched arm." References to the anatomy of God (including finger, hand, and arm) do not always function as a synecdoche that points to God per se, but rather a literary device that emphasizes the presence of YHWH, His creative power, and His conscious involvement in human affairs.[73] The reference to the strong arm of God should also be seen in the context of the overall motif of the battle between YHWH and Pharaoh in the exodus narrative, a fact underlined by parallel terminology in both Hebrew and Egyptian.[74] Because YHWH is a God of liberation, Israel is to keep the Sabbath day (Deut 5:15b).

---

[72] Similarly, one can note that "remembering" will (and should) lead to action in the mindset of the authors of the Hebrew Bible. God hears the suffering of His people in Egypt and *remembers* them and, as a consequence, the plan of liberation is set in motion. Cf. Exodus 2:24–25. Interestingly, when God *remembers* Noah and his family He sends a wind to dry up the waters (Gen 8:1). A similar pattern can also be observed in Genesis 19:29: God *remembers* Abraham and in consequence takes Lot out of the city of Sodom.

[73] Gerald A. Klingbeil, "The Finger of God in the Old Testament," *ZAW* 112 (2000): 409–416. Cf. also David L. Baker, "The Finger of God and the Forming of a Nation: The Origin and Purpose of the Decalogue," *TynBul* 56 (2005): 1–24, who emphasizes the "finger of God" reference as a marker for the forming of a covenant people.

[74] James K. Hoffmeier, "The Arm of God Versus the Arm of the Pharaoh in the Exodus Narratives," *Biblica* 67 (1986): 378–387; idem, *Israel in Egypt: The Evidence for the Authenticity of the Exodus Tradition* (New York: Oxford University Press, 1997), 151–153; and Manfred Görg, "Der starke Arm Pharao's—Beobachtungen zum Belegspektrum einer Metapher in Palästina und Ägypten," in *Hommages à François Daumas*, ed. Hartwig Altenmüller (Montpellier: Université de Montpellier, 1986), 323–330, all have indicated the military aspect and parallelism of terminology

As already noted, creation is not far away from the Sabbath commandment in Deuteronomy 5, even considering the difference of the motivation clauses of Exodus 20:11 and Deuteronomy 5:15. In a sense, the liberation of Israel out of the land of Egypt is the starting point of a new creation, not dissimilar from the creation account in Genesis. Israel, as a liberated people, is God's new creation. This concept occurs frequently in the prophets and is often associated with the new creation after the exile (e.g., Isa 40:26; 42:5; 43:1, 7, 15; Mal 2:10). This new creation is rooted in God's election (Gen 12:1–3).[75] In this sense, the Sabbath links the cosmic creation to the establishment of a people who are to reflect the holiness of YHWH (Exod 19:6), which is another link to the Sabbath (cf. Exod 20:8).[76]

Conclusions: Creation and Liberation for Community

The study of the Sabbath command in two occurrences of the Decalogue in the Pentateuch has challenged us to look beyond the words, toward the larger context and usage. The fourth commandment is neither the only nor the most important commandment of the Decalogue (even though it is by far the largest, but then length does not always equal importance). Rather, the entire package needs to be appreciated as part and parcel of a covenant document that looks back to creation and reminds the immediate audience that its very existence is the result of another divine creative event—namely, the exodus from slavery and servanthood to liberty and freedom. It appears as if the Sabbath command were the meeting point of both concepts. One particular element that has not yet been handled in detail involves the community aspect of the Sabbath

---

between both Hebrew and Egyptian texts. For the iconography of the king with a raised (right) hand and ready to smite, see Othmar Keel, *Die Welt der altorientalischen Bildsymbolik und das Alte Testament*, 5th ed. (Göttingen: Vandenhoeck & Ruprecht, 1996), 397–404. Siegried Kreuzer, "Die Mächtigkeitsformel im Deuteronomium: Gestaltung, Vorgeschichte und Entwicklung," *ZAW* 109 (1997): 188–207; and idem, "Die Verwendung der Mächtigkeitsformel außerhalb des Deuteronomiums," *ZAW* 109 (1997): 369–384, discusses the phrase in regard to its literary origin, which he understands as a clear marker for the so-called Deuteronomist.

[75] For further discussion, see Seock-Tae Sohn, *The Divine Election of Israel* (Grand Rapids, MI: Eerdmans, 1991); J. Guillén Torralba, *La fuerza oculta de Dios: La elección en el Antiguo Testamento* (Valencia-Córdoba: Publicaciones del Monte de Piedad y Caja de Ahorros de Córdoba, 1983).

[76] The link of holiness between creation and Israel and its religious institutions and practice has also been noted in Philip Peter Jenson, *Graded Holiness: A Key to the Priestly Conception of the World* (Sheffield: JSOT Press, 1992). Cf. also John G. Gammie, *Holiness in Israel* (Minneapolis, MN: Fortress, 1989).

commandment, which is also visible in other commandments. Even though the verbal forms used in the Sabbath commandment are singular forms, the effects and impact of Sabbath keeping involve communities, beginning with a family, its animals, its servants (suggesting a leveling effect of Sabbath observance—social barriers do not bind when mankind is obliged to God), and includes also the stranger in the sphere of influence of the particular Sabbath keeper.

This community is an echo of the lost paradise where mankind and God shared uninhibited and unfettered fellowship. It also prefigures restored community that God's people will enjoy with one another, but even more so with the nations, the people, and the tribes who can hear the voice of a holy God in a text that links humanity's origins with the liberation of a people (and individuals who make up the people) who have tasted and seen God in action in their lives. Finally, the Sabbath command in the Decalogue reminds us that time—created time at that—is not ours but belongs to the Creator. The explicit command, "But the seventh day is the Sabbath of the Lord, your God" (Exod 20:10a and Deut 5:14a) is a reminder of lordship and ownership and again points back to creation. This resonates well in a time and culture where time is understood in terms of accomplishments, ticked-off job lists, or lost (or gained) time.[77] This time is God's time and reminds us of a rhythm that is distinct from our own rhythm of modernity or postmodernity. God's time is holy time and challenges us to look to the only one who is able to make us holy.

---

[77] See the very helpful comments found in Chilton, *Redeeming Time*, 1–20.

CHAPTER 3

"Bread of the Presence" and Sabbath as Culminating Expressions of Covenant Holiness

Roy Gane

Introduction

In Exodus 25:30 the Lord requires a unique presentation offering of bread, called "bread of the Presence" (*lekhem panim*; literally, "bread of the Face"), to be regularly placed before Him (literally, "to my face") on the table in the outer sanctum of the Israelite tabernacle.[1] Leviticus 24:5–9 provides the details:

> You will take choice flour and bake it as twelve pierced loaves. Each loaf will consist of two tenths of an ephah. You will place them in two stacks, six to a stack, on the pure table before the Lord. You will place pure frankincense on each stack, and it will be a token portion for the bread; it is a food gift for the Lord. He will regularly set it out Sabbath after Sabbath before the Lord, from the Israelites, as a permanent covenant. It will belong to Aaron and his sons, and they will eat it in a holy place. For it is most holy to him from the Lord's food gifts, as a permanent portion.[2]

---

[1] Cf. Exodus 35:13; 39:36; 40:23.

[2] From a prepublication draft translation of Leviticus by Roy Gane and William Gilders for the *Common English Bible*.

This concise ritual prescription brings together several key elements: food, divine Presence, sanctuary, Sabbath, covenant, and holiness. The token food gift is offered to the divine Presence in His sanctuary. Renewed every Sabbath, it represents a permanent covenant, and it is most holy.

These elements are profoundly interrelated. The deity is inherently holy (Lev 11:44–45; 19:2; 21:8), and holiness of anything else is derived from Him. It is His Presence that makes the tabernacle structure a sanctuary, a sacred space (cf. Exod 25:8; 40:34–35; Lev 9:23–24). The bread is holy because it is offered to Him at the sanctuary, so it is a kind of sacrifice. He assigns the bread to priestly personnel who are holy because He has authorized them to have a special connection to Himself (Lev 8). They are to place fresh bread on the table every Sabbath, the day that is holy because the Lord reserved this weekly unit of time as special in relation to Himself (e.g., Gen 2:2–3; Exod 20:8–11; 31:12–17). The fact that the twelve loaves of holy bread, one loaf for each of the twelve tribes of Israel,[3] are from the Israelites indicates that they are the offerers, on whose behalf the priests present the bread as a "permanent covenant." Therefore, this covenant must be between God and the Israelites, whom He has joined to Himself as a holy nation (Exod 19:3–6; 24:3–8).

That which binds together the elements of Leviticus 24:5–9 is the concept of holiness, which characterizes divine and human persons, space, time, and food. It is not surprising that holiness is dominant here, given that this passage is part of the section of Leviticus that explicitly emphasizes the need for holiness in every aspect of Israelite life (Lev 17–27), to the extent that many scholars refer to it as the "Holiness Code."[4]

---

[3] For twelve as the standard number of the tribes of Israel, corresponding to the number of the sons of Jacob/Israel, see Genesis 49:28; Exodus 24:4; 28:21; 39:14, etc. However, Jacob gave Joseph a double inheritance in that the descendants of his two sons, Manasseh and Ephraim, each became a separate tribe (Gen 48), resulting in an actual total of thirteen tribes. Nevertheless, later the Lord separated out the tribe of Levi for special holy service so that the Levites were counted separately from the other twelve tribes and did not receive a territorial inheritance in the promised land (Exod 32:28–29; Num 1:47–53; 2:33; 3:1–4:49; 18:1–32).

[4] However, Erhard Blum, "Issues and Problems in the Contemporary Debate Regarding the Priestly Writings," in *The Strata of the Priestly Writings: Contemporary Debate and Future Directions*, ed. Sarah Shectman and Joel S. Baden (Zürich: Theologischer Verlag Zürich, 2009), 33–39, does not see the need for a sharp and diachronic distinction between a "P" (Priestly) source and "H" (Holiness) or "HS" (Holiness School) authorship or redaction. Rather, he explains the distinctive rhetoric of admonition in passages found in Leviticus 11 and 17–26 (cf. some other minor expansions, such as Lev 3:17; 7:22–27; 10:6–11; 16:29–34) as necessary to emphasize the idea that every aspect of Israel's life is subject to the demands of the holy realm, an understanding that is essential to the overall conception of "P," in contexts where this is not self-evident.

This chapter will first summarize what we can learn about the meaning of the "bread of the Presence" from its unique ritual aspects and then further explore the meaning of the bread and its significance in light of the placement of Leviticus 24:5–9 within the book and in comparison with a parallel passage in Exodus (31:12–17). Both of these literary units culminate expressions of the covenant between the Creator, whose holy power is commemorated by the Sabbath, and the faulty people whom He seeks to make holy and among whom He promises to dwell.

Unique Ritual Aspects of the Bread to Acknowledge the Creator-in-Residence

The "bread of the Presence," the only Israelite presentation offering (a ritual genre common elsewhere in the ancient Near East from very early times), is also the only Israelite offering designated "of the Presence" or that represents a "permanent covenant" between the Lord and His people.[5] Moreover, its renewal is the only regular (*tamidh*) activity at the sanctuary to be performed weekly, on the Sabbath, rather than daily.

While the expression "of the Presence" highlights the fact that the Lord resides with Israel, there is no prescription in Leviticus 24 for an accompanying libation, which we would expect with an ancient Near Eastern presentation offering. Thus, the ritual statement limits the anthropomorphism associated with the concept of divine residence.

Although the bread, on which frankincense is placed, represents a "permanent covenant," the ritual shows that the Lord does not consume this offering from Israel, the lesser party to the covenant. He instructs His priests to eat the bread when they replace it on the Sabbath, and He retains only the frankincense (apparently burned for Him when the priests eat the bread), which humans could not eat. In this way, the ritual avoids the excessive anthropomorphism of ancient Near Eastern care and feeding of gods. Unlike those so-called deities, the Lord does not need human food (cf. Ps 50:12–13).

Ancient Near Eastern presentation offerings were placed before gods twice daily, corresponding to human mealtimes. By contrast, the Israelite priests are to arrange the "bread of the Presence" before the Lord only once

---

[5] For further discussion of unique aspects of the "bread of the Presence" offering against their ancient Near East background, see Roy Gane, "'Bread of the Presence' and Creator-in-Residence," *VT* 42 (1992): 179–203; cf. Gane, *Leviticus, Numbers*, NIVAC (Grand Rapids, MI: Zondervan, 2004), 416–417, 420–423.

per week, on the Sabbath. This does not mean that the metabolism of Israel's God operates at one-fourteenth the speed of that of other deities. He does not need food at all. It is true that sacrifices regularly (*tamidh*) burned up on the outer altar every morning and evening are called His "food" (*lekhem*; Num 28:2; cf. Lev 21:6, 8, 17, 21–22, including other sacrifices), but He receives it only as an aroma in the form of smoke (Lev 1:13; Num 28:2, 6, 8). So there is no danger of supposing that He consumes food on the altar as humans do. On the other hand, humans do eat bread laid out on tables, so it is the "bread of the Presence" offering that needs to avoid a degree of anthropomorphism that could lead to mythic notions about God. Therefore, the Israelite version of cultic bread-laying replaces daily mealtimes, which would indicate that humans feed their deity, with the weekly Sabbath, which serves as a reminder that the Lord is the Creator (cf. Exod 20:11; 31:17). As the Creator, He feeds humans because He is also the Sustainer of all that He has created.[6] Through an apparently minor modification of ancient Near Eastern practice, the "bread of the Presence" expresses an opposite theological statement.

So why risk confusion by having a presentation offering at all? Should not God's people avoid theological "slippery slopes" altogether? Nevertheless, the "bread of the Presence" is needed to affirm some crucial concepts: God dwells with His people, has established a permanent covenant with them, and continually provides for them as their Creator-in-Residence.[7] So rather than "throwing the baby out with the bath water," the Lord establishes a balanced representation of His relationship to Israel that expresses His truth while carefully avoiding error.

Literary Placement of Leviticus 24:5–9 and Parallel to Exodus 31:12–17

Having identified some basic aspects of Leviticus 24:5–9 within its Israelite and ancient Near Eastern ritual contexts, we now turn to investigation of its literary context. As mentioned above, the "bread of the Presence" instructions appropriately appear within the literary environment of

---

[6] Job 12:10; Psalm 104:14–15; 145:15–16; Daniel 5:23. Cf. the sample of manna kept in the sanctuary (Exod 16:33–34), which reminds Israel of the food (*lekhem*, Exod 16:15) that the Lord provided for the Israelites in the wilderness.

[7] "The bread functions within the context of the tabernacle. Thus, we expect the theological statement provided by the bread and its ritual to emphasize aspects of the meaning of the tabernacle. This is, in fact, the case. Both the bread and the tabernacle are tied to the covenant and to creation" (Gane, "Bread of the Presence," 202).

holiness that dominates the latter part of Leviticus. However, scholars have struggled to understand how Leviticus 24 is more closely connected to the preceding and following material and how its two parts (Lev 24:1–9 and Lev 24:10–23) relate to each other.[8] Leviticus 23 and 25 provide instructions regarding sacred times: Sabbath and annual festivals (Lev 23) and sabbatical and jubilee years (Lev 25). But the intervening chapter 24 contains legislation concerning olive oil for the lampstand (Lev 24:1–4; mainly reiterating Exod 27:20–21) and bread for the table (Lev 24:5–9) in the tabernacle, followed by a narrative concerning an episode of brawling and blasphemy by a half-Israelite and half-Egyptian man that called forth his capital condemnation and additional legislation from God (Lev 24:10–23).

There are obvious connections between the pericopes regarding the olive oil (Lev 24:1–4) and the bread (Lev 24:5–9). Both these perishable materials that need to be replenished are provided by the Israelites to be regularly (*tamidh*) used before the Lord (*lifne YHWH*) at pure (adj. from root *thr*) items of furniture located opposite each other in the outer apartment of God's earthly residence.[9] But what do these passages have to do with the preceding and following sections?

Several factors contribute to literary cohesion between Leviticus 24:1–9 and the preceding and following chapters (Lev 23; 25). First, the two pericopes in Leviticus 24:1–9, where the Israelites are permanently responsible for providing the oil for the light and the bread for the table, logically follow chapter 23, which highlights their responsibility for maintaining the festivals. Thus, Leviticus 23:1–24:9 is united by the "responsibility of *the people* to maintain *the public* cult."[10]

Second, there is continuation of cyclical time from the weekly Sabbath and yearly festival observances of Leviticus 23 to the daily oil and weekly bread rituals of chapter 24 (vs. 1–9) and then to the sabbatical and

---

[8] E.g., Gordon J. Wenham, *The Book of Leviticus*, NICOT (Grand Rapids, MI: Eerdmans, 1979), 308–309; John E. Hartley, *Leviticus*, WBC (Dallas, TX: Word, 1992), 396–397; Jacob Milgrom, *Leviticus 23–27: A New Translation with Introduction and Commentary*, AB (New York: Doubleday, 2001), 2081–2082; cf. references in Wilfried Warning, *Literary Artistry in Leviticus* (Leiden: Brill, 1999), 92–93.

[9] Hartley, *Leviticus*, 398; Warning, *Literary Artistry*, 95. Note that both the light/lamps (rather than the oil) and the bread are arranged (verb from the root ʿrk; Lev 24:3–4, 8). See Milgrom, *Leviticus 23–27*, 2082–2083 regarding the question of why Leviticus 24 does not deal with the people's obligation to supply the daily incense on the inner, golden altar, which Exodus 35:8 implies.

[10] Milgrom, *Leviticus 23–27*, 2082; cf. Jacob Milgrom, *Leviticus: A Book of Ritual and Ethics*, Continental Commentary (Minneapolis, MN: Fortress, 2004), 288.

jubilee year cycles of chapter 25.[11] More specifically, the idea of Sabbath in Leviticus 24:8, where the "bread of the Presence" is renewed Sabbath by Sabbath, provides an important link between chapter 24 and the preceding and following chapters, where "Sabbath" (*shabbath*) appears several times (Lev 23:3, 11, 15–16, 32, 38; 25:2, 4, 6, 8; cf. 26:2, 34–35, 43).[12] Third, the sanctuary light (Lev 24:1–4) recollects God's creation of light (Gen 1:3–5, 14–16), the basis for delineating units of time, which makes cyclical religious observances possible (Lev 23:1–24:9; 25; see further below).

More difficult is the question of why Leviticus 24:10–23 (blasphemer and ensuing legislation), which does not involve cyclical time or maintenance of the public cult, is inserted in chapter 24 after verses 1–9. The placement of Leviticus 24:10–23 identifies the divine name as the ultimate sanctum in an overall progression of entities in Leviticus 19–24 that shows ascending holiness in proximity to God's presence: laypersons (Lev 19–20), priests (Lev 21:1–22:16), sacrificial animal victims offered at the outer altar (Lev 22:17–33), sacred times (Lev 23), oil and bread presented in the outer sanctum (Lev 24:1–9), and finally, the name of the deity YHWH (Lev 24:10–23—blasphemed), who is enthroned above the ark in the holy of holies (Exod 25:22; Num 7:89; 1 Sam 4:4; 2 Sam 6:2, etc.).[13] The progression

---

[11] Christophe Nihan, *From Priestly Torah to Pentateuch: A Study in the Composition of the Book of Leviticus* (Tübingen: Mohr Siebeck, 2007), 98–99, 512; cf. Nobuyoshi Kiuchi, *Leviticus*, AOTC (Nottingham: Apollos, 2007), 436; Mathilde Frey, "The Sabbath in the Pentateuch: An Exegetical and Theological Study" (PhD diss., Andrews University, 2011), 242.

[12] Warning, *Literary Artistry*, 93–94, who also observes that the "bread of the Presence" offering, consisting of stacks of loaves with frankincense placed on them, is a "food gift" (*'isheh*) for the Lord (Lev 24:7; cf. v. 9). This supplies the Sabbath "food gift" that is lacking in Leviticus 23, where "food gifts" are prescribed for the annual festivals, but not for the weekly Sabbath in verse 3 (ibid., 94). Note, however, that although the Israelite ritual system centered at the sanctuary honored the Sabbath, Sabbath rest itself preceded and was independent of that ritual system, fulfilling a moral requirement to accept God's work as that of the Creator (Gen 2:2–3; Exod 16:22–30; 20:8–11; cf. Gane, *Leviticus, Numbers*, 393–395, 754–755).

[13] See Gane, "Bread of the Presence," 192 n. 41. This approach has limitations. The progression is weakened by the fact that it involves a mixture of different kinds of entities (persons, animals, time, objects, divine name) and does not adequately explain why the section on sacred times, including the weekly Sabbath and the annual festivals, occupies its present position in Leviticus 23. Moreover, a progression of ascending sanctity does not always operate within a given section. For example, the sanctity of the Sabbath (Lev 23:1–3) is by no means inferior to that of the annual festivals (Lev 23:4–44). However, other scholars have subsequently acknowledged the importance of the divine name in Leviticus 24. Nihan, *From Priestly Torah to Pentateuch*, 99 (cf. p. 513), observes "that the center of 24:10–23 is constituted by the blasphemy of the divine Name (vs. 10–16) . . . and that *the divine Name is, with the Sabbath, the other major sanctum outside the sanctuary and its belongings which can be desecrated by the Israelites*. Hence, possibly, the reason for the inclusion of the account of

is most clearly seen in movements of topics from laypersons to priests and from items associated with the outer altar to those that are located in the outer sanctum and finally in the holy of holies.

Regarding a rationale for placement of Leviticus 24:10–23, Jacob Milgrom prefers the solution provided by Mary Douglas's a ring structure of Leviticus, in which 24:10–23 balances 10:1–5, the narrative of failure by Nadab and Abihu.[14] However, this leaves unexplained the relationships between Leviticus 24:10–23 and the immediately preceding and following units.[15]

Rather than emphasizing continuity between Leviticus 24:1–9 and 24:10–23, Nobuyoshi Kiuchi accounts for placement of the latter unit as providing an important contrast:

> Therefore, on the whole, the first part of this chapter presents the positive and spiritual side of the divine-human relationship through the symbolism of the ritual in the Holy Place, while the second part relates its negative side by reporting a blatant act of blasphemy.[16]

So the fact that Leviticus 24:10–23 appears to be jarringly out of place by recounting a violation of holiness, in opposition to the prevailing theme of Leviticus,[17] precisely captures the intended rhetorical effect. This contrasting passage would be a warning for the people as a whole in the second part of the book, which concerns their responsibilities for holy living, just as the narrative of Nadab and Abihu (Lev 10) serves to warn the priests and assert God's holiness (Lev 10:3) in the first part of the book, which concentrates on ritual worship.[18]

24:10–23 between 23:1–24:9 and ch. 25." Emphasis original. Michael Hildenbrand, *Structure and Theology in the Holiness Code* (North Richland Hills, TX: Bibal, 2004), 244, notes that the name YHWH appears seven times in Leviticus 24:1–9, thereby emphasizing the name before the half-Egyptian blasphemes it.

[14] Milgrom, *Leviticus 23–27*, 2082, citing Mary Douglas, "The Forbidden Animals in Leviticus," *JSOT* 59 (1993): 11.

[15] Cf. Leigh M. Trevaskis, "The Purpose of Leviticus 24 within its Literary Context," *VT* 59 (2009): 306–307.

[16] Kiuchi, *Leviticus*, 444.

[17] Nehama Leibowitz, *Studies in Vayikra (Leviticus)* (Jerusalem: World Zionist Organization, 1983), 243, points out that "the story of the blasphemer stood in direct contrast to the theme of holiness that distinguishes the whole book emphasising how life devoid of sanctity may debase man."

[18] Allen P. Ross, *Holiness to the LORD: A Guide to the Exposition of the Book of Leviticus* (Grand Rapids, MI: Baker, 2002), 444–445. The book of Numbers also uses positive-negative contrasts to provide warnings, e.g., Numbers 15:22–29—expiability of inadvertent sin, in contrast to verses

Leigh M. Trevaskis expands on the contrast between Leviticus 24:1–9 and 24:10–23:

> Within Lev 24 an ideal Israel is represented by the symbolic prescriptions of Lev 24:1–9: 12 tribes 'regularly' committing themselves to living under YHWH's sovereign rule. However, as is characteristic of H, the narrative concerning the blasphemer (vv. 10–23) extends this ideal to everyday life within Israel. The holiness of the community required each of its members, even the "sojourner," to adhere to YHWH's law.... By observing the prescribed festivals Israel would continue living under YHWH's rule and within his presence. That is, the symbolic 'ideal Israel' (Lev 24:1–9) would materialise through adherence to YHWH's rule. Within the same analogy, Israel would experience the fate of the blasphemer (Lev 24:10–23), presumably by death or exile (cf. Lev 26:33, 38), if she rebelled against YHWH.[19]

The oil and bread are from the Israelites (Lev 24:2, 8), which means that these items are presented to the Lord on behalf of the people and represent them in this sense. Additionally, the "bread of the Presence" offering consists of twelve loaves in two stacks, with six loaves in each stack (Lev 24:5–6), which most likely means that one loaf is presented on behalf of each tribe (cf. Num 7:2–3, 84, 86–87; 17:2, 6 [MT vs. 17, 21], etc.).[20] Compare the names of the twelve tribes engraved on two onyx stones, with six names on each stone, which are attached to the shoulder pieces of the high priest's ephod (vest) and serve as a reminder for the Israelites before the Lord (Exod 28:9–12).[21] Therefore, Trevaskis, interprets the loaves as symbolic representations of

---

30–36—inexpiability of defiant sin and execution of Sabbath wood-gatherer. The movement from ritual worship in Leviticus 24:1–9 to life in the wider community in verses 10–23 reflects this movement between the two halves of Leviticus (Trevaskis, "The Purpose of Leviticus 24," 307).

[19] Trevaskis, "The Purpose of Leviticus 24," 312.

[20] Rather than emphasizing that the loaves are offered to God, Hartley, *Leviticus*, 402, focuses on the benefit that God returns to them: "The table with the twelve loaves of bread on it represented the twelve tribes in fellowship with God. That is, God served as the host, having a meal prepared for the twelve tribes at his place of residence. This meal was eaten weekly by the priests as representatives of the people inside the holy chamber in the presence of God."

[21] Wenham, *The Book of Leviticus*, 310; cf. references in Trevaskis, "The Purpose of Leviticus 24," 300 n. 19. For division of the twelve tribes themselves into two groups, see Deuteronomy 27:12–13, where six tribes are to stand on Mt. Gerizim and the other six on Mount Ebal for a recitation of covenant blessings and curses.

their presenters.²² If so, perhaps the weekly renewal of the bread could be taken to represent a kind of renewal of the Israelites each Sabbath.

Regarding the crimes of the Israelite-Egyptian blasphemer (Lev 24:10–11), the ensuing legislation concerning the same categories of faults (blasphemy and assault) applies to any member of the Israelite community, whether citizen or resident alien (Lev 24:15–22). Therefore, his fate is clearly a warning to all and he could be taken to represent what everyone else would be like if they were to behave similarly (cf. Num 15:32–36—wood-gatherer who violated the Sabbath).²³

For the present chapter, it is particularly significant that the instructions regarding the "bread of the Presence" (Lev 24:5–9), which is renewed each Sabbath and represents a "permanent covenant" between the Lord and His people (Lev 24:8), immediately precede a narrative about serious moral failure in rebellion against God (Lev 24:10–23). The only other passage in the Pentateuch where God speaks of a "permanent covenant" between the Lord and the Israelite nation as a whole during the wilderness period is Exodus 31:12–17.²⁴ Here Sabbath observance is not only a sign of the relationship between the Lord and Israel, but also constitutes a "permanent covenant" (Exod 31:13, 16–17).

Sabbath and "permanent covenant" are uniquely linked in Leviticus 24:8 and Exodus 31:16,²⁵ but scholars' suggestions regarding the relationship between the bread and blasphemer pericopes have prompted recognition of a further parallel. Just as the instructions for the two stacks of "permanent covenant" bread changed on the Sabbath are followed by a narrative of failure, so the Sabbath legislation in Exodus 31:12–17 and the notice that God gave Moses two tablets of witness (or testimony) to the covenant stipulations (Exod 31:18) are directly followed by the narrative of the catastrophic golden calf apostasy and its aftermath (Exod 32:1–34:9). At God's command, some Israelites (Levites) executed about three thousand rebels (Exod 32:26–28),²⁶ just as Israelites were

---

²² Trevaskis, "The Purpose of Leviticus 24," 312.

²³ Cf. Frey, "The Sabbath in the Pentateuch," 130–131.

²⁴ This passage contains language and concepts characteristic of the "Holiness" portion of Leviticus that includes chapter 24 (Gane, "Bread of the Presence," 200; Israel Knohl, *The Sanctuary of Silence: The Priestly Torah and the Holiness School* [Minneapolis: Fortress, 1995], 15–16, 105). Earlier, God had given circumcision to Abraham, with his household and descendants, as a "permanent covenant" (Gen 17:13).

²⁵ Gane, "Bread of the Presence," 199.

²⁶ The Lord also sent a plague (Exod 32:35), but the body count is not recorded.

responsible for executing the blasphemer (Lev 24:23). So in Exodus, as in Leviticus, Sabbath and "eternal covenant" immediately precede rebellion and its consequences.

Using the unique parallel between Leviticus 24:8 and Exodus 31:16 as a base point and reading forward and backward from there in both books, we can identify a remarkable succession of mostly parallel thematic developments in Exodus 19 to 40 (the end of the book) and the entire book of Leviticus. The following table selectively highlights key themes in portions of material that vary in length, without attempting to analyze these portions into smaller literary units (e.g., as discrete divine speeches or laws).

Parallel Thematic Developments in Exodus and Leviticus			
Exodus	Content	Leviticus	Content
chap. 19	narrative of God's glory appearing on Mt. Sinai to make **covenant** with people He wants to make **holy**		
20:1–21	God gives Ten Commandments (**covenant** stipulations, including **Sabbath**; vs. 8–11)		
20:22–26	instructions for sacrificial worship (regarding altar)	chaps. 1–7	instructions for sacrificial worship at **sanctuary** (regarding rituals and priestly portions)
		chaps. 8–10	narrative of consecration and inauguration of **sanctuary**, and **failure** by Nadab and Abihu
chaps. 21–23	instructions for **holy** living (including **holy** times: sabbath years of land, **Sabbath**, and annual festivals; 23:10–12, 14–17)	chaps. 11–15	instructions for (physical ritual) pure living (compatible with **sanctuary**)
chap. 24	narrative of **covenant** ratification by sacrifice; elders and Moses in God's presence	chap. 16	instructions to annually purge **sanctuary**, with high priest in God's presence

Parallel Thematic Developments in Exodus and Leviticus			
Exodus	Content	Leviticus	Content
25:1–9	instructions to provide materials for **sanctuary**	chaps. 17–22	instructions for **holy** living
25:10–31:11	instructions to prepare **sanctuary**		
31:12–17	instruction for **holy Sabbath** as sign that God makes Israelites **holy** (v. 13), as **"permanent covenant"** (v. 16), and as sign of **Creation** (v. 17)	chap. 23	instructions for **holy** times: **Sabbath** and annual festivals
		24:1–4	instructions to provide olive oil for light from pure lampstand in **sanctuary** "from evening until morning" (cf. **creation** days in Gen 1, "evening … morning")
31:18	God gives to Moses two tablets of witness/testimony (to the **covenant** stipulations)	24:5–9	instructions to provide **holy** "bread of the Presence" representing Israelite tribes (twelve loaves in two stacks) on pure table in **sanctuary**, renewed regularly on **Sabbath** as **"permanent covenant"** (v. 8)
32:1–6	narrative of **failure** by Israelites: apostasy with golden calf ("god who brought them from Egypt," 32:4)	24:10–12	narrative of **failure** by Israelite-Egyptian: assault and blasphemy
32:7–34:9	divine response, including condemnation of rebels, and Moses' intercession to spare nation	24:13–14	divine condemnation of rebel
34:10–28	God renews **covenant**, with instructions (including **holy** times: **Sabbath** and annual festivals, vs. 18, 21–23) in response to the failure	24:15–22	instructions (penalties for blasphemy and assault) in response to the failure

Parallel Thematic Developments in Exodus and Leviticus			
Exodus	Content	Leviticus	Content
34:29–35:1	Moses relays God's instructions to Israelites (his face shining from encounter with God)	24:23	Moses relays God's instructions to Israelites (who execute blasphemer)
35:2–3	instruction for **holy Sabbath**	25:1–7	instructions for **holy sabbath** years of land
		25:8–55	instructions for **holy** jubilee years with release of land and freedom for debt servants
		chap. 26	**covenant** blessings and curses, holding Israelites accountable for **holy** living
35:4–19	instructions to provide materials for **sanctuary**	chap. 27	dedications to **sanctuary** **END OF LEVITICUS**
35:20–40:33	narrative regarding preparation of **sanctuary**		
40:34–38	God's glory moves to **sanctuary** **END OF EXODUS**		

It would require many pages to unpack this table thoroughly. Here we focus on the parallel portions shaded in gray (Exod 31:12–18; Lev 23:1–24:9), which contain the Sabbath and "bread of the Presence" pericopes, which we will examine in terms of their internal relationships and then their relationships to other parts of Exodus and Leviticus.

Relationships within Exodus 31:12–18 and Leviticus 23:1–24:9

There is a direct parallel between the legislation for the weekly Sabbath in Exodus 31:12–17 and the beginning of Leviticus 23, which reminds Israelites to keep the Sabbath holy by abstaining from work (Lev 23:3). Placement of the Sabbath here, before the instructions regarding the annual festivals (including ceremonial sabbaths; Lev 23:7–8, 21, 25, 32, 35–36) that occupy the rest of the chapter, serves as a reminder that it is the archetype of holy time.

The ideas of covenant and creation provide implicit but strong parallels between Exodus 31:12–17 and the instructions to provide olive oil for the lampstand (Lev 24:1-4). Regarding the concept of "covenant," Sabbath is a "permanent covenant" in Exodus 31:16, and Leviticus 24:3 specifies the location of the lamp outside the inner veil of the witness/testimony (to the covenant). Regarding creation, in Exodus 31:17, Sabbath is a sign that the Lord created heaven and earth in six days and rested on the seventh day. The lampstand is connected to creation in several ways. First, its regular (*tamidh*) cycle is uniquely "from evening until morning" (Lev 24:3; cf. Exod 27:21), reminiscent of the "evening . . . morning" cycles of the six days of creation in Genesis 1 (vs. 5, 8, 13, etc.), by contrast with the "morning . . . evening" (or "between the two evenings") cycles of all other daily regular rituals (Exod 29:39; 30:7-8; Lev 6:20 [MT v. 13]; Num 28:4).[27]

Second, the lampstand provides light, which the Lord caused to appear on the first day of Creation, and which provides the basis for measuring time (Gen 1:3-5). So by supplying olive oil from their land for the lamps, the Israelites acknowledge that God lit our world, keeps it lit with lights in the heavens, and is the originator and ruler of time. The Hebrew word for "light" or "luminary" (*ma'or*) in Leviticus 24:2 is the same as the word for "light" or "luminary" to describe the sun and moon on the fourth day of creation in Genesis 1:14-16.[28] There the sun and moon mark appointed times (plural of *mo'edh*, Gen 1:14), days, and years, without which the sacred calendar of festivals to be observed in the promised land (Lev 23) would not be possible.

Third, given the creation connections already mentioned, the seven lamps of the lampstand (Exod 25:37; 37:23; Lev 24:4 only refers to plural "lamps") can be taken to correspond to the seven days of creation.

Moving on to Leviticus 24:5-9, we have already pointed out that "permanent covenant" and "Sabbath" link this passage concerning the "bread of the Presence" to Exodus 31:12-17, where Sabbath commemorates creation (Exod 31:17). Insofar as the bread represents the Israelites, it would acknowledge that God created them, as He created light, and in a sense He could be regarded as renewing them on the Sabbath. The bread also evokes the idea of creation because it is basic food (cf. *Sirach* 29:21), as

---

[27] Not including the weekly regular ritual of the "bread of the Presence" (Lev 24:8).

[28] On this and other connections between the sanctuary/temple and creation (including the pre-fall garden of Eden), see Richard M. Davidson, "Cosmic Metanarrative for the Coming Millennium," *JATS* 11 (2000): 109-110. For a list of links between the sanctuary/temple and creation, see Moshe Weinfeld, "Sabbath, Temple and the Enthronement of the Lord—The Problem of the Sitz im Leben of Genesis 1:1-2:3," in *Mélanges bibliques et orientaux en l'honneur de M. Henri Cazelles*, ed. A. Caquot and M. Delcor (Kevelaer: Butzon & Bercker, 1981), 501-512.

implied by the fact that the Hebrew word *lekhem* ("bread") often refers to food in general (Gen 3:19; 31:54; 43:32; Exod 2:20, etc.). The Lord created food in the beginning (Gen 1:29–30) and His creative power continues to provide food for all (cf. Ps 104:14–15; 145:15–16).[29]

Thus far we have found that the concepts of Sabbath, creation, and covenant link Exodus 31:12–17 to Leviticus 23:1–24:9. In Exodus 31, we can add verse 18 to this set of parallels because it reports that when God finished speaking with Moses on Mt. Sinai, He gave him the two tablets of witness/testimony, comprising the covenant document. For the Israelites to be holy, they must comply with all of the Lord's commandments, including those recorded on the tablets (cf. Exod 19:5–6; Lev 20:7–8; Num 15:40), and Sabbath is a sign that the Lord makes His people holy (Exod 31:13). Thus, it is the Lord who gives them the ability to follow His requirements. The Sabbath connection preempts a notion of legalistic self-help by reminding God's people that in order to enjoy the covenant benefits they must rely on empowerment by their Creator and rest from self-dependence.[30]

Exodus 31:12–18 and Leviticus 23:1–24:9 in Relation to Earlier Units

Here we look at the previous context of Exodus 31:12–18 in the book of Exodus and then the previous context of Leviticus 23:1–24:9 in the book of Leviticus. Exodus 19–24 consists of narrative units and divine speeches concerning the Lord's covenant with the Israelites, whom He wants to live holy lives in harmony with His commandments, including the Sabbath and other holy times.[31] Then divine speeches in Exodus 25:1–31:11 concern instructions for setting up the sanctuary, God's holy dwelling place (including its priesthood; Exod 28–29) among His people.

Just after the tabernacle instructions, the Lord concisely recapitulates the themes of Exodus 19–24 in Exodus 31:12–17, which reminds the Israelites what His dwelling among them will entail. For one thing, they are not to work on the Sabbath, the temple of time, even to build His sanctuary,

---

[29] Gane, "Bread of the Presence," 202–203. While humans now work land to obtain their food (*lekhem,* Gen 3:19), agricultural toil is futile without the divine power that keeps nature operating. God's provision does not depend on agriculture or even land, as shown by the creative way He supplied Israel with manna (Exod 16), a memorial sample of which was kept in the inner sanctum of the sanctuary (Exod 16:32–34; cf. 26:33; Heb 9:4).

[30] Reclamation from sin also requires dependence on the Creator, as David recognized when he prayed: "Create in me a clean heart, O God, and renew a right spirit within me" (Ps 51:10 [MT v. 12]).

[31] The narrative of Exodus 16 regarding weekly cessation of manna provides background to subsequent laws regarding the Sabbath.

the temple of space.³² Furthermore, they are to recognize that their Creator and covenant Lord sanctifies them in accordance with His desire for them to be His "kingdom of priests and a holy nation" (Exod 19:6). By implication, their holiness would bring them into harmony with Himself and His holy dwelling.

Turning now to Leviticus, in chapters 1–16 the Lord gives instructions relevant to the sanctuary, including directions for sacrificial worship, separation of physical ritual impurity from the holy domain, and annual purgation of the sanctuary from sins and impurities. Then Leviticus 17–22 teaches all Israelites how to live comprehensively holy lives in order to emulate the character of the holy deity, who resides among them (see Lev 19:2; 20:26; 21:8).³³ Continuing the theme of the people's reception of and participation in holiness, Leviticus 23 reiterates the Sabbath command and extends the topic of holy time to the annual festivals. These festivals involve ritual activities at the sanctuary that celebrate gracious activities of the divine covenant Lord on behalf of Israel, including His deliverance of the Israelites from Egypt (Lev 23:5–6, 42–43) and His provision for their needs through the agricultural cycle that He has created and maintains (Lev 23:10–11, 16–17, 39).

Subsequently, Leviticus 24:1–9 focuses on holiness in the sanctuary (light from the lamps and bread on the table), including a reminder of the Sabbath and the covenant holiness of the people (twelve loaves as a "permanent covenant"). So just as Exodus 31:12–17 briefly recapitulates earlier themes of the book of Exodus, the "bread of the Presence" pericope (Lev 24:5–9) encapsulates earlier themes of Leviticus. Explicit or implicit references or connections to the covenant, the Sabbath, the people's holiness, and the sanctuary in

---

[32] Nahum M. Sarna, *Exodus: The Traditional Hebrew Text with the New JPS Translation*, JPSTC (Philadelphia, PA: Jewish Publication Society, 1991), 201, comments on Exodus 31:12–17: "The concluding—and, appropriately, the seventh—literary unit within the pericope of the instructions for the Tabernacle is devoted to the observance of the law of the Sabbath. Correspondingly, the resumption of the Tabernacle narrative in chapter 35 commences with the Sabbath law. This structural pattern is intended to make an emphatic statement about the hierarchy of values that informs the Torah: The Tabernacle enshrines the concept of the holiness of space; the Sabbath embodies the concept of the holiness of time. The latter takes precedence over the former, and the work of the Tabernacle must yield each week to the Sabbath rest." For the rabbinic idea that Exodus 31:12–17, coming just after instructions for construction of the tabernacle, indicates that work on the tabernacle does not override the Sabbath, see the commentaries of Rashi and Ibn Ezra on Exodus 31:13 (for additional references, see Knohl, *The Sanctuary of Silence*, 16 n. 20). On the Sabbath as a "sanctuary in time," see Abraham J. Heschel, *The Sabbath: Its Meaning for Modern Man* (New York: Farrar, Straus and Young, 1951), 27–29.

[33] Leviticus 17–18 do not explicitly refer to holiness, but they clearly relate to this theme.

these passages summarize and climax the expressions of God's ideal for His people up to this point in both books. In Exodus and Leviticus, His ideal remains constant. Holiness is the paramount theme of this ideal: the holy deity wants to have a covenant connection with the Israelites and dwell among them, the people whom He makes holy, as signified by their observance of holy time, especially the Sabbath.

Not only does God want to reside among the Israelites in His holy dwelling, but He also wants to dwell in their holy lives. As the above table shows, there is a thematic parallel between the sanctuary and holy living that is implied by a structural literary parallel between Exodus 25:1–31:11, regarding establishment of the sanctuary, and Leviticus 17–22, regarding holy living. Not only are the sanctuary and its priests consecrated to the Lord (Lev 8), but also all Israelites are to be consecrated to Him (Lev 11:44–45; 19:2; 20:7, 26; 21:8; cf. Exod 19:6). This connection serves as a harbinger of Paul's statements that Christians are God's temple (1 Cor 3:16–17; 2 Cor 6:16; Eph 2:19–22; cf. 1 Cor 6:19).

While the "permanent sign" pericopes are parallel, the "bread of the Presence" in Leviticus 24:5–9 is more directly connected to the sanctuary than the Sabbath is in Exodus 31:12–17. The association between the latter and the sanctuary is primarily due to the fact that this passage immediately follows instructions for constructing the tabernacle, which can be taken to infer that the Sabbath is a holy unit in the dimension of time corresponding to a holy unit in the dimension of physical space.[34] Since holiness is defined in relation to God (e.g., Exod 15:11; 28:36; Lev 11:44–45; 19:2), the Sabbath is the special time of divine Presence just as the sanctuary is the special place of the Presence where the "bread of the Presence" is located.

There are also indirect links between the Sabbath and the sanctuary through the creation theme, which is involved with both of them.[35] For example, just as God *sabbathed* (ceased/rested) on the seventh day of creation and made it holy (Gen 2:2–3), thereby introducing the concept of holiness in the Bible,[36] the sanctuary (with its priesthood), consecrated in seven days (Exod 29:35–37; Lev 8:33–35), is His resting place (Ps 132:8, 13–14).

---

[34] On the Sabbath in Exodus 31:12–17, especially including the connection between the sanctuary and the Sabbath as places of divine meeting in space and time, see Frey, "The Sabbath in the Pentateuch," 193–224.

[35] See discussion and references in Gane, "Bread of the Presence," 200–201; and Frey, "The Sabbath in the Pentateuch," 196.

[36] Sarna, *Exodus*, 201.

However, Exodus 31:12–17 does not contain a direct internal reference to the sanctuary.

On the other hand, within Leviticus 24:5–9 the "bread of the Presence" is directly linked to the sanctuary because there it is presented to the Lord by His priest. Additionally, as noted above, the description "of the Presence" uniquely identifies the bread as belonging to the divine resident of the sanctuary.

Two additional factors connect the bread to the sanctuary. First, unlike other offerings, the bread is a fixture in the sanctuary. Not only does it remain on the golden table throughout the week, but it is also the only food offering item included in Exodus 35 and 39 in lists of components of the sanctuary and its equipment (Exod 35:13; 39:36). The bread belongs to the table as olive oil does to the lamps and incense to the incense altar (cf. Exod 35:14–15; 39:37–38), all of which are used in regular (*tamidh*) service for the Lord. In fact, the bread is even more closely associated with its item of furniture than the oil and incense are to theirs in the sense that the bread is transported on its table ("the regular bread," Num 4:7).[37]

Second, the twelve loaves in the outer sanctum symbolize the divine covenant by displaying items of the same number as the tribes of Israel, the lesser party to the covenant. The terms of this covenant are recorded in a document, the Ten Commandments, contained in the "ark of the covenant" (Num 10:33; 14:44, etc.; cf. 1 Kgs 6:19; 8:6) or "ark of the witness/testimony (to the covenant stipulations)" (Exod 25:21–22, 33–34, etc.) housed in the inner sanctum of the sanctuary (Exod 26:33–34). So the bread offering represents Israel before the Lord in a symbolic physical environment that implies their accountability to the terms of His covenant with them.[38]

Exodus 31:12–18 and Leviticus 23:1–24:9 in Relation to Later Units

After the lofty summations of God's holy ideal in Exodus 31:12–18 and Leviticus 24:5–9, Israelites fall over cliffs of corporate and individual failure in Exodus 32:1–6 and Leviticus 24:10–12, respectively.[39] These

---

[37] On the importance of the table, see Milgrom, *Leviticus 23–27*, 2091–2092.

[38] Cf. Trevaskis, "The Purpose of Leviticus 24," 303–304, who refers to other elements of the sanctuary.

[39] Hildenbrand, *Structure and Theology*, 250, points out that repetition of the root *qdsh*, "holy," three times in Leviticus 24:9 strengthens the contrast with the following narrative that involves desecration of the divine name. We can add that the root *qdsh* also appears three times in Exodus 31:12–17 (vs. 13, 14, 15), just before the golden calf narrative, and does not reappear until the

events provide negative examples of what holy living in faithfulness to God's covenant is not. In Exodus, the failure is idolatry (with associated wild amusement) and in Leviticus it is assault and blasphemy. Both sets of faults repudiate the lordship of YHWH, the Creator (Exod 20:11; 31:17),[40] and both are connected to Egypt. In Exodus 32:4, the golden calf is heralded as the deity who brought the Israelites from Egypt, and in Leviticus 24:10 the brawling blasphemer is identified as half Egyptian. Throwing off YHWH's covenant, rebellious members of His community choose to return to the ways of Egypt (cf. Exod 32:1–6, etc.).[41] The Lord responded to the challenges in Exodus and Leviticus by condemning rebels and ordering their execution by the community, and also by giving additional instructions to counter such failure to comply with holy living in the future (Exod 32:7–35:1; Lev 24:13–23).[42]

Next in both books are units of further divine legislation regarding sabbatical principles: Exodus 35:2–3 concerns the weekly Sabbath and Leviticus 25:1–7 provides detailed instructions for a sabbatical fallow year every seventh year (previously introduced in Exod 23:10–11 just before a reminder of the weekly Sabbath in Exod 23:12).[43] Then Leviticus 25 introduces super-sabbatical jubilee years that should recur every fiftieth year after seven sabbatical-year cycles (7 x 7 = 49 years), when debt servants would be free from their obligations and could reclaim ownership of their ancestral agricultural land (Lev 25:8–55).

Leviticus 26 brings the book to a rhetorical climax by outlining blessings for obedience to the Lord and curses for disobedience. This chapter

---

Sabbath command in Exodus 35:2.

[40] On the nature and significance of assault and blasphemy in Leviticus 24:10–23, see Gane, *Leviticus, Numbers*, 417–418, 426. A permanent and serious physical blemish or disfigurement (Heb. *mum*) disqualifies a priest from holy officiation (Lev 21:16–23; cf. Lev 22:17–25 for analogous disqualification of an animal's fitness for sacrifice), implying that such a condition caused by assault "detracts from holiness by partially defacing the live human image of God. In a sense, assault is analogous to blasphemy, which also violates holiness" (ibid., 426); cf. Hildenbrand, *Structure and Theology*, 256–257.

[41] Later during the wilderness wandering, rebellious Israelites regretted leaving Egypt and wanted to physically return to that place of slavery from which the Lord had graciously delivered them (Num 11:5, 18, 20; 14:2–4; 20:5; 21:5).

[42] The community-wide scope of the golden calf fiasco, which annulled the newly contracted covenant (cf. Exod 32:15–16, 19; cf. chap. 24), initially called forth God's terminal condemnation of the entire nation (Exod 32:10), but in response to Moses' intercession (Exod 32:11–13), the Lord granted corporate amnesty (Exod 32:14) and renewed the covenant (Exod 34, esp. v. 10).

[43] Note that Exodus 23:10–12, 14–17 briefly outline sacred times on which Leviticus 23 and 25 elaborate.

recapitulates covenant conditions and holds the Israelites accountable for holy living in accordance with God's commands. The introduction to the blessings and curses gives special prominence to the Lord's prohibition of idolatry, keeping His Sabbaths, and respecting His sanctuary (Lev 26:1–2).[44] If the people persist in rebellion against God, including in failure to give the land its sabbatical rest, they will go into exile and it will rest without them (Lev 26:33–35, 43). In this way, Leviticus 26 combines the sabbatical theme of chapter 25 with a warning against covenant disloyalty.

Both Exodus and Leviticus conclude with sections concerning the sanctuary. In Exodus, the reiteration of the command to donate materials for the tabernacle (Exod 35:4–19) is followed by a narrative stream that describes the construction of the sanctuary (Exod 35:20–40:33) and the movement of divine glory into His new residence (Exod 40:34–38). Formerly the Lord spoke to Israel and Moses from Mount Sinai (Exod 19), but now He would speak to Moses from the sanctuary (Lev 1:1, etc.), which has replaced the mountain as the place of theophany.

Leviticus ends with a unit on dedications of various items to the Lord, which belong to the sanctuary (Lev 27). Scholars have been puzzled by the anticlimactic placement of this section after the covenant blessings and curses (Lev 26), which seem to bring the book to a logical conclusion (with subscript in Lev 26:46, reiterated in Lev 27:34). Although some interpreters have viewed Leviticus 27 as integrated into the structure of the book in various ways,[45] critical scholars have generally regarded it as an appendix.[46]

---

[44] Cf. renewal of the covenant in Exodus 34:10–28, which includes the prohibition of idolatry and commands to keep the Sabbath and to appear before the Lord at festivals (at the sanctuary). Leviticus 26:1–2 forms an *inclusio* with Leviticus 19:3–4, which also reiterates the requirements to keep God's Sabbaths and abstain from idolatry (although here these accompany a command to respect one's mother and father, rather than the sanctuary). Thus, the beginnings of Leviticus 19 and 26 frame the core of the portion of Leviticus that explicitly deals with holy lifestyle.

[45] E.g., William H. Shea, "Literary Form and Theological Function in Leviticus," in *The Seventy Weeks, Leviticus, and the Nature of Prophecy*, ed. F. Holbrook (Washington, DC: Biblical Research Institute, 1986), 147–149; Mary Douglas, "Poetic Structure in Leviticus," in *Pomegranates and Golden Bells: Studies in Biblical, Jewish, and Near Eastern Ritual, Law, and Literature in Honor of Jacob Milgrom*, ed. D. P. Wright, D. N. Freedman, and A. Hurvitz (Winona Lake, IN: Eisenbrauns, 1995), 250–251, 253; John H. Walton, "Equilibrium and the Sacred Compass: The Structure of Leviticus," *BBR* 11 (2001): 299–304.

[46] E.g., Milgrom, *Leviticus 23–27*, 2401–2402, 2407–2409, although he acknowledges the role of chapter 27 in closing the overall structure of the book in its final form. Cf. Wenham, *The Book of Leviticus*, 4–5, 336; Hartley, *Leviticus*, xxxiv–xxxv, 479. While Nihan, *From Priestly Torah to Pentateuch*, 94, regards Leviticus 27 as an appendix to the whole book, he finds it to be "a logical and necessary supplement" relating to preservation of the distinction between the sacred and the profane, a theme that runs through chapters 17–27.

Now we see that the placement of Leviticus 27 makes logical literary sense to complete the progression of thematic parallels with Exodus (cf. especially donations in Exod 35:4–19).

This brief sketch of themes in Exodus and Leviticus that follow the reports of failures in Exodus 32 and Leviticus 24 reveals that the Lord's concerns did not change. In spite of human faults, He wanted to restore and maintain the covenant with people who would become holy through their connection with Him and harmony with His principles, including by keeping His Sabbath and related sabbatical observances for the land He was giving them. They were not worthy to enjoy intimate proximity to His beneficent, holy presence dwelling among them in a sanctuary they constructed, but His grace overcame their unworthiness.

Conclusion

The "bread of the Presence" pericope in Leviticus 24:5–9, which is thematically connected to the preceding units in Leviticus 23:1–24:4, occupies a strategic literary position and culminates instructions for holiness that appear throughout earlier portions of the book. The bread represents God's "permanent covenant" with the Israelites, whom He wants to make holy, as signified by their Sabbath observance, so that He can dwell among them as their resident Creator-Provider and covenant Lord.[47] Following the ideal expression of holiness through the passage regarding the bread, a narrative about a man who rebelled against the Lord and disturbed the peace (Lev 24:10–12) implicitly warns God's people that their relationship with God is conditional. The covenant would be permanent for them only if they kept their side of it.[48]

Leviticus reminded the Israelites of the same dynamics of divine-human relationship already found in the book of Exodus. Just after God's instructions for building His sanctuary and His culminating formulation of the Sabbath as a "permanent covenant" between Himself as the Creator and the people whom He was making holy (Exod 31:12–17), the Israelites violated the first of His covenant stipulations (Exod 20:3–6; first and second of the Ten Commandments) by worshipping a metallic image of a creature instead of their Creator (Exod 32:1–8).

---

[47] Cf. the role of bread in the "new covenant" Lord's Supper (Matt 26:26; 1 Cor 11:23–24, 26).

[48] On covenant jeopardy, see John H. Walton, *Covenant: God's Purpose, God's Plan* (Grand Rapids, MI: Zondervan, 1994), 94–107.

Both in Exodus and Leviticus, God's plan for the covenant, holy living, the Sabbath, and the sanctuary continued from initial formulation and development to summary and then to renewal and further development after members of the human party to the covenant failed. Their failures highlighted human weakness, the conditionality of the covenant, and their existential need for the persistence of divine grace. Christians can learn much from the Lord's approach to the Israelites. It is true that theocratic regulation of the land (including through sabbatical and jubilee years) and the sanctuary/temple with its observances (including festivals centered there) no longer exist. However, the eternal creation Sabbath continues in the "new covenant" era as a vital part of Christian holy living (e.g., Matt 24:20).[49]

---

[49] See Roy Gane, "The Role of God's Moral Law, Including Sabbath, in the 'New Covenant,'" https://adventistbiblicalresearch.org/sites/default/files/pdf/Gane%20Gods%20moral%20law.pdf (accessed April 17, 2020).

CHAPTER 4

THE PUNISHMENT OF THE SABBATH BREAKER IN NUMBERS 15:32-36

Daniel K. Bediako

Introduction

Numbers 15:32-36 describes the stoning of a man who was found gathering wood on the Sabbath day. This passage recalls the fourth commandment, which requires rest on the Sabbath from routine work (Exod 20:8-11), including the gathering of manna (Exod 16:22, 26-27), cooking (Exod 16:23-25, 29-30), and the kindling of fire (Exod 35:2-3). A violation of the Sabbath regulation was punishable by death (Exod 31:14-15). The incident of the wood-gatherer is one of several instances in the book of Numbers where the penalty is inflicted on persons who disregard the covenant relationship of Yahweh with Israel.[1] The death penalty and its implementation in the OT have received several interpretations. For many, the regulation seems harsh or even unjust. The present study argues that to seek to understand the law solely from the viewpoint of ethics means to lose sight of its covenantal significance (cf. Exod 19-24).

Numbers 15 has long been considered one of the most difficult passages in the book of Numbers.[2] The scholarly discussion centers around three

---

[1] For example, Numbers 11:31-33 narrates the death of a multitude of the Israelites when they despised the manna and demanded meat (Num 11:4-6). The ten spies who brought discouraging reports (Num 13:32-33) fell in the plague (Num 14:36-38). The death of Korah and company, who rebelled against Moses and Aaron, is recounted in Numbers 16:1-40. Finally, Numbers 25:1-18 records the death of twenty-four thousand at Baal Peor.

[2] Jonathan Burnside, "'What Shall We Do with the Sabbath-Gatherer?' A Narrative Approach to a 'Hard Case' in Biblical Law (Numbers 15:32-36)," *VT* 60 (2010): 60.

main questions: How does chapter 15 relate to chapters 13–14 and 16–17? What connection is there between the discernable units within chapter 15? And how should the statement "Because it had not been explained what should be done to him" (*ki lo ʾporash mah-yeʿaseh lo*, Num 15:34) be understood?[3] The first two questions require some analysis of structure and the thematic connections within chapters 13–17. The third question requires grammatical analysis of Numbers 15:32–36 within its immediate context and the larger context of the fourth commandment. A fourth question this study raises borders on theodicy:[4] Why would a Sabbath breaker be stoned to death, and what continuity/discontinuity is there between the Christian church and the OT regarding the death penalty? This study attempts to answer these questions.

Numbers 15 and Its Context

The book of Numbers covers a period of about thirty-nine years and records select events and interventions of Yahweh that colored the exodus from Egypt, particularly the journey through the desert from the foot of Mt. Sinai to their encampment in the plains of Moab (Num 1:1; 10:11; Deut 1:3). These narratives depict both the historicity of the exodus and the centrality of the covenant. Overall, the book underscores the necessity of obedience and the tragedy of disobedience to Yahweh and His Word.

One author has proposed that the two censuses in Numbers 1 and 26 provide the major indicators of outline and theme in the book,[5] with respect to its immediate audience: chapters 1–25 (first generation)[6] and

---

[3] Unless otherwise indicated, quotations from Scripture are taken from NKJV.

[4] For the purposes of this study, the term "theodicy" is used with reference to how God deals with the problem of evil, rather than confining it to the question of why there is evil and suffering in the world. For a recent discussion of theodicy, see for example Edward P. Meadors, "'It Never Entered My Mind': The Problematic Theodicy of Theistic Determinism," *BBR* 19.2 (2009): 185–214.

[5] On the difficulty in discovering the structure of the book of Numbers, see Thomas Römer, "Egypt Nostalgia in Exodus 14–Numbers 21," in *Torah and the Book of Numbers*, ed. C. Frevel, Th. Pola, and A. Schart (Tübengen: Mohr Siebeck, 2013), 68. Some scholars would organize the material around three major geographical markers—Sinai, Kadesh, and the plains of Moab, e.g., Dennis Cole, *Numbers*, NAC (Nashville, TN: Broadman & Holman, 2000), 36; G. B. Gray, *A Critical and Exegetical Commentary on Numbers*, ICC (Edinburgh: T&T Clark, 1903); Philip J. Budd, *Numbers*, WBC (Waco, TX: Word Books, 1984); and Elmer A. Martens, "Numbers, Theology of," *NIDOTTE* 4:985.

[6] The first section begins with the census of the generation that left Egypt and their organization for the wilderness sojourn (chaps. 1–10). Then follows a series of rebellions (Num 11:1–14:45; 15:32–36; 16:1–17:13; 21:4–9) interspersed with Yahweh's provision for forgiveness and cleansing

chapters 26–35 (second generation).⁷ Within chapters 1–25, chapters 11–25 constitute a cycle of rebellion and death, with the events of chapters 13–17 occupying a central place.⁸

Source-critical scholars generally hold that chapter 15 has little connection to what precedes (chaps. 13–14) and what follows (chaps. 16–17), a conclusion influenced by the assumption that chapter 15 is a later addition from the postexilic period based either on Leviticus 4–5, 17–26, or Ezekiel 46.⁹ But a closer look at the narratives reveals strong thematic connections within Numbers 13–17. In these chapters, ten out of twelve spies incite Israel to rebel against Yahweh and His appointed leadership (chap. 13). Consequently, Yahweh destines the first generation to death in the wilderness (chap. 14) while reiterating His promise of the land of Canaan (chap. 15). Although the first generation "will not see the land" (Num 14:23), they are still required to be faithful to the covenant relationship and to instruct their children in the law (cf. Num 14:20, 40–43; 15:37–41). In such a context, any open rebellion was punishable, be it a direct infringement of

---

through the ministration of the priests (Num 15:1–31; 18:1–19:1–22), as well as assurance of hope through military success (Num 21:1–3, 21–35) and prophetic blessings (chaps. 22–24). Although much of chapters 11–25 records the complaints, rebellions, and punishments of the first generation, these chapters also imply that Yahweh had "great compassion" for that generation (cf. Neh 9:16–21). The story of the first generation ends with the final rebellion of the people and the death of the remainder of its members in Numbers 25.

⁷ D. T. Olson, *The Death of the Old and the Birth of the New: The Framework of the Book of Numbers and the Pentateuch* (Chico, CA: Scholars Press, 1985), 55; idem, *Numbers*, Interpretation: A Bible Commentary for Teaching and Preaching (Louisville, KY: John Knox, 1996), 3–7; and idem, "Numbers, Book of," *Dictionary of the Old Testament: Pentateuch*, ed. T. Desmond Alexander and David W. Baker (Downers Grove, IL: InterVarsity, 2003), 612. Cole, *Numbers*, 37–65, has proposed a three-part structural outline of the book with in-depth thematic and theological analyses, but his structure basically builds upon the bi-partite division proposed by Olson.

⁸ Cf. Cole, *Numbers*, 240.

⁹ E.g., Gray, *Critical and Exegetical Commentary*, 169–170; Budd, *Numbers*, 166–173; Reinhard Achenbach, "Complementary Reading of the Torah in the Priestly Texts of Numbers," in *Torah and the Book of Numbers*, ed. C. Frevel, Th. Pola, and A. Schart (Tübengen: Mohr Siebeck, 2013), 202–222; J. Wellhausen, *Die Composition des Hexateuchs und der historischen Bücher des Alten Testaments* (Berlin, 1963), 175–178; A. Kuenen, *An Historico-Critical Inquiry into the Origin and Composition of the Hexateuch* (London, 1886), 96; Israel Knohl, *The Sanctuary of Silence: The Priestly Torah and the Holiness School* (Minneapolis, MN: Augsburg, 1995), 53; C. Nihan, "The Priestly Laws of Numbers, the Holiness Legislation, and the Pentateuch," in *Torah and the Book of Numbers*, ed. C. Frevel, Th. Pola, and A. Schart (Tübengen: Mohr Siebeck, 2013), 109; P. Grelot, "La Dernière Étape de la Rédaction Sacerdotale," *VT* 6 (1956): 174–189; M. Noth, *A History of Pentateuchal Traditions* (Englewood Cliffs, NJ: Prentice-Hall, 1972), 114; idem, *Numbers*, OTL (Philadelphia, PA: SCM, 1968), 116; J. Sturdy, *Numbers* (Cambridge: Cambridge University Press, 1976), 108–112; and Baruch A. Levine, *Numbers 1–20: A New Translation with Introduction and Commentary*, AB (New York: Doubleday, 1993), 103–108.

the covenant stipulations as exemplified by the Sabbath (Num 15:32–36) or insurrection against the appointed leadership (chaps. 16–17).

Further elements underscore the thematic unity of the material in Numbers 13–17. First, the statement in chapter 15:2—"When you have come into the land you are to inhabit"—provides a link with the events of chapters 13–14 where, after the rebellion following the scouting of the land (Num 13:2), Yahweh still promises the land to their "little ones" (Num 14:31).[10] Notwithstanding Israel's rejection of the land and the consequent condemnation of the first generation (chap. 14), chapter 15 emphasizes Yahweh's grace in giving the second generation the hope of inheriting the land (Num 15:2–3, 18–19).[11] Second, the delineation of the various sacrifices in Numbers 15:1–21 picks up and builds on the theme of the land as one "flowing with milk and honey" (Num 13:27; 14:8).[12] In this land, Israel will be blessed so abundantly that they will accompany the animal sacrifices with bounteous produce of the land (Num 15:1–21). Third, Numbers 15:22–31 implies that while Yahweh graciously offers forgiveness of sins through animal sacrifices, these sacrifices do not expiate deliberate and defiant sin such as that of the spies in chapters 13–14 (cf. Lev 6:1–7).[13] Nonetheless, God can forgive such sin without the offering of sacrifices, especially when the perpetrator repents (e.g., 2 Sam 12:9–10, 13–14). Fourth, the tassel regulation in Numbers 15:37–41 evokes the narrative of the spies through the use of certain words. In Numbers 15:39, Israel is called to look (*ra'ah*) at the tassels and remember God's law so that they do not explore (*tur*) and promiscuously pursue (*zanah*) after their own eyes (*'ayin*). This recalls Numbers 13:32–33 and 14:33, where the spies are said to have explored (*tur*) the land, seen (*ra'ah*) the giants, felt as grasshoppers in their own eyes (*'ayin*), and led Israel into rebellion (*zanah*).[14] Thus, the instruction on the use of tassels (Num 15:37–41), while following directly from the wood-gatherer's

---

[10] Cf. Budd, *Numbers*, 168; Cole, *Numbers*, 56; and Ronald B. Allen, "Numbers," in *EBC*, vol. 2 (Grand Rapids, MI: Zondervan, 1990), 823.

[11] Martens, "Numbers," 990; Budd, *Numbers*, 167; Olson, *Death of the Old*, 170–174; idem, "Numbers, Book of," 615; and Roy Gane, *Leviticus, Numbers*, NIVAC (Grand Rapids, MI: Zondervan, 2004), 620.

[12] For example, Achenbach, "Complementary Reading," 209, has observed that the motif of an immense grape cluster in Numbers 13:23 is picked up by the gift of wine in Numbers 15:5, 7, 10, 24.

[13] "The thrust of the entire passage reaches its climax in the broader context of Israel's rebellion in rejecting the Promised Land and hence rejecting God. The nation's defiance was an example of a sin of 'a high hand' in that they had symbolically raised their fists in defiance of God, and for this there was no means of sacrifice that could deliver them from judgment" (Cole, *Numbers*, 252).

[14] See also Jacob Milgrom, *Numbers*, JPSTC (New York: The Jewish Publication Society, 1990), 126.

incident, concludes both chapter 15 and chapters 13–15.[15] Fifth, it has been suggested that by gathering wood on the Sabbath the man openly rejects the freedom from slavery and prefers a life of servitude in Egypt,[16] a choice that Israel had already made in Numbers 14:2–4. The decision to gather wood on the Sabbath may serve to express the man's displeasure with the condemnation of the first generation and his choice to reject the covenant relationship (Num 14:22–29). Sixth, the two acts of rebellion in chapters 15–17 seem to illustrate further the twofold theme of chapters 13–14: breaking of the covenant (Num 13:31; 14:9–11) and rejection of the leadership (Num 14:4). As the wood-gatherer's incident (chap. 15) is a demonstration of displeasure with Yahweh's judgment in response to the breaking of the covenant, so the rebellion of Korah and company (chaps. 16–17) expresses dissatisfaction with Yahweh's chosen leaders. Roy Gane has noted that chapter 15,

> with its thematic balance between God's justice and mercy and its strong warning against disloyalty, simultaneously makes Korah's revolt (ch. 16) appear more shocking and unreasonable to the listener/reader and places the Lord in a better light than if the narrative moved directly from one rebellion and divine judgment (ch. 14) to the next (ch. 16).[17]

Together, the three acts of rebellion in chapters 13–17 serve as examples of defiant sins (Num 15:29–31),[18] all of which occurred during the sojourn in the wilderness of Paran (cf. Num 13:3, 26; 15:32; 20:1).

Scholars have also questioned the unity within chapter 15.[19] Some consider the chapter as a strange collection of cultic laws,[20] part of which

---

[15] Cf. Budd, *Numbers*, 178; Joel S. Baden, "The Structure and Substance of Numbers 15," *VT* 63 (2013): 361; and David L. Stubbs, *Numbers*, Brazos Theological Commentary on the Bible (Grand Rapids, MI: Brazos Press, 2009), 141.

[16] Tzvi Novick, "Law and Loss: Responses to Catastrophe in Numbers 15," *HTR* 101 (2008): 5, 13; and Mathilde Frey, "The Sabbath in the Pentateuch: An Exegetical and Theological Study" (PhD diss., Andrews University, 2011), 125, 130. Frey also summarizes her observations on Numbers 15:32–36 in "The Woodgatherer's Sabbath: A Literary Study of Numbers 15:32–36," *JAAS* 13.1 (2010): 1–11.

[17] Gane, *Numbers*, 620; and idem, "Loyalty and Scope of Expiation," *ZABR* 16 (2010): 261.

[18] See also Budd, *Numbers*, 174; Gane, *Numbers*, 622; and Stubbs, *Numbers*, 140.

[19] For a summary of views, see Baden, "Structure and Substance," 351–354; Achenbach, "Complementary Reading," 205; Novick, "Law and Loss," 3–5; Frey, "The Sabbath in the Pentateuch," 119; and A. Noordtzij, *Numbers*, Bible Student's Commentary (Grand Rapids, MI: Zondervan, 1983), 138.

[20] Levine, *Numbers 1–20*, 386; Gray, *Critical and Exegetical Commentary*, 168; Noth, *Numbers*,

is "the displaced conclusion of another legal section."[21] However, there is thematic unity within the chapter.

The introductory clause of Numbers 15:32 ("While the children of Israel were in the wilderness") should not lead to the conclusion that the Sabbath narrative (vs. 32–36) is a later addition to chapter 15 and, therefore, out of place in time.[22] Although the phrase "in the wilderness" can be used in the generic sense (e.g., Exod 5:1; Num 14:33), it often refers to a specific wilderness (e.g., Gen 21:20; Exod 15:22; 16:2; 18:5; Num 10:12; 20:1). In Numbers 15:32, the reference is probably to the "wilderness of Paran" (cf. Num 13:3, 26). Moreover, the transitional statement of Numbers 15:32a seems necessary because of the switch in genre from legal instructions in vs. 3–31 to a narrative in vs. 32–36. The transitional statement implies that the instructions of vs. 1–31 were given in the wilderness of Paran where the incident of the spies occurred, and that while still in that wilderness the wood-gatherer rebelled despite earlier warnings (vs. 22–31).

Numbers 15:1–21 records various sacrifices and offerings. Numbers 15:22–31 contains legal prescriptions for inadvertent sins (vs. 22–29) and defiant sins (vs. 30–31) applicable to both native and alien (vs. 29–30). Inadvertent (unintentional) sins, committed either by the congregation (vs. 22–26) or by an individual (vs. 27–29), can be atoned for (vs. 25–28). However, defiant (deliberate and rebellious) sins are not expiable through animal sacrifices (vs. 30–31).[23] Numbers 15:30 defines such sins as

---

114; Sturdy, *Numbers*, 108; Gordon J. Wenham, *Numbers* (Leicester: InterVarsity Press, 1981), 126; S. Chavel, "Numbers 15:32–36—A Microcosm of the Living Priesthood and Its Literary Production," in S. Shectman and J. S. Baden, eds., *The Strata of the Priestly Writings: Contemporary Debate and Future Directions* (Zurich: Theologischer Verlag, 2009), 45–56; and Eryl Davies, *Numbers*, New Century Bible (Grand Rapids, MI: Eerdmans, 1995), 149–150.

[21] Milgrom, *Numbers*, 405. See also Novick, "Law and Loss," 8. Baden, "Structure and Substance," 356–357, argues that the manna story of Exodus 16 originally stood before Numbers 15:17–21, but see note 30. See also Joel S. Baden, "The Original Place of the Priestly Manna Story in Exodus 16," *ZAW* 122 (2010): 491–504; cf. Achenbach, "Complementary Reading," 225.

[22] E.g., Novick, "Law and Loss," 8; Milgrom, *Numbers*, 405; and Noordtzij, *Numbers*, 138.

[23] Gane, *Numbers*, 625, notes that there are two kinds of intentional sins: (1) non-defiant, deliberate sins that are expiable by mandatory purification or reparation offerings preceded by voluntary confession and any required reparation (Lev 5:1, 5–6; 6:1–7; Num 5:5–8), and (2) "high-handed" defiance against God and His covenant that are inexpiable by sacrificial offerings (Num 15:30–31). See also Roy Gane, *Cult and Character: Purification Offerings, Day of Atonement, and Theodicy* (Winona Lake, IN: Eisenbrauns, 2005), 204–213; Timothy R. Ashley, *The Book of Numbers*, NICOT (Grand Rapids, MI: Eerdmans, 1993), 288; A. Schenker, "Das Zeichen des Blutes und die Gewissheit der Vergebung im Alten Testament," *MTZ* 34 (1983): 205; and idem, "Interprétations récentes et dimensions spécifiques du sacrifice *ḥaṭṭāt*," *Bib* 75 (1994): 65, 69.

high-handed (*beyadh ramah*) and blasphemous (*gadhaf*).²⁴ Defiance and blasphemy constitute an affront against Yahweh—a rebellion against His authority and His covenant.²⁵ Since atonement is not available for such sin, the perpetrator is to be "cut off" (*karath*) bearing their own guilt (Num 15:31).²⁶ Within the context of cultic legislation of offerings for the expiation of inadvertent sins versus death for defiant sins (Num 15:22–31), the incident of the wood-gatherer (Num 15:32–36) provides an example of defiant rebellion and the application of the death penalty (Num 15:30–31).²⁷ As an example of the terminal punishment resulting from defiant violation of the covenant (Num 15:22–31), this incident provides immediate basis within chapter 15 for the prescription of the use of tassels (Num 15:37–41).²⁸ Although verses 37–41 evoke the narrative of the spies (Num 13–14),²⁹ the wearing of the tassels would serve as a constant reminder for Yahweh's

---

²⁴ On the metaphor of "high hand," Milgrom, *Numbers*, 125, notes, "The original setting of this metaphor is seen in the statues of ancient Near Eastern deities who were sculpted with an uplifted or outstretched right hand, bearing a spear, war ax, or lightning bolt. Similarly, the mighty acts of the God of Israel are described as being performed 'by a mighty hand and an outstretched arm' (Deut 4:34; 5:15; 26:8) or by this very expression, 'with an upraised hand' (33:3; Exod 14:8). The upraised hand is therefore poised to strike; it is a threatening gesture of the Deity against His enemies or of man against God Himself. Thus, this literary image is most apposite for the brazen sinner who commits his acts in open defiance of the Lord (cf. Job 38:15). The essence of this sin is that it is committed flauntingly. However, sins performed in secret, even deliberately, can be commuted to the status of inadvertencies by means of repentance."

²⁵ Cf. Gane, *Numbers*, 625; and Caspar J. Labuschagne, "The Meaning of *beyad rama* in the Old Testament," in *Von Kanaan bis Kerala: Festschrift for J. P. M. van der Ploeg*, ed. W. C. Delsman et al. (Neukirchen-Vluyn: Neukirchener, 1982), 146.

²⁶ There is no unanimity with regards to the nature of *karath* ("cut off") punishment (e.g., Milgrom, *Numbers*, 125; Stubbs, *Numbers*, 140; Dale A. Brueggemann, "Numbers," in *Cornerstone Biblical Commentary*, ed. Philip W. Comfort [Carol Stream, IL: Tyndale, 2008], 320; and Cole, *Numbers*, 253). Whatever specific meaning it carried, *karath* could involve death (e.g., Exod 31:14; Lev 20:17). In Numbers 15:31, the use of the phrase "bear his guilt" may imply that here *karath* punishment refers to the death penalty. In Leviticus 20:2–3 a person is both stoned to death and "cut off," showing that the latter could go beyond the former, likely indicating loss of an afterlife, which could include loss of his line of descendants. See Donald Wold, "The Biblical Penalty of Kareth" (PhD diss., University of California, Berkeley, 1978).

²⁷ See also Ashley, *The Book of Numbers*, 291; Cole, *Numbers*, 47, 254; Gane, *Numbers*, 622; Olson, *Death of the Old*, 95; Budd, *Numbers*, 175–176; Allen, "Numbers," 830; Baden, "Structure," 360; W. H. Bellinger Jr., *Leviticus and Numbers*, NIBC (Peabody, MA: Hendrickson, 2001), 237; and Glen S. Martin, *Exodus, Leviticus, Numbers*, Holman Old Testament Commentary (Nashville, TN: Broadman and Holman, 2002), 319. Cf. Frey, "The Sabbath in the Pentateuch," 120.

²⁸ See also Stubbs, *Numbers*, 141; and Adriane Leveen, *Memory and Tradition in the Book of Numbers* (Cambridge: Cambridge University Press, 2008), 107.

²⁹ Cf. Novick, "Law and Loss," 8.

covenant and His law, including the Sabbath (Num 15:32–36), and thereby deter the people from rebellion either as individuals (Num 15:30–36) or as a nation (Num 13–14).[30]

The foregoing description of the thematic unity within chapters 13–17 in general and within chapter 15 in particular argues against conceiving chapter 15 as an anthology of scarcely related legal material.[31] The issues involved in the Israelites' rebellion are multi-faceted, so Numbers 15 provides an effective multi-faceted response. We now turn to the punishment of the wood-gatherer.

Dealing with the Wood-Gatherer

As one scholar notes, "Numbers 15:32–36 has long been regarded as problematic. The decision seems, at face value, to be grossly *unjust* and there are questions as to why it was seen as a *hard case* in the first place and why an oracular procedure was needed to resolve it."[32] The discussion in the previous section has shown that Numbers 15:32–36 is a case of deliberate rejection of Yahweh and His commands. The stoning of the wood-gatherer cannot be deemed "unjust," given that he presumptuously disregards Yahweh's authority despite the stern warning against defiance.

---

[30] There are further explicit thematic connections within Numbers 15. Yahweh assures Israel that they will inherit the land of Canaan (Num 15:2, 18) and will worship Him with the produce of the land (Num 15:1–21). It is unnecessary, therefore, to suppose (as does Baden, "Structure," 356–357) that Numbers 15 makes logical flow only when we place Exodus 16 between Numbers 15:16 and Numbers 15:17. The reference to grain and drink offerings in the section dealing with inadvertent sins and the corresponding sacrifices (Num 15:22–29) clearly presupposes Numbers 15:1–21 (Cf. Gray, *Critical and Exegetical Commentary*, 179; and Cole, *Numbers*, 61). The stoning of the wood-gatherer in Numbers 15:32–36 is an example of the penalty resulting from defiance as pronounced in verses 30–31, while the tassel regulation in verses 37–41 is intended to discourage defiance as in the case of the wood-gatherer. So Yahweh not only wishes that Israel observe *kol-mitswoth ha'eleh* ("all these commandments") (Num 15:22), but He also provides the tassels to remind them of *kol-mitswoth* ("all the commandments") (Num 15:39). The references to *'ezrakh*, "native"; *ger*, "alien"; and *kol-ha'edah*, "all the congregation"; as well as the use of the verb *'asah*, "made/do" are further markers of textual unity in the chapter. Finally, Frey demonstrates that Numbers 15:22–36 displays a chiastic structure that attests to the unity of these verses. In this structure the phrase *kol-ha'edah*, "all the congregation" occurs six times: once each in A and A¹ and twice each in B and B¹. The center of the chiasm emphasizes the singularity of the law for both native and alien (X and X¹).

[31] See also Gane, "Loyalty," 248–262, who also indicates that there is cohesion both in Numbers 15 and within chapters 13–17, and that the literary cohesion can be described as reflecting the contrast between loyalty and disloyalty.

[32] Burnside, "'What Shall We Do with the Sabbath-Gatherer?,'" 60. Emphasis supplied.

As to why the incident is treated as a "hard case," scholars have answered in diverse ways.[33] Jacob Milgrom suggests this incident provides the precedent for the principle that all work on the Sabbath is punishable by death,[34] implying that the prescription in Exodus 31 is based on Numbers 15:32–36.[35] Earlier, J. Weingreen similarly thought that Numbers 15:32–36 "presented a new situation for which no legal precedent or principle could be invoked."[36] This passage then constitutes an elementary form of a later rabbinic principle known as "fence around the law," which sought to prohibit acts that, though not harmful in themselves, could lead to breaking the law.[37] However, the internal historical claims of the biblical text disallow the conclusion that Numbers 15 predates Sabbath laws in the book of Exodus.[38]

Anthony Phillips finds Weingreen's view to be anachronistic and, instead, suggests the question in Numbers 15:34 was whether the gathering of wood constituted labor, which was prohibited on the Sabbath.[39] Several versions of this view have been espoused.[40] Timothy R. Ashley, for example, thinks the issue was "whether a man who was *gathering sticks . . . on the Sabbath*, presumably to make a fire in contravention of the law, was as guilty as if he had actually built the fire."[41] Still, some suggest that though the congregation understood that wood-gathering profaned the Sabbath, they could not tell whether it was punishable by death or by some lesser penalty.[42] In other words, "the deliberation would have been to deter-

---

[33] Cf. Novick, "Law and Loss," 2 n. 4.

[34] Milgrom, *Numbers*, 408–409.

[35] Ibid., 126.

[36] J. Weingreen, "The Case of the Woodgatherer (Numbers 15:32–26)," *VT* 16 (1966): 362.

[37] The gathering of wood is a prelude to the kindling of fire, and thus reveals a culpable intent (Weingreen, "The Case of the Woodgatherer," 362).

[38] In fact, recent critical scholarship tends to accept that Numbers 15 presupposes the Sabbath laws in Exodus and Leviticus. See C. Frevel, Th. Pola, and A. Schart, eds., *Torah and the Book of Numbers* (Tübengen: Mohr Siebeck, 2013).

[39] Anthony Phillips, "The Case of the Woodgatherer Reconsidered," *VT* 19 (1969): 125–128, finds Numbers 15:32–36 as an illustration of the extension of Sabbath principles to all forms of domestic activity. Cf. Noth, *Numbers*, 117.

[40] Budd, *Numbers*, 175; and Richard E. Friedman, *Commentary on the Torah with a New English Translation* (New York: HarperCollins, 2001), 479.

[41] Ashley, *The Book of Numbers*, 291; and Stubbs, *Numbers*, 140–141. Cf. Noordtzij, *Numbers*, 139.

[42] Novick, "Law and Loss," 2 n. 4, cites Y. Gilat, *Meqerei Talmud 2: Talmudic Studies Dedicated*

mine whether this sin might be covered by an offering so they did not have to execute the man or if it was a brazen sin for which no offering was possible."[43] Quite apart from the incongruity of such interpretation with Exodus 31, which enjoins the death penalty for the profanation of the Sabbath,[44] a close reading reveals that the issue in Numbers 15:32–36 was neither whether wood-gathering constituted work nor whether some penalty lesser than death could apply.

Numbers 15:32 reports that some people found the man "gathering wood/sticks" (*meqoshesh 'etsim*) on the Sabbath. The Hebrew verb *qashash* ("gather") may be related to the noun *qash* ("stubble"). In Exodus 5:7, 12 *qashash* is used for the gathering of stubble (*leqoshesh qash*), and in 1 Kings 17:10–12 it is used in connection with the gathering of firewood (*meqoshesheth 'etsim*). Zephaniah 2:1 uses the verb with reference to the coming together of people. The use of *qashash* in Numbers 15 is closer to its use in Exodus 5 and 1 Kings 17. In each instance, gathering stubble or wood is physical work. The arrest of the wood-gatherer and placing him under guard are indications that the congregation understood his activity to have constituted a direct infraction of the Sabbath regulation regarding work, even if it was near-domestic work (cf. Exod 16:22–23; 35:2–3).[45] Whereas of his own will the man refused to rest on the Sabbath from labor, he was now caused, against his will, to "rest" (*nuakh*) in "custody" (*mishmar*) (Num 15:34). In the *Qal* stem, the verb *nuakh* means "settle" or "rest," as one rests on the Sabbath day (Exod 20:11). It is suggested that by the use of the *Hiphil* form of *nuakh*, Numbers 15:34 identifies the Sabbath as the day of rest; the culprit is made to rest "for, indeed, it was Sabbath, the day of rest."[46] However, this conclusion is problematic because the usage of the verb (that is, *nuakh* in the *Hiphil* form) is not limited to Sabbath contexts (e.g., Lev 24:12). While there is a link between Sabbath rest and *nuakh*, Numbers 15:32–36 does not indicate that the culprit was

---

to the Memory of Professor Eliezer Shimshon Rosenthal, ed. M. Bar-Asher and D. Rosenthal (Jerusalem: Magnes, 1993), 208–210. See Olson, *Numbers*, 95; and Levine, *Numbers 1–20*, 399.

[43] Brueggemann, "Numbers," 320.

[44] Since the profanation of the Sabbath was punishable by death (Exod 31), it is quite unlikely that the congregation would consider sacrificial offering as a possible solution. Cf. Novick, "Law and Loss," 14; and J. Stackert, "Compositional Strata in the Priestly Sabbath," *JHS* 11 (2011): 19.

[45] Even domestic work was forbidden by the Sabbath commandment ("You shall not do any work," Exod 20:10; cf. 16:22–23; 35:2–3), in contrast to the ceremonial sabbaths (except for the Day of Atonement), on which only occupational work was forbidden.

[46] Frey, "The Sabbath in the Pentateuch," 125.

made to rest because it was a Sabbath day. In the *Hiphil*, *nuakh* often means "to place" or "to put," and when it is used together with *mishmar*, as in Leviticus 24:12, it means to "put" in "custody."[47]

While the gathering of sticks would generally be intended for fire in biblical times, the reason for the gathering of sticks in Numbers 15 is not stated. If the intent was to build a fire,[48] then the wood-gatherer was arrested and detained on two counts—"working" and intending to "kindle fire"—neither of which would be allowed on the Sabbath day.[49] The man did not need to build a fire, whether for cooking or for warmth:

> This happened sometime during the period when the Israelites were in the desert (15:32), where the climate was warm and the people had manna to eat (Ex. 16:35). So a fire for warmth or cooking would not have been urgent even if it were not Sabbath. It looks as though this man was going out of his way to violate the Sabbath command of the Decalogue (Ex. 20:8–11), of which the people were reminded every weekend when they received a double portion of manna on Friday and none on the Sabbath (16:22–30).[50]

It would appear that the wood-gatherer had no good reason to engage in the activity. The larger context of rebellion against Yahweh and His

---

[47] The noun *mishmar* may refer to a "guard house" (Gen 40:3–4; 41:10; 42:17,19; Lev 24:12), placing someone under guard (Lev 24:12; Num 15:34), or may denote "guarding" or a "guard" (Num 3:7; 2 Kgs 11:5; Jer 51:12).

[48] Weingreen, "The Case of the Woodgatherer," 362; and Levine, *Numbers 1–20*, 399.

[49] The prohibition of the kindling of fire in Exodus 35:3 seems to have been applicable only during the wilderness sojourn. In Exodus 16:22–30, where Yahweh prohibits preparation of food on the Sabbath, He miraculously preserves from decay the food prepared on Friday. After Israel enters Canaan and the manna ceases, there is no direct evidence that the people refrain from cooking and/or heating their food on the Sabbath. Nonetheless, Friday has always been known as the preparation day (Mark 15:42). The preparation for the Sabbath must have included preparation of food. Sabbath-keeping Christians would do well to finish the preparation of food on Friday where necessary. What should be avoided on Sabbath is work that could be done before Sabbath, such as gathering firewood or parts of cooking that are laborious, whereas heating it up in a cold climate would be acceptable. Moreover, it appears that the kindling of fire referred to in Exodus 35 is not necessarily for the preparation of food; fire was also kindled to give warmth (Isa 44:16; 47:14). Ellen G. White, *Patriarchs and Prophets* (Washington, DC: Review and Herald, 1958), 408, writes, "During the sojourn in the wilderness the kindling of fires upon the seventh day had been strictly prohibited. The prohibition was not to extend to the land of Canaan, where the severity of the climate would often render fires a necessity; but in the wilderness, fire was not needed for warmth."

[50] Gane, *Numbers*, 622.

covenant (Num 13–17), and the immediate context of warning against defiant sins (Num 15:29–31) suggest that the incident in Numbers 15:32–36 was a case of rebellion by which the man expressed dissatisfaction against Yahweh's judgment in chapter 14. There is a connection between the gathering of wood on the Sabbath (Num 15) and the gathering of stubble in Egypt (Exod 5), especially on the basis of the use of *qashash* in both passages and Israel's preference for a life of slavery in Egypt in Numbers 13–14:

> The telling link that Num 15 draws between the Israelite slaves who were forced to gather straw to make bricks and the man gathering wood on Sabbath reveals the intention of the text to show that the Israelite man, even though freed from slavery, consciously chose to act against the law of freedom and thereby placed himself back into the position of a slave.[51]

The bold defiance of the wood-gatherer constituted an affront against the authority of Yahweh for which no animal sacrifice was possible (Num 15:30–31).

If the gathering of wood constituted a violation of the fourth commandment (Exod 20), and if such a violation—including the gathering of manna (Exod 16), cooking (Exod 16), and the building of fire (Exod 35) on the Sabbath—was punishable by death (Exod 31), would the wood-gatherer's fate still be unclear to Moses and the congregation, so as to require the intervention of Yahweh? The meaning of the clause "because it had not been explained what should be done to him" (*ki loʾ porash mah-yeʿaseh lo*, Num 15:34) needs to be understood within the specific context of Numbers 15:32–36. The verb *parash* in *Qal* may mean "clarify" or "give a clear decision" (Lev 24:12).[52] It occurs two times in the *Pual*, and seems to convey the meaning "to be explained" or "to be made clear" (Num 15:34; Neh 8:8; cf. Ezra 4:18). The use of the same root in Leviticus 24:12 in a similar context (though in the *Qal* stem) allows the observation that in Numbers 15:34, the wood-gatherer was held in custody because "what should be done to him" was yet to be "explained," "made clear," or "decided."[53] The clause *mah-yeʿaseh lo* occurs also in Exodus 2:2–4, where Moses' sister is said to have stayed behind to see what would happen to the baby.[54]

---

[51] Frey, "The Sabbath in the Pentateuch," 125.

[52] *HALOT* (2 vols.) 2:976.

[53] Cf. Levine, *Numbers 1–20*, 399.

[54] Cf. 1 Samuel 17:26, where the similar construction *mah-yeʿaseh leʾish* means, "What should be done for the man."

In itself, *mah-yeʿaseh lo* in Numbers 15:34 could imply an uncertainty on the part of the congregation, either regarding the fate of the man or the kind of punishment to be meted out, or it could express the congregation's anticipation for Yahweh's verdict.

A rabbinic interpretation, for example in *b. Sanhedrin* 78b, is that while Moses and the elders knew that the death penalty had to apply, they were not certain about the mode of execution. Some modern commentators espouse this view,[55] while others find it unconvincing.[56] One scholar seems to read too much into the text when he suggests that the congregation's uncertainty resulted from their own doubt as to whether the covenant law, which prohibits work on the Sabbath, was still valid and applicable to the first generation, who had already been condemned to death (Num 14:20–23). Thus, "although the wood-gatherer acts alone, he gives expression, through his action, to the doubt of the entire people."[57] The judgment in Numbers 14 could have roused a spirit of rebellion among the people as exemplified by the wood-gatherer in chapter 15, yet there is no textual basis to interpret verse 34 to mean that the entire congregation doubted the relevance and applicability of the covenant law to the first generation.[58]

One could argue that placing the wood-gatherer under guard was unavoidable because the elders of the congregation would not be in a position to judge the case immediately, since the incident occurred on the Sabbath. While this is reasonable, it must be pointed out that there is no indication in the text that the leadership of the congregation intended to judge the case after the Sabbath hours. It is thus instructive that the congregation does not make any attempt to formally judge the case. Perhaps rather than ask *why* the leaders could not decide on the case despite the apparent clarity of the already known Sabbath-profanation penalty, we may ask *whether* they intended to take a decision other than Yahweh's specific pronouncement on the case. Not in a single instance in the book of Numbers did the congregation apply the death penalty as a result of their own judgment (cf. Num 14:10). The profanation of the Sabbath and defiant sin in Exodus 31:14

---

[55] E.g., Martin, *Exodus, Leviticus, Numbers*, 319; and Clyde M. Woods and Justin M. Rogers, *Leviticus–Numbers*, The College Press NIV Commentary (Joplin, MS: College Press, 2006), 273–274. Cf. Achenbach, "Complementary Reading," 226.

[56] Cf. Weingreen, "The Case of the Woodgatherer," 361–364; Novick, "Law and Loss," 2 n. 4; and Wenham, *Numbers*, 131–132.

[57] Novick, "Law and Loss," 5.

[58] For further refutation of Novick's view, see Frey, "The Sabbath in the Pentateuch," 129–130.

and Numbers 15:30–31, respectively, require the application of the "cut off" (*karath*) punishment, which was a divinely exacted terminal punishment for certain sins against Yahweh (cf. Num 9:13; 19:13, 20).[59] The congregation may thus have known that the wood-gatherer deserved the death penalty, but decided to wait for the pronouncement of Yahweh as in the case of the blasphemer in Leviticus 24. Since there is no indication of the congregation's trial of the man, the *Pual* form *porash* may best be understood as a divine passive—he was put in custody "because it had not been declared *by Yahweh* what should be done to him," not necessarily because the elders/judges could not reach a consensus on his fate or the mode of punishment.

Pragmatically, even if the congregation was supposed to decide on the case and mode of punishment based on earlier legal prescriptions, certain factors may possibly have discouraged the attempt. First, as a case of defiant affront against Yahweh, the congregation may have so wondered at the wood-gatherer's blatant profanation of the Sabbath that they would only think of referring the case to Yahweh. Second, given the context in which the authority of Moses and Aaron is specifically questioned (Num 14:4; 16:2–3), their reliance upon Yahweh's judgment in a case of defiance against Himself was only appropriate.

That in Numbers 15:34 the congregation anticipates Yahweh's verdict, as suggested by the use of *porash*,[60] is confirmed by verse 35, where He directs that "the man must surely be put to death."[61] The mode of punishment then follows: "The whole congregation" (*kol-ha'edah*) must "stone" (*ragam*) the man "outside" (*khuts*) the camp.[62] The fact that Yahweh's verdict in verse 35 spells out both the penalty and the mode of execution could be further indication that the congregation had not decided on the case.

---

[59] Milgrom, *Numbers*, 405–408; Gane, *Numbers*, 621; Stubbs, *Numbers*, 140; and Chavel, "Numbers 15:32–36," 50.

[60] *HALOT* (2 vols.) 2:976, translates *porash* in Numbers 15:34 as "to be explained, decided." This may support the argument that the congregation may have intended to wait for the Lord's decision.

[61] This statement, which conveys the death penalty, is recurrent in the Pentateuch (e.g., Exod 19:12; 21:12; Lev 20:2; 24:16; Num 35:16–18).

[62] As with the Rabbinic interpretation (cf. *b. Sanhedrin* 78b), Chavel, "Numbers 15:32–36," 50, has argued that Numbers 15:32–36 adds the new information that the people are to punish the man by stoning him; the law in verses 30–31 tells only how he will be punished by God through *karath* punishment. See also Michael Fishbane, *Biblical Interpretation in Ancient Israel* (Oxford: Oxford University Press, 1985), 100.

Numbers 15:36 reports the execution of the sentence. The verb *ragam*, whose infinitive absolute is used with imperatival force in verse 35, always involves the use of stones and probably depicts the vivid casting of stones. The OT prescribes stoning as the mode of executing the death penalty in many instances.[63] It usually took place outside the camp or the city—probably to avoid contamination or to signify the horribleness of taking human life.[64] It could also signify rejection by the community. Although it is commonly understood that stoning was prescribed "because it supposedly does not shed blood, and thus does not bring blood-guilt on the community,"[65] it appears such was the most appropriate mode of inflicting the death penalty as a communal activity. The entire congregation participated in the execution of the wood-gatherer, thereby signifying their corporate identity and responsibility as a covenant community, poised to obey Yahweh and fulfill His demands (Exod 24:7). The threefold repetition of "all the congregation" (*kol-ha'edah*) in Numbers 15:32–36 conveys the covenantal implications of the sin of the wood-gatherer.

Burnside has lamented the inadequacy of earlier studies on Numbers 15:32–36, as these attempt to understand the text from the viewpoint of the modern legal system, and have yielded only "anachronistic results."[66] He discards the "semantic and literal" approach to biblical Sabbath-profanation laws in favor of a "narrative and visual" approach, and then reads Numbers 15:32–36 against Exodus 5:7–19. As to why "gathering materials on the Sabbath [was] regarded so seriously," he answers that "'gathering' on the seventh day of the week evoked the Israelites' regular activity under the lordship of Pharaoh."[67] Suffice it to say that this alternative approach to reading biblical Sabbath laws disregards Genesis 2:1–3 as the backdrop of subsequent Sabbath laws (e.g., Exod 20; 31; 35).[68] With the earlier Sabbath texts in the books of Genesis and Exodus in view, the incident of the wood-gatherer evokes a "literal" rather than an "imagistic"

---

[63] See e.g., Exodus 21:28–32; Leviticus 20:2–5; 20:27; 24:15–16; Deuteronomy 13:7–11; 21:18–21; 22:23–24; and Joshua 7:25.

[64] Cf. Levine, *Numbers 1–20*, 399–400; and Budd, *Numbers*, 176.

[65] Ashley, *The Book of Numbers*, 292. See also Budd, *Numbers*, 176; and Milgrom, *Numbers*, 126.

[66] Burnside, "'What Shall We Do with the Sabbath-Gatherer?,'" 60.

[67] Ibid., 55. On the relationship between Numbers 15:32–36 and Egyptian slavery, see also Novick, "Law and Loss," 5, 13; and Frey, "The Sabbath in the Pentateuch," 125, 130.

[68] See Burnside, "'What Shall We Do with the Sabbath-Gatherer?,'" 56.

regulation. For that matter, Numbers 15:32–36 deserves a "semantic and literal" reading as done in this study.[69]

Death Penalty, the Sabbath, and the Christian Church

The OT prescribes the death penalty by stoning in several cases, including (1) profaning the Sabbath by working (Exod 31:14–15; 35:2), (2) idolatry (Lev 20:2; Deut 13:6–10; 17:2–5), (3) sorcery (Lev 20:27), (4) blasphemy (Lev 24:16; cf. 1 Kgs 21:10), (5) rebellion against parents (Deut 21:18–21), (6) sex with a woman betrothed to another man (Deut 22:20–24), (7) failure to confine a dangerous ox that consequently gores a human (Exod 21:28–29), and (8) taking things that are dedicated to God through the ban (Josh 7:24–25). A cursory reading of the death penalty passages indicates that stoning was a major form of capital punishment required by the law.[70] However, death by stoning may not have been a special form of punishment, aside from the fact that it could involve as many people as possible—sometimes "all the congregation"—in inflicting the punishment (Lev 24:16; Num 15:36). The NT also contains references to stoning. Jesus saved an adulteress from being stoned to death (John 8:3–11). While the OT does not specifically state that adulterers/adulteresses must be stoned (cf. Lev 20:10), the incident in John 8:3–11 suggests that stoning was understood as the mode of punishment in some other cases where capital punishment was instructed (e.g., Exod 21:16; 22:19; Lev 20:13; 24;17–20). Several attempts were made to stone Jesus for blasphemy (John 8:59; 10:32–33). And Stephen was stoned to death on grounds of blasphemy (Acts 6:11–14; 7:59–60).

In general, the death penalty instruction is connected to infringements on the commandments of God, especially the Ten Commandments. The worship of other gods, disregard for the *name* of Yahweh, profaning His Sabbath by working, and disregard for human dignity (including murder, attacking parents, and wrongful sexual acts) are the areas covered by the death penalty law.[71] The Pentateuch appears to be harsh in its institution

---

[69] In fact, Burnside's "imagistic" reading of Numbers 15:32–36 into Exodus 5 seems influenced by semantics, particularly the use of the verb *qashash* in both texts.

[70] Other modes of capital punishment included shooting with arrows (Exod 19:13), burning (Lev 20:14), and hanging (Deut 21:22–23; Ezra 6:11).

[71] The list includes (1) worship of false gods that includes witchcraft and sorcery (Exod 22:18; Lev 20:27; Deut 13:15; 1 Sam 28:9) and human sacrifice (Lev 20:2–5); (2) blasphemy (Lev 24:14–16, 23); (3) false prophecy (Deut 18:20); (4) profaning the Sabbath by working (Exod 31:14; 35:2);

and application of death penalty.⁷² However, this is to be understood in at least two ways. First, as God creates a new people for Himself and for a unique mission, there is the need to tighten the boundaries in the covenant relationship (Gen 9:6; Lev 24:16; Num 15:36).⁷³ In this covenant relationship, the Ten Commandments stand at the center, and this would explain why the death penalty regulation centers around these commandments. Although after Israel's possession of the land of Canaan we find examples of infringements that should have attracted the penalty of death but did not (e.g., Judg 17:4–5; 20:12–13), there are instances where the sentence was meted out as required (e.g., 1 Sam 28:9; 1 Kgs 2:29–32; 2 Kgs 23:20). Second, and in light of the theocratic leadership in Israel, the death penalty instruction has crucial theodical significance: by requiring the congregation to stone the culprit, God both intended to curb defiant sins among His covenant people and to grant the desire of the perpetrator, per his or her act, to be removed from the covenant community. Thus from the perspective of God's covenant with Israel and His plan of redemption for humanity, this "strange" command to apply the death penalty can be understood as an indispensable divine intervention and God's gracious action to preserve the covenant which would culminate in the coming of the Messiah and Savior.

Within the context of Numbers 13–17, the narrative of the wood-gatherer needs to be understood in connection with the significance of the Sabbath in the covenant relationship and Yahweh's dealing with the problem of sin.

The significance of the Sabbath is marked by it being the universal symbol of Yahweh's creatorship, ownership, and redemption/blessing (Gen 2:1–3; Exod 20:8–11; Isa 58:13–14). Israel is thus required to remember the Sabbath in order to keep it holy (Exod 20:8–11). Numbers 15:32–36 demonstrates

---

(5) disregarding human dignity, including murder (Exod 21:12–14; Lev 24:17, 21), kidnapping (Exod 21:16), attacking, cursing or disobeying a parent (Exod 21:17–17; Deut 21:18–21), failure to confine a dangerous animal that subsequently kills a human (Exod 21:28–29), human sacrifice (Lev 20:2–5), perjury in capital cases (Deut 19:16–19), and disrespect for the decision of a judge or a priest (Deut 17:12); and (6) some wrong sexual acts, including bestiality (Exod 22:19; Lev 20:16), incest (Lev 18:6–18; 20:11–12, 14, 17, 19–21), adultery (Lev 20:10; Deut 22:22), homosexual acts (Lev 20:13), prostitution by a priest's daughter (Lev 21:9), false claim of virginity (Deut 22:13–21), and sex between a man and a woman betrothed to another man (Deut 22:23–24).

⁷² On the theodicy issue of such punishments, see Roy Gane, *Old Testament Law for Christians: Original Context and Enduring Application* (Grand Rapids, MI: Baker Academic, 2017).

⁷³ Interestingly, this seems to be the case at the beginning of the Christian church, where Ananias and his wife Sapphira are struck dead for lying to God and the church (Acts 5:1–11).

that Sabbath-keeping is the litmus test for Israel's loyalty toward Yahweh's covenant. Frey has observed that

> the focus of the text [Num 15:32–36] is placed upon the specific role of the whole congregation, with one law for both the native and the alien. . . . The Sabbath narrative involves the whole congregation, despite the fact that the rebellious act of wood-gathering on Sabbath was the sin of one individual person and not that of the community. This shows that the Sabbath contains a decisive meaning for the covenantal relationship between the whole congregation and YHWH. The sin of one individual performed on the Sabbath affected and disturbed the life of the whole community.[74]

As the sign of the covenant, the Sabbath constitutes the essence of the relationship between Yahweh and Israel (Exod 31:12–17; Jer 17:21–27).[75] Prophets such as Amos, Hosea, Isaiah, and Jeremiah decried the abuse of the Sabbath throughout Israel's history. Jeremiah 17 indicates that the Sabbath plays such a central role in the covenant relationship that the national fate of Israel depends on the observance of the Sabbath (cf. Lev 26). Not only is the Sabbath the day to remember the covenant relationship, but it is also the ultimate example of Yahweh's faithfulness in delivering Israel from Egypt (Deut 5:15).[76] Indeed, "Israel as a community is in part defined by its adherence to the Sabbath."[77]

The introductory clause of Numbers 15:32 ("While the children of Israel were in the wilderness") impresses upon the reader that only one example of defiant sin is here being cited, and, in light of the breach of the covenant in the immediate context, the choice of a Sabbath incident testifies to the central position it occupies in the covenant relationship.[78] One author is correct in observing that the placement of the Sabbath narrative between the laws regarding sins (Num 15:17–31) and that of the

---

[74] Frey, "The Sabbath in the Pentateuch," 123.

[75] Cf. Gerhard F. Hasel, "The Sabbath in the Pentateuch," in *The Sabbath in Scripture and History*, ed. Kenneth A. Strand (Washington, DC: Review and Herald, 1982), 21–37.

[76] See also Cole, *Numbers*, 254.

[77] Robert Alter, *The Five Books of Moses: A Translation with Commentary* (New York: Norton, 2004), 759.

[78] Cole, *Numbers*, 242–243; Chavel, "Numbers 15:32–36," 50–51; and Frey, "The Sabbath in the Pentateuch," 123.

tassels (Num 15:37–41) is determined by the "ultimate significance of the Sabbath."[79] The reason for the tassel regulation that follows the Sabbath narrative is for Israel to "remember" the commandments (Num 15:39), as they would "remember" the Sabbath day (Exod 20:8). Considering the significant role of the Sabbath, one can conclude that the wood-gatherer's decision to profane it signified his determination to despise the authority of Yahweh as the covenant Lord in the most presumptuous way. Thus "the vehemence" of the death penalty relating to the Sabbath "is predicated on the notion that the Sabbath is the ultimate sign of the covenant between God and Israel, so that one who violates the Sabbath violates the covenant and renounces solidarity with the covenanted people."[80]

The Pentateuch, as seen also in Numbers 13–17, shows that Yahweh deals with the problem of evil by making Himself accessible among humans, which means entering into a covenant relationship with them (Exod 19–24) and coming very close to them by dwelling among them (Exod 25). Explicit commands and warnings were intended to discourage the perpetration of evil and thereby maintain the purity of the divine-human relationship (Exod 19–24; Num 15:30–31, 37–41). And sacrificial offerings in the sanctuary served as means both of worship and expiation for non-defiant sins and cultic impurities (Num 15:3–29). However, defiant sins were too serious to be expiated through animal sacrifices (Num 15:30–31). In such cases, the covenant community of Israel was to be purged of evil through the infliction of the death penalty on the perpetrator (Deut 17), though God can forgive the repentant perpetrator without animal sacrifices (2 Sam 12:9–10, 13–14). The death penalty is thus to be understood in the context of the covenant relationship.

As enshrined in the covenant provisions, willful deviations on the part of Israel were punishable. This explains, for example, the judgment of Yahweh against the first generation that rejected the covenant by refusing to go into the land of Canaan (Num 13–14). Similarly, the incidents of the wood-gatherer and Achan are typical examples illustrating that, as a covenant community, the sin of the individual affected the congregation as a whole, and thus needed to be dealt with (Num 15:32–36; Josh 7:1, 10–26). In both cases, the involvement of the entire congregation in inflicting the

---

[79] Chavel, "Numbers 15:32–36," 51. See also Achenbach, "Complementary Reading," 227, who has observed that "the Sabbath is the basis of the whole of the sacral regulations in the Torah and the Sabbath Commandment is valid everywhere at every time (Gen 2:2–3)."

[80] Alter, *The Five Books of Moses*, 491.

penalty underscored the detrimental effect these incidents had on the well-being of the covenant community.

In the case of Numbers 15:32–36, the divine intervention through retributive punishment served to curb the contagion of defiance among God's people, thereby saving generations of Israel from following the destructive path of the wood-gatherer, as the covenant community learned first-hand the harsh consequence of intentional straying from the authority of God. In fact, the wood-gatherer knew that union with God in a covenant relationship marked with Sabbath observance means life and freedom, and disunion with the covenant God means death. Again, he was aware that in the covenant relationship, rebellion meant utter rejection of divine sovereign rule over the perpetrators and the covenantal communal life. Consequently, the act of gathering wood on the Sabbath was an outward expression of his desire to remove himself from the covenant relationship. A high-handed sin such as the wood-gatherer's could only be dealt with through the death sentence, cutting off the perpetrator from the presence of God and the covenant community.

The Israelite nation was a theocracy, a system of state organization and government in which God was the supreme authority who exercised His authority through His agents, priests, prophets, or kings. In a theocracy, there is no distinction between religion and state, so that in ancient Israel all legal, political, and social provisions were essentially religious, with the Torah serving as the basic law of the nation. A key aspect of the theocracy in Israel included the physical presence of God through His sanctuary (Exod 25:8) and, with it, the physical holiness of the covenant land (Lev 18:24–30; 25:23; Isa 24:5; Jer 2:7; Ezek 36:17; Zech 2:16). In a sense, the death penalties that were inflicted in response to defiant sins were done to cleanse the land and its people (Num 35:33–34; Deut 21:1–9).

The OT death penalty was a legal requirement applicable within the Israelite theocratic kingdom. For this reason, a move away from the theocratic structure would imply discontinuation of the application of this penalty. And this is the picture we find from the beginning of the NT church. Jesus' proclamation of the kingdom of God/heaven pointed toward a break away from the physical, Israelite kingdom to a spiritual Israel without political boundaries, the Christian church comprising both Jews and Gentiles (e.g., Matt 5–7, 18). Consequent to Jesus' first advent, there is a separation of church and state, even though believers have obligations toward the state (Matt 22:21; John 18:36; Rom 13:1). In His reaction against the Pharisees, Jesus seems to imply that although capital punishment could be inflicted by the state, it would not prevail within the community of His believers, given His impending sacrifice and the effects it would cause (John 8:3–12). Jesus' comments regarding the "eye-for-eye" and "tooth-for-tooth" regulation (cf. Exod 21:22–27) may also be understood in similar light (Matt 5:38–48).[81] Finally, Jesus' death and the influx of Gentile believers that followed marked the transition from the theocracy to the experience of the new community of faith.[82] Indeed, Jesus' death ended the requirement not only for blood sacrifice (of animals) but also blood recompense (that is, capital punishment) in the community of faith (Heb 9:14), though those who reject the gift of salvation in Jesus or willfully disobey Him shall face the "fiery indignation" (Heb 10:27; cf. vs. 26–31). Thus, the picture of God's dealing with evil in the OT reaches a climax in the NT in Christ's substitutionary death that atones for human sins (Mark 10:45; Heb 9:28) and requires the ultimate destruction of those who reject the offer of forgiveness through Him (John 3:16–18; Rev 14:9–12).

In the new covenant community that Jesus inaugurated, the application of the death penalty discontinues, following both the atoning sacrifice of Jesus and the church's discontinuity with the theocratic structure of Israel.[83] Thus, while the church treats sins—including defiant sins—with repulsion, in the NT the legislation of the death penalty as instituted in the OT is not applicable within the church. Outside the church, however, Paul may imply that secular governments inflict the death penalty against persons who have committed crimes deserving death (Acts 25:10–11; Rom 13:1–4).

The discontinuity of corporal punishment relating to an OT commandment is not to be interpreted to mean that the church, as the new community of faith, does not have to keep that commandment. As noted earlier, the death penalty regulation is related to infringements on the law, especially the Ten Commandments. Yet the NT is clear that these commandments are still in force, even beyond Christ's death (Matt 5:17–20; Rom 3:31). Jesus commands, "If you love Me, keep My commandments"

---

[81] See also Craig L. Blomberg, *Matthew*, NAC (Nashville, TN: Broadman & Holman, 1992), 113–114.

[82] See Richard Davidson, "Israel and the Church: Continuity and Discontinuity—II," in *Message, Mission, and Unity of the Church: Studies in Adventist Ecclesiology*, vol. 2, ed. Angel Manuel Rodriguez (Silver Spring, MD: Biblical Research Institute, 2013), 411.

[83] The instant deaths of Ananias and Sapphira do not constitute cases of death penalty in the Christian church. The incident constituted a direct affront against the Holy Spirit and resulted in death (Acts 5:1–11), comparable to the instant deaths of the youths following Elisha's curse (2 Kgs 2:23–24).

(John 14:15)! He also warns, "Whoever therefore breaks one of the least of these commandments, and teaches men so, shall be called least in the kingdom of heaven; but whoever does and teaches them, he shall be called great in the kingdom of heaven" (Matt 5:19). The worship of other gods, blasphemy, adultery, and homosexuality are still considered sinful acts in the church (e.g., 1 Cor 6:9–11; 1 Tim 1:8–11). And as Christ Himself observed the Sabbath, so did the disciples after His ascension, even as He expected all His followers to keep observing the Sabbath (Matt 24:20). What this means is that while there is continuity between the NT church and the OT congregation with regards to seventh-day Sabbath-keeping (Luke 4:16–17; Acts 13:14–15, 42–45; 16:11–15; 17:2; 18:4; Heb 4:4–9), there is discontinuity in the application of the death penalty that resulted from Sabbath-breaking.

Believers in Christ constitute a covenant community, though this community is not a religio-political entity as was the nation of Israel (2 Cor 3:4–6). As a covenant community, the church disciplines its erring members (1 Cor 5; cf. Matt 18:17; 1 Tim 1:20). And the basis for church discipline recalls the basis for the death penalty in the OT—namely the curbing of sin to cleanse the community and deter others from evil (e.g., Deut 17:7–12; 19:19–20; 22:21–24; Josh 7:13). The metaphors of the body of Christ (1 Cor 12:12–27) and the body temple (1 Cor 3:16–17; 6:19) illustrate that, as was the case in ancient Israel, the impurity of one member affects the well-being of the whole (cf. 1 Cor 5:5–8). The church's way of dealing with such impurity is to expel the individual from membership (1 Cor 5). Thus, sins from which Israel was purged by means of the death sanction are by the church dealt with through expulsion from membership (e.g., Lev 20:10–11; 1 Cor 5:1–5).[84]

Paul's instruction in 1 Corinthians 5 sets forth the church's practice of disfellowshipping. Although verse 5 has received differing scholarly interpretations,[85] Paul clearly states in this chapter that it was the responsibility

---

[84] Beyond expulsion from the church, however, some cases are handled by state government through criminal justice (e.g., Rom 13:1–7; 1 Pet 2:13–14).

[85] See e.g., Barth Campbell, "Flesh and Spirit in 1 Cor 5:5: An Exercise in Rhetorical Criticism of the New Testament," *JETS* 36 (1993): 331; Hans Conzelmann, *1 Corinthians: A Commentary on the First Epistle to Corinthians*, Hermeneia (Philadelphia, PA: Fortress, 1975), 97; H. Olshausen, *A Commentary on Paul's First and Second Epistles to the Corinthians* (Minneapolis, MN: Klock & Klock, 1984), 90; Adela Yarbro Collins, "The Function of 'Excommunication' in Paul," *HTR* 73 (1980): 254–263; Gerald Harris, "The Beginnings of Church Discipline: 1 Corinthians 5," *NTS* 37 (1991): 1–21; A. C. Thiselton, "The Meaning of *SARX* in 1 Corinthians 5:5: A Fresh Approach in the Light of Logical and Semantic Factors," *SJT* 26 (1973): 218; and Brian S. Rosner, "Temple and Holiness in 1 Cor 5," *TynBul* 42 (1991): 137–145.

of the Corinthian church to expel the member who slept with his father's wife (1 Cor 5:1–2, 4–5, 7, 13).[86] This goes to emphasize the fact that the execution of discipline in the community of faith is a corporate responsibility (cf. Num 15:35).[87] The exhortations in 1 Corinthians 5 seem to be based on the concept of the church as the temple of God (1 Cor 3:16–17) and prepare the believer to understand that church discipline is redemptive (2 Cor 2:5–11). Here, it is hoped that through disfellowshipping, with its accompanying disgrace and grief, the incestuous man may come back to his senses, turn away from evil, and ultimately be saved.[88] In this regard, church discipline is corrective-redemptive.

Beyond church disfellowshipping, however, the NT is replete with warnings against sins that will lead to eternal destruction (Matt 13:41–42, 49–50; 2 Thess 1:9–10; Heb 10:26–31; 2 Pet 3:3–7; Rev 14:9–11; 19:19–21). The list includes idolatry, blasphemy, adultery, homosexuality, murder, etc.—similar sins that attracted the death penalty (1 Cor 6:9–11; Gal 5:19–21; cf. Rev 22:14–15). The OT death penalty was both punitive-destructive and redemptive: punitive-destructive because the perpetrator was sentenced to death, and redemptive because this served to deter others from defiance in the community of faith as they participated in God's mission (e.g., "and all Israel shall hear and fear," Deut 21:21).[89] The eternal destruction of the wicked thus fulfills the punitive-destructive aspect of the death penalty associated with certain sins, including the profanation

---

[86] E.g., F. F. Bruce, *1 and 2 Corinthians* (London: Oliphants, 1971), 55; John Ruef, *Paul's First Letter to Corinth* (Philadelphia, PA: Westminster, 1977), 40; James T. South, "A Critique of the 'Curse/Death' Interpretation of 1 Corinthians 5:1–8," *NTS* 39 (1993): 539–561; R. C. H. Lenski, *The Interpretation of St. Paul's First and Second Epistles to the Corinthians* (Minneapolis, MN: Augsburg, 1961), 216–217; Brian S. Rosner, "'Drive Out the Wicked Person': A Biblical Theology of Exclusion," *Evangelical Quarterly* 71 (1999): 31–34; Jerome Murphy-O'Connor, "The First Letter to the Corinthians," in *New Jerome Biblical Commentary*, ed. Raymond E. Brown (Englewood Cliffs, NJ: Prentice Hall, 1990), 803; Leon Morris, *The First Epistle to the Corinthians: An Introduction and Commentary* (Grand Rapids, MI: Eerdmans, 1958), 88; Eugene Walter, *The Epistle to the Corinthians* (New York: Crossroad, 1981), 54; Gordon D. Fee, *The First Epistle to the Corinthians*, NICNT (Grand Rapids, MI: Eerdmans, 1987), 209; Nigel Watson, *The First Epistle to the Corinthians* (London: Epworth, 1992), 49; and Craig L. Blomberg, *1 Corinthians*, NIVAC (Grand Rapids, MI: Zondervan, 1994), 105.

[87] Martin, *Exodus, Leviticus, Numbers*, 319.

[88] See Daniel Bediako, "Spirit and Flesh: An Interpretation of 1 Corinthians 5:5," *Cultural and Religious Studies* 1 (2013): 21–26.

[89] It also served to remove damage to the corporate community as consequences of one person's or one group's actions (cf. Deut 13).

of the Sabbath (Exod 31; Num 15). Thus, the wood-gatherer's experience, like those others who suffered similar destruction, foreshadows the eschatological punishment of individuals who, despite all warnings, reject or renounce the covenant relationship with God and are consequently eternally cut off from the presence of God and the community of believers. And we could infer further that the predication of the death penalty upon disobedience regarding the Ten Commandments is indication also that the final, destructive judgment will involve those who deliberately infringe upon God's law (cf. Matt 13:41; Rom 3:31; 1 Tim 1:8–11; Rev 14:4–12), including the Sabbath commandment (Heb 10:25–31).[90]

Conclusion

The narrative of the wood-gatherer in Numbers 15:32–36 appears in a context of warning against defiant sins (Num 15:30–31, 37–41). Sandwiched between two incidents of corporate rebellion against the authority of Yahweh (chaps. 13–14) and His chosen leaders (chaps. 16–17), the narrative emphasizes that individual cases of defiance against Yahweh have adverse implications for the entire congregation. The death penalty was a covenant-related provision within ancient Israel through which to handle such cases. The narrative also demonstrates that defiant sins perpetrated within the covenant community are dealt with openly and require the participation of the congregation as a whole. This same principle underlines Paul's instruction to expel the evildoer from church membership in 1 Corinthians 5, though repentance was still possible. The punitive-destructive aspect of the death penalty foreshadows the final judgment where "those who practice lawlessness" will be destroyed (Matt 13:41).

---

[90] Interestingly, Numbers 15:22–36 forms the OT background to Hebrews 10:24–31 (William L. Lane, *Hebrews 9–13*, WBC [Dallas, TX: Word, 1991], 292, finds allusion in Hebrews 10:24–31 to Numbers 15:22–31, without referring to the incident of the wood-gatherer in Numbers 15:32–36; see also F. F. Bruce, *The Epistle to the Hebrews*, rev. ed. [Grand Rapids, MI: Eerdmans, 1990], 261 n. 132). This is demonstrated in Hebrews 10 by the use of not only key terminologies, but also the concept of the death penalty, as it was connected especially with the breaking of the Ten Commandments. Using the example of the narrative of the Sabbath wood-gatherer in Numbers 15, Hebrews 10 shows that "forsaking" Sabbath worship "gathering/assembling" constitutes an intentional sin (i.e., believers "sin willfully" by so doing) and that for such willful acts there is no "sacrifice for sins" but, like the wood-gatherer who died "without mercy," the perpetrator should expect "a fearful . . . judgment . . . a fiery indignation" on the coming "Day" of the Lord. Both Numbers 15 and Hebrews 10 present the Sabbath commandment as having a decisive meaning for the covenant relationship between God and His people and warn against deliberate infringement on God's law.

All said, Numbers 15:32–36 presents the gracious gift of the Sabbath commandment as having a decisive meaning for the covenant relationship, as it is the sign of the everlasting covenant between God and His people (cf. Exod 31; Isa 58). In light of this study of the narrative of the wood-gatherer, it is suggested that the breaking of the Sabbath may be dealt with through church discipline, but also that disregard for the Sabbath, together with the other commandments, constitutes willful disobedience to God that, if the perpetrator does not repent, is ultimately punishable by destruction in the everlasting fire at the eschaton. The offer of grace in Christ is still available. Those who believe in Him will relate to Him in love, which includes obedience to His commandments.

CHAPTER 5

THE SABBATH IN THE PSALMS AND WISDOM LITERATURE

Richard M. Davidson

Introduction

In previous scholarly studies that presented a biblical theology of the Sabbath, the OT Hymnic/Wisdom literature had usually been either entirely overlooked or else only cursorily treated.[1] While it is true that few references/allusions to the Sabbath appear in the OT Psalms and Wisdom literature, those few references/allusions make a significant contribution to the overall theology of the Sabbath in Scripture. In this study, primary attention is given to the only explicit reference to the Sabbath in the Psalms and Wisdom literature: Psalm 92. This is followed by an exploration of other possible allusions to the Sabbath in this portion of the biblical canon.

The Sabbath in Psalm 92

Psalm 92 is the only psalm in the Hebrew Psalter expressly connected with the Sabbath.[2] Its superscription reads: "A Psalm. A Song for the Sabbath"

---

[1] See, e.g., Kenneth A. Strand, ed., *The Sabbath in Scripture and History* (Washington, DC: Review and Herald, 1982), which contains full chapters on "The Sabbath in the Pentateuch" and "The Sabbath in the Prophetic and Historical Literature," but does not even mention the explicit reference and possible allusions to the Sabbath in OT Hymnic/Wisdom literature. Psalm 92, with its superscription specifically referring to the Sabbath, is not even included in the Scripture index.

[2] In the LXX and later Jewish liturgical tradition (see *m. Tamid* 7, 3–4), along with Psalm 92

(*mizmor shir leyom hashabbath*). Critical scholars have tended to regard this superscription as a later addition totally unrelated to the content of the psalm. On the other hand, conservative Christian scholarship has provided strong evidence for accepting the superscriptions of the psalms as original and not later additions, providing historically reliable information about the psalms they introduce.[3] Jewish tradition clearly regarded the superscription to Psalm 92 as significant, as this psalm was chanted to accompany the wine libation following the Tamid offering every Sabbath in Second Temple times.[4] "The connection of the Psalm to the Sabbath even in postbiblical tradition is so strong, however, that there can be no doubt: in the time of early Judaism Psalm 92 was (also) understood as containing a Sabbath theology."[5]

Whether or not the superscription of Psalm 92 is original to the psalm, a "final form" canonical reading of the psalm must take seriously the claims of the superscription and the force of Jewish liturgical tradition, and read the entire Psalm with the Sabbath in view. "The title and liturgical tradition ask the reader to read it [Psalm 92] with a sabbath repertoire (a referential context of norms and allusions; the 'familiar territory' of a text).... [T]he ancient liturgical wisdom... asks us to read it with the Sabbath in mind."[6]

(Psalm 91 in LXX), six additional psalms are associated with the other days of the week, in this order for each of the weekdays: Psalm 24 (Ps 23 in LXX); Psalm 48 (Ps 47 in LXX); Psalm 82 (Ps 81 in LXX); Psalm 94 (Ps 93 in LXX); Psalm 81 (Ps 80 in LXX); and Psalm 93 (Ps 92 in LXX). The LXX superscriptions for the six weekdays are clearly later additions to the Hebrew text.

[3] See, e.g., Franz Delitzsch, *Commentary on the Old Testament: Psalms* (Grand Rapids, MI: Eerdmans, [n.d.]), 1:20–23; *SDABC* 3:615–617; H. C. Leupold, *Exposition of the Psalms* (Grand Rapids, MI: Baker, 1959), 5–10; Gleason Archer, *A Survey of Old Testament Introduction*, rev. ed. (Chicago, IL: Moody, 1994), 488–493; and Daniel J. Estes, *Handbook on the Wisdom Books and Psalms* (Grand Rapids, MI: Baker, 2005), 142–144. Jerome L. Skinner, "The Historical Superscriptions of Davidic Psalms: An Exegetical, Intertextual, and Methodological Analysis" (PhD diss., Andrews University, 2016).

[4] See *m. Tamid* 7, 3–4. The Psalm was also sung at the service connected with the Mincha or evening sacrifice (*b. Ros. Hash.* 31a). In today's synagogue service, it is sung yet a third time on Sabbath as the psalm of the day.

[5] In German, "Dennoch ist die Verbindung des Psalms mit dem Sabbat auch in der nachbiblischen Tradition so stark, daß kein Zweifel daran bestehen kann: Psalm 92 wurde in frühhjüdischer Zeit (auch) sabbat-theologisch verstanden." Erich Zenger, "Kanonische Psalmenexegese und christlich-jüdischer Dialog: Beobachtungen zum Sabbatpsalm 92," in *Mincha: Festgabe für Rolf Rentdorff zum 75. Geburtstag*, ed. Erhard Blum (Neukirchen-Vluyn: Neukirchener, 2000), 255.

[6] Marvin E. Tate, *Psalm 51–100*, WBC (Waco, TX: Word, 1990), 471.

This study argues that Psalm 92 contains both sabbatic literary features and theological content intertextually related to major sabbatic themes and motifs elsewhere in the Hebrew Bible, and thus the superscription appropriately connects this psalm to the Sabbath, and that the Second Temple practice linking the psalm with the Sabbath is consonant with the psalm's literary and thematic structure in its canonical form.

Sabbatic Literary Features

Numerous literary aspects of Psalm 92 highlight the number seven, thus providing evidence of the appropriateness of linking this psalm with the Sabbath in the canonical superscription. This psalm is one of only two psalms in the Hebrew Psalter where the Tetragrammaton (*YHWH*) is repeated seven times,[7] and Psalm 92 is the only one where "the Tetragrammaton is [predominantly] used in 'direct' address, unbuffered by any preposition."[8] One scholar notes that Psalm 92 contains seven different epithets for the wicked and seven positive qualities of the righteous.[9] A closer look at the text confirms this observation. The seven epithets for the wicked are concentrated in Psalm 92:8–12:

1. "wicked" (v. 8a [ET v. 7a])
2. "evildoers" (v. 8b [ET v. 7b])
3. "your enemies" (v. 10a [ET v. 9a])
4. "your enemies" (v. 10b [ET v. 9b])
5. "evildoers" (v. 10c [ET v. 9c])
6. "my enemies" (v. 12a [ET v. 11a])
7. "my evil assailants" (v. 12b [ET v. 11b])

The seven positive qualities of the righteous are concentrated in Psalm 92:13–16:

1. "flourish like the palm tree" (v. 13a [ET v. 12a])
2. "grow like a cedar in Lebanon" (v. 13b [ET v. 12b])

---

[7] The only other psalm in the Hebrew Psalter that repeats the Tetragrammaton seven times is Psalm 19, in its exaltation of the Torah of the Lord.

[8] Dan Vogel, "A Psalm for Sabbath? A Literary View of Psalm 92," *JBQ* 28 (2000): 215. Vogel claims that all seven occurrences of the Tetragrammaton in Psalm 92 are used in direct address without preposition. Actually, five of the seven are in the vocative of direct address; the first occurrence (Ps 92:2 [ET v. 1]) does attach the preposition, but the second part of the sentence moves to the vocative; and the sixth occurrence is in the construct chain "house of the Lord."

[9] Jacob Bazak, "Numerical Devices in Biblical Poetry," *VT* 38 (1988): 335.

3. "transplanted in the Lord's own house" (v. 14a [ET v. 13a, NLT])
4. "flourish in the courts of our God" (v. 14b [ET v. 13b])
5. "bring forth fruit in old age" (v. 15a [ET v. 14a, RSV])
6. "fresh" (v. 15b [ET v. 14b, NKJV])
7. "flourishing" (v. 15b [ET v. 14b, NKJV])

The midpoint and climax of the psalm (v. 9; ET v. 8) is flanked by seven poetic verses on either side.[10] Furthermore, the overall structure of the psalm contains five stanzas (or strophes), each with six lines (or cola), except for the climactic middle stanza, which contains seven.[11] In Psalm 92:10 (ET v. 9), the psalmist gains the number seven by means of an anadiplosis (see Chart 1 below for the depiction of this stanza division). "Certainly the unmistakable strophe-schema too, 6.6.7.6.6., is not without significance. The middle of the psalm bears the stamp of the sabbatic number."[12]

The text of Psalm 92 is an intricately wrought chiasm. This not only reveals the poem's unity and central thrust, but further underscores its "sevenness." We will take up the details of this chiastic structure below, but here we note that the Hebrew poetry divides into seven sections. There are the five stanzas, each with six cola except the middle stanza, which has seven. The central stanza has two matching thematically and structurally related tricola (vs. 8, 10 [ET vs. 7 and 9]) forming a frame for the central verse in the poem (v. 9 [ET v. 8]), which contains the only colon standing alone without any parallelismic counterpart. Thus, with the three-part central stanza and four flanking stanzas, the psalm is comprised of seven thematic/structural sections.[13]

---

[10] Bazak, "Numerical Devices in Biblical Poetry," 335. See also Vogel, "A Psalm for Sabbath," 214.

[11] The division of the psalm into five stanzas is supported by poetic metrical analysis, as well as by grammatical-syntactical, terminological, and thematic evidence. As for the poetic meter, the psalm scans evenly with each stanza (except the middle one) containing three bicola (for a total of six cola) with a predominating meter of 3:3. The middle stanza (Ps 92:8–10 [ET vs. 7–9]) contains two matching tricola (Ps 92:8 and 10 [ET vs. 7 and 9]) that scan 3:3:3 and a central single colon that scans as four beats, for a total of seven cola. For the layout of poetic meter of the psalm (and scanning similar to my own), see Tate, *Psalm 51–100*, 460. Evidence beyond the poetic meter supporting the five-stanza division (three English verses for each stanza) is presented below.

[12] Franz Delitzsch, *Commentary on the Old Testament: Psalms*, 3:67.

[13] See Vogel, "A Psalm for Sabbath," 211–221, for an alternative analysis of the psalm yielding seven stanzas. Utilizing Hebrew verse numbers, the stanzas of Psalm 92 are the following: I (vs. 2–5), II (v. 6), III (vs. 7–8), IV (v. 9), V (vs. 10–12), VI (vs. 13–15), and VII (v. 16). Although Vogel presents some important evidence to support his structural analysis, and correctly recognizes the apex of the chiasm in verse 9, in the end the author of this study does not find his overall structure convincing. Most problematic is his positing of very uneven stanza divisions, with single verses on one side of

The numerous patterns of sevens running structurally and terminologically throughout the psalm link its literary form and features to a septenary motif. These septenary patterns are so striking that the superscription may be regarded as accurately reflecting the sabbatic character of the poem.

Sabbatic Chiastic Structure

Before examining the themes that correspond with Sabbath theology, let us note in more detail the structure of Psalm 92. Terminological and thematic parallels between the matching parts of the six outer sections, coupled with the thematic/structural parallels between the opening, concluding, and central sections, suggest a septenary, chiastic macro-structure to the psalm.[14]

Let us look in more detail at the inverted parallelism of the chiasm. Starting at the outer members, A and A^1 (stanzas 1 and 5), each stanza climaxes with the same central Hebrew verb *lehaggidh* ("to proclaim or show") that occurs only in these stanzas, and emphasizes the same theological motif of proclaiming attributes of the Lord's (Yahweh's) character: "To proclaim [*lehaggidh*] your steadfast love in the morning and your faithfulness at night" (Ps 92:3 [ET v. 2]) and "to proclaim [*lehaggidh*] that the Lord is upright; He is my Rock, and there is no unrighteousness in him" (Ps 92:16 [ET v. 15]). In both of these outer members there is no finite verb, unlike the other matching sections of the chiasm.

In the matching members, B and B^1 (stanzas 2 and 4), the emphasis is upon the Lord's (Yahweh's) creative/re-creative works. Terminologically, only in these two sections in the psalm does the psalmist directly address the Lord using the second masculine singular completed action: "You have made me glad by your work" (Ps 92:5 [ET v. 4]) and "You have exalted my horn" (Ps 92:11 [ET v. 10]). Each section begins with this unique direct address/description, and each section ends with a broadening to an indefinite, generalized subject that is also unique to these matching sections: "A senseless/brutish man [*'ish ba'ar*] does not know" (Ps 92:7 [ET v. 6]) and "A righteous man flourishes" (Ps 92:13 [ET v. 12]). In section B (stanza 2) God's cosmic creative works are particularly in view, while in section B^1 (stanza 4) His personal re-creative/sustaining works are pronounced (see below for discussion).

---

the inverted parallelism matched with several (up to four) verses on the other side. He also does not recognize crucial terminological parallels and boundaries of the different stanzas.

[14] The author of this study initially presented this chiastic structure of Psalm 92 in a paper for the Society of Biblical Literature meetings in New Orleans, November 1988, and subsequently this structure was adopted essentially without change by Tate, *Psalm 51–100*, 468.

Chart 1
The Chiastic Literary Structure of Psalm 92

[Hebrew text of Psalm 92, arranged in 5 stanzas with chiastic structure A–B–C–D–C¹–B¹–A¹]

¹ מִזְמוֹר שִׁיר לְיוֹם הַשַּׁבָּת׃

A — ² טוֹב לְהֹדוֹת לַיהוָה וּלְזַמֵּר לְשִׁמְךָ עֶלְיוֹן׃
³ לְהַגִּיד בַּבֹּקֶר חַסְדֶּךָ וֶאֱמוּנָתְךָ בַּלֵּילוֹת׃
⁴ עֲלֵי־עָשׂוֹר וַעֲלֵי־נָבֶל עֲלֵי הִגָּיוֹן בְּכִנּוֹר׃

B — ⁵ כִּי שִׂמַּחְתַּנִי יְהוָה בְּפָעֳלֶךָ בְּמַעֲשֵׂי יָדֶיךָ אֲרַנֵּן׃
⁶ מַה־גָּדְלוּ מַעֲשֶׂיךָ יְהוָה מְאֹד עָמְקוּ מַחְשְׁבֹתֶיךָ׃
⁷ אִישׁ־בַּעַר לֹא יֵדָע וּכְסִיל לֹא־יָבִין אֶת־זֹאת׃

C — ⁸ בִּפְרֹחַ רְשָׁעִים כְּמוֹ עֵשֶׂב וַיָּצִיצוּ כָּל־פֹּעֲלֵי אָוֶן לְהִשָּׁמְדָם עֲדֵי־עַד׃

D — ⁹ וְאַתָּה מָרוֹם לְעֹלָם יְהוָה׃

C¹ — ¹⁰ כִּי הִנֵּה אֹיְבֶיךָ יְהוָה כִּי־הִנֵּה אֹיְבֶיךָ יֹאבֵדוּ יִתְפָּרְדוּ כָּל־פֹּעֲלֵי אָוֶן׃

B¹ — ¹¹ וַתָּרֶם כִּרְאֵים קַרְנִי בַּלֹּתִי בְּשֶׁמֶן רַעֲנָן׃
¹² וַתַּבֵּט עֵינִי בְּשׁוּרָי בַּקָּמִים עָלַי מְרֵעִים תִּשְׁמַעְנָה אָזְנָי׃
¹³ צַדִּיק כַּתָּמָר יִפְרָח כְּאֶרֶז בַּלְּבָנוֹן יִשְׂגֶּה׃

A¹ — ¹⁴ שְׁתוּלִים בְּבֵית יְהוָה בְּחַצְרוֹת אֱלֹהֵינוּ יַפְרִיחוּ׃
¹⁵ עוֹד יְנוּבוּן בְּשֵׂיבָה דְּשֵׁנִים וְרַעֲנַנִּים יִהְיוּ׃
¹⁶ לְהַגִּיד כִּי־יָשָׁר יְהוָה צוּרִי וְלֹא־(עַלְתָה) [עַוְלָתָה] בּוֹ׃

Moving to the next level of the inverse parallelism, members C and C¹ (Ps 92:8 and 10 [ET vs. 7 and 9] in the central stanza) are terminologically interlocked by the double use of the expression "all workers of evil" (*kol-poʿale ʾawen*), which appears in the psalm only in these verses. In both these parallel sections of the central stanza, the prominent theme is divine judgment in the destruction of enemies with an implicit connotation of the deliverance/redemption of the righteous. As will be discussed, member C (Ps 92:8 [ET v. 7]) focuses upon past destruction/redemption, while member C¹ (Ps 92:10

The Sabbath in the Psalms and Wisdom Literature

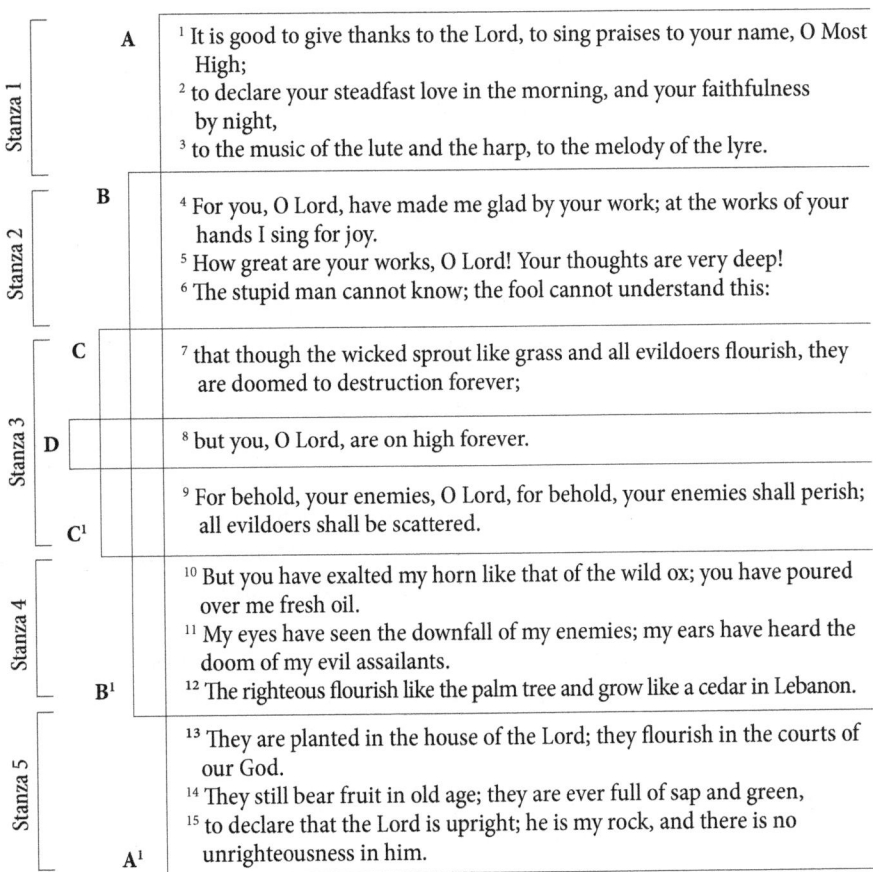

[ET v. 9]) speaks with assurance about God's work of future destruction/redemptive work. Both sections contain echoing phraseology from Exodus and conquest literature (Num 10:35; Deut 7:23; Judg 5:31) that describes Israel's deliverance/redemption from her enemies.

The central section of the Psalm, member D (Ps 92:9 [ET v. 8]), reiterates the dominant motif of the introduction and conclusion of the psalm, the exaltation of Yahweh: "But you, O Lord, are exalted forever." Verse 9 (ET v. 8) is comprised of only four Hebrew words. As has been noted, this distinctive prosodic structure makes it visually, metrically, and thematically pivotal. Unlike all the other verses of Psalm 92, this verse has but a single clause: There is no *ethnachta*, no caesura. Nor is there a main clause. Thus, the verse itself acts as a caesura, a pause between the first and last three stanzas.[15]

This is the only poetic line standing alone without a matching parallel line, thus forming the climactic peak of the septeniary chiastic structure.

Sabbatic Themes

If the literary features of Psalm 92 point to its sabbatic character by highlighting the "sevenness" of the psalm, what about the theological content? Most commentators have seen no relationship between the theological themes of Psalm 92 and the Sabbath. One scholar describes the situation, which still holds true among critical scholars: "Scholarly opinion is well-nigh unanimous that . . . there is absolutely no connection between the content of the psalm and the Sabbath day."[16] Scholars such as Hermann Gunkel and Sigmund Mowinckel have classified the literary genre of Psalm 92 as an "individual thanksgiving hymn," totally separated from any liturgical, cultic setting.[17]

A few scholars have recognized the cultic background of this psalm, although they have not connected it in any way to the Sabbath. So C. A. Briggs finds Psalm 92 "eminently suited for worship whether in the temple or synagogue."[18] N. H. Snaith goes further in stating that this psalm "was definitely written for the service of the Temple."[19] And Artur Weiser argues that the psalm "itself originated in the public worship of the cult community."[20]

---

[15] Vogel, "A Psalm for Sabbath," 218.

[16] Nahum M. Sarna, "The Psalm for the Sabbath Day [Psalm 92]," *JBL* 81 (1962): 158–159.

[17] Hermann Gunkel and J. Begrich, *Einleitung in die Psalmen* (Gottingen: Vandenhoeck and Ruprecht, 1966), 83–84, 274–280; Sigmund Mowinckel, *The Psalms in Israel's Worship* (Oxford: Basil Blackwell, 1962), 2:29, 37; cf. Claus Westermann, *The Psalms: Structure, Content and Message* (Minneapolis, MN: Augsburg, 1980), 72–73; Bernhard W. Anderson, *Out of the Depths: The Psalms Speak for Us Today* (Philadelphia, PA: Westminster, 1974), 176.

[18] C. A. Briggs, *The Book of Psalms*, ICC (New York: Charles Scribner's Sons, 1907), 2:283.

[19] N. H. Snaith, *Studies in the Psalter* (London: Epworth, 1934), 73.

[20] Artur Weiser, *The Psalms*, OTL (Philadelphia, PA: Westminster, 1962), 614.

Sarna summarizes the evidence for the liturgical character of Psalm 92.[21] He then argues that the contents of Psalm 92 correspond to and describe two major themes of the biblical Sabbath: creation and the socio-moral motif.[22] Other scholars have recognized major Sabbath themes in the psalm. "Apparently decisive . . . in the history of the interpretation of this Psalm—apart from the title of the Psalm—was the fact that a certain subject matter was connected with this Psalm, which corresponded to the religious interpretation of meaning of the Sabbath."[23] Maier points particularly to the theological dimensions developed in rabbinic interpretations connecting the weekly Sabbath with the eschatological "World Sabbath" of the whole creation. Erich Zenger builds on Maier's remarks and further correlates Psalm 92 with the Sabbath theology elsewhere in the Hebrew Bible, emphasizing the themes of eschatology (the weekly Sabbath as pointing to the eschatological era when deliverance from all pharaonic powers will be a reality, harking back to the Sabbath commandment in Deuteronomy 5), and sanctuary (the Sabbath as a spiritual, eternal, sanctuary par excellence, based upon the linkage between the Sabbath texts of Exodus 31:12-13 and 35:1-3).[24] Pinchas Kahn suggests that Psalm 92 traverses "the same sequence of teachings of the Sabbath commandments in Exodus and Deuteronomy"—that is, the twofold themes of creation and redemption (including a future dimension).[25]

Whereas for these scholars Psalm 92 coincidentally contained themes dominant in Israel's Sabbath theology and therefore was later pressed into liturgical service as a Song for the Sabbath, the author of this study finds more than this in the text. If one takes the superscription of the psalm as historically accurate and organically connected with the psalm from its inception,[26] then the psalm was actually composed to correspond to various Sabbath themes elsewhere in the Hebrew Bible. Even if the inscription

---

[21] Sarna, "The Psalm for the Sabbath Day," 158.

[22] Ibid., 167-168.

[23] All translations are original (with thanks to Chris Vogel, for ensuring fluency and accuracy). The original reads, "Entscheidend war offenbar . . . , daß auslegungsgeschichtlich mit diesem Psalm—auch abgesehen von seiner Überschrift—eine bestimmte Thematik verbunden wurde, die der religiösen Sinndeutung des Sabbat entsprach." J. Maier, "Zur Verwendung der Psalmen in der synagogalen Liturgie (Wochentag und Sabbat)," in *Liturgie und Dichtung: ein Interdisziplinäes Kompendium*, ed. Hg von H.-J. Becher and R. Kaczynski (St. Ottilien: Verlag Erzabtei, 1983), 69.

[24] Zenger, "Kanonische Psalmenexegese," 255-260.

[25] Pinchas Kahn, "The Expanding Perspectives of the Sabbath," *JBQ* 32 (2004): 243-244.

[26] See note 3 above for scholars providing evidence for this position.

were added later, a "final form" canonical approach to the psalm includes the superscription, and this superscription asks the reader to read the psalm with the Sabbath in mind, with a "sabbath repertoire"[27] of themes and allusions, or "Sabbath thoughts" (*Sabbatgedanken*).[28]

There are seven Sabbath themes in Psalm 92, each developed successively in the seven sections of the psalm, and corresponding to the major theological Sabbath motifs in the Hebrew Bible. There is strong internal and intertextual evidence to support the conclusion that the psalm in its canonical form is intertwined with literary sabbatic features and intertextually linked theological Sabbath motifs, thus constituting a highly artistic work either composed by the psalmist for use on the Sabbath (most likely), or canonically to be read with this Sabbath perspective in view. In what follows, this study argues that Psalm 92, the only psalm linked explicitly with the Sabbath in the Psalter, was from its inception, or at least canonically, envisioned as the psalm for the Sabbath par excellence, encompassing the cultic worship mode, prevailing mood, primary motivations, and essential theological meaning of the biblical Sabbath for God's people.

This study works through each stanza successively, highlighting the "sabbath repertoire" of sabbatic themes and allusions for each stanza, and relating these themes to the corresponding aspects of Sabbath theology elsewhere in the Hebrew Bible (see Chart 2 for summary). The opening stanza of Psalm 92 (vs. 2–4 [ET vs. 1–3]) provides the cultic context and sets the tone for the remainder of the psalm. The hymnic introduction and reference to elaborate instrumental accompaniment involving instruments used in temple worship[29] all point to a congregational worship setting at the sanctuary.[30] The implied praxis or mode for Sabbath theology is thus communal worship and praise at the house of God.

The theme is joyous exultation! The worshippers praise and sing (Ps 92:2 [ET v. 1]); they declare the "covenant love" (*khesedh*) and "covenant faithfulness" (*'emunah*) of the Lord (Ps 92:3 [ET v. 2]). Making such declaration in praise is *tov*, which in Hebrew means not only "good" and "fitting," but also "beautiful." This opening word of the psalm (after the superscription) "shows to what a high degree the aesthetic and artistic and the ethical and religious aspects of the worshiping life are here

---

[27] Tate, *Psalm 51–100*, 471.

[28] Dieter Schneider, *Das Buch der Psalmen*, 3 vols. (Wuppertal: Brockhaus Verlag, 2008), 2:227.

[29] See 1 Chronicles 13:8; 15:16, 20–21, 28; 25:1, 6; and 2 Chronicles 5:12.

[30] See especially Weiser, *The Psalms*, 614–615, for elaboration of this point.

comprehended as a unity by those who are subject to the vivid impression produced by the glory of God."[31]

From every line of this first stanza comes evidence of the prevailing mood: the thanksgiving, singing, and instrumental accompaniment are all part of exuberant celebration. This stanza constitutes a thematic counterpart to the keynote of joy in the observance of the Sabbath as set forth in Isaiah 58:13–14.

> The Sabbath is the day that God has hallowed, and that is to be consecrated to God by our turning away from the business pursuits of the working days (Isa. lviii.13 sq.) and applying ourselves to the praise and adoration of God, which is the most proper, blessed Sabbath employment.[32]

In Isaiah 58:13–14 Yahweh promises that "if . . . you call the Sabbath a delight [ʿonegh] . . . then you will find your joy [ʿanagh] in the Lord." The Hebrew Bible has various words for joy, happiness, pleasure, and delight, each of which appears numerous times. But the noun ʿonegh occurs only one other time, where it describes the palaces of royalty (Isa 13:22). As a verb, ʿanagh appears only ten times, and denotes not just that which brings delight, but in particular that which delights because of its surpassing quality—that which satisfies and pleases because it has a delicate beauty or regal charm. In short, it describes "exquisite delight."[33]

In the first stanza of Psalm 92, the psalmist catches this vision of exquisite delight. If the psalm in its canonical form is shaped in conscious reference to the theology of the Sabbath, this opening stanza may be seen to canonically point to the prevailing mood of exultation that according to Isaiah 58 is to lie at the heart of the Hebrew understanding of the Sabbath.

Already in this first stanza there are also hints of the motivation that underlies Sabbath exultation, found in the deep meaning and message of the Sabbath. The psalmist rejoices in the name—the character—of the Most High: His character of "steadfast covenant love" (khesedh), of "covenant faithfulness and stability" (ʾemunah). Beholding the character of God has put a song in his heart. A hint that God's creative activity is a motivation for Sabbath joy may also be implied by the reference to "morning" and "night" (Ps 92:3 [ET v. 2]), perhaps alluding to the rhythm of evening and

---

[31] Weiser, The Psalms, 615.

[32] Delitzsch, Commentary on the Old Testament: Psalms, 3:67.

[33] BDB (1979), 772.

morning in creation week (Gen 1:5, 8, 13, 19, 23, 31).[34] But this motivation from creation becomes explicit in the next stanza.

The stanzas that follow the initial one in Psalm 92 appear to elaborate on the various motivations or reasons for the joyous exultation for the Sabbath, and at the same time highlight other major motifs of OT Sabbath theology. The second stanza (Ps 92:5-7 [ET vs. 4-6]) begins with the word "for, because" (*ki*), a preposition that emphasizes motivation or cause, which provides the "statement of the ground of this commendation of the praise of God."[35] This verse highlights the first motivation for Sabbath joy (Ps 92:5 [ET v. 4]): "For [or because] you have made me glad by your work; at the work of your hands I sing for joy." Psalm 92:6 (ET v. 5) continues: "How great are your works, Oh Lord." The Hebrew expression for "work[s] of your hands" (*ma'ase yadhekha*) elsewhere in the Psalms consistently refers to creation (Ps 8:3, 6; 19:1; 102:25; 138:8, etc.), and the parallel "your works" (*ma'asekha*) also can refer to the creation motif (see especially Prov 8:22). Some have shown in detail how the creation motif suffuses this section of the psalm.[36]

By means of the pervasive creation motif in the second stanza, the psalmist links the exultation and praise of worship on the Sabbath with the divine work of creation. Emerging from this stanza is an implicit allusion to, or at least correspondence with, the Sabbath as the memorial of creation, capturing the motivation of the Sabbath embedded in Genesis 2:2-3 and Exodus 20:8-11. The song for the Sabbath is thus ultimately rooted in the acknowledgment of the God of creation, and linked to the Sabbath He set aside as a memorial of His creation.

Psalm 92:7 (ET v. 6) has been translated by some modern versions as referring to the verses that follow (hence punctuated with a colon), but the poetic structure of the poem indicates that this verse is part of the second stanza and refers to what precedes—that is, the creative works (and deep thoughts) of God. Hence, the poetic line should be punctuated by a full

---

[34] Frank-Lothar Hossfeld, Erich Zenger, Linda M. Maloney, and Klaus Baltzer, *Psalms 2: A Commentary on Psalms 51–100*, Hermeneia (Minneapolis, MN: Fortress, 2005), 445.

[35] Delitzsch, *Commentary on the Old Testament: Psalms*, 3:67. The mood of celebration is also highlighted in Exodus 31:16–17. The same verb '*asah* ("do/make") is used both for Israel's "observance" of the Sabbath (Exod 31:16) and God's "making" of the heavens and earth (Exod 31:17). Instead of translating '*asah* with such a bland term as "observe," as in most modern versions, NAU and NIV more aptly reflect the nuance of the original by translating as "celebrate." Thus, Israel is not merely to "observe" the Sabbath, but to joyously "celebrate" it!

[36] Sarna, "The Psalm for the Sabbath Day," 159–165; Tate, *Psalm 51-100*, 466–470.

stop.³⁷ One scholar captures the nuances of the verse: "A brutish man [*'ish baʿar*] remains unconscious, and a fool doth not discern this,"³⁸ and points out that the Hebrew *'ish baʿar* literally means "a man of animal nature, *homo brutus*."³⁹ In the context of the Sabbath and the modern debate over creation and evolution, it is tempting to suggest that the psalmist wrote more than he knew and beyond his time, intimating that those who regard humankind as only evolved from the brute animals will never grasp the significance of the Sabbath as a memorial of creation by God. And conversely, those who understand the Sabbath will not be led astray into regarding humanity as having evolved through naturalistic mechanisms rather than being directly created by God.

The central stanza (Ps 92:8–10 [ET vs. 7–9]) leads us into the second motivation for joyous worship on the Sabbath day. Here we have an implicit indication of, or at least correspondence with, the fact that the Sabbath is not only a celebration of creation but also of redemption/deliverance from the enemies. The redemption has two temporal aspects.

Psalm 92:8 [ET v. 7] focuses upon the past. Although some English versions translate this verse in the future tense, the most precise rendering refers to a particular event that has taken place in the past.⁴⁰ For example, the NASB: "When the wicked sprouted up like grass, and all the workers of iniquity flourished, it came to pass that they were absolutely destroyed." The historical event referred to in this verse (as well as verses 9–10) is most probably the exodus when God delivered Israel from their enemies, which was the time of redemption par excellence for ancient Israel.⁴¹ This is confirmed by the strong intertextual links between Psalm 92:8–10 [ET vs. 7–9] and several passages related to Israel's exodus and conquest. The "exaltation" (*rum*) of the Lord harks back to Yahweh's exaltation (*rum*) in the Song of Moses (Exod 15:2). The reference to Israel's enemies being "scattered" (*prd* in the Hitpael stem, Ps 92:10 [ET v. 9]) probably alludes to Moses' statement repeated whenever the camp of Israel set out in the wilderness: "Rise up, O Lord! Let Your enemies be scattered" (Num 10:35, using the cognate term

---

³⁷ Correctly punctuated in such modern English versions as the KJV, NKJV, NET, and NJB.

³⁸ Delitzsch, *Commentary on the Old Testament: Psalms*, 3:65.

³⁹ Ibid.

⁴⁰ Sarna, "The Psalm for the Sabbath Day," 159–160, and Delitzsch, *Commentary on the Old Testament: Psalms*, 3:65, summarize the syntactical data to support this preferred translation of the infinitive with the preposition followed by the imperfect consecutive.

⁴¹ E. J. Kissane, *The Book of Psalms* (Dublin: Brown and Nolan, 1964), 430, 432.

puts). The Hebrew expression translated "to be destroyed" (Ps 92:8 [ET v. 7], *shmd* in the Niphal stem) is used elsewhere in a positive sense for Israel only in Deuteronomy 7:23, describing the conquest. An almost exact parallel to Psalm 92:10 [ET v. 9] appears in the context of the extended conquest in the song of Deborah: "Thus let all your enemies perish, O Lord!" (Judg 5:31).

The redemption/deliverance motif implicitly connected with, or at least corresponding to, the Sabbath in Psalm 92 echoes the explicit mention of this motivation for Sabbath celebration in the Sabbath commandment of Deuteronomy 5.[42] According to Deuteronomy 5:15, each Sabbath God called for Israel to remember in a special way that He had redeemed them from their bondage in Egypt, from the threat of their enemies. This sabbatic motif of redemption and liberation is elsewhere in the Pentateuch extended to the ultimate in the sabbatical year and the jubilee (Exod 21:1–6; 23:10–12; Deut 15:1–18; Lev 25:1–55). The redemptive/deliverance motif is also underscored in the larger context of Isaiah 58, where God's people are to extend the redemptive, liberating work to those around them (Isa 58:6–12). This motif becomes the heart of Christ's redemptive work in His Sabbath miracles in the NT.

Stanza 3 of Psalm 92 not only emphasizes the past redemptive activity of God in language of the exodus/conquest, but looks forward to a cosmic consummation of redemption/deliverance in the ultimate destruction of all God's enemies (Ps 92:10 [ET v. 9]): "For surely your enemies, O Lord, surely your enemies will perish; all evildoers will be scattered." This verse alludes to the cosmic conflict that will find ultimate consummation in the last days, the "final victory of good over evil."[43] Here the psalm implicitly anticipates, or at least is in correspondence with, the eschatological character of the Sabbath, as the sign of the everlasting covenant between God and Israel, a

---

[42] See Zenger, "Kanonische Psalmenexegese," 258, who writes, "On the weekly-celebrated Sabbath Israel rehearses the hope that someday an eternal world Sabbath will come, during which the end of all pharaonic power and danger will be celebrated. It is *these* connotations of the Sabbath as a feast of the deliverance from all pharaonic powers which can be heard in Psalm 92, if one hears the statements about the righteous judgment of YHWH over the enemies before the background of the exodus, which according to Deuteronomy 5:12–15 should be remembered on the Sabbath day." In German, "Am wöchentlich gefeierten Sabbat übt Israel die Hoffnung ein, daß einmal ein ewiger Weltensabbat kommen wird, an dem das Ende aller pharaonischen Macht und Bedrohung gefeiert werden kann. Gerade *diese* Konnotationen vom Sabbat als dem Festtag der Befreiung von allen pharaonischen Mächten können in Psalm 92 mitgehört werden, wenn man seine Aussagen über das gerechte Gericht JHWHs an den Feinden vor dem Hintergrund des Exodus, der gemäß Dtn 5,12–15 am Sabbat-Tag erinnert werden soll, hört."

[43] Delitzsch, *Commentary on the Old Testament: Psalms*, 3:69.

test of Israel's obedience in the context of judgment at the eschatological new exodus (Exod 31:16–17; Ezek 20:12, 20; Isa 56:1–2; Rev 12:17; 14:7).[44]

At the heart of this divine work of deliverance and destruction of God's enemies, and at the heart of the entire psalm, Psalm 92:9 [ET v. 8] reveals the focal point in the song for the Sabbath: "But You, O Lord, are exalted forever." The exaltation—yes, vindication—of Yahweh is paramount in the theology of this psalm. The motif of the exaltation of God's character in stanza 1 has already been discussed, and it reappears at the conclusion of the psalm. The expression "Forever" (le'olam), which occupies the climactic position in the central poetic line of the psalm, highlights the eschatological character of this exaltation/vindication of Yahweh.[45]

The fourth stanza of the Song for the Sabbath (Ps 92:11–13 [ET vs. 10–12]) brings us to the here and now: the song's lyrics describe present personal experience.[46] Images of the abundant, victorious life of covenant blessings come fast and glorious in this stanza. In Psalm 92:11 (ET v. 10) there is the exalted horn like the wild ox, symbols of power and victory, echoing passages from Israel's salvation history with allusions to the coming Messiah's ultimate fulfillment (Num 23:22; 24:8; Deut 33:17; 1 Sam 2:1, 10).[47] There is the "anointing" with oil, utilizing the term *balal*, which elsewhere (when used in connection with oil) always refers to the "mixing" or "mingling" of oil with cakes or flour for the grain offering (see Exod 29:40; Lev 2:4–5; 7:10, 12; 14:10, 21; 23:13; Num 7 [12x]; Num 28 [7x], etc.). Thus, the psalmist is like fine flour mixed with oil to be offered to Yahweh.[48] The

---

[44] For a discussion of the eschatological character of the Sabbath passages in Torah, see, e.g., Zenger, "Kanonische Psalmenexegese," 255–260.

[45] Ibid., 257.

[46] In Psalm 92:11 (ET v. 10) the perfect verb form is employed, in the sense of our English perfect, denoting a past action with continuing effect in the present: "But my horn You *have exalted* like a wild ox; I *have been anointed* with fresh oil" (NKJV). In Psalm 92:12 (ET v. 11), the juxtaposition of the perfect aspect (in the sense of action with continuing present results) combines with the imperfect aspect (describing a present condition): "My eye also *has seen* my desire on my enemies; my ears *hear* my desire on the wicked who rise up against me" (NKJV). In Psalm 92:13 (ET v. 12) the imperfect aspect continues the sense of present condition: "The righteous [lit. 'a righteous one'] *flourish* like the palm tree, and *grow* like a cedar in Lebanon" (NRSV).

[47] For further discussion of the Messianic allusions in Numbers 23–24 and Deuteronomy 33, see, e.g., Richard M. Davidson, "The Eschatological Literary Structure of the Old Testament," in *Creation, Life, and Hope: Essays in Honor of Jacques B. Doukhan*, ed. Jiří Moskala (Berrien Springs, MI: Old Testament Department, Seventh-day Adventist Theological Seminary, Andrews University, 2000), 354–357.

[48] See Derek Kidner, *Psalms 73–150*, Kidner Classic Commentaries (London: Inter-Varsity, 1975; repr., Downers Grove, IL: InterVarsity, 2014), 336; Leupold, *Exposition of the Psalms*, 663.

imagery of victors "*soaked in freshening oil*" also connotes "a process of revivification, beautification, and consecration."[49]

In Psalm 92:12 (ET v. 11), the psalmist also personalizes Yahweh's exploits, and describes the present experience of defeating his (which are also Yahweh's) enemies. Intertextual parallels are found in other psalms (Ps 112:8; 59:11 [ET v. 10]; 54:7).[50] In Psalm 92:13 (ET v. 12), a righteous one is described as flourishing like the graceful date palm, which yields some six hundred pounds of dates in a single season (see also Prov 11:28).[51] He "grows" or "increases" (*saghah*) like the majestic and mighty cedar of Lebanon (see intertextual parallels in Ps 104:16; Ezek 17:22–23 [with messianic allusions]; 27:5).

In short, this section of Psalm 92 summarizes the ongoing covenant blessings of pre-eminence, strength, victory, and fertility God had promised in Deuteronomy 28 and Leviticus 26 as He establishes them as His "holy people" (Deut 28:9). It describes God's work of sanctification or "making holy" of His people. It is instructive to note that in Leviticus 26:2, keeping the Sabbath is placed in direct juxtaposition with the covenant blessings that follow (Lev 26:3–14), and at the heart of the parallel list of covenant blessings in Deuteronomy 28 is the establishing of "a holy people" (Deut 28:9). The song of Psalm 92 may be viewed as the melodic counterpart of Exodus 31:13: "You shall keep my Sabbaths, for this is a sign between me and you throughout your generations, that you may know that I, the Lord, sanctify you." Just as the Lord rested on the seventh day after creating the earth and was "refreshed," or literally "took on new life" (*npsh* in the Niphal, Exod 31:17), so He offers the worshipper the gifts of this same life, ever new.[52] Stanza 4 of Psalm 92 uplifts the God who acts in the present in the life of the individual worshipper, Yahweh the Sanctifier.

The final stanza of Psalm 92 (vs. 14–16 [ET vs. 13–15]) takes us from the present to the eschatological future. The stanza break is indicated between verses 13 and 14 (ET vs. 12 and 13) by several features: (1) the overall poetic metrical structure of the psalm, (2) the grammatical moves from the singular "righteous one" to the plural "they," (3) the move from the simple "budding, sprouting" of the righteous (Qal imperfect of *parakh*)

---

[49] Vogel, "A Psalm for Sabbath," 219.

[50] See the discussion in Kidner, *Psalms 73–150*, 336.

[51] Delitzsch, *Commentary on the Old Testament: Psalms*, 3:71.

[52] This revitalizing refreshment also has a humanitarian perspective, as the offer of "taking on new life" (*nafash* in the Niphal) is extended to the "son of your maidservant and the stranger" in Exodus 23:12.

to the causative "showing buds or sprouts, flourishing" (Hiphil imperfect of *parakh*), and (4) a shift of scene to the sanctuary ("the house of the Lord") in the setting of eschatological, paradisiacal imagery that follows.

Psalm 92:14 (ET v. 13) literally reads, "Transplanted [*shethulim*, Qal passive of *shathal*] into the house of the Lord, they will flourish in the courts of our God" (see the NLT, which more accurately translates *shethulim* as "transplanted" and not simply "planted" as in most other modern versions). Although parts of Mitchell Dahood's analysis of technical terms for the afterlife in the Psalms based upon Ugaritic parallels have been questioned, he has set forth weighty evidence (supplementing the earlier work of Julian Morgenstern) that "transplant" (*shathal*) is here a technical term referring to the eschatological entrance into the future life in the heavenly palace and courtyard of God.[53]

This interpretation is strengthened by analysis of the language of Psalm 92:14–15 (ET vs. 13–14), describing the temple courts "as paradise" and the "primal fertility of creation."[54] This eschatological interpretation is further strengthened by the intertextual linking of many of the rare terms and distinctive descriptions in these verses with passages in eschatological contexts referring to the age to come. The only other use of the root *nuv* (in the Polel stem) translated "bear fruit" (Ps 92:15) is in the description of the eschatological age in Zechariah 9:17. There is the eschatological picture of those Gentiles who keep Sabbath being brought "into the house of the Lord" (Isa 56:5; cf. Ps 92:14) and the days of God's people, when He creates the new heavens and new earth, being "as the days of a tree" (Isa 65:22; cf. Ps 92:15 and the link with the Sabbath in Isa 66:22–23). The adjective "luxuriant" (*ra'anan*) is found in the eschatological context of Hosea 14:9 (ET v. 8; also the eschatological judgment context of Ps 52:8–9). The accompanying adjective "full of oil or sap" (*dashen*) is found in both of its other two occurrences in the Hebrew Bible in an eschatological context (Ps 22:30; Isa 30:23).

There is thus sufficient evidence to conclude that in this last stanza of Psalm 92, continuing the imagery of palm and cedar, God promises that the righteous will be "transplanted" (either by translation or resurrection) to the heavenly sanctuary and paradise of God. There they will still bring forth fruit in old age; they will be ever "fresh and flourishing" (Ps 92:15 [ET v. 14]). In light of a parallel in Psalm 73:24, which reads, "Afterward you will receive

---

[53] Mitchell Dahood, *Psalms*, AB (Garden City, NY: Doubleday, 1968), 2:338; 1:3–4; cf. Julian Morgenstern, "Psalm 48," *HUCA* 16 (1941): 81–82.

[54] Tate, *Psalm 51–100*, 468, 470.

me to glory," and which has likewise been shown to refer to the heavenly afterlife,[55] it is appropriate to refer to this stanza as a song of glorification.

This final stanza thus implies that the Sabbath is a celebration in anticipation of glorification—a foretaste of the eschaton. We have the melodic counterpart to the description of the continuation of the weekly Sabbath in the context of the eschatological consummation, alluded to in Sabbath passages of Torah,[56] and made explicit in Isaiah 66:23: "'From one month to the next and from one Sabbath to the next, all people will come to worship me,' says the LORD" (NET).[57]

The Jewish Mishnah recognizes the eschatological vision of Psalm 92: "It is the psalm for the hereafter, for the day that will be wholly Sabbath and rest for eternity."[58] Contemporary scholars have caught the eschatological flavor of the psalm, especially its final verses: "The Sabbath is a proleptic glimpse of the eternal life of the coming age: 'Those who observe the Sabbath experience an earnest of the coming redemption.' . . . So it is with the righteous in Psalm 92:13–16; they both anticipate and experience the paradisaical life."[59]

How does the Sabbath song of Psalm 92 end? What is the central point that encapsulates the ultimate meaning of the Sabbath? The last verse of the psalm reiterates the underlying theme that has surfaced again and again. It is all toward one end: "to show that the Lord is upright ["straight," *yashar*]; he is my rock [*tsur*], and there is no unrighteousness ["injustice," *'awlatha*] in him." All three key words in this final declaration converge in the Song of Moses, appearing together in a single verse in Deuteronomy 32:4. Thus, the psalmist echoes the focus of Moses' final song. The focal point of the Sabbath in Psalm 92 is the same as the focus of all the life of Israel for Moses: a revelation of the character of God.

---

[55] Dahood, *Psalms*, 2:194–195.

[56] See Zenger, "Kanonische Psalmenexegese," 255–260.

[57] The NET (also NLT) more accurately translates "month" instead of "New Moon." The noun *khodhesh* in the Hebrew Bible "occurs 283x, its most common meaning being 'month.' . . . . A second meaning . . . is new moon" (J. A. Naudé, "חדש *khdsh*," *NIDOTTE* 5:38). Although many English versions translate the Hebrew *khodhesh* used in Isaiah 66:23 as "New Moon," the standard Hebrew lexicons agree that in connection with the special grammatical construction of this verse, the preferred translation for *khodhesh* here is "month," not "New Moon." So *BDB* (1979), 191: "*As often as* month (comes) in its month"; cf. *HALOT* 1:219: "From month to month."

[58] *m. Tamid* 7, 4.

[59] Tate, *Psalm 51–100*, 470, citing Jon D. Levenson, *Sinai and Zion: An Entry into the Jewish Bible* (Minneapolis, MN: Winston, 1985), 183–184. Cf. Zenger, "Kanonische Psalmenexegese," 255–260.

Psalm 92 may rightly be described as a "theodicy psalm."[60] One scholar captures the essential message of the psalm:

> It praises God, the Creator of the world, as the Ruler of the world, whose rule is pure lovingkindness and faithfulness, and calms itself, in the face of the flourishing condition of the evil-doers, with the prospect of the final issue, which will brilliantly vindicate the righteousness of God.[61]

Throughout the psalm, Yahweh is shown to be just what the Sabbath reveals Him to be: the Creator, the Redeemer, the Sanctifier, the Glorifier. In the final analysis, the message of the psalm, the meaning of the Sabbath, is not ultimately about the glorification of man, but about the glorification and vindication of God: "You, O Lord, are exalted forever" (Ps 92:9 [ET v. 8])!

The chiastic sabbatic structure of Psalm 92 may be summarized as follows:

Chart 2
The Chiastic Sabbatic Structure of Psalm 92

EXALTATION
(God's Character)
D

v. 9
(1 colon)

REDEMPTION C — v. 8 (3 cola) / v. 10 (3 cola) — **C¹ REDEMPTION**
(God's Work in the Past) / (God's Work in the Future)

CREATION B — vs. 5-7 (6 cola) / v. 11-13 (6 cola) — **B¹ SANCTIFICATION**
(God's Creative Works) / (God's Re-creative Work)

EXULTATION A — vs. 2-4 (6 cola) / v. 14-16 (6 cola) — **A¹ GLORIFICATION**
(God's Character) / (God's Character)

---

[60] Hossfeld et al., *A Commentary on Psalms 51–100*, 445.

[61] Delitzsch, *Commentary on the Old Testament: Psalms*, 3:66–67.

Other Possible Allusions to the Sabbath

Psalm 104

Although Psalm 104 does not explicitly mention the Sabbath, there is good evidence to suggest that sabbatic theology is found in this psalm. Numerous scholars have recognized that this psalm follows the same basic order as the six days of creation in Genesis 1: For example, Walter Zorn writes, "A summary of the creation account is contained in the psalm, similar to the record in Genesis chapter one. . . . Following the order of creation as given in Genesis, he [the psalmist] shows how God, in successive stages, was preparing for the welfare and comfort of his creatures."[62] W. T. Purkiser comments, "The major section of the psalm is given to the present magnificence of the creative acts described in Genesis 1. The order of topics follows that of the original creation account, beginning with light and concluding with man."[63] Derek Kidner likewise argues that "the structure of the psalm is modeled fairly closely on that of Genesis 1, taking the stages of creation as starting-points for praise."[64] Other similar statements could be multiplied.[65]

---

[62] Walter D. Zorn, *Psalms*, The College Press NIV Commentary, vol. 2 (Joplin, MO: College Press, 2004), 264, 266.

[63] W. T. Purkiser, "Psalms," in *Beacon Bible Commentary*, ed. Ralph Earle, W. T. Purkiser, and A. F. Harper, vol. 3 (Kansas City, MO: Beacon Hill, 1967), 356.

[64] Kidner, *Psalms 73–150*, 368, nuances his analysis with the following observation: "But as each theme is developed it tends to anticipate the later scenes of the creation drama, so that the days described in Genesis overlap and mingle here."

[65] See, e.g., Willem A. VanGemeren, "Psalms," in *EBC*, vol. 5 (Grand Rapids, MI: Zondervan, 1991), 657: "The poetic version of Creation [in Psalm 104] is complementary to the prosaic of Genesis 1." Again, note the comments of Leupold, *Exposition of the Psalms*, 722: "What is its relation to the creation account found in Gen. 1? This psalm is not based directly on this Scripture passage, but it does show familiarity with it and may well be regarded as a free treatment of the known facts of creation with particular attention to various other factors that the concise account of Gen. 1 could not have brought into the picture." Throughout his commentary on the psalm, Leupold refers to the days of creation in Genesis 1. He points out that verse 2a "parallels the work of the first day of creation" (ibid., 724) and verses 2b–4 constitute "a reference to the work of the second day of creation" (ibid.). He continues, "On the third day of God's great creative work dry land and water were separated. This aspect of creation is now under consideration (vs. 5–9)" (ibid., 725). Regarding verses 13–18, he writes: "The work of the second half of the third day of creation interests the writer chiefly in this section, except that he combines with it the thought of the living beings that come into existence on the sixth day inasmuch as vegetation is the primary article of diet of these beings. So the sixth day gets only incidental attention" (ibid., 727). Regarding verses 19–23, Leupold comments, "In the pattern that the writer is following we have arrived at the fourth day's work of creation, the work of providing the heavenly bodies in their various functions" (ibid., 728). The description of verses 24–36 is seen as "a part of the work of the fifth day when the birds of the heaven and fish of the sea were brought into being" (ibid., 729). For earlier, critical studies of

More than noting with a general statement the linkages between Genesis 1 and Psalm 104, Kidner points out the linkages in his comments on specific verses, and also provides the following helpful summary of the correspondences between the two creation accounts:[66]

Day 1 (Gen 1:3–5) light Ps 104:2a
Day 2 (Gen 1:6–8) the firmament divides the waters Ps 104:2b–4
Day 3 (Gen 1:9–10) land and water distinct Ps 104:5–9 (+10–13?)
    (Gen 1:11–13) vegetation and trees Ps 104:14–17 (+18?)
Day 4 (Gen 1:14–19) luminaries as timekeepers Ps 104:19–23 (+24)
Day 5 (Gen 1:20–23) creatures of sea and air Ps 104:25–26 (sea only)
Day 6 (Gen 1:24–28) animals and man Ps 104:21–24 (anticipated)
    (Gen 1:29–31) food appointed for all creatures Ps 104:27–28 (+29–30)

What is surprising about this analysis, and most other modern commentaries, is not what is said, but what is overlooked. They point out the development of thought in Psalm 104:2–30 that so closely parallels the six consecutive days of creation in Genesis 1. But in commenting upon the final verses of Psalm 104 (vs. 31–35), there is little or no attempt to connect this last section of the psalm with the Genesis creation account. If the first six sections of Psalm 104 (vs. 1–30) have a clear parallel, section by section, with the sequence of the six days of creation, why is there no recognition of the possibility that the last section (Ps 104:31–35) might parallel the seventh day of creation, the Sabbath?

Fortunately, what has been largely—if not entirely—overlooked by more recent commentators has been recognized by that classic nineteenth OT commentary by Delitzsch, who labels this psalm as a "Hymn in Honour of the God of the Seven Days."[67] He then summarizes its contents: "The Psalm is altogether an echo of the heptahemeron (or history of the seven days of creation) in Gen. i.1–ii.3. Corresponding to the seven days it falls

---

the relationship between Genesis 1 and Psalm 104, which conclude that Psalm 104 is directly dependent upon Genesis 1, see H. Gunkel, *Die Psalmen*, 4th ed. (Göttingen: Vandenhoeck und Ruprecht, 1926), 453; and P. Humbert, "La relation de Genèse 1 et du Psaume 104 avec la liturgie du Nouvel-An israëlite," *Revue des sciences philosophiques dt théologiques* 15 (1935): 1–27.

[66] Adapted from Kidner, *Psalms 73–150*, 368. The verses marked with + in parentheses are those verses that Kidner sees as developing a theme further. See also Richard M. Davidson, "The Creation Theme in Psalm 104," in *The Genesis Creation Account and Its Reverberations in the Old Testament*, ed. Gerald A. Klingbeil (Berrien Springs, MI: Andrews University Press, 2015), 149-188.

[67] Delitzsch, *Commentary on the Old Testament: Psalms*, 3:125.

into seven groups. . . . [I]t begins with the light and closes with an allusion to the divine Sabbath."[68]

Delitzsch articulates the thematic parallels between the first six sections of Psalm 104 and the first six days of creation week, with similar results as the summary of Kidner presented above.[69] Then he comes to the final section, Psalm 104:31–35, in which he finds a clear allusion to the Sabbath: "The poet has now come to an end with the review of the wonders of the creation, and closes in this seventh group . . . with a sabbatic meditation."[70]

This "sabbatic meditation" begins with the poet's wish: "May the glory of the Lord endure forever; May the Lord rejoice in His works" (Ps 104:31). The psalmist

> wishes that the glory of God, which He has put upon His creatures, and which is reflected and echoed back by them to Him, may continue for ever, and that His works may ever be so constituted that He who was satisfied at the completion of His six day's work may be able to rejoice in them.[71]

Especially significant in linking this final stanza of the poem to the Sabbath is the close relationship between the reference to the poet's rejoicing in Yahweh (Ps 104:34) and the reference to Yahweh's rejoicing in creation (Ps 104:31): "Between the 'I will rejoice,' ver. 34, and 'He shall rejoice,' ver. 31, there exists a reciprocal relation, as between the Sabbath of the creature in God and the Sabbath of God in the creature."[72] The eschatological

---

[68] Delitzsch, *Commentary on the Old Testament: Psalms*, 3:127-128. Like Kidner, Delitzsch clarifies that the psalm does not rigidly treat each day of creation in each successive section: "It is not, however, so worked out that each single group celebrates the work of a day of creation; the Psalm has the commingling whole of the finished creation as its standpoint, and is therefore not so conformed to any plan" (ibid.).

[69] For Delitzsch, *Commentary on the Old Testament: Psalms*, 3:128, Psalm 104:1-30 is divided into six groups. Group 1 (vs. 1–4) "begins the celebration with the work of the first and second days." Group 2 (vs. 5–9) includes the depiction of "primordial waters" and "the coming forth of the dry land on the third day of creation" (ibid., 130). In the third group (vs. 10–14b), the poet is "passing on to the third day of creation" (ibid., 131). In the fourth group (vs. 14c–18) there is continued discussion of the third day, and "the fifth decastich [vs. 19–23], in which the poet passes over from the third to the fourth day, shows that he has the order of the days of creation before his mind" (ibid., 133–134). In verses 24–30, the sixth group: "Fixing his eye upon the sea with its small and great creatures, and the care of God for all self-living beings, the poet passes over to the fifth and sixth days of creation" (ibid., 134).

[70] Ibid., 136.

[71] Ibid.

[72] Ibid.

implication of the sabbatical meditation is also captured in the poet's linkage of rejoicing in creation with the destruction of the wicked:

> When the Psalmist wishes that God may have joy in His works of creation, and seeks on his part to please God and to have his joy in God, he is also warranted in wishing that those who take pleasure in wickedness, and instead of giving God joy excite His wrath, may be removed from the earth . . .; for they are contrary to the purpose of the good creation of God, they imperil its continuance, and mar the joy of His creatures.[73]

The link between the final stanza of Psalm 104 and the Sabbath of Genesis 2:2–4 is finally receiving some attention in more recent scholarship. Without explicitly mentioning the Sabbath, one scholar writes,

> The psalm empowers poet and hearer to imitate God by taking time to enjoy the creation (Gen. 2:2–3). Such moments of 'resting' in the creation are crucial not only for human recreation but also for the survival of the world itself, for it can entice one out of the mode of using and into the mode of revering.[74]

Another writer remarks, concerning the concluding prayer of the psalm, "Just like God is experiencing Sabbath joy over his creation, so the prayer will rejoice in Jahwe."[75]

Two Seventh-day Adventist scholars have explored the allusion to the Sabbath in Psalm 104:31–35. In his doctoral dissertation on the literary structure of the Genesis creation narratives, Jacques Doukhan points out the thematic parallels between Genesis 1:1–2:4a and Psalm 104 (with similar conclusions to Kidner and Delitzsch).[76] With regard to the relationship between the seventh day of creation week and Psalm 104:31–32, he notes the thematic correspondence of the glory of God in creation[77] and allusion to the

---

[73] Delitzsch, Commentary on the Old Testament: Psalms, 3:136.

[74] Virgil Howard, "Psalm 104," Interpretation 46, no. 2 (April 1992): 178.

[75] Schneider, Das Buch der Psalmen, 3:39. The German reads, "Wie Gott sich seiner Schöpfung gegenüber in der Sabatfreude befindet, so will der Betende sich freue(n) in Jahwe."

[76] See Jacques B. Doukhan, The Genesis Creation Story: Its Literary Structure (Berrien Springs, MI: Andrews University Press, 1978), 84–87.

[77] Doukhan, The Genesis Creation Story, 85 n. 4, indicates that the glory of God "belongs especially in the Psalms to the imagery of God as king of the earth, i.e., its Creator (see Ps 145:11; 19:2; 29:2–3, etc.). On the other hand, this concept is clearly associated with the theophany on Sinai

revelation on Sinai in verse 32. Doukhan draws the implication: "This reference to Sinai in direct association with the very concern of creation points to the Sabbath."

Doukhan also indicates the presence of terminological linkages between the account of each day of creation week in Genesis and the respective section of Psalm 104. With regard to specific terminological parallels between the seventh day of Genesis 2:1–3 and Psalm 104:31–32, both employ the term "earth" (ʾerets) (Gen 2:1; Ps 104:32) and the same Hebrew root ʿsh (from which come the verb "to make" [three times in Gen 2:2–3] and the noun "works" [Ps 104:31]). Doukhan also points to the fact that both the introduction and conclusion of Psalm 104 (vs. 1, 33, and nowhere else in the Psalm) bring together the two names employed for God in Genesis 1 and 2: *Elohim* (used alone only in Gen 1:1–2:4a and together with the Tetragrammaton in Gen 2:4b–25) and *Yahweh* (used with *Elohim* in Gen 2:4b–25), which may imply the poet's recognition of the unity and complementarity of the two accounts of creation in Genesis 1–2.[78]

The other Adventist scholar to call attention to the Sabbath allusion in Psalm 104 is William Shea. In his article on creation in the *Handbook of Seventh-day Adventist Theology*, Shea examines the correspondences between the creation week of Genesis 1:1–2:4a and Psalm 104.[79] He sets forth the parallels between the first six days of creation week and Psalm 104 in a way similar to that presented by Delitzsch, Kidner, Leupold, and others. Then he elaborates on the parallels between the seventh day of creation week and the final verses of Psalm 104:

> In Genesis the account of Creation week goes on to describe the seventh day. The psalm has something similar. On the Sabbath we recognize that God is our Creator; we honor Him in the commemoration of Creation. That is the first thing mentioned in Psalm 104:31. When God finished His creation, He said that it was "very good." In Psalm 104 He rejoices in His works (verse 31).[80]

Shea's major contribution to the Sabbath theology of Psalm 104 may be in elaborating on the significance of what is described in verse 32: "He

---

(see Exod 24:16–17)."

[78] Doukhan, The Genesis Creation Story, 89-90.

[79] William H. Shea, "Creation," in *Handbook of Seventh-day Adventist Theology*, ed. Raoul Dederen (Hagerstown, MD: Review and Herald, 2000), 430–431.

[80] Ibid., 431.

looks at the earth, and it trembles; He touches the mountains, and they smoke" (NASB). Indeed, "This is the picture of a theophany, the manifestation of God's personal presence. This is what happens on the Sabbath when the Lord draws near to His people and makes Himself known. Struck with reverential awe, they render Him worship."[81] As Shea points out, that worship is depicted in the final verses of the psalm:

> Human beings bring worship and honor and glory and praise to God (verse 33). This is not a onetime occurrence: The psalmist promises to carry on this activity as long as life lasts. The praises of the Lord are on the lips of the psalmist continually. Silence is another part of worship. In verse 34 the psalmist asks that silent meditation upon the Lord may be pleasing to God. Finally, this reflection upon worship ends with rejoicing (verse 35).[82]

There appears to be sufficient evidence to conclude with a high degree of probability that Psalm 104 not only refers to the first six days of creation week, but also, in its final stanza, alludes to the seventh-day Sabbath of Genesis 2:1–3. Significant insights into Sabbath theology and praxis emerge from Psalm 104:31–35, including themes of God's glorification and rejoicing in His created works, the presence of God (theophany) leading to both reverential awe and joyous intimacy between the Creator and His creation, exuberant singing and praise in worship of God, silent meditation on the Lord, and the eschatological end of the wicked who refuse to give God praise.

Job 38–42

When Yahweh comes to Job at the end of the book that bears his name, He delivers the longest divine speech of the Scriptures, and it is centered in creation. Several OT scholars have noted the parallels between the final speech of Yahweh in Job 38–41 and the account of creation in Genesis 1. One writes, "The portrayal of creation in chapters 38–41 is reminiscent of Genesis 1, not only in its similar catalogue of the regions of the cosmos and their denizens, but in its light/darkness alternations. The sequence of day/night/day/night in Genesis 1 is partly paralleled in chapters 38–41."[83] Another comments similarly, "Yahweh's first speech [38:4–39:30] consists

---

[81] Shea, "Creation," 431.

[82] Ibid.

[83] J. Gerald Janzen, *Job*, Interpretation: A Bible Commentary for Teaching and Preaching (Atlanta, GA: John Knox, 1985), 229.

of dozens of questions about the cosmos. They begin with creation and advance in a pattern that approximates the first chapter of Genesis."[84]

Thematic parallels between the Genesis creation narrative and Job 38–42 indicate more than correspondences only with the first six days of creation. There is "a pattern in seven steps" corresponding to all seven days of creation week, including the Sabbath:

> Day One: Dialectic darkness-light (Job 38:2–3)
> Day Two: Basis of the earth; delimitations of the earth with regard to heaven (Job 38:4–7)
> Day Three: Delimitation of waters with regard to the earth (Job 38:8–11)
> Day Four: Dominion of light over darkness—connotation of time (Job 38:12)
> Distinction between light and darkness (Job 38:19)
> The mystery of the light (Job 38:24)
> Creation of the stars (Job 38:31–32)
> Rule of heaven on the earth (Job 38:33–38)
> Day Five: Theme of animals (Job 38:39–39:30). But the passage is mostly concerned with birds (see vv. 38:41; 39:13–18, 26–30).
> Day Six: Man in relation to God (Job 40:1–5)
> Man compared with God (Job 40:6–14, especially vv. 9–10)
> Animals are here presented in connection with man (cf. especially Job 40:15)
> Theme of dominion of animals by man (Job 40:24; 40:33–34; 41:1–10a)
> Idea of a relationship with the animals (Job 41:4)
> Day Seven: Response of Job:
> Confession of faith in the creative power of God (Job 42:1–3)
> Closeness of relationship and repentance (Job 42:5–6)[85]

---

[84] Robert L. Alden, *Job*, NAC (Nashville, TN: Broadman & Holman, 1993), 369. Cf. other commentators who have pointed out some reference to the Genesis creation narratives in Job 38–42: Samuel R. Driver and George B. Gray, *A Critical and Exegetical Commentary on the Book of Job*, ICC (Edinburgh: T&T Clark, 1958), 327; and Robert Gordis, *The Book of God and Man: A Study of Job* (Chicago, IL: University of Chicago Press, 1966), 301.

[85] Doukhan, *The Genesis Creation Story*, 90–92.

What is significant for our purposes is Job's response, which highlights sabbatic motifs contained in Genesis 2:1–3. Job's confession of faith in the creative power of God (Job 38:2–3) echoes humankind's imitating God's rest on the seventh day in memorial of creation. Job's statement in Job 42:5 implies his realization of a closer intimacy with Yahweh: "I have heard of You by the hearing of the ear, But now my eye sees You." This corresponds to the intimacy between Yahweh and His creatures on the Sabbath implied in Genesis 2:1–3, as Yahweh makes the Sabbath holy by His presence.[86] In the response of Job, we find the counterpart of God's original plan for humans epitomized by the Sabbath: humble dependence upon God's creative power, and divine-human intimacy.

Proverbs 8 and 9

The figure of Wisdom in Proverbs 8:21–31 moves beyond personification to a hypostasis of the pre-incarnate Son of God, "Master-craftsman" or Co-Creator with Yahweh, who at the beginning of creation is installed into the office of "Mediator" between Yahweh and "His inhabited world . . . the sons of men" (Prov 8:30–31).[87]

While Proverbs 8:22–31 does not follow the detailed order of the six days of creation as in Genesis 1, Psalm 104, and Job 38–41, nonetheless there is a general movement from the "beginning" (Prov 8:22, using the same word as found in Gen 1:1), emphasizing creating of the foundations of the earth, to the end of creation week, when Wisdom rejoices with Yahweh and with human beings (Prov 8:31). The terminology of twofold "rejoicing" in Proverbs 8:30–31—Wisdom rejoicing with Yahweh and with the sons of men—recalls the twofold "rejoicing" in the sabbatic meditation of Psalm 104:31, 34. The language of Wisdom's mediatorship between Yahweh and humans depicts the same divine-human intimacy implied by the actualizing of God's holiness on the first Sabbath through the divine presence (Gen 2:3). Proverbs 8:32–34 contains a twofold blessing that may possibly echo the blessing of the seventh day ina Genesis 2:3 (although the Hebrew terms are not the same).

Proverbs 9:1 continues the depiction of Wisdom: "Wisdom has built her house, she has hewn out her seven pillars." The reference to Wisdom's

---

[86] See Richard M. Davidson, *Flame of Yahweh: Sexuality in the Old Testament* (Peabody, MA: Hendrickson, 2007), 51–53, for discussion of the intimacy of Sabbath and marriage implied in God's actualizing the holiness of both by His presence.

[87] See Richard M. Davidson, "Proverbs 8 and the Place of Christ in the Trinity," *JATS* 17 (2006): 33–54.

building "denotes bringing something into existence through a particular type of craftsmanship."[88] "Fundamentally, 'building' always has to do with 'creating' and 'bringing into existence,' and is connected with the idea of a functioning creative power."[89] The "house of Wisdom," in light of the preceding context of Wisdom's creation of the world, may be a reference to the creation mentioned in Proverbs 8. "The house of Wisdom is the 'habitable world' (viii 31)."[90]

Although numerous suggestions have been given for the "seven pillars" of Wisdom's house,[91] given the preceding immediate context of creation it seems best to interpret the seven pillars as the seven days of creation week. "The nature of Wisdom's house of seven pillars is uncertain.... The significance of 'seven' here is also not elucidated. Some have connected it to the seven planets, but a more reasonable explanation is that it refers to the seven days of creation (note Wisdom's role in creation in 8:22–31)."[92] If the "seven pillars" refer to the seven days of creation, then it is possible that the feast described in Proverbs 8:2–6 may imply the celebration of rejoicing connected with the Sabbath after the completion of creation. This is plausible, although not certain.

Proverbs does seem to allude to the seventh day of creation, more probably in 8:30–31—with reference to the intimacy between Yahweh and the sons of men at the conclusion of creation—and possibly with reference to the "seven pillars" of Wisdom (the seven days of the week) and the accompanying celebratory feast. Intimacy and celebration are motifs that occur elsewhere in biblical Sabbath theology, and if present here in Proverbs, further underscore and enhance the joy and beauty of the Sabbath according to God's design.

---

[88] Bruce K. Waltke, *The Book of Proverbs: Chapters 1–15*, NICOT (Grand Rapids, MI: Eerdmans, 2004), 431.

[89] S. Wagner, "בנה banah," *TDOT* 2:168.

[90] R. B. Y. Scott, *Proverbs, Ecclesiastes*, AB (Garden City, NY: Doubleday, 1965), 76. See also Allen P. Ross, "Proverbs," in *EBC*, vol. 5 (Grand Rapids, MI: Zondervan, 1991), 947–948: "She [wisdom] has prepared a house and established it on seven pillars. This is probably a reference to the inhabitable world (8:31), which is spacious and enduring. For the equation of a house with the world, see 8:29; Job 38:6; and Psalm 104:5."

[91] For the range of suggestions, see, e.g., R. N. Whybray, *Proverbs*, New Century Bible Commentary (Grand Rapids, MI: Eerdmans, 1994), 142–144.

[92] Duane Garrett, *Proverbs, Ecclesiastes, Song of Songs*, NAC (Nashville, TN: Broadman & Holman, 1993), 115.

Conclusion

Few references/allusions to the Sabbath appear in the OT Psalms and Wisdom literature, but the ones that are present make a significant contribution to a biblical theology of the Sabbath. Psalm 92, with its intricate sabbatic literary features, appears to have been either from its inception, or at least canonically, envisioned as the psalm for the Sabbath par excellence. It includes a "sabbath repertoire" of motifs and intertextual allusions that encompasses the mood and mode of Sabbath praxis along with a full-orbed theology of the Sabbath. Other possible allusions to the Sabbath in the Psalms and Wisdom literature, including Psalm 104, Job 38–42, and Proverbs 8–9, expand the horizons of Sabbath theology only hinted at elsewhere in the OT, especially with the motifs of divine-human intimacy, exuberant celebration and worship, God-centered meditation, humble dependence upon the Creator, and the eschatological implications of the Sabbath.

CHAPTER 6

THE SABBATH IN THE PROPHETS

Laurentiu G. Ionescu and Gerhard Pfandl

Introduction

The OT "writing prophets" were God's spokespersons from the eighth to the fifth century B.C. Because Israel was a theocracy with God as King over the nation, His prophets were empowered to speak to the nation on His behalf. Against the background of Israel's covenant with God, the prophets primarily addressed the local and national situation by warning about the future consequences of Israel's sinful behavior. Their exhortations were meant to ensure God's blessings rather than His judgments.

Israel as a community of faith was rooted in a cultural and theological tradition going back to Abraham, offering moral principles and values, and providing standards for behavior and action. The prophets' frequent critiques inspired, guided, and supported individual and social action. At the same time, the OT prophets consistently warned God's people against breaking the precepts found in the Torah. Although the noun "Sabbath" appears infrequently in the Prophets,[1] the few passages in which it does occurs challenge God's people to restore the true spirit of the Sabbath.

---

[1] There are thirty-three occurrences, in twenty-eight verses across six books: eight times in Isaiah (Isa 1:13; 56:2, 4, 6; 58:13[2x]; 66:23[2x]); seven times in Jeremiah (Jer 17:21, 22[2x], 24[2x], 27[2x]); fifteen times in Ezekiel (Ezek 20:12, 13, 16, 20, 21, 24; 22:8, 26; 23:38; 44:24; 45:17; 46:1, 3, 4, 12); and once each in Lamentations (Lam 2:6), Hosea (Hos 2:11 [Heb v. 13]), and Amos (Amos 8:5).

The Sabbath and the Main Theological Themes

The Sabbath is linked to concepts that are significant from both theological and ethical perspectives. One notable feature of Israel's prophets' preaching is how often their sermons sound like unavoidable verdicts. These oracles do not warn or threaten; they simply announce judgments. For Claus Westermann, this "announcement of judgment" is not a rhetorical rarity or an experiment in homiletical virtuosity, but one of the "basic forms of prophetic speech."[2] Over the past century, commentators have contributed new perspectives on the Sabbath, with the primary shift being toward seeing Sabbath as a gift and blessing rather than as a restrictive and limiting institution. The following sections will present the Sabbath in the context of some theological themes that appear frequently in the Prophets.

The Sabbath as a Sign

> Moreover, I also gave them My Sabbaths, to be a sign between them and Me, that they might know that I am the LORD who sanctifies them (Ezek 20:12).[3]

The context refers to God's covenant faithfulness in bringing Israel out of Egypt (Ezek 20:10). On the way to the promised land they stopped in the wilderness of Sinai, where God gave them His laws, statutes, and judgments (Ezek 20:11). At the same time, He gave them His Sabbaths (Ezek 20:12). Although Ezekiel repeatedly uses the plural "Sabbaths" (Ezek 20:12, 13, 16, 20, 24; 23:38; 44:24), these Sabbaths do not include the ceremonial Sabbaths (Lev 23) or the sabbatical years (Exod 23:11), as some scholars assume.[4] Ezekiel has in mind the seventh-day Sabbath, as the reference to the purpose of the Sabbath in Ezekiel 20:12 indicates: "that they might know that I *am* the LORD who sanctifies them." This echoes Exodus 31:13: "Surely My Sabbaths [pl.] you shall keep, for it *is* a sign between Me and you throughout your generations, that *you* may know that I *am* the LORD who sanctifies you." That these Sabbaths are seventh-day Sabbaths is clearly indicated in Exodus 31:16–17, where God says, "Therefore the children of Israel shall keep the Sabbath [sg.], to observe the Sabbath throughout their generations

---

[2] Claus Westermann, *Basic Forms of Prophetic Speech*, OTL (Louisville, KY: Westminster, 1991), 66.

[3] All biblical quotations are from the NKJV, unless otherwise indicated.

[4] Daniel E. Block, *The Book of Ezekiel: Chapters 1–24*, NICOT (Grand Rapids, MI: Eerdmans, 1997), 632.

as a perpetual covenant. It is a sign between Me and the children of Israel forever; for in six days the LORD made the heavens and the earth, and on the seventh day He rested and was refreshed." Thus, prior to the building of the tabernacle (Exod 36–40), God reminded the Israelites that work on the sanctuary was not to interfere with observance of the Sabbath.

God's purpose in giving the seventh-day Sabbath was threefold: First, it was a sign that the Lord had created the world in six days and rested on the seventh day (Exod 31:17). Second, the Sabbath was a sign to remind the Israelites of God's covenant with them (Exod 31:16). Third, at Sinai, the Sabbath also became a sign that God had set them apart and sanctified them for His service (Ezek 20:12; Exod 31:13).

While in Exodus 20:8 God commands His people to keep the Sabbath holy (e.g., to sanctify it), in Ezekiel 20:12 the Sabbath is a reminder that God had sanctified His people. Not only will the Israelites know this, but "the nations also will know that I, the LORD, sanctify Israel, when My sanctuary is in their midst forevermore" (Ezek 37:28). God declared the keeping of the Sabbath a sign that He had consecrated Israel to Himself as a holy people to be His witnesses to the nations (Isa 44:8). "Through the Jewish nation it was God's purpose to impart rich blessings to all peoples. Through Israel the way was to be prepared for the diffusion of His light to the whole world."[5]

The rationale for Sabbath observance has several dimensions. First, in the exodus narrative, it is related to "God as the Creator"; Israel is called upon to imitate God's own pattern of activity and rest in creating the world (Exod 20:8–11). Second, in Deuteronomy the reason for Sabbath observance is related to the history of Israel as slaves in Egypt. It is the release from bondage that is to be remembered. Here, we may find equally rich applications for the Sabbath as the command of "God the Redeemer" (Deut 5:12–15). Third, references to the Sabbath in the Prophets highlight the theme that the Sabbath reasserts Israel's own identity as the people of the covenant God, as the people called and sanctified by God for His purposes (Ezek 20:12; Exod 31:13). Here, we can explore the command as given by "God the Sanctifier" whose concern goes beyond "mere" humanity and even "mere" deliverance, to an ongoing process of development in obedience.[6]

Idolatry and profanation of the Sabbath were some of the reasons Israel ended up in exile (Ezek 20:16; Neh 13:17–18). After the return from exile,

---

[5] Ellen G. White, *Christ's Object Lessons* (Washington, DC: Review and Herald, 1941), 286.

[6] Fuller Seminary, "Sabbath," *The Next Faithful Step* (blog), https://www.fuller.edu/next-faithful-step/resources/sabbath (accessed February 26, 2020).

the Jews determined that never again would they go into exile. Idolatry was banished from the land and the Sabbath was surrounded with thirty-nine special Sabbath laws to make sure no one would profane the Sabbath again.[7] Israel's strict obedience to the Sabbath command was often misunderstood by others. For example, when the Romans met the Jews and noticed their strict adherence to the law of abstaining from labor on the Sabbath, their reaction was contempt: "The Sabbath is a sign of Jewish indolence, was the opinion held by Juvenal, Seneca and others."[8] Contrary to this perception, Scripture presents the Sabbath as "a sign of sanctification" (Ezek 20:12).

One perspective of Sabbath keeping focuses on the formal aspects. Thus, keeping the Sabbath can be perceived as following a long list of prohibitions. The other perspective is that Sabbath observance is a way of connecting with God. The relational aspect of Sabbath observance is the heart of the message of the prophets. The prophets' rebuke of Israel is not connected to the formal aspects of the worship, but refers to their attitudes and experiences. For example, when Isaiah 1:13–14 proclaims the displeasure of the Lord against Sabbath keeping and the sacrifices, it is "because of the attitude of the people of Judah, not because these ordinances were no longer to be observed."[9] This text indicates that the Sabbath could be "abused, if it regressed into formal ritualism when emptied of a true relationship with God."[10]

Sabbath Not to Be Defiled

> Yet the house of Israel rebelled against Me in the wilderness; they did not walk in My statutes; they despised My judgments, 'which, if a man does, he shall live by them'; and they greatly defiled My

---

[7] Although the Torah does not list the activities prohibited on the Sabbath, rabbis in the Babylonian Talmud, Shabbat 49a, state that the Torah hints at the banned activities. The thirty-nine activities forbidden on Sabbath are sowing, plowing, reaping, binding sheaves, threshing, winnowing, selecting, grinding, sifting, kneading, baking, shearing wool, washing wool, beating wool, dyeing wool, spinning, weaving, making two loops, weaving two threads, separating two threads, tying, untying, tearing, trapping, slaughtering, flaying, salting meat, curing hide, scraping hide, cutting hide up, writing two letters, erasing two letters, building, tearing a building down, extinguishing a fire, kindling a fire, hitting with a hammer, taking an object from the private domain to the public, and transporting an object in the public domain (m. *Shabbat*, 7:2).

[8] Abraham J. Heschel, *The Sabbath: Its Meaning for Modern Man* (New York: Farrar Straus and Giroux, 1951), 4.

[9] Daniel K. Bediako, "Sabbath in the Book of Isaiah," *Asia-Africa Journal of Mission and Ministry* 6 (2011): 162.

[10] Christopher J. H. Wright, "Sabbath," *ABD* 5:852.

Sabbaths. Then I said I would pour out My fury on them in the wilderness, to consume them (Ezek 20:13).

In Isaiah, Jeremiah, Ezekiel, Hosea, and Amos, the mention of the Sabbath is not always within the context of positive exhortation. In Jeremiah 17, for example, the Lord instructs the prophet to visit all the gates of Jerusalem and warn the people not to carry any burdens in or out of the city or out of their houses on the Sabbath (Jer 17:21-22, 27). A similar transgression of the Sabbath took place in Nehemiah's time (Neh 13:15-22). Most likely, these burdens included "the grain, wine, fruits, fish, and other articles that were brought into the city from the country by those coming to the Temple to worship. Also included were the wares of the city, which were sold on the holy day of rest."[11] Thus the people of Jerusalem practiced a loose Sabbath observance, something God strongly condemned. God, therefore, warned the people, "But if you will not heed Me to hallow the Sabbath day, such as not carrying a burden when entering the gates of Jerusalem on the Sabbath day, then I will kindle a fire in its gates, and it shall devour the palaces of Jerusalem, and it shall not be quenched" (Jer 17:27). Because Judah failed to reform their practices, in 586 B.C., Nebuchadnezzar, king of Babylon, besieged and conquered Jerusalem: "He burned the house of the LORD and the king's house; all the houses of Jerusalem, that is, all the houses of the great, he burned with fire" (2 Kgs 25:8-9).[12]

All the prophets condemn the misuse or neglect of the Sabbath (Isa 1:13; Ezek 20:13, 16, 21, 24; Hos 2:11). Their speeches emphasize the intensity of guilt, using such harsh words as "profaned," "defiled," and "despised" (e.g., "You have despised My holy things and profaned My Sabbaths" [Ezek 22:8]). Israel's practices constituted not only a legal offense, but also a personal offense against God: "Moreover they have done this to Me: They have defiled My sanctuary on the same day and profaned My Sabbaths" (Ezek 23:38, cf. 20:16).

According to the sages, three acts of God characterized the seventh day: He rested, He blessed, and He hallowed the seventh day (Gen 2:2-3). The consensus among the rabbis was that God works on the Sabbath, for otherwise providence itself would weekly go into suspension or abeyance. Around the end of the first century A.D., four eminent rabbis (Rabban

---

[11] *SDABC* 4:424.

[12] See the tractate "Shabbath," in *The Babylonian Talmud*, ed. I. Epstein (London: Socino, 1952), 151, 589, 642-643, 786-787, etc.

Gamaliel II, R. Joshua, R. Eleazar b. Azariah, and R. Akiba) discussed the issue and concluded that although God works constantly, He cannot rightly be charged with violating the Sabbath law since the entire universe is His domain (Isa 6:3) and He never carries anything outside it. In other words, God fills the whole world (Jer 23:24) and lifts nothing to a height greater than His own stature.[13] The debates regarding proper Sabbath keeping reflect the deep theological inquiries within Judaism and, in time, developed into a system of tradition and legislation that tried to regulate all aspects linked to Sabbath observance.

In the terms of the *halakhah* (Jewish law that evolved since biblical times), the Sabbath is *yom tov*, holy time, while the workday is *yom khol*, profane time. According to the rabbinic understanding, "the Sabbath is a day of rest, which in a technical sense means not engaging in the kind of work one would perform to build the temple. It is the day when sleep is good, not only sleep, but also feasting and studying, making love, chatting, walking, and of course praying and glorifying God."[14]

The regular "weekday is a day during which one performs what is analogous to the work of building the temple: a day of cutting, dragging, carrying, engraving, and transforming elements of the material world from something they are now to something they will be because of the work of your hands."[15] This is labor with an end in mind, preparing this world to be a place where the next world may be. By contrast, on Sabbath "one does not talk on it in the same manner in which one talks on weekdays. Even thinking of business or labor should be avoided."[16] Thus, the Sabbath day is not a prospective day, a day of planning the future, but a retrospective, contemplating day.

As a holy day, the Sabbath was to be kept holy by the people and free from all profanation (Exod 20:10–11; Lev 23:3; Isa 56:2, 4, 6; 58:13), and special offerings were prescribed for its observance (Num 28:9–10; 1 Chr 23:3; 2 Chr 2:4). It was to be a day of complete rest and cessation from toil and business. Abraham Heschel suggests that Judaism has always been oriented more to time than to space. He memorably depicts Sabbath as the creation of hallowed time, or "a palace in time."[17] From this perspective, "the day of the

---

[13] D. A. Carson, *The Gospel According to John* (Leicester: InterVarsity, 1991), 247.

[14] Peter Ochs, "The Way Sabbath Complements the Weekday," *Pro Ecclesia* 23, no. 3 (2014): 267.

[15] Ibid.

[16] Heschel, *The Sabbath*, 12.

[17] Ibid., 21.

Lord is more important to the prophets than the house of the Lord,"[18] so that profaning the Sabbath day is worse than profaning the temple.

The distinction between secular and holy time implies different forms of experience and behavior. Failing to distinguish between these times seems to have been a problem not only with the laity, but also with the priests: "Her priests have violated My law and profaned My holy things; they have not distinguished between the holy and unholy, nor have they made known the difference between the unclean and the clean; and they have hidden their eyes from My Sabbaths, so that I am profaned among them" (Ezek 22:26). The problem was not ignorance or lack of information on Sabbath keeping, but a disdainful attitude against God and His law. Such an attitude made any spiritual reforms in Israel impossible.

Losing the distinction between holy and secular affected not only the practice of Sabbath keeping, but also the attitude about the Sabbath day. One of the fiercest denunciations of the prophets was against the unethical behavior in commercial trading. Instead of celebrating the Sabbath as a day of joy and rest, the people perceived the Sabbath day as an obstacle to their business. "Hear this, you who swallow up the needy, and make the poor of the land fail, saying: 'When will the New Moon be past, that we may sell grain? And the Sabbath, that we may trade wheat? Making the ephah small and the shekel large, Falsifying the scales by deceit, that we may buy the poor for silver, and the needy for a pair of sandals—Even sell the bad wheat?'" (Amos 8:4-6).

The loss of the distinction between holy and profane, and the transgression of the Sabbath culminated into a system of social injustice that contributed to Israel's exile (Jer 17:27; 2 Chr 36:21; Ezek 20:21-24; Amos 8:5-6). As Jeremiah laments, the Lord "has done violence to His tabernacle, *As if it were* a garden; He has destroyed His place of assembly; The LORD has caused the appointed feasts and Sabbaths to be forgotten in Zion. In His burning indignation He has spurned the king and the priest" (Lam 2:6). This drastic measure aimed at a change of attitude: keeping the Sabbath as an experience of joy and delight.

Sabbath as a Day of Delight

God's words about the Sabbath in Isaiah 58 may serve as a guide for Sabbath keeping. The command to keep the Sabbath holy receives material specification in the command to rest, to desist from all work. This serves

---
[18] Heschel, The Sabbath, 79.

to remind humanity of the activity of the one whose good work precedes, accompanies, and succeeds any human work. To keep the Sabbath holy is to cease the rhythm of our weekly endeavors and to recognize and focus upon the work of the one who neither slumbers nor sleeps. It is to do justice to God's law in a different mode of activity, in acts of contemplation, confession, fellowship, and prayer that represent a different ordering of our ordinary work. Sound theology might helpfully begin with these activities as it seeks to respect the Sabbath commandment.

Isaiah 58 appears in a section that some Bible translations title as "False and True Worship." The Lord tells the people that their spiritual disciplines are not true spiritual disciplines, but rather self-centered practices that strike the pose of worship. The "fast" that the Lord chooses is one of justice for the poor: letting the oppressed go free, bringing the homeless into our homes, and sharing our bread with the hungry. When we act as the Lord chooses, we will be "like a watered garden" (Isa 58:11), restored and nourished. It is in this context that the Sabbath is addressed:

> If you turn away your foot from the Sabbath, *From* doing your pleasure on My holy day, And call the Sabbath a delight, The holy *day* of the LORD honorable, And shall honor Him, not doing your own ways, Nor finding your own pleasure, Nor speaking *your own* words, Then you shall delight yourself in the LORD; And I will cause you to ride on the high hills of the earth, And feed you with the heritage of Jacob your father. The mouth of the LORD has spoken (Isa 58:13-14)

The traditional translation "turn away your foot from the Sabbath" is misleading. Why would you call the Sabbath a delight after turning your foot from the Sabbath? The Hebrew preposition *min* ("from") also has the meaning "on account of, because of"[19] as in Deuteronomy 7:7-8: "The LORD did not set His love on you nor choose you because [*min*] you were more in number than any other people, for you were the least of all peoples; but because [*min*] the LORD loves you, and because [*min*] He would keep the oath which He swore to your fathers." Speaking of the suffering Messiah, Isaiah 53:5 says, "He *was* wounded for [*min*] our transgressions." The word "for" in this phrase has the meaning of "because of" (JPS) or "on account of" (LXX). Thus, a better translation of the first part of Isaiah 58:13 is "If because of the Sabbath, you turn your foot from doing

---

[19] DCH 5:337.

your *own* pleasure on My holy day" (NAS, NAU). Then the next phrase—"And call the Sabbath a delight"—makes more sense.[20]

What is meant by "doing your pleasure"? The Hebrew noun *khefets* is generally translated as "delight, pleasure" (1 Sam 15:22; 18:25; Ps 1:2), or "wish, desire" (1 Kgs 5:22-24; Prov 3:15), but it also has the meaning of "matter, affairs"[21] as in Ecclesiastes 3:1: "For everything there is a season, and a time for every matter [*khefets*] under heaven" (RSV).[22] When we apply this meaning to our phrase in Isaiah 58:13, "God is not speaking against pleasure here, but against working, doing business on Sabbath."[23]

God further instructs His people not to do their own ways. The Hebrew word for "way" is *derekh*. Generally, it refers to the road, path, or way on which one is walking (Gen 16:7; Josh 2:7; 2 Kgs 25:4). Frequently we read of "the way of the Lord" (Judg 2:22; 2 Kgs 21:22; Prov 10:29), which is a metaphor for "doing righteousness and justice" (Gen 18:19). Because "doing one's way" does not really make sense, we look for another meaning and discover that *derekh* can also mean a "venture, mission, errand," or "manner"[24] (1 Kgs 2:3; 2 Chr 13:22). Thus, God is telling His people not to walk in their own ways, doing their own business on Sabbath.

As indicated by italics in the NKJV, the words *"your own"* in the last phrase of verse 13 ("nor speaking *your own* words") are not in the Hebrew text. The Hebrew literally says, "Nor speaking a word [*davar*]." This does not mean the Sabbath keeper must be silent on Sabbath. *Davar* generally refers to a speech (1 Sam 16:18; 1 Kgs 3:10), a report (1 Kgs 10:6; 2 Chr 9:5), or some matter (Gen 21:11; Dan 1:14). In 1 Samuel 21:8, David says to Ahimelech, "Is there not here on hand a spear or a sword? For I have brought neither my sword nor my weapons with me, because the king's business [*davar*] required haste." "Business" is also the more likely meaning in Isaiah 58:13. Thus we find that "God is asking us to refrain not only from 'finding business,' but from 'talking business' or making deals in Sabbath."[25] This translation of the phrases in verse 13 fits nicely with the fourth commandment, which prohibits labor and commerce on Sabbath.

---

[20] This translation of the text is found in the New American Standard Bibles (1977, 1995), and in the Jewish *Tanakh* translation.

[21] *DCH* 3:288.

[22] See also Eccl 5:8; 8:6.

[23] Ed Christian, "Sabbath Is a Happy Day!," *JATS* 13, no. 1 (2002): 87.

[24] *DCH* 2:465.

[25] Christian, "Sabbath Is a Happy Day," 87.

This understanding of the text was especially important in the time of Nehemiah, when he saw "*people* in Judah treading wine presses on the Sabbath, and bringing in sheaves, and loading donkeys with wine, grapes, figs, and all *kinds of* burdens, which they brought into Jerusalem on the Sabbath day" (Neh 13:15). He warned them against selling food on the Sabbath and eventually closed the gates of the city to stop this commerce on the Sabbath.

But the Sabbath command does not end with "you shall do no labor" (Exod 20:10); it requires the community "to keep it holy" (Exod 20:8).[26] While God's people must rest from regular workday activities, they will pursue everything that promotes the public and private worship of God (e.g., Ezek 46:1–4), excluding everything that detracts from this pursuit (Isa 58:13–14). To the prohibition of labor, therefore, is added the blessing of delight and the accent of sanctity. This should push out all unnecessary thoughts about worldly employments and recreations. Not only the hands celebrate the day; the tongue and the soul keep the Sabbath. It is not only that Sabbath keeping is commanded, nor that it is a habit of highly effective people or devoutly religious people; it cultivates our bond with God who loves us.

Heschel poetically summarizes the intention of Isaiah 58:13–14 as follows:

> He who wants to enter the holiness of the day must first lay down the profanity of clattering commerce, of being yoked to toil. He must go away from the screech of dissonant days, from the nervousness and fury of acquisitiveness and the betrayal in embezzling his own life. He must say farewell to manual work and learn to understand that the world has already been created and will survive without the help of man. Six days a week we wrestle with the world, wringing profit from the earth; on the Sabbath we especially care for the seed of eternity planted in the soul. The world has our hands, but our soul belongs to Someone Else. Six days a week we seek to dominate the world; on the seventh day we try to dominate the self.[27]

This is not a call to make a few small changes. It is a call for transformation both of individuals and of a nation. Significant personal restoration

---

[26] The Pharisees mistakenly treated the Sabbath in terms of inactivity. This resulted from a negative emphasis on what was forbidden on the day, rather than a positive emphasis on what was required on it. This kind of thinking robs the day of its God-given purpose.

[27] Heschel, *The Sabbath*, 2.

is once again offered. But, community restoration is promised as well.[28] The challenge is to engage in meaningful observance that does not trample on the Sabbath or use it for self-interest. That will result in delighting in the Lord, riding upon the heights of the earth, and being fed with the heritage of Jacob. To delight in the Lord through observing the Sabbath and the true fast fulfills the desire of the human heart to be in communion with God. This juxtaposition of the true fast and Sabbath observance clearly indicates that worship of God and care for the neighbor are not to be separated.

Sabbath as Inclusive and Universal

> For thus says the LORD: 'To the eunuchs who keep My Sabbaths, And choose what pleases Me, And hold fast My covenant, even to them I will give in My house and within My walls a place and a name better than that of sons and daughters; I will give them an everlasting name that shall not be cut off. Also the sons of the foreigner who join themselves to the LORD, to serve Him, and to love the name of the LORD, to be His servants—everyone who keeps from defiling the Sabbath, and holds fast My covenant— even them I will bring to My holy mountain, and make them joyful in My house of prayer. Their burnt offerings and their sacrifices will be accepted on My altar; for My house shall be called a house of prayer for all nations' (Isa 56:4–7).

Isaiah 40–55 is called the book of consolation for God's people, Israel. Chapter headings in English translations indicate the tenor of this book, such as "Israel assured of God's help" (Isa 41), "God's blessing on Israel" (Isa 44), "Israel refined for God's glory" (Isa 48), and "God redeems Jerusalem" (Isa 52). The exile to Babylon would come (Isa 39:6), but God would not forsake His people; He would bring them back to Jerusalem (Isa 51:11). The emphasis is on Abraham's seed (Isa 41:1), and on the Servant's seed (Isa 53:10)—the Israelites. If you were born an Israelite, you belonged to the elect community. The Gentiles, particularly the Ammonites and Moabites, as well as the eunuchs were to be excluded from Israel (Deut 23:1–6). Despite some

---

[28] See also Bediako, "Sabbath in the Book of Isaiah," 172, who notes, "As does Isaiah 56, Isaiah 58 reveals that Sabbath-keeping epitomizes righteousness, so that proper Sabbath-keeping will have to characterize the aftermath of the exile. That Sabbath-keeping encapsulates covenantal faithfulness explains why Judah's prosperity and continual inheritance of the land are contingent upon proper Sabbath-keeping (Isa 58:12–14). In this regard, Sabbath-keeping plays an integral role in the future restoration and mission of God's people (Isa 58:12–14; cf. 56:2–7; 66:18–24)."

exceptions, membership in the Israelite community was not a matter of individual decision and choice; membership implied genealogy and ethnicity.

The new section in the book of Isaiah (Isa 56–66) seems to reverse the exclusivity that characterizes covenant membership. Isaiah 56:1–8 is a divine oracle that addresses the issue of foreigners and eunuchs in Israel. Here, "a purebred Israelite may be on the outside while a foreigner, even a eunuch, may be on the inside."[29] These two groups of people, foreigners and eunuchs, receive a divine oracle, which changes their status regarding membership in the covenant community. The prophet claims the divine authority to announce such a change against what seems to have been the normal practice—namely, not to allow foreigners and eunuchs to be included into the community of worshippers.

It is quite clear that this prophecy envisions a dramatic change. Once God's rule from Mount Zion is established and revealed to the world, history will change. And while God's universal rule may be the most salient aspect of this change, this is also a time when formerly excluded categories of people, such as the foreigners and eunuchs, can rejoice in the blessings of the covenant of God. To the despairing eunuch, the Lord promises a "monument and a name" that are superior to "sons or daughters."

The prophet's main point in Isaiah 56:2–8 is that God not only cares for Israelites, but also for Gentiles. God's house is to become a place for all peoples, as He is going to gather Gentiles as well as Israelites. Eunuchs, who were excluded from the temple in the old covenant (Deut 23:1), will also be accepted. The terms of relationship between God and human beings will be changed, and a new covenant will be made.

It bears mentioning that the motif of the "pilgrimage of the nation" to Mount Zion in Isaiah 60–62, with its vindictive overtone, finds its counterpart in a significantly more balanced version in Isaiah 2:1–4 that can explain the inclusion of the foreigners. The nations come to Mount Zion not to be exploited or submitted to the God of Israel (and His people), but to receive a Torah that would teach them to unlearn war. The contribution of Israel as a community is not to implement just another form of hegemonic rule, but to establish universal peace. The messianic kingdom is open to new participants.

While in the past, the vast majority belonged to the community by birth, in the future God promises that others will be included. This presupposes to destroy the distinction between religion and ethnicity. This

---

[29] R. Reed Lessing, *Isaiah 56–66*, Concordia Commentary (Saint Louis, MO: Concordia, 2014), 26.

prefigures Paul's statement in the epistle to Galatians: "There is neither Jew nor Greek, there is neither slave nor free, there is neither male nor female; for you are all one in Christ Jesus" (Gal 3:28).

The new perspective introduces new conditions. To "love the name of the LORD" could be the call to exclusive Yahweh worship, meaning that the foreigner, too, should not have any other gods apart from Him. In this worshipping context, the Sabbath celebration is a key marker of the new identity. So, "the seventh day is like a palace in time with a kingdom for all."[30] The universality of salvation in the context of true worship and Sabbath keeping is the theme of the concluding segment of the great controversy in the book of Revelation (e.g., Rev 14).

The inclusion of strangers (that is, Gentiles), the universality of worship, Sabbath observance, and the messianic kingdom are elements that open another important theme in the prophetic literature: the Sabbath and eschatology.

Eschatology and the Sabbath

> And it shall come to pass *That* from one New Moon to another, And from one Sabbath to another, All flesh shall come to worship before Me, says the LORD (Isa 66:23).

The focus of OT eschatology is on the coming of the Messiah and the messianic kingdom which He was to establish here on earth. God's plan was to place Israel "in Palestine at the crossroads of the ancient world, and provided them with every facility for becoming the greatest nation on the face of the earth."[31] Ellen G. White tells us, "God withheld from them nothing favorable to the formation of character that would make them representatives of Himself. Their obedience to the law of God would make them marvels of prosperity before the nations of the world."[32] According to Deuteronomy 28:1–14 God intended to set Israel "on high above all nations of the earth"; they were to become "the head and not the tail" of all the nations. The condition for this was the keeping of God's commandments, the center of which was the Sabbath (Deut 5:12–15; 28:13). The result would be that "all people of the earth" would recognize their superiority and call them "blessed" (Mal 3:12).

---

[30] Heschel, *The Sabbath*, 21.

[31] *SDABC* 4:27.

[32] White, *Christ's Object Lessons*, 288.

God promised them great temporal and spiritual wealth as a reward for representing the principles of heaven to the world (Deut 28:1-14).

Unfortunately, God's plan never came to full fruition. Although the era of David and Solomon seemed to mark the beginning of the fulfillment of God's glorious plan for Israel, the subsequent history of Israel with its division into the northern and southern kingdoms brought it to a halt. "In spite of the bold and zealous efforts of such prophets as Elijah, Elisha, Amos, and Hosea, the northern kingdom rapidly deteriorated and was eventually carried into Assyrian captivity."[33] More than a century later, Judah was also carried into captivity, this time to Babylon. In both cases, one of the reasons for their exiles was their attitude toward God's commandments, including the Sabbath commandment (Jer 17:21-23, 27; Amos 8:2-6).

Nevertheless, God did not forsake His people in exile. He sent them messages of encouragement and promises of renewed blessings. Judah was to be restored and the covenant renewed (Jer 31:2-6, 23, 31-34). These promises were to have "met fulfillment in large measure during the centuries following the return of the Israelites from the lands of their captivity. It was God's design that the whole earth be prepared for the first advent of Christ, even as today the way is preparing for His second coming."[34] All of it, of course, was dependent on Israel's response to God's condition of obedience. Because Israel failed to live up to God's requirements, many of these promises were never literally fulfilled, including the promise of the messianic kingdom in Isaiah 65-66.

The description of new heavens and a new earth in Isaiah 65:17-25 refers to the messianic kingdom God wanted to establish, had Israel heeded the messages of the prophets and fulfilled God's purpose following the restoration from captivity.[35] "Heaven and earth are employed as figures to indicate a complete renovation or revolution in the existing course of affairs."[36] With the first advent of the Messiah the blessings would have

---

[33] *SDABC* 4:31.

[34] Ellen G. White, *Patriarchs and Prophets* (Mountain View, CA: Pacific Press, 1943), 703-704.

[35] *SDABC* 4:332.

[36] Edward J. Young, *The Book of Isaiah*, 3 vols. (Grand Rapids, MI: Eerdmans, 1972), 3:514. See also Daniel K. Bediako, "Isaiah's 'New Heavens and New Earth' (Isa 65:17; 66:22)," *JAAS* 11, no. 1 (2008): 1-20, who argues that the eschatology presented in Isaiah 65-66 is not apocalyptic eschatology on par with, say, Revelation 21, but rather a postexilic eschatology (that is, an extended period of time following the return from Babylonian captivity) and that the creation of "new heavens and new earth" (Isa 65:17; 66:22)—which semantically equates the creation of "Jerusalem and her people" (Isa 65:18)—is a hyperbolic expression of the certainty of the redemption of Judah from the Babylonian captivity and their restoration to "the heritage of Jacob" (Isa 58:14).

been in every sense so great that they could only be described as "the creation of a new heaven and a new earth."³⁷ Yet death and sin would still have been present: "No more shall an infant from there *live but a few* days, Nor an old man who has not fulfilled his days; For the child shall die one hundred years old, But the sinner *being* one hundred years old shall be accursed" (Isa 65:20). That means children would still be born, but there would be no infant death, and sinners would die at one hundred years old. In other words, longevity would be one of the blessings of this new age.

The next verse makes clear that Isaiah 66:23 does not refer to the future new heaven and earth in Revelation 21:1: "And they shall go forth and look Upon the corpses of the men Who have transgressed against Me. For their worm does not die, And their fire is not quenched. They shall be an abhorrence to all flesh" (Isa 66:24). This is a picture of the destiny of those who refuse to accept the Messiah—they will be destroyed. This is further evidence that this text does not apply to the future new heaven and earth, where every trace of sin will have been removed.

Nevertheless, while Isaiah 65:17–66:24 refers primarily to the messianic age that would have been established had the Jewish nation accepted its divine mandate, these prophecies apply in principle but not in detail to the earth made new in Revelation 21. The order in the natural world will be changed (Isa 65:25) and the Sabbath will be observed,³⁸ but the present Jerusalem will be replaced by the heavenly Jerusalem (Rev 21:2), and "there shall be no more death, nor sorrow, nor crying. There shall be no more pain, for the former things have passed away" (Rev 21:4).

In his vision about the new temple (Ezek 40–45) in the messianic age, the prophet describes in detail the various parts of the temple, as well as a new plan for the division of the land (Ezek 45). And there are references to Sabbath worship in the temple (Ezek 44:24; 45:17; see also 46:1, 3–4, 12). What we observe about Isaiah's prophecy in chapters 65 and 66 also applies to Ezekiel 40–45. Had the people been faithful after their return from Babylon, this prophecy would have been literally fulfilled: "A comparison with other prophecies relating to the restoration leads us to the belief that the prophet is here describing a literal state with a literal temple and a literal capital. It is hard to conceive how the Jews, to whom this prophecy was addressed, could have understood it otherwise."³⁹

---

³⁷ Young, *Book of Isaiah*, 514.

³⁸ Ellen G. White, *The Desire of Ages* (Oakland, CA: Pacific Press, 1898), 283.

³⁹ *SDABC* 4:715.

Conclusion

The Sabbath in the Prophets is a sign that God sanctifies His people, that He has set them apart to be His witnesses to the nations. The Sabbath was to be a holy and special day, a day conducive to finding true delight. It presented Israel with an opportunity to subdue selfishness and cultivate the habit of doing things that were pleasing to God and that contributed to the well-being of others. True Sabbath observance was to lead to the work of reform pictured in Isaiah 58:5–12.[40] Unfortunately, the people failed to truly understand the meaning of the Sabbath and had to bear the consequences.

The prophets had an important reason to warn against the profanation of the Sabbath. The command to observe the Sabbath, after all, does not merely point back to the beginning of all creation, nor simply to the rhythm of human life. Rather, as Karl Barth observes, "the holy day with its reminder of the special history of the covenant and salvation undoubtedly points us to the ultimate consummation of this history."[41] In this consummation lies the goal not only of all our theology, but of all creation. The Sabbath is, finally, a weekly eschatological party, a sojourn in the qualities of eternity as they come to expression in each day of worship.

---

[40] SDABC 4:307.

[41] Karl Barth, *Church Dogmatics: The Doctrine of Creation* III.4 (Edinburgh: T&T Clark, 1961), 56.

Thematic Perspectives

CHAPTER 7

THE ORIGIN OF THE SABBATH

Martin Pröbstle

Introduction

The search for the origin of the Sabbath has a long history. Scholars have sought answers to a number of specific questions: Did the Sabbath originate in Israel or outside of Israel? Does its origin have to be explained extra-biblically or is it preserved in the OT? And if its origin is found in the Hebrew Bible, did the Sabbath debut when Israel already existed, at the exodus or sometime during the monarchy, or long before Israel existed, at creation?

In addressing these questions, this study argues that the best explanation is that Sabbath originated at creation as described in Genesis 2:1–3, and that this text should be understood to mean that at the end of the week of creation, God established the Sabbath for humanity as a perpetually recurring institution with the rhythm of a seven-day cycle.

After a summary look at the Hebrew terminology relevant to the Sabbath question, the first part of this study offers a critical brief survey of the main proposals for the origin of the Sabbath. The extra-biblical and socioeconomic hypotheses are investigated—especially the widely held opinion in critical scholarship that the Sabbath derives from a Babylonian full moon day that was associated in the exilic or postexilic period with an Israelite socioeconomic seven-day period. A careful consideration of these proposals finds them to be unconvincing and inconclusive.

Using a text-oriented and canon-based exegetical approach,[1] the second part of this study supports the thesis that the origin of the Sabbath

---

[1] A text-oriented and canon-based exegetical approach focuses primarily on the written text as we have it in its canonical form and the linguistic and literary data the text provides, as well as its

begins, chronologically, with God's rest from His creation activity on the seventh day. Based on this approach, Genesis 2:1–3 not only documents this idea, but represents the seventh-day Sabbath as an ordinance for humanity with its individual statements (God rested on, blessed, and sanctified the seventh day). In arguing for such a position, this study also looks closely at the validity of the reasons raised against it, and shows that the "seventh day" in Genesis 2:1–3 can be identified with the Sabbath, and that there is some biblical evidence that the Sabbath may have been known in pre-Mosaic times. Hence, the OT represents the Sabbath as not originally an Israelite institution, but as an institution for all humanity.

Hebrew Terminology

As a preliminary task, we must first consider Sabbath terminology in the OT. In reference to the Sabbath, Hebrew uses the nouns *shabbath* and *shabbathon*. The verb *shavath*, which utilizes the same consonants (*shbt*), seems to be related to these nouns.

The noun *shabbath* ("sabbath, day of rest") occurs 111 times in the Hebrew Bible. It usually refers to the seventh day, which is a day of rest (e.g., Exod 16:27; 20:10; 31:15; 35:2; Lev 23:3; Deut 5:14), and by counting from one Sabbath to another it can refer to a week (Lev 23:15–16).[2] In a secondary and extended use, *shabbath* refers to the "sabbath year" when the land is not in use for agriculture (Lev 25:2, 4, 6; 26:34, 43; 2 Chron 36:21), so that it can be used to refer to the "period of seven years" (Lev 25:8).[3]

The noun *shabbathon* ("sabbath [feast]") occurs eleven times and probably designates "one individual and particular" *shabbath*,[4] often in

---

textual relations within the canonical corpus, without inquiring too much about its genesis and development or the inner dynamics of its author(s). Manfred Oeming, *Contemporary Biblical Hermeneutics: An Introduction* (Aldershot: Ashgate, 2006), 55, describes the basic conviction of interpreters using text-oriented approaches as follows: "The interpreter should not lose himself in an obscure reconstruction of history, nor in an author's inner life only guessed at, nor in the chaos of personal subjectivity. Only the concentration on the text itself brings security and objectivity."

[2] In Leviticus 23:15–16 the term *shabbath* still refers to the seventh day, but by counting the Sabbaths until "seven sabbaths" are complete, one *de facto* counts seven "sabbath-weeks." This is the only occurrence in which *shabbath* in the Hebrew Bible implicitly refers to a week. Only here, the Septuagint renders the term *shabbath* not as *sabbatōn* but as *hebdomados* ("the number seven" > "period of seven days" > "week"), confirming that each week of seven days ends with a Sabbath (see Jacob Milgrom, *Leviticus 23–27*, AB [New York: Doubleday, 2001], 1998–1999).

[3] Cf. *DCH* 8:258–261; *HALOT* 4:1409–1411.

[4] *HALOT* 4:1411.

regard to special regulations: the first Sabbath after the manna fell (Exod 16:23), the annual Feast of Trumpets (Lev 23:24), the first and eighth day of the Feast of Tabernacles (Lev 23:39), and the sabbatical year (Lev 25:5). The superlative expression *shabbath shabbthon* refers to the Day of Atonement (Lev 16:31; 23:32), the sabbatical year (Lev 25:4), and the seventh-day Sabbath itself (Exod 31:15; 35:2; Lev 23:3).

The verb *shavath* ("to cease, stop") occurs seventy-one times in the Hebrew Bible. In connection with the Sabbath, the Qal stem of *shavath* takes on the meaning of "to rest" and "to keep, observe (the Sabbath)."[5] It then occurs with the preposition "in/on" (Heb. *be*) in the temporal sense, meaning "on/in the seventh day" (Gen 2:2–3 [plus "from work"]; Exod 16:30; 23:12; 31:17; 34:21) and "in plowing time" and "in harvest time" (Exod 34:21). The verb *shavath* appears in this context in parallel to the verbs *nuakh* ("to rest") (Exod 23:12) and the Niphal of *nafash* ("be refreshed") (Exod 23:12; 31:17), as well as in opposite to *ʿasah* ("make") (Exod 31:17) and *ʿavadh* ("work") (Exod 34:21). The land that is not farmed can also keep Sabbath (Lev 26:34–35; 2 Chron 36:21). The verb *shavath* occurs twice with the object *shabbath*—once referring to the Day of Atonement (Lev 23:32) and once referring to the seventh year of agricultural rest for the land (Lev 25:2; 26:35)[6]—but it does not occur with *shabbath* for observing the seventh-day Sabbath. Other verbs are used with the object *shabbath* to express observance of the weekly Sabbath, namely *shamar* ("keep") (Exod 31:13–14, 16; Lev 19:3, 30; 26:2; Isa 56:2, 4, 6), *ʿasah* ("do/make") (Exod 31:16), and *qadash* ("consecrate") (Ezek 20:20; 44:24).

The identical consonants of the verb and noun, and their frequent combination and use in overlapping contexts, beg the question: Is there a link between the noun *shabbath* and the verb *shavath*?

---

[5] Cf. *DCH* 8:254–256; *HALOT* 4:1407. The noun *mishbath* ("cessation")—the root *shbt* with prefixed *mem*—occurs only once in the OT (Lam 1:7, if not emended) and refers to the destruction of Jerusalem by the Babylonians.

[6] Qumran literature shows a very similar use and meaning of the verb and nouns of the root *shbt*. See *DCH* 8:255–256; and Lutz Doering, "שָׁבַת *šābat*," in *Theologisches Wörterbuch zu den Qumrantexten*, ed. H. J. Fabry and U. Dahmen (Stuttgart: Kohlhammer, 2016), 3:840–850. In Qumran texts the noun *shabbath* designates the weekly Sabbath (approx. 150 times), the week (twenty-two times), a week of years (two times), the Day of Atonement (three times), and the Sabbath year (four times) (ibid., 842).

The Quest for the Origin of the Sabbath

The history of research of the origin of the Sabbath is inextricably bound with the trends in OT scholarship in general and the assumed literary-critical history of the text and the surmised historical, sociological, and religious processes in ancient Israel in particular. Etymological considerations have often played a role in the search for the origin of the Sabbath. Demonstrating where the noun *shabbath* comes from would mean being a step closer to the source of the biblical Sabbath day. Of course, etymological study has its dangers and limits when it comes to the meaning of words in their actual context, and thus there remains reasonable skepticism about the explanatory power of etymological interpretations.[7]

The main proposals for the derivation of the noun *shabbath* and the origin of the weekly Sabbath are as follows:[8]

Babylonian Origin

In pursuing an extra-biblical origin of the Sabbath, a Babylonian connection is the hypothesis most often advocated. Over time several different proposals have been forwarded.[9] Most popular is the suggestion that the

---

[7] See the classic treatise by James Barr, *The Semantics of Biblical Language* (Oxford: Oxford University Press, 1961), 107–160.

[8] For overviews of the different hypotheses, see J. H. Meesters, *Op zoek naar de oorsprong van de Sabbat* (Assen: Van Gorcum, 1966), 4–83; Niels Erik A. Andreasen, *The Old Testament Sabbath: A Tradition-Historical Investigation* (Missoula, MT: Society of Biblical Literature, 1972), 1–16, 100–04; idem, "Recent Studies of the Old Testament Sabbath: Some Observations," *ZAW* 86 (1974): 453–455; Gnana Robinson, *The Origin and Development of the Old Testament Sabbath: A Comprehensive Exegetical Approach* (Frankfurt am Main: Lang, 1988), 6–24; Léo Laberge, "Sabbat, étymologie et origins: étude bibliographique," *ScEs* 44 (1992): 185–204; Samuele Bacchiocchi, "Remembering the Sabbath: The Creation-Sabbath in Jewish and Christian History," in *The Sabbath in Jewish and Christian Traditions*, ed. T. C. Eskenazi, D. J. Harrington, and W. H. Shea (New York: Crossroad, 1991), 70–74; Gerhard F. Hasel, "Sabbath," *ABD* 5:850–851; idem, "The Origin of the Biblical Sabbath and the Historical-Critical Method: A Methodological Text Case," *JATS* 4/1 (1993): 34–37; Alexandra Grund, *Die Entstehung des Sabbats: Seine Bedeutung für Israels Zeitkonzept und Erinnerungskultur* (Tübingen: Mohr Siebeck, 2011), 2–9; and Ottilia Lukács, *Sabbath in the Making: A Study of the Inner-Biblical Interpretation of the Sabbath Commandment* (Leuven: Peeters, 2020), 3–12.

[9] At an earlier time, the Akkadian *shab/pattu(m)* was believed to mean the same as the Hebrew *shabbath*, namely "day of rest" (see Wilhelm Lotz, *Questiones de historia Sabbati* [Leipzig: Hinrichs, 1883]), but it soon became evident that the *shab/pattu(m)* was the full moon day, the fifteenth day of the month, and not a weekly recurring day. Also, the Sabbath and the *shab/pattu(m)* had been connected with the evil (taboo) days, the *umu lemnutu*, which prohibited certain types of work and seemed to appear at a seven-day cycle (see S. Langdon, "The Derivation of šabattu and Other Notes," *ZDMG* 62 [1908]: 29–32). But again, these evil days do not constitute a consistent seven-day cycle because they fell on the first, seventh, fourteenth, nineteenth, twenty-first, and

Hebrew *shabbath* derives from the Akkadian *shabattu(m)* or *shapattu(m)*,[10] the day of the full moon or the fifteenth day of the lunar month.[11] It is said that in pre-exilic times the Sabbath was indeed a full moon festival, similar to the *shab/pattu(m)*, and that the weekly cycle of Sabbath rest days developed from the seven weeks between Passover and the Feast of Weeks/Pentecost (Lev 23:15-16). After much critique, this thesis by Meinhold lay at rest[12]

---

twenty-eighth of the month, and also because seven-day periods do not accord with the lunar month of twenty-nine and one-half days. J. T. Nichols, "The Origin of the Hebrew Sabbath," *The Old and New Testament Student* 12 (1891): 36-42, suggests that these "Akkadian sabbaths" were connected to the moon worship and, by intercalation, conformed to the lunar month and had been received into Hebrew tradition via the migrating ancestors, Nahor and his family, which should explain why the Hebrew Sabbath supposedly "also is intimately connected with the changes and celebrations connected with the moon, indicating that the Sabbath had originally its source in moon worship" (ibid., 42). At the exodus, Moses allegedly fixed the time of Sabbath observance to an interval of seven days (idem, "The Development of the Sabbat among the Hebrews," *The Old and New Testament Student* 12 [1891]: 207-209). However, such conjecture is hardly convincing. Another hypothesis is to derivate the seven-day week from the Mesopotamian time unit *ḫamushtu(m)*, which at first was considered to be a fifty-day period, approximately seven weeks. The sabbath was then supposedly the last day of these alleged Babylonian weeks (see Hildegard Lewy and Julius Lewy, "The Origin of the Week and the Oldest West Asiatic Calendar," *HUCA* 17 [1942-1943]: 1-152) or the last day of the entire period, namely the fiftieth day in a pentacontad calendar (see J. Morgenstern, "The Chanukka Festival and the Calendar of Ancient Israel," *HUCA* 20 [1947]: 1-136). However, it has become evident that *ḫamushtu(m)* is rather a fifth of a month or five days and was used only administratively in trading and judicial issues, particularly in eighteenth-century Kültepe, but not for civil purposes (Kemal Balkan, "The Old Assyrian Week," in *Studies in Honor of Benno Landsberger on His Seventy-Fifth Birthday, April 21, 1965*, ed. H. G. Güterbock and Th. Jacobsen [Chicago: University of Chicago Press, 1965], 159-174; cf. Naphtali H. Tur-Sinai, "Sabbat und Woche," *BiOr* 8 [1951]: 24).

[10] See *AHw* 1172a; *CAD* 17:449-450.

[11] Johannes Meinhold, *Sabbat und Woche im Alten Testament: Eine Untersuchung* (Göttingen: Vandenhoeck und Ruprecht, 1905); idem, "Die Entstehung des Sabbats," *ZAW* 29 (1909): 81-112; idem, *Sabbat und Sonntag* (Leipzig: Quelle & Meyer, 1909); idem, "Zur Sabbatfrage," *ZAW* 36 (1916): 108-110; and idem, "Zur Sabbathfrage," *ZAW* 48 (1930): 121-138. Meinhold builds his hypothesis upon the previous work by Theophilus G. Pinches, "Šappattu, the Babylonian Sabbath," *PSBA* 26 (1904): 51-56, who shows that the fifteenth of the month is called *shab/pattu(m)*, and H. Zimmern, "Sabbath," *ZDMG* 58 (1904): 199-202; idem, "Nochmals Sabbath," *ZDMG* 58 (1904): 458-460, who infers from this that the Sabbath in Israel could have been originally a full moon day. Theophile James Meek, "The Sabbath in the Old Testament: Its Origin and Development," *JBL* 33 (1914): 201-212, claims that he came independently to the same conclusion and introduced it to the English-speaking scholarship. Wellhausen had already surmised a connection between the Sabbath and the moon phases (Julius Wellhausen, *Prolegomena zur Geschichte Israels*, 6th ed. [Berlin: Reimer, 1905], 108).

[12] In 1974, Andreasen, "Recent Studies," 455, could still declare that "the well-known position of J. Meinhold (the pre-exilic sabbath was a festival on the day of the full moon, whereas the postexilic sabbath was a weekly day without work), though once influential, is now generally abandoned."

until it was revived by A. Lemaire and especially G. Robinson.[13]

Robinson hypothesizes that while the word *shabbath* originated from the Akkadian *shab/pattu(m)*, the origin of the weekly Sabbath is not found in Mesopotamia, but rather in Israel itself. Because the seventh day is called the day of rest in Exodus 34:21a, he argues that the Sabbath evolved from *Mazzot*, the Week of Unleavened Bread, that this week with its rest day was expanded into seven weeks to include the time of plowing (Exod 34:21b), and moreover that this weekly Sabbath ultimately affected the temporal structuring of the entire year.[14] The origin of the Sabbath is thus said to rest in Exodus 34:21, which used the pre-exilic regulation concerning a day of rest in Exodus 23:12. In other words, only the name *shabbath* is derived from a pre-exilic full moon day, while the Sabbath origin is found in the *Mazzot*. It is said that the seven days of the Feast of Unleavened Bread (Exod 24:18, 21) and its theological meaning, the remembrance of Yahweh's salvation, "generated in Israel the new temporal unit of the week."[15] This hypothesis, with some variation, enjoys popularity particularly among German-speaking scholars.[16] In the

---

The main reasons for abandoning Meinhold's full moon thesis were (1) the lack of plausibility of how and why the Sabbath as full moon day could become a weekly seventh day; (2) why such a central and identity-forming Israelite institution as the Sabbath was taken from another, even Babylonian culture; (3) the renewed view that the (pre-monarchic) commands to rest in Exodus 23:12 and 34:21 should be understood as true Sabbath commandments and conform to the Sabbath texts in the prophets, which, for the most part, are considered pre-exilic; and (4) the resulting increasing tendency to perceive the origin of the Sabbath as being much older than the time when Israel had contact with the Babylonian culture, be it pre-exilic, pre-monarchic, or even Mosaic.

[13] André Lemaire, "Le sabbat à l'époque royale israélite," *RB* 80 (1973): 161–185; Robinson, *The Origin and Development of the Old Testament Sabbath*, which was originally presented as a dissertation in 1975; idem, "The Idea of Rest in the Old Testament and the Search for the Basic Character of the Sabbath," *ZAW* 92 (1980): 32–42.

[14] See also Eckart Otto, "Feste und Feiertage II. Altes Testament," *TRE* 11 (1982): 96–106.

[15] Ernst Haag, "שָׁבַת *shavath*," *TDOT* 14:390. See also the extensive treatment in Haag, *Vom Sabbat zum Sonntag: eine bibeltheologische Studie* (Trier: Paulinus, 1991), 7–28.

[16] See, e.g., Frank-Lothar Hossfeld, *Der Dekalog: Seine späten Fassungen, die originale Komposition und seine Vorstufen* (Göttingen: Vandenhoeck & Ruprecht, 1982), 247–252; Erich Zenger, "Die Feier des Sonntags: Alttestamentlich-jüdischer Sabbat und neutestamentlich-christlicher Sonntag," *Lebendige Seelsorge* 33 (1982): 249–253; Timo Veijola, "Die Propheten und das Alter des Sabbatgebotes," in *Prophet und Prophetenbuch: Festschrift für Otto Kaiser zum 65. Geburtstag*, ed. V. Fritz, K. F. Pohlmann, and H. Ch. Schmitt (Berlin: de Gruyter, 1989), 246–264; Ludger Schwienhorst-Schönberger, *Das Bundesbuch (Ex 20,22–23,33): Studien zu seiner Entstehung und Theologie* (Berlin: de Gruyter, 1990), 389–391; idem, "Die Zehn Gebote (III): Sabbat- und Elterngebot," *BL* 65 (1992): 112–113; Eckart Otto, "שֶׁבַע *sheva'*," *TDOT* 14:356 (cf. idem, *Deuteronomium 1–11*, vol. 2, 4,44–11,32 [Freiburg: Herder, 2012], 738–739); Corinna Körting and Hermann Spieckermann, "Sabbat. I. Altes Testament," *TRE* 29 (1999): 518–521; Michaela

work by A. Grund it has found its most detailed literary-historical and literary-critical argumentation to date.[17]

Grund's main thesis is that the Sabbath was originally the day of the full moon (supporting the thesis of Meinhold and Robinson), which was celebrated monthly in alternation with the new moon festival (she refers to 2 Kgs 4:22–23; Isa 1:13; 66:23; Ezek 45:17; 46:1–3; Hos 2:13; Amos 6:3; 8:4; Lam 2:6). She suggests that the pre-exilic conception of time was basically elliptical, as exemplified by the rhythm of festivals. As the social time in Israel was oriented according to the agricultural year with two polar foci in spring and autumn, so the monthly unit had two focal points in the new moon and the full moon sabbath. Using Exodus 23:12 and 34:21, Grund believes that the "seventh day," which had not yet been designated as *shabbath* and did not exhibit any cultic elements, was an agricultural day of rest. It was in exilic times that this rest day was combined with the full moon Sabbath day.[18] Grund thus regards the Sabbath as an invention of the priestly redactors who associated the term *shabbath* with the increasingly

---

Bauks, "Le Shabbat: un temple dans le temps," *ETR* 77 (2002): 473–490; Friedhelm Hartenstein, "Der Sabbat als Zeichen und heilige Zeit: Zur Theologie des Ruhetages im Alten Testament," in *Das Fest: Jenseits des Alltags*, ed. M. Ebner (Neukirchen-Vluyn: Neukirchener, 2003), 103–131; Klaus Bieberstein, "Vom Sabbat und Siebten Tag zum Sabbat am Siebten Tag: Zur Vorgeschichte des christlichen Sonntags," in *Sonntäglich: Zugänge zum Verständnis von Sonntag, Sonntagskultur und Sonntagspredigt; Festgabe für Ludwig Mödl zum 65. Geburtstag*, ed. U. Roth, H. G. Schöttler, and G. Ulrich (München: Don Bosco 2003), 23–29; Matthias Köckert, *Leben in Gottes Gegenwart: Studien zum Verständnis des Gesetzes im Alten Testament* (Tübingen: Mohr, 2004), 117–120; M. Albani, "Israels Feste im Herbst und das Problem des Kalenderwechsels in der Exilszeit," in *Festtraditionen in Israel und im Alten Orient*, ed. E. Blum and R. Lux (Gütersloh: Gütersloher, 2006), 111–156; Corinna Körting, "Sabbat," *Das Wissenschaftliche Bibellexikon im Internet*, https://www.bibelwissenschaft.de/de/stichwort/25732; Walter Bührer, *Am Anfang ...: Untersuchungen zur Textgenese und zur relativ-chronologischen Einordnung von Gen 3* (Göttingen: Vandenhoeck & Ruprecht, 2014), 123–128; Jörg Jeremias, *Theologie des Alten Testaments* (Göttingen: Vandenhoeck & Ruprecht, 2015), 380 n. 2; and Martin Prudký, "'Keeping Sabbath': Variability and Stability of a Prominent Identity-Marking Norm," in *The Process of Authority: The Dynamics in Transmission and Reception of Canonical Texts*, ed. J. Dušek and J. Roskovec (Berlin: de Gruyter, 2016), 41–60; Julia Rhyder, "Sabbath and Sanctuary Cult in the Holiness Legislation: A Reassessment," *JBL* 138 (2019): 731–732; see also Jacob L. Wright, "Shabbat of the Full Moon and the Origins of the Seven-Day Week," 2015 Torah and Biblical Scholarship Essays, http://thetorah.com/shabbat-of-the-full-moon; idem, "How and When the Seventh Day Became Shabbat," 2015 Torah and Biblical Scholarship Essays, http://thetorah.com/how-and-when-the-seventh-day-became-shabbat.

[17] Grund, *Die Entstehung des Sabbats*; idem, "'Und das Volk ruhte am siebten Tag' (Ex 16,30): Sabbat, Gebot und Identität in der priesterlichen Komposition," in *Identität und Gesetz: Prozesse jüdischer und christlicher Identitätsbildung im Rahmen der Antike*, ed. E. Bons (Neukirchen-Vluyn: Neukirchener, 2014), 51–72.

[18] Grund, *Die Entstehung des Sabbats*, 299.

important day of rest, which has developed from a full moon day to a repetitive seventh day,[19] and used the verb *shavath* for the respective obedience of this day.[20]

A number of considerations dampen the excitement for the Babylonian/ *Mazzot* origin hypothesis of the Sabbath. First, suggestions as to how the noun *shabbath*, with the doubling of the middle radical, derived from *shab/pattu(m)* with the doubling of the third radical seem strenuous.[21]

Second, while *shabbath* refers to a weekly day, *shab/pattu(m)* refers to the monthly day of the full moon.[22] It is highly doubtful whether any biblical passages can legitimately be interpreted in a way that indicates *shabbath* originally referred to the full moon.[23] Since Hebrew has its own term for "full

---

[19] Ron H. Feldman, "The 364-Day 'Qumran' Calendar and the Biblical Seventh Day *Sabbath*: A Hypothesis Suggesting Their Simultaneous Institutionalization by Nehemiah," *Henoch* 31 (2009): 342–365, who accepts a full moon tradition behind the Sabbath, believes that the origin of the perpetual seventh-day Sabbath is post-exilic and connected to the implementation of a 364-day calendar, possibly by Nehemiah. For Feldman, "it may even be the case that the 364-day year was a catalyst for the conception of the perpetual weekly Sabbath, rather than vice-versa as is almost universally assumed" (ibid., 365); cf. Feldman, "'New Moon after New Moon and Sabbath After Sabbath': The Tension Between Culture and Nature in the Cycles of Sabbath and Moon in Ancient Jewish Calendars" (PhD diss., Graduate Theological Union, 2004), 159–169.

[20] A development from another kind of lunar day with no Babylonian origin is suggested by Ina Willi-Plein, "Anmerkungen zu Wortform und Semantik des Sabbat," *ZAH* 10 (1997): 201–206. She proposes an alternative to the derivation of the Sabbath from the full moon day. For her, the Sabbath is in fact the *Leermondtag* or empty moon (ibid., 205)—that is, the moonless night (or nights) with its corresponding day (or days) at the last day of the month just before the new moon, so that the combination of the new moon and Sabbath in some biblical texts (e.g., Amos 8:5) is said to refer to the beginning and the end of the lunar month; see also Christoph Dohmen, "'Der siebte Tag soll ein Sabbat sein,'" *WUB* 17 (2000): 44; idem, *Exodus 1–18* (Freiburg: Herder, 2015), 199; and idem, *Exodus 19–40* (Freiburg: Herder, 2004), 116–117. Norman H. Snaith, *The Jewish New Year Festival: Its Origin and Development* (London: SPCK, 1947), 103–130, proposes that in pre-exilic Israel the month began at the full moon and the Sabbath was in fact the day of the new moon.

[21] The most promising proposal yet seems to be by Hans Rechenmacher, "*šabbat[t]* Nominalform und Etymologie," *ZAH* 9 (1996): 203, who supposes that the doubling of the second radical is due to the tendency to keep the vowel of the open, unaccented syllable. Still, this is an intelligent assumption, which in fact can be neither verified nor disproven.

[22] This is the main point of critique forwarded by Meesters, *Op zoek naar de oorsprong*, 202, and Haag, *TDOT* 14:389.

[23] William W. Hallo, "New Moons and Sabbaths: A Case-Study in the Contrastive Approach," *HUCA* 48 (1977): 11, warns, "There is nothing in the biblical evidence that the sabbatical conception depended in any way on the luni-solar calendar." See also Roland de Vaux, *Ancient Israel: Its Life and Institutions* (London: Darton, Longman and Todd, 1961), 475–483, who concludes after surveying the different theories of sabbath origin: "One thing is certain: it is useless to try to find the origin of the sabbath by connecting it in some way with the phases of the moon" (ibid., 480). Matitiahu Tsevat, "The Basic Meaning of the Biblical Sabbath," *ZAW* 84 (1972): 456–458, believes

moon"—*keseh/kese'* (Ps 81:4 [ET 3];[24] Prov 7:20; with conjecture in Job 26:9, see NASB)—why should *shabbath* have referred to it at earlier times, all the more so since *keseh/kese'* may be a loanword from the Akkadian and also appears in the languages of the surrounding cultures of Israel?[25]

Third, if, as hypothesized, the Sabbath is connected to the new moon, then one would expect a prohibition of work on the new moon. However, the OT does not prohibit work on the new moon day.[26]

Fourth, the new moon and the Sabbath, which appear together in texts that are often dated late in the history of Israel, do not appear as a pair in the rather old festival calendars of Exodus and Deuteronomy. This is against one's expectation if the full moon hypothesis should be true.[27] Again, the Sabbath appears in some texts without connection to the new moon (2 Kgs 11:4–12; 16:18; Lam 2:6; Jer 17:19–27). And in some of the texts in which the Sabbath appears together with the new moon, the two are part of a more complete time reference specifying daily, weekly (Sabbath), monthly (new moon) and yearly activities (1 Chron 23:31; 2 Chron 2:3; 8:13; 31:3; Neh 10:34; Ezek 45:17; Hos 2:13). Hence, texts in which only the time references of the Sabbath and the new moon appear should not be understood as referring to two lunar phases, but to holidays of different frequencies (2 Kgs 4:23; Isa 1:13; 66:23; Ezek 46:1, 3; Amos 8:5).[28]

---

that "the dichotomy between the sabbath on the one hand and nature on the other hand was not unintentional," suggesting that the "content [of the Sabbath], displacing the various ideas and phenomena associated with natural time, is the idea of absolute sovereignty of God, a sovereignty unqualified even by an indirect cognizance of the rule of other powers" (ibid., 458). Cf. Meesters, *Op zoek naar de oorsprong*, 33–34; and Ernst Kutsch, "Der Sabbat–ursprünglich Vollmondtag?" in *Kleine Schriften zum Alten Testament*, ed. Ernst Kutsch (Berlin: de Gruyter, 1986), 71–77, who rejects a connection to the full moon day and instead maintains that there was already a pre-exilic seventh-day Sabbath.

[24] "ET" stands for "English text," and indicates where the numbering of chapters or verses in the English translation deviates from the Hebrew text.

[25] Volker Wagner, *Profanität und Sakralisierung im Alten Testament* (Berlin: de Gruyter, 2005), 20–21.

[26] This has already been pointed out by Felix Mathys, "Sabbatruhe und Sabbatfest: Überlegungen zur Entwicklung und Bedeutung des Sabbat im Alten Testament," *ThZ* 28 (1972): 249–250, but with different conclusions.

[27] Wagner, *Profanität und Sakralisierung*, 20.

[28] See Gerhard F. Hasel, "'New Moon and Sabbath' in Eighth Century Israelite Prophetic Writings (Isa 1:13; Hos 2:13; Amos 8:5)," in *"Wünschet Jerusalem Frieden": Collected Communications to the XIIth Congress of the International Organization for the Study of the Old Testament, Jerusalem 1986*, ed. M. Augustin and K. D. Schunck (Frankfurt am Main: Lang, 1988), 37–64.

Fifth, it is the reconstruction of the literary history with its focus on the prehistory (*Vorlagen*) and different stages of the texts which makes suggestions like those of Robinson and Grund possible in the first place. In literary-critical analysis, the texts in Exodus 23:12 and 34:21 are generally regarded as older than the Decalogue, thus making it much more difficult to argue for the presence of the Sabbath in Exodus 23:12 and 34:12.[29] However, in a text-oriented approach, the *Privilegrecht* (Exod 34:11–26) does not rival or antecede the Decalogue but reinstates the meanwhile broken covenant of the Decalogue (Exod 20:1–17) and the Book of the Covenant (Exod 20:22–23:33). The texts in Exodus 23:12 and 34:21 could then be seen as extensions of the general principle of the Decalogue's Sabbath commandment.

Sixth, no evidence is provided for a pre-exilic seven-day rhythm fromwhich the Sabbath could have developed. In fact, the week cycle does not find any correlation in astronomical or climatic events, nor is there acceptable evidence that it had been used elsewhere in ancient cultures before the Babylonian exile—in contrast to the frequent topos of a period of seven days.[30] The logical conclusion seems that the continuous

---

[29] The dependency of Sabbath origin hypotheses on the current understanding of the development of the Israelite culture and the biblical text has been elaborated by Hasel, "The Origin of the Biblical Sabbath," 17–46. It has also been noted by Cornelius Houtman, *Exodus*, vol. 3, HCOT (Leuven: Peeters, 2000), 43.

[30] See an excursus on the number seven and its symbolism in the ANE in Grund, *Entstehung des Sabbats*, 29–43. After reviewing seven-day time units in Ugaritic and Mesopotamian epics, seven-day life cycle celebrations and seven-day annual festivals, as well as other seven-day periods in the ANE and in Israel, Grund concludes there is no continuous rhythm of six days plus a seventh day to be found outside of Israel: the weekly cycle with its seventh day is "without real analogy" in the ANE (ibid., 42) and "the rhythmization of time through the seventh day is an independent development" (ibid., 43). Grund does not include in her survey the so-called "planetary week," in which the seven days of the week are governed by seven heavenly bodies that the ancients called planets and worshipped as gods (Sun, Moon, Mars, Mercury, Jupiter, Venus, Saturn)—thus a *dies saturni*, "Saturn's day," from which the English "Saturday" is derived. Such a planetary week has its roots in the planetary hours of the Babylonian horoscopic astrology and was introduced via Hellenistic Mithraic astrology into the Roman West as early as the first century BC. It had permeated the Roman Empire by the beginning of the third century AD. See F. H. Colson, *The Week: An Essay on the Origin and Development of the Seven-Day Cycle* (Cambridge: Cambridge University Press, 1926); Solomon Gandz, "The Origin of the Planetary Week or The Planetary Week in Hebrew Literature," *Proceedings of the American Academy for Jewish Research* 18 (1948–1949), 213–254, esp. 215–218; Samuele Bacchiocchi, *From Sabbath to Sunday: A Historical Investigation of the Rise of Sunday Observance in Early Christianity* (Rome: The Pontifical Gregorian University Press, 1977), 241–247; S. Douglas Waterhouse, "The Planetary Week in the Roman West," in *The Sabbath in Scripture and History*, ed. Kenneth A. Strand (Washington, DC: Review and Herald, 1982), 308–322; and Eviatar Zerubavel, *The Seven Day Circle: The History and Meaning of the Week* (New York: Free Press, 1985), 12–19. There is

seven-day rhythmic cycle with a special seventh day is independent of the ancient Near Eastern context and should be traced back to the creation week reported in Genesis 1:3–2:3.

In the end, the derivation of the word *shabbath* from *shab/pattu(m)*, or any other Mesopotamian word, is merely a hypothesis,[31] and the supposed development of the Sabbath from the *Mazzot* feast, or from other special days, is merely highly sophisticated conjecture. W. W. Hallo's final assessment still stands: "Here, then, two of the great contrasts between biblical Israel and its Near Eastern matrix meet: sabbatical cycles versus lunar calendars, and divine authority versus royal authority. The legacy of these contrasts is with us to this day."[32]

Kenite Origin

A. Kuenen suggests that the biblical Sabbath is derived from the day of Saturn of the nomadic Kenites, whom Moses met in the Sinai region. The Kenites supposedly considered this day as a taboo day on which they would not light their furnaces.[33] However, the textual support for this

---

almost a total absence of the planets both in biblical literature and Jewish literature of the late Second Temple period (see Reimund Leicht, "Planets in Ancient Hebrew Literature," in *Giving a Diamond: Essays in Honor of Joseph Yahalom on the Occasion of His Seventieth Birthday*, ed. W. van Bekkum and N. Katsumata [Leiden: Brill, 2011], 16–18), which shows that—at least until the Roman time—the Hebrew tradition had not been interested in astral entities.

[31] See also Gotthard G. G. Reinhold, "Die Zahl Sieben als Zahl der Vollendung: Der Sabbat; Antworten auf die Frage nach seinem Ursprung," in *Die Zahl Sieben im Alten Orient: Studien zur Zahlensymbolik in der Bibel und ihrer altorientalischen Umwelt*, ed. Gotthard G. G. Reinhold (Frankfurt: Lang, 2008), 27–34. The suggestion that the Hebrew word *shabbath* derives from the Akkadian *sebutum* ("seventh"), which supposedly would refer to the seventh day and thus to a week, is without foundation and difficult to explain etymologically (i.e., how to derive the doubling of the middle consonant and *sh* [shin] from *s* [samekh]). In another, novel approach, Koot van Wyk, "Seven Day Cycles and Seventh-day Sabbath in Cuneiform Texts," *Korean Journal of Christian Studies* 84 (2012): 25–48, proposes a reversal of the direction of influence so that the seventh day and the seventh-day cycle in Babylonian texts should stem from the influence of the exiled Israelites on the neo-Assyrian and neo-Babylonian culture. However, his hypothesis is based on an analysis of only a few cuneiform texts, mainly from 542–522 BC, and it seems rather odd that the Hebrew culture in exile would leave such a heavy mark on the dominant Babylonian tradition.

[32] Hallo, "New Moons and Sabbaths," 17; cf. Abraham Joshua Heschel, *The Sabbath: Its Meaning for Modern Man* (New York: Farrar, Straus, and Giroux, 1951), 10 and U. Cassuto, *A Commentary on the Book of Genesis*, Part 1: *From Adam to Noah* (Jerusalem: Magnes, 1961), 68, who goes so far as to say that "the Israelite Sabbath was instituted in *opposition* to the Mesopotamian system." See also Tsevat, "Basic Meaning," 447–459, who argues that the Sabbath is grounded in God's structuring of time.

[33] A. Kuenen, *De voonaamste Godsdiensten: De Godsdienst van Israël tot den Ondergang van den*

view (an alleged fire taboo in Exodus 35:3 and Numbers 15:32; and the mention of *Kiyyun*, which is similar to Akkadian *kayyamanu*, "Saturn," in Amos 5:26) is highly speculative at best, and extra-biblical support for a seven-day week and a dedicated Saturn day among the Kenites is simply nonexistent.[34]

Arabic Origin

D. Nielsen suggests that the term *shabbath* is related via the Akkadian *shabattu(m)* to the Arabic *thabat*, "to sit," which designates an interval between the moon phases when the moon rests in its stations (Akkadian *shubtu*)—four days each month—on which the ancient Arabs worshipped the moon.[35] The four lunar phases were supposedly "copied" by the ancient Israelites, who developed them into seven-day cycles with the Sabbath as the day of worship. However, it could not be demonstrated that the Akkadian *shabattu(m)* was used for a seven-day cycle or the four lunar phases, nor that it is "a linguistic variant" of *shubtu* as Nielsen suggested,[36] nor that ancient Israel was cultically influenced by the ancient Arabs.

Social and Socio-Economic Origins in Israel

Some suggest that the Sabbath emerged from sociological and economic considerations in Israel. H. Webster proposes that Israel adopted a "rest day," similar to the days of rest or cessation of labor found in various cultures in different regions and periods. M. P. Nilsson believes that "the sabbath had once been the proper market-day" because they would rest from work and gather together—a festive day.[37] Ernst Jenni follows Webster and suggests that the Sabbath evolved from "work-free market

---

Joodschen Staat, vol. 1 (Haarlem: Kruseman, 1869). Kuenen's proposal has been accepted by B. D. Eerdmans, "Der Sabbat," in *Vom Alten Testmanet: Karl Marti zum 70. Geburtstage gewidmet*, ed. Karl Budde (Gießen: Töpelmann, 1925), 79–83; Karl Budde, "Antwort auf Johannes Meinholds 'Zur Sabbathfrage,'" *ZAW* 48 (1930): 138–145; and H. H. Rowley, "Moses and the Decalogue," *BJRL* 34 (1951): 81–118.

[34] See, e.g., the critique by Johannes Botterweck, "Der Sabbat im Alten Testament," *ThQ* 134 (1954): 143; de Vaux, *Ancient Israel*, 478–479.

[35] Dietlef Nielsen, *Die altarabische Mondreligion und die mosaische Überlieferung* (Strasbourg: Trübner, 1904), 52–88 (with summary on 87–88).

[36] Ibid., 69.

[37] Hutton Webster, *Rest Days: A Study in Early Law and Morality* (New York: Macmillan, 1916), 88–92, 101–123; Martin P. Nilsson, *Primitive Time-Reckoning: A Study in the Origins and First Development of the Art of Counting Time among the Primitive and Early Culture Peoples* (Lund: Gleerup, 1920), 335.

days,"[38] while Volker Wagner believes it was originally a weekly day of rest on which no work or trade was allowed.[39]

However, there are no parallels of periodically recurring seven-day cycles of rest or market days in ancient Near Eastern cultures. Furthermore, how the sabbaths would have evolved from irregular or otherwise regular market days has not been demonstrated, and this is difficult to imagine, for "the sabbath is quite unlike a market day, since trade was actually forbidden."[40]

For Fritz Stolz the Sabbath originated as the last day of a creation festival week that celebrated the original creation week and was later repeated throughout the year.[41] Opposed to this, F. Mathys believes the Sabbath was originally merely a social institution with no festive character, which, only under the influence of a Canaanite fertility cult in connection with the new moon, developed into a feast in popular Israelite folk religion.[42] Neither of these suggestions gained much support, because there is no evidence for either a creation festival or a social Sabbath in Israel.

So far, we can summarize that none of the suggested extra-biblical or extra-Israelite origins of the Sabbath or of the noun *shabbath* has been convincing.[43] Therefore, this study turns to the most promising suggestion: that the noun *shabbath* has Hebrew roots, and that the best explanation of the origin of the Sabbath can be found within the Hebrew Bible.

---

[38] Ernst Jenni, *Die theologische Begründung des Sabbatgebotes im Alten Testament* (Zürich: Evangelischer Verlag, 1956), 7–16.

[39] Wagner, *Profanität und Sakralisierung*, 24–25. Cf. de Vaux, *Ancient Israel*, 480; Rainer Kessler, "Das Sabbatgebot: Historische Entwicklung, kanonische Bedeutung und aktuelle Aspekte," in *Religion und Gestaltung der Zeit*, ed. D. Georgi, H. G. Heimbrock, and M. Moxter (Kampen: Kok Pharos, 1994), 94; and Uwe Becker, *Sabbat und Sonntag: Plädoyer für eine sabbattheologisch begründete kirchliche Zeitpolitik* (Neukirchen: Neukirchener, 2006), 262–266.

[40] Milgrom, *Leviticus 23–27*, 1960. See also the critique of the transition theory from a social-ethical to a religious-ritual understanding of the Sabbath by Rüdiger Bartelmus, *Auf der Suche nach dem archimedischen Punkt der Textinterpretation: Studien zu einer philologisch-linguistisch fundierten Exegese alttestamentlicher Texte* (Zürich: Pano, 2002), 159–200.

[41] Fritz Stolz, "Sabbat, Schöpfungswoche und Herbstfest," *Wort und Dienst* 11 (1971): 159–175.

[42] Mathys, "Sabbatruhe und Sabbatfest," 241–262 (esp. 248–249).

[43] Similar assessments of the extra-biblical suggestions have been given by Andreasen, *Old Testament Sabbath*, 8–9 and Houtman, *Exodus*, 40–42. After a short overview of the most important suggestions on the extra-biblical origin of the Sabbath, Werner H. Schmidt, *Die Zehn Gebote im Rahmen alttestamentlicher Ethik* (Darmstadt: Wissenschaftliche Buchgesellschaft, 1993), 87, concludes that "so far, despite manifold investigations, the origin of the week with its closing day of rest remains obscure."

Hebrew Origin

Some believe that the Sabbath has to be regarded as a unique Israelite innovation, without giving any detail about its original development.[44] In an extensive study of the literary and redactional development of the Sabbath, Ottilia Lukács presupposes a pre-exilic Sabbath and identifies Exodus 34:21 as "core commandment," or the oldest form of the Sabbath commandment, from which the development of the Sabbath as identity marker began during exilic times.[45] However, she does not discuss where the Sabbath originally comes from.

Others attempt to derive *shabbath* from the Hebrew *sheva'* ("seven").[46] This seems attractive since the Sabbath as the seventh day has a close relation to the number seven. However, while the final consonant Taw in *shabbath* could be explained as a feminine ending, the disappearance of the final guttural consonant Ayin in *sheva'* is difficult to explain in the Hebrew language.[47]

The most obvious etymological interpretation of the noun *shabbath*, however, is to relate it to the Hebrew verbal root *shbt*.[48] Their similarity, based on identical consonants, simply cannot be denied. Yet their relation remains

---

[44] Mayer Gruber, "The Source of the Biblical Sabbath," *JANESCU* 1, no. 2 (1969): 14–20; reprinted in idem, *The Motherhood of God and Other Studies* (Atlanta, GA: Scholars Press, 1992), 111–119, who surveys and rejects various ideas on how the Sabbath originated. See also William W. Hallo, *Origins: The Ancient Near Eastern Background of Some Modern Western Institutions* (Leiden: Brill, 1996), 127–134; idem, "New Moons and Sabbaths," 1–18.

[45] Lukács, *Sabbath in the Making*, 12, 65, 178–183, 293–296; see also idem, "The Inner-Biblical Interpretation of the Sabbath Commandment," in *"Hiszek, hogy megértsem!": Konferenciakötet*, ed. Gér András László, Jenei Péter, and Zila Gábor (Budapest: Károli Gáspár Református Egyetem, 2015), 37–45.

[46] This suggestion had already been proposed by Theophilus of Antioch (ca. AD 170–180), Lactantius (ca. AD 300), and in recent times by H. Hirschfeld, "Remarks on the Etymology of Šabbāth," *JRAS* 53 (1896): 353–359; Charles C. Torrey, "Recent Hebrew Lexicography," *AJSL* 33 (1916–1917): 53; Johannes Hehn, *Siebenzahl und Sabbat bei den Babyloniern und im Alten Testament: eine religionsgeschichtliche Studie*, Leipziger semitistische Studien 2/5 (Leipzig: Hinrichs, 1907), 91–98; and idem, "Zur Sabbatfrage," *BZ* 14 (1917): 210–213.

[47] This is why Hirschfeld and Hehn resort to the Akkadian language, in which the final guttural could more easily vanish, which is of no help since the Akkadian *shabattu(m)* has no relation to the number seven (see the critique by Andreasen, *The Old Testament Sabbath*, 103; and Grund, *Entstehung des Sabbats*, 3–4).

[48] Fritz Stolz, "שבת *shbt*," *TLOT* 3:1297.

disputed.⁴⁹ Some believe that the noun (*shabbath*) is deverbalized—that is, derived from the verb (*shavath*)⁵⁰—while others hold that the verb is denominalized—that is, derived from the noun.⁵¹ Still others see no etymological connection between the verb and the noun.⁵² Then again, in the absence of any plausible, alternative explanation, such a relation receives additional weight.

In the debate about the etymological provenance of the Hebrew noun *shabbath*, one should reckon with the possibility that "the seventh day, in analogy to its uniqueness and distinctiveness as a genuine institution of faith in Yahweh, has been designated with an equally unique and distinctive linguistic term."⁵³ *Shabbath* could very well be a unique word creation.

Even if it should emerge at this point that it is not possible to demonstrate beyond doubt *how* the noun is etymologically derived from the verb, the linkage between *shbt* and *shabbath* remains the most plausible conclusion to the etymological question, especially since the biblical text in Genesis 2:2 uses the root *shbt* to describe one of God's activities on the seventh day, and later on in the Decalogue this seventh-day of the creation week is identified as *shabbath* (Exod 20:10; cf. 16:26). The divine nonactivity on creation's seventh day gave rise to the name given to it. The seventh day became known as day of "*shbt*-ing," hence as *shabbath*.

---

⁴⁹ *HALOT* 4:1407.

⁵⁰ de Vaux, *Ancient Israel*, 475–476, who states that "the simplest etymology is from the Hebrew verb *shabath*" (ibid., 475); Ernst Kutsch, "Sabbat," *RGG* 5 (1961): 1259; Dohmen, *Exodus 19–40*, 116–117.

⁵¹ R. North, "The Derivation of Sabbath," *Bib* 36 (1955): 185–187.

⁵² *Shabbath* is usually regarded as a loan word from the Akkadian. See, e.g., W. H. Schmidt, *Die Schöpfungsgeschichte der Priesterschrift: Zur Überlieferungsgeschichte von Genesis 1,1–2,4a und 2,4b–3,24*, 2nd ed. (Neukirchen-Vluyn: Neukirchener, 1967), 156; Robinson, "The Idea of Rest in the Old Testament," 40; Rechenmacher, "šabbat[t] Nominalform und Etymologie," 199–203; Otto, *Deuteronomium 1–11*, 739; Grund, *Entstehung des Sabbats*, 43–49; and idem, "'Und das Volk ruhte am siebten Tag,'" 55–56.

⁵³ Josef Wehrle, *Der Dekalog: Text, Theologie und Ethik* (Berlin: LIT Verlag, 2014), 100. Haag, *TDOT* 14:388, had already expressed the same idea: "Israel designated the seventh day, in accordance with its unique quality as a genuine institution of the Yahweh faith, with an equally unique expression, the noun šabbāt, deriving it from the verb šābat used in ancient Israelite commandment concerning the day of rest (Ex. 34:21)." Haag and Wehrle suggest that the noun *shabbath* was derived from the verb *shavath* by medial doubling (in some sort of intensive way) and a feminine ending indicating abstractness (Haag, *TDOT* 14:388; Wehrle, *Der Dekalog*, 100n390).

The Seventh Day of the Creation Account

If, as suggested, the origin of the Sabbath is to be found within the Hebrew Bible (and if there is an etymological link between the noun *shabbath* and the verbal root *shbt*), it is Genesis 2:1–3 that first presents itself as the text describing the origin of the Sabbath. If the Sabbath is introduced at creation, it consequently should be understood as a universal institution for humanity. However, others are less convinced that the origin of the Sabbath is found at creation and instead look to Exodus 16:23–30 and Exodus 20:8–11 for the Sabbath's debut.[54] Such an understanding often hinges on the view that the creation account supposedly stems from the so-called priestly source,[55] dating from post-exilic times. At best, this makes Genesis 2:1–3

---

[54] E.g., Harold H. P. Dressler, "The Sabbath in the Old Testament," in *From Sabbath to Lord's Day: A Biblical, Historical, and Theological Investigation*, ed. D. A. Carson (Grand Rapids, MI: Zondervan, 1982), 23, believes that "the Sabbath originated in Israel as God's special institution for His people." He also asserts, "As a sign of the covenant the Sabbath can only be meant for Israel, with whom the covenant was made. It has perpetual function, i.e., for the duration of the covenant" (ibid., 30).

[55] Because in a literary-critical framework the Sabbath is regarded as a late invention, most Sabbath texts, including Genesis 2:1–3, are attributed to the priestly source; a few scholars assign some (parts of) Sabbath texts to H (i.e., the Holiness Code). See, e.g., Klaus Grünwaldt, *Exil und Identität: Beschneidung, Passa und Sabbat in der Priesterschrift* (Frankfurt am Main: Hain, 1992), 122–219; Israel Knohl, *The Sanctuary of Silence: The Priestly Torah and the Holiness School* (Minneapolis, MN: Fortress, 1995), 14–9, 162–63; Yairah Amit, *Hidden Polemics in Biblical Narrative* (Leiden: Brill, 2000), 229–240; Aaron Schart, "The Sabbath: In the Law, in the Prophets, and in Mark," *Verbum et ecclesia* 25 (2004): 256–258; Saul M. Olyan, "Exodus 31:12–17: The Sabbath According to H, or the Sabbath According to P and H?" *JBL* 124 (2005): 201–209; Baruch J. Schwartz, "The Sabbath in the Torah Sources" (paper presented at the Annual Meeting of the Society of Biblical Literature, San Diego, CA, November 19, 2007), 1–14; Thomas Krüger, "Schöpfung und Sabbat in Genesis 2,1–3," in *Sprachen-Bilder-Klänge: Dimensionen der Theologie im Alten Testament und in seinem Umfeld: Festschrift für Rüdiger Bartelmus zu seinem 65. Geburtstag*, ed. Ch. Karrer-Grube et al. (Münster: Ugarit-Verlag, 2009), 156; Jeffrey Stackert, "Compositional Strata in the Priestly Sabbath: Exodus 31:12–17 and 35:1–3," *JHS* 11 (2011): 2–20; idem, "The Sabbath of the Land in the Holiness Legislation: Combining Priestly and Non-Priestly Perspectives," *CBQ* 73 (2011): 240–242; idem, "How the Priestly Sabbaths Work: Innovation in Pentateuchal Priestly Ritual," in *Ritual Innovation in the Hebrew Bible and Ancient Judaism*, ed. N. MacDonald (Berlin: de Gruyter, 2016), 79–111; Bill T. Arnold, "Genesis 1 as Holiness Preamble," in *Let Us Go Up to Zion: Essays in Honour of H. G. M. Williamson on the Occasion of His Sixty-Fifth Birthday*, ed. I. Provan and M. J. Boda (Leiden: Brill, 2012), 334–336; Christophe Nihan, "Das Sabbatgesetz Exodus 31,12–17, die Priesterschrift und das Heiligkeitsgesetz: Eine Auseinandersetzung mit neueren Interpretationen," in *Wege der Freiheit: Zur Entstehung und Theologie des Exodusbuches; Die Beiträge eines Symposions zum 70. Geburtstag von Rainer Albertz*, ed. R. Achenbach, R. Ebach, and J. Wöhrle (Zurich: Theologischer Verlag Zurich, 2014), 131–149; David Daniel Frankel, "The Priestly Conception of the Sabbath in Exodus 16," *BZ* 59 (2015): 208–231; and Christoph Berner, "Der Sabbat in der Mannaerzählung Ex 16 und in den priesterlichen Partien des Pentateuch,"

an etiology of the Israelite Sabbath, or simply the theological conclusion of God's works of creation, which at first has nothing to do with the Sabbath. Whether the Sabbath is purposed for all humanity or for Israel alone obviously depends on the interpretation of Genesis 2:1–3.[56]

The issues that seem to make Genesis 2:1–3 a less likely candidate for the origin of the Sabbath are the absence of the noun "Sabbath," the absence of the evening-morning formula, the absence of humanity, and the absence of any command about keeping the seventh day as Sabbath.[57] We will address these issues to see if Genesis 2:1–3 can or cannot legitimately be regarded as witness to the origin of the Sabbath.

Is the "Seventh Day" the Sabbath Day?

The word *shabbath* occurs for the first time during the Exodus story in the sections of the manna (Exod 16:23–30), the Decalogue (Exod 20:8–11), and the Sabbath laws (Exod 31:13–17; 35:2–3). There is no mention of *shabbath* in the creation account of the seventh day (Gen 2:2–3). This has led some to the assumption that the "seventh day" of creation should not be equated with the Sabbath day,[58] although most

---

ZAW 128 (2016): 562–578.

[56] A wide array of scholars who adhere to a historical-critical approach focus on literary-critical and source-critical questions regarding Genesis 2:1–3, observing closely its structural and linguistic features, and draw conclusions about its priestly-theological impact (or, respectively, its contribution to the theological mindset of H), but they seem less interested in analyzing as meticulously the biblical-theological or canonical contribution of this text. This is the reason why for the following issues in the present essay the discussion takes place more among those scholars who struggle with the question whether Genesis 2:1–3 has or has not a decisive influence for a biblical theology of the Sabbath and, if it has, what this influence might exactly be, and how Genesis 2:1–3 plays into the question of covenantal (dis)continuity and the universality and permanence of the Sabbath, touching on the even larger issue of its impact on Christian life and ethics.

[57] See, e.g., Schmidt, *Die Schöpfungsgeschichte der Priesterschrift*, 157; Dressler, "The Sabbath in the Old Testament," 27–30; and Andrew T. Lincoln, "From Sabbath to Lord's Day: A Biblical and Theological Perspective," in *From Sabbath to Lord's Day: A Biblical, Historical, and Theological Investigation*, ed. D. A. Carson (Grand Rapids, MI: Zondervan, 1982), 346–349.

[58] See, e.g., Dressler, "The Sabbath in the Old Testament," 28, who argues that "unless the reader equates 'seventh day' and 'Sabbath,' there is no reference to the Sabbath here"; and Lincoln, "From Sabbath to Lord's Day," 347–349. Although Haag does not argue that the seventh day is not the Sabbath, he still does not treat Genesis 2:1–3 in his monograph *Vom Sabbat zum Sonntag*. A similar separation between the seventh day of creation and the Sabbath but a different theological conjecture is proposed by Samuel A. Meier, "The Sabbath and Purification Cycles," in *The Sabbath in Jewish and Christian Traditions*, ed. T. C. Eskenazi, D. J. Harrington, and W. H.

believe that the two are identical. The question therefore is: Is the seventh day of the creation account indeed the Sabbath, even if the proper name is not used in Genesis 2:1–3?

The mere mention of six days plus a highlighted seventh day is not enough to conclude that the seventh day needs to be a Sabbath. Periods of seven days (as one unit or as 6+1 days) are frequently found in the Hebrew Bible—and in Near Eastern tradition—without requiring the seventh day to be the Sabbath.[59] Still, "everyone reading this section [Gen 2:1–3] sees it as relating to the Sabbath day."[60] Why?

The Seventh Day is the Sabbath Day

The correspondence between the narrative of the seventh day at creation and the Sabbath commandments is most remarkable. It does not limit itself to thematic parallels but includes common terminology ("work," "do," "bless," "sanctify," "seventh day"), as the following comparison shows:[61]

Shea (New York: Crossroad, 1991), 3–11. He argues that the seventh day is not named "Sabbath" because it was only a day of rest for God, but not for humans who had become God's substitute to manage creation, in accordance with other ancient Near Eastern myths (ibid., 5–6). The seventh day "is therefore the first day of humanity's labor" (ibid., 5). He further conjectures that the seven-day period of purification and sanctification in priestly legislation provided the original context for the seven-day creation cycle with the sanctification of its "seventh day" (ibid., 6–10). However, there is basically unanimous agreement that the biblical creation account does not conform to polytheistic creation stories.

[59] See E. Otto, "שֶׁבַע sheva'," *TDOT* 14:354–356; Amit, *Hidden Polemics*, 224–226; and Grund, *Entstehung*, 29–43. Time units of seven days occur in the biblical tradition at several points: wedding feasts (Gen 29:27–28; Judg 14:12), festivals (Exod 12:15, 19; 13:6–7; 23:15; 34:18; Lev 23:6–8, 34–42; Num 28:17, 24; 29:12; Deut 16:3–4, 13, 15; 2 Chr 30:21–23; Ezra 6:22; Neh 8:18; Ezek 45:23, 25), as well as days of mourning (Gen 50:10; 1 Sam 31:13; 1 Chr 10:12; Job 2:13; Ezek 3:15–16; Dan 10:2 [3x7 days]; cf. 2 Sam 12:18), and various cultic time periods, such as at the consecration of the priests (Exod 29:30, 35; Lev 8:33–35; Ezek 44:26), the sanctification of the altar (Exod 29:37; Ezek 43:25–26), the dedication of the temple (1 Kgs 8:65–66; 2 Chr 7:8–9), in diagnosing skin diseases or mold in fabrics or houses (Lev 13:4–5, 21, 26, 31, 33, 50, 54; 14:8; cf. Num 12:14–15), impurity after child birth (Lev 12:2), after genital discharges (Lev 15:13, 19, 24, 28), or after touching a dead body (Num 6:9; 19:11, 14, 16; 31:19), and the days a newborn animal must live before it can be used as sacrifice (Exod 22:29 [ET 30]; Lev 22:27). Seven days appear several times in the flood narrative (Gen 7:4, 10; 8:10, 12) and there are also other, erratic periods of seven days (Gen 31:23; Exod 7:25; Judg 14:12, 17–18; 1 Sam 10:8; 13:8; 2 Kgs 3:9; 1 Chron 9:25; Isa 30:26). The specific unit of 6+1 days, often used in cultic seven-day periods, especially in festivals, is also connected with the time the cloud of God's glory covered Mount Sinai (Exod 24:15–16) and is found in the 6+1 days in battle (Josh 6:1–20; 1 Kgs 20:29) or in feasting (Esth 1:5, 10).

[60] Amit, *Hidden Polemics*, 226.

[61] Cf. Grund, "'Und das Volk ruhte am siebten Tag,'" 63. Lukács, *Sabbath in the Making*, 58–60, compares the phraseology of the different Sabbath commandments in the Pentateuch (Exod 20:8–9; 23:12; 31:15; 34:21; 35:2; Lev 23:3; Deut 5:13–14) and demonstrates that these texts

Genesis 2:2–3	Exodus 20:8–11	Deuteronomy 5:12–15
… his work [*mela'kh-to*], which he had done [*'asah*] (2:2a)	do [*'asah*] all your work [*kol-mela'khtekha*] (20:9)	do [*'asah*] all your work [*kol-mela'khtekha*] (5:13)
… all his work [*kol-mela'khto*], which he had done [*'asah*] (2:2b)	not do [*'asah*] any work [*kol-mela'khah*] (20:10)	not do [*'asah*] any work [*kol-mela'khah*] (5:14)
on the seventh day [*bayyom hashevi'i*] (2:2, twice); rested [*shavath*] on the seventh day [*bayyom hashevi'i*]	the seventh day [*yom hashevi'i*] is a Sabbath of the Lord (20:10); rested [*nuakh*] on the seventh day [*bayyom hashevi'i*] (20:11)	the seventh day [*yom hashevi'i*] is a sabbath of the Lord (5:14)
blessed [*barakh*, Piel] **the seventh day** [*yom hashevi'i*] (2:3)	blessed [*barakh*, Piel] **the Sabbath day** (20:11b)	
sanctified [*qadhash*, Piel] it, because in it He rested [*shavath*] (2:3)	sanctified [*qadhash*, Piel] it (20:11b)	

The seventh day of creation is unquestionably referred to as Sabbath. Hence, in Exodus 20:11 it can be said that Yahweh rested "on the seventh day" and "therefore Yahweh blessed *the Sabbath* and sanctified it," referring back to Genesis 2:3, where it states that "God blessed *the seventh day* and sanctified it because in it he rested."[62] The variation in vocabulary between

---

follow the same word order and employ the same terms for working and for work as well as for the act of resting and for the Sabbath day. Hence, the seventh day of Genesis 2:2–3 is connected through the Sabbath commandment in the Decalogue to the other Sabbath commandments in the Pentateuch.

[62] Exodus 20:11 is also linked to Genesis 2:3 by the reverse order of God's activities of creation, blessing, and sanctification: "made – rested – blessed the sabbath day and made it holy" (Gen 2:3) is inverted by "blessed the seventh day and sanctified it – rested – created and made" (Exod 20:11). See Matthew Haynes and P. Paul Krüger, "Creation Rest: Exodus 20:8–11 and the First Creation Account," *OTE* 31 (2018): 109. Otto, *Deuteronomium 1–11*, 702, believes that the word *zkr* ("remember") in Exodus 20:8 already serves as literary link between the Sabbath commandment and the creation story. There is a suggestion that a supposed long form of the ending of the creation story (Gen 1:31–2:4a) shows the exact same number of words as the Sabbath commandment (Exod 20:8–11)—that is, fifty-five words—and thus the two texts are intertextually

the texts are not significant enough to allow a different conclusion.[63] One should also not forget that the "seventh day" and the Sabbath are identified as the same day in several other instances (Exod 16:27, 29; 20:10; 31:15; 35:2; Lev 23:3; Deut 5:14). Furthermore, the grammatical construction of the phrase "the seventh day" (noun *yom* without article + ordinal with article)[64] occurs only seven times in the OT, of which three instances are in Genesis 2:3, Exodus 20:10, and Deuteronomy 5:14.[65] This is a clear morphological link between the creation narrative and the Sabbath commandment.

A further hint that the seventh day in Genesis 2:2-3 refers to the Sabbath is the verb *shavath* that is used twice in these verses: instead of any other verb for God's activity on the seventh day (such as *nuakh* ["rest"] in Exodus 20:11), the text uses the rather unusual verb *shbt* ("cease"), with its obvious assonance to the noun *shabbath* ("Sabbath"), which is especially visible in the pronunciation of the perfect *shavath* in verse 3. This allusion exists independently from whatever the exact relation between the two may be.[66]

There is yet another argument why the seventh day is linked with the Sabbath day. Just as creation took six days—each day introduced by "God said"—followed by the seventh day, so there are six "the Lord spoke to Moses" sections concerning the tabernacle instructions (Exod 25:1; 30:11, 17, 22, 34; 31:1), followed by a seventh section about the Sabbath, which is also introduced by the formula "the Lord spoke to Moses" (Exod 31:13–17).[67] The seventh day of creation therefore correlates with

---

linked (see Alfred Marx, "La fin du récit sacerdotal de la création: Gn 2,4a ou Gn 2,3?" *VT* 67 [2017]: 587–588). However, such a conclusion seems far-fetched.

[63] Genesis 2:1-3 differs from the Sabbath commandment in Exodus 20:8-11 in the following points: (1) the use of the verb *shavath* ("cease") instead of *nuakh* ("rest"), (2) the use of the divine name *Elohim* instead of *YHWH*, and (3) the mention of "the seventh day" instead of "the Sabbath day." See Lukács, *Sabbath in the Making*, 123–125.

[64] The phrase is a construct word group (literally "the day of the seventh" > "the seventh day"). In the Hebrew Bible, the determinate numeral word group in which both noun and ordinal have the article occurs 116 times, almost always with the preposition "on" (e.g., "on the seventh day" in Gen 2:2; Exod 16:5, 22, 29), except for once with the preposition "for" ("for the third day" in Exod 19:11).

[65] The other cases are found in Genesis 1:31; Exodus 12:15; and Leviticus 19:6; 22:27.

[66] See Amit, *Hidden Polemics*, 226; and Jan Christian Gertz, *Das erste Buch Mose (Genesis): Die Urgeschichte Gen 1–11* (Göttingen: Vandenhoeck & Ruprecht, 2018), 76.

[67] Peter J. Kearney, "Creation and Liturgy: The P Redaction of Ex 25–40," *ZAW* 89 (1977): 375–378, who observes that "the seventh speech (Ex 31:12-17) effortlessly recalls the seventh day of creation by prescribing the day of rest, to be observed because of what God had done that seventh day (Ex 31:17)" (ibid., 378). Cf. John H. Sailhamer, *The Pentateuch as Narrative: A*

the Sabbath in the instructions for the building of the tabernacle. In fact, there are terminological links between Exodus 31:13–17 and Genesis 2:1–3: God's six-day creation and His rest on the seventh day (Exod 31:17), as well as the holiness of the Sabbath (Exod 31:14–15). Again, the seventh day of creation is identified as the Sabbath day (Exod 31:15, 17).

The common language is significant enough to reach the conclusion that the seventh day in Genesis 2:1–3 is in fact the Sabbath day spoken of in Exodus 20:8–11.[68] In a literary-critical framework this is regarded as evidence of the priestly redactor who inserted the idea of the Sabbath day into creation,[69] in an obvious attempt to link the Sabbath to the creation story in the final text. However, for those who use a text-oriented approach, it is evident that the Sabbath commandment resorts to the language of the creation account because creation was naturally before the exodus, and thus the seventh day existed before the Sinaitic Sabbath command was given.[70]

Absence of *Shabbath* in Genesis 2:1–3

Nevertheless, the question why the noun *shabbath* is not mentioned in the creation account is a valid one. God's naming parts of creation is an important component of the first three days of creation (Gen 1:5, 8, 10). He could have easily given the seventh day a special name, but He did not—or at least the writer does not mention it. Why is the word "Sabbath" not introduced here?

First of all, the word "Sabbath" need not necessarily be mentioned in order to have an essential text or theological statement about the Sabbath.[71]

Biblical-Theological Commentary (Grand Rapids, MI: Zondervan, 1992), 298–299.

[68] Indeed, many scholars perceive such connections and consequently conclude that Genesis 2:1–3 speaks about the weekly Sabbath day.

[69] See, e.g., Samuel A. Meier, "The Sabbath and Purification Cycles," 6.

[70] See Ernst-Joachim Waschke, "Zum Verhältnis von Ruhe und Arbeit in den biblischen Schöpfungsgeschichten Gen 1–3," in *"Gerechtigkeit und Recht zu üben" (Gen 18,19): Studien zur altorientalischen und biblischen Rechtsgeschichte, zur Religionsgeschichte Israels und zur religionssoziologie; Festschrift für Eckart Otto zum 65. Geburtstag*, ed. R. Achenbach and M. Arneth (Wiesbaden: Harrassowitz, 2009), 71–72; cf. idem, "Das Sabbatgebot und die Gottebenbildlichkeit des Menschen: Überlegungen zu zwei verschiedenen Traditionen und ihrem theologischen Zusammenhang," in *Mensch und König: Studien zur Anthropologie des Alten Testaments; Rüdiger Lux zum 60. Geburtstag*, ed. A. Berlejung and R. Heckl (Freiburg: Herder, 2008), 13–24.

[71] Compare the similar reasoning by Rolf Rendtorff, *The Covenant Formula: An Exegetical and Theological Investigation* (Edinburgh: Clark, 1998), 3–4, in regard to texts about the covenant. Specific terms are important and vital guides to detect theological themes, but "they are by no

Genesis 2:1–3 is such a text, as are Exodus 23:12 and Exodus 34:21. In other words, the absence of the word *shabbath* does not constitute a sign that a text is not about the Sabbath. Genesis 2:1–3 is as clearly about the Sabbath as Genesis 1:14–16 is clearly about the sun and the moon, even though the terms "sun" (*shemesh*) and "moon" (*yareakh*) are not used there.

In Genesis 2:2–3, the day in question is called "the seventh day" three times. In an almost poetic arrangement of three consecutive lines of seven words (Gen 2:2a, 2b, 3a), the expression "seventh day" occurs at the midpoint—that is, at the end of the first part of each line, "like a threefold refrain."[72] In the creation context, the designation "seventh day" is fitting. It points to the fulfillment of the series of the previous six days. One would logically expect that another day, the day after the sixth day, would be called the "seventh day." Since the seventh day will acquire the name "Sabbath" in the book of Exodus, we know that we are supposed to identify the seventh day of creation with the Sabbath all along.

Other less convincing proposals have been put forward as to why the term "Sabbath" is missing from the creation account. Umberto Cassuto argues that the term "seventh day" rather than "Sabbath" was used to distinguish it from the Babylonian *shabattu(m)* or *shapattu(m)*, which was determined by the phases of the moon.[73] However, such a view presupposes that the creation account in Genesis 1:1–2:4a serves also as a polemic piece against Near Eastern religious conceptions, placing its origin or last redaction in a Babylonian context, often attributed to the priestly source. Cyrus H. Gordon suggests that the name Sabbath is intentionally absent as a counter-polytheistic device so that the Israelite readers would not associate "Sabbath" with the god Saturn, which in Hebrew is called *Shabbetai*.[74] However, there is no evidence that Sabbath and Saturn would have been linked in OT times.[75] Benno Jacob believes the word "Sabbath" is missing in Genesis 2:1–3 "because it is not applicable to God, of whom alone is spoken here," for God's rest is different from humans' rest inasmuch as humans follow a recurring rhythm of work and rest, while God worked for six days and after ceasing from work on the seventh day did not take

---

means always used where today's reader would expect them" (ibid.).

[72] Cassuto, *A Commentary on the Book of Genesis*, 61.

[73] Ibid., 68; Gordon Wenham, *Genesis 1–15*, WBC (Dallas, TX: Word, 1987), 35–36.

[74] Cyrus H. Gordon, "The Seventh Day," *UF* 11 (1980): 299–301; idem, "The Biblical Sabbath: Its Origin and Observance in the Ancient Near East," *Judaism* 31 (1982): 15.

[75] See previous remarks regarding the Kenite origin hypothesis.

up creation work again on the following days.[76] It seems, however, strange that one should expect that God would continue works of creation on the eighth day, when it is reported that He rested on the "Sabbath"—all the more so since there is no second week of creation activities reported. The use of the term "Sabbath" does not imply that divine creation will continue after the seventh day. Jan C. Gertz argues that the noun "Sabbath" is not used here because the creation account has a "universal focus," but "the Sabbat is a privilege of Israel."[77] However, even though the term "Sabbath" appears for the first time in an Israelite context, there is no reason not to assume that at least the "Sabbath principle" (the seventh day of rest in a weekly cycle), if not the term "Sabbath," was known before Israel. If such is the case, and Genesis 2:2–3 supports this, as does Gertz, then the "Sabbath principle" should not be considered an Israelite institution.

Why Is the Day Formula Absent?

The noticeable absence of the day formula—"there was evening and there was morning, day X"—that has been used for the first six days of creation (Gen 1:5, 18, 13, 19, 23, 31) gives rise to the idea that the seventh day in some way anticipates or foreshadows "the eternal rest that God would provide for his people,"[78] instead of being a memorial of creation, pointing to the creation and to the Creator. The absence of the day formula would indicate "the non-literal nature of the seventh day in particular" and be a sign that "the scheme of the creation week is a literary device."[79] It is thus argued that the Sabbath at creation has never been intended to be an ordinance that has to be kept by humans.[80]

However, there are other, better reasons why the day formula is omitted in Genesis 2:1–3. First of all, the phrase "seventh day" is repeated three

---

[76] Benno Jacob, *Das erste Buch der Tora: Genesis* (Berlin: Schocken, 1934), 66.

[77] Gertz, *Das erste Buch Mose*, 76–77.

[78] Joseph A. Pipa, "The Christian Sabbath," in *Perspectives on the Sabbath: 4 Views*, ed. C. J. Donato (Nashville, TN: Broadman and Holman, 2011), 121.

[79] Lincoln, "From Sabbath to Lord's Day," 347.

[80] For Dressler, "The Sabbath in the Old Testament," 29, "that God ceased from working on the seventh day to 'rest' and be 'refreshed' . . . can only indicate that the goal of creation is not mankind, that the crown is not man, but that all creative activities of God flow into a universal rest period," significantly indicated by the absence of the evening-morning formula, which means that Sabbath is "an Israelite institution based on the heavenly pattern and eschatological in its ultimate purpose and goal" (ibid., 27).

times in Genesis 2:2–3, making it obsolete to insert the day formula.[81] The absence of the day formula also indicates that the seventh day is indeed the climax and goal of creation.[82] It marks the end of the week, thus "creating" a new, not astronomically determined, time cycle of seven days. The rhythm of the creation days is a 6+1 pattern. The first day of creation concerns time, and the unit of a day is created. Literally, the first day formula is "there was evening and there was morning, day one" (Gen 1:5). The following days 2 to 6 end appropriately with the same formula, with a slight difference when it comes to the day number, which is expressed as an ordinal (second day, third day, etc.). The ordinal numbers imply that a series has begun with day 1 and 2 and finds its fulfillment in the seventh day, when the day numbering stops and the end of the weekly cycle is reached.

It is interesting to note that the day formula for the sixth day also differs from the previously used day formula. The one for the sixth day uses the article—"*the* sixth day" (Gen 1:31)—and is not followed by another day formula for the seventh day. The temporal framework of creation thus emphasizes the 6+1 pattern. The seventh-day stands apart and does not need to be counted because it is the goal of the seven-day time unit.[83]

Each day formula has the literary function of closing the present day and anticipating another day of creation as the series must continue. Because the seventh day does not receive a day formula, the series of creation days has clearly ended; there will not be an eighth day of creation.[84] In other words, the seventh day is on God's mind right from the beginning when He creates light on day one. Every day formula drives the series forward to this seventh day. The entire creation story is thus structured with the seventh day in view.

---

[81] See Bernd Janowski, "Tempel und Schöpfung: Schöpfungstheologische Aspekte der priesterschriftlichen Heiligtumskonzeption," *JBT* 5 (1990): 57n86.

[82] It is usually agreed upon that Genesis 2:1–3 is inseparable from the creation account in Genesis 1:1–2:4a. The seven-day structure (see previous discussion), the obvious *inclusio* around the words "God created" (*bara' 'elohim*) in Genesis 1:1 and 2:3b, and the similar vocabulary (see esp. Gen 2:1) show that the seventh day is part of the creation account. See, e.g., Howard N. Wallace, "Genesis 2:1–3: Creation and Sabbath," *Pacifica* 1 (1988): 235–250.

[83] Cf. Dohmen, *Exodus 19–40*, 118–119. Slightly different, H. Ross Cole, "The Sabbath and Genesis 2:1–3," *AUSS* 41 (2003): 7n8, suggests that the day formula is missing in Genesis 2:1–3 because the account of the seventh day "stands outside the parallel structure of the first six days," in which the forming of the first three days parallels the filling or fullness of the next three days and the day formula connects the two halves of the weekdays.

[84] For further arguments, see Daniel Bediako, "Genesis 1:1–2:3 in the Light of Textlinguistics and Text-Oriented-Literary Studies" (PhD diss., Adventist International Institute of Advanced Studies, Cavite, Philippines, 2009), 233–236.

This conclusion gains additional support by the fact that the seventh day breaks with other formulas used in the first six days of creation: the speech introductory formula "God said" (Gen 1:3, 6, 9, 11, 14, 20, 24, 26, 28, 29), the divine command formula in the jussive (Gen 1:3, 6, 9, 11, 14–15, 20, 24) and cohortative (Gen 1:26), the execution formula "it was so" (Gen 1:7, 9, 11, 15, 24, 30), and the approval formula "God saw that it was good" (Gen 1:4, 10, 12, 18, 21, 25, 31 ["very good"]). These characteristic elements of the first six days are missing from the report of the seventh day. Hence, the absence of the day formula on the seventh day is not a sign of this day's symbolic nature, but rather fits perfectly the purpose of letting the Sabbath stand out as the climactic conclusion of the creation account and highlighting its otherness and holiness.[85]

A further theological reason might apply to the absence of the day formula. If darkness (as well as other terms) in Genesis 1:2 (also in Gen 1:4–5) is considered to have negative theological overtones in relation to negativeness, non-existence, and nothingness,[86] the absence of the day formula, which includes the dark period ("evening"), could also be interpreted as having theological overtones. In this case, the nothingness that existed before creation is completely eliminated on the seventh day because existence, fullness, and meaningfulness have been fully established with the seventh day.[87]

Is the Seventh Day a Creation Ordinance?

Creation ordinances are timeless mandates or principles that God gave humans in the garden of Eden and that define universal human nature.[88]

---

[85] See also the chapters by Mathilde Frey and Lael Caesar in this volume.

[86] See Jacques Doukhan, *The Genesis Creation Story: Its Literary Structure* (Berrien Springs, MI: Andrews University Press, 1980), 64–73. See also the similar conclusion by David T. Tsumura, *Creation and Destruction: A Reappraisal of the Chaoskampf Theory in the Old Testament* (Winona Lake, IN: Eisenbrauns, 2005), 35, that the phrase *tohu wavohu* in Genesis 1:2 "simply means 'emptiness'... explaining the initial situation of the earth as 'not yet.'"

[87] Similarly, but with a different tone, Bruce K. Waltke, *An Old Testament Theology: An Exegetical, Canonical, and Thematic Approach* (Grand Rapids, MI: Zondervan, 2007), 187, attributes a theological reason for the seventh day "having no evening or night. God's rest is conceptualized as having no darkness, a negative theological symbol for oppression and death. On that day the horrific primordial chaos is banished forever."

[88] See the definition of the essence of creation ordinances and a summary list by John Murray, *Principles of Conduct: Aspects of Biblical Ethics* (Grand Rapids, MI: Eerdmans, 1957), 27: "We have had occasion already to refer to the commandments or mandates given to man in the state

Two of these, work and marriage, are not much disputed (more on this below). But the question that concerns us here is whether the seventh-day Sabbath should also be regarded among the creation ordinances. If the Sabbath is referred to by the "seventh day" in Genesis 2:2–3, as has been shown above, does this mean that God initiated a recurring weekly rest on the seventh day at creation? Or did He establish/command the Sabbath for the first time for humans (that is, the Israelites) after the exodus, and in the Decalogue simply appealed to His personal day of rest at creation as an analogy for Sabbath keeping? Is the Sabbath only a "Jewish Sabbath"? The observation that the seventh day at creation is indeed the Sabbath mentioned later in the Pentateuch does not answer the question of the origin of the recurring seventh-day Sabbath. We need to find out whether or not the seventh day of creation is the starting point from which God desired humans to keep a regular seventh-day Sabbath.

Genesis 2:2–3 does not contain any (explicit) command from God to keep the seventh day or even recognize it. In fact, humanity is not even mentioned or involved with the seventh day, despite the fact that the first two human beings had been created on the day before, on the sixth day. For some, this absence of humanity or any command in this text presents sufficient reason to believe that the seventh day was not instituted as a recurring seventh day of rest until God commanded Israel to keep the Sabbath after their exodus from Egypt.

The creation story in Genesis 1:1–2:3 is concerned with the activities of God and so, naturally, the final day of that week is also about God's Sabbath keeping. The entire focus is on God. This might be one of the reasons why there is no command given concerning the seventh day.

The first explicit command to keep the Sabbath is given in the wilderness of Sin (Exod 16:23–30) and at Sinai (Exod 20:8–11). However, this does not imply that there was no knowledge of a Sabbath commandment before the exodus. Of the Ten Commandments in Exodus 20, only the one concerning murder is mentioned previously (Gen 9:5–6). Nevertheless, we

---

of integrity. These creation ordinances, as we may call them, are the procreation of offspring, the replenishing of the earth, subduing of the same, dominion over the creatures, labour, the weekly Sabbath, and marriage. When we consider them and seek to assess their significance, we discover how relevant they are to the elementary instincts of man and to the interests that lay closest to his heart, how inclusive they are in respect of the occupations which would have engaged man's thought and action, and how intimately related they are one to another.... There is a complementation of these mandates and they interpenetrate one another." Of course, whether the weekly Sabbath rightly belongs to the creation ordinances, as Murray suggests, has yet to be decided in this study.

assume they were all in force from the time of creation until Sinai, even though the biblical narrative contains only a few indications that they were: Cain was held accountable for murder (Gen 4:6–11); Lamech's bigamy and brutal retaliatory murder are portrayed as the excessive outcome of the line of Cain, who started bloodshed and fratricide, and are juxtaposed to the righteous line with Enoch and Lamech (Gen 4:19–24); God hindered Pharaoh and Abimelech from touching Abraham's wife (Gen 12:17–19; 20:3–6); the divine messengers punished the Sodomites with blindness and then death by fire for their sexual violence and perversion (Gen 19:1–25); and Joseph counted adultery as sin against the Lord (Gen 39:9).[89] Also, the divine judgment that the antediluvian generation was wicked and corrupt (Gen 6:5, 11–13) must have been based on some kind of moral law. These examples for other commandments give enough reason to argue that the absence of an explicit Sabbath commandment is not evidence that there was no Sabbath commandment. Rather, the Sabbath was known before the exodus—as were all other commandments of the Decalogue.[90]

Nevertheless, the salient question is whether Genesis 2:2–3 provides enough evidence that the seventh day should be recognized as a creation ordinance. In the light of this question, this study will first take a closer look at the divine activities mentioned in the text.[91]

God Blessed the Seventh Day

The blessing of the seventh day is the third creation blessing God pronounces. It is a continuation of His blessings on the fifth day (of sea creatures and birds) and on the sixth day (of humans, animals implied). The divine blessing (expressed in "God blessed...") is a perlocutionary act that entails what is mentioned immediately afterwards as command or

---

[89] For more examples see Jo Ann Davidson, "The Decalogue Predates Mount Sinai: Indicators from the Book of Genesis," *JATS* 19 (2008): 61–81, who finds all the Ten Commandments attested or alluded to in the Genesis narratives. Cf. Skip MacCarty, "The Seventh-Day Sabbath," in *Perspectives on the Sabbath: 4 Views*, ed. C. J. Donato (Nashville, TN: Broadman and Holman, 2011), 12.

[90] In his discussion of the Decalogue, Waltke, *An Old Testament Theology*, 420, states, "as with other commandments, the Book of Covenant [Exod 20–24] codified, not inaugurated, Israel's Sabbath observance (cf. Exod 16:23); indeed, the practice is as old as creation."

[91] See also Roy Gane, "Sabbath and the New Covenant," *JATS* 10 (1999): 311–315; idem, "The Role of God's Moral Law, Including Sabbath, in the 'New Covenant'" (2003 paper published by the Biblical Research Institute, June 3, 2004), 12–14, https://adventistbiblicalresearch.org/sites/default/files/pdf/Gane%20Gods%20moral%20law.pdf; and Ángel M. Rodríguez, "The Biblical Sabbath: The Adventist Perspective" (paper presented at Adventist-Catholic Conversation, Genève, Switzerland, May 2002), 2–3, https://adventistbiblicalresearch.org/sites/default/files/pdf/Sabbath-Catholic_2002.pdf.

activity: the blessing for fish and birds is to be fruitful, multiply, and fill (Gen 1:22); the blessing for humans is to be fruitful and multiply, to fill the earth and subdue it, and to exercise dominion (Gen 1:28); and the blessing for the seventh day is that God sanctified it (Gen 2:3). In fact, God's blessings culminate on the seventh day: fish and birds are blessed with physical fertility, male and female human beings are blessed with physical fertility and spiritual elevation, and the blessing of the seventh day is one of spiritual exaltation for its blessing is one of sanctity.[92] The blessings indicate the continuation or perpetuation of the God-blessed item. Regarding the seventh day, this means that from creation onward the seven-day cycle is repeated and the reappearance of the seventh day is a perpetuated phenomenon.[93] The divine blessing of the seventh day is thus a guarantee of its permanent function; it "brings about the continuing, life-promoting validity of this ordinance, that is, the steady recurrence and life-sustaining effect of the sanctified seventh day after a series of six working days."[94] It is only in connection with humanity that the intention of blessing the seventh day

---

[92] Cassuto, *A Commentary on the Book of Genesis*, 65. Stackert, "How the Priestly Sabbaths Work," 91–94, suggests that the blessing of the seventh day in Genesis 2:3 is oriented toward agricultural fertility. He infers such an idea from matching the blessing of the seventh day with the other blessings during creation week and from a supposed connection to the sabbatical year law in Leviticus 25:20–21 and the manna narrative in Exodus 16. However, Stackert is reading an (Israelite) agricultural context backwards into Genesis 2:2–3, which is possible only if one assumes that Genesis 1:1–2:4a has been composed at such an agricultural time or afterwards (in or after the Babylonian exile). But such agricultural context is not present in Genesis 1:1–2:4a (earliest references might be Gen 2:15 and 3:17–19) and does not fit the universal tone of the creation account. Furthermore, he misses the facts that (1) the agricultural/manna blessing rests on the sixth and not on the seventh year/day; (2) the kind of blessing depends to a large degree on the object of blessing, meaning that a different kind of object to be blessed involves a different kind of blessing so that the blessing of the seventh day has a different impact than the blessing of living beings; and (3) in the creation report the divine blessing is immediately followed by the essence of such blessing, which is fertility for the living beings (Gen 1:22, 28) and sanctity for the seventh day (Gen 2:3).

[93] See J. G. Murphy, *A Critical and Exegetical Commentary on the Book of Genesis*, ICC (Andover, MA: Draper, 1866), 71: "The solemn act of blessing and hallowing is the institution of a perpetual order of seventh-day rest: in the same manner as the blessing of the animals denoted a perpetuity of self-multiplication, and the blessing of man indicated further a perpetuity of dominion over the earth and its products. The present record is a sufficient proof that the original institution was never forgotten by man." Cf. Gane, "The Role of God's Moral Law," 13; see also Bührer, *Am Anfang*, 122–123, who recognizes the blessing's goal of perpetuation, but argues that the end of the creation story is "not an etiology of the Sabbath" and cannot be so, since the noun *shabbath* is not mentioned and the Sabbath is an order limited to Israel.

[94] Janowski, "Tempel und Schöpfung," trans. Martin Pröbstle, 59. Cf. Benno Jacob, *The First Book of the Bible: Genesis*, trans. and abridged by E. I. Jacob and W. Jacob (Jersey City, NJ: KTAV, 1974), 13: "If God has blessed the seventh day, he has equipped it with the power to do good as his blessing over beast and man equipped them with fertility."

can ever be fulfilled. "The blessing gives the day, which is a day of rest, the power to stimulate, animate, enrich and give fullness of life. It is not the day in itself that is blessed, but rather the day in its significance for the community. In the context of creation it is for the world and humankind."[95] Hence, the act of blessing the seventh day presupposes that from now on—from the seventh day of creation on—every seventh day brings blessings to the humans.

God Sanctified the Seventh Day

On the seventh day, God added to the value of "good" and "very good" the value of holiness.[96] The sanctifying of the seventh day is expressed by the Piel form of the verbal root *qdsh* (Gen 2:3). Indeed, this is the only Genesis reference of the verb *qdsh*[97] (which becomes a key root in Exodus and Leviticus), possibly indicating the special position of the seventh day long before there was anything else designated as holy, including the people of Israel. This particular verbal form in the Piel means that in a declarative sense God pronounced the seventh day as holy, transferring it into a state of holiness,[98] into the realm of God.[99] Such sanctification anticipates the commandment that humans should keep the Sabbath holy (Exod 20:8).[100] Actually, God's command is to treat or observe the Sabbath as holy.[101] The proper response to God's consecration of the Sabbath is to respect the divine presence and not to profane it. Humans can only keep something

---

[95] Claus Westermann, *Genesis 1–11* (Minneapolis, MN: Augsburg, 1984), 172.

[96] Israel C. Stein, "Sacred Space and Holy Time," *JBQ* 34 (2006): 244.

[97] The root *qdsh* occurs elsewhere in Genesis only in reference to Kadesh (Gen 14:7; 16:14; 20:1) and a cult prostitute (Gen 38:21–22).

[98] The standard lexica are unanimous: "to declare holy" or "to transfer something to the state of holiness" (*HALOT* 3:1073); "make inviolable, make holy, set apart, purify, sanctify" (*DCH* 7:192); or "declaring something/someone holy" (W. Kornfeld, "קדש *qdsh*," *TDOT* 12:528); "putting something into a state of holiness" (J. A. Naudé, "קדשׁ *qdsh*," *NIDOTTE* 3:884).

[99] David J. A. Clines, "Alleged Basic Meanings of the Hebrew Verb *qdš* 'be holy': An Exercise in Comparative Hebrew Lexicography" (paper presented at the International Organization for the Study of the Old Testament, Stellenbosch, September 4–9, 2016), 14–15.

[100] The "anticipation" of the Sabbath command at Sinai should not be mistaken for the main focus of Genesis 2:1–3. Andreasen, "Recent Studies," 466, points out that "though the creation sabbath anticipates the sabbath institution, perhaps as preparation, its main direction is towards creation and the creator."

[101] *DCH* 7:192, lists Exodus 20:8 with the meaning "observe as holy, keep holy religious feasts, assemblies and times." See also Deuteronomy 5:12; Jeremiah 17:22, 24, 27; Ezekiel 20:20; 40:24; and Nehemiah 13:22.

holy if God, the source of all holiness, has sanctified it first. The command given at Sinai ("Keep the holiness of the Sabbath," Exod 20:8) then presupposes that God had already made the day holy, which He did at the time of creation (Gen 2:3; cf. Exod 20:11).

This conclusion goes against the view that God sanctified the seventh day and was looking forward to its first-time introduction as Sabbath at Sinai, as if to say that God really did not do anything at creation that would have affected the seventh day right away.[102] Again, another approach to discard the immediate effect of God's blessing and sanctifying the seventh day places a purely proleptic or eschatological value[103] on the seventh day of creation. On the basis that blessing is explained as sanctifying, and sanctifying means separation, one scholar proposes that the seventh day is separated to be an "eschatological, proleptic sign indicating some future rest" and claims that "the statement in Genesis 2:3 is to be understood not in terms of blessing the Sabbath . . . but in terms of the ultimate rest for the people of God," while the blessing of the Sabbath is only given at Sinai (Exod 20:11).[104] Such a view, however, imposes an artificially contrived dichotomy between the seventh day and the Sabbath, for which textual evidence has not been provided. It is simply unconvincing to say that although Genesis 2:3 and Exodus 20:11 mention explicitly that "God

---

[102] Contra Richard J. Griffith, "The Eschatological Significance of the Sabbath" (ThD diss., Dallas Theological Seminary, 1990), 33, who compares the Piel of *qdsh* in Genesis 2:3 with the Hiphil of *qdsh* in Jeremiah 1:5 to illustrate that sanctification/separation and the actual taking effect of the assigned task could be chronologically far apart. Cole, "The Sabbath and Genesis 2:1-3," 10, rightly critiques this view and points to the fact that the Piel of *qdsh* stresses the result while the Hiphil of *qdsh* stresses the process. Hence, the two are not interchangeable.

[103] This approach comes close to the suggestion of an "open end" or "eschatological aspect" of Genesis 2:2-3 by scholars who adhere to the idea that the creation account stems from a priestly source and looks forward to the Sabbath commands in the Sinai narrative. See also Rudolf Borchert, "Stil und Aufbau der priesterlichen Erzahlung" (Theol. diss., Heidelberg University, 1957), 126; Gerhard von Rad, *Genesis*, OTL, rev. ed. (Philadelphia, PA: Westminster, 1972), 62; Odil H. Steck, *Der Schöpfungsbericht der Priesterschrift: Studien zur literarkritischen und überlieferungsgeschichtlichen Problematik von Genesis 1,1–2,4a*, 2nd ed. (Göttingen: Vandenhoeck & Ruprecht, 1981), 196–197; and Erich Zenger, *Gottes Bogen in den Wolken: Untersuchungen zu Komposition und Theologie der priesterlichen Urgeschichte* (Suttgart: Katholisches Bibelwerk, 1983), 100–101.

[104] Dressler, "The Sabbath in the Old Testament," 29. See also Lincoln, "From Sabbath to Lord's Day," 348; Richard H. Lowery, *Sabbath and Jubilee* (St. Louis, MO: Chalice, 2000), 90. Cf. Pipa, "The Christian Sabbath," 121, who connects the idea of a future rest with the absence of the day formula; but see Howard N. Wallace, "Rest for the Earth? Another Look at Genesis 2:1-3," in *The Earth Story in Genesis*, ed. N. C. Habel and S. Wurst (Sheffield: Sheffield Academic, 2000), 51–52, who argues that "each term brings its own nuance to the text," so also the term "seventh day" in Genesis 2:2-3.

blessed the seventh day" at creation, this act of blessing had no outcome at that time, and instead to believe that God blessed the Sabbath only at Sinai, although this is never mentioned in the text. Rather, when God blessed and sanctified the seventh day at creation, it had an immediate effect; the Sabbath did not become operative only at the time of the exodus. This immediate effect is exactly what the Piel form of *qdsh* in Genesis 2:3 expresses: God declared the seventh day holy, *and it was holy*—very similar to His creation by word, with which He commanded all things into existence.

It should also be clear that the holiness of the seventh day does not pertain only to the historic seventh day of creation week. It makes no sense to make this first seventh day holy without further effect on subsequent seventh days. The sanctification of the seventh day must have a perpetual aspect, similar to its blessing. Indeed, by blessing and declaring holy the seventh day, God initiated the seven-day cycle.

Another pertinent question arises: For whom did God sanctify the seventh day? It was the first human couple, who were created the day before the seventh, and who were again in focus in the following narrative in Genesis 2:4b–25. Most naturally then, the consecration of the seventh day was for Adam and Eve to appreciate this day as set apart by God for the enjoyment of His presence. Genesis 2:3 states that God put the Sabbath into a state of holiness, and because holiness is only acquired in relation to God, who is the source of all holiness, the activity of sanctifying conveys the idea that this day is sacred by virtue of God's special presence (cf. Exod 3:5; 29:43; Lev 19:2).[105] It is truly God's day, by right of ownership, which is why He calls this day "my Sabbath," or in the plural "my Sabbaths."[106]

---

[105] Daniel C. Timmer, *Creation, Tabernacle, and Sabbath: The Sabbath Frame of Exodus 31:12–17; 35:1–3 in Exegetical and Theological Perspective* (Göttingen: Vandenhoeck & Ruprecht, 2009), 73–74, surmises that the seventh day does not serve as cultic sacred time but "in part" represents "the perfection and purpose of God's creation" and as such symbolizes "the goal to which humans are directed as terminus of their probation." In his view, the Sabbath does not constitute a set apart time in which humans can enjoy God's presence, but with its "telic character" (ibid., 70) it sets an attainable goal *if* humans are obedient to God. Humans first need to become holy—that is, pass their test of loyalty to God—before they can enter the rest symbolized by the holy "seventh day." However, he misses the character of the Sabbath as a gift, in which "His holiness, first of all, means His presence" (Jiří Moskala, "The Sabbath in the First Creation Account," *JATS* 13/1 [2002]: 61), which is given freely to humanity. See also Mathilde Frey, "The Sabbath in the Pentateuch: An Exegetical and Theological Study" (PhD diss., Andrews University, 2011), 69–72, 277–279.

[106] Exodus 31:13; Leviticus 19:3, 30; 26:2; Isaiah 56:4; Ezekiel 20:12–13, 16, 20–21, 24; 22:8, 26; 23:38; 44:24. The similar phrase "Sabbath to the Lord" also points to God as sovereign owner of the Sabbath (Exod 16:25; 20:10; 35:2; Lev 23:3; 25:2; Deut 5:14). An interesting case in point is observed

God's Rest as Example for Humans Created in the "Image of God"

Some believe that the absence of reference to humans in Genesis 2:1–3 suggests that God's behavior does not constitute an example for humanity,[107] or that the seventh day has only to do with God and "His own triumphant rest."[108] However, the anthropomorphic description of God ceasing from work, even refreshing,[109] and resting on the seventh day serves as "a divine role model set for man," especially in the light of the fact that God is presented in the first six days of creation as the transcendent Creator who is so different from created beings.[110] Such a connection between God's resting on the seventh day and the mandate for humans to rest on the seventh day seems obvious.[111] If God is described like a human,

---

by Milgrom, *Leviticus 23–27*, 1962: "Moses' rebuke of the Israelites who sought to gather manna on the sabbath: ... 'today is a sabbath of YHWH; you will not find it in the field' (Exod 16:25). This highly anthropomorphic expression is clear: God is resting on this day; the Sabbath is his day off."

[107] Timmer, *Creation, Tabernacle, and Sabbath*, 71; and Wayne G. Strickland, "Response to Willem A. VanGemeren," in *Five Views on Law and Gospel*, ed. G. L. Bahnsen et al. (Grand Rapids, MI: Zondervan, 1999), 76–77, 81–82.

[108] Lincoln, "From Sabbath to Lord's Day," 348.

[109] Compare the Niphal of *npsh* ("breathe freely") in Exodus 31:17 (God "refreshed" on the seventh day) and in Exodus 23:12 (human beings "may refresh themselves" on the seventh day).

[110] Stanley L. Jaki, "The Sabbath-Rest of the Maker of All," *AsTJ* 50, no. 1 (Spring 1995): 37–38, who believes that the divine role model is set in opposition to the Babylonian conception in which the gods rested permanently after the creation of humans as servants/slaves.

[111] In the past, rarely would a scholar who espoused source-critical views and maintained that Genesis 2:1–3 does not establish Sabbath observance turn from his or her previously held ideas. An interesting example is Johann Philipp Gabler (1753–1826), the "father of modern biblical theology," especially considering his way of reasoning. Gabler first follows Eichhorn and claims that Genesis 2:1–3 is part of merely a poet's painting ("Dichtergemälde"), that there was no Sabbath observance before Moses, and that the Sabbath is entirely Mosaic or Jewish (Johann Gottfried Eichhorn, *Urgeschichte: Erster Theil*, ed. J. P. Gabler [Altdorf: Monath & Kussler, 1790], 234–256). Five years later, Gabler abandons his previous position and asserts that "the exegetical feeling" speaks in favor of the explanation that Genesis 2:1–3 does refer to the inauguration of the Sabbath (Johann Philipp Gabler, *Neuer Versuch über die Mosaische Schöpfungsgeschichte aus der höhern Kritik: Ein Nachtrag zum ersten Theil seiner Ausgabe der Eichhorn'schen Urgeschichte* [Altdorf: Monath & Kussler, 1795], 19–25). He states, "If you read Gen 2:3 completely unbiased, no doubt the idea suggests itself that this is about the establishment of the Sabbath and that the author, with the words [citing the Hebrew of Gen 2:3a], does not only make the following seventh day after six creation days to a festive day for God Himself, but that he let God, in remembrance of his rest from creation, determine and solemnly inaugurate every seventh day of the week to a festive day for the humans" (ibid., 19–20). Gabler points out that "the irresistible power of the exegetical feeling at this point deserves all respect and attention" (ibid., 21), and concludes that the view that Genesis 2:1–3 establishes the recurring weekly Sabbath observance from creation onward, which he previously rejected, "deserves our preference" (ibid.). What convinces Gabler, then, is what the text obviously wants to say, without imputing it any other intention by any hypothetical (source-critical) argument.

ceasing from work and resting, "the call for human Sabbath-keeping is implicit in the creation of human beings in the image of God."[112]

Among other things, the image of God (*imago Dei*)[113] is often understood to also include the imitation of God (*imitatio Dei*), for humanity's responsibility as God's earthly representative implies like actions.[114] The first activity after God created humans in His image and blessed them was that He completed His work and rested on the seventh day. Hence, since God ceased from work and rested on the seventh day, humans should "imitate" the divine behavior and cease from work and rest on the seventh day.[115]

It is unthinkable that God rested on the seventh day yet the humans whom He created the day before would not emulate His resting but would be working on this day, cultivating and keeping the garden (Gen 2:15), subduing the earth (Gen 1:28).[116] Rather, they would have rested together with God, having the opportunity to enjoy the sanctity of the day—that is, the presence of their God. We can assume that they naturally would have experienced this first seventh day as a day of companionship and worship

---

[112] Cole, "The Sabbath and Genesis 2:1–3," 12.

[113] This study will not elaborate on the meaning and the significance of the *imago Dei* and its various interpretations. For a starting point, see Gunnlaugur A. Jónsson, *The Image of God: Genesis 1:26–28 in a Century of Old Testament Research* (Stockholm: Almqvist & Wiksell, 1988); J. Richard Middleton, *The Liberating Image: The Imago Dei in Genesis 1* (Grand Rapids, MI: Brazos, 2005); Catherine L. McDowell, *The Image of God in the Garden of Eden: The Creation of Humankind in Genesis 2:5–3:24 in Light of the* mīs pî pīt pî *and* wpt-r *Rituals of Mesopotamia and Ancient Egypt* (Winona Lake, IN: Eisenbrauns, 2015); and Beth Felker Jones and Jeffrey W. Barbeau, eds., *The Image of God in an Image Driven Age: Explorations in Theological Anthropology* (Downers Grove, IL: InterVarsity, 2016).

[114] The imitation of God is definitely given as an ethical rationale of the Sabbath commandment. See Patrick D. Miller, *The Ten Commandments* (Louisville, KY: John Knox, 2009), 125–127.

[115] Hasel, "Sabbath," *ABD*, 5:851, states: "The sequence of 'six working-days' and a 'seventh [sabbath] rest-day' indicates universally that every human being is to engage in an *imitatio Dei*, 'imitation of God,' by resting on the 'seventh day.' 'Man' (*'ādām*), made in the *imago Dei*, 'image of God,' (Gen 1:26–28) is invited to follow the Exemplar in an *imitatio Dei*, participating in God's rest by enjoying the divine gift of freedom from the labors of human existence and thus acknowledging God as his Creator." Georg Fischer, *Genesis 1–11* (Freiburg im Breisgau: Herder, 2018), 163, comments that the pragmatics of the narrative dictate that God's "resting should even become a *model for the humans*. He and they, so to speak, live 'synchronized in unison.'" Cf. also Amit, *Hidden Polemics*, 228.

[116] Gane, "The Role of God's Moral Law," 12; cf. Krüger, "Schöpfung und Sabbat," 167, who infers from the Sabbath commandment that the humans first needed to work six days before they could celebrate the Sabbath so that "it is not to be expected that they would have a sabbath on the first day after their creation"; and Matthew Haynes and P. Paul Krüger, "Creation Rest: Genesis 2:1–3 and the First Creation Account," *OTE* 30 (2017): 681–682, who maintain that "as God rests, humans are busily going about all of the functions that they were created to fulfil."

of God—how appropriate for the first full day of their lives. At the same time, "the reason why He refrains from further activity on the seventh day is that He found the object of His love and has no need for further works."[117] The seventh day ensures time for mutual relationship.

The New Testament underscores this line of thought. Jesus declares that "the Sabbath was made for man, and not man for the Sabbath" (Mark 2:27). Such an assertion refers back to the "making" of the Sabbath, which took place at creation[118] and not at Sinai, and attributes to it a beneficial purpose for humans.[119] The conclusion is inescapable: What God did on the seventh day was for humans. He intended the seventh day to serve His crowning creation. They could rest from their work and enjoy companionship. On the first seventh day, however, the humans did not need to rest from six work days, simply because they did not work yet. The most likely purpose of this first Sabbath was for humans to have communion with God and worship their Creator, who had just given them life and the gift of partnership. Joy of contemplation and enjoying creation must be part of the Sabbath celebration.[120]

Does ceasing from work to rest imply a mandate to worship? Later on in the Hebrew Bible, when Israel as God's holy people have been chosen and the sanctuary/temple has been given, the Sabbath rest includes activity in

---

[117] Karl Barth, *Church Dogmatics*, vol. 3, Part 1: *The Doctrine of Creation*, ed. G. W. Bromiley and T. F. Torrance (Edinburgh: T&T Clark, 1958; repr. 2004), 215.

[118] The verb *egeneto* ("made"), which occurs in Mark 2:27, is used twenty times in the LXX of Genesis 1.

[119] Cf. Haag, *Vom Sabbat zum Sonntag*, 127–128; Joel Marcus, *Mark 1–8*, AB (New York: Doubleday, 2000), 242; Adela Yarbro Collins, *Mark: A Commentary*, Hermeneia (Minneapolis, MN: Fortress, 2007), 203; MacCarty, "The Seventh-Day Sabbath," 21; and Pipa, "The Christian Sabbath," 122. Contra D. A. Carson, "Jesus and the Sabbath in the Four Gospels," in *From Sabbath to Lord's Day: A Biblical, Historical, and Theological Investigation*, ed. D. A. Carson (Grand Rapids, MI: Zondervan, 1982), 65 and Lincoln, "From Sabbath to Lord's Day," 350, who recognize the beneficial purpose of the Sabbath but claim that the temporal origin is not in view in the saying of Mark 2:27.

[120] See John Calvin, *Commentaries on the First Book of Moses Called Genesis*, vol. 1 (Grand Rapids, MI: Eerdmans, 1948), 106: God "dedicated every seventh day to rest, that his own example might be a perpetual rule. The design of the institution must be always kept in memory: for God did not command men simply to keep holiday every seventh day, as if he delighted in their indolence; but rather that they, being released from all other business, might the more readily apply their minds to the Creator of the world. Lastly, that is a sacred rest, which withdraws men from the impediments of the world, that it may dedicate them entirely to God.... So far as the Sabbath was a figure of this [spiritual] rest, I say, it was but for a season; but inasmuch as it was commanded to men from the beginning that they might employ themselves in the worship of God, it is right that it should continue to the end of the world."

individual and communal worship. Leviticus 23:3 points to the seventh day as a festival of the Lord:[121] "The seventh day is a sabbath of complete rest, a holy convocation."[122] Grammatically, the "holy convocation" or "proclamation of holiness" (*miqra' qodhesh*) stands in apposition to the "Sabbath of complete rest" (*shabbath shabbathon*), bringing resting and holiness close together conceptually.[123] The instruction on the Sabbath is sandwiched between the heading of the section on sacred festive days (Lev 23:2) and the introduction to the different sacred festive days (Lev 23:4).[124] This arrangement shows that while the Sabbath belonged to the festive calendar, and thus a sacred assembly is implied and (compared to the other days of the week) additional sacrifices had to be brought on it (Num 28:9–10), it also stood apart from the cultic festivals by originating in the 6+1 day creation cycle. The "liturgical performance"[125] of Psalm 92 on the Sabbath day and the psalm's formative Sabbath theology is another clear indication for worship on Sabbath in Israel.[126] An early cultic practice on the Sabbath day is seen in 2 Kings 4:23,[127] and texts like Isaiah 1:13 and Hosea 2:11 imply that the Sabbath day in Israel was a festive day with assembly and sacrifices. Theologically, the Sabbath rest is and needs to be filled with worship.[128] To be sure, the Sabbath is essentially a day of work stoppage,

---

[121] See Gerhard F. Hasel, "The Sabbath in the Pentateuch," in *The Sabbath in Scripture and History*, 33.

[122] The LXX renders here "a holy calling [of a meeting] for the Lord."

[123] A festival is only truly holy by abstinence from the workaday life: "Holiness mandates cessation from labor" (Milgrom, *Leviticus 23–27*, 1978).

[124] The essential words of the heading in Leviticus 23:2 ("[as for] the fixed times of YHWH [*mo'adhe YHWH*] which you shall proclaim as sacred occasions [*miqra'e qodhesh*], these are my fixed times [*mo'adhay*]"—reappear in the introduction in verse 4 ("These are the fixed times of YHWH [*mo'adhe YHWH*], the sacred occasions [*miqra'e qodhesh*], which you shall proclaim at their fixed times [*bemo'adham*]"). For the translation, see Milgrom, *Leviticus 23–27*, 1947.

[125] Frank-Lothar Hossfeld and Erich Zenger, *Psalmen 51–100* (Freiburg: Herder, 2000), 631.

[126] See Richard M. Davidson, *A Love Song for the Sabbath* (Hagerstown, MD: Review and Herald, 1988), 11–14, 23–24; and idem, "The Sabbath in the Old Testament Psalms and Wisdom Literature" (paper presented at the Symposium on the Sabbath, Universidad Adventista del Plata, October 13, 2010).

[127] Erich Spier, *Der Sabbat* (Berlin: Institut Kirche und Judentum, 1992), 18.

[128] Contra Heather McKay, *Sabbath and Synagogue: The Question of Sabbath Worship in Ancient Judaism* (Leiden: Brill, 1994); cf. the earlier version of this part of her 1992 dissertation in idem, "New Moon or Sabbath?" in *The Sabbath in Jewish and Christian Traditions*, ed. T. C. Eskenazi, D. J. Harrington, and W. H. Shea (New York: Crossroad, 1991), 12–27; cf. also idem, "From Evidence to Edifice: Four Fallacies about the Sabbath," in *Text as Pretext: Essays in Honour of Robert Davidson*, ed. R. P. Carroll (Sheffield: JSOT, 1992), 179–199. After scanning the Sabbath

a day of rest, but it is also a day of rest to enjoy God and celebrate Him. The human being was created as *homo liturgicus*—as a person who loves, believes, and worships—and the day of rest provides the most beneficial temporal space for it.

One might expect that Adam and Eve would continue to imitate God's example in the next seven days, working six days and resting on the seventh day. Such a pattern of work and rest is put into writing in the Sabbath command. That we discover it for the first time in written form in the Sabbath command does not imply, however, that such behavior does not have its origin in creation.

The pattern of six workdays and one rest day is found in all seven Sabbath laws in the Pentateuch (Exod 20:8–11; 23:12; 31:13–17; 34:21; 35:2–3; Lev 23:3; Deut 5:12–15), and also in the manna narrative (Exod 16:26, 29–30). In fact, this work-rest pattern is the only content these Sabbath texts all have in common. This suggests that God's six days of labor and His seventh day of rest serve as an example pattern for humanity, because it is such a pattern from creation that all texts exhibit. Since God gave the first humans the command to work (Gen 1:28; 2:15), we have to assume that God also gave them the command to rest.

Creation Ordinances of Work, Marriage, and Sabbath

As mentioned above, creation ordinances are timeless mandates or principles that God established prior to the fall of humans and are therefore part of God's design prescribed for all people. Two such ordinances seem quite obvious and, as ordinances, are not much disputed, and both have a specific relation to the Sabbath: work and marriage.

First, God gifted humans with work. He placed the first humans in the garden of Eden and gave them the dignified task to cultivate and keep it

---

texts in the Hebrew Bible, McKay sums up her findings: "The only places where the word 'sabbath' is used in the Hebrew Bible in reference to actual worship are in details of the sabbath sacrifice at Numbers 28:9–10 and in the title of Psalm 92, the former referring to actions of priests and the latter implying a group of singers, not, however, identified in the text" (idem, *Sabbath and Synagogue*, 18). Thus, she concludes "there are no texts about regular sabbath worship for the ordinary worshipper in the Hebrew Bible," with the exception of future sabbath worship mentioned in Ezekiel 46 and Isaiah 66:23 (ibid.). McKay attempts to distinguish between Sabbath observance and actual Sabbath worship. Her thesis is that the Sabbath was a day of communal worship only from the third century AD onward. Her argument is basically an *argumentum ex silentio*. She uses the apparent silence about worship on Sabbaths among ancient Israelites to build her case of a very late introduction of communal worship on Sabbath. However, the OT evidence does not preclude any worship on Sabbath. In fact, it is reasonable to believe that if priests and singers celebrate Sabbath, the ordinary people would also do so.

(Gen 2:15).[129] After the fall and outside of the garden, God still commanded humans to work (Gen 3:23; cf. 2:5; 3:18–20). If work is an ordinance of creation that was in effect before and after the fall, it is virtually consequential that the seventh-day rest from work should be regarded as a creation ordinance as well. Labor and rest, work and Sabbath, go hand in hand; both are divine inventions of creation. If God wanted humans to work, He must have also wanted them to rest. As already stated above, the divine mandate for work implies the mandate for rest. This is why God's example of six days of work plus one day of rest serves humanity as a paradigm for the weekly work-rest cycle that differentiates between "time and holy time" and "the everyday and the solemn."[130]

Second, God gifted humans with marriage. He created them male and female (Gen 1:26–28) and intended them to have a monogamous marriage of equal partners (Gen 2:18–24). Sin certainly left its mark on marriage, which can be seen from the divine pronouncement concerning Eve in Genesis 3:16, however this statement is interpreted.[131] Yet, in principle this ordinance was not changed after the fall. Significant is that marriage and the seventh day of creation relate to each other. For one, the climax of the second pericope of the creation account (Gen 2:4–25) is clearly the divinely blessed intimacy between man and woman in sanctified relationship, while the climax of the first pericope (Gen 1:1–2:3) is the creation of sacred time in which God and humans, while resting from work, enjoy intimacy in sanctified time. If Genesis 2:24 is understood as a mandate, and most interpreters do, Genesis 2:2–3 should be as well. It is a mandate to take the opportunity, which God created for the Sabbath day, to foster

---

[129] This task was originally given to Adam (Gen 2:15), but of course includes Eve as well, just as the instructions stated immediately in the next two verses about eating the fruit from all the trees except from the tree of knowledge applied also to Eve (Gen 2:16–17). We can safely assume that Eve got knowledge of all divine instructions for the humans.

[130] Westermann, *Genesis 1–11*, 171: "The time which God created is structured; days of work have their goal in a day of rest. . . . The sanctification of the Sabbath institutes an order for humankind according to which time is divided into time and holy time, time for work and time for rest. . . . By sanctifying the seventh day God instituted a polarity between the everyday and the solemn, between days of work and days of rest, which was to be determinative for human existence. This is a gift of the creator to his people and is not merely an anticipation of the Israelite Sabbath."

[131] For major positions on the meaning of Genesis 3:16, see Richard M. Davidson, *Flame of Yahweh: Sexuality in the Old Testament* (Peabody, MA: Hendrickson, 2007), 60–65. See also the overview of translations and interpretations of Genesis 3:16 in recent times as well as in antiquity, the rabbis, and the church fathers by Joel N. Lohr, "Sexual Desire? Eve, Genesis 3:16, and תשוקה," *JBL* 130 (2011): 227–246. Cf. also Janson C. Condren, "Toward a Purge of the Battle of the Sexes and 'Return' for the Original Meaning of Genesis 3:16b," *JETS* 60 (2017): 227–245.

and maintain the divine-human relationship. Further, on the first Sabbath in world history the intimacy of the man and woman in Eden finds its full potential. The eve of the Sabbath was their wedding night, and "God who hallows that first Sabbath with his presence, at the same time hallows the marriage bed on the Sabbath as Adam and Eve share sexual intimacy with each other."[132] Thus, Sabbath and marriage are two creation ordinances to strengthen relationships. The relational paradigm of Genesis 2:24 confirms the relational dimension of the seventh day.

In sum, the creation ordinances of work and marriage are closely related to the seventh day, suggesting that the seventh day is a creation ordinance as well: "Just as the ordinances of work and marriage are permanent, so is the ordinance of the Sabbath."[133]

Was the Sabbath Kept by the Patriarchs?

Another question arises: If the seventh-day Sabbath rest had been instituted at creation, did the Hebrew Bible know of the Sabbath before Sinai?

The biblical evidence that the patriarchs kept the Sabbath is circumstantial at best.[134] After creation, the "seventh day" is not mentioned again until the people of Israel arrive in the wilderness of Sin in Exodus 16. This should not come as a surprise, since Sabbath observance apparently was not an issue in this time. We also need to note that the absence of the weekly Sabbath in the patriarchal narratives does not have any repercussions regarding its nature as a creation ordinance. As John Murray states,

> The silence of Genesis subsequent to Genesis 2:2, 3 proves nothing as to the desuetude of the institution during patriarchal times, nor does it prove ignorance of the ordinance on the part of the patriarchs. But even if we suppose that the remembrance of this institution did pass away and that the patriarchs did not

---

[132] Davidson, *Flame of Yahweh*, 53.

[133] Pipa, "The Christian Sabbath," 120.

[134] Jewish tradition has it that Adam (*Gen. Rab.* par. XVI, on Gen 2:15), Abraham (*b. Yoma* 28b: Abraham kept the seven laws of Noah, circumcision, and the written and the oral Torah; cf. *Gen. Rab.* par. LXIV on Gen 26:1) and Jacob (*Gen. Rab.* par. LXXIX, on Gen 33:18) kept the Sabbath, that Israel knew the Sabbath in Egypt (*Exod. Rab.* par. I, on Exod 2:11) and in the wilderness (*Mid. Tanh.* B sec. 24) before the Torah was given at Sinai. Cf. Sarit Kattan Gribetz, "Between Narrative and Polemic: The Sabbath in Genesis Rabbah and the Babylonian Talmud," in *Genesis Rabbah in Text and Context*, ed. S. G. Gribetz et al. (Tübingen: Mohr Siebeck, 2016), 33–61, esp. 59.

observe the weekly sabbath, it is no more difficult to explain this lapse from the creation ordinance than it is to explain the lapse from the principle of monogamy so clearly implied in Genesis 2:24. It is precarious to base too much on silence. But even if the silence indicates declension, ignorance, and non-observance, this does not remove the creation ordinance nor does it disestablish its binding obligation.[135]

Even if at first glance the Sabbath and Sabbath observance do not seem to be present between creation and manna, there are still a few texts, apart from Genesis 2:2–3, that could serve as evidence of a Sabbath before Sinai.

"Seven Days"

A weekly cycle with a possible seventh-day Sabbath as climax and boundary of the week might have been known, since there are some references to a period of seven days: the seven days mentioned in the flood story (Gen 7:4, 10; 8:10, 12), the wedding week (Gen 29:27–28), the distance of a seven-day journey (Gen 31:23), the length of a death ritual (Gen 50:10; cf. 50:3), a period of seven days between the first and the second plague (Exod 7:25), and the length of the first feast of unleavened bread (Exod 12:15, 19; 13:6–7). Of course these texts are not conclusive, but they are at least clues to the knowledge of a weekly cycle.

Genesis 26:5

Genesis 26:5 is a conspicuous text that deserves our attention. In retrospect of Abraham's life, the Lord encouraged Isaac and declared He would fulfill His oath and give to his descendants "all these lands" (Gen 26:3). He gave the reason: "because Abraham obeyed my voice and kept my charge, my commandments, my statutes, and my laws" (Gen 26:5). The various designations imply differentiation as well as comprehensiveness or totality of the precepts that Abraham received or had been passed on to him.[136]

---

[135] Murray, *Principles of Conduct*, 34–35.

[136] Samuel Greengus, "The Anachronism in Abraham's Observance of the Laws," *HUCA* 86 (2015): 18–19. For a similar listing of different terms for God's instructions see Leviticus 26:46; Deuteronomy 11:1; 1 Kings 2:3; 2 Kings 17:13, 34; Nehemiah 9:13; Psalm 19:8–10 [MT vs. 7–9]; and Psalm 119. A clustering of four law terms can only be found in Genesis 26:5; Deuteronomy 11:1; and Nehemiah 9:13.

How does Genesis 26:5 relate to Abraham's life?[137] The first part of God's declaration ("Abraham obeyed my voice") obviously refers back to Genesis 22:18 ("because you have obeyed my voice"). Genesis 22:18 and 26:5 are the first two instances in the OT where it is said that someone obeyed the voice of the Lord, and both statements are given as reasons for the promises of an abundant family, the gift of the land, and the blessing for the nations—in that order (Gen 22:17–18; 26:4–5). The second part of God's statement, with its four terms for laws, does not find any terminological reference point in Abraham's life.[138] Furthermore, the occasions on which the patriarch obeyed or worshipped God do not provide sufficient reason for why these terms are used.[139] Rather, Abraham exemplified by his

---

[137] See Andrew Hugh Bruno, "The Relationship between Genesis 26:5 and the Patriarchal Narrative of Abraham," *Churchman* 130 (2016): 241–264, who especially compares Genesis 26:5 to Genesis 22:18. John H. Sailhamer, "The Mosaic Law and the Theology of the Pentateuch," *WTJ* 53 (1991): 249–254, surveys the proposed solutions on how Abraham knew of the law, then discards all of them and rather suggests that Abraham's keeping the law in Genesis 26:5 means nothing else than Abraham was believing in God (Gen 15:6). Sailhamer's solution raises the question why Genesis 26:5 did not mention something similar to Genesis 15:6 and why the author needed to list four different law terms. Regardless of the disputable connection between faith and obedience, Genesis 26:5 is primarily about Abraham and the law(s).

[138] This series of unique words in the Abraham narrative prompts scholars who adhere to the historical-critical method to surmise a Deuteronomistic or post-Deuteronomistic background (Claus Westermann, *Genesis 12–36* [Minneapolis, MN: Augsburg, 1985], 424–425; and David M. Carr, *Reading the Fractures of Genesis: Historical and Literary Approaches* [Louisville, KY: John Knox, 1996], 157–159), or priestly background to Genesis 26:5 (Gordon Wenham, *Genesis 16–50*, WBC [Dallas, TX: Word, 1994], 190). For them, the laws referred to here were not yet notified in Abraham's time. H. Seebass, *Genesis II*, vol. 2: *Vätergeschichte II (23,1–36,43)* (Neukirchen-Vluyn: Neukirchener, 1999), 281, puts it this way: "The strangeness of the expressions appears to indicate that not Abraham becomes the paradigm for Torah loyalty, because there was no Torah yet, but contrariwise that (the vocabulary of) Torah loyalty is put into his life of following God."

[139] The Abraham cycle (Gen 11:27–25:11) records the following acts of obedience by Abraham in response to specific commands of the Lord: He departed as the Lord had spoken to him (Gen 12:4; cf. v. 1), moved his tent through the land (Gen 13:18; cf. v. 17), prepared the animals for the covenant offering (Gen 15:10; cf. v. 9), circumcised himself and every male of his household (Gen 17:23–27; cf. vs. 9–14), prayed to God on behalf of Abimelech (Gen 20:17; cf. the indirect command in v. 7), named his son Isaac and circumcised him on the eighth day (Gen 21:3; cf. 17:12, 19), sent Hagar and Ishmael away (Gen 21:14; cf. v. 12), and took Isaac to offer him to God (Gen 21:3–10; cf. v. 2). Furthermore, he served the Lord by building altars to Him, or planting a tamarisk tree (Gen 21:33), and calling on His name (Gen 12:7–8; 13:4, 18; 22:9, 14). One may add that he gave a tithe to "the priest of the most high God" (Gen 14:18). Except for circumcision and the tithe, these acts of obedience are very specific. They may rightfully be called "obligation," maybe even "commandments," but hardly "statutes and laws" (Gen 26:5); contra John H. Walton, *Genesis*, NIVAC (Grand Rapids, MI: Zondervan, 2001), 553.

life the response to God's law for Israel, because the law was in his heart[140] and presumably he knew its basic principles.[141]

The four legal terms in Genesis 26:5, each appearing here for the first time in the Hebrew Bible, are used in Exodus and subsequent books often—but not exclusively—to refer to God's revelation of the law at Sinai. Here is the list of their occurrences in the book of Exodus:

1. *mishmereth* ("obligation, charge") appears first in Genesis 26:5, then in Exodus 12:6; 16:23, 32–34; etc.
2. *mitswah* ("command") appears first in Genesis 26:5, then in Exodus 15:26; 16:28; 20:6; 24:12 etc.
3. *khuqqah* ("statutes") appears first in Genesis 26:5, then in Exodus 12:14, 17, 43; 13:10; 27:21; 28:43; 29:9 etc.
4. *torah* ("law, instruction") appears first in Genesis 26:5, then in Exodus 12:49; 13:9; 16:4, 28; 18:16, 20; 24:12 etc.

It is conspicuous that in several places the Sabbath is connected to one of these words. In the manna narrative, God wants to test the people, to see "whether they will walk in My law [*torah* pl.] or not" (Exod 16:4). The test is connected to the seventh day. God wants to observe if the Israelites would put aside the second portion of the sixth day "for safekeeping" (*mishmereth*) until the next morning so that they could observe Sabbath,

---

[140] Victor P. Hamilton, *The Book of Genesis: Chapters 18–50*, NICOT (Grand Rapids, MI: Eerdmans, 1995), 194. Sailhamer, *The Pentateuch as Narrative*, 187, suggests that "Abraham acted in accordance with the Law, particularly Deuteronomy, yet the writer has never assumed that Abraham actually had a knowledge of the law itself," and gives as an example Abraham's course of action in war in Genesis 14, which "followed quite closely the stipulations of Deuteronomy 20."

[141] Even before the various laws of God were put into writing on Mount Sinai and thus the written law entered into history, God must have made known to the forefathers and patriarchs His will (orally), which they passed on (orally or in writing) to the next generation. See, for example, God's order to perform the circumcision as a covenant sign (Gen 17:10–14). So there was a handing down of some divine instructions from one generation to the next, most likely not as extensive as the later written law; there was an oral tradition of the laws of God. See Greengus, "The Anachronism in Abraham's Observance," 28–35, who argues "that God was a universal law-giver; that such laws already appear in the covenant with Noah; and that Abraham is implied to have known and followed these universal laws in pre-Mosaic times" (cf. Sailhamer, "The Mosaic Law," 251). According to Jewish tradition, the plural "laws" in Genesis 26:5 suggests that Abraham observed both the oral and the written Torah before God revealed the written Torah to Moses; see R. W. L. Moberly, "The Earliest Commentary on the Akedah," *VT* 38 (1988): 55. In allusion to Genesis 26:5, the *Book of Jubilees* 21:5 mentions that Abraham, in his final blessing, urges his children to keep "God's commandments, ordinances, and judgements" which he learned from "the books of my forefathers and in the words of Enoch and in the words of Noah" (*Jubilees* 21:10–11) (see Greengus, "The Anachronism in Abraham's Observance," 28).

"a holy Sabbath to the Lord" (Exod 16:23). When some Israelites fail and nevertheless want to gather manna on the seventh day, the Lord complains, "How long do you refuse to keep my commandments [*mitswah*, pl.] and my laws [*torah*, pl.]?" (Exod 16:28), using two words of Genesis 26:5 in the exact same forms (which in the OT occurs only in Genesis 26:5 and Exodus 16:28). This terminological link is striking. The least one can say is that the seventh-day Sabbath belongs to God's commandments and laws, which Abraham kept. It would not be unfounded to suggest that Abraham might indeed have kept the seventh-day Sabbath.

In reference to the Ten Commandments, which include the Sabbath commandment, God uses the words *torah* and *mitswah* again: "I will give you tablets of stone, and the law [*torah*] and commandment [*mitswah*] which I have written, that you may teach them" (Exod 24:12). Within the Decalogue the reference to "my commands" (*mitswah*, pl., Exod 20:6) must refer primarily to the Ten Commandments, including the one on the Sabbath. Since the Sabbath commandment is the only law of the ten that explicitly points to a time before Abraham—namely to creation (Exod 20:11)—it seems likely to be one of the laws Abraham might have observed.

Exodus 5:5

When Moses and Aaron came to lead Israel out of Egypt, their people suffered under the abuse of the pharaoh's exploitation of labor. Exodus 5 provides insight into Egypt's system of slavery: heavy, exhausting work with demands to fulfill an unreasonable daily quota (Exod 5:8, 13, 18). It is easily conceivable how such a "'no Sabbath' environment"[142] caused the Israelites to neglect the commandment to keep a day of rest. Judging from Pharaoh's rhetoric, the workload was harsh and intolerable, and the draconian decree ensured that the Israelites would not get any rest. It is the issue of rest that Moses and Aaron obviously raised.

In indignation, the royal despot reproaches the troublemakers, "You allow them to rest [Hiphil of the verb *shbt*: 'causing them to cease'] from their forced labors" (Exod 5:5).[143] The verbal root *shbt* evokes the Sabbath,

---

[142] Walter Brueggemann, *Sabbath as Resistance: Saying No to the Culture of Now* (Louisville, KY: John Knox, 2014), 5. For Brueggemann, Exodus 5 reports Pharaoh's relentless rhetoric as manager of an inexhaustible production schedule (ibid., 2–6) so that "in this system there can be no Sabbath rest" (ibid., 4). See also idem, "Sabbath as Alternative," *WW* 36 (2016): 252–253, 255–256.

[143] Translation according to *HALOT* 4:1408. *DCH* 8:258 translates as "You cause to desist/make rest/give rest from arduous labor."

and the idea of ceasing from work is elsewhere linked with Sabbath rest (Gen 2:2–3; Exod 16:30; 23:12).[144] "The author implies that pharaoh wants to prevent the Israelites from resting on the Sabbath."[145] In fact, in the Hebrew Bible the grammatical construction of the verb *shbt* with the preposition "from" (*min*) followed by a word for work occurs only in Genesis 2:2–3 and Exodus 5:5,[146] thus creating a unique link between Moses' and Aaron's undertaking to cause the Israelites to rest from their work and God's example of resting from all His work.[147]

A further terminological link of Exodus 5 to the Sabbath is the use of the noun "work" (*ma'aseh*), which in close connection with the verb "rest" (*shavath*) occurs only in Exodus 5:4, 13 and in Exodus 23:12, which commands believers to "rest" (*shavath*) on the Sabbath after six days of "work" (*ma'aseh*).[148] Interestingly, Exodus 23:12 is unique in that it is the only Sabbath text that uses *ma'aseh* instead of the regular *mela'khah* for the six weekdays of "work." This might be regarded as an intentional adaption referring back to the forced labor of the Israelites in Egypt mentioned in Exodus 5.

Exodus 16:28

Exodus 16 records the first occurrence in the OT of both the nouns *shabbath* ("Sabbath," v. 25) and *shabbathon* ("Sabbath feast," v. 23). However,

---

[144] Waldemar Janzen, *Exodus*, Believers Church Bible Commentary (Waterloo: Herald, 1989), 398; William C. Propp, *Exodus 1–18*, AB (New York: Doubleday, 1999), 254; and especially the comprehensive studies by Gershon Hepner, *Legal Friction: Law, Narrative, and Identity Politics in Biblical Israel* (New York: Lang, 2010), 671–685; and Mathilde Frey, "Sabbath in Egypt? An Examination of Exodus 5," *JSOT* 39 (2015): 249–263. Usually, commentators note the connection between Exodus 5:5 and the Sabbath rest that is later explicitly commanded by God in Exodus 16 and 20. See, for example, Dohmen, *Exodus 1–18*, 199.

[145] Hepner, *Legal Friction*, 672.

[146] In extra-biblical Hebrew, such a construction is also found in two Qumran texts in 4Q216 [Jubilees=4QJubᵃ] 2:17 ("And He gave us a great sign, the Sabbath day, that we should work six days, but *keep Sabbath* [Qal stem of *shbt*] on the seventh day *from all work*"), which is a reference to Exodus 31:13–15, and in 4Q422 [4QParaphrase of Genesis and Exodus] 1:7 ("And He rested [Qal stem of *shbt*] on the seventh day *from all His work* which He had been doing"), which is a reference to Genesis 2:2–3. In both texts, an early biblical interpreter uses the verb *shbt* with the preposition "from" (*min*) followed by the word for "work" to refer to a Sabbath text.

[147] See Frey, "Sabbath in Egypt?" 257, 260. To express the idea of merely ceasing or stopping work, without a reference to the Sabbath, the construction *shbt* with a word for work as a direct object (without the preposition *min*) is used (2 Chr 16:5; Neh 4:5 [ET v. 11]; 6:3; and also in *Sirach* 38:8).

[148] Frey, "Sabbath in Egypt?" 260–261.

in this chapter there is also a hint of previous knowledge of the Sabbath.[149] First, God uses His instruction concerning the seventh day—that is, the prohibition of going out to gather manna because none will fall—as a test of loyalty to His law (Exod 16:4). The Sabbath is seen here as part of God's law, but it is not clear from this text whether it was known before or given at this very moment. The second and more explicit indication is that when some Israelites failed to keep the Sabbath and went out anyway to find manna, God reprimanded them with the words, "How long do you refuse to keep My commandments and My laws? (Exod 16:28, NKJV). The question "How long?" (*'adh-'anah*) occurs twelve times in the Hebrew Bible and always asks about the end of a prolonged negative activity or attitude.[150] In Exodus 16:28, it implies that the Israelites had a history of antagonistic behavior toward God's commandments and laws.[151] The Sabbath instruction clearly belongs to these. Inasmuch as there are no instances reported in which the Israelites did not keep the divine law—neither their grumbling at Pi Hahiroth (Exod 14:9–12) nor at Marah (Exod 15:24) qualifies as refusal to keep God's instructions—one has to suppose that God's question refers to their behavior during their servitude in Egypt, when under the pressure of a ruthless pharaoh they bent their principles and did not keep the day of rest until Moses and Aaron tried to reinstitute it (Exod 5:4–5). God's command given in the wilderness of Sin (thirty days after the exodus from Egypt and twenty days before Sinai), not to go out on Sabbath but to rest on this day, is obviously given to let the Israelites relearn what a day of rest means. It is also the first explicit commandment given to them after their exodus.

---

[149] Brevard S. Childs, *The Book of Exodus*, OTL (Philadelphia, PA: Westminster, 1974), 290: "The existence of the Sabbath is assumed for the writer"; contra Dressler, "The Sabbath in the Old Testament," 24, who argues that the first occurrences of the term Sabbath in Exodus 16:22–30 "allows the view that the institution of the Sabbath was unknown to the people of Israel at this time."

[150] The question *'adh-'anah* ("how long?") is directed to God (Ps 13:2 [2x], 3 [2x]; Jer 47:6; Hab 1:2) or to human (Exod 16:28; Num 14:11; Josh 18:3; Ps 62:4; Job 18:2; 19:2). Compare the similar questions *'adh-matay* ("how long?") (Exod 10:3, 7; Num 14:27; 1 Sam 1:14; 16:1; 2 Sam 2:26; 1 Kgs 18:21; Neh 2:6; Ps 6:4; 74:10; 80:5; 82:2; 90:13; 94:3 [2x]; Prov 1:22; 6:9; Isa 6:11; Jer 4:14, 21; 12:4; 23:26; 31:22; 47:5; Dan 8:13; 12:6; Hos 8:5; Hab 2:6; Zech 1:12) and *'adh-mah* ("how long?") (Num 24:22; Ps 4:3; 74:9; 79:5; 89:47). Both *'adh-matay* and *'adh-mah* have a similar function to *'adh-'anah* in that they ask for the termination of an untenable situation.

[151] The Israelite behavior towards God's instruction is also the theme in Exodus 15:26, which refers to divine commandments (*mitswoth*) and statutes (*khuqqim*) after another statute (*khoq*) and regulation (*mishpath*) has been established (Exod 15:25). What these commandments comprise, however, is not said.

Conclusion

The perennial question of the origin of the Sabbath has two focal points: the search for a possible extra-biblical origin, and the sifting of biblical references and indicators of the Sabbath. The results of the quest for the origin of the Sabbath in extra-biblical cultures are varied, but in the end unconvincing, since the conclusions proposed are all based on literary-critical and historical-critical hypotheses on how cultures and literature developed. Actual evidence is meager or inconclusive, and arguments are often conjectural.

A text-oriented, canon-based approach toward biblical passages finds the origin of the Sabbath either at creation (Gen 2:1–3), which would give the Sabbath perpetual validity for all humanity, or after the exodus from Egypt (Exod 16:23–29), which would restrict the Sabbath to Israel and to the time of God's covenant with them.

The main arguments for an origin at creation are as follows: (1) The "seventh day" is demonstrably the Sabbath day; (2) God's blessing and sanctifying of the seventh day includes a beneficial purpose for humans; (3) God's ceasing of work after six days and resting on the seventh day is an exemplary pattern for humans who are created in His image; (4) the mandate to work (Gen 1:28; 2:15) implies the mandate to rest on the seventh day; (5) the ordinance of marriage with its focus on partnership (Gen 2:24) completes the ordinance of the seventh-day Sabbath with its focus on divine-human relationship; (6) Jesus pinpoints the making of the Sabbath at creation (Mark 2:27); (7) there are hints that the weekly cycle and the Sabbath were known in the time between creation and Sinai (Gen 26:5; Exod 5:4–5; 16:28). The Sabbath fits perfectly the storyline of Genesis and Exodus: Abraham and the Israelites were aware of the Sabbath, which came under attack during the oppression of Egypt's exploitative labor practices. God needed to reinstitute Sabbath rest for Israel first in Egypt, then again in the manna experience, before anchoring it perpetually in the center of the Ten Commandments given at Sinai. Thus, although a Sabbath command is not mentioned in the creation account, the text implies it powerfully.

In conclusion, the genesis of the Sabbath is rooted in Genesis 2:1–3. The Sabbath has a perpetual function far beyond Israel and the covenant with Israel. The Sabbath is not a divine invention for Israel and, in view of the biblical evidence, should not be simply considered as a Hebrew or Jewish festival. Rather, because its origin lies in creation, the universality of creation justifies the universality of the Sabbath for all humanity. Particularly through God's activities on the seventh day, the Sabbath has been awarded divine authority.[152]

---

[152] See Hasel, "The Origin of the Biblical Sabbath," 19–20, for seven implications of the question of whether the Sabbath is a divine or human invention.

CHAPTER 8

THE SABBATH AT CREATION: CHARACTER AND THEOLOGY

Lael O. Caesar

Introduction

As the topic suggests, the biblical doctrines of Sabbath and creation are inextricably linked. Clarification of one is commentary on the other. Conversely, confusion about either likely signifies confusion about both. But given the number and wide variation of references to "Sabbath" in the Hebrew Bible,[1] it may be appropriate to ask which Sabbath is being here considered. It also helps to note that the creation referred to here is the one involving a week of days, which we know yields a different understanding of Sabbath than the one in which the Genesis creation story represents many millennia during which life forms developed on earth.

By way of example, Kenneth Hein defends the Roman Catholic understanding of the Sabbath, *inter alia*, on the basis of the Roman Catholic doctrine that "the spiritual soul of each human being is created directly by God." The body/soul dualism is how the church's creation doctrine remains intact in the face of the success of neo-Darwinian evolutionary theory.[2] Hein's defense is a response to Jacques B. Doukhan's

---

[1] Translations marked with an asterisk [*] are the author's; beyond this, and except as otherwise indicated, Scripture quotations are from the NASB. Gerhard F. Hasel, "Sabbath," *ABD* 5:849–856, mentions that the Hebrew noun *shabbath* ("sabbath") occurs 111 times in the OT. However, a quick review of seven different English versions reveals wide variation in translation of terms into the English word "Sabbath"—from a low of 75 times in 59 verses (JPS), through 135 times in 116 verses (NET), 137 times in 116 verses (KJV), 138 times in 116 verses (NASB), 138 times in 117 verses (ESV), 151 times in 137 verses (NLT), to 157 times in 134 verses (NRSV).

[2] Kenneth Hein, "A Catholic Response to J. B. Doukhan," in *The Sabbath in Jewish and Christian*

exposition on "Loving the Sabbath as a Christian," which includes the statement that "the idea of creation is in Seventh-day Adventist theology incompatible with evolution."[3] One understanding of the biblical Sabbath sees the rule of tooth and claw as a tragedy subsequent to and disruptive of God's perfect creation, while another sees nature's rule of kill or be killed as essential to the process of creation's establishment. Philosophical readings of the Genesis creation account that understand it as one more idiosyncratic reflection of ANE worldviews also tend to produce their own distinct Sabbath theologies.[4] In a not dissimilar vein, John Walton's exhaustive familiarity with ancient Near East thought[5] has shown him that their functional orientations on creation are in clashing, cognitive contrast with the material orientation of today's traditional Bible readers. He concludes that for Israel and the rest of the ANE world, "creation was an activity of bringing functionality to a nonfunctional condition rather than bringing material substance to a situation in which matter was absent."[6]

Whatever the variety of its readings, Genesis 1:1–2:3 is still recognized "as a discrete literary composition with its own structure, style, and dynamic. It is a pericope that can be excised from its present context without damage to its internal coherence and integrity."[7] This chapter will not excise the story from context, but will consider particularly its last three verses (Gen 2:1–3) in relation to such issues as the functional versus material dichotomy, the days as we know them versus the multiplied millennia controversy, and the overall theology of the institution of the Sabbath as taught through the creation report.

Traditions, ed. Tamara C. Eskenazi, Daniel J. Harrington, and William H. Shea (New York: Crossroad, 1991), 169–175.

[3] Jacques B. Doukhan, "Loving the Sabbath as a Christian: A Seventh-day Adventist Perspective," in *The Sabbath in Jewish and Christian Traditions*, ed. Tamara C. Eskenazi, Daniel J. Harrington, and William H. Shea (New York: Crossroad, 1991), 149–168. Hein's response also cites the historical-critical method as a basis for his differences with Doukhan's Seventh-day Adventist doctrinal formulations on Sabbath keeping.

[4] See, e.g., Bernhard W. Anderson, ed., *Creation in the Old Testament* (Philadelphia, PA: Fortress, 1984).

[5] See John Walton, *Ancient Near Eastern Thought and the Old Testament* (Grand Rapids, MI: Baker, 2006).

[6] John Walton, *The Lost World of Genesis One* (Downers Grove, IL: InterVarsity, 2009), 53.

[7] Bernhard W. Anderson, "Introduction: Mythopoeic and Theological Dimensions of Biblical Creation Faith," in *Creation in the Old Testament*, ed. Bernhard W. Anderson (Philadelphia, PA: Fortress, 1984), 14–15.

Is There a Sabbath Here?

Although the Bible's only creation account concludes its first section (Gen 1:1–2:3) without mentioning the noun "Sabbath,"[8] Samuele Bacchiocchi points to the last three verses (Gen 2:1-3) as a place where "the Sabbath is explicitly related to creation."[9] For him, the Bible's three other explicit references to seventh-day Sabbath rest (Exod 20:11; 31:17; Heb 4:4) are all dependent on Genesis 2:1–3.

For Harold H. P. Dressler, any reference to the Sabbath in Genesis 2:1–3 remains doubtful: "Unless the reader equates 'the seventh day' and 'Sabbath,' there is no reference to the Sabbath here."[10] Genesis 2:1-3 speaks of the seventh day and uses the verb translated "rest" (*shavath*), but there is no substantive, "Sabbath" (*shabbath*) in the passage.

Dressler's emphasis on the absence of the noun is part of his dismissal of the Sabbath as universal creation ordinance. He sees the Sabbath as but one element of God's covenant with His people Israel: "The biblical view is unequivocal: the Sabbath originated in Israel as God's special institution for His people."[11] The quotation is drawn from an article in which Robert Johnston elaborates on idiosyncratic claims for a Jewish Sabbath as found in Exodus Rabbah 25:11. Dressler's negations contrast with Laurence A. Turner's schematic recognition of the essential significance and intentional location of the seventh day in relation to creation week. Turner's diagram shows how days 1, 2, and 3 have their balancing counterparts in days four through six, while day 7 is counterpoint to all that goes before:

---

[8] See Harold H. P. Dressler, "The Sabbath in the Old Testament," in *From Sabbath to Lord's Day*, ed. D. A. Carson (Grand Rapids, MI: Zondervan, 1982), 21–41, esp. 28.

[9] Samuele Bacchiocchi, *Divine Rest for Human Restlessness* (Rome: The Pontifical Gregorian University Press, 1980), 61.

[10] Dressler, "The Sabbath in the Old Testament," 28.

[11] Ibid., 23. In support of this view Dressler (ibid., 36 n. 16) cites Robert M. Johnston, "Patriarchs, Rabbis, and Sabbath," *AUSS* 12 (1974): 95: "The Sabbath was Israel's own bride and belonged to no other. Ex. 16:29 was interpreted in an exclusive sense: The Lord hath given *you*—Israel—the Sabbath, but hath not given it to the heathen. This then, was the prevailing conception ... of what had become normative Rabbinic Judaism." However, this quotation acknowledges precisely what Johnston is establishing—that this position was not biblical; rather, it was part of the aggregate of traditions that became "normative Rabbinic Judaism."

Day 1: Day Night	Day 4: Sun Moon/Stars
Day 2: Sea Sky	Day 5: Fish Birds
Day 3: Land Vegetation	Day 6: Animals Humans

Day 7: Rest and Sanctification[12]

A reading of the creation story that dismisses or fails to properly appreciate the seventh day converts human beings into its narrative climax. But the full seven-day report is a narrative on God's commitment to restful, spiritual relationship with humanity and all His creation. He accomplishes this by the acts of the seventh day. Seventh-day Sabbath rest, communion, and intimacy easily transcend in value and significance the alternate proposal whose sixth-day climax is the birth of humans.[13] According to Genesis 2:1–3, God distinguishes the seventh day from the rest by not working on that day,[14] the day that eight OT verses explicitly identify as Sabbath (*shabbath*, noun—Sabbath).[15] Two other verses ordain seventh-day rest as God's intention for His people (Exod 23:12; 34:21). The OT linkage of "seventh day," "rest," and "Sabbath" is hardly in dispute. And whereas the present study seeks a basic understanding of biblical material that may illuminate the issue of the Sabbath in relation to creation, Genesis 2:1–3—the first passage to link "rest" (*shavath*) and "seventh day"—seems a reasonable point of departure.

Seven-Day Continuities

Niels-Erik Andreasen speaks of the creation report as involving a "six-seven day scheme."[16] Multiple elements in the passage under review (Gen 2:1–3) confirm the integrity of this scheme. This chapter focuses on three such elements:

---

[12] For diagram, see Laurence Turner, "A Theological Reading of Genesis 1," in *In the Beginning: Science and Scripture Confirm Creation*, ed. Bryan W. Ball (Nampa, ID: Pacific Press, 2012), 67.

[13] Ibid.

[14] Cf. Exodus 20:11; 31:17.

[15] The verses are Exodus 16:26, 29; 20:10–11; 31:15; 35:2; Leviticus 23:3; Deuteronomy 5:14.

[16] Niels Erik A. Andreasen, *The Old Testament Sabbath: A Tradition-Historical Investigation* (Missoula, MT: Society of Biblical Literature, 1972), 65: "six-seven day."

1. Six-seven day continuities that demonstrate the integrity of the seven-day scheme
2. Six-day continuities important to the six-day aspect of the six-seven day scheme but absent from the seventh-day report
3. Four seventh-day distinctive traits that mark the uniqueness of the seventh day within the six-seven day scheme

Six elements sequentially link the material in Genesis 2:1–3 to that of Genesis 1:1–31, and emphasize that the latter is the logical context of the former. The six are as follows:

1. A presumption of earlier information: The seventh-day report (Gen 2:1–3) does not commence as if introducing a new phenomenon. Rather, the initial words presume familiarity with a report of earlier activity. The passage announces the completion of that earlier effort: "The heavens and earth and all their host were now completed" (Gen 2:1).*
2. Seventh after 1 to 6: Events in this passage are part of something larger involving an ordinal sequence of days; the day of this passage's events is thrice identified as the seventh in that series of days (Gen 2:2–3).
3. God (*'elohim*) as agent of action: According to Gen 2:2–3, the creating intelligence who is present on the seventh day of the sequence is the same as conducted the creative work of the earlier days in the sequence: on the seventh day God (*'elohim*) does not work as He had before (Gen 2:2);[17] God (*'elohim*) blesses the seventh day because it is the day on which He (*'elohim*—third iteration) rests from His creative work (Gen 2:3).
4. Genesis 2:1 as culminative of creation acts ("Thus the heavens and the earth were completed, and all their hosts"): This announcement, immediately following the sixth day's termination statement (Gen 1:31), both acknowledges the summary word of the previous verse and suggests that the creation account does not end with Genesis 1:31. Confirmation of this suggestion in the following verse supports a strongly temporal adverbial rendering of the clause introduced by the ubiquitous and flexible *waw* conjunction: "Thus, by the seventh day, . . ." (Gen 2:2).*[18]

---

[17] Samaritan, LXX, and Syriac all read "sixth day," to escape the implication of "on the seventh day God ended His work," that God was still working on the seventh.

[18] The first verse would read, "The heavens and earth and all their host were now completed."

5. Genesis 2:2 as culminative of the Creator's work: The culminative character of verse 1 does not make verse 2 redundant. Verse 1 marks the end of the first segment of a bipartite account.[19] Verse 2 increases our information while introducing a personal aspect that complements the impersonal neutrality of verse 1. By repeating the verb "complete" (*kalah*) and adding the subject "God" (*'elohim*), it makes clear that the events mentioned in the previous verse were the result of divine design and link not only to the work in general but to the introductory superscript in particular. The God who created everything is the Creator of earth's first week: "God completed the work." The announcement features a double affirmation and confirmation: "By the seventh day, God had completed His work which He had done" (Gen 2:2a);* "and He rested on the seventh day from all His work which He had done" (Gen 2:2b). The first announcement ("The heavens and earth and all their host were now completed," Gen 2:1*) may be read as part and parcel of the ongoing account of creation week. But in Genesis 2:2a the verb of completion is reused, transformed into the active voice. Now the text names God as the subject of the verbal action, acknowledged as the unique personal agent of the entire account. We may enumerate as follows:

   a. the six days' work is first affirmed as excellent (*tov me'odh*, Gen 1:31);
   b. the sixth-day termination formula follows ("evening and morning, a sixth day," Gen 1:31);
   c. next comes the statement on culmination of creation acts ("The heavens and earth and all their host were now completed," Gen 2:1); and finally,
   d. a double confirmation on the seventh day as the signal of creation's completion. This is because the seventh day climaxes the full six-seven day scheme ("by the seventh day, God had brought to a close the work He had been doing," Gen 2:2*).

The second, taken in the temporal adverbial sense, would read, "Thus, by the seventh day God had finished his work of creation"* or NLT's "On the seventh day God had finished his work of creation"; or "By the seventh day God had brought to a close the work he had been doing."*

[19] The "six-seven day scheme" of Andreasen, *The Old Testament Sabbath*, 65, reflects this bipartite reality. The creation story includes a six-day, as well as a seven-day narrative, with the six, the one, and the seven all essential to the integrity of the narrative. Thus, from a "literary point of view," the creation narrative is "a unity" (ibid.). And because it is a report on the seventh day, its literary integrity points toward validation of both the narrative on the earlier six days, as well as the entire pericope on the week (Gen 1:1–2:3).

6. Genesis 2:3 as a rational, climactic ordinance: The final verse of the seventh-day report is also the final verse of the creation pericope of Genesis 1:1–2:3, and does more than forcefully reiterate that God has honored the seventh day. The verse also explains why and how the blessing comes to be placed on that particular day. God bestows His blessing on that day because it constitutes a unique feature of the week's process—the feature of rest. God rests from all His work on that day. The seventh day—while clearly similar to the first through sixth days as part of the first week of earth's history, and as part of the creation story—is clearly different, unique in its character as part of the creation week. The report on its establishment differs in the presence of elements not hitherto apparent in the narrative of the creation week. To these we shall later turn. Here we have first sought to show how integral it is to the creation week account.

Six-Day Continuities

Though the seventh day is an unmistakable part of the seven-day week, it is also unique. Within the six-seven day scheme a number of elements highlight the difference between the seventh day and the rest of the week by their absence from the Sabbath report contrasted with their prominence in the narrative on days 1–6. Following their enumeration, we reflect on what their presence/absence may imply for continuity, discontinuity, uniqueness and integration in relation to the seven-day week, and to our study on the Sabbath at creation.

Six-Day Continuities: The Overall Account

1. First to be noted should probably be the account's divine speech introduction, "And God said" (*wayyo'mer 'elohim*). The first six days include ten of these, as well as one infinitive construct "saying" (*le'mor*). But there is no divine speech introduction for the seventh day. Its absence obtrudes all the more because of its presence on all other days, and its quadruple repetition on the sixth, the day preceding the seventh.
2. As the divine speech introduction (*wayyo'mer 'elohim*) is absent from day seven, so also is the content of any such speech. Day seven displays none of the jussive, imperative, or cohortative articulations that pervade the week. Nor are there any simple perfects or imperfects, for that matter. The seventh day of the week reports no "God said X."

3. A third notable omission from the Sabbath narrative is the confirmatory "and it was so" (*wayehi khen*), which, in two forms, is found seven times through the first six days of creation week.
4. No statement of bringing into being appears in the seventh-day narrative. By contrast, words of reification and naming are consistently present through the rest of the week, as, for example, when God identifies light as day (*yom*, Gen 1:5) after dividing light from darkness. Thirteen verbs of such agency proliferate through the text with God as subject, whether as Creator, Divider, Maker, Namer (Gen 1:1–8), or otherwise.
5. The six-day account features seven repetitions of a note of divine affirmation on the goodness of the created work: "and God saw that it was good" (e.g., Gen 1:4, 10, 12, 18, 21, 25, 31). No equivalent affirmation occurs on the seventh day.
6. Finally, a climactic ordinal and chronological determinative marks off every day but one of that original week: "and there was evening and there was morning, day $\underline{X}$." Every day of creation week but one, the seventh, is marked by this definitive, concluding announcement.

Because, for Dale Ratzlaff, the literary pattern of the creation account exposes a "precise and well-thought-out construction," this sixth omission could hardly have been accidental.[20] Remarkably, he gives no attention to the multitude of other departures from the formulae of days 1–6 that are observable in the seventh day's report. Broader attention to the variations between Genesis 1:1–31 and 2:1–3, whether by omission or insertion, permits us to savor the complex relationships of distinctiveness and continuity, separateness and harmony, otherness and unity that characterize the bipartite narrative, within its septenary structure, on the first week of earth's history.

Six-Day Continuities: Tripartite Sequences

The six omissions from day seven all contribute to the clear and logical progression of God's creative miracle during days 1–6 of creation week. The six may be further recognized as a pair of integrally related threefold sequences. In the first of these tripartite sequences, the divine speech

---

[20] Dale Ratzlaff, *Sabbath in Crisis* (Applegate, CA: Life Assurance Ministries, 1990), 20. Gerhard von Rad, *Genesis*, OTL, rev. ed. (Philadelphia, PA: Westminster, 1972), 63, notes that "the concluding formula ('and it was evening and it was morning...') is lacking, and that too, like everything else in this chapter, is intentional." In his own chapter on "The Seventh Day in Genesis," Ratzlaff includes seven references to the fact that the word 'Sabbath' is missing from Genesis 2:1–3 (ibid., 17–26).

introduction ("God said") is followed by speech content ("Let . . ."), and fulfillment confirmation ("and so it was"). In the second, God named (divine reification), God was pleased (rational approval), and the day ended (temporal closure). We may also highlight the internal consistency and logical equivalence of triplets A and B by viewing them in juxtaposition:

Triplet A	Triplet B
1. God said	God named (reification)
2. Let . . .	God was satisfied (rational approval)
3. It was so	End of the day (temporal closure)

Statements of rational approval in line 2 of triplet B [B2] equate in function to reports of direct speech in A2. In both instances, second lines serve to validate actions God reportedly performs in line 1. Triplet A is concerned with God speaking (Gen 1:3, 6, 9, 11, 14, 20, 24, 26). In triplet B, He is involved with dividing (day 1, Gen 1:4), naming (day 3, Gen 1:10), putting (day 4, Gen 1:17–18), creating (day 5, Gen 1:21), or making (day 6, Gen 1:25). In both triplets A and B, line 2 affirms or validates line 1: God's Word goes forth when and as He wills. Note though, that the concreteness of most verbs in B should not be allowed to distort the report's literary and theological balance.[21] The satisfaction expressed in B2 does not exceed the fulfillment represented in line A2 when the very words of God confirm and validate the simple divine speech introduction "And God said."

Psalm 33 emphasizes the great significance of triplet A, line 2: "By the word of the Lord the heavens were made," the psalmist states, "and by the breath of his mouth all their host. For he spoke and it was done; he commanded, and it stood fast" (Ps 33:6, 9).

Walton's detailed response to this traditional view of God thus bringing things into existence by His Word is that the text is simply not addressing material creation. Instead, Walton resolves to read the text within the "cognitive environment" of its time.[22] The three sources which alone

---

[21] Robert Davidson, *Genesis 1–11*, Cambridge Bible Commentary (Cambridge: Cambridge University Press, 1973), 19, speaks of "a certain roughness" and von Rad, *Genesis*, 53–54, speaks of the "decisive terminological unevenness" that attempts to blend God's "speaking" with God's "making." The reality our text conveys is that of Scripture's masterful control of paradox, from the very beginning, on the otherness of God and the validation of material creation, on His incomprehensible inaccessibility and transcendence matched to the immanence of one who, notwithstanding the grandeur of His holiness, is never far from every one of us (Acts 17:27).

[22] John Walton, *Genesis 1 as Ancient Cosmology* (Winona Lake, IN: Eisenbrauns, 2011), 6.

may now grant us access to this ancient environment are surviving texts, archaeological artifacts, and available iconography from those times.[23] Walton accepts that "all literature is dependent on the culture from which it emerges."[24] Also, that "the more we discover from the ancient world . . . , the more the distinctives of ancient Israel diminish—or, perhaps better, change categories."[25] He warns against a whole spectrum of beliefs about the text: from one extreme that sees it as "entirely distinctive,"[26] "the very words of God,"[27] to another that takes it as "human, northwest Semitic texts"[28] with "nothing distinctive to offer."[29] Walton's goal is to find "commonalities that resulted from a shared cultural environment," while also understanding "the nature of the Israelite 'stamp' that shaped its own cosmology."[30] He concludes that the Genesis creation story "is not an account of material origins but an account of functional origins, specifically focusing on the functioning of the cosmos as God's temple."[31]

Walton's faithfulness to his theory may be illustrated by his discussion of the meaning of "create" (*bara'*). He comments that "even when the object [of *bara'*] is something more tangible (sea creatures in Gen 1:21), the point is not necessarily physical manufacturing as much as assigning roles."[32] Concerning Genesis 1, he comments that the creation of the great sea monsters is the first use of *bara'* since verse 1, "perhaps emphasizing that *tannin* is not some primeval chaos monster that must be overcome, but a creature being given its role. . . . Yet it ought to be viewed as a cosmic creature rather than a marine specimen."[33]

---

[23] Walton, Genesis 1, 6.

[24] Ibid., 12.

[25] Ibid., 15. According to Walton, *Ancient Near Eastern Thought*, 293, Pentateuchal law was "essentially a self-revelation of Deity," while ANE law was "essentially a self-glorification of the king."

[26] Walton, *Genesis 1*, 15.

[27] Ibid., 14.

[28] Ibid.

[29] Ibid.

[30] Ibid., 16.

[31] Walton, *Lost World*, 93.

[32] Walton, *Ancient Near Eastern Thought*, 183.

[33] John Walton, "Genesis," in Zondervan Illustrated Bible Backgrounds Commentary, vol. 1, ed. John Walton (Grand Rapids, MI: Zondervan, 2009), 20.

Walton's language betrays uncertainty about his position on *bara'*. His "not necessarily" and "perhaps emphasizing" are at least appropriate. His earnest effort to render the product of *bara'* as functional and not material in Genesis 1 includes the claim that "grammatical objects of the verb are not easily identified as material items, and even when they are, it is questionable that the context permits objectifying them."[34] This seems to say that some objects of *bara'* are identifiable, though it may involve some difficulty. But an examination of the biblical data he has compiled hardly bears out this claim. His list of almost fifty objects of *bara'* begins with Genesis elements—"the heavens and the earth" (Gen 1:1; 2:4), "the great sea monsters" (Gen 1:21), man and woman (Gen 1:27), humanity (Gen 5:1-2)—and continues with "unprecedented wonders" (Exod 34:10), a generation to come/people not yet born (Ps 102:18), people (created by God's "Spirit" [*ruakh*]—Ps 104:30), cloud by day and fire by night (Isa 4:5), stars (Isa 40:26), and rivers/springs and flora (Isa 41:18-20).

Walton's difficulty in objectifying streams and flora in the desert may be consistent with the denial that God created vegetation on the third day of creation week. But this faithfulness to his theory is no less troubling for seeming to be consistent. For his doubt about God creating cloud by day and fire by night provokes its own wonder over his beliefs about the wilderness wanderings (Exod 13:22; Deut 1:33). His uncertainty about the material reality of God's wonders (*nifla'oth*) in Exodus 34:10 raises questions about his understanding of God's dealing with Pharaoh and Egypt at the time of the Exodus. For it was through His wonders wrought upon them, He promised, that they would be obliged to let His people go free (Exod 3:20). The Bible does not, and Pharaoh and the Egyptians did not, hold any doubt about the physical, objective, material reality of the blood, frogs, lice, and flies that overran the land at God's command (Exod 7:14–8:31). By way of example, when desperation drove Pharaoh to beg for relief from the frogs, Moses did not simply wave an arm to heaven and cause them to vanish: "Moses cried to the LORD concerning the frogs which He had inflicted upon Pharaoh. And the LORD did according to the word of Moses" (Exod 8:12-14). The wonder of the frogs involved utterly material, visible, palpable swarms of hopping frogs that turned by God's command into material heaps of visible, palpable, vile smelling dead frogs.

Moreover, the wonder of the destroying angel whose visitation compelled the stubborn Pharaoh to let Israel go was no less real for being

---

[34] Walton, *Genesis 1*, 128.

supernatural (Exod 12:29–32). The Creator of Genesis is the Maker of things "visible and invisible, whether thrones or dominions or rulers or authorities" (Col 1:16), and no cognitive environment in ANE thought may deny Him this power. Walton's theory of inspiration may be the subject of some other study, but his doubts over his theory are fully justified by the evidence of Scripture, history, and creation. His efforts to explain away *bara'* as functional and not material are quite futile. As Norman Geisler pointedly states, "The word *create* (*bara* [sic]) is used in connection with three great events in Genesis 1: the creation of matter (v. 1), living things (1:21), and human beings (1:27)."[35]

Psalm 33 revisits and reiterates this function of the verb "create" (*bara'*). The multi-leveled allusions to the Genesis account in Psalm 33:6, 9 are difficult to overlook. Links with Genesis include the thematic, philosophical, and ideological. But their most intriguing connection relates to a distinctive syntactical sequence that appears in the OT only in context of God's miraculous creative power.[36] In terms of theme, the passage deals with the creation of the heavens and the earth. Philosophically, the author is persuaded that the process was miraculous. Ideologically, he sees this miracle as the work of a God who is orderly and omnipotent, utterly in control of the process of creation. However, it is the unique syntax of Psalm 33:9 that most fascinatingly signals its direct linkage with the Genesis story, and most effectively underlines the value of the triplet A.

Elucidating that connection, we find that triplet A, repeated six times through Genesis 1,[37] is similar in construction to an Exodus report on the supernatural intervention that liberates Israel from Egyptian slavery. When Moses cowers before God's commissioning word the Lord reminds him of His omnipotence. "What is that in your hand?" He asks. "A staff," answers

---

[35] Norman Geisler, *Systematic Theology*, vol. 2: *God and Creation* (Minneapolis, MN: Bethany House, 2003), 441. Tremper Longman III and Raymond B. Dillard, *An Introduction to the Old Testament*, 2nd ed. (Grand Rapids, MI: Zondervan, 2006), 52, state:: "Creation in Babylon is the result of divine sexual activity and conflict, whereas in Genesis God is sovereign, self-sufficient, and supreme. In the Near East, the creation comes from preexistent stuff, while in the Bible creation is from nothing."

[36] Except in Isaiah 63:8, a verse that is grammatically and thematically distinct from the circumstances of Genesis, etc. Though God speaks (*'mr*) and *wayehi* follows, the subject of *wayehi* is God Himself ("and he became . . ."), unlike the *wayehi khen* ("and it was / became so") of Genesis, Exodus, and Psalms passages.

[37] See Genesis 1:3, 6–7, 9, 11, 14–15, 24.

Moses (Exod 4:2). "Then he said [*wayyo'mer*]: Throw it on the ground. So he threw it on the ground, and it became [*wayehi*] a serpent" (Exod 4:3).[38] This verbal combination of *wayyo'mer* and *wayehi* is particularly rare in the OT, more notably so because of how ubiquitous these forms (*wayyo'mer* and *wayehi*) and their roots (*'mr, hyh*) are in the OT.[39] In fact, Genesis 1, Exodus 4, and Psalm 33 present *wayyo'mer* and *wayehi* in a narrative relationship that is nowhere else encountered in the OT.

And Psalm 33:9 supplies a rather conspicuous syntactical connection with the Genesis creation report. Where Genesis features a non-specific substantive "so" (*khen*) as part of the predicate with the verb "to be" (*hayah*),[40] Exodus 4:3 features a standard substantive "serpent." The openness and indeterminacy of the term "so" in Genesis ("and so it was") highlights, with a force not apparent in the Exodus account, the awesome truth of God's transcendent authority in the creative miracle. It was "so," Genesis repeatedly states, in a manner that conveys the mystery of realia materializing out of oblivion, coming into visibility and palpability, taking form, and conforming to their purpose exactly and completely as decreed. The material adequacy of all this is readily accessible through triplet B with its verbs of dividing, making, putting, etc. But the psalmist chooses to persuade by using the much less palpable language of triplet A. Yet, the forcefulness of pausal *wayehi*, the synonymous parallelism of the verse's second stich that makes use of "command" (*tsawah* D stem)—another verb of speaking, the strident insistence of independent personal pronouns ("He Himself"—*hu'*, twice)—all these elements of solidity unite in compelling contrast with the grand abstraction of the verse's predicate, lacking as it does any explicit substantive that characterizes the verse's predicate.

Added to all this, for good measure, is the fact that in the overwhelming majority of instances, the root *'mr* is rendered as "say," not "speak." Though "speak" is also a legitimate translation, Psalm 33:9 confronts us with a verb whose complement is usually a speech report, leaving us with the syntactically pregnant rendering: "For he said [A1], and so it was [A3]."

---

[38] At the seventh plague God commands (*wayyo'mer*): "Stretch out your hand toward the sky, that hail may fall [*wayehi*] on all the land of Egypt" (Exod 9:22). And again at the ninth He speaks (*wayyo'mer*): "Stretch out your hand toward the sky, that there may be [*wayehi*] darkness" (Exod 10:21). However, because these are indirect volitive purpose clauses, they sustain more of a visual similarity to Genesis, and less of the compelling syntactical equivalence found in the narrative sequence of Exodus 4:2, and, particularly, Psalm 33:9.

[39] The specific form *wayyo'mer* occurs 2,081 times, and *wayehi*, 776 times. The root *'mr* appears 5,298 times, and *hyh* is present 3,548 times.

[40] Some may wish, with reason, to identify *khen* as an adverb ("thus").

Which naturally provokes the question: What did he say? By which means the text invites us to acknowledge the incomparable consequence, and thorough gratification, of our triplet's A2. In Psalm 33:9, and by his own peculiar omission, one biblical writer eloquently affirms the force of another's design, the Genesis creation design of triplet A. His use of A1 and A3 as separate components is in itself confirmation of A2 as a distinct entity. His employment of A1 and A3, absent A2, compels acknowledgement of the essential value, and the fulfilling and completing character of the implied component.

"Saying" (*'amar*) and the Sabbath at Creation

As Exodus 4:3 demonstrates, the link between the Sabbath at creation and God's wonders at the time of the exodus is more than incidental. The narrative connection among Exodus 4, Genesis 1, and Psalm 33 is conspicuous for uniqueness, particularly with reference to the syntactical relationship they exhibit between "and He said" (*wayyo'mer*) and "and it was/became" (*wayehi*). It may further be emphasized that as with the Genesis creation narrative, Moses' call and the signs that accompany it are dominated by the root *'mr* ("to say"). The miracles of Moses' initial call are all introduced by *'mr*. We have already commented on Exodus 4:3, but we may begin with verse 2: The Lord said (*wayyo'mer*), "What is that in your hand?" The Lord said, "Throw it on the ground." The Lord said, "Stretch out your hand and grasp it by its tail." The Lord said, "Now put your hand into your bosom." The Lord said, "Put your hand into your bosom again" (Exod 4:2–7). In each of these instances the verb is the same *wayyo'mer* [even to precision of form] that narrates the Genesis creation story of days 1–6.

This verb *wayyo'mer* is the paramount verb in triplet A above, underlining its value to the report of days 1–6, and the relationship between the works and wonders of God at creation week and the exodus liberation. Of all the verbs employed in the creation narrative, it is the root *'mr* that dominates. It is the most used. It is used from first to last. It frames the report at Genesis 1:3 and 1:29, introducing the chapter's first and last recorded speeches. Its paramount character in triplet A only highlights its indisputable importance for the whole account. For in the logical and rhetorical parallelism of the two threefold accounts (triplets A and B), this verb of God's saying (triplet A) stands alone over against all the doings of His hands (triplet B), including "to make" (*'asah*—three times: Gen 1:7,

16, 25) and "to create" (*bara'*—four times: Gen 1:21 [once] and Gen 1:27 [thrice]).

What seems quite remarkable, then, is that the term *'mr*, so strongly associated with God's creative miracles, should be entirely absent from the verses that report on the event of the last day of creation week. This absence supplies one of the text's early indicators that accessing its full message requires sensitivity to its features of both distinctiveness and continuity that simultaneously mark off and integrate the two contrasting segments of its septenary structure. We have spoken at length of elements of the first six days' reportage that are absent from the seventh day's announcement. Their absence is no compositional deficiency. Instead, these absences eloquently convey the purpose of the pericope of Genesis 1:1–2:3 to demonstrate the otherness of the seventh day's character within the continuity of earth's first week.

Six Day Continuities: "Saying" (*'amar*) and "Work" (*mela'khah*)

The significance of omitting *'mr* from day seven seems related to the presence and role of the term "work" (*mela'khah*), a term that requires attention at this point. Its treatment would also be appropriate in the following section on seventh-day distinctives, because it is unique to the report on that day. But given its rhetorical relation to the six-day distinctive *'mr*, it seems most appropriate to discuss it now.

We have seen that *'mr* is the principal term used to structure the shape, and express the language of, the first six days of creation's work. The verb "to say," made concrete through the components of triplets A and B, is the divine means for initiating, prosecuting, and bringing to final fruition all the creative efforts of Genesis 1:1–31. To cite the psalmist again, with regard to divine creation, it is the principal, yea, the unique verb, of work: The heavens were made by the Lord's Word. And the poet is unequivocal about the divine means of labor: He said (*ki hu' 'amar*) and so it was (*wayehi*, Ps 33:9). Simply put, the passage's use of *'mr*, and the psalmist's understanding and reiteration of that usage,[41] show, independently and together, that this is the word, par excellence, for introducing and bringing to pass God's work during the first six days of the creation week.

This is very likely then why *'mr* itself, and so much of the narrative structure that it dominates, has been omitted from the seventh

---
[41] Along with the usage in Exodus 4:2–7.

day's report.⁴² Genesis 1:1–2:3 is a unified pericope reporting on a single theme—the origins of earth's creation order. The text informs that this creation order was supernaturally brought into being in a week of seven days. But the activities of the first six days and the manner of their reporting in Genesis 1:1–31 differ from the content and shape of Genesis 2:1–3. What our study strives for here is a proper respect for literary and rhetorical differences. Appreciating the six-seven day scheme, we better access the report by properly respecting its two distinct yet interrelated portions of the one creation account in context of the whole that is greater than the sum of its parts. It helps to be alert to what, and how much, is absent from Genesis 1:1–31 in relation to Genesis 2:1–3, and vice versa.

As such, we find that Genesis 1 elements missing from elsewhere are as essential where they do occur as they would be a violation if occurring elsewhere. For example, except for when it points back to the six days of work, the passage on the seventh day rest excludes all the terms of labor encountered in triplets A and B that represent six-day work. The summary of Genesis 2:1 on the end of the week's work⁴³ explains why: those terms (*'mr, bdl, qr', ntn, br', 'sh*) that constituted the divine means of work in days 1–6 do not belong to or represent the experience that God depicts as rest for Him and His creation. In Genesis 2:1–2, the text's skilled integration of form and function, of content and style, yields an announcement of transparent import. Merely stating that God completes His work and rests (Gen 2:2) is not enough. Nor is stating and repeating,⁴⁴ nor even employing exhaustive epithet. Beyond the content of words, the stylistic strategy of omission terminates the usage of all those components that, as features of work, were employed in configuring the six-day report. The account on rest is the more transcendently accomplished by dispensing with the rhetorical tools so fundamental to shaping the account on work. Only two of the six verbs of work in days 1–6 appear on day seven. And they only appear in reference to what happened on days 1–6 that distinguishes that

---

⁴² "With the lack of reference to divine speech the text shows that God's activity changes on the seventh day" (Mathilde Frey, "The Sabbath in the Pentateuch: an Exegetical and Theological Study" [PhD diss., Andrews University, 2011], 23). Which is to say that God's seventh-day activity is different from that of days 1–6.

⁴³ "The heavens and earth and all their host were now completed" (Gen 2:1).*

⁴⁴ "By the seventh day God had completed His work that He had done, and He rested on the seventh day from all His work that He had done" (Gen 2:2*). And verse 3 seems to add further reiteration, again mentioning God's rest on that day. Limits of appreciation for the seventh-day Sabbath among exegetes, religious and people of faith may well point to our failure to value as we might the broad and deep significance of rest—specifically, divine Sabbath rest.

period from day seven: "His work that He did" (Gen 2:2), "that He created and made" (Gen 2:3). The author will therefore avail himself of no divine speech introduction ("God said") to advance his account. Again, neither the frequent jussive, nor the occasional imperative, nor the unique cohortative of divine reported speech (Gen 1:27) encumbers the narrative. Also, no fulfillment confirmation ("and so it was") accompanies the description of God's seventh-day ordaining. And whereas God's unique word of work ('mr) does not occur here, neither do we expect any of the other proofs of work accomplished (statements of reification, rational approval, or temporal closure).

The distinction between day seven and its preceding days is signaled, taught, and maintained with meticulous particularity: as God desists from work on the seventh, so is that truth conveyed by laying aside, on the seventh, the rhetorical tools that so effectively served for the literary labor of the first six.

According to Genesis 2:2, what God accomplished during the six days of creating things was His "work" (*mela'khah*): "By the seventh day God had completed His work [*mela'khah*] that He had done, and He rested on the seventh day from all His work [*mela'khah*] that He had done."*[45] And Genesis 1 and Psalm 33:6, 9 both show that "saying" ('mr) is how God realizes His creation miracle. Beyond this, Genesis 2:2 states, and verse 3 reiterates, that God desists—rests—on the seventh day from His work (*mela'khah*) that He has been doing and making. The text is quite insistent on this. It is God's *mela'khah*, thrice affirmed within two verses (Gen 2:2–3), that He has made and from which He desists on the seventh day.

Six Day Continuities: "Work" (*mela'khah*) and Similar Terms

Study of the term *mela'khah* in the OT exposes one distinctive property that sets it apart from other oft-used terms for service and work frequently associated with it, such as *ma'aseh* and *'avodha*. Most frequently occurring of the three is *ma'aseh*, appearing in 220 verses, and as applicable as *mela'khah* (167 times) or *'avodha* (145 times) to matters of general labor, specialized skill, or cultic service. Despite their similarity, OT usage, including the commandment statements of Exodus 20 and Deuteronomy 5,

---

[45] See Jacques B. Doukhan, *Genesis*, Seventh-day Adventist International Bible Commentary (Nampa, ID: Pacific Press, 2016), 68, who argues against a pluperfect rendering. It may be that God's seventh-day rest is to be seen as the sabbatical finishing touch to His week of work (*mela'khah*), demonstrating the inadequacy and incompleteness of six-day laborious existence, absent the sanctifying benediction of seventh-day rest.

consistently sets *mela'khah* over against Sabbath rest, whether as divine modeling or as human prescription.

The three terms all bear the most affirming of connotations: Your [God's] works [*ma'asekha*] are wonderful [*nifla'im*] (Ps 139:14), praised from generation to generation (Ps 145:4). The Lord "is righteous with respect to all his deeds [*'al kol ma'asayw*]" (Dan 9:14). As to *'avodha*, Moses informs the Levite rebels who hanker after the priesthood that their work (*'avodha*) in the service of the tabernacle is a divinely bestowed honor (Num 16:9). The Levites, he later explains, are a gift the Lord has taken for Himself, to do the service (*'avodha*) of the tabernacle (Num 18:6).

Sometimes *ma'aseh* can be negative. God's *ma'aseh* is wonderful, but those of the heathen are not.[46] Again, Israel is not to conform to patterns of conduct in Egypt or Canaan (Lev 18:3), whence they come and whither they are going (Deut 27:15; cf. Jer 25:6). By contrast, Leviticus 25:39 cites the single OT prohibition involving unmodified *'avodha*, where Israelites are forbidden to subject their brethren to slave service.

Twelve times the Pentateuch presents celebrants with freedom from a modified type of work (*mele'kheth 'avodha*) in connection with the cult. These involve any of six different religious feast days: Unleavened Bread (first and seventh [last] days, Lev 23:7-8; Num 28:18, 25), the Day of Shavuot (Lev 23:21; Num 28:26), Rosh Hashanah (Lev 23:25; Num 29:1), and Sukkot (first and eighth [last] days) (Lev 23:7-8, 21, 25, 35-36; Num 28:18, 25-26; 29:1, 12, 35).

Besides these divine and insistent notes of liberation from "laborious work," the Bible contains one other group of texts on the matter of prohibition from work. In these cases, the prohibition is (1) clearly associated with the others, (2) readily distinguishable from the others, (3) foundational to the others, and (4) stronger than all the others. The eight texts in this group make use of the very term, *mela'khah*, that features in all other work prohibitions. But while other prohibitions are from "laborious work," these eight that relate specifically to seventh-day Sabbath rest are categorical and unmodified. Thus, seventh-day Sabbath rest is distinguishable from all others by its absolute prohibition of any kind of work on the Sabbath. That prohibition remains inseparably linked with the creation rest day by its use of *mela'khah* in the absolute, as opposed to the *mele'kheth 'avodha* of other ritual Sabbaths.

---

[46] "You shall not bow down to their gods in worship or follow their practices [*ma'asehem*], but shall tear them down and smash their pillars to bits" (Exod 23:24).

Evidently, the fullest, purest, most complete rest from labor that the OT offers is seventh-day, creation Sabbath[47] rest: (1) It is related to other ritual rests—they have *mela'khah* in common; (2) it is distinguishable from other rests—they are modified forms of its basic principle; (3) by the same token, it is seen to be foundational to them—they build on and derive from it; and (4) it is stronger than all others except Yom Kippur[48]—it is categorical. Its strength is its originality: it is the first of Sabbaths. Its authority is its source and model: God Himself. Its beginnings are un-improvable: it comes from a flawless time. And its application is universal, given at the beginnings of humanity and earth history. A review of the entire OT canon in its use of terms for work and proposals for rest strongly bolsters the message of Genesis 1:1–2:3: that the creation Sabbath institution is earth's earliest and purest. The stipulation on rest that informs every cultic work prohibition in the OT is founded on the concept of rest God instituted for earth and humanity at the beginning of earth's history. These four truths may only be set aside by the argument that the Creation account is of limited application—a mere Jewish thing invented for Abraham's descendants. But such a claim remains outside the biblical evidence.

The use of *mela'khah* also speaks to the Genesis teaching on the significance of the seventh day in relation to the remaining days of the week. Ratzlaff has made much of differences observed between treatment of creation days 1–6, and day seven. Finding the literary pattern of the creation account a "precise and well-thought-out construction,"[49] he reacts, in a chapter on "The Seventh Day in Genesis," with seven references to the fact that the concluding formula on "the evening and the morning" is absent from day seven.[50] He does fail to give attention to the multitude

---

[47] As contrasted with first-day rest, usually explained as resurrection Sabbath.

[48] The relative theological significance of Yom Kippur is suggested by the fact that it is the only occasion in the OT, besides the multiple and consistent seventh-day Sabbath prohibitions, that fully parallels creation Sabbath abstention. On the annual Day of Atonement, as on the weekly Sabbath, *mela'khah* is absolutely forbidden (see Lev 23:28, 30–31; Num 29:7). Yom Kippur's soul searching may thus be seen to be, *inter alia*, a cultic acknowledgement and reminder of, a reflection and meditation on, and a turning again toward a time of original, unspoiled purity, harmony, and wholeness: "For the Israelite, Kippur symbolized the purification of the world, a true re-creation. This is why Daniel uses the expression 'evenings and mornings' (Dan 8:14), a phrase that occurs strictly in the context of Creation (Gen 1:5, 8, 13, 19, 23, 31)" (Jacques B. Doukhan, *Secrets of Daniel: Wisdom and Dreams of a Jewish Prince in Exile* [Hagerstown, MD: Review and Herald, 2000], 130).

[49] Ratzlaff, *Sabbath in Crisis*, 20.

[50] Ibid., 17–26.

of other departures from the formulae of days 1–6 that we have noted here. Expanding his awareness of difference in reportage would no doubt improve his explanation of the significance of such difference.[51] Ratzlaff has construed the difference between days 1–6 and day seven as a basis for Old versus New Covenant theology. In such an equation, the creation miracle of the first six days would correspond to the period of Israel's dishonor of and disobedience to God. More consistently, and as the text teaches, the difference between days 1–6 and day seven is, in the first instance, the difference between divine work and divine rest.[52] Beyond this, as Exodus 20 and Deuteronomy 5 make clear, day seven differs from days 1–6 in teaching what God means for humanity to do on day seven by contrast with days 1–6. The Sabbath is the day of no *mela'khah*, of abstention from what should be the norm, based on the divine pattern, of six days of *mela'khah*.

Seventh-Day Distinctives: Genesis 2:1–3

The seventh day of the creation week report stands out as much by the uniqueness of its introductions as by omission of elements that, before that, seemed indispensable to the narrative. Their absence in the continued story shows the exceptional character of this final episode (day seven) within this thoroughly integrated story. Having commented on those omissions and also on common features (continuities), we turn to an examination of seventh-day distinctives.

Seventh-Day Distinctives: "Rest" (*shbt*), "Finish" (*klh*)

Rest (*shbt*) is a new thing to the Genesis story when it appears in Genesis 2:2. So is holiness (*qdsh*, D stem, Gen 2:3). So is use of the term *mela'khah*, already discussed. So too is a verb of completion (*klh*, Gen 2:1–2). The creation narrative that reports God's six days of miracle and summarizes those deeds at the end of the sixth includes a consistent, six-time refrain to mark the end of each of those days. But despite the

---

[51] Ratzlaff, Sabbath in Crisis, 51–72, gives extensive attention to the ceremonial Sabbaths, but shows no awareness of the distinctions here addressed.

[52] Divine work is awkwardly impugned, in Ratzlaff's equation, as analogical to human sin (days 1–6) versus divine salvation (day 7). Arguments that Jesus fulfills the Sabbath concept of rest are intended to set grace over against works. They amount to setting the seventh day over against the first six (ibid., 276, 289–290). However, Sabbath sacredness as a blessing from Eden does not "put Adam and Eve" where they do not belong (ibid., 290). Rather, it keeps the blessedness of the Sabbath where it belongs.

breadth of its range of actions and the steady repetition that marks each new cycle of the day, the story uses no verb of completion until the seventh-day report. Whereupon, that note on completion is insisted upon: "They were completed" (*wayyekhullu*, Gen 2:1); God (*ʾelohim*) had completed His work (*wayekhal*, Gen 2:2). And rest attracts the same attention. Completion and rest require equal insistence: "And He rested" (*wayyishboth*, Gen 2:2); "He rested" (*shbt*, Gen 2:3). The two appear not in tandem, but in sequence. Completion reasonably precedes rest. Rest signals completion. The advent of rest confirms completion. Thus the double articulation on completion precedes the earliest statement on rest. And the double statement on rest follows, rhetorically as logically, the declaration of completion. "One could not affirm that God's work was finished, until He showed that it was by ceasing . . . from it."[53] And there was no better way than by resting for God to affirm that His work was finished and that He had ceased from it.

This new note on completion has been linked, in our text, to the most basic of six-day ordinal continuities. The author achieves his linkage by a delicate touch that subtly varies the standard summary on day six. Hitherto, the narrator has identified each day as but another in the ordinal sequence: day one (Gen 1:5), second day (v. 8), third day (v. 13), fourth day (v. 19), fifth day (v. 23).[54] The sixth day's difference is subtle but significant, being a difference of demarcation. By introducing the definite article (that is, "*the* sixth day"), the report lends increased specificity and limitedness to a previously indefinite substantive, and prepares the reader for the climax of greatest particularity: day seven.[55]

The seventh day comes to us regaled with multiple ascendancies, including its use of the article. Only two days of the week enjoy articular definition. They are the sixth and the seventh. Like those before it, day 6 is only named at its end. Day 7 is different from the start, being named by way of introduction: Variously rendered as "by the seventh day" or "on the seventh day" (*bayyom hashevi'i*, Gen 2:2),[56] the text exhibits a need to

---

[53] H. L. Ellison, "Genesis," in *International Bible Commentary*, 2nd ed, ed. F. F. Bruce (Grand Rapids, MI: Zondervan, 1986), 116.

[54] Note that the ordinary Semitic order is one, second, third, etc. (E. A. Speiser, *Genesis: Introduction, Translation, and Notes*, AB [New York: Doubleday, 1964], 6).

[55] On this use of the definite article, see GKC sec. 126.5(a). A number of translations have ignored the distinction (KJV, NIV, RSV, NRSV), except the JPS (1917).

[56] For the various interpretations, see Andreasen, *The Old Testament Sabbath*, 63–64, 64 n. 2, who supports the suggestion that the verb *wayekhal* ("and he finished") should be rendered in the pluperfect ("God had ended . . ."). See also the NIV, and Nahum Sarna, *Genesis*, JPSTC

employ promptly, and much, the phrase "the seventh day." Not only is the seventh day the only one throughout the week that is named by way of introduction, but it is the only day whose identification is repeated—and thrice in two verses. Articular attention to the sixth is preparatory and anticipatory to the unveiling of the day that follows, the truly unique seventh.

Along with the article (days 6 and 7), the feature of blessing (days 5, 6, 7) also contributes to the buildup that comes to its climax on the seventh day. Both of these find their full purpose in day seven. A graduated piling up of details of moment attends the advance of creation week. Divine speech introductions populate all the days, but rise to a crescendo of four on the sixth day; blessings bestowed through three days come to their apex on the Sabbath. Articular identification, first introduced on day six, is fully explained by the distinctiveness of day seven. These elements combine to bring the creation report to its inexorable and triumphant culmination in the seventh of the days, the day of rest, blessedness, and holiness.

Seventh-Day Distinctives: "Sanctify" (*qdsh*)

Completeness, definiteness, and blessing notwithstanding, there may well be no term in the entire pericope that signals the otherness of the seventh day as effectively as "sanctify" (*qdsh*). This particular distinctive of the week's unique seventh day holds its own uniqueness as a word with no synonyms.[57] The Piel form appearing here stands for bringing "something/someone into the condition of holiness/consecration," as well as "declaring something/someone holy." Some lexicographers find no better example of this sanctification than the Sabbath of creation (Gen 2:3; Exod 20:11).[58] "Sanctification is grounded in the holiness of God."[59] And the author's implication is clear: at the end of earth's first week, the God of holiness declares the seventh day as Sabbath, and a partaker of His virtue. Once that has been done, it is done, inspiring one scholar's assertion: "The sabbath [sic] has been a holy day since creation."[60] This is very different from

---

(Philadelphia, PA: Jewish Publication Society, 1989), 15, who translate the preposition (*b*ᵉ) as "by." Speiser, *Genesis*, 5, prefers the view that God brought "to a close the work that he had been doing." Consistent OT usage of *mela'khah* as non-sabbatical activity requires the pluperfect rendering of *wayekal* ("By the seventh day God had completed . . .").

[57] H. Ringgren and W. Kornfeld, "קדש *qdsh*," *TDOT* 12:521–543.

[58] Ibid.

[59] Martin H. Manser et al., *Zondervan Dictionary of Bible Themes* (Grand Rapids, MI: Zondervan, 1999), #6745.

[60] Patrick D. Miller, *Deuteronomy* (Louisville, KY: John Knox, 1990), 80.

claiming that the seventh-day Sabbath is somehow a peculiarly Jewish phenomenon.

Seventh-Day Distinctives: The Blessing of a Day

As already noted, blessing is not unique to the seventh day of creation week. Sea monsters and winged birds are blessed on the fifth (Gen 1:21–22). And the man and woman formed in God's image are blessed on the sixth (Gen 1:27–30). And yet blessing is new on the seventh. For it is the tangible realia that have been blessed on previous days. No day has been blessed. And so, in further confirmation of the day's uniqueness from the outset of earth history, God blesses it. The sacredness of the seventh day, a divine act distinguishable from *mela'khah*, the work of the week, is also a deed of the deity. Turner emphasizes:

> On days one through three God names his creation. On days five and six he blesses it. But on the seventh day he both blesses and sanctifies the day itself. No physical part of the heavens and earth is sanctified, not even human beings who were created in the image of God. The only thing sanctified in the whole of creation is the seventh day.[61]

J. N. Andrews and L. R. Conradi offer comment on God's rest upon blessing and sanctifying the day:

> The blessing and sanctification of the seventh day . . . , relate, not to the first seventh day of time, but to the seventh day of the week for time to come, in memory of God's rest on that day from the work of creation.[62]

Of paramount importance here is the authors' sense of the significance of divine rest, blessing, and sanctifying in relation to the seventh day. The text of Genesis cannot alone expose the fullest understanding of the holy rest of the seventh day. Momentous truths must necessarily be presented from multiple perspectives. But the text at face value already reveals the Sabbath as distinctly valuable to the Creator. Walton says:

---

[61] Turner, *A Theological Reading of Genesis 1*, 73. Interestingly, Frey, "Sabbath in the Pentateuch," 20, points out that the phrases "on the seventh day" and "the seventh day" occur "within three consecutive parallel lines each consisting of seven words."

[62] J. N. Andrews and L. R. Conradi, *History of the Sabbath and First Day of the Week*, 4th ed., (Washington, DC: Review and Herald, 1912), 25.

If the Israelites along with the rest of the ancient Near East, thought of existence and therefore creation in functional terms, and they saw a close relationship between cosmos and temple, then those are part of the face value of the text and we must include them in our interpretation.[63]

Jacques Doukhan responds that Walton is right about such terms as "create" (*bara'*) and "good" (*tov*) having a functional sense. He also is right to claim that there are biblical connections between the temple and creation. However, any such linkages derive their functional, theological validity from their basis in a historical, material reality—namely, Genesis 1–2.[64] And that material, historical reality is affirmed as much in God's acts of blessing and Sabbath as it is in His creation of bird, bee, fish, and tree. For as the birds of the air are material products of His word (*br'*, Gen 1:21), and the man and the woman the products of His hand (*br'*, v. 27; *ytsr*, 2:7; *bnh*, v. 22), so is the blessed seventh day of rest yet one more deed of the God who is author of things visible and invisible (Col 1:16).

God's process of blessing the seventh day powerfully confirms the distinction between the labor (*mela'khah*) of the week, now completed, and the rest (*shbt*) of the seventh day now blessed. For whereas, during the week of work, saying (*'mr*) has been the requisite manner of blessing (Gen 1:22, 28–30), God shows the seventh to be a new order of phenomenon apart from every materially accessible, and every humanly calculable category, by blessing without saying (*'mr*).

Generally understood, to bless is to invest with advantage or benefit. Anyone is better for being blessed. Abraham, once blessed, could be the agent of advantage to the whole world (Gen 12:1–3). The advantage of blessing may be fertility, prosperity, protection, deliverance, healing, preservation, empowerment, exaltation, favor, or, possibly, all the above, as well as unquantifiable spiritual benefits besides. God's blessing may or may not be tangible, and with discernible, measurable effects. The more powerful the blessing deity, the more important the blessing.[65]

Thus the blessing on the seventh day is to be understood in context of the creation week. The God who blesses this day is the one who has just made every other day of the week and formed a whole new world pulsing

---

[63] Walton, *Lost World*, 104.

[64] Jacques B. Doukhan, "A Response to John H. Walton's *Lost World of Genesis One*," *AUSS* 49 (2011): 198.

[65] Michael L. Brown, "ברך *barakh*," *NIDOTTE* 1:758.

with vigor and swarming with its indescribable variegation of creeping, leaping, soaring, flawlessly healthy life. The hosts of heaven come to be by the breath of His mouth (Ps 33:6). His action in blessing is an intentional divine embrace of creatures of His that now swarm upon the oceans' swells and flocks that flood the skies. The uniqueness of His blessing on the seventh day is directed to the advantage of all—every element and entity, palpable and invisible, that He engendered during creation's miracle week.

This uniqueness of day seven does not come on the basis of constraint, convenience, or creaturely request; it comes not by majority vote or general acclamation; it does not arise out of subsequent exegetical logic. The uniqueness of day 7 comes exclusively by declaration and investment of the God of holiness. As Abraham Joshua Heschel recognizes, "The Sabbath is a presence of God in the world."[66] His declaration of the seventh day as holy is both a signal that He has given it His presence, and acknowledgement that His presence makes it so. It is because God enters and makes it partaker of His virtue that the Sabbath may be declared holy. And this truth is strongly insisted upon in Exodus.

Seventh-Day Distinctives: Exodus Elaborations

Biblically speaking, Exodus 16 is the first occasion after Genesis 2:1–3 that God will speak about the seventh day rest. Together with Exodus 20:8–11, it provides extended comment on the significance of the institution of seventh-day rest in Genesis 2:1–3.[67] The divine voice that spoke in Genesis is the very voice that speaks explanatorily on the identical subject in Exodus 20:8–11. Commentators consistently acknowledge that the appeal of the Exodus passage[68] is an appeal to the universality of the Genesis story—specifically of its Sabbath sacredness.[69] The two passages are historically, thematically, and theologically inseparable, despite much effort to separate the one from the other, dismiss the first as merely functional and not material, or relegate

---

[66] Abraham J. Heschel, *The Sabbath: Its Meaning for Modern Man* (New York: Farrar, Straus, Giroux, 1951), 60.

[67] When the seventh day comes up again in Exodus, "it is with explicit reference to what God did at the beginning" (Sigve K. Tonstad, *The Lost Meaning of the Seventh Day* [Berrien Springs, MI: Andrews University Press, 2009], 76).

[68] To which the NT points us in Luke 23:56–24:1.

[69] Terence E. Fretheim, "Genesis," in *New Interpreter's Bible*, ed. Leander E. Keck et al. (Nashville, TN: Abingdon, 1994), 347, is typical: "Exodus 20:11 and 31:17 . . . appeal to Genesis in order to claim that Sabbath observance belongs to the creation as God intended it to be; hence its importance for all peoples, not just Israel." See also Walton, *Lost World*, 146, who notes that "the fourth commandment directs people to observe the sabbath [sic] based on God's rest in Genesis 1 [sic]."

the second to parochial status as the peculiar property of a singular ethnic group. The relation of expanding explanation between Exodus 20:8–11 and Genesis 2:1–3 is hardly unique to truth in general or Scripture in particular, where revelation progresses and doctrine must be grasped by uniting precept to precept and line to line (Isa 28:10).[70]

Scripture makes more and more explicit the divine purpose and desire with regard to the creation Sabbath. Exodus 16 identifies seventh-day Sabbath rest as divine law ("How long do you refuse to keep my *mitswoth* and my *toroth*," Exod 16:28),* and this when the Sinai theophany is still weeks ahead (Exod 16:1; 19:1). Exodus 20:8–11 insists on the universality of the creation Sabbath, applicable to parent, child, local, foreigner, servant, and livestock (Exod 20:10). The Leviticus clarification that God's seventh-day Sabbath was given and established for holy coming together (Lev 23:3) comes as no surprise, given that the Lord specifically came together with Adam and Eve by deliberately imparting His presence to that day. Neither Exodus nor Leviticus deserves to be read as of limited, local application, or as adding to the import of God's original action. Rest and worship are, from the beginning, unavoidable implications of God's creation Sabbath actions. He makes the first clear by His words and action. His loving compulsion leaves no doubt about the second. And that compulsion is underlined by proper creaturely response: Moses in the desert must show reverence because the place he is standing is "holy ground" (Exod 3:5). And woes against his own unworthiness well up in Isaiah's breast and burst from his lips at the sight of the divine throne room where awe abounds and unfallen intelligences cry "Holy! Holy! Holy!" before the Lord (Isa 6:1–4). Isaiah's Lord is the very one who, at the climax of creation week, explicitly invests Himself in the creation Sabbath, to make it holy time—different and distinct, reverential time—separate, set apart, unique. Creation's seventh-day Sabbath has never been like the week's other days. They have never been holy, and it has never been other than holy.

Genesis 2:1–3 documents *shbt* as a verb of rest (*shavath*), not as substantive (*shabbath*). This is hardly an inadequacy or lack as some have tried to argue. For the name and number of the day on which God acts by resting, blessing, and sanctifying are not in dispute. The day, by name and number, is the seventh. Its specialness has been established from the

---

[70] The passage (Isa 28:9–13) includes a warning to those who will not listen to or heed the Lord's offer of rest. The warning may perhaps be more pertinent than often realized: contempt for this basic divine offer and requirement causes one to "stumble backward, be broken, snared, and taken captive" (v. 13).

dawn of earth's history. Exodus 20:8–11 shows that its specialness stands independent of the existence of nations, or the permanence or abolition of deals between God and any of these. The origins and validity of the creation Sabbath institution are biblically unrelated to nationality, dispensation, or sin: Israel is not to observe the Sabbath based on ethnicity or Jacob by another name, but because "in six days the LORD made the heavens and the earth, the sea and all that is in them, and rested on the seventh day; therefore the LORD blessed the Sabbath day and made it holy" (Exod 20:11). Equally, the historical fact involved in God's statement of the Sabbath as a sign between Him and Israel (Exod 31:17) does not depend on what is thought of Israel. Whether or not Israel is properly valued as God's OT church (Acts 7:38), the text's statement of fact is that "in six days the LORD made heaven and earth, but on the seventh day He ceased *from labor,* and was refreshed." Creation Sabbath values increase rather than diminish for today's Christians as we properly appreciate the fact, the moment, and the God of our creation, and His rationale for our keeping the seventh-day Sabbath holy. Biblical creation Sabbath theology is only secondarily Israel theology.[71] But what we think and say about Israel cannot reduce in any particular the validity of seventh-day Sabbath rest.

Tragic and distorted things have been said and thought about Israel, with baleful and long-lasting effect on Sabbath theology and practice. Justin Martyr, speaking to Trypho, the Jew, circa AD 150–160, of a new law with "perpetual Sabbath," encourages that "if there is any perjured person or a thief among you, let him cease to be so; if any adulterer, let him repent; then he has kept the sweet and true sabbaths of God."[72] Christians too would practice circumcision, keep the Sabbaths, and observe all the feasts if they did not know that these had been given to the Jews "on account of your transgressions and the hardness of your hearts."[73] More disturbingly, God foresaw that the Jews would kill His Son and therefore gave them the sign of circumcision so

> that you may be separated from other nations, and from us; and that you alone may suffer that which you now justly suffer; and

---

[71] See Tonstad, *The Lost Meaning,* 114.

[72] Justin Martyr, *Dialogue with Trypho,* Early Christian Writings, comp. Peter Kirby, chap. XII, accessed November 12, 2019, http://www.earlychristianwritings.com/text/justinmartyr-dialoguetrypho.html.

[73] Ibid., chap. XVIII. He may here be confusing Creation Sabbath with Sabbaths of the Levitical economy ("I also gave them statutes that were not good" Ezek 20:25).

that your land may be desolate, and your cities burned with fire; and that strangers may eat your fruit in your presence, and not one of you may go up to Jerusalem."[74]

Ultimately, these sorry distortions of whom God is thought to be provided ancient roots for today's delight and confidence that "what eclipses the seventh day, according to NT theology, is the *eighth day*, and its observance."[75] Again, that "what God's people need far more than rest or even restoration is resurrection for when one rises from the dead, one finally shakes off the weariness of the old fallen mortal flesh and needs, and studies Sabbath no more."[76] And "the attributes of Sabbath were not transferred to the Lord's Day, they were transcended by the Lord's Day."[77] The limits of this study permit only the comment that such theology inherently impugns the exhaustive flawlessness of God's original creation, ignoring the truth that God's program of redemption is His necessary and horribly painful "plan B" strategy to restore us to the perfection in which He created us.[78]

The Sabbath at creation was not instituted to be replaced, for there is no replacing the divine lordship over us and all His created works as celebrated in the Sabbath (Mark 2:28; Luke 6:5). Turner knows that "the highlight of God's achievement, and the point to which all creation moves, is the blessing and sanctification of the seventh day."[79] God's blessing and sanctification of the day serve for much more than abstract theological categories of lordship with its logical demand for obedience, as opposed to liberation and salvation with its consequent import of gratitude. Sabbath and law versus Sunday and resurrection freedom misses the sheer love expressed in God's intimate involvement with His newly minted creation that gives birth and worth to the Sabbath: "When God ceases the work of creating, hallowing the seventh day, we see God coming into an enduring relationship with Creation."[80] The mystery of the incarnation expresses

---

[74] Martyr, Dialogue with Trypho, chap. XVI.

[75] Ben Witherington, "The Case for the Christian Sabbath—Part Seven," February 1, 2011, http://www.patheos.com/blogs/bibleandculture/2011/02/01the-case-for-the-christian-sabbath-part-seven

[76] Ibid.

[77] Ibid.

[78] Ellen G. White, *Education* (Mountain View, CA: Pacific Press, 1903), 15.

[79] Turner, *A Theological Reading of Genesis 1*, 67.

[80] Tonstad, *The Lost Meaning*, 32.

the heart of a God who has always cared enough to wish to be with His people (Exod 25:8). And God does this first, not when sin has blighted His creation and deliverance is necessary; for God is not an emergency room physician: He is a lover.

He is just as surely Lord of all. One scholar concludes that "the imperative of the Ten Commandments may not remedy what the indicative of the first Sabbath rest fails to accomplish."[81] This is surely not to be taken to mean that the God of Sinai is superior or inferior to the God of Genesis. The Sabbath of Sinai is the same as the blessed and sanctified day of rest of Genesis. Also, God's veiling of Himself for the sake of preserving sin-blighted mortals[82] need not be projected backward onto the flawless canvas of Eden. The Sabbath of Eden needed and knew no shadow. It was all light and glory and intimacy and majesty and presence, if the joyful shout of morning stars (Job 38:7) is any indicator.

Seventh-Day Distinctives: "Create" (*bara'*) . . . "to Make" (*la'asoth*)

The concluding phrase of the seventh-day report, as well as the concluding phrase of Genesis' first pericope, has been apprehended as "pleonastic" or difficult "in the Hebrew."[83] Scholars may emend, overlook, or explicate the phrase. Andreasen sees no need for emendation;[84] nor did the medieval scribes whom Nahum Sarna cites.[85] The line is apparently calculated as a concluding embrace that draws together the work of six days and the rest of the seventh, registering a final note on the exhaustive nature of the divine authority over all creation. It is conclusion "with a certain fullness of expression."[86] The pericope's introduction brings to view a grand and independent statement of principle, that everything was created by God (Gen 1:1).[87] And the reader is reminded again of the grandeur of that opening as the narrative ends. To close with notes of power commensurate to those of its opening, the passage employs *br'* and *'sh*, the two principal verbs of "making" used in

---

[81] Tonstad, The Lost Meaning, 97.

[82] As in the sanctuary, burning bush, pillar of cloud and fire, or the incarnation.

[83] See Andreasen, *The Old Testament Sabbath*, 64; Sarna, *Genesis*, 15.

[84] Andreasen, *The Old Testament Sabbath*, 64.

[85] Ibn Janah and Ramban connect the verbs *la'asoth* and *shavath* (cease) to render: "He ceased to perform all His creative work." The rendering would fail to account for the then superfluous preposition *min* (as in *mikkol mela'khto*). See also Sarna, *Genesis*, 15.

[86] H. C. Leupold, *Exposition of Genesis*, vol. 1 (Grand Rapids, MI: Baker, 1956), 104.

[87] See von Rad, *Genesis*, 48.

the creation narrative (Gen 1:1, 7, 16, 21, 25, 26, 27 [3x], 31).[88] Their usage here is grammatically precise.[89] But their rhetorical force may be their most compelling feature. In what is perhaps the best NT equivalent to that force, John exhaustively affirms that "All things came into being through Him, and apart from Him nothing came into being that has come into being" (John 1:3).

Sabbath at Creation: Summary and Theological Reflections

This study has mainly looked at Genesis 2:1–3 as a passage that deals specifically with the topic of the Sabbath at creation. It has also noted elaborations on that topic from the book of Exodus. The Genesis report on the institution of the Sabbath is integral to and inseparable from earth's creation story. Analysis of the literary association between reports on the two parts of the six-seven day scheme (Gen 1:1–2:3) includes study of (1) elements unique to days 1–6, (2) elements unique to the seventh day, and (3) elements continuous through all seven days. All three groups demand attention: study of the first group constitutes an overview of things not seen—of what is *not* found—in the seventh-day report. These absences from day seven are a calculated contrast with days 1–6, highlighting difference, and designed as instructive of the otherness of the seventh day: "a day wholly granted to [rest] as opposed to other days."[90] Exodus 20:11 and 31:17 support the view that the divine command to rest on Sabbath, the seventh day of the week, is grounded on the divine behavior of six days of work and a seventh day of rest as it took place on creation week. Reference to the Sabbath as a sign (Exod 31:17) in no way affects the historicity of creation or the sanctity of the day for all who count themselves God's people.[91]

---

[88] Frey, "Sabbath in the Pentateuch," 22–23.

[89] See GKC sec. 114.4; Leupold, *Exposition of Genesis*, 104; B. Jacob, *The First Book of the Bible: Genesis*, abridged ed. (New York: KTAV, 1974), 13. Frey, "Sabbath in the Pentateuch," 21, notes, "Thus the overall literary framework shows a double framing and reinforces the literary unity of the first creation account."

[90] Karl Barth, *Church Dogmatics*, vol. 3, Part 1: *The Doctrine of Creation*, ed. G. W. Bromiley and T. F. Torrance (Edinburgh: T&T Clark, 1958; repr. 2004), 217.

[91] God gave the day "the power and special determination to have for the creature *mutatis mutandis* the same content and meaning, to be for it a day of the same conduct, as for Himself" (ibid.). Deuteronomy 5 expands application of seventh-day Sabbath rest to human eventualities, ultimately demonstrated by Christ's own rest after His work of delivering us all from sin (Heb 4:3, 9–11).

The parallel triplets of sequences formed by six-day elements absent from day 7 reflect a paradox of divine transcendence and immanence. They do this through a contrast between the unassailable authority of the divine word ("God said . . . and so it was") and the dynamic communion with His creation as heard in verbs of putting, dividing, making, and creating. That celebration of paradox is itself already, and uniquely, preparatory to the mystery of the seventh. For in that seventh God the exalted draws that creation nearer to Himself than at any point through the rest of the week. In the seventh, the God who "said . . . and so it was" invests Himself in time—an entire day, declaring it participant in His virtue. And, as Exodus 20 makes us know, He donates that time as a gift of freedom to all humanity and all creation.

The combination of divine ordering and order that separate humanity from work on the Sabbath is, first of all, an astonishing divine bequest. For by desisting from work on the seventh day, in accordance with God's own model, we live in the image of the one who created us to be like Him, and gave us the pattern and rhythm of Sabbath rest. "Keeping the Sabbath holy is an emulation of God's actions at the time of creation."[92] And as one scholar sees it,

> God's resting is a divine act that builds into the very created order of things a working/resting rhythm. Only when that rhythm is honored by all is the creation what God intended it to be. The sabbath is thus a divinely given means for all creatures to be in tune with the created order of things. Even more, sabbath-keeping is an act of creation-keeping. To keep the sabbath is to participate in God's intention for the rhythm of creation. Not keeping the sabbath is a violation of the created order; it returns one aspect of that order to chaos.[93]

God's gift of the Sabbath is not, moreover, a conditioned bequest. Its absolute character obtrudes, in that we enter into that rest with Him before we are able to work with Him or for ourselves. Humanity has no need to live, nor do creatures of God's providence deserve to, by the confused notion that existence—ours or that of the cosmos—depends upon ourselves. When the authority of the command is respected, slaves and animals are no longer at the beck and call of human masters. Nor are masters subject

---

[92] Jeffrey H. Tigay, *Deuteronomy*, JPSTC (Philadelphia, PA: Jewish Publication Society, 1996), 68.
[93] Fretheim, *Genesis*, 230.

to the unpredictable whim of economic circumstance. While humanity is invited to rest, it is also true that "to the tacit annoyance of many readers and expositors, there is no corresponding invitation to action as participation in God's creative work."[94] There is elsewhere, of course, unmistakable command to work (Exod 20:9), but it must be a resounding irony that humanity sometimes so wills to work, and simultaneously so wills to ignore, dismiss, or even oppose the Sabbath. For the order to work surely does not surpass, either in authority or in intensity, the combination of divine order and invitation to the fellowship of God's rest (Exod 20:8; cf. Gen 2:3).

Nor are human beings capable of supporting the tyrannical misconception of responsibility for their own existence. The current order, in which the infant comes into the world to first be cared for, before she may ever serve, is one with the ordaining of Eden's God who, preempting the breeding of a farce—that our labor must keep the world spinning—began all human history with a holiday, as, true to form, He still begins life with freedom from care. Grasping that plan, we may the better savor the miracle-working power of His word ('mr) and also enjoy our personal release from the burden of our labor. All this is why God, on the Sabbath day, enjoins humans not to work.

Rest—textually speaking, total desisting from *mela'khah*—is apparently prerequisite to experiencing Sabbath blessing or Sabbath blessedness. Conversely, the causal relation between divine blessing and divine rest points to the conclusion that divine blessing is the natural, predictable, and guaranteed result of entering into God's Sabbath rest. Moreover, Exodus 20:8 asserts that this seventh-day Sabbath belongs to God. In His owner's prerogative He dictates how it is to be used. Philological, ethical, legal, political, theological, or other arguments may supply no adequate basis for disregarding God's instructions on use of this day without first denying His ownership of the day. Nor is God's owner's prerogative over us any less (Ps 24:1) than His possessive authority over the seventh day.

The labels of the days of creation week are through seventh. And the seventh is the day of the Sabbath institution. The significance of "seven" to the remainder of the biblical corpus is no indeterminate mystery. It manifestly derives from the seventh day of creation week. Hence, indisputably, the combination of seventh and rest, of seventh and *shabbath* that pervades the Bible. The OT exposes the theological import of that name,

---

[94] Barth, *Church Dogmatics*, 225.

and the literary force of that naming in all subsequent employment of the phrase "the seventh day." United to the activities of blessing and sanctifying divinely applied to that first seventh day, Exodus 20 makes clear that this impact is particularly to be felt in cultic and covenant context. Indeed, every employment of the phrase "the seventh day," following Genesis 2:2–3, has that passage, and that naming, as—at the very least—its implicit referent.

Our focus here on the Sabbath at creation may limit our exploration of its later observation but may yet permit this minimum concession: it is God Himself who calculatedly insisted on the multiple combinations of seventh and *shabbath* in Israel's annual feasts, seventh years, and jubilees, predicating all upon His Sabbath institution of the last day of creation week. By this means God sought to explicate something of the inexhaustible depth of meaning designed into that first seventh-day rest. His levitical elaborations were meant to communicate to everyone the value of His original Sabbath. They multiplied the lessons of its import and increased the possibilities for better experiencing it. Thus the message of the day on whose foundation all were erected would be better savored through weeks, and years, and generations. They deepened human understanding of the truths inherent in creation's Sabbath, beginning with the most basic: that the Lord of life wills humanity's first engagement as undistracted intimacy with Him.[95] This basic truth also holds its negative corollary: that the world, for its perfect functioning, is not dependent upon human input. And the varied nuances of *shabbath* would also intensify the longing for return to the place where that bliss of restful communion was first known. It would prove the reliability of that heritage—of collective belief in a time when the man and the woman reaped without sowing and made love and not war. By it God would confirm the validity of the dream that that time would come again.

The Sabbath of creation has never been dispensed with; nor can it, whether the length of the week be modified or not. Discussions on which day is the Sabbath too often fail to recognize that the creation Sabbath may be modified by theologies of covenant or other on only one basis: by denying the historicity of the report.[96] The simple, methodical transparency of the

---

[95] Barth, *Church Dogmatics*, 227.

[96] See Emil Brunner, *The Christian Doctrine of Creation and Redemption* (Philadelphia, PA: Westminster, 1952), 6–7; John Paul II, *Dies Domini*, apostolic letter, May 31, 1998, chap. 1, https://w2.vatican.va/content/john-paul-ii/en/apost_letters/1998/documents/hf_jp-ii_apl_05071998_dies-domini.html. See also Barth, *Church Dogmatics*, ix–x, who argues a distinction between

report counters every attempt to convert it into some extended metaphor or allegory, dependent for its interpretation on the literary genius of the individual reader. As one scholar states, the text's "theological force is not an extrinsic category which was later imposed by religious interpreters, but is constitutive of the literature itself."[97] That text straightforwardly reports a supernatural event by which life and order on this earth began existence in six ordinary and consecutive days a few millenia ago. The realia of that creation materialize in response to the divine jussive, "Let there be . . ."—a miraculous, unique, experimentally non-demonstrable event, and one, as such, not subject to scientific corroboration. Many students of Scripture freely acknowledge this as the message of the text. Says Rolf Rendtorff, "This first chapter of the Bible [referring to 1:1–2:3] constitutes an impressive, self-contained account of the coming into being of the world and of human beings."[98] And Brevard Childs would declare: "Genesis serves the community of faith and practice as a truthful witness to God's activity on its behalf in creation and blessing, judgment and forgiveness, redemption and promise."[99]

Like multiple other biblical accounts—the flood, the Babel interruption, the call of Abraham, the birth of Isaac or John the Baptist, the incarnation of Jesus, His death and resurrection, His ascension and second coming, etc.—fiat creation is not more or less established on the basis of studies of the physical universe or human biology.[100] Walton has seriously compromised his analysis by his inappropriate deference to such studies. His functional explanation of the Genesis creation story "stands in good harmony with evolution."[101]

The precious truth of creation as taught in Genesis includes the indispensability of the witness of the Sabbath, the seventh day of the week, as a token of God's perfection—the perfection of His lordship as Creator; the perfection of His love in and for His creation. It is a token to be cherished

---

dogmatics (i.e., expounding the faith of the text) and reliability (i.e., resisting the historicity of said text). In process of Barth's attempt to validate first-day worship, he admits that those who ventured this "apparent revolution" were going "against its divine order in creation" (ibid., 228).

[97] B. S. Childs, *Introduction to the Old Testament as Scripture* (Philadelphia, PA: Fortress, 1979), 157.

[98] Rolf Rendtorff, *The Canonical Hebrew Bible: A Theology of the Old Testament* (Leiden: Brill, 2005).

[99] Childs, *Introduction to the Old Testament*, 158.

[100] Ibid.

[101] Doukhan, "A Response," 204.

by all humanity, for the sake of all humanity, for the sake of all the earth, for the sake of Him who would have His children revel forever in the incomparable assurance that we are not contingent, we are not alone, nor are we mere servants of economic necessity. We are children of the Author of Creation. And we share dominion with our Lord and life source, in the first instance, by resting serenely in Him because it is in Him that we live, and by Him that we move, and through Him and Him alone that we will ever have our being (see Acts 17:28, KJV). Taken seriously, as the text means for us to take it, the Bible's creation Sabbath also provides ample response to that dualism that seeks to separate things spiritual from things temporal, the soul from the material, and the spirit from the body. For in acknowledging the biblical link between Sabbath and Creation, we acknowledge, equivalently, the linkage between things palpable and impalpable, between things physically accessible and realities that transcend the material. Celebration of the Sabbath within the context of this linkage is humanity's most proper biblical means of affirming, *inter alia*, such truths as the source and agency of our origins, the fact of our creatureliness, the manner of our coming into being, the idyllic perfection of our beginnings, the spiritual dignity of our existence from the first, the validity of rest as an original, integral, and essential part of human existence, and the regularity of rest.

Sabbath at Creation: Conclusion

In the end, all questions on the Sabbath at Creation present us, as they always have, with the inescapable problem of what is meant by *the Bible*, because it is the Bible's creation story to which we refer. Accepted as God's authoritative word, the infallible revelation of His will, standard of character, revealer of doctrine, and test of experience,[102] the Bible holds far reaching implications for our attitudes to the data here analyzed, and to the concepts that flow from our conclusions about it. At a minimum, we accept the Creator's lordship, and proudly display His sign.[103] Alternatively, human genius has not ended its search for other interesting, non-literal approaches to the interpretation of the text. Following that history may lead us interminably on, but we answer, instead, with the dialogue that

---

[102] Ellen G. White, *The Faith I Live By* (Hagerstown, MD: Review and Herald, 1958; repr. 2000), 293.

[103] "As an invitation and commandment it also makes it plain, of course, that on man's part it will involve decision—obedience or disobedience. Will the human race keep the Sabbath or not? Will it enter into its promised rest or not?" (Barth, *Church Dogmatics*, 227).

concludes H. C. Leupold's comments on Genesis 2:1–3: "Is this a strictly factual account," he enquires, "reporting what actually transpired in the manner in which it transpired?"[104]

And Leupold poses a further question: "Does the value of this account lie 'in the broad basic truths it embodies' . . . or in the details by which these truths are conveyed?"[105] Whereupon he repudiates the idea of alternatives between "broad basic truths" and "details" that convey these truths. The division, like Walton's adversarial juxtaposition of functionality and the material, is at best unfortunate. For it is the reliability of the details that gives credence to the broader principles: "Faith in inspiration, as taught by the Scriptures allows for no other possibility";[106] faith in God's actions during earth's first week of life teaches sane principles of living, the balance of labor and rest; faith in God's original act of will to share communion with us on that first Sabbath anchors His promise to never leave or forsake us (Deut 31:8; Matt 28:20; Heb 13:5); faith in God's declaration of the holiness of that first Sabbath enlightens the prophetic assurance of our own sanctification through His holy Sabbath (Ezek 20:12); faith in His explicit self-investment in the day He made for us (Mark 2:28) gives sense to His wilderness sanctuary and the incarnation of His Son by which He may dwell among us (Exod 25:8; John 1:14). And it is faith in His first and precious condescension that gives flawless context to His climactic promise of soon return, that where He is we soon shall also be (John 14:3), so that from one Sabbath to another, we shall, at last, all come together, to continue the worship before Him, in spirit and in truth, that was first begun in that garden of Paradise so long, long ago (Isa 66:23).

---

[104] Leupold, *Exposition of Genesis*, 104.

[105] Leupold, Exposition of Genesis, 104.

[106] Ibid., 104–105.

CHAPTER 9

THE SABBATH AND THE NEW COVENANT[1]

Roy Gane

Introduction

Is literal rest on the seventh-day Sabbath a part of the "new covenant" experience to be enjoyed by Christians today? An answer to this question is reached through biblical exegesis that investigates the Sabbath's scope of applicability.

The following interrelated sub-questions delineate the main sections of the study:

1. Is the seventh-day Sabbath a *universal* institution, or was it only for the literal Israelites?

2. Does the seventh-day Sabbath have an *ongoing* literal application, or was it a temporary type that lost its literal significance when it met its antitype?

3. Does the seventh-day Sabbath have *theological significance* for the present phase of the divine covenant (that is, the "new covenant") or did it only have theological significance as part of the obsolete "old covenant"?

Following consideration of these questions in order, this study will conclude by formulating an answer to the overall question.[2]

---

[1] This study was originally published in *JATS* 10/1–2 (1999): 311-332. It has been updated and edited for the present volume. The author is grateful to Jonatas Leal, his research assistant, for supplementing and updating resources cited here.

[2] All biblical quotations are from the NRSV, unless otherwise indicated.

Universal Sabbath or Only for Israelites?

This section explores the first sub-question: Is the seventh-day Sabbath a *universal* institution, or was it only for the literal Israelites?

The short answer to this question is: The seventh-day Sabbath is universal because it was instituted at creation for the benefit of all human beings, before the nation of Israel existed. This answer is based upon exegesis of Genesis 2:2–3,[3] which reads: "And on the seventh day God finished the work that he had done, and he rested on the seventh day from all the work that he had done. So God blessed the seventh day and hallowed it, because on it God rested from all the work that he had done in creation." God rested—that is, ceased[4]—His work at the end of creation week because His work was done, not because He was tired (cf. Isa 40:28; Ps 121:3–4).[5]

---

[3] The issue of the universality of the Sabbath is related to the question of its historical origins. After summarizing more than a century of investigation into a possible extra-Israelite origin of the sabbath, Gerhard F. Hasel, "Sabbath," *ABD* 5:849–856 concludes that "the quest for the origin of the sabbath outside of the OT cannot be pronounced to have been successful" (ibid., 851). Hence, Genesis 2:1–3 is still the best place to look for the origin of the Sabbath.

[4] The Hebrew word translated "rested" here is the verb from the root *shbt*, which means "cease," "desist," or "rest" in the sense of desisting from labor (*BDB*, s.v. *shbt*; cf. John Skinner, *A Critical and Exegetical Commentary on Genesis*, 2nd ed., ICC (Edinburgh: T & T Clark, 1930), 36–37; E. Haag, "שָׁבַת *shavath*," *TDOT* 14:382). Although the precise etymological relationship between this verb *shavath* and the noun *shabbath* is elusive, the two words are used in biblical Hebrew as if they were from the same root (Gerhard F. Hasel, "The Sabbath in the Pentateuch," in *The Sabbath in Scripture and History*, ed. Kenneth Strand (Washington, DC: Review and Herald, 1982), 24. Exodus 20:11 uses another Hebrew verb, *nuakh*, to refer to God's "rest" on the seventh day of creation. While this word is sometimes used with reference to rest from weariness or pain (see, e.g., Isa 14:3; 28:12), this meaning is not necessarily present. The basic meaning of the word seems to be the idea of settling down (see, e.g., Gen 8:4; Num 11:25–26; 2 Sam 21:10). See F. Stolz, "נוח *nuakh*," *TLOT* 2:723; Leonard J. Coppes, "נוח *nuakh*," *TWOT* 2:562. In fact, "the term's general concept is progression away from agitated movement and motion to a state of settlement marked by stability and security" (Matthew Haynes and Paul Krüger, "Creation Rest: Exodus 20:8–11 and the First Creation Account," *OTE* 31/1 [2018]: 107). Thus, Exodus 20:11 refers to God's repose at the end of creation, but does not express the idea that He was weary (cf. Gnana Robinson, "The Idea of Rest in the Old Testament and the Search for the Basic Character of Sabbath," *ZAW* 92 [1980]: 33–37; *BDB*, s.v. *nuakh*).

[5] The idea that God does not sleep (Ps 121:3–4), which affirms the constancy of His care, appears to be contradicted in the Bible by the idea that He can be called upon to arise from sleep (Pss 7:6; 35:23; 44:23; 59:4). However, Bernard Batto, "When God Sleeps," *Bible Review* 3 (1987): 21–23, has pointed out that the sleeping deity is an image that expresses the omnipotence of God, who can sleep because He has supreme authority. Batto finds this to be the essential significance of Jesus sleeping in a boat on the Sea of Galilee during a storm (ibid., 21–23; see Matt 8:23–27; Mark 4:35–41; Luke 8:23–27).

On the seventh day He stopped to celebrate what could be regarded as the "birthday" of the world.

There is evidence that God intended not only to celebrate, but also to provide an example for human beings. Exodus 31:17 refers to God being "refreshed" as a result of His rest on the seventh day of creation. The verb translated "refreshed" here is the Niphal of the root *npsh*, which is used only three times in the Hebrew Bible (Exod 31:17; 23:12; 2 Sam 16:14). In 2 Samuel 16:14, the verb *npsh* describes David and his people recovering from fatigue induced by their flight from Absalom. Exodus 23:12 reiterates the Sabbath command given in the Ten Commandments (Exod 20:8–11):

> Six days you shall do your work, but on the seventh day you shall rest, so that your ox and your donkey may have relief, and your homeborn slave and the resident alien may be refreshed (Exod 23:12).

In this context, "rest" (verb *nuakh*) on the seventh-day Sabbath clearly relieves the fatigue of human beings and animals (cf. Deut 5:14) and refreshes (verb *npsh*) them. Now the question arises: If the verb *npsh* describes relief from fatigue in Exodus 23:12 and 2 Samuel 16:14, why does Exodus 31:17 use the same word with reference to God being "refreshed"? The answer lies in the purpose of Exodus 31:12–17, which is to have God's people follow His example by resting on the seventh day of the week.[6] Even though God did not need rest from fatigue, the Bible here speaks of Him anthropomorphically[7] as receiving some kind of refreshing benefit[8] in order to show people how to rest on the seventh day, as a result of which *they would* gain relief from fatigue (Exod 23:12).

Lest it should seem strange that God would do something as an example for human beings, consider two similar cases:

1. In the Israelite ritual system, the blood of a sacrificial animal was drained out and applied to the sides or horns of the altar in the courtyard (see e.g., Lev 1:5; 4:25) or to the area of the outer sanctum and the horns of the incense altar (Lev 4:6–7), with the remainder disposed of by pouring it

---

[6] Umberto Cassuto, *A Commentary on the Book of Exodus* (Jerusalem: Magnes, 1967), 245, 404; Walter A. Elwell and Barry J. Beitzel, "Sabbath," *Baker Encyclopedia of the Bible*, ed. Walter A. Elwell (Grand Rapids, MI: Baker, 1988), 1874; John H. Sailhamer, *The Pentateuch as Narrative* (Grand Rapids, MI: Zondervan, 1992), 309.

[7] That is, ascribing human characteristics to the deity.

[8] Nahum Sarna, *Exodus: The Traditional Hebrew Text with the New JPS Translation*, JPSTC (Philadelphia, PA: Jewish Publication Society, 1991), 202.

out at the base of the outer altar (Lev 4:7). The blood did not go up to God in smoke along with the meat as a "pleasing aroma" (see e.g., Lev 1:9). Why not? Because the meat constituted a "food gift" to God (cf. Num 28:2)[9] and God had commanded the Israelites not to eat meat without draining out the blood because the blood represents life (Lev 17:10–12; cf. Gen 9:4).[10] By not eating blood with their meat, the Israelites acknowledged that they did not have ultimate control over life. But God did have such control. So why did He not show it by accepting blood with His meat? Apparently because He wanted to be an example to His people, thereby practicing what He preached.

2. Jesus asked John the Baptist to baptize Him, but John recognized that Jesus did not need baptism (Matt 3:13–14). Baptism symbolizes purification from sin (Rom 6:1–5), but Jesus was sinless (Heb 4:15). Nevertheless, Jesus insisted that John baptize Him, saying to him: "Let it be so now; for it is proper for us in this way to fulfill all righteousness" (Matt 3:15). So Jesus went through the motions of baptism because it is part of a righteous human life, even though the righteousness that He already possessed transcended the fallen state and did not require baptism.

Thus far, we have found that God's rest served as an example for human Sabbath observance. But did this example begin to operate thousands of years after creation, or did God intend for human beings to follow His example from the beginning? Jesus succinctly answers the question by declaring that "the sabbath was made for humankind." (Mark 2:27).[11] He viewed the original purpose of the Sabbath as providing benefit to human beings.[12] This means that when God rested on the seventh day of creation, He did not simply intend to benefit Himself.

---

[9] The word translated "offering by fire" in Leviticus 1:9 and elsewhere is better rendered "food gift." On this interpretation of the Hebrew word *'isheh*, see Jacob Milgrom, *Leviticus 1–16: A New Translation with Introduction and Commentary*, AB (New York: Doubleday, 1991), 161–162. The rendering "offering by fire" is not appropriate for several reasons, including the fact that some offerings given this designation are not burned (Lev 24:6, 9, "bread of the presence"). Furthermore, the "purification offering" (so-called "sin-offering"), which is burned, is never given this designation. Compare also Deuteronomy 18:1, where priests eat the Lord's "food gifts." They could not eat an "offering by fire" because it would be burned up on the altar.

[10] See more regarding the prohibition of the consumption of meat with its blood in Roy Gane, *Old Testament Law for Christians: Original Context and Enduring Application* (Grand Rapids, MI: Baker, 2017), 350–352.

[11] "The statement in v. 27 is often compared to that of Rabbi Simeon ben Menasya (ca. A.D. 180): 'The Sabbath is delivered over for your sake, but you are not delivered over to the Sabbath'" (James A. Brooks, *Mark*, NAC [Nashville, TN: Broadman & Holman, 1991], 67).

[12] Ibid.; Jacques Doukhan, *Genesis*, Seventh-Day Adventist International Bible Commentary (Nampa, ID: Pacific Press, 2016), 69.

It is true there is nothing in the text of Genesis 2 that explicitly tells us the Sabbath was made for human beings, as Jesus later declared. Nor does Genesis state that the Sabbath is to be an ongoing, cyclical event, occurring on each seventh day. However, Genesis did not need to explicitly state these things because the context makes them clear. Consider the following contextual factors:

1. According to Genesis 2:3, God blessed the seventh day and made it holy (Gen 2:3). Thus, God must have endowed this day with a special relationship to Himself, who alone is intrinsically holy (1 Sam 2:2).[13] But how can a day be holy? A day is a unit of time, which is not a material substance, so it cannot be made holy by application of a holy substance, such as anointing oil (Lev 8:10–12). The only way for someone to make/treat time as holy is by altering behavior. Thus, God altered His behavior on the seventh day of creation, the archetype of the weekly Sabbath,[14] and proclaimed the day holy. One scholar points out, regarding the Sabbath in Genesis 2:1–3: "It is not an institution which exists or ceases with its observance by man; the divine rest is a fact as much as the divine working, and so the sanctity of the day is a fact whether man secures the benefit or not."[15]

But what sense would it make to say that God *blessed* the day if He intended this unit of holy time to benefit only Himself? Elsewhere in the creation story, God's blessings were outgoing, for the benefit of His creatures (Gen 1:22, 28).[16] So could we imagine that on the seventh day God rested and admired His handiwork while man toiled in the garden (cf. Gen 2:15)? The blessing must be for created beings living in the world where the seventh day operated.[17] In order to receive the blessing, these beings would consecrate the

---

[13] Jacques Doukhan, *Genesis*, Seventh-Day Adventist International Bible Commentary (Nampa, ID: Pacific Press, 2016), 69. Gordon Wenham, *Genesis 1–15*, WBC (Dallas, TX: Word, 1998), 36, points out that making a day holy is unusual. According to him, the Piel of *qdsh*, which is usually factitive ("make holy"), has a declarative sense in Genesis 2:3. However, elsewhere in the creation account, God's declarations bring about new realities.

[14] Hasel, "The Sabbath in the Pentateuch," 23.

[15] Skinner, *A Critical and Exegetical Commentary*, 35.

[16] On the relationship between the divine blessing upon animals in Genesis 1:22 and upon humanity in Genesis 1:28, Paul Kissling, *Genesis*, College Press NIV Commentary (Joplin, MO: College Press, 2004), 130, comments, "God's blessing on humankind parallels the blessing on water creatures and birds in verse 22, but here God addresses them directly in speech, showing the different status of humankind."

[17] Skinner, *A Critical and Exegetical Commentary*, 35; Gerhard von Rad, *Genesis: A Commentary*, rev. ed., OTL (Philadelphia, PA: Westminster, 1972), 62; Kenneth A. Mathews, *Genesis 1–11:26*, NAC (Nashville, TN: Broadman & Holman, 1996), 180.

day as God did, by altering their behavior.[18] The blessing results from activity that acknowledges the consecration. "The Sabbath is a constant source of well-being to the man who recognizes its true nature and purpose."[19]

2. God made human beings in His image (Gen 1:26–27) and commissioned them to continue the work of creation by being fruitful and multiplying (v. 28). He also gave them the work of having dominion/responsibility over the earth (Gen 1:26–28; 2:15).[20] If human beings are made in God's image and are to *emulate God* by working on their level as God worked on His (cf. Lev 19:2), it would stand to reason that they should also emulate God by resting from their work as God rested from His.[21]

3. On each of the first six days of creation, God did something that had *ongoing* results for our world. Thus, we expect that what He did on the seventh day would also have earthly ongoing results.[22]

4. God set up cyclical time even before man was created (Gen 1:3–5, 14–18). According to Genesis 1:14, God made heavenly luminaries, chiefly the sun and moon (v. 16), to mark earthly time as "signs" and "seasons"—appointed times, days, and years. So when Genesis 2:3 says that God blessed and hallowed the seventh day, this blessing and consecration could be on-going in a *cyclical* sense, applying to each subsequent seventh day.[23] In fact, the seventh-day Sabbath provides a plausible explanation for the origin of the week, which is not defined by the movement of heavenly bodies.[24]

---

[18] See Jacques Doukhan, "Loving the Sabbath as a Christian: A Seventh-Day Adventist Perspective," in *The Sabbath in Jewish and Christian Traditions*, ed. Tamara Eskenazi, Daniel Harrington, and William Shea (New York: Crossroad, 1991), 156.

[19] Skinner, *A Critical and Exegetical Commentary*, 38.

[20] Benjamin B. Phillips, "A Creature among Creatures or Lord of Creation? The Vocation of Dominion in Christian Theology," *Journal of Markets & Morality* 14 (2011): 133–146, provides a good overview of dominion as a vocation from a Christian perspective.

[21] Cf. Sailhamer, *The Pentateuch as Narrative*, 96–97.

[22] Bruce K. Waltke and Cathi J. Fredericks, *Genesis: A Commentary* (Grand Rapids, MI: Zondervan, 2001), 71–72.

[23] Doukhan, *Genesis*, 70, suggests the possibility that in Genesis 2:1–3 the biblical author "preferred not to use the word *shabbath* simply to avoid having it confused with other *Shabbath* feast days in the Hebrew calendar (Lev 23:32, 39; Isa 1:13). Unlike the other 'Sabbaths,' which were linked to the fourth day of creation week's astronomically computed 'seasons' and 'feasts,' the seventh-day Sabbath is given here as an independent time that is separate from all these feasts and relates only to the event of God's sovereign work of creation."

[24] Cf. Cassuto, *A Commentary on the Book of Exodus*, 244. Sarna, *Exodus*, 111, points out the significance of the Sabbath's uniqueness as a unit of time and delineator of the weekly cycle:

The creation story does not contain a command for human beings to observe the Sabbath. But neither does it contain commands to abstain from idolatry, adultery, murder, or any of the other Ten Commandments (cf. Exod 20).[25]

In Genesis 1–2 God was concerned with setting up the ideal order of relationships rather than commanding protection of existing relationships. For human beings, He instituted the Sabbath, marriage, and work.[26] These three institutions embody principles that were later expressed in the Ten Commandments (cf. Exod 20:3–17).

According to Genesis 3, when Adam and Eve showed disrespect for God's lordship by eating the fruit of a forbidden tree (Gen 3:6), their marriage and work suffered as a result of the curse of sin (Gen 3:16–19). But there is an important omission in Genesis 3: the Sabbath is not affected by any curse resulting from the fall. Unlike the other two creation institutions, the Sabbath remains a little piece of paradise.[27] As such, its value is enhanced by the deterioration around it. Now that work is exhausting, ceasing from labor on the Sabbath provides needed rest. More importantly, now that human beings are cut off from direct access to God, they need a reminder of His lordship even more than they did before the fall.

While the fall made marriage and labor difficult and reduced joy in these things, it did not take away human responsibility with regard to any of the creation institutions or the principles that they embody. When Cain murdered Abel, showing disrespect for the life given by God through the marriage of Adam and Eve, God held him accountable (Gen 4:9–15). Genesis does not say that the sixth commandment was formulated as such before Cain killed Abel, but Cain was a murderer anyway because

---

"There is nothing analogous to it in the entire ancient Near Eastern world. This is surprising since seven-day units of time are well known throughout the region. Yet the Sabbath is the sole exception to the otherwise universal practice of basing all the major units of time—months and seasons, as well as years—on the phases of the moon and solar cycle. The Sabbath, in other words, is completely dissociated from the movement of celestial bodies. This singularity, together with Creation as the basis for the institution, expresses the quintessential idea of Israel's monotheism: God is entirely outside of and sovereign over nature."

[25] Jo Ann Davidson, "The Decalogue Predates Mount Sinai: Indicators from the Book of Genesis," *JATS* 19/1–2 (2008): 61–81.

[26] O. Palmer Robertson, *The Christ of the Covenants* (Phillipsburg, NJ: Presbyterian and Reformed, 1980), 68–81.

[27] Susannah Heschel, "Introduction to Heschel," in Abraham J. Heschel, *The Sabbath*, paperback ed. (New York: Farrar, Straus and Giroux, 2005), xv, observes that "strict adherence to the laws regulating Sabbath observance doesn't suffice; the goal is creating the Sabbath as a foretaste of paradise. The Sabbath is a metaphor for paradise and a testimony to God's presence."

he violated the order God had set up. Just as we cannot say that the obligation to abstain from murder could not exist before the sixth of the Ten Commandments was given to Israel, so we cannot say that the Sabbath could not exist as a human responsibility before the fourth commandment was given.

It is true that the Pentateuchal narratives do not mention the seventh day as a day of ceasing from work between the time God rested on the seventh day of creation (Gen 2:2–3) and the time He commanded the Israelites to observe Sabbath in the wilderness on the way to Mount Sinai (Exod 16:23–30). But neither do the early Pentateuchal narratives record the specific obligation to refrain from taking God's name in vain. This is stated in the third of the Ten Commandments (Exod 20:7) and illustrated in a later narrative (Lev 24:11–16, 23). The early silence does not constitute evidence that God did not expect people to live according to the implications of the creation order.

To summarize thus far, the context of Genesis 2:2–3 indicates that when God ceased/sabbathed on the seventh day of creation week, He did not abruptly stop setting up ongoing life for human beings on planet Earth and start doing something *ad hoc* exclusively for Himself. By His own example He created the Sabbath as the capstone and delineator of the ongoing weekly cycle for human beings. He created the world, vegetation, and non-human life by speaking. He created human beings in His image by forming dust, breathing His breath into nostrils, and using a rib (Gen 1:26–27; 2:7, 21–22). And then He created the blessed and holy Sabbath by "sabbathing" Himself.[28]

It is clear that God instituted the Sabbath for all human beings on planet Earth because He instituted it in the beginning, long before Israel existed, along with basic elements of human life such as marriage and labor. The fact that the Sabbath shows up as one of the Ten Commandments that God gave to Israel at Sinai does not negate the universality of the Sabbath, but rather supports it because the other nine commandments are universal principles applicable beyond the boundaries of the literal Israelite nation (cf. e.g., Rom 7:7).

---

[28] Cf. Hasel, "The Sabbath in the Pentateuch," 22–26; and idem, "Sabbath," 851. Sailhamer, *The Pentateuch as Narrative*, 71, adds, "The author likely also intends the reader to understand the account of the seventh day in the light of the 'image of God' theme of the sixth day. If the purpose of pointing to the 'likeness' between human beings and their Creator was to call on the reader to be like God (e.g. Lev 11:45), then it is significant that the account of the seventh day stresses the very thing the writer elsewhere so ardently calls on the reader to do: 'rest' on the seventh day (Ex 20:1–8)."

This interpretation of the Sabbath in Genesis 2 agrees with that of a Presbyterian scholar, who writes:

> His blessing of this day had a significant effect on the world. Furthermore, the reference to God's blessing the day should not be interpreted as meaning that God blessed the day with respect to himself. It was with respect to his creation, and with respect to man in particular that God blessed the Sabbath day. As Jesus pointedly indicated, "the Sabbath came into being [ἐγένετο] for the sake of man [διὰ τὸν ἄνθρωπον; Mark 2:27). Because it was for the good of man and the whole of creation, God instituted the Sabbath.
>
> Neither antinomianism nor dispensationalism may remove the obligation of the Christian today to observe the creation ordinance of the Sabbath. The absence of any explicit command concerning Sabbath-observance prior to Moses does not relegate the Sabbath principle to temporary legislation of the law-epoch. The creational character of God's sabbath-blessing must be remembered. From the very beginning, God set a distinctive blessing on the Sabbath… God blessed man through the Sabbath by delivering him from slavery to work.[29]

God invested the Sabbath with additional significance when He reaffirmed it for the Israelite nation. In addition to its function as a reminder of creation (Exod 20:11), the Sabbath became a reminder of God's deliverance of His people from Egypt (Deut 5:15). The latter event is thematically related to the former.[30] God delivered His people from Egypt because they were His, by virtue of His creative power, which was displayed in the ten plagues on Egypt and in His miraculous protection and provision for the Israelites in the wilderness.[31] Thus, God's deliverance was a manifestation

---

[29] Robertson, *The Christ of the Covenants*, 68–69.

[30] The concept of rest is not exclusive to Exodus 20:8–11, but is also implicit in Deuteronomy 5:14–15, where the Sabbath commandment is repeated. Hasel, "Sabbath," 852, finds that "the soteriological and freedom-from-slavery emphasis in Deut 5:14c–15a and the creation freedom-from-labor emphasis in Exod 20:11a indicate that one is dependent on the other and that both are humanitarian in essence. Man is to rest on the seventh day because YHWH, as rest-providing Creator, sets an example of rest for human beings and because YHWH, as liberating Redeemer, sets an example of rest from slavery so that all are able to rest (Exod 5:5)."

[31] Mathilde Frey, "The Sabbath in the Pentateuch: An Exegetical and Theological Study" (PhD diss., Andrews University, 2011), 133–188, provides a systematic contextual exegesis and close

of the ongoing divine creative power that Daniel proclaimed to King Belshazzar: "the God in whose hand is your very breath, and to whom belong all your ways" (Dan 5:23).

Because of its importance, the Sabbath was honored in the worship system of the Israelites. This is to be expected. It would be surprising if the Sabbath were not honored in this way. Additional sacrifices were offered at the Israelite sanctuary/temple on the Sabbath (Num 28:9–10). The "bread of the presence" on the golden table inside the sacred tent was changed every Sabbath "as a covenant forever" (Lev 24:8). This bread is the only offering at the sanctuary that is referred to in this way as an eternal covenant. It is no accident that it was renewed every Sabbath. The only other reference to an "eternal covenant" between God and the Israelites as a whole during the wilderness period is in Exodus 31:16–17, where the Sabbath, the memorial of creation, is called an eternal covenant. Thus, the "bread of the presence" offering, consisting of twelve loaves plus frankincense, was placed upon the golden table every Sabbath to acknowledge the dependence of the twelve tribes of Israel upon God as their resident Creator-Provider.[32]

The fact that the Sabbath was an important part of Israelite worship does not mean that it was only for the Israelites. It is true that the earthly sanctuary/temple and its rituals have given way to Christ's glorious heavenly ministry (Heb 7–10). It is also true that for most Christians, the Sabbath does not represent the redemption of their literal ancestors from Egypt. But the honored place of the Sabbath in the worship system of Israel at a particular phase of the divine covenant does not wipe out its significance for people living at other times and places.

Ongoing Sabbath or Temporary Type?

The second sub-question is: Does the seventh-day Sabbath have an *ongoing* literal application, or was it a temporary type that lost its literal significance when it met its antitype? The short answer to this question is: The ongoing applicability of the Sabbath, which God instituted at creation, has not ceased because the Sabbath has never functioned as a temporary type.

If God instituted the Sabbath for human beings before the fall (Gen 2:2–3; see above), the function/applicability of the Sabbath cannot be

---

reading of the Pentateuchal Sabbath texts, including Exodus 20:8–11 and Deuteronomy 5:12–15.

[32] See Roy Gane, "'Bread of the Presence' and Creator-in-Residence," *VT* 42 (1992): 179–203.

dependent upon its belonging to the system of temporary types that God set up after the fall in order to lead human beings back to belief in Him. That is to say, the Sabbath cannot be a temporary type because it pre-existed the need for temporary types.

Even if the Sabbath had originated as a human institution when God gave it to the Israelites, it would not necessarily follow that the Sabbath functioned as a temporary type to be superseded by the Christian "rest" experience. It is true that in Hebrews 4, Sabbath rest is used to symbolize a life of peaceful rest, involving all days of the week, which results from believing in God. Perhaps it could be said that as a microcosm of such a life, the Sabbath in a broad sense "typifies" such a life.[33] This idea is simply an extension of the significance that the Sabbath has had since God rested at the end of the creation week. But this does not mean that the Sabbath is a temporary, historical/horizontal kind of type like the Israelite sacrificial system. Nor does the fact that human beings imitate God by keeping the Sabbath indicate that the Sabbath is a temporary vertical type like the Israelite sanctuary. Examination of the biblical evidence yields the conclusion that the Sabbath is neither a historical/horizontal type nor a vertical type. As such, the Sabbath is fundamentally different from the Israelite festivals, at which rituals functioning as types constituted the essence of observance.

Sabbath as a Historical/Horizontal Type?

A historical/horizontal type consists of something that prefigures something in the future, which constitutes its antitype.[34] When the antitype commences, the type becomes obsolete. Thus, for example, the Levitical

---

[33] Richard M. Davidson agrees (in personal communication with the author).

[34] See more about typology in Richard M. Davidson, *Typology in Scripture: A Study of Hermeneutical τύπος Structures* (Berrien Springs, MI: Andrews University Press, 1981); idem, "The Eschatological Hermeneutic of Biblical Typology," *TheoRhema* 6 (2011): 5–48; Leonhard Goppelt, *Typos: The Typological Interpretation of the Old Testament in the New* (Grand Rapids, MI: Eerdmans, 1982); W. Edward Glenny, "Typology: A Summary of the Present Evangelical Discussion," *JETS* 40 (1997): 627–638; Walter C. Kaiser, *The Uses of the Old Testament in the New* (Eugene, OR: Wipf and Stock, 2001); Daniel Treier, "Typology," in *Dictionary for Theological Interpretation of the Bible*, ed. Kevin Vanhoozer (Grand Rapids, MI: Baker, 2005), 823–827; Peter J. Leithart, *Deep Exegesis: The Mystery of Reading Scripture* (Waco, TX: Baylor University Press, 2009); G. K. Beale, *The Right Doctrine from the Wrong Texts? Essays on the Use of the Old Testament in the New* (Grand Rapids, MI: Baker Academic, 1994); and idem, *Handbook on the New Testament Use of the Old Testament: Exegesis and Interpretation* (Grand Rapids, MI: Baker Academic, 2012).

priesthood was superseded by the greater Melchizedek priesthood of Jesus Christ (Heb 7–10). The Levitical priesthood functioned as a type in one era and ceased to function when its antitype, Christ's priesthood, began to function in the next era. Another example is the ritual of Passover, which Christ fulfilled and therefore superseded when He died on the cross (see John 19:14). Sacrificing literal sheep at the time of Passover can no longer point forward to Christ's death because that event is now in the past.

In the case of a historical/horizontal type, the type has significance, and then the antitype replaces it. The type and antitype do not function at the same time. A crucial test of whether or not the Sabbath functions as a historical type of a God-given life of "rest" is: Can the Sabbath function *at the same time* as the life of rest? The answer that arises from Hebrews 4 is yes. In this chapter, God's "rest" has not suddenly become available for Christians; it was available all along and was not fully appropriated in OT times only because of unbelief.[35] Because the life of rest was available in the OT, at the same time when the Sabbath was in operation for the Israelites, the Sabbath cannot be a historical type of the life of rest. The following paragraphs provide the exegetical basis for the conclusion that in Hebrews 4 the life of rest was available in OT times.

Hebrews 4:3, 5 quotes Psalm 95:11, where God says of the rebellious generation who left Egypt and rebelled at Meribah (Exod 17:2–7): "They shall not enter my rest." The reason why the ancient Israelites did not enter God's rest was not because such rest was available only to future Christians when type met antitype, but because they did not believe.[36] If they had

---

[35] Donald Guthrie, *Hebrews: An Introduction and Commentary*, TNTC (Downers Grove, IL: InterVarsity, 1983), 114–115; Harold Attridge and Helmut Koester, *The Epistle to the Hebrews: A Commentary on the Epistle to the Hebrews*, Hermeneia (Philadelphia, PA: Fortress, 1989), 123; William L. Lane, *Hebrews 1–8*, WBC (Dallas, TX: Word, 1998), 97.

[36] F. F. Bruce, *The Epistle to the Hebrews* (Grand Rapids, MI: Eerdmans, 1964), 74–75, makes this interesting comment: "It was not because the 'rest' of God was not yet available that the wilderness generation of Israelites failed to enter into it; it had been available ever since creation's work was ended. When we read that God 'rested on the seventh day from all his work which he had made' (Gen. 2:2), we are to understand that He *began* to rest then; the fact that He is never said to have completed His rest and resumed His work of creation implies that His rest continues still, and may be shared by those who respond to His overtures with faith and obedience. This interpretation that views the divine sabbath as beginning from the moment when creation's work came to an end and going on to the present time is paralleled in Philo and is implied by our Lord's words in John 5:17, 'My Father worketh even until now, and I work'. It differs from another interpretation that was widespread in the early Church, according to which the seventh day of Gen. 2:2f. is a type of the seventh age of righteousness that is to follow six ages of sin's domination. The identification of the rest of God in the Epistle to the Hebrews with a coming millennium on earth has, indeed, been ably defended; but it involves the importation into the epistle of

believed, they would have entered God's rest. "The reason why these men did not gain entrance was their own unbelief, not any failure on God's part to have the Rest ready."[37] The next generations could also have entered God's rest, but because of unbelief they stopped short of completely subduing Canaan and therefore failed to enjoy peace from striving against their enemies (Judg 1–3).

Hebrews 4:8 says, "For if Joshua had given them rest, God would not speak later about another day." Although rest was available as a result of the conquest under Joshua, it was not attained then because of unbelief, and God had to make a later appeal through the psalmist (Ps 95:7–8), which is quoted in Hebrews 4:7: "Today, if you hear his voice, do not harden your hearts." If God's rest would only become available when the seventh-day Sabbath and the Israelite worship system would lose their significance, why would God appeal to the Israelites through the psalmist to have this rest experience?

Hebrews 4 does not contradict the fact that there were some OT people who believed and *temporarily* enjoyed God-given rest. Joshua 23:1 says of the Israelites in the later years of Joshua: ". . . when the LORD had given rest to Israel from all their enemies all around . . ." David is another such example, as in 2 Samuel 7:1: "Now when the king was settled in his house, and the LORD had given him rest from all his enemies around him." But this rest for the Israelites and for David did not last because of their failure.

Of course, permanent rest in the ultimate sense will come only when God abolishes the present evil era (Rev 20–22). This rest is still future; it did not commence at the beginning of the Christian era.[38] But although Hebrews 4 refers to several kinds or aspects of rest, it emphasizes a rest that human beings can begin to enjoy in the present era:

---

a concept that in fact is alien to it." While the author of the present study agrees with Bruce that the divine spiritual rest experience described in Hebrews 4 has been available to human beings since they were created, he finds that Bruce has not clearly defined the relationship between literal rest *on* the seventh day and the continuous rest experience that *begins on* the seventh day. Genesis 2:2–3 says that God rested "on" the seventh day. This passage does not say God *began to* rest on the seventh day. Thus, Genesis 2:2–3 defines the seventh day as a unit of time during which rest occurs. It is true that God has not resumed His work of creation in the sense described in Genesis 1–2, but He does work, as shown by John 5:17, which is cited by Bruce. Therefore, the author interprets Genesis 2:2–3 as describing God's literal seventh-day rest, which serves as an example of literal rest to human beings. But this literal rest symbolizes a continuous "rest" experience available to human beings ever since the first Sabbath.

[37] James Moffatt, *A Critical and Exegetical Commentary on the Epistle to the Hebrews*, ICC (Edinburgh: T&T Clark, 1924), 51.

[38] Ibid., 53.

The emphasis, therefore, seems to be on that 'rest' that comes when the life is submitted to God. The whole discussion is reminiscent of the words of Jesus as recorded in Matthew 11:28, R.S.V.: "Come to me . . . and I will give you rest" . . . through the experience of personal salvation the individual might enjoy that 'rest' here and now through grace while preparing for the full experience ultimately in the kingdom of glory.[39]

Hebrews 4 appeals to Christians to succeed where people in OT times failed.[40] The condition for entering and remaining in God's rest is belief, and that is still true during the Christian era—or else Hebrews 4 would not need to make its appeal to "make every effort to enter that rest, so that no one may fall through such disobedience as theirs." It is those who have believed who are entering[41] God's rest (Heb 4:3). The Christian era does not change the basic dynamic of entering God's rest through belief (cf. Eph 2:8–9).[42]

To summarize the discussion of Hebrews 4, we do not find in this passage the kind of discontinuity between the OT and NT eras that we find in connection with the Israelite Levitical priesthood or the sacrifices officiated by that priesthood (see above).[43] The Sabbath and the rest of believers can function in the same era. If the Israelites had believed, the rest experience and the Sabbath would have functioned together at the same time. The fact that this was possible shows that the Sabbath did not function

---

[39] Roy Graham, "A Note on Hebrews 4:4–9," in *The Sabbath in Scripture and History*, ed. Kenneth A. Strand (Washington, DC: Review and Herald, 1982), 344.

[40] Erhard H. Gallos, "*Katapausis* and *Sabbatismos* in Hebrews 4" (PhD diss., Andrews University, 2012), 294–306.

[41] *Eiserchometha*, present tense in Greek (see W. F. Arndt and F. W. Gingrich, *A Greek-English Lexicon of the New Testament and Other Early Christian Literature* (Chicago: University of Chicago Press, 2000), 293–294.

[42] Harold Attridge, "'Let Us Strive to Enter That Rest': The Logic of Hebrews 4:1–11," *HTR* 73 (1980): 284, overlooks the basic continuity between the rest available in OT times and the rest available to Christians when he attempts to establish a type-antitype relationship between the exodus generation and the Christian community. It is true that the exodus generation serves as a negative *example* to Christians and a warning that Christians may also fail because of unbelief. But just because history has the potential of repeating itself through an analogous group of people does not mean that a type-antitype dynamic is present.

[43] For an introduction to the issue of continuity and discontinuity between the testaments, see John S. Feinberg, ed., *Continuity and Discontinuity: Perspectives on the Relationship between the Old and New Testaments, Essays in Honor of S. Lewis Johnson Jr.* (Wheaton, IL: Crossway, 1988).

as a temporary type that could only be fulfilled when the Christian era commenced.

The Sabbath and God's "rest" are not mutually exclusive, but rather, they are complementary.[44] Insofar as keeping the seventh-day Sabbath expresses and helps maintain belief in God (see below), it contributes to the experience of entering God's rest. Therefore, when God offered His "rest" to the Israelites, He offered the Sabbath along with it. The Sabbath was supposed to be part of God's "rest," and there is no indication in the Bible that this has changed.

At first glance, Colossians 2:16-17 might appear to contradict the conclusion reached from exegesis of Hebrews 4. Colossians 2:16-17 reads:

> 2:16 Therefore do not let anyone condemn you in matters of food and drink or of observing festivals, new moons, or sabbaths.
>
> 2:17 These are only a shadow of what is to come, but the substance belongs to Christ.

In Colossians 2:17, "shadow" means "temporary type." So does this mean that the "sabbaths" mentioned in verse 16 functioned as temporary types?

The issue here is ritual observance of special holy days. "Festivals, new moons, or sabbaths" inverts the order found in Numbers 28-29, and therefore appears to cite[45] this calendar of ritual offerings on holy days, which includes sacrifices on Sabbaths (Num 28:9-10), new moons (Num 28:11-15) and festivals (Num 28:16-29:40). These offerings were part of the Israelite worship system. But it was the rituals performed on the days, not the days themselves, that functioned as the shadowy types. Food and drink in this context have typological significance, so they refer to sacred ritual meals (e.g., Lev 7:15-16; Deut 12:6-7; 16:2-8).[46] It is such ritual observance[47] at the festivals, new moons, and Sabbaths that constitutes the "shadow"/type; it is

---

[44] Cf. Sigve K. Tonstad, *The Lost Meaning of the Seventh Day* (Berrien Springs, MI: Andrews University Press, 2009), 290.

[45] See Pancratius C. Beentjes, "Discovering a New Path of Intertextuality: Inverted Quotations and Their Dynamics," in *Literary Structure and Rhetorical Strategies in the Hebrew Bible*, ed. L. J. de Regt, J. deWaard, and J. P. Fokkelman (Assen: Van Gorcum, 1996), 31-50.

[46] See also Gane, *Old Testament Law for Christians*, 357-358.

[47] The words translated "of observing" by the NRSV in Colossians 2:16 are the combination of a preposition and noun, "in the matter of," literally "in the part of" (*en merei*) (Arndt and Gingrich, *A Greek-English Lexicon*, 507).

not the days themselves. There is no evidence that new moon days, for example, had typological significance of their own; it was the special sacrifices offered on new moon days (Num 28:11–15) that served as a "shadow."

In Colossians 2:16–17, Paul affirms the same basic message that was decided at the Jerusalem council (Acts 15): People do not need to practice the Jewish rituals in order to be Christians. The rituals were historical types pointing forward to the better, truly efficacious ministry of Jesus Christ, which has already begun and to which our focus should be directed.

So what about the prohibition of labor on the Sabbath, which is part of the Ten Commandments? Was this part of the ritual system that functioned as a shadow of things to come? No. It is true that the ritual system honored the Sabbath, but Sabbath rest itself is not a historical shadow/type (see above), and abstaining from work on the Sabbath existed before any ritual system was needed (see also above). Moreover, even for the Israelites, keeping Sabbath rest was never dependent upon the operation of the sanctuary/temple or its services. It could be observed wherever God's people found themselves.[48]

By recognizing the temporary nature of the Israelite ritual element that had been added by God to the Sabbath, Paul implies an affirmation of the underlying universality of the Sabbath, which can be kept by anyone apart from the Israelite ritual system. Paul does not touch the original function of the Sabbath itself. If he had, we can be sure there would have been a major uproar in the Christian church, calling for a council like the one in Jerusalem that dealt with the controversy over circumcision (Acts 15).[49]

Sabbath as a Vertical Type?

If the Sabbath does not function as a temporary historical/horizontal type, is it possible that it functioned as a temporary vertical type, like the Israelite sanctuary on earth that served as a copy of God's temple in heaven above (Exod 25:9; Heb 8:5; cf. Ps 11:4)? Could human, earthly rest on the seventh day be a copy of divine heavenly rest? The following factors, taken together, indicate that the Sabbath was not such a temporary vertical type:

---

[48] For instance, the Essenes in Qumran strictly observed the Sabbath even though they were disconnected from the temple in Jerusalem (see "Damascus Document" in Geza Vermes, *The Complete Dead Sea Scrolls in English* [London: Penguin, 2004], 141–142).

[49] Walter Specht, "The Sabbath in the New Testament," in *The Sabbath in Scripture and History*, ed. Kenneth Strand (Washington, D.C.: Review and Herald, 1982), 111.

1. That human beings imitate God in some respect does not indicate the existence of a temporary vertical type. In Leviticus 19:2, for example, God commands the Israelites to be holy as He is holy. The fact that the rest of Leviticus 19 consists of laws governing divine-human and human-human relationships indicates that the aspect of holiness in view is that of character. This call to emulate God's character is repeated in 1 Peter 1:16, quoting Leviticus 19:2. It is clearly a timeless command.[50]

2. In Genesis 2:2-3, God rests on the seventh day in connection with His creation of this world. There is no indication that the Sabbath was originally a heavenly institution that was then copied on earth in the same way that the earthly sanctuary was a copy of an original heavenly temple.

3. If the Sabbath were a temporary vertical type, we would expect some indication in the Bible regarding the end of its typical significance as we have in the case of the earthly sanctuary. The earthly temple lost its significance when the original heavenly temple took the place of the earthly as the location toward which worship should be directed (Heb 7–10). But there is no such indication that a similar dynamic applies to the Sabbath.[51]

Sabbath and the Israelite Festivals

If literal observance of the seventh-day Sabbath does not function as a temporary type and therefore should be maintained, should we also be obliged to keep elements of the Jewish festivals that do not function as temporary types?

The short answer is: No. It is true that not every activity connected with the Israelite worship system functioned as a temporary type. For example, the priestly blessing (Num 6:23–27) and prayers and music offered at the temple (1 Sam 1:10–11; 2:1–10; 1 Kgs 8:22–54; 1 Chr 6:31–46; 16:4–37, 41–42; 25:1–31) were simply part of the ongoing religious experience and did not function as types. But the rituals, which constituted the essence of observance of the festivals, did function as historical temporary types. According to the Bible, all of the Israelite spring festivals met their antitypes at the beginning of the Christian era. Christ died as the antitype of the Passover lamb (John 19:14). Christ rose as the "first fruits of those who have died" (1 Cor 15:20)—that is, as the antitype of the festival raised sheaf

---

[50] Roy Gane, *Leviticus, Numbers*, NIVAC (Grand Rapids, MI: Zondervan, 2004), 335–351.

[51] Ibid., 393–395.

(so-called "wave sheaf") of barley (Lev 23:11).[52] The Festival of Weeks, known as Pentecost, when the Festival, met its antitype in the early Christian harvest of souls through the outpouring of the Holy Spirit (Acts 2).

If the spring festivals were temporary types, it stands to reason that the autumn festivals, when even more sacrifices were offered (see Num 29), also functioned as temporary types.[53] There is no room in the present chapter to identify the antitypes of the autumn festivals, which would require more discussion than the antitypes of the spring festivals. However, the point relevant to this chapter has been made: Unlike the Sabbath, the essence of festival observance is constituted by ritual that functions as type.

Even if the Festival of Booths (so-called Festival of Tabernacles), which was the last of the autumn festivals (Lev 23:33–43; Num 29:12–38), has not yet met its antitype, this does not mean that Christians should be required to keep it today.[54] According to the NT, Christian worship is directed toward Christ in the heavenly sanctuary (Heb 7–10) rather than toward the resident Shekinah in an earthly sanctuary having human priests and a yearly cycle of national festivals.

The Israelite festivals were part of and owed their existence to the Israelite worship system. This system was grounded in the experience of the Israelite nation within its historical and agricultural context and limited to that phase of the covenant in which God's election of literal Israel operated.[55]

We could not, of course, fully keep the biblical festivals even if we wanted to, because that would require us to make pilgrimages to a temple in Jerusalem, where sacrifices would be offered (Exod 23:14–17; 34:22–24; Lev 23; Num 28–29). Following the destruction of the Second Temple in AD 70, the Jews developed adapted versions of the festivals that do not require sacrifices or pilgrimage. In this way, the Jews can continue to keep the festivals. These observances are based on important elements of the

---

[52] See Leviticus 23:11b, "on the day after the sabbath the priest shall raise it." Christ rose on Sunday, the day after the Sabbath (John 20:1).

[53] Ángel M. Rodríguez, *Israelite Festivals and the Christian Church* (Silver Spring, MD: Biblical Research Institute, 2005), 1–18.

[54] Edwin E. Reynolds, "The Feast of Tabernacles and the Book of Revelation," *AUSS* 38, no. 2 (2000): 245–268.

[55] For more on the Israelite Festivals, see, e.g., R. K. Harrison, "Feasts and Festivals of Israel," in *Baker Encyclopedia of the Bible* (Grand Rapids, MI: Baker, 1988), 783–788; M. O. Wise, "Feasts," in *Dictionary of Jesus and the Gospels*, ed. Joel B. Green and Scot McKnight (Downers Grove, IL: InterVarsity, 1992); E. E. Armerding, "Festivals and Feasts," in *Dictionary of the Old Testament: Pentateuch*, ed. T. Desmond Alexander and David W. Baker (Downers Grove, IL: InterVarsity, 2003), 300–313.

biblical festivals, to which postbiblical traditional liturgical and didactic elements have been added.

If a modern Christian wishes to participate in a Jewish festival occasion such as the Passover Seder, Yom Kippur (Day of Atonement), or Sukkot (Booths), he/she may find personal enrichment and edification. But we should not confuse the Jewish postbiblical adaptations with the mandatory biblical forms of the ancient Israelite festivals, which no longer exist.

The Israelite festivals have been carried on by the Jews because these observances commemorate the historical events that formed their nation, thereby keeping their heritage alive. As Christians, we share their heritage in the sense that we recognize the way God used the Israelites to reveal Himself and His purposes to the world. However, biblical events such as the exodus from Egypt, which is remembered in the Passover service, did not happen to our ancestors. Those events were limited to the experience of a particular people. But that limited exodus pointed forward to a universal exodus that belongs to all human beings equally: our exodus from sin and the control of Satan through the sacrificed body and blood of Jesus Christ, our Passover Lamb (1 Cor 5:7).[56] To keep this universal exodus alive, Jesus gave all Christians the Last Supper/Communion service, a Christian Passover that replaces the biblical Israelite Passover (Matt 26:26–29; 1 Cor 11:23–26). Since this service utilizes only bread and wine and does not require a human priest officiating at a temple, it can continue to function following the destruction of the Second Temple.

Jesus created the Christian Passover on the occasion of the biblical Passover, while the Second Temple was still standing, well before the Jews adapted the festivals for their own purposes. If Christ meant for Christians to keep altered forms of the festivals other than Passover, we would expect Him to have taught us what to do, as He did at the Last Supper.

There is a fundamental difference between ancient Israelite and Christian worship. The center and focus of the Israelite worship system was God dwelling among His people on earth, the resident Shekinah enthroned above the cherubim in the holiest apartment of the sanctuary/ temple (Exod 25:22; 1 Sam 4:4; 2 Sam 6:2; 2 Kgs 19:15, etc.). The sacrifices, festivals, songs, and prayers of the Israelites were directed toward God in His earthly dwelling place. They knew, of course, that God also lives in heaven (Ps 11:4) and that an earthly building cannot contain Him (1 Kgs 8:27;

---

[56] Elizabeth F. Lund, "'Out of Egypt:' The Exodus Motif in the New Testament" (PhD diss., Assemblies of God Theological Seminary, 2018).

cf. Isa 6:1), but their worship reached heaven via the earthly sanctuary/temple. Notice the wording in Solomon's dedicatory prayer: "Hear the plea of your servant and of your people Israel when they pray toward this place; O hear in heaven your dwelling place; heed and forgive" (1 Kgs 8:30). So Israelites prayed horizontally toward the temple, and they believed that from there the prayers went vertically to heaven. Notice that Daniel prayed horizontally toward Jerusalem even when the temple lay in ruins (Dan 6:10).

Unlike the Israelites under the Sinaitic covenant, Christians under the "New Covenant" are to orient their worship directly to the heavenly temple, where Christ ministers as their high priest (Heb 7–10). Christians do not need an earthly temple or mediation by earthly priests. By faith in the mediation of Christ, we can send our prayers vertically from wherever we are directly to God's "throne of grace" (Heb 4:16).[57]

To conclude this section, there is a basic difference between the Sabbath and the Israelite festivals.[58] The festivals were limited to the Sinaitic/Israelite phase of God's covenant by several factors:

1. The essence of festival observance involved rituals functioning as temporary historical types.

2. For their full observance, the festivals were dependent upon continuation of the Israelite ritual system.

3. The festivals were rooted in the particular national religious experience of the Israelite people.

By contrast, observance of the seventh-day Sabbath is not subject to any of these limitations. It is not a temporary type, it is not dependent upon continuation of the Israelite ritual system, and it is universal in origin (see above). Therefore, there is no reason to believe that the Sabbath was restricted to the Sinaitic phase of God's covenant.

Sabbath as Part of the "New Covenant"?

The third sub-question is: Does the seventh-day Sabbath have *theological significance* for the present phase of the divine covenant (that is, the "new covenant") or did it only have theological significance as part of the obsolete "old covenant"? Whereas the previous sub-question challenged

---

[57] Frank B. Holbrook, *The Atoning Priesthood of Jesus Christ* (Berrien Springs, MI: Adventist Theological Society Publications, 1996).

[58] H. Ross Cole, "The Sacred Times Prescribed in the Pentateuch: Old Testament Indicators of the Extent of their Applicability" (PhD diss., Andrews University, 1996).

the present applicability of the Sabbath on the basis of typology, the present question challenges its continuing relevance on the basis of covenant theology.

The short answer is: As a sign of the ongoing dependence of human beings upon their Creator and His work, the seventh-day Sabbath continues to have significance for the "new covenant." The fact that the Sabbath functioned during the "old covenant" period does not mean that the Sabbath became obsolete with that phase of the divine covenant. Rather, there is a sense in which the significance of the Sabbath is restored under the "new covenant."[59]

When God reaffirmed the Sabbath for Israel, the Sabbath was more than a commandment; according to Exodus 31:13, 17 (cf. Ezek 20:12), the Sabbath functioned as a sign of the covenant relationship by which He sanctified the Israelites.[60] This function applied to Israel a principle that had been inherent in the Sabbath since creation. On the seventh day of creation, God sanctified the Sabbath (Gen 2:2–3), a unit of time. Why? In order to affect those who observe this special time. How would they be affected? They would emulate their holy Creator and acknowledge their ongoing connection with Him. Because they would belong to God, who is intrinsically holy, they would gain holiness from Him. In other words, the Sabbath would be a sign that God makes people holy, just as God explicitly said in Exodus 31:13 with particular reference to the Israelites. From the beginning, His desire has been for all people to enjoy a holy relationship with Him.

The divine-human relationship signified by the Sabbath is one in which human beings are dependent upon God and His work. Thus, those who rest on the Sabbath acknowledge "that I, the LORD, sanctify you" (Exod 31:13) and "that in six days the LORD made heaven and earth" (Exod 31:17). The Sabbath is not simply the immovable "birthday of the world," it recognizes the dependence of the world—and more particularly the human beings who have dominion over the world—on God who created the world.

Our dependence on God is not only based upon what He did for us thousands of years ago. According to the Bible, He continues to sustain His creatures. Speaking to King Belshazzar, Daniel referred to "the God

---

[59] Gudmundur Olafsson, "God's Eternal Covenant and the Sabbath," *JATS* 16 (2005): 155–163.

[60] Roy Gane, "Sabbath and Sanctification," *JATS* 22 (2011): 3–15.

in whose power is your very breath, and to whom belong all your ways" (Dan 5:23; cf. Ps 114:14–15; 145:15–16; Job 12:10).

God will always be our Creator and Sustainer. Therefore, the basic meaning of the Sabbath, which encapsulates this divine-human relationship,[61] is timeless; it cannot become obsolete as long as human beings inhabit planet Earth.

It is true that God expressed the Sabbath to the Israelites in the form of a law.[62] It is also true that the Israelite phase of the covenant, which emphasized law, was defective and had to be replaced by the "new covenant." But this does not mean that the Sabbath became obsolete along with the Israelite "old covenant." This conclusion is based upon examination of the relationship between the "old" and "new" covenants. The "old covenant" was defective because Israel's response to God's covenant initiative was defective, not because God gave the "old covenant" to Israel as a faulty means of salvation by works.

There was nothing wrong with the covenant God offered to Israel.[63] Like earlier phases of the covenant, it was based upon grace. This is shown by the fact that God first saved Israel by grace, and then He gave His commandments to them. In Exodus 20, obedience to the Ten Commandments (Exod 20:3–17) is a response to the prior grace of "the LORD your God, who brought you out of the land of Egypt, out of the house of slavery" (Exod 20:2).

Earlier OT covenants were also based upon grace. God first saved Noah from the flood (Gen 7:1–8:19) and then formally inaugurated the covenant by giving Noah an ongoing covenant promise (Gen 8:21–22), blessings and commandments (Gen 9:1–7), and a sign of the promise (Gen 9:8–17). God first gave Abraham a military victory, keeping him safe as He saved Lot from His captors (Gen 14), and then God formally inaugurated the covenant with him (Gen 15, 17).

To Israel, as to Noah and Abraham, God offered salvation by grace through faith, as in the Christian era (Eph 2:8). There has never been a different way of salvation. The divine covenants are unified and function as phases of cumulative development in God's overall plan.[64]

---

[61] Cf. Cassuto, *A Commentary on the Book of Exodus*, 244.

[62] Gane, *Old Testament Law for Christians*, 248–255.

[63] Peter M. Van Bemmelen, "The Everlasting Covenant," *JATS* 24, no. 1 (2013): 92–106.

[64] Robertson, *The Christ of the Covenants*, 27–52 and John H. Walton, *Covenant: God's Purpose, God's Plan* (Grand Rapids, MI: Zondervan, 1994), 49–50.

It is true that Christ has eclipsed the Mosaic law in the sense that He is a more glorious revelation of God's character (2 Cor 3). But this means that Christ's revelation sheds greater light on the divine principles that constitute God's law. Christ magnified God's law (cf. Matt 5:17-48); He did not replace law as a means of salvation because God has never offered salvation on that basis.

While no amount of our own works can purchase our salvation (cf. Isa 55:1-3), our works are a necessary part of the faith response that accepts the gift of salvation that God freely gives to us. Real, living faith works through love (Gal 5:6). If faith does not have works, it is dead faith (Jas 2:26), not the kind of faith through which we can be saved by grace (Eph 2:8). Living in harmony with God's principles results from forgiveness. As Jesus said to the woman caught in adultery, "Neither do I condemn you. Go your way, and from now on do not sin again" (John 8:11).

Does not the idea that obedience to God is necessary contradict the dynamic of salvation by grace (Eph 2:8)? No, because obedience is a gift of grace. According to Romans 5:5, the Holy Spirit pours love into our hearts. Thus, God gives us love, the principle upon which law keeping is based (Matt 22:36-40), as a gift. The fact that the Holy Spirit was available to people in OT times (see e.g., Neh 9:20) indicates that the gift of love by the Spirit is not restricted to the Christian era.

Deuteronomy 6 informs us that God wanted the Israelites to respond to His prior grace by having an internalized, heart relationship with him. He commanded them, "You shall love the LORD your God with all your heart, and with all your soul, and with all your might. Keep these words that I am commanding you today in your heart" (Deut 6:5-6). Upon this principle of love for God and upon the principle of love for fellow human beings (Lev 19:18) all of God's OT commandments were based (Matt 22:36-40).

So God offered to the Israelites a covenant of grace and internalized love.[65] But it takes two parties to make a covenant. The good covenant became a defective "old covenant" because the divine-human relationship became dysfunctional due to human failure to have a heart relationship with God. This is clear from Jeremiah 31:31-34, which first mentions the "new covenant":

---

[65] Ronald Hals, *Grace and Faith in the Old Testament* (Minneapolis, MN: Augsburg, 1980); Skip MacCarty, *In Granite or Ingrained? What the Old and New Covenants Reveal about the Gospel, the Law, and the Sabbath* (Berrien Springs, MI: Andrews University Press, 2007).

> The days are surely coming, says the LORD, when I will make a new covenant with the house of Israel and the house of Judah. It will not be like the covenant that I made with their ancestors when I took them by the hand to bring them out of the land of Egypt—a covenant that they broke, though I was their husband, says the LORD. But this is the covenant that I will make with the house of Israel after those days, says the LORD: I will put my law within them, and I will write it on their hearts; and I will be their God, and they shall be my people. No longer shall they teach one another, or say to each other, "Know the LORD," for they shall all know me, from the least of them to the greatest, says the LORD; for I will forgive their iniquity, and remember their sin no more.

From this passage we can see that the difference between the "old covenant" and the "new covenant" is not the difference between "law" and "grace." Rather, it is the difference between failure to internalize God's law, resulting in disobedience, and successful internalization of God's law, resulting in obedience. It is harder to break the law when it is internalized; sin against law in the heart would be a "myocardial infraction."[66]

When the Israelites were disobedient and failed to receive sanctification from the Lord, any Sabbath keeping they did would have been a hypocritical outward form (cf. Isa 58). But by accepting God's grace and internalizing His law, including the Sabbath, the people could become holy as God is holy (Lev 19:2). Thus the Sabbath could be a true sign of a real sanctification experience (Exod 31:13; Isa 58).

> In obeying the fourth commandment, the believer does not negate the value of grace. On the contrary, the awareness of grace is implied. Through obedience to God's law, the believer expresses faith in God's grace. This principle is particularly valid when it applies to the Sabbath, because in it not only the divine law but also divine grace are magnified.[67]

---

[66] The key to the success of the "new covenant" is found in verse 34: "For I will forgive their iniquity, and remember their sin no more." The "new covenant" is based upon forgiveness. It is the sacrificial atonement of the incarnate Christ that draws all men to Him (see John 12:31), demonstrating the supreme love of God (John 3:16) and the utter dependence of human spiritual life upon divine grace. Whereas Israel at Sinai began covenant life with a clean slate, as a neonatal nation (cf. Exod 24:3b, 7b; Ezek 16), "new covenant" people begin from the humbling posture of accepting forgiveness. Such people know their weakness because they know they have fallen.

[67] Doukhan, "Loving the Sabbath as a Christian," 155.

By restoring sanctification, the "new covenant" restores the Sabbath to its true significance. Instead of being a hypocritical "tour de farce," the Sabbath points to a living reality: people who are allowing God to sanctify them keep the sanctified day.[68] During His ministry, Jesus showed Christians how to live under the "new covenant."[69] He did not wait to begin teaching Christians how to live until He had officially inaugurated the "new covenant" era with His broken body and spilled blood. So Jesus' example regarding the seventh-day Sabbath has prime relevance for Christians today. Luke 4:16 says, "When he came to Nazareth, where he had been brought up, he went to the synagogue on the sabbath day, as was his custom."

If Jesus had simply participated in Jewish worship on the Sabbath, the significance of His example would be limited.[70] But the fact that He took so much trouble to restore the Sabbath to its rightful place shows that it was of great importance for Him and therefore should be important for Christians.[71] Jesus risked controversy and danger by healing people on the Sabbath (see e.g., Mark 3:1–6; John 5:2–18; 9:1–41), thereby stripping away hypocritical human tradition and showing by example the purpose of the Sabbath as it was originally created by God's own example (Gen 2:2–3; see above): "The sabbath was made for humankind, and not humankind for the sabbath" (Mark 2:27).

It is no accident that Jesus made a point of healing people on the Sabbath,[72] thereby lifting their burdens and giving them rest from their suffering. His healing was a manifestation of His ongoing divine creative power. When Jesus was persecuted for healing on the Sabbath, He responded, "My Father is still working, and I also am working" (John 5:17).[73] Because of the divine creative work, human beings can have rest (cf. Ps 121:3–4).

---

[68] Gane, "Sabbath and Sanctification," 3–15.

[69] See Specht, "The Sabbath in the New Testament," 105.

[70] Compare His circumcision, done to Him when He was eight days old (Luke 2:21). The Jerusalem Council, guided by God, determined that circumcision was no longer relevant so that Gentiles could become Christians directly without first becoming Jewish (Acts 15).

[71] Kenneth A. Strand, "Sabbath," in *Handbook of Seventh-Day Adventist Theology*, vol. 12, electronic ed., Commentary Reference Series, ed. Raoul Dederen (Hagerstown, MD: Review and Herald, 2001), 502-505.

[72] Doukhan, "Loving the Sabbath as a Christian," 152.

[73] Kim Papaioannou, "John 5:18: Jesus and Sabbath Law—A Fresh Look at a Challenging Text," *JATS* 20 (2009): 244-261.

Moreover, Jesus' miracles provide "snapshots" of God's ideal for the world as He created it and to which He will restore it:

> Some see miracles as an implausible suspension of the laws of the physical universe. As signs, though, they serve just the opposite function. Death, decay, entropy, and destruction are the true suspensions of God's laws; miracles are the early glimpses of restoration. In the words of Jurgen Moltmann, "Jesus' healings are not supernatural miracles in a natural world. They are the only truly 'natural' things in a world that is unnatural, demonized and wounded."[74]

Under the "new covenant" phase of the divine covenant, God restores the world and human beings to the sinless ideal He had for them in the beginning (Rev 21–22). Since the Sabbath was part of the "covenant of Creation," before human sin arose, it is appropriate that the Sabbath continues into the sinless "new earth."

Evidence that the Sabbath will continue as a day of worship into the eschatological era is found in Isaiah 66:22–23: "For as the new heavens and the new earth, which I will make, shall remain before me, says the LORD; so shall your descendants and your name remain. From new moon to new moon, and from sabbath to sabbath, all flesh shall come to worship before me, says the LORD." The context of these verses shows that Isaiah envisioned the eschaton through the lens of God's plan to use literal Israel to gather all nations to Himself at Jerusalem (cf. Isa 66:18–21). As shown by comparison with the book of Revelation, God will still gather all nations to Himself (Rev 7:9–10). Since the Sabbath was universal from the beginning, there is no reason why it should be regarded as an obsolete element in Isaiah's eschatological description.

Isaiah 66:23 mentions ongoing eschatological worship on new moon days along with worship on sabbaths. Like sabbaths, new moons were honored by extra sacrifices in the Israelite ritual system (Num 28:11–15). This does not mean that new moon days cannot be worship days apart from the ritual system (see the same point above regarding the Sabbath). According to Genesis 1:14, before sin or the ritual system existed, God created and appointed the sun and the moon "to separate the day from the night; and let them be for signs and for seasons and for days and years." The term translated "seasons" here is *mo'adhim*, which refers to "appointed

---

[74] Philip Yancey, *The Jesus I Never Knew* (Grand Rapids, MI: Zondervan, 1995), 182–183.

times."⁷⁵ In passages such as Leviticus 23:2, 4, 37, 44, this word refers to regular, cyclical times of worship. In Genesis 1:14, the term could not include the Sabbath because the weekly cycle is not marked by movements of the sun or moon in relation to the earth as are days, months, and years. But new moons would fit well into the category of "seasons" (*moʿadhim*) in Genesis 1:14. Thus, eschatological observance of regular worship at new moons could revive a potential that was recognized at creation.⁷⁶ But we must make two qualifications here:

1. Isaiah 66:23 mentions sabbaths and new moons as days of worship. But whereas sabbaths by definition are days of rest, new moons are not. Sabbaths are constituted as sabbaths by cessation of ordinary weekly activity. New moons are constituted as such by the position of the moon in relation to the earth (see Gen 1:14). So Isaiah 66:23 does not inform us that new moons will be observed as eschatological days of *rest*.

2. Since God sanctified the Sabbath and instituted cessation of labor on this day by His example (Gen 2:2–3), which He subsequently reinforced by His command (Exod 20:8–11), the Sabbath is naturally a day of worship. But the Bible does not give us this kind of indication that we should observe new moons as days of worship in the Christian era. It is true that new moons were honored by additional sacrifices at the Israelite sanctuary (Num 28:11–15), but that appears to be all the attention they received. In fact, while the cultic calendar of Numbers 28 includes new moons because it lists the sacrifices, the list of cyclical appointed worship times in Leviticus 23 passes directly from seventh-day sabbaths (v. 3) to yearly festivals (vs. 4–43), without mentioning new moons at all. The implication seems to be that the new moons did not function as special days of worship except for the addition of some sacrifices.

To summarize this section, the "old covenant," as opposed to the "new covenant," was not a different means of salvation established by God during OT times, but rather was a relationship with Israel that was defective due to failure of the human party. So the "new covenant" does not supersede the "old covenant" by abolishing all aspects of what God offered to the Israelites, including His re-affirmation of the Sabbath. Rather, the "new covenant" fulfills the only ideal God has ever had for His people: a heart relationship with Him. As an important sign of the divine-human

---

⁷⁵ See *BDB*, s.v. *moʿedh*; K. Koch, "מועד *moʿedh*," *TDOT* 8:167–173.

⁷⁶ Compare the monthly cycle of the tree of life (Rev 22:2).

relationship, the Sabbath is restored to its full significance under the "new covenant."

Conclusion

The seventh-day Sabbath as a day of rest was given to the human race at creation, before there was a nation of Israel and before humanity needed redemption from sin. Therefore, the applicability of the Sabbath is not limited to the Israelite worship system or to the period of salvation history during which ritual observances functioned as temporary types. The Sabbath is for all human beings, whether or not they are sinners and whether or not they are Israelites. The Sabbath did not become obsolete along with the elective covenant with Israel, which became dysfunctional due to human failure. To the contrary, the Christian "new covenant" restores the significance of the Sabbath, when God's people have the experience of which the Sabbath has always been a sign: sanctification by God, the Creator who sanctified the Sabbath in the first place.

CHAPTER 10

The Sabbath in the Old Testament: Day of Rest or Day of Worship?

Elias Brasil de Souza

Introduction

Following an extensive study about the Sabbath,[1] one scholar concludes that

> for non-priestly Jews what the Hebrew Bible prescribes is rest on the Sabbath. They have no religious duties peculiar to the Sabbath. Some texts indicate that special Sabbath activities were required from the priests in the Jerusalem Temple. The priests had to work on the Sabbath, as on other days, and in some texts (Num 28–29; Ezek 45–46) they are instructed to offer extra sacrifices on each Sabbath day.[2]

In the same vein, another argues that

> Moses commanded the Jews to stay home and observe the Sabbath as a day of rest rather than a day of corporate worship. Sabbath corporate worship was mandated for the priesthood in the tabernacle/temple compound but not for individual Jews elsewhere.[3]

---

[1] Although "sabbath" may also refer to other religious festivals such as the Day of Atonement (Lev 16:31), the Festival of Trumpets (Lev 23:24), and the Feast of Booths (Lev 23:39), the present study deals with the seventh-day Sabbath.

[2] Heather A. McKay, *Sabbath and Synagogue: The Question of Sabbath Worship in Ancient Judaism*, ed. R. van den Broek, H. J. W. Drijvers, and H. S. Versnel (Boston, MA: Brill Academic, 2001), 247.

[3] Arnold G. Fruchtenbaum, "Messianic Congregations May Exist Within the Body of Messiah,

Thus, the task before us is to evaluate this claim in light of the biblical text. Is the biblical Sabbath merely a day of rest, or is worship also an integral part of what the Sabbath was (and is) meant to be? Although the definition of worship may be debated, from a biblical perspective worship may involve not only rites and rituals but also the study and explanation of Scripture done in recognition of or in obedience to God.[4] This study argues that the Sabbath, since its inception, was meant to be a day of worship as much as it was meant to be a day of rest. This study examines some of the main lines of evidence, discussed under six subheadings: Sabbath and Creation, Sabbath and Holy Time, Sabbath at Sinai, Sabbath and Sanctuary Building, Sabbath and Sanctuary/Temple Worship, and Sabbath under the New Covenant. Finally, a closing section summarizes and concludes the study.

Sabbath and Creation

The Sabbath emerges for the first time in the biblical canon as the climax of God's creation work. According to the biblical text:

> Thus the heavens and the earth, and all the host of them, were finished. And on the seventh day God ended His work which He had done, and He *rested* on the seventh day from all His work which He had done. Then God *blessed* the seventh day and *sanctified* it, because in it He rested from all His work which God had created and made (Gen 2:1–3).[5]

This climactic conclusion of the creation account comes through as a doxology that conveys the divine origin of the Sabbath by means of the three actions God performed in regard to the seventh day. As the text says, God rested (*shavath*), blessed (*barakh*), and sanctified (*qadhash*). It is important to note that God not only "rested" on the Sabbath, but also

---

as Long as They Don't Function Contrary to the New Testament Culture in Pieces: Essays on Ancient Texts in Honour of Peter Parsons," in *How Jewish Is Christianity?*, ed. Stanley N. Gundry and Louis Goldberg (Grand Rapids, MI: Zondervan, 2003), 124.

[4] McKay, *Sabbath and Synagogue*, 3, works with a very narrow definition: "Reading, studying and explaining sacred texts I do not necessarily regard as worship, unless given a place in a planned session of worship." Such a minimalist definition flies in the face of a number of psalms, which invite study and meditations of the Torah as actions pleasing to God (Josh 1:8; Pss 19:7–14; 1:1–3; 119:11, 15–16, 148).

[5] All biblical quotations are from the NKJV, unless otherwise indicated. Emphasis supplied.

"blessed" and "sanctified" it. Such divine actions put the seventh day above the other six days and indicate that it is to be devoted to sacred purposes.[6] Besides, such divine actions are fraught with the notion of worship insofar as they evoke similar actions later on in the context of the tabernacle.

As God blesses (*barakh*) the Sabbath—the sacred time—upon completing His act of creation, so Moses blesses (*barakh*) the people after completing the work of the tabernacle, the sacred space (Exod 39:43). And concerning the idea of holiness (*qadhash*), it occurs here for the first time and "occupies such an important place in the description of religious worship and godly life."[7] In fact, from the root *qdsh*—used here to designate the holiness of the Sabbath—comes the noun *miqdash*, which designates the sanctuary as the place of worship par excellence. Thus, prior to appointing a place of worship specifically designated as *miqdash*, God appointed a time of worship by sanctifying (*qadhash*) the seventh day of the week. The rationale for this lies in the fact that God is not only Lord over space, but also Lord over time. As the creation account shows, God created space by separating waters above from waters below, then water from dry land, and eventually planted the Garden of Eden, a space for humans to entertain communion with Him. In the same vein, after creating six units of time, God brought them to a climax when He separated (sanctified) the seventh day. The Sabbath then became the special time for communion between the Creator and human beings with significant repercussions for the created order.

To sum up, Genesis 2:1–3 implies that there is more to the Sabbath than simply "rest." Because God blessed and sanctified it, the seventh day has a doxological nature that calls for the worship of the Creator:

> The Sabbath passage [Gen 2:1–3] is the creation story's doxology: a hymn of praise that is not so much an assertion of the oneness of Deity as a call to Israel to acknowledge that oneness, to affirm the lordship of that One over ourselves, over our person and our property, over our time and activity—which is to say, the uses to which we put time.[8]

---

[6] Robert Jamieson, A. R. Fausset, and David Brown, *Commentary Critical and Explanatory on the Whole Bible*, vol. 1 (Oak Harbor, WA: Logos, 1997), 18.

[7] Herbert E. Ryle, *The Book of Genesis in the Revised Version with Introduction and Notes*, The Cambridge Bible for Schools and Colleges (Cambridge: Cambridge University Press, 1921), 25–26.

[8] Herbert C. Brichto, *The Names of God: Poetic Readings in Biblical Beginnings* (Oxford: Oxford

Sabbath and Holy Time

According to the OT worship system, God sanctified places, people, and objects—the place of the sanctuary/temple, the cultic personnel involved with the ritual services, and the objects related to the ritual system were made holy. But even before sanctifying places, people, and objects, God sanctified time. It is interesting to note that like the sanctuary/temple, its cultic objects, and personnel, the Sabbath could also be defiled (*khalal*). But how and in what ways can one speak of the defilement of something so intangible and abstract as time? As the sanctuary was devoted to God as His exclusive dwelling, so the Sabbath was devoted to God in that it was the day blessed and sanctified by the Creator.

Given its close connection with the sanctuary, the special place for worship, the Sabbath may be properly regarded as the special time for worship. Significantly, not only are the Sabbath and the sanctuary/tabernacle closely connected in several passages (Exod 31:12-17; 35:1-3; Lev 19:30), but "the Mosaic covenant was sealed by the observance of the Sabbath and by the tabernacle and its laws (Exod 24:1-18; 25:8-10)."[9] And on every Sabbath, twelve newly baked loaves of bread were set in order before the Lord (Lev 24:8) as a memorial of the covenant.[10] Thus, improper activities carried out on the Sabbath defiled it as if it were a portion of sacred space—hence the promise of blessings to those who refrained from defiling the Sabbath (Isa 56:1-7). Indeed, it appears that the very act of not performing improper activities on the Sabbath coupled with a proper attitude toward the Sabbath, including calling the seventh day "a delight," was tantamount to honoring (*kavedh*) the Lord (Isa 58:13), an attitude akin to that of worship (Pss 22:23; 50:23; 86:12; Isa 43:23; 66:5).[11]

It bears mentioning that the ritual service of the tabernacle unfolded according to a calendar of sacred times. The Israelite festivals followed a timetable determined by the month, which in Israel was regulated by the moon. But unlike the ceremonial feasts and other aspects of the sanctuary service, the weekly Sabbath was a sacred time set apart with no connection to the cycle of nature:

University Press, 1998), 69.

[9] Lamar E. Cooper, *Ezekiel*, NAC (Nashville, TN: Broadman and Holman, 1994), 379.

[10] See discussion under "Sabbath and the Tabernacle Rituals" in this study. See also the study of Roy Gane on the "Bread of Presence" in this volume.

[11] See C. Dohmen and P. Stenmans, "כבד *kavedh*," *TDOT* 7:19-20.

All regularly recurring events in ancient Israel were bound up with the cyclical changes of nature—the seasons or the revolutions of the moon or the sun. The impact of the climactological and astronomical divisions of time on the economic, social, and religious life of Israel, as anywhere in the ancient Near East, was overwhelming and elicited significant responses. Man who structured social time in accordance with the natural divisions of time was likely to be in harmony with nature. The structure all but guaranteed that the rhythm of society and culture should beat in unison with the rhythm of heaven, earth, and underworld.

For the Sabbath, however, there is no room in this physico-human periodicity. Having no bond with nature other than the change of day and night, the sabbatical cycle is indifferent to the harmony of the universe. It represents a neutral structuring of empty time.[12]

The same scholar continues,

The celebration of the Sabbath is an act completely different from anything comparable in the life of ancient Israel. The Sabbath is an isolated and strange phenomenon, not only in the world but also in Israel itself.[13]

Interestingly, another scholar has noted that

the authors of Scripture were well aware that the theology of paganism was chained to the natural rhythms of time, even to the celestial deities personified as Sun, Moon, Stars, and Constellations, which lorded it over the cycles of days and night, months and seasons and years; personified powers of nature that are demoted in Genesis to mere artifacts, lamps rising and setting on command of the one creator.[14]

Although attempts have been made to track the origins of the Sabbath outside of Scripture, no consensus has emerged. As one scholar summarizes,

---

[12] Matitiahu Tsevat, "The Basic Meaning of the Biblical Sabbath," *ZAW* 84 (1972): 457–458

[13] Ibid., 458.

[14] Brichto, *The Names of God*, 400.

no hypothesis whether astrological, menological, sociological, etymological, or cultic commands the respect of a scholarly consensus. Each hypothesis or combination of hypotheses has insurmountable problems. The quest for the origin of the sabbath [sic] outside of the OT cannot be pronounced to have been successful. It is, therefore, not surprising that this quest has been pushed into the background of studies on the Sabbath in recent years.[15]

It appears that the weekly Sabbath occupied a central place in the life of ancient Israel. As a day sanctified by the Creator, the Sabbath stands in the biblical canon as a memorial to creation. And to ancient Israel, the Sabbath was also the sign of the covenant. So most naturally the Sabbath has been understood as a day of rest—as clearly enjoined in the commandment—and a day of worship.

Sabbath and Sinai

As Israel marched through the wilderness—prior to the ratification of the covenant, the tabernacle, and the giving of the law—the Sabbath was already in force. Indeed, it is in connection with the manna narrative that the noun *shabbath* occurs for the first time in the OT (Exod 16). God provided sufficient food every day, but on the sixth day He gave them twice as much manna so that they would not need to gather food on the Sabbath. Those who disobeyed incurred God's displeasure. One should note, however, that the cessation of work on the Sabbath was not an end in itself. As one scholar perceptively suggests, "The importance is not simply in the abstention of activity but on what this abstention allows Israel to concentrate: the Lord's presence in its midst."[16] In other words, on the Sabbath the people were free to reflect on and respond to the great act of redemption performed by the Lord in their behalf.[17]

---

[15] Gerhard F. Hasel, "Sabbath," *ABD* 5:851. See also the contribution of Martin Pröbstle, "Origin of the Sabbath," in this volume.

[16] Michael H. Burer, *Divine Sabbath Work*, ed. Richard S. Hess (Winona Lake, IN: Eisenbrauns, 2012), 33.

[17] The subsequent association of the Sabbath with joy finds its root in the manna experience, as noted by Brevard S. Childs, *The Book of Exodus: A Critical, Theological Commentary*, OTL (Louisville, KY: John Knox, 2004), 290: "In the verses which follow [Exod 16:31–36] Moses explains in detail the nature of the sabbath and what it entails. It stems from a command of God; it is a day of special rest; it is set apart from the ordinary and dedicated to God. In anticipation

Thus, the manna is explicitly associated with the liberation of the people from Egyptian bondage (Exod 16:32) and subsequently memorialized by its deposit before "the Testimony" (Exod 16:34). As the exodus narrative unfolds, the interconnections of the seventh day, the covenant, and the tabernacle further indicate that the meaning of the Sabbath was not exhausted by the mere cessation of work.

Indeed, a close look at the tabernacle narrative shows important connections between Sabbath and tabernacle, which further underscores the Sabbath as a day of worship. In the narrative of the Sinaitic covenant there appears an interesting allusion to the Sabbath that seems to link it with worship: "Now the glory of the Lord rested on Mount Sinai, and the cloud covered it six days. And on the seventh day He called to Moses out of the midst of the cloud" (Exod 24:16). A few observations are important in regard to this passage:

First, there is a succession of six days concluded by a seventh. Although this passage makes no explicit reference to the Sabbath, it appears to evoke the creation week made of six days followed by the climactic seventh day. As the seventh day of the creation week comes to a climax with divine rest, blessing, and sanctification, the seventh day of the Sinai theophany comes to a climax with a call for Moses to come from the midst of the cloud to sight "the glory of the Lord," which was like "a consuming fire" (Exod 24:17).

Second, this passage belongs to the literary unit formed by Exodus 19–24. This unit reports the ratification of the Sinaitic covenant, the Sabbath commandment in the context of the Ten Commandments, along with other religious, ethical, and social laws. Moreover, this literary section sets the foundation for Israel's cult and worship, as indicated by the following details: Mount Sinai was fenced all around, access to it was restricted to a few individuals, and only Moses was allowed to climb the mountaintop. Such apparent gradation of holiness proleptically points to the tabernacle with its gradation of sacred space composed of courtyard, holy place, and most holy place.[18]

---

for this special day, Israel is encouraged to be prepared. The manna can be baked or boiled—its properties are indeed wonderful—and kept in any form desired. When the people took Moses' advice, it did not spoil or become rancid. There is a festive ring in Moses' speech which continues in v. 25. The sabbath is not a day to go hungry and mourn. Rather Israel is to eat, for 'today' is God's special day. Later tradition expanded greatly on the theme of the joy of the sabbath, but the kernel of the theme is already present in the manna story."

[18] See Ángel M. Rodríguez, "Sanctuary Theology in the Book of Exodus," *AUSS* 24 (1986): 127–145. U. Cassuto, *A Commentary on the Book of Exodus* (Jerusalem: Magnes, 1997), 484,

Third, it is important to note that Moses came out of the cloud on the seventh day in order to receive instructions to build the tabernacle—as reported in the next major literary unit of Exodus (chaps. 25–31). Interestingly, it was most likely on the seventh day that God commanded Moses, "And let them make Me a sanctuary [*miqdash*], that I may dwell among them. According to all that I show you, that is, the pattern of the tabernacle and the pattern of all its furnishings, just so you shall make it" (Exod 25:8–9). It seems fitting that during sacred time (Sabbath) God issued the order for Moses to construct the sacred space (sanctuary).[19]

Thus, it seems that the linkage of the "seventh day" with the covenant and the Hebrew ritual system further reinforces the notion that the Sabbath is not only a day of rest, but a day of worship. In addition, since it is rooted in creation, the Sabbath obviously precedes the earthy tabernacle and extends its validity beyond it. As one scholar aptly states,

> According to this passage the holy place, the holy period of time, the mediator of the holy are basic to the structure of the cultic event. Though it is only in this event that the holy place is founded (Sinai and the tent of the meeting which derives from it and which prefigures the temple in Jerusalem), the holy period is nevertheless already there ("six days . . . and on the seventh day").[20]

Sabbath and Sanctuary Building

Further connections between Sabbath and worship may be inferred from certain literary strategies reflected in the tabernacle account in Exodus. First, it should be noted that at the end of the directives to build the tabernacle comes an instruction about the Sabbath: "Therefore the children of Israel shall keep the Sabbath, to observe [*la'asoth*] the Sabbath"

---

states, "The Tabernacle is a kind of miniature Sinai, which can be transported from place to place, in order to accompany the children of Israel in their wanderings and to serve as a palpable token of the Divine Presence in their midst throughout their journeyings. Just as the Lord had revealed Himself to them on Mount Sinai in the awe-inspiring theophany of the third month, even so He manifests Himself to them now, and will reveal Himself in the future, in the sanctuary that they have made to Him."

[19] Thus, Abraham J. Heschel, *The Sabbath: Its Meaning for Modern Man* (New York: Farrar, Straus and Young, 1951), 29, argues that the Sabbath is a kind of sanctuary in time, and William H. C. Propp, *Exodus 19–40*, AB (New York: Doubleday, 2006), 692, adds that the tabernacle is a Sabbath in space.

[20] Claus Westermann, *Genesis 1–11: A Continental Commentary* (Minneapolis, MN: Fortress, 1994), 172.

(Exod 31:16). This recalls Genesis 2:3: "Because in it He rested from all His work which God had created and made [*la ʿasoth*]." So there is a close connection by means of the Hebrew prepositional phrase *la ʿasoth*, which as a *Leitwort* links both passages together.[21] One may further inquire about the reasons for the juxtaposition of this piece of Sabbath legislation with the construction of the tabernacle. According to rabbinic and medieval Jewish commentators, this juxtaposition shows that work for the sanctuary does not supplant the Sabbath.[22] Whatever the case may be, the formula "You shall keep My Sabbaths and reverence My sanctuary: I am the Lord" (Lev 19:30; 26:2) explicitly integrates Sabbath and sanctuary. But the fact that the Sabbath is mentioned before the sanctuary in the two occurrences of this formula may indicate that the former has precedence over the latter.

The instructions to build the tabernacle, reported in the book of Exodus, can be divided into seven sections. All of them are introduced by a formula of direct speech in which God speaks to Moses, thus echoing the seven days of creation.

1. "Then the Lord spoke to Moses, saying..." (Exod 25:1)
2. "Then the Lord spoke to Moses, saying..." (Exod 30:11)
3. "Then the Lord spoke to Moses, saying..." (Exod 30:17)
4. "Moreover the Lord spoke to Moses, saying..." (Exod 30:22)
5. "And the Lord said to Moses..." (Exod 30:34)
6. "Then the Lord spoke to Moses, saying..." (Exod 31:1)
7. "And the Lord spoke to Moses, saying..." (Exod 31:12)[23]

And the connection becomes explicit because the seventh section deals with the Sabbath:

> Speak also to the children of Israel, saying: "Surely My Sabbaths you shall keep, for it is a sign between Me and you throughout your generations, that you may know that I am the Lord who sanctifies you. You shall keep the Sabbath, therefore, for it is holy to you. Everyone who profanes it shall surely be put to death; for whoever does any work on it, that person shall be cut off from among his people. Work shall be done for six days, but the seventh is the

---

[21] Shimon Bakon, "Creation, Tabernacle and Sabbath," *JBQ* 25 (1997): 79–85.

[22] Israel Knohl, *The Sanctuary of Silence: The Priestly Torah and the Holiness School* (Minneapolis, MN: Fortress, 1995), 16.

[23] Emphasis supplied.

Sabbath of rest, holy to the Lord. Whoever does any work on the Sabbath day, he shall surely be put to death" (Exod 31:12–15).

This passage "shows that the Sabbath is regarded as more important than the building of the Tabernacle because the Israelites were to keep the Sabbath even during its construction, and it shows that the regular worship of God and his presence among them will be grounded in the Sabbath."[24]

Now let us consider Exodus 40, which reports the completion of the tabernacle and its consequent dedication. This final chapter is also divided into seven sections. Each section concludes with the resumptive formula stating that Moses executed the work as "the Lord had commanded [*tsiwwah*]."

1. "Thus Moses did; according to all that the Lord had commanded him, so he did" (Exod 40:16)
2. ". . . as the Lord had commanded Moses" (Exod 40:21)
3. ". . . as the Lord had commanded Moses" (Exod 40:23)
4. ". . . as the Lord had commanded Moses" (Exod 40:25)
5. ". . . as the Lord had commanded Moses" (Exod 40:27)
6. ". . . as the Lord had commanded Moses" (Exod 40:29)
7. ". . . as the Lord had commanded Moses" (Exod 40:32)[25]

The seventh and concluding formula is followed by a depiction of God's glory filling the tabernacle and the cloud resting above it: "Then the cloud covered the tabernacle of meeting, and the glory of the LORD filled the tabernacle. And Moses was not able to enter the tabernacle of meeting, because the cloud rested [*shakhan*] above it, and the glory [*kavodh*] of the LORD filled the tabernacle" (Exod 40:34–35).

It is not surprising that in connection to the seventh formula God is portrayed as taking His rest inside the tabernacle as He rested on the seventh day of creation. While the verb "rest" does not occur in these verses, the concept is certainly present. The resting of the cloud and the filling of the tabernacle with glory depict the Lord's resting in the tabernacle. Elsewhere the Hebrew Scriptures explicitly designate the temple/tabernacle as a resting place (*menukhah*) for the Lord (Ps 132:7–8). So God's rest in connection to the tabernacle points to the manifestation of His presence inside His earthly dwelling. God's rest in the context of the sanctuary

---

[24] Burer, *Divine Sabbath Work*, 36.

[25] Emphasis supplied.

means that He accepted the construction work carried out by Moses and took residence inside the tabernacle.

It bears noting that the two series of sevens (Exodus 25–31 and Exodus 40) are somehow theologically connected. The first one focuses on the construction of the tabernacle while the second one centers on its inauguration. But while the first ends by emphasizing the sacred time (Sabbath) for humans to rest, the second concludes by depicting the sacred space (tabernacle) in which God's glory rests. Furthermore, while the first one climaxes by emphasizing the perpetual sign of the covenant inscribed in the sacred time (Sabbath), the second one concludes with a focus on the sacred space (tabernacle) that epitomizes God's covenantal presence among His people. Indeed, the two series of sevens indicate the tight interconnection between the Sabbath and tabernacle. In this context, God's rest certainly moved the people to respond with worship. Although rest is not exclusive of worship, it points to the divine presence that invites worship.

One should also note that in the context of the covenant, the Sabbath also pointed to the redemption of Israel in Egypt (Deut 5:15). As stated, one explicit purpose for the exodus was to provide God's people with an opportunity to worship (Exod 9:1), a reality that began to be realized in the momentous experience at Sinai. There God made a covenant with the people and made the Sabbath into the covenant sign. Thus, the connection of the Sabbath with the exodus, the purpose of which was worship, indicates that the seventh day should not be dissociated from the worship experience of the event it was supposed to memorialize. Subsequently, as the nation found rest in the land, the occasion arose to set up a permanent dwelling for the Lord. Significantly, the biblical narrative also links the construction of the the temple with the rest (*menukhah*) God gave to the nation (1 Kgs 8:56; see also 1 Kgs 5:4; 1 Chr 22:9–10, 18–19; 23:25; 28:2). The connection between rest and the covenant/sanctuary/temple indicates that rest provides the condition and environment for worship. Thus the Sabbath, being a day of rest, must also have been understood as a day of worship.

Sabbath and Sanctuary/Temple Worship

Sabbath as a Holy Convocation

The Sabbath day was to be a holy convocation: "Six days shall work be done, but the seventh day is a Sabbath of solemn rest, a *holy convocation*. You shall do no work on it; it is the Sabbath of the Lord in all your dwellings" (Lev 23:3).²⁶ The designation of the Sabbath day as a "holy convocation" most likely indicates that the community was convoked for corporate worship and celebration.²⁷ In addition, it should be noted that the five feasts mentioned in Leviticus 23 are also holy convocations, which certainly involved corporate worship: the Feast of Unleavened Bread or Passover (Exod 12:16; Lev 23:7-8; Num 28:18, 25), the Feast of Weeks or Pentecost (Lev 23:21; Num 28:26), the Feast of Trumpets (Lev 23:24; Num 29:1), the Day of Atonement (Lev 23:27; Num 29:7), and the Feast of Tabernacles or Booths (Lev 23:35-36; Num 29:12).²⁸ It is interesting to note that the parallel lists of holy convocations contained in Leviticus and Numbers are introduced with specific instructions about the celebration of the weekly Sabbath as a day of holy convocation. That is, before the annual feasts are set out, the people are reminded of the weekly holy convocation, the Sabbath. This does not mean that the weekly Sabbath should be taken as a ceremonial law like the annual feasts. Rather, this indicates that the weekly Sabbath sets the tone for the pentateuchal laws about the festivals²⁹ in that the Israelites were to observe the festivals in the same way they celebrated the Sabbath.³⁰

Although one scholar argues that the Sabbath in Leviticus 23:3 functioned as a day of corporate worship only for the priests, such a restrictive interpretation of the phrase "holy convocation" does not seem compelling.³¹ Indeed, the latter were already involved in the ritual activities of the sanctuary and were permanently "convoked" by default. Most likely, the phrase "holy convocation" designates the Sabbath as a day of corporate worship, as recognized by several commentators.³²

---

²⁶ Emphasis supplied.

²⁷ Baruch A. Levine, *Leviticus*, JPSTC (Philadelphia, PA: Jewish Publication Society, 1989), 154. See also Leland Ryken et al., *Dictionary of Biblical Imagery* (Downers Grove, IL: InterVarsity, 2000), 747.

²⁸ David B. W. Phillips, "Holy Convocation," in *The Lexham Bible Dictionary*, ed. John D. Barry et al. (Bellingham, WA: Lexham, 2016).

²⁹ See Gordon J. Wenham, *The Book of Leviticus*, NICOT (Grand Rapids, MI: Eerdmans, 1979), 301-302 and Levine, *Leviticus*, 154.

³⁰ According to Burer, *Divine Sabbath Work*, 38, "this placement of the Sabbath command at the head of legislation involving the festival calendar for Israel indicates a strong connection between the Sabbath and these festivals that Israel is to observe, because they all involve the sanctification of time."

³¹ Fruchtenbaum, "Messianic Congregations," 25.

³² Levine, *Leviticus*, 154; Armor D. Peisker, "The Book of Leviticus," in *Genesis–Deuteronomy*, *The Wesleyan Bible Commentary*, vol. 1, ed. Charles W. Carter (Grand Rapids, MI: Eerdmans,

By this we do not need to posit that every Sabbath the entire nation would come to worship in the tabernacle. It may be hypothesized that such holy convocation was primarily intended for tribal leaders and elders. At this point, one is reminded of the revelation at Sinai when only Moses, Aaron, and the seventy elders of Israel as representatives of the nation were allowed to access the mountain to experience that worshipful encounter with the Lord. In light of this event, it is not illogical to understand the holy convocations related to the Sabbath day as primarily intended for representatives of tribes, clans, and/or families.

In this connection, it bears noting that even during times of religious apostasy when the northern kingdom plunged into Baal worship, as was the case during Ahab's reign, the Sabbath seems to have remained an occasion of assembling for worship. From the narrative of the resurrection of the Shunammite's son, it appears that the husband was surprised to see his wife going to see the prophet Elisha: "Why are you going to him today? It is neither the New Moon nor the Sabbath" (2 Kgs 4:23). Seemingly, as the question suggests, it was customary for the Shunammite to leave her home on Sabbath to see the prophet.[33] Although no more details are given, it is likely that she would attend some kind of cultic activity led by the prophet. Indeed, it seems that prophets led the worship services when it was impossible to have the service of priests or Levites.[34] Assuming that such an encounter most likely would have involved other people, it is reasonable to suppose that the Sabbath was an occasion not only of cessation from work, but also a time for sacrifices and prayers.[35] One plausible suggestion is that this was a time "when the godly in Israel were in the habit of sitting at the feet of a religious teacher and having him instruct them."[36] The text indicates that even under

---

1967), 352; and Walter C. Kaiser Jr., "The Book of Leviticus," in *New Interpreter's Bible*, vol. 1, ed. Leander E. Keck (Nashville, TN: Abingdon, 1994–2004), 1157.

[33] According to T. R. Hobbs, *2 Kings*, WBC (Dallas, TX: Word, 1998), 51-52, the question may imply one of several elements: "Elisha might have received visitors only on feast days or sabbaths. The visit of the woman would then be out of order. The woman herself might have visited the prophet on a regular basis on such days. Another possibility is that festive days and sabbaths were those on which no work was done, therefore the woman would be free to make journey on those days only." The question, however, seems to imply that the woman used to do such journeys on new moons and Sabbaths. This is corroborated by other passages that mention the Sabbath in connection with sacrifices and festivals (2 Chr 2:4; Isa 1:13; Hos 2:11).

[34] J. Rawson Lumby, *The Second Book of the Kings with Introduction and Notes*, The Cambridge Bible for Schools and Colleges (Cambridge: Cambridge University Press, 1891), 40.

[35] SDABC 2:869.

[36] Cyril J. Barber, *The Books of Kings: The Righteousness of God Illustrated in the Lives of the People*

challenging circumstances in Israel, the Sabbath seems to have been a day devoted to prayers, sacrifices, and the teaching of Scripture.

Sabbath and the Tabernacle Rituals

Two specific procedures set the Sabbath apart as a singular day in the course of the sanctuary services. Every Sabbath the bread of the presence was renewed (Lev 24:5–9) and additional sacrifices were offered (Num 28:9–10). The ritual renewal of the bread of the presence every Sabbath connected the bread to the Sabbath, and thus to creation.[37] The expression "bread of the presence" (*lekhem panim*) points to the fact that bread was placed in the presence of the Lord. This "emphasizes the theocentric nature of the cult: Rituals are performed with reference to YHWH."[38] In addition, the "'bread of the presence' is the only offering designated as *bᵉrit 'ōlām* 'an eternal covenant' (Lev. xxiv 8). Thus, it uniquely symbolizes the relationship itself between YHWH and his people, not serving merely as an instrument of that relationship."[39] Although space constraints do not allow further elaboration on the profound implications of this concept for the ritual service and theology of the tabernacle, clearly the seventh-day Sabbath was a special time in the services of the sanctuary. On Sabbath, the priests as representatives of the people brought the twelve loaves of bread and set them on the table in two rows of six each. In this way Israel reaffirmed its relationship with the Lord as Creator and Provider. That Israel expressed such a worshipful response to God as Creator and Provider precisely on the Sabbath day is a telling indication that the seventh day functioned also as a day of worship.

But in addition to the renewal of the bread of the presence, some special sacrifices were offered on the Sabbath day and so the regular services of the sanctuary changed on the seventh day:

> And on the Sabbath day two lambs in their first year, without blemish, and two-tenths of an ephah of fine flour as a grain offering, mixed with oil, with its drink offering—this is the burnt offering for every Sabbath, besides the regular burnt offering with its drink offering (Num 28:9–10).

---

of Israel and Judah (Eugene, OR: Wipf and Stock, 2004), 2:108.
[37] Roy Gane, "'Bread of the Presence' and Creator-in-Residence," *VT* 42, no. 2 (1992): 179–203.
[38] Ibid., 181.
[39] Ibid., 192.

Such change in the sanctuary service every seventh day most likely points to the Sabbath "as a special day of worship within the cultic system of the sanctuary."[40] This by no means indicates that the theological and practical relevance of the Sabbath would have been restricted to the ritual system. Rather, it shows that the worship system of ancient Israel could not operate without regard for the Sabbath, the origins of which go back to creation (Gen 2:1–3).

Sabbath and Temple Worship

Attention must now be turned to a few passages in the historical books and the Psalms. At the outset, it bears noting David's instructions to the Levites

> to stand every morning to thank and praise the Lord, and likewise at evening; and at every presentation of a burnt offering to the Lord on the Sabbaths and on the New Moons and on the set feasts, by number according to the ordinance governing them, regularly before the Lord (1 Chr 23:30–31).

In addition to other sacrifices and cultic occasions, it is significant that praises should accompany the Sabbath sacrifices as well. Another significant passage for this study links the Sabbath to the temple worship envisioned by Solomon:

> Behold, I am building a temple for the name of the Lord my God, to dedicate it to Him, to burn before Him sweet incense, for the continual showbread, for the burnt offerings morning and evening, on the Sabbaths, on the New Moons, and on the set feasts of the Lord our God. This is an ordinance forever to Israel (2 Chr 2:4; cf. 8:13).

The above passages certainly refer to the extra offerings of the Sabbaths (Num 28:9–10), which, as noted in the previous section, shows that the Sabbath was a day of worship as much as it was a day of rest inasmuch as it was fully integrated into the liturgical activities of the temple.

Another reference to the Sabbath occurs in 2 Kings 16:17–18, which mentions the "Sabbath pavilion" (*mesakh hashabbath*),[41] dismantled by King

---

[40] Mathilde Frey, "The Sabbath in the Pentateuch: An Exegetical and Theological Study" (PhD diss., Andrews University, 2011), 251.

[41] The Septuagint translates the expression as *themelion tēs kathedras* ("base of the throne"),

Ahaz along with other cultic implements because of the king of Assyria.[42] Apparently the word *musakh* refers to a "*covered* structure"[43] and may be related to *masakh*, which occurs "in connection with the several entrance screens in the tabernacle complex (Ex 39:34–40)."[44] Commentators have struggled to understand this passage and ascertain the meaning and role of the "Sabbath pavilion" in the temple. According to one opinion, it might have designated "a covered place, stand or hall in the court of the temple, to be used by the king whenever he visited the temple with his retinue on the Sabbath or on feast-days."[45] Indeed, the reference to the removal of the "king's outer entrance" (2 Kgs 16:18) may refer to the entryway by which the king would have access to the temple (1 Kgs 10:5) and was supposed to be opened only on the Sabbath and the New Moon (cf. Ezek 46:1–2).

Admittedly, the interpretation of the "Sabbath pavilion" in 2 Kings 16:17–18 is fraught with exegetical and linguistic difficulties. But however one understands the specific meaning of the term and the function of that structure, it seems evident that the Sabbath was important enough to deserve a special structure associated with the temple service. It follows from this that the Sabbath was not only an occasion in which the Israelites refrained from work, but a day that was honored and "sanctified" within the supreme cultic institution of the nation.

After brief consideration of the historical books, attention must now turn to the book of Psalms. At first glance, it seems striking that a biblical work so devoted to worship hardly mentions the Sabbath—and even more so considering the fact that worship in the Psalms largely presupposes a sanctuary/temple setting. In this connection, two observations are in order.

First, it should be noted that not only the Sabbath but also the annual feasts are seldom mentioned in the Psalms. In spite of a sustained focus on temple worship, the psalmists hardly mention—either in the superscriptions or in the body of their compositions—the liturgical setting in which such worship took place. As a matter of fact, some superscriptions mention

---

which may read the Hebrew as *musadh hasheveth*. However, there is no attestation for such a reading in extant Hebrew manuscripts and other ancient versions.

[42] For a summary of possible interpretations, see the entry "Sabbath Canopy" in Moisés Silva and Merrill Chapin Tenney, *The Zondervan Encyclopedia of the Bible, Q-Z* (Grand Rapids, MI: Zondervan, 2009), 225.

[43] *BDB*, s.v. *musakh*.

[44] R. D. Patterson, "סכך *sakhakh*," *TWOT* 624.

[45] Carl F. Keil and Franz Delitzsch, *Commentary on the Old Testament* (Peabody, MA: Hendrickson, 1996), 3:289.

the occasion or circumstances of composition of their respective psalms, but there is hardly any connection between an individual psalm and its worship setting.[46] This may indicate that the same psalm could be used on more than one cultic occasion, which in turn would explain why most psalms give more attention to the temple than to the weekly Sabbath and the annual feasts.

Second, in spite of the paucity of references and/or allusions to the Sabbath in the book of Psalms, there are some indications that the psalmists were not oblivious to the seventh day as a day of worship. Several lines of evidence may be suggested at this point:

1. The frequent references and allusions to creation and the commandments across the Psalter certainly includes the Sabbath, which, among the Ten Commandments, is the one that explicitly points to and is validated by creation. In addition, the connection of the Sabbath to the exodus in Deuteronomy 5:12–26 links the Sabbath to the psalms celebrating the deliverance from Egypt.

2. The concept of "rest" evoked in Psalm 95:11, although admittedly not referring exclusively to the seventh day, most likely alludes to the Sabbath in order to make its point: "So I swore in My wrath, 'They shall not enter My rest'" (Ps 95:11). By calling it "my rest," God links this "rest" with His rest on the seventh day of creation week. Moreover, the use of this psalm at the beginning of worship services on Friday evening in the synagogue indicates that the Jewish tradition understood the connection of this psalm to the Sabbath day.[47] A similar idea, attested in the Christian tradition, links the notion of rest implied in Psalm 55:6 with the "rest of the Sabbath on which God rested from all the works of his world"[48] (cf. Heb 3:7–11).

3. Another allusion to the Sabbath likely occurs in Psalm 118:24: "This is the day the Lord has made; we will rejoice and be glad in it." Older commentators entertain the idea that "the day that the Lord has made" could

---

[46] Psalms 120–134, the "Songs of Ascents," for example, may indicate some cultic or worship settings. However, it is not clear whether these compositions serve either pilgrimage to the temple or return from exile. Most scholars, however, seem to favor the view that these psalms were sung as worshippers went up to Jerusalem to celebrate the major annual feasts. See, e.g., Robert Davidson, *The Vitality of Worship: A Commentary on the Book of Psalms* (Grand Rapids, MI: Eerdmans, 1998), 405.

[47] Marvin E. Tate, *Psalms 51-100*, WBC (Dallas, TX: Word, 1998), 499.

[48] Martin R. P. McGuire, "The Christian Funeral Oration," in *Funeral Orations*, trans. Leo P. McCauley et al. (Washington, DC: The Catholic University of America Press, 1953), 320.

refer to the Sabbath.[49] Although largely abandoned by modern commentators,[50] this view has some exegetical support. The use of the definite article in the phrase "the day" (*hayyom*), along with the qualifying expression "the Lord has made it," may indicate that this is the Sabbath day, the seventh day, which God made as the apex of the creation week. Psalm 118 reflects some kind of corporate celebration within the temple, and some commentators have suggested a connection with the Passover.[51] Indeed, the tone of victory over the enemy harks back to the exodus. However, none of the various festival days or ceremonial Sabbaths of the Hebrew cultic system could be understood as being made by God like the Sabbath, which God set apart and rested in. When the Sabbath reoccurs at the heart of the Ten Commandments, it is grounded in both creation (Exod 20:8–11) and liberartion (Deut 5:12–15).[52] The allusions to the exodus (Exod 3:7–8) and the similarities with the Song of Moses (cf. Ps 118:14 with Exod 15:2; Ps 118:15–16 with Exod 15:6; and Ps 118:28 with Exod 15:2) may well point to the Sabbath as a celebration of redemption (Exod 3:7–8), which is consistent with the Sabbath commandment as articulated in Deuteronomy 5. Thus, there seems to be some exegetical support to understand "the day the Lord has made" as referring to the Sabbath.

---

[49] See Matthew Henry, *Matthew Henry's Commentary on the Whole Bible: Complete and Unabridged in One Volume* (Peabody, MA: Hendrickson, 1994), 913; C. H. Spurgeon, *Psalms*, Crossway Classic Commentaries (Wheaton, IL: Crossway, 1993), 172; H. D. M. Spence-Jones, ed., *Psalms*, The Pulpit Commentary 3 (London: Funk and Wagnalls, 1909), 94; Albert Barnes, *Notes on the Old Testament: Psalms* (London: Blackie and Son, 1870–1872), 173–174; J. W. Burn, "Psalm 110–120," in *Psalms 88–150*, The Preacher's Complete Homiletic Commentary 2 (London: Funk and Wagnalls, 1892), 252; William S. Plumer, *Studies in the Book of Psalms: Being a Critical and Expository Commentary, with Doctrinal and Practical Remarks on the Entire Psalter* (Philadelphia, PA: Lippincott, 1872), 1012–1013; David Brown, A. R. Fausset, and Robert Jamieson, *A Commentary, Critical, Experimental, and Practical, on the Old and New Testaments: Acts–Revelation*, vol. 6 (London: William Collins and Sons, [n.d.]), 334; and Robert Haldane, *Exposition of the Epistle to the Romans; With Remarks on the Commentaries of Dr. MacKnight, Professor Moses Stuart, and Professor Tholuck* (New York: Robert Carter and Brothers, 1858), 709–710.

[50] Although not endorsing this view, Samuel Terrien, *The Psalms: Strophic Structure and Theological Commentary* (Grand Rapids, MI: Eerdmans, 2003), 786, mentions it. On the other hand, Derek Kidner, *Psalms 73-150: An Introduction and Commentary*, TOTC (Downers Grove, IL: InterVarsity, 1975), 450, mentions this possibility but rejects it altogether. Older commentators confidently interpreted this passage as a reference to the seventh-day Sabbath.

[51] J. A. Motyer, "The Psalms," in *New Bible Commentary: 21st Century Edition*, ed. D. A. Carson et al., 4th ed. (Leicester, England: InterVarsity, 1994), 564.

[52] For an explanation of the differences in the language of the Sabbath command in Exodus and Deuteronomy, see Gerald A. Klingbeil, "The Sabbath Law in the Decalogue(s): Creation and Liberation as a Paradigm for Community," *Revue biblique* 117, no. 4 (2010): 491–509.

4. Finally, it must be noted that the superscription to Psalm 92—"A Song for the Sabbath Day"—makes the only explicit reference to the Sabbath in the Psalter. But it is not surprising "that the Sabbath should be the one day with a special psalm."[53] Although scholars date the superscription to the post-exilic period,[54] there is evidence to suggest that the superscriptions of the Psalms were incorporated early into the Hebrew text and probably refer to even earlier historical traditions.[55] The superscriptions in the Septuagint (with the challenges they posed to the Greek translators) and their attestation in the extant psalms of the Dead Sea Scrolls suggest that they may be older than admitted by critical scholars.[56] For the purpose of this study, it must be noted that the liturgical note that links this psalm with the Sabbath also appears in the Septuagint. This suggests that such a connection was already present in the Hebrew Vorlage used by the Greek translators.

A further line of evidence comes from later Jewish tradition. As attested in the *Mishnah* tractate *Tamid* 7:4, in the second temple a choir of Levites chanted a specific psalm each day of the week to open and close the daily sacrificial activities: Psalm 24 on Sunday, Psalm 48 on Monday, Psalm 82 on Tuesday, Psalm 94 on Wednesday, Psalm 81 on Thursday, Psalm 93 on Friday, and Psalm 92 on the Sabbath.[57] It is striking that in the Hebrew Psalter only Psalm 92 has the superscription making the liturgical connection. This contrasts with the Septuagint, which has superscriptions

---

[53] John Goldingay, *Baker Commentary on the Old Testament: Psalms 90–150*, vol. 3, ed. Tremper Longman III (Grand Rapids, MI: Baker Academic, 2006), 53.

[54] Terrien, *The Psalms*, 655.

[55] Greg W. Parsons, "Guidelines for Understanding and Proclaiming the Psalms," *BSac* 147 (1990): 172n17 and Gleason L. Archer, Jr., *Survey of Old Testament Introduction*, rev. ed. (Chicago, IL: Moody, 1974), 451–452.

[56] *SDABC* 1:616 presents the following arguments in support of the historical reliability of the superscriptions: "(1) because their antiquity can be proved to go back to a time at least as early as the second century B.C. by their presence in the LXX (in fact they must have gone back to a time far preceding the date of that version, because the translators of the LXX did not understand many of the expressions); (2) because they have come down to us as a part of the Hebrew text itself; (3) because Hebrew lyrics from the earliest times had superscriptions attached to them; and (4) because the superscriptions provide certain helpful backgrounds for a fuller understanding of the meaning and message of the psalms thus introduced."

[57] Jacob Neusner, *The Mishnah: A New Translation* (New Haven, CT: Yale University Press, 1988), 872–873. See Peter L. Trüdinger, *The Psalms of the Tamid Service: A Liturgical Text from the Second Temple* (Leiden: Brill, 2004), 1–2. For a reflection on the joy of Sabbath as a day of worship, see Richard M. Davidson, *A Love Song for the Sabbath* (Washington, DC: Review and Herald, 1988).

in five of these seven psalms (Pss 24 [ET 23];⁵⁸ 48 [ET 47]; 94 [ET 93]; 93 [ET 92]; 92 [ET 91]). So the question naturally emerges as to why the Hebrew Psalter has a liturgical superscription only for Psalm 92. Most likely, "at the time of the final redaction of the Book of Psalms only Ps 92 was sung in the temple in connection with the Tamid offering on the Sabbath, the recitation of the other six not yet having been instituted."⁵⁹ If so, the association of Psalm 92 with Sabbath worship must date to a time prior to the final edition of the Hebrew Psalter. It thus can be further suggested that the association of the psalm with the Sabbath liturgy may reach back to the pre-exilic period. Indeed, the mention of "the house of the Lord" and "the courts of our God" (Ps 92:5) suggest a setting in pre-exilic times when the first temple was still standing. Although none of the aforementioned arguments may be decisive in itself, their cumulative forces indicate that the Sabbath was regarded as a day of worship since pre-exilic times.⁶⁰

Sabbath in Classical Prophecy

Explicit references to the Sabbath as a day of worship occur in two important prophetic sections: Isaiah 66 and Ezekiel 40–48. In an eschatological oracle Isaiah delivers the promise that "'from one New Moon to another, and from one Sabbath to another, all flesh shall come to worship [*lehishtakhawoth*] before Me,' says the Lord" (Isa 66:23). The Hebrew verb translated as "worship" (*shakhah*) means to "bow down, prostrate oneself"⁶¹ and clearly conveys the idea of the nations bowing in worship before the Lord on the Sabbath day. For such a promise to make sense, the Sabbath must have already been observed as a day of worship in ancient Israel. As the context shows, the prophetic message announces the restoration of Jerusalem (Isa 66:10–11) and the recreation of heaven and earth (Isa 66:22). In this context, cultic life would be restored with the universal acquiescence of the nations as they join Israel for worship on the Sabbath.⁶² This passage was subsequently taken up and expanded at the close of the

---

⁵⁸ "ET" stands for "English text," and indicates where the numbering of chapters or verses in the English translation deviates from the Hebrew text.

⁵⁹ Nahum M. Sarna, "Psalm for the Sabbath Day (Ps 92)," *JBL* 81, no. 2 (1962): 156.

⁶⁰ Although not conceding as much, Davidson, *The Vitality of Worship*, 307, recognizes that "at least we know that, from an early period in Jewish tradition, its natural home was the Sabbath."

⁶¹ *BDB*, s.v. *shakhah*.

⁶² For insights on this passage, see Daniel Bediako, "Isaiah's 'New Heavens and New Earth' (Isa 65:17; 66:22)," *JAAS* 11, no. 1 (2008): 1–20 and Anne E. Gardner, "The Nature of the New Heavens and New Earth in Isaiah 66:22," *ABR* 50 (2002): 10–27.

biblical canon in reference to the eschatological restoration of the created order (Rev 21–22).

In the same vein, Ezekiel speaks of worship on the Sabbath when YHWH returns to the eschatological temple and sets His presence there: "Likewise the people of the land shall worship [*wehishtakhawu*] at the entrance to this gateway before the LORD on the Sabbaths and the New Moons. The burnt offering that the prince offers to the LORD on the Sabbath day shall be six lambs without blemish, and a ram without blemish" (Ezek 46:3–4). The section to which this passage belongs (Ezek 40–48) brings a message of hope to the people in exile as it lays out the plan to rebuild the temple and reinstate the cultic service. It is a vision report given twenty-five years after the deportation of Jehoiachin and fourteen years after the fall of Jerusalem (Ezek 40:1).[63]

Among the several elements of cultic service to be reestablished, the Sabbath and the special sacrifices to be performed thereon are mentioned. "On Sabbaths and new moon festivals the citizens of the restored community of faith shall gather and pay homage to Yahweh by prostrating themselves at the entrance of the inner gate."[64] The gate referred to here is the eastern gate of the outer wall. This gate—through which the glory of the Lord would reenter the temple—was to remain closed on weekdays, but on Sabbath and new moons it became the place where people would gather to worship the Lord. This new situation contrasts with the apostasy described earlier when Ezekiel is shown people around this area worshipping the sun:

> So He brought me into the inner court of the Lord's house; and there, at the door of the temple of the Lord, between the porch and the altar, were about twenty-five men with their backs toward the temple of the Lord and their faces toward the east, and they were worshiping the sun toward the east (Ezek 8:16).

But in the eschatological temple shown to Ezekiel, that area would become a place of worship to the Lord. Every Sabbath the people would gather at the eastern gate to "worship"—that is, to bow down (*hishtakhawu*) "before the LORD" (*lifne* YHWH). In doing so, they turn their back to the sun in a complete reversal of the apostasy.

---

[63] Daniel I. Block, *The Book of Ezekiel, Chapters 25-48*, NICOT (Grand Rapids, MI: Eerdmans 1999), 495.

[64] Ibid., 671.

The Sabbath under the New Covenant

This study would have been incomplete without some considerations about the relevance of the Sabbath for Christians living under the new covenant. This is already implied in the previous section where it was noted that according to Isaiah 66, the Sabbath will remain a day of worship in the age to come. Space does not allow a full discussion of all the ramifications and implications of this fascinating topic, but a few points should be noted.

Clearly, in the OT the Sabbath is used as the sign of the covenant between God and Israel. However, prior to this specification of the Sabbath in relation to the covenant, the Sabbath emerges in the creation account as the day sanctified and blessed by the Creator. In other words, the Sabbath was inscribed in the order of creation.[65] Therefore, the Sabbath emerges with a universal scope that, by virtue of its chronological and canonical placement in Scripture, transcends geographic and ethnic distinctions or particularities. Thus, before the Sabbath became related to the experience of Israel under the old covenant, it was given to the human race at creation.[66]

> Rest-day holiness is something God bestowed onto the seventh day. God manifested himself in refraining from work and in rest as the divine Exemplar for humankind. The sequence of "six working-days" and a "seventh [sabbath] rest-day" indicates universally that every human being is to engage in an imitatio Dei, "imitation of God," by resting on the "seventh day." "Man" (*'ādām*), made in the imago Dei, "image of God," (Gen 1:26–28) is invited to follow the Exemplar in an imitatio Dei, participating in God's rest by enjoying the divine gift of freedom from the labors of human existence and thus acknowledging God as his Creator.[67]

And precisely because it was supposed to be a universal institution, the Sabbath was subsequently given to Israel, whose ultimate purpose was to be a blessing to "all the families of the earth" according to the promise originally made to Abraham (Gen 12:3) and unfolded throughout Scripture.

---

[65] In the words of Childs, *The Book of Exodus*, 416, the "sanctification of the Sabbath . . . is built into the very structure of the universe."

[66] As Burer, *Divine Sabbath Work*, 31, states, "because of God's actions of blessing the day at the end of creation, God's activity here is understood to be paradigmatic for the world in general and Israel in particular. Thus the day becomes a medium through which humanity and Israel can experience the blessing of God in the form of rest and freedom."

[67] Hasel, "Sabbath," *ABD* 5:851.

This being the case, the Sabbath cannot be reduced to a legal prescription embedded in the old covenant because it flows with full force into the new covenant, as can be inferred from an examination of Jeremiah 31:30–34, the *locus classicus* of the new covenant.[68]

For the purpose of this study, it suffices to focus on two aspects of Jeremiah 31:30–34. First, God promises to put "My law in their minds, and write it on their hearts" (Jer 31:33). Interestingly, the passage speaks of a "new covenant," not a new law. And it must be noted that the new covenant law contrasts with the old in terms of the medium (flesh versus tablets of stone), not content, which remains the same. Indeed, the context requires that the law that will be inscribed in the hearts and minds of God's new covenant people must be the same law that had been in force in the old covenant. Such law, so extolled and revered throughout the OT (e.g., Ps 119), may be understood as God's instructions for His people to live holy and joyful lives, as encapsulated in the Ten Commandments (Exod 20; Deut 5), the center of which is the Sabbath. Thus, as God promised through Jeremiah, the new covenant would be different from the old in that the law formerly inscribed on tablets of stone would now be inscribed on the tablets of the heart. And the law must remain the same because as the psalmist acknowledges, "All your words are true; all your righteous laws are eternal" (Ps 119:160, NIV). Significantly, the eternality of God's laws and ordinances is often connected with the order of creation: "Your word is settled in heaven. Your faithfulness *endures* to all generations; You established the earth, and it abides" (Ps 119:89–90).

Second, because it finds its ultimate guarantee in the order of creation, the promise of the new covenant has a bearing on the Sabbath, as can be inferred from Jeremiah 31:35–37:

> Thus says the Lord, Who gives the sun for a light by day, The ordinances [*khuqqoth*] of the moon and the stars for a light by night, Who disturbs the sea, And its waves roar (The Lord of hosts is His

---

[68] This passage has been an object of intense study and debate among covenant and dispensational theologians. See, e.g., Christopher Cone, ed., *An Introduction to the New Covenant* (Hurst, TX: Tyndale Seminary Press, 2013); Peter J. Gentry and Stephen J. Wellum, *Kingdom through Covenant: A Biblical-Theological Understanding of the Covenants* (Wheaton, IL: Crossway, 2012). To keep the focus of the present discussion, the intricacies of this debate must be avoided. It suffices to say that the author of this study accepts in general lines the Christological approach to the OT prophecies related to Israel, as explained by Hans K. LaRondelle, *The Israel of God in Prophecy: Principles of Prophetic Interpretation* (Berrien Springs, MI: Andrews University Press, 1983).

name): "If those ordinances [*khuqqim*] depart From before Me, says the Lord, Then the seed of Israel shall also cease From being a nation before Me forever." Thus says the Lord: "If heaven above can be measured, And the foundations of the earth searched out beneath, I will also cast off all the seed of Israel For all that they have done, says the Lord."

As emphasized in the passage, the stability of the laws (*khuqqim*)[69] that govern the cosmos is the guarantee that God would establish a new covenant with His people. Thus, since the ordinances of the sun, moon, and stars—which God established on the fourth day of creation (Gen 1:14–19)—will stand forever to the point of serving as a guarantee for the fulfillment of the new covenant, it follows that the Sabbath command (Gen 2:1-3), grounded in the seventh day of creation, will do as well.

Conclusion

This study has suggested that the Sabbath cannot simply be reduced to a day of rest in OT times, as suggested by some biblical scholars. The literary and theological contours of the biblical text reveal that the notion of worship has resided in the Sabbath since it was instituted at creation. God's action of blessing and sanctifying the seventh day set it apart from the other weekdays, and later would set it over the sacred times of the Hebrew cultic calendar. An examination of the Sabbath in the context of creation, Sinai, and the sanctuary/temple shows that at both the literary and conceptual levels the Sabbath is inextricably connected to the notion of worship. The narratives of the Sinaitic covenant and the construction of the tabernacle contain literary structures that focus on the seventh element as the occasion in which God reveals His glory. Such literary strategies not only link the Sabbath with covenant and sanctuary, but implicitly point to the Sabbath as a special time of worship.

In the ritual system of the tabernacle/temple, the Sabbath was a day of holy convocation, which appears to have been a gathering of people around the sanctuary to render corporate worship to the Lord. In addition, on Sabbath some ritual services changed, marking the distinctiveness of

---

[69] As Helmer Ringgren, "חקק *khaqaq*," *TDOT* 5:141, notes, the term *khuqqim* (statutes) as used in Jeremiah 31:36 refers to the order of creation, described in the previous verse. In Deuteronomy 5:1 the word pair *khuqqim* and *mishpatim* (statues and judgments) refers to a variety of laws, beginning with the Decalogue (Deut 5:6–22).

the seventh day for the Hebrew cultus. In this connection, it should be reiterated that the Psalter may contain implicit references to the Sabbath in connection with several psalms reflecting on creation and the commandments. Even the idea of rest occasionally mentioned or implied in some individual psalms may presuppose the Sabbath. However, the only psalm devoted to the Sabbath makes an explicit connection between the seventh day and the cultic service (Ps 92).

Similarly, Isaiah and Ezekiel announced that one significant aspect of God's eschatological work of salvation involves the Sabbath. The nations will flow to Jerusalem to worship the Lord from Sabbath to Sabbath. Another aspect of God's plan entails the restoration of proper worship, which takes place on Sabbath. That the Sabbath plays such a prominent role as a day of worship in these prophetic/eschatological passages suggests that it must have played a similar role during the tabernacle and temple times.

Coming back to the question of whether the Sabbath was a day of rest or a day of worship, we should note that the OT does not support this dichotomy. Indeed, the Sabbath was a day in which, according to God's own example at creation, every Israelite should cease from work and rest in the Lord. However, such rest certainly did not exclude worship either at home or in the sanctuary/temple, as the notion of holy convocation seems to imply. Indeed, the overall perception of the Sabbath conveyed by the OT texts surveyed here shows the Sabbath as having been closely connected to worship since its inception at creation. And that remained so throughout the history of ancient Israel, as conveyed by the literary, ritual, and prophetic dimensions of the OT.

Finally, since the Sabbath belongs to the order of creation and will be in force as a day of worship in the eschatological new earth, it remains God's appointed day of worship for new covenant believers as well.

CHAPTER 11

ISRAELITE FESTIVALS, SABBATH YEAR, JUBILEE, AND THE SABBATH FOR CHRISTIANS

Michael Sokupa

Introduction

A number of studies focus on biblical festival calendars.[1] How does the seventh-day Sabbath in the calendric texts relate to the feasts? Some interpret the festivals exclusively within the OT context.[2] Others view the festivals as not applicable to Christians beyond the death of Christ.[3] There are those who find continued relevance of the festivals to Christians, hence proposing their celebration.[4] In this study, we shall look at the purpose, function, typological and theological meaning of the festivals, their

---

[1] This term is used in this study as a collective term for the Jewish festivals, the Sabbath Year, and the Jubilee. The major calendric texts are Leviticus 23 and Numbers 28–29.

[2] See Karl William Weyde, *The Appointed Festivals of YHWH: The Festival Calendar in Leviticus 23 and the Sukkot Festival in Other Biblical Texts* (Tübingen: Mohr Siebeck, 2004); and Roger T. Beckwith, *Calendar and Chronology, Jewish and Christian: Biblical, Intertestamental and Patristic Studies* (Leiden: Brill, 2001).

[3] See Daniel Fuchs, *Israel's Holy Days in Type and Prophecy* (Neptune, NJ: Loizeaux Brothers, 1985).

[4] See Samuele Bacchiocchi, *God's Festivals in Scripture and History: Part 1: The Spring Festivals* (Berrien Springs, MI: Biblical Perspectives, 2007), who evaluates the festivals to determine continuity or discontinuity. He further develops his research as a basis for proposing the celebration of the festivals today.

relationship to the Sabbath in the biblical calendar, and the relevance of the seventh-day Sabbath for Christians.

An Overview of Biblical Festivals

The OT calendar contained several festivals that celebrated the goodness of God in various ways. Each feast had a set of prescribed rituals assigned to it. Some festivals resonated with the agricultural cycles of the community. In a number of these festivals, the Lord demanded rest from customary work. A closer look at the festival list and ritual prescriptions aids in showing how the seventh-day Sabbath is set apart from these festivals and their prescribed rest days.

There are seven annual feasts listed in the calendric passages of the OT: the Passover, the Feast of Unleavened Bread, the Feast of Firstfruits, the Feast of Weeks/Pentecost, the Feast of Trumpets, the Day of Atonement, and the Feast of Tabernacles/Booths (see, e.g., Lev 23). The table below displays some important ritual and sabbath-related prescriptions that are important for consideration.

Table 1: Sabbath and Festivals in Leviticus 23

Festival/Time	Ritual Activity	Type of Sabbath
Sabbath (Lev 23:3)	Silent about sacrifices	Weekly seventh-day Sabbath, a "Sabbath to the Lord"; no work must be done
Passover (fourteenth day of first month) (Lev 23:5)	Silent about sacrifices	Not prescribed
Feast of Unleavened Bread (fifteenth to twenty-first days of first month) (Lev 23:6–8)	Eating of unleavened food for seven days, presentation of offering to the Lord for seven days	No customary work on first and seventh days of the feast
Feast of Firstfruits (no date is given) (Lev 23:10–14)	Raising of the sheaf of the firstfruits, one lamb, grain and drink offerings accompanying the burnt offering	Not prescribed, but presentation is made on the "day after the Sabbath"

Feast of Weeks/ Pentecost (fiftieth day from the Feast of Firstfruits) (Lev 23:15–21)	Bread offering, nine lambs, one bull, two rams, one goat, grain and drink offerings accompanying the burnt offering	Ceremonial sabbath, no customary work; feast takes place after seven Sabbaths/weeks from the "day after the Sabbath" when the Feast of Firstfruits occurred
Feast of Trumpets (first day of seventh month) (Lev 23:24–25)	Blowing of trumpets, food offering	Ceremonial sabbath, no customary work
Day of Atonement (tenth day of seventh month) (Lev 23:27–32)	Food offering, fasting	Ceremonial sabbath, no manner of work
Feast of Tabernacles/ Booths (fifteenth to twenty-second days of the seventh month) (Lev 23:34–36, 39–43)	Food offering, dwelling in booths	Ceremonial sabbath, no customary work on first and eighth days of the feast

Notice that in Leviticus 23 the seventh-day Sabbath is distinguished from the seven festivals.[5] Leviticus 23:2 and 23:4 have a common introductory phrase: "these are My feasts" (v. 2) and "these are the feasts of the Lord" (v. 4).[6] The double introduction sets apart the weekly Sabbath (mentioned in v. 3) from the rest of the festivals. Again, at the beginning of the chapter, the weekly Sabbath is referred to as "Sabbath to the LORD" (Lev 23:3). The seven "appointed feasts" that follow (Lev 23:4, 37) are "besides the LORD'S [weekly] Sabbaths" (Lev 23:3, 38 ESV). The language of Leviticus 23:3 echoes Genesis 2:1–3, thus linking the Sabbath in Leviticus 23 with the

---

[5] Roy Gane, *Leviticus, Numbers*, NIVAC (Grand Rapids, MI: Zondervan, 2004), 388, argues convincingly that the two introductions in Leviticus 23:1–4 are significant. The first (Lev 23:1–2) introduces the entire chapter, and the second (Lev 23:4) emphasizes the introduction after the Sabbath command (Lev 23:3). According to him, "this suggests that although the weekly Sabbath is a sacred time, it is distinguished from the yearly festivals" (ibid.). See also Jacob Milgrom, *Leviticus 23–27*, AB (New York: Doubleday, 2001), 1955; Mathilde Frey, "The Sabbath in the Pentateuch: An Exegetical and Theological Study" (PhD diss., Andrews University, 2011), 240. For Ross Cole, "The Sacred Times Prescribed in the Pentateuch: Old Testament Indicators of the Extent of Their Applicability" (PhD diss., Andrews University, 1996), 140, "the weekly Sabbath in Lev. 23:2–3 is set apart from the festal list of vs. 4–38 but at the same time is presented as a model upon which the others are based." He further argues that "the absence of any reference to the cultus in Lev 23:2–3 indicates that in contrast to the situation with the annual festivals, the proclamation of the weekly Sabbath as holy time has validity quite apart from cultic observances prescribed for it" (ibid., 141).

[6] Unless otherwise indicated, citations of Scripture are taken from the NKJV.

original Sabbath of creation in Genesis. In Leviticus 23, apart from the Passover, the other festivals have ritual sacrificial offerings and some reference to the Sabbath or work-free celebration.

The table below, based on Numbers 28–29, in some respects duplicates the Leviticus 23 calendar; in other ways, it complements it. One significant addition in Numbers 28 is the mention of the prescribed offerings for the weekly Sabbath.

Table 2: Sabbath and Festivals in Numbers 28–29

Festival	Ritual Activity	Type of Sabbath
Sabbath (Num 28:9–10)	Four lambs, grain and drink offerings accompanying the burnt offering	Focus is on weekly Sabbath offerings; "rest" is not mentioned
New Moon (Num 28:11–15)	Two bulls, one ram, seven lambs, one goat, grain and drink offerings accompanying the burnt offering	Not prescribed
Passover (fourteenth day of first month) (Num 28:16)	Silent about sacrifices	Not prescribed
Feast of Unleavened Bread (fifteenth through twenty-first of first month) (Num 28:17–25)	Eating of unleavened bread for seven days, presentation of food offering to the Lord for seven days (two bulls, one ram, seven lambs, one goat)	No customary work on first and seventh days of the feast
Feast of Weeks/Pentecost (Num 28:26–31)	Two bulls, one ram, seven lambs, one goat, new grain offering and drink offering accompanying the burnt offering	Ceremonial sabbath, no customary work
Feast of Trumpets (first day of seventh month) (Num 29:1–6)	Blowing of trumpets, one bull, one ram, seven lambs, one goat, grain and drink offerings accompanying the burnt offering	Ceremonial sabbath, no customary work
Day of Atonement (tenth day of seventh month) (Num 29:7–11)	One bull, one ram, seven lambs, one goat, fasting, grain and drink offerings accompanying the burnt offering	Ceremonial sabbath, no work

Feast of Booths (fifteenth through twenty-second day of seventh month) (Booths) (Num 29:12–38)	Food offerings for eight days (seventy-one bulls, fifteen rams, 105 lambs, eight goats in total), grain and drink offerings accompanying the burnt offerings	Ceremonial sabbath on first and eighth days of feast, no customary work

The calendar of Numbers 28–29 contains a more elaborate list of sacrifices, including that prescribed for the Sabbath. The ritual prescription is perhaps one of the reasons the Sabbath is included in the list of festivals. This is evident from the fact that the idea of "rest," so integral to the Sabbath, is not even mentioned in this text. Sacrificial elements do not feature in the earlier references to the weekly Sabbath (Gen 2:2; Exod 16:23; 31:15). The Sabbath predates all feasts and serves as a reminder of God's creation. The temporary, ritual prescription for the weekly Sabbath (Num 28:9–10) does not make it a festival that would lose its significance after the death of Christ. When these ritual prescriptions would fall away (Col 2:16–17; Heb 10:1), the Sabbath would remain (Heb 4:4–9). The next sections focus on the festivals in more detail.

The Passover

The first Passover was instituted just before the tenth plague fell upon Egypt. It was by God's design that the Passover would mark the beginning of the religious calendar for Israel (Exod 12:2). The stated purpose and instruction for the Passover to the Israelites was "so this day shall be to you a memorial; and you shall keep it as a feast to the Lord throughout your generations. You shall keep it as a feast by an everlasting ordinance" (Exod 12:14).

According to Samuele Bacchiocchi, the "Passover ritual, like that of the other feasts, was designed to place the individual in contact with the event, not merely through its symbolism but primarily by recreating in the believer the same attitude as that of those who experienced the event."[7] The commemoration of the Passover, according to this argument, was event-oriented. And the event is in the past. So, we may ask whether the original purpose of the festivals carries through to the present.

Bacchiocchi argues that the Passover, for example, is "a commemoration of the historic deliverance of God's people from the Egyptian

---
[7] Bacchiocchi, *God's Festivals*, 36–37.

bondage."[8] This may be the original purpose. It is further "typical of the Messianic deliverance of God's people from the bondage of sin."[9] Finally, it is "prophetic of the final deliverance of the great multitude of the redeemed out of all nations."[10]

Bacchiocchi's position on the continuity of the festivals is clear:

> Christ's sacrifice as our Paschal Lamb, however, does not render the celebration of Passover unnecessary. Christ fulfilled the sacrificial typology of the Passover, not by terminating the observance of the feast, but by transforming it so that the festival could fittingly celebrate His redemption from sin.[11]

As he further argues, "by choosing the bread and the wine (non-sacrificial elements of the Passover meal) as the emblems of His atoning death, Jesus detached the new Passover from the sacrificial system and transformed it into a fitting memorial of His redemption."[12]

Bacchiocchi's argument seems to be over-reaching, in that nowhere in Scripture does Christ talk about a new Passover. One scholar offers a convincing argument against the permanence of the Passover: "The incidental New Testament references to Passover, the Feast of Unleavened Bread, and Pentecost do not show that they are permanent or universally applicable institutions."[13] The fulfillment of the Passover type by the coming of the antitype is buttressed by Paul in 1 Corinthians 5:7. However, the colliding of the two events should be one giving way to the other rather than the continuation of the same institution. The book of Hebrews shows how the fulfillment took place: the OT sacrificial system was functional for a certain time; it foreshadowed, and has given way to, the sacrifice of Jesus Christ.

The purpose of the Passover must also be discussed alongside its function within the entire system of festivals. One scholar aptly points out that

---

[8] Bacchiocchi, *God's Festivals*, 121.

[9] Ibid.

[10] Ibid.

[11] Ibid., 122.

[12] Ibid., 123.

[13] For the development of the argument against continuity, see Ross Cole, "Passover and Pentecost: Optional or Obligatory," https://adventistbiblicalresearch.org/materials/theology-festivals/passover-and-pentecost-optional-or-obligatory (accessed October 19, 2016).

the festivals were exclusively celebrated at the temple.[14] This means that in the absence of the temple the celebration of the festivals is meaningless and outside the boundaries that were set for them. Another writer also makes a case against Christians observing the festivals. He cautions, "This example [that Jesus and the disciples kept Jewish festivals] cannot be used as an argument to justify the Christian celebration of the feasts since Jesus and the early Christians kept not only the Jewish festivals but also other cultural and ceremonial practices, such as circumcision."[15] While it may be significant that Jesus is portrayed as the lamb in several NT passages (John 1:29; 1 Pet 1:19; Rev 7:14; 12:11), the connection between the lamb as a sacrificial sin offering and the Passover lamb needs to be explained.[16] The imagery of Christ as the lamb and sin-bearer may not be so obvious in the Passover narrative. However, the deliverance theme does tie up the Passover imagery with the redemptive work of Christ. Therefore, Christ provides a way of escape from death and slavery (John 11:26; Rom 6:14; Heb 2:15).

The Feast of Unleavened Bread

The Feast of Unleavened Bread has its purpose preambled by a reminder of the exodus event: "Remember this day in which you went out of Egypt, out of the house of bondage" (Exod 13:3). This reminder is followed by specific instructions on how to observe the feast (Exod 13:4–8). Then the purpose of the feast is given: "It shall be as a sign to you on your hand and as a memorial between your eyes, that the Lord's law may be in your mouth; for with a strong hand the Lord has brought you out of Egypt, you shall therefore keep this ordinance in its season from year to year" (Exod 13:9–10). The Israelites were not only to avoid the use of leaven in food, but also to make sure it was not in their possession during the seven-day festival period (Exod 13:6–7). They had to eat unleavened bread for the duration of the festival. There are other similar instructions regarding the feast (Exod 12:15–20; Lev 23:6–8; Num 28:17–25; Deut 16:3–4).

There are two applications to the symbol of leaven in the NT: it is the symbol of sin (1 Cor 5:6–8; Gal 5:9) and the kingdom of God (Matt 13:33).

---

[14] Ángel Rodriguez, *Israelite Festivals and the Christian Church*, Biblical Research Institute Release 3 (Washington, DC: Biblical Research Institute, 2005). See Deuteronomy 16:5, 16 and Hosea 9:5 as a biblical basis for this argument.

[15] See Jacques Doukhan, "Should We Observe the Levitical Festivals? A Seventh-day Adventist Perspective—Part 1," *Ministry*, April 2010, 7–8.

[16] Laszlo Gallusz, *The Throne Motif in the Book of Revelation* (London: T&T Clark, 2014), 160.

In 1 Corinthians 5:6–7 Paul points to leaven as sin. In the same passage is a reference to Jesus as "Christ, our Passover." Paul concludes the passage with the words, "Therefore let us keep the feast, not with old leaven, nor with the leaven of malice and wickedness, but with the unleavened bread of sincerity and truth" (1 Cor 5:8). While Paul uses festival language with the symbols, there is no hint in the text that he is advocating for the continuity of the feast as it was originally instituted. He is pointing to the "unleavened bread of sincerity and truth," which ties up with the current issues he was dealing with in the Corinthian congregation. The context of 1 Corinthians 5 is not festivals but immorality in the church. Paul uses the symbolisms of Passover and unleavened bread to point to the release from the slavery of sin.

The nature of the Feast of Unleavened Bread interlocks with the Passover in both purpose and function. There is a clear distinction between the two feasts in terms of prescribed offerings and ritual activities. But they both point to the same event. Their connection is also demonstrated in Paul's application of the symbolism (1 Cor 5). It is therefore fitting to see the two festivals and their symbolism point to Christ and His sacrificial death that brings liberation from the slavery of sin.

The Feast of Firstfruits

This festival has as its main purpose the celebration of the barley harvest. When the festival was first instituted it pointed forward: "When you come into the land which I give you, and reap its harvest, then you shall bring a sheaf of the firstfruits of your harvest to the priest. He shall wave the sheaf before the Lord, to be accepted on your behalf; on the day after the Sabbath the priest shall wave it" (Lev 23:10–11). When Israel settled in Canaan, they celebrated this feast every spring, bringing their sheaf offering to the priest as a way of giving thanks to God for the first produce in the agricultural calendar. The Feast of Firstfruits is listed after the Passover and the Feast of Unleavened Bread (Lev 23:4–11) but the sheaf offering could have taken place during the seven-day period of the Feast of Unleavened Bread:

> Leviticus 23 does not specifically state that the sheaf offering was to be elevated in the first month. However, verses 5–16 clearly imply that this ritual took place during the seven-day period of the Passover and Unleavened Bread, which took place in the first month (Exod 12:2; 12:8; 34:18). Moreover, we read elsewhere (Exod 9:31–32; Josh 2:6; 3:15; 4:19) that barely ripens in the first month of the Israelite year (i.e., Abib/Nisan corresponding to

March/April of the Julian calendar). The famous Gezer Calendar commonly dated to the 10th century BC supports this.[17]

The sheaf was to be raised by the priest before the Lord on the "day after [morrow of] the Sabbath" (Lev 23:11, 15). There are at least two views on the "Sabbath" here. Some view it as referring to the seventh-day Sabbath.[18] Others take it to mean a ceremonial sabbath.[19]

There are some typological and theological links that can be gleaned. First, it is important to note the Hebrew words *re'shith* ("beginning" or "firstfruits") and *bikkurim* ("firstfruits") used for the Feast of Firstfruits and Feast of Weeks/Pentecost respectively. However, the distinction between these terms is not maintained in the translations beginning with the LXX, in which the word *aparche* is used for both Hebrew terms. When Paul refers to Christ as the firstfruits in 1 Corinthians 15:20–23, to which firstfruits is he referring?

Christ at His resurrection became the firstfruits of those who died (1 Cor 15:20). The day of His resurrection also comes "after the Sabbath," symbolically linking it to the fulfillment of the Feast of Firstfruits.[20] The Sabbath preceding the resurrection of Christ as firstfruits of the dead was a high Sabbath that overlapped both the seventh-day Sabbath and the ceremonial Sabbath on the same day. The feast, as it was originally intended, had implications for the agricultural setting as well as typological nuance for the raising of Christ, the firstfruits of the dead.

The Feast of Weeks/Pentecost

The Feast of Weeks, as detailed in Leviticus 23:15–21, was closely connected to the main grain harvest (that is, wheat). The purpose of the feast was a thanksgiving to God for the blessing of the harvest. Like the Feast of Firstfruits, the Feast of Weeks was tied to the harvest within the agricultural setting.

---

[17] Daniel Bediako, "The Sheaf Offering and Resurrection Sunday," *AAMM* 16 (2017): 121.

[18] Laid R. Harris, "Leviticus," *EBC* (Grand Rapids, MI: Zondervan, 1990), 624; Bediako, "The Sheaf Offering and Resurrection Sunday," 122–126.

[19] *SDABC* 1:804. See also Ellen G. White, *Patriarchs and Prophets* (Washington, D.C.: Review and Herald, 1958), 539; idem, *Desire of Ages* (Mountain View, CA: Pacific Press, 1940), 77; and Bradford Maris, "A Proposed Solution to 'the Most Long-Lasting Schism in the History of the Jewish People': A Fresh Look at השבת in Leviticus 23:11," *AUSS* 56/1 (2018): 47–62.

[20] See further arguments in Bediako, "The Sheaf Offering and Resurrection Sunday," 127–130.

The typological links to the Feast of Weeks may not be as defined as that of the Passover. However, there are some hints on how this feast reaches its fulfillment in the NT—Pentecost in Acts 2, where the idea of the harvest is hinted: "Then those who gladly received his word were baptized; and that day about three thousand souls were added to them. . . . And the Lord added to the church daily those who were being saved" (Acts 2:41, 47). The celebration of the Feast of Weeks occurred on the fiftieth day following the Feast of Firstfruits, counting from one "day after the Sabbath" to another "day after the Sabbath," with seven Sabbaths/weeks in the interval (Lev 23:15–21). The resurrection of Christ and the outpouring of the Holy Spirit occurred exactly on the days of these feasts, leading to the conclusion that

> the death of Christ during the Feast of Passover/Unleavened Bread, His being 'raised' from the dead on the day 'after the Sabbath' (i.e., the day of the raising of the sheaf offering), and the outpouring of the Holy Spirit on the Day of Pentecost—the fiftieth day following Christ's resurrection—even as the ritual of Pentecost followed the fiftieth day from the sheaf ritual, cannot be merely coincidental. Indeed, type was being fulfilled by the anti-type.[21]

The link between the Feast of Weeks and the giving of the law at Sinai has also been cited.[22] Historically the Jews have celebrated the giving of the law based on its chronological connection to the Feast of Weeks.

The Feast of Trumpets

The blowing of the trumpets (Num 29:1) is central to this feast and its purpose. Numerous suggestions have been offered concerning the meaning of the blowing of trumpets.[23] The purpose of the festival in the calendric texts (Lev 23:24–25; Num 29:1–6) where the feast is prescribed is not obviated.

The function of the Feast of Trumpets seems to be linked to the Day of Atonement. The blowing of the trumpets set the stage in preparation

---

[21] See further arguments in Bediako, "The Sheaf Offering and Resurrection Sunday," 130.

[22] See Bacchiochi, *God's Festivals*, 180.

[23] "War" is one option to the interpretation of the purpose of the blowing of trumpets. See Richard Booker, *Jesus in the Feasts of Israel: Restoring the Spiritual Realities of the Feasts of the Church* (South Plainfield, NJ: Bridge, 1987), 77. The purpose may also be "to awaken us" (Edward Chumney, *The Seven Festivals of the Messiah* [Shippensburg, PA: Destiny, 1994], 100–101).

for the Day of Atonement. Are there indications of continuity in purpose and function of the Feast of Trumpets through the NT and the present? In the first place, this feast, like the others, points to the sacrifice and work of Christ, at whose first advent all sacrifices ceased. There are also some typological and theological connections that need to be noted. The book of Revelation seems to provide the most allusions to the Feast of Trumpets. The language chosen by the author gives evidence to an "order of the annual festal calendar of the Hebrew Cultus."[24] "The Feast of Trumpets is closely associated in Jewish thought with the New Moon festivals that were celebrated at the beginning of each month" and comes "as the climax of a seven-month series of mini-Feasts of Trumpets."[25] The seventh trumpet in the book of Revelation represents the Feast of Trumpets itself, and "within the seventh trumpet (Rev 11:18) we find the first explicit use of judgment terminology in Revelation. In Jewish thought the seventh-month Feast of Trumpets ushered in the time of judgment that led to the Day of Atonement."[26] This connects the function of the Feast of Trumpets to the ushering in of the next festival, the Day of Atonement.

The Day of Atonement

The purpose of the Day of Atonement is "to make atonement for you before the Lord your God" (Lev 23:28). That this is a day of judgment is evidenced by the fact that "any person who is not afflicted in soul on that same day shall be cut off from his people" (Lev 23:29). The details of the observance of the Day of Atonement are given in Leviticus 16. The sanctuary was defiled by both defiant sins and the forgiven sins.[27] Once a year there was a cleansing of the sanctuary from "ritual impurities and sins of the Israelites (Lev 16:16, 19, 33)."[28] The outcome of the cleansing of the sanctuary was forgiveness to the loyal and condemnation to the rebellious.[29] This dual effect of the cleansing is paralleled by the eschatological cleansing of the sanctuary in Daniel 8:14. While Leviticus 16 portrays the

---

[24] Jon Paulien, "The Role of the Hebrew Cultus, Sanctuary, and Temple in the Plot and Structure of the Book of Revelation," *AUSS* 33/2 (1995): 257.

[25] Ibid., 259.

[26] Ibid., 259.

[27] Ibid., 131.

[28] Roy Gane, "Judgment as Covenant Review," *JATS* 8/1–2 (1997): 183. There are two categories of sins in view: confessed sins (Lev 4:26, 31, 35) and sins of rebellion (Lev 20:3; Num 19:13, 20).

[29] Ibid., 184.

annual Day of Atonement that reconciled God to His people, the cleansing of the sanctuary in Daniel 8:14 has a cosmic sweep and a climactic effect. "It is a one-time eschatological climax to a cosmic struggle over lordship and worship."[30]

The function of the Day of Atonement within the calendar is such that it connected the calendar of feasts to the sanctuary services in a more direct way. The other festivals are seen to be connected to each other and even to form a unit, but were not directly linked to the sanctuary services. While the offering of sacrifices was required at the sanctuary on other festival days, the Day of Atonement provided a direct connection for all the festivals as a unit to the sanctuary.

The Day of Atonement had a typological and theological significance. The typological nature of the sanctuary is evidenced in the intertextual relationship between Hebrews 8:5 and Exodus 25:40.[31] The Hebrews text points to a new covenant priestly ministry in the heavenly sanctuary (Heb 8:1).[32] Christ's appointment as High Priest requires Him to "offer both gifts and sacrifices" (Heb 8:3). Only a high priest could minister in the Holy of Holies on the Day of Atonement (Lev 16:3–4).

The central argument of the book of Hebrews sets the earthly sanctuary and its priestly services as both repetitious and limited (Heb 9:6). There is an indication in Hebrews 9:22–23 that the Day of Atonement is typologically fulfilled in the heavenly sanctuary by Christ. The author of Hebrews states that the nature of the earthly sanctuary indicates that it was symbolic (Heb 9:9–10). In contrast to the earthly sanctuary, Christ ministers in a more "perfect tabernacle not made with hands, that is, not of this creation" (Heb 9:11). The heavenly sanctuary is not new; in fact the earthly sanctuary was built from the pattern of the heavenly (Exod 25:8), but its function comes as a fulfillment of the earthly sanctuary and all its functions (Heb 9:23–28). Therefore, the typological significance of the Day of Atonement is seen in the fulfillment of the sacrificial functions of the earthly sanctuary in Jesus Christ.

---

[30] Roy Gane, "Judgment as Covenant Review," *JATS* 8/1–2 (1997): 184.

[31] Richard Davidson, "The Eschatological Hermeneutic of Biblical Typology," *Theo Rhema* 6.2 (2011): 35; idem, *Typology in Scripture* (Berrien Springs, MI: Andrews University Press, 1981), 367–368.

[32] Christ's ministry in the heavenly sanctuary has two phases to it: 1) His intercessory ministry (Heb 7:25; Dan 8:11–12; Rom 8:24) and 2) His work of judgment which is symbolized by the Day of Atonement (Lev 16; Dan 7:5–27; 8:13–14).

There may be some allusions to the Day of Atonement in the book of Revelation (Rev 11:1–2, 18–19).[33] "The visions of the second half of Revelation, furthermore, portray a division of all humanity into two groups . . . such a division along spiritual lines took place also in relation to lots cast over the two male goats on Yom Kippur."[34]

The Feast of Tabernacles/Booths

The purpose of this feast was "that your generations may know that I made the children of Israel dwell in booths when I brought them out of the land of Egypt" (Lev 23:43). There is an element of joy that accompanies this feast: "Seven days you shall keep a sacred feast to the Lord your God in the place which the Lord chooses, because the Lord your God will bless you in all your produce and in all the work of your hands, so that you surely rejoice" (Deut 16:15). The Feast of Booths was a reminder that the God who provided for them in the wilderness when they lived in booths is the same God who provides abundant harvest.

The function of this festival, in the context of the calendric texts, is first demonstrated by its inclusion in the list of the major biblical calendars (Lev 23; Deut 16; Num 28–29). It is commemorative of the exodus event (Lev 23:43).[35] It is a joyful celebration at the end of the harvest (that is, other crops).[36]

The typological and theological perspective of the Feast of Tabernacles hinges on one explicit reference to the feast in the NT (John 7:2). The brevity of this reference speaks volumes of the way we should view the festivals. The absence of any elaborate theological development of the Feast of Tabernacle's themes by the NT authors is an indicator that while we may study the feasts individually and draw meaning for today, the NT does not present these festivals as having continuing relevance for Christians, once the type has met the antitype in Christ. Having said that, we need not close the door for allusions and echoes of the Feast of Tabernacles in the NT.[37]

---

[33] Paulien, "The Role of the Hebrew Cultus," 256.

[34] Ibid., 257.

[35] J. C. Rylaarsdam, "Feast of Booths," IDB (New York: Abingdon, 1962), 457.

[36] *SDABC* 1:805. Since it came after the Day of Atonement, "all misunderstandings had been cleared up, all sins confessed and put aside. The Israelites were happy and their happiness found expression in the Feast of Tabernacles" (ibid., 805).

[37] In a brief homily, Richard Davidson, "Christmas Festival of Lights," *AUSS* 44/2 (2006): 200, suggests connections between the annual Feast of Tabernacles and the birth of Christ. Further exploration of this allusion could throw significant light into the festival events around the time of Christ.

Does Peter's spontaneous response to the appearance of Moses and Elijah ("let us make three tabernacles: one for You, one for Moses, and one for Elijah" [Mark 9:5]) invoke the Feast of Tabernacles? This is unlikely, as Peter excludes not only himself but also the rest of the disciples from dwelling in the booths. His proposal departs radically from the spirit of the Feast of Tabernacles that includes everyone dwelling in the booths. Thus, Peter's suggestion should not be taken as an indication of the continuity of this festival for Christians. The observations made against such allusions point to the danger of stretching the festival typology beyond the scope of the text. Therefore, it may be beneficial to study individual festivals that are not explicitly discussed typologically by the biblical authors in the light of the rest of the festivals.

The New Moon

In Hebrew, the phrase translated "new moon" (*rosh khodesh*) literally means "head of the month." The new moon seems to have been celebrated on the same level as the festivals. Its celebration was introduced by the blowing of trumpets. The day was a day of rejoicing (Num 10:10), with sacrifices (Num 28:11–15; 1 Chr 23:31)[38] and probably fellowship meals (1 Sam 20:18). It was a common practice to consult a prophet on the new moon (2 Kgs 4:23). It is interesting that in this passage both the Sabbath and the new moon are mentioned. It may be observed that on both the new moon and the Sabbath all work was suspended, among other things. In times of apostasy, Israel still wanted to experience the joy that came with the observance of the festivals, but God gave a stern warning to remove the joy of the new moons from Israel in the times of apostasy (Hos 2:11). This pronouncement of the cessation of the feasts, including the New Moon, was due to Israel's adulterous relationship with other gods (Hos 2:13).[39]

In Isaiah 1:13–14, Israel's feasts are viewed as "'empty', 'abhorrent', and its sacred liturgy a 'trampling' in God's courts."[40] In this passage the New Moon feast is clustered with "vain offerings," the Sabbath, and the appointed feasts. God would not accept the sacrifices and holy convocations on these days because of the people's iniquities (Isa 1). The purposes

---

[38] See Sara Japhet, *1–2 Chronicles* (Louisville, KY: Westminster, 1993), 420, who notes that the word *tamid* used in 1 Chronicles 23:31 is a "terminological mark of the regular service."

[39] Hans Walter Wolff, *Hosea*, Hermenia (Philadelphia, PA: Fortress, 1974), 38.

[40] Brevard Childs, *Isaiah* (Louisville, KY: Westminster, 2001), 19.

of the new moon are expressed eschatologically in Isaiah 66:23.[41] Again the new moon is paired with the Sabbath in this passage within the context of acceptable worship. There are some who have attempted to connect the Sabbath with the moon,[42] arguing that the Sabbath was originally based on a lunar calendar. This system assigns a specific date for each Sabbath every month. The arguments are untenable.[43] Tying the weekly Sabbath to the lunar calendar removes the distinction between the seventh-day Sabbath and the festivals.

Sabbath Year

The sabbatical year for the land is introduced in Leviticus 25:1–7. The purpose of the sabbath year was to provide rest for the land (Lev 25:3–4). For subsistence, the people had to depend on what grows naturally from the land (Lev 25:6). One scholar observes that there is a similarity between Leviticus 25 and Leviticus 23: the former follows naturally from the latter.[44] He further observes that "Leviticus 23 describes religious observances which take place annually; Lev 25 those that take place super-annually. Both chapters begin with a 'sabbath': Lev 23:1–4 describes the Sabbath day, Lev 25:1–7 describes the Sabbath year."[45] It may further be observed that both chapters have the agricultural cycle in focus, in celebrating the harvest and regulating and preserving land fertility.[46] Since the sabbatical year occurred every seventh year, it was a "sabbath of years" (Lev 25:8).

Jubilee

If the sabbatical year was a "sabbath of years," the year of Jubilee was a "sabbath of a sabbath of years" (that is, a year following seven weeks/sabbaths of years [Lev 25:8–9]). Leviticus 25 introduces the Jubilee as the

---

[41] Skip McCarty, *In Granite or Ingrained? What the Old and New Covenants Reveal about the Gospel, the Law, and the Sabbath* (Berrien Springs, MI: Andrews University Press, 2007), 214.

[42] See the discussion in Ángel Rodriguez, "What about a Lunar Sabbath?," https://adventistbiblicalresearch.org/ material/theology-sabbath/whataboutalunarSabbath? (accessed January 21, 2017).

[43] See the discussion in Gerhard Pfandl, "Weekly Sabbath or Lunar Sabbath: Are Adventists Keeping the Wrong Sabbath?," https://adventistbiblicalresearch.org/sites/default/files/pdf/Weekly%20Sabbath%20or% 20Lunar%20Sabbath_0.pdf (accessed April 17, 2017).

[44] John S. Bergsma, *The Jubilee from Leviticus to Qumran: A History of Interpretation* (Leiden: Brill, 2007), 82.

[45] Ibid.

[46] Ibid.

fiftieth year that follows the seventh sabbatical year (the forty-ninth year). There are instructions about the observance of Jubilee that specify the time and outcomes of observing the year of Jubilee (Lev 25:8–13). During this year, there was no agricultural activity. Further, an inherited property that had been sold was returned to the owner. The word "jubilee" comes from the Hebrew word *yovel*, meaning "ram's horn." A trumpet (Heb. *shofar*) was blown at the commencement of Jubilee to usher it in (Lev 25:9). The instructions concerning the Jubilee year include the statement "you shall not oppress one another," which occurs twice (Lev 25:14, 17). The purpose for this instruction unfolds in Leviticus 25:25–55, where a description is given on how one could fall prey to debt and eventually slavery. This section of the chapter is outlined as follows:

The Outline of the Jubilee Year Section (Lev 25:8–55)
    1. Instructions for Its Observance (vv. 8–13)
    2. Implications for the Sale of Property (vv. 8–13)
    3. Encouragement for Its Observation (vv. 18–22)
Implications of the Jubilee for the Redemption of Property (vv. 23–55)
    1. Statement of Principle (vv. 23–24)
    2. The Stages of Destitution (vv. 25–55)
        a. The loss of lands (vv. 25–28)
        b. The loss of home (vv. 29–34)
        c. The loss of independence (vv. 35–38)
        d. The loss of freedom ('slavery') (vv. 39–46)
            i. True slavery forbidden for Israelites (vv. 39–43)
            ii. True slavery permitted for non-Israelites (vv. 44–46)
        e. The loss of freedom to a foreigner (vv. 47–55).[47]

The section begins with instructions on the observance of the Jubilee, followed by conditions and implications for land sales. There are instructions regarding a poverty-stricken Israelite, who may slide from selling land (Lev 25:25–28) and house (Lev 25:29–34) to dependency on charity (Lev 25:35–38), and finally to selling oneself to a fellow Israelite (Lev 25:39–43) or, in the worst case, to a foreigner (Lev 25:47–55). The Jubilee provides a means to ensure that the land is not permanently lost by an Israelite. This is based on the fact that the land belongs to the Lord and must not be sold permanently (Lev 25:23). "Like the rest of the sabbatical

---

[47] Bergsma, *The Jubilee from Leviticus to Qumran: A History of Interpretation* (Leiden: Brill, 2007), 84.

provisions, the Jubilee proclaimed the sovereignty of God over time and nature; and obedience to it would require submission to that sovereignty hence the year is dubbed 'holy,' 'a Sabbath to Yahweh' to be observed."[48]

While there are indications of kinship redemption in the OT (Ruth 4; Jer 32), there is no clear reference of the observance of Jubilee laws in the OT. Some allusions to the Jubilee year may be found in Isaiah 37:30. Many Israelites were deported from their land and taken into captivity. There was a time in which there was nothing to return to (Isa 5:8; Mic 2:2, 9).

Luke 4:16–30 quotes Isaiah 61, which has Jubilee elements. "Scholars are agreed that Jesus made use of jubilary imagery, though there is division over exactly what he meant by it."[49] There are three views that seek to connect the Jubilee observance with the teachings of Jesus: "(1) Jesus explicitly called for observance of Jubilee, perhaps connected with a specific year. (2) Jesus deliberately used Jubilee concepts but without calling for a general observance in a particular year, as a way of expressing his prophetic call for justice according to covenant norms. (3) Jesus used images associated with Jubilee symbols, though not consciously so."[50] One scholar argues that Jesus did not deliberately use jubilary images to interpret the coming kingdom nor did He identify a specific year as a Jubilee year. She traces the evidence for jubilary images in the gospel narratives (Matt 11:2–6; 18:21–35; Luke 14:12–24), and concludes that the Jubilee is portrayed as a model or image of the kingdom of God.[51] The year of Jubilee with its provisions was given and implemented in a theocratic context. Therefore, any application of the system should be done with caution. The statement of Christ in Luke 4:18–19 seems to have the Jubilee as its backdrop; this text could be the fulfillment of the jubilary principles. While the celebration of Jubilee is not required for Christians, there are lessons and principles that may provide a helpful guide on matters of social justice and equity in contemporary society.

Festivals in the New Testament

Jesus went to Jerusalem to celebrate the Feast of Tabernacles (John 7:2, 10). On the last day of the feast Jesus called out and said, "If anyone thirsts, let him come to Me and drink" (John 7:37). The Lord's Supper or

---

[48] Christopher J. H. Wright, "Jubilee, Year of," *ABD* 3:1029.

[49] Ibib., 1028.

[50] R. D. Kaylor, *Jesus the Prophet: His Vision of the Kingdom of Earth* (Louisville, KY: Westminster, 1994), 84.

[51] S. H. Ringe, *Jesus, Liberation, and the Biblical Jubilee: Images for Ethics and Christology* (Philadelphia, PA: Fortress, 1985), 84.

Communion Service appropriates elements of the Feast of Unleavened Bread. The bread and wine symbolize His body and blood that inaugurates the new covenant (Matt 26:17–30; Mark 14:12–26; Luke 22:1–23). There is a clear instruction for the continuation of the Lord's Supper initiated by Jesus Himself, as believers come together in remembrance of Him (1 Cor 11:23–26). The death of Christ is connected to the Passover (1 Cor 5:8), in which Christ becomes our Passover Lamb that has been sacrificed. Christ also resurrected as Firstfruits of those who are dead; this links His resurrection to the raising of the sheaf offering that occasioned the Feast of Firstfruits (1 Cor 15:20–23). Together, the references and allusions in the NT demonstrate that the OT feasts and sacrifices have been replaced by something new:[52]

> The NT represents both continuity and innovation regarding religious festivals. On the one hand, Jesus and his disciples are described as participating in statutory Jewish Festivals. But there is an element of fulfilment and abrogation as well as observance of OT festivals.[53]

The death and resurrection of Christ provides a reference point for the fulfillment of significant elements of the festivals.

The commandment to keep the Sabbath holy (Exod 20:8; Deut 5:12) has generated debate and several questions have been raised. The word *sabbaton* occurs sixty-eight times in the NT: (eleven times in Matthew, twelve in Mark, twenty in Luke, ten in Acts, thirteen in John, and once each in 1 Corinthians 16 and Colossians 2). Of the sixty-eight references, twenty-four are in the plural form. Both in singular and plural, *sabbaton* refers to the Sabbath.[54]

For the purposes of this study, the most relevant reference from the Gospels is in Matthew 12, which links the Sabbath with an illustration from the sacrificial services by the priests. In this reference, the disciples were hungry and, walking through the fields, they plucked heads of grain and ate (Matt 12:1–8). This act was condemned by the Pharisees because it

---

[52] Leland Ryken et al, "Feast, Feasting," *Dictionary of Biblical Imagery* (Downers Grove, IL: InterVarsity, 1998), 278-280.

[53] Idem, "Festival," *Dictionary of Biblical Imagery* (Downers Grove, IL: InterVarsity, 1998), 282.

[54] James H. Moulton and George Milligan, *The Vocabulary of the Greek Testament* (London: Hodder and Stoughton, 1930), 567, who note that "in the Pentateuch and elsewhere the plural *ta sabbata* is used both for 'the Sabbath' and 'the sabbaths.'"

occurred on the Sabbath, and they confronted Jesus about the behavior of His disciples. Jesus appealed to Numbers 28:9–10 in defense of the disciple's action, pointing out that the priests meet a need that seems to violate the Sabbath without incurring guilt.[55] The priests had to offer sacrifices morning and evening on Sabbath (Num 28:9–10). In engaging in this work on Sabbath they were not condemned because they were serving in obedience to God's own command for their office. Therefore, "man's traditions about the Sabbath were wrong, for they contradicted God's own law."[56] Possible parallels between this Sabbath controversy passage and Colossians 2:16 may be seen in the following arguments:

1. In ritual contexts, priestly activities in the offering of sacrifices are condoned on the Sabbath.
2. The comparison between Christ and the temple in the context of the Sabbath controversy may point to a similar situation in Colossians where the focus may be on the sacrificial services on Sabbath, in comparison with Christ's sacrifice rather than the time element.[57]

The Practical Significance of the Festivals and the Sabbath for Christians

Some Christians view the observance of Jewish festivals as contrary to the injunction of the apostle Paul in Colossians 2:16–17 and other Pauline passages.[58] Others see value in celebrating Jewish festivals in a Christian context.[59] There are those who see a symbiotic connection between Israel,

---

[55] S. Westerholm, "Sabbath," *Dictionary of Jesus and the Gospels*, ed. Joel B. Green et al. (Downers Grove, IL: InterVarsity, 1992).

[56] Warren W. Wiersbe, *The Bible Exposition Commentary: New Testament*, vol. 1 (Colorado Springs, CO: Victor, 1989), 42.

[57] Mxolisi M. Sokupa, "*Skia tōn mellontōn in Colossians 2:17: An Interpretation* (PhD diss., Adventist International Institute of Advanced Studies, 2009), 152. In examining the ritual elements within the context of the arguments in Colossians and other parallel passages (Rom 14:5–6; Gal 4:10; Heb 10:1), it seems evident that the focus is more on the sacrificial elements than time. Time is used as an index but the issues are around sacrifice.

[58] Tony Costa, "The Sabbath and Its Relation to Christ and the Church in the New Testament," *SBJT* 20.1 (2016): 128.

[59] Martha Zimmerman, *Celebrating Biblical Feasts in Your Home or Church* (Bloomington, MN: Bethany House, 2004) offers suggestions on how to celebrate biblical festivals as a Christian. The author indicates that her suggestions are "to be used as tools to help our families honor God" (ibid., 16).

Christ, and the church and therefore maintain that the Jewish festivals are a "telescopic picture" of the connection between the three.[60] This topic brings up a number of questions relating to continuity and or discontinuity of the festivals and the Sabbath. This study has explored the meaning of the seven Festivals, New Moon, sabbath year, and Jubilee in relation to the Sabbath. A critical question among others is whether Christians should observe the Sabbath as well as the festivals and sabbatical years.

The weekly Sabbath is the seventh day, sanctified by the Lord at creation (Gen 2:1–3). Observing the seventh-day Sabbath requires, among other things, a complete cessation from work (Exod 20:12–13). On the other hand, the observance of the festivals—with the exception of the Day of Atonement—required rest from customary work. While Leviticus 23 lists the seventh-day Sabbath among the feasts without listing its sacrificial requirements, Numbers 28 adds the sacrificial elements to the Sabbath. These sacrificial requirements may have been the reason for including the Sabbath in the calendar of feasts. Further, the inclusion of the weekly Sabbath in the calendric texts may be necessary as there are combinations of "seventh," "sabbath," and "rest" in the annual feasts and sabbatical years that are considerably predicated on the features of the seventh-day Sabbath (Gen 2:1–3; Exod 20:8–11).

The feasts were also celebrated by assembling together for fellowship and by participating in sacrifice and offerings. The aim of these celebrations was to affirm the covenant relationship with God and to actively anticipate the promised Messiah. The temporary nature of these sacrifices is indicated by their temple-centeredness. The weekly Sabbath, on the other hand, was not observed exclusively at the temple. Its observance was not dependent on sacrifices and the temple; its observance began at creation, when God rested on the seventh day of the creation week. The weekly Sabbath predated the nation Israel and their festivals; the feasts and sacrifices would cease, and Israel itself would also cease to be a special nation, but the seventh-day Sabbath would continue because its original purpose was universal and permanent.

---

[60] Albert Bailey, *Ancient Bible Feasts: A Telescopic View of Israel, Christ and the Church* (Bloomington, IN: Author House, 2015).

Conclusion

This study focused on the main calendric texts, discussing the meaning of the Sabbath and the festivals. The two main elements that were highlighted are the prescribed sacrifices and instructions about rest. It is evident that all the festivals had required sacrificial offerings. Without the sacrifices and the temple within the confines of a theocratic nation, the festivals would not stand. All sacrifices pointed forward to the ultimate sacrifice of Jesus Christ (Col 2:16–17; Heb 10:1). Since Christ offered Himself, the sacrifices and festivals (with their ceremonial sabbaths and rituals) that pointed forward to the Messiah have been fulfilled. There is therefore no need for Christians to observe the festivals.

The two introductory phrases at the beginning of Leviticus 23 (vs. 2, 4) clearly set the seventh-day "Sabbath to the LORD" (Lev 23:3) apart from the festivals. In the same chapter, these "appointed feasts" (Lev 23:4, 37) are "besides the LORD'S [weekly] Sabbaths" (Lev 23:38). Numbers 28 indicates that an additional burnt offering was required on the Sabbath, but these sacrifices are a temporal element that would find fulfillment in Christ. Unlike the festivals, the seventh-day Sabbath was established and sanctified by God at creation and serves to remind humanity—hence their celebration—of God's work of creation. On this day, humans are expected to emulate God by resting and fellowshipping with Him. The death and resurrection of Christ does not invalidate the Sabbath. Rather, it affirms God's creatorship and His love for humans—a love that must be reciprocated by humans in obeying the Lord, including recognizing His ownership through keeping the Sabbath. Thus, Christians are still under obligation to observe the seventh-day Sabbath.

The study of the Sabbath in the context of the calendric texts has distinguished the seventh-day Sabbath from the festivals with their ceremonial sabbaths on the basis of their purpose, function, and typological and theological application. The Sabbath predates the feasts and its purpose and function was already established as a day of rest. There are a number of festivals where rest is prescribed, but none of the festivals are defined by it. Therefore, it is a grave mistake to lump together the weekly Sabbath established at creation and the festivals that pointed forward to, hence reached fulfillment in, Christ's death, resurrection, and ministry. Against those who have interpreted the Sabbath as another feast that ended with the festivals after the death and resurrection of Christ, the evidence of Scripture clearly demonstrates the validity of the Sabbath beyond the festivals.

CHAPTER 12

TORAH'S SEVEN VIBRANT DIMENSIONS OF SABBATH REST

Richard M. Davidson

Introduction

Seventh-day Adventists have conducted much careful research to substantiate the permanence and universality of the seventh-day Sabbath.[1] The objective of such study with regard to the Sabbath largely has been to show which is the right *day*—the validity of the Saturday Sabbath instead of Sunday—but comparatively little has been written dealing with the right *way* to keep the Sabbath. Adventists have generally refrained from making a (legalistic) list of Sabbath prohibitions, paralleling the thirty-nine rabbinic categories of activity prohibited on the Sabbath.[2] However, with few

---

[1] See, e.g., J. N. Andrews, *History of the Sabbath and the First Day of the Week*, 3rd. ed. (Battle Creek, MI: Review and Herald, 1887; reprint, TEACH Services, 1998); Carlyle B. Haynes, *From Sabbath to Sunday* (Washington, DC: Review and Herald, 1928); M. L. Andreasen, *The Sabbath* (Washington DC: Review and Herald, 1942); Samuele Bacchiocchi, *From Sabbath to Sunday: A Historical Investigation of the Rise of Sunday Observance in Early Christianity* (Rome: Pontifical Gregorian University Press, 1977); and Kenneth A. Strand, ed., *The Sabbath in Scripture and History* (Washington, DC: Review and Herald, 1982).

[2] See the tractate *Shabbat* in the Talmud, and the thirty-nine classes of work listed in the Mishnah, tractate *Shabbat* 7:2. To be fair to the rabbinic understanding, this list was not arbitrarily chosen, but based upon biblical statements regarding Sabbath observance and inferences drawn from these and related passages. In the Talmudic tractate, the basic thirty-nine categories of prohibited kinds of work are sub-divided into more detailed examples of prohibited activities. The purpose of these prohibitions was (at least theoretically) to eliminate distractions so that one may more fully enjoy the "exquisite delight" of the Sabbath day. As far as the author has been able to determine, Jewish tradition is not encumbered with the misunderstanding of the word

exceptions, Adventist writings have not showcased the joyous experiential significance of Sabbath observance for a vibrant spiritual life.[3]

In contrast to most Seventh-day Adventist literature, a number of writers from observant (and messianic) Jewish traditions have given careful thought and expended creative energy in describing the experiential joy and blessing of Sabbath celebration.[4] In recent years, a growing

---

khefets in Isaiah 58:13, which English versions have often translated as "pleasure," but which Jewish translations have rightly recognized as referring to one's ordinary business pursuits/affairs (see NJPS; cf. *HALOT* 1:340, which translates as "business"; note the business context in the earlier occurrences of this noun in this chapter [Isa 58:2–3]). The Jewish tradition has recognized the "exquisite delight" of the Sabbath even though, as did many scribes and Pharisees in Jesus' day (and as do some Sabbath-keeping Christians today), in reality some have turned the Sabbath into a legalistic burden and not a delight.

[3] Exceptions might include, among others, treatments of Sabbath experience in Samuele Bacchiocchi, *Divine Rest for Human Restlessness: A Theological Study of the Good News of the Sabbath for Today* (Rome: Pontifical Gregorian University Press, 1977); Sakae Kubo, *God Meets Man: A Theology of the Sabbath and Second Advent* (Nashville, TN: Southern Publishing, 1978); John Brunt, *A Day For Healing: The Meaning of Jesus' Sabbath Miracles* (Washington, DC: Review and Herald, 1981), 55–63; Roy Branson, ed., *Festival of the Sabbath* (Takoma Park, MD: Association of Adventist Forums, 1985); Gerita G. Liebelt, *From Dilemma to Delight: Creative Ideas for Happy Sabbaths* (Hagerstown, MD: Review and Herald, 1986); Richard M. Davidson, *A Love Song for the Sabbath* (Washington, DC: Review and Herald, 1988); Clifford Goldstein, *A Pause for Peace* (Boise, ID: Pacific Press, 1992); Celeste P. Walker, *Making Sabbath Special* (Nampa, ID: Pacific Press, 1999); Des Cummings Jr., *Original Love: Experience Peace, Meaning and Harmony through Sabbath Rest* (Fallbrook, CA: HART Books, 2001); and Sigve K. Tonstad, *The Lost Meaning of the Seventh Day* (Berrien Springs, MI: Andrews University Press, 2009).

[4] See especially, Abraham J. Heschel, *The Sabbath: Its Meaning for Modern Man* (New York: Farrar, Straus and Giroux, 1951; New York: Harper & Row, 1966); Isidor Grunfeld, *The Sabbath: A Guide to Its Understanding and Observance*, 5th ed., rev. and expanded (Jerusalem: Feldheim, 2003); Abraham E. Millgram, *Sabbath: Day of Delight* (Philadelphia, PA: Jewish Publications Society of America, 1965); and Samuel H. Dresner, *The Sabbath* (New York: Burning Bush, 1970). See also Malka Drucker, *Shabbat: A Peaceful Island* (New York: Holiday House, 1983); Pinchas H. Peli, *The Jewish Sabbath: A Renewed Encounter* (New York: Schocken, 1988); Rabbi Shimon Finkelman, *Shabbos* (New York: Mesorah Publications, 1990); Dov P. Elkins, ed., *A Shabbat Reader: Universe of Cosmic Joy* (New York: UAHC Press, 1998); Josef Erlich, *Sabbath* (Syracuse, NY: Syracuse University Press, 1999); Francine Klagsbrun, *The Fourth Commandment: Remember the Sabbath Day* (New York: Harmony, 2002); Yehoshua Rubin, *Spiritual Awakenings: Illuminations on Shabbat and the Holidays* (New York: Urim Publications, 2003); Judith Shulevitz, *The Sabbath World: Glimpses of a Different Order of Time* (New York: Random House, 2010); and Joe Lieberman, *The Gift of Rest: Rediscovering the Beauty of the Sabbath* (New York: Howard Books, 2011). From a messianic Jewish perspective, see, e.g., Barry and Steffi Rubin, *The Sabbath: Entering God's Rest* (Baltimore: Lederer Books, 1998); Rabbi A. Steinsaltz, *The Miracle of the Seventh Day: A Guide to the Spiritual Meaning, Significance, and Weekly Practice of the Jewish Sabbath* (San Francisco, CA: Jossey-Bass, 2003); Lauren F. Winner, *Mudhouse Sabbath* (Brewster, MA: Paraclete, 2003); Bonnie S. Wilks, *Sabbath: A Gift of Time* (Southlake, TX: Gateway, 2018); Arnold G. Fruchtenbaum, *The Sabbath* (San Antonio, TX: Ariel, 2012); D. T. Lancaster, *From Sabbath to Sabbath: Returning the Holy Sabbath to the Disciples of Jesus* (Marshfield, MO: First Fruits of Zion, 2016).

number of Christians who do not personally observe the seventh-day Sabbath have nonetheless discovered in the Sabbath a paradigm for vibrant Christian spirituality.[5] However, most of the literature written by Jewish and Christian authors (including Seventh-day Adventists) about the spiritual values of the Sabbath contain little substantial biblical foundation for the conclusions drawn.[6]

The present study focuses on the Torah (Pentateuch), the foundational divine revelation given to Moses. This study does not discuss the various general biblical principles of Sabbath observance.[7] Rather, it focuses on the

---

[5] This trend was spearheaded by such authors as Tilden Edwards, *Sabbath Time: Understanding and Practice for Contemporary Christians* (New York: Seabury, 1982); and Marva J. Dawn, *Keeping the Sabbath Wholly: Ceasing, Resting, Embracing, Feasting* (Grand Rapids, MI: Eerdmans, 1989). In 1989 Dawn lamented that "so many of the books and articles describing the disciplines of the spiritual life contain no mention whatsoever of observing the Sabbath" (p. xii). But in the last twenty years a number of books by (mostly evangelical) Christians have appeared which highlight the spiritual experience to be found in the Sabbath. See, e.g., Don Postema, *Catch Your Breath: God's Invitation to Sabbath Rest* (Grand Rapids, MI: CRC Publications, 1997); Wayne Muller, *Sabbath: Finding Rest, Renewal, and Delight in Our Busy Lives* (New York: Bantam, 1999); Martha W. Hickman, *A Day of Rest: Creating a Spiritual Space in Your Week* (New York: Avon Books, 1999); Dorothy Bass, *Receiving the Day: Christian Practices for Opening the Gift of Time* (San Francisco, CA: Jossey-Bass, 2000); Phillip L. Button, *Sabbath Living* (Baltimore, MD: Publish America, 2004); Lynne M. Baab, *Sabbath Keeping: Finding Freedom in the Rhythms of Rest* (Downers Grove, IL: InterVarsity, 2005); Mark Buchanan, *The Rest of God: Restoring Your Soul by Restoring Sabbath* (Nashville, TN: Thomas Nelson, 2006); Kathleen Casey, *Sabbath Presence: Appreciating the Gifts of Each Day* (Notre Dame, IN: Ave Maria, 2006); Norman Wirzba, *Living the Sabbath: Discovering the Rhythms of Rest and Delight* (Grand Rapids, MI: Brazos, 2006); Kerry W. Kent, *Rest: Living in Sabbath Simplicity* (Grand Rapids, MI: Zondervan, 2009); Dan B. Allender, *Sabbath* (Nashville, TN: Thomas Nelson, 2009); idem, *Upside Down Living: Sabbath* (Harrisburg, VA: Herald, 2016); Walter Brueggemann, *Sabbath as Resistance: Saying No to the Culture of Now* (Louisville, KY: John Knox, 2014); Rob Muthiah, *The Sabbath Experiment: Spiritual Formation for Living in a Non-Stop World* (Eugene, OR: Cascade, 2015); A. J. Swoboda, *Subversive Sabbath: The Surprising Power of Rest in a Nonstop World* (Grand Rapids, MI: Baker, 2018); Anita Amstutz, *Soul Tending: A Journey into the Heart of the Sabbath* (Nashville, TN: Skylight Paths, 2018).

[6] Several of the major works which do contain biblical substantiation for their practical suggestions regarding Sabbath rest are cited in this study.

[7] Davidson, *Love Song for the Sabbath*, 87–108, endeavors to set forth these basic principles in a positive way, based largely on Isaiah 58 and Psalm 92. These principles include, among others: (1) exquisite delight (the Sabbath is a day for joy!), (2) holiness (wholly for the Lord—all of it, all of us, all the time), (3) honor (eliminating any distractions that will keep us from focusing attention upon the honored guest, the Lord of the Sabbath, while asking the practical question: Will this activity enhance or detract from attention upon the honored guest of the Sabbath?), (4) service (humanitarian, redemptive activity), (5) worship, (6) meditation upon God's character, and (7) rest. The present chapter does not attempt to treat all of these (and other) biblical principles for Sabbath observance, but rather focuses upon the last principle (rest), examining the multiple positive experiential dimensions of Sabbath rest found in the Pentateuch. For other Adventist treatments of basic Sabbath-keeping principles, see, e.g., Bacchiocchi, *Divine Rest for Human*

principle of rest, exploring seven vibrant dimensions of Sabbath rest that emerge from the Torah.[8]

According to the Torah, Sabbath is a verb! There are seven different verbs used in the Pentateuch to describe Sabbath observance. Each verb leads to a different positive dimension of Sabbath rest. This study invites the reader to savor each vibrant dimension of rest connected with the Sabbath. Inasmuch as this study concerns the practical, positive, experiential aspects of Sabbath observance, it cites case studies from the author's and others' experiences. It draws especially on the Jewish faith tradition, which for millennia has been cultivating the delicate artistry of joyful Sabbath observance.[9] The author has had opportunity to personally experience how practicing Jews apply the Torah's positive Sabbath-observance principles in their homes and synagogues, and has dialogued with orthodox and messianic Jewish believers, discovering that many of the beautiful Jewish Sabbath traditions are actually rooted in Scripture, especially in the Torah. This study focuses upon those biblical dimensions of Sabbath rest as encapsulated in the key verbs of Pentateuchal passages describing Sabbath rest.

This exposition of Scripture is placed within a canonical, redemptive, Christocentric context, in which the Decalogue ("Ten Words") of Exodus 20 and Deuteronomy 5 is interpreted as encompassing ten promises. According to Hebrew grammar, all "Ten Words" can either be translated as negative commands (prohibitions) or as emphatic promises.[10] The Decalogue begins with a preamble in which Yahweh identifies Himself, followed by a historical prologue in which He declares His past redemption of His people: "I am the Lord your God, who brought you out of the land

---

Restlessness, 131–226; and Kubo, *God Meets Man*, 5–69.

[8] This chapter is largely adapted, revised, and expanded from Richard M. Davidson, "Sabbath, Spirituality and Mission: Torah's Seven Dimensions of Sabbath Rest," in *Encountering God in Life and Mission: A Festschrift Honoring Jon Dybdahl*, ed. Rudi Maier (Berrien Springs, MI: Department of World Mission, Andrews University, 2010), 3–19.

[9] There is also much that can be learned from Christians who have kept the seventh-day Sabbath down through the centuries, but the author's experience has brought him in contact with the positive spiritual values of the Sabbath through encounters with observant (and messianic) Jews, and thus this chapter concentrates on their contributions for illustrations in this chapter, without denying the positive contributions of others. This study does not seek to be an exhaustive treatment of positive Sabbath values; rather, it is only illustrative.

[10] In the Torah the Decalogue is never in Hebrew called the "Ten Commandments" but rather the "Ten Words." For further discussion and substantiation of the possibility of translating each "Word" as an emphatic promise rather than a negative prohibition, see, e.g., Davidson, *Love Song for the Sabbath*, 35–37; cf. the standard Hebrew grammar which supports this possibility: E. Kautzsch, ed., *Gesenius' Hebrew Grammar* (Oxford: Clarendon, 1910), par. 113bb, 113ee.

of Egypt, out of the house of slavery" (Exod 20:2; Deut 5:6). In effect, God says, "I am Yahweh who has redeemed you by the blood of the Lamb. You are already saved and now I promise you power to enable you to keep My law."[11] If one recognizes that the Decalogue starts with this preamble and historical prologue, then all "Ten Words" that follow become promises![12] From a Christian perspective, Christ provides the motivation and power to effectuate those promises in our lives. Duty becomes a delight. Wholistic Sabbath rest finds its ultimate experiential meaning in Jesus Christ.

What follows is an exploration of seven positive experiential values of Sabbath rest as they emerge from the key verbs in passages describing Sabbath observance in the Pentateuch.

Physical, Work-Free Rest

As a first dimension of Sabbath rest, God offers humans *physical* rest. Genesis 2:2 indicates that God "rested [*shavath*] on the seventh day from all His work which He had done."[13] The verb *shavath* means "to cease, stop."[14] Already implicit in Genesis 1–2, and explicit in the fourth "Word" of the Decalogue, we are invited to follow God's example, to cease from our weekday work, and rest on the *shabbath* (Exod 20:10).[15] For twenty-four golden hours we do not have to work. We are free from the tyranny of toil.

Recent scientific studies have shown that human physiology involves seven-day (septacircadian) rhythms. We are wired for one day of rest in seven! The heart rate; the production of steroid hormones; the swelling after surgery; a variety of immune reactions; the rise in the cortical hormones in human mothers' milk; and fluctuations in blood pressure, red blood cell count, body temperature, and concentrations of body chemicals—all these,

---

[11] For further discussion of the suzerainty covenant structure of the Decalogue, which highlights grace preceding law, see Davidson, *Love Song for the Sabbath*, 35–39.

[12] Note how Ellen G. White, apparently without any knowledge of Hebrew grammar, describes the Decalogue positively as consisting of ten promises: "'The Ten Commandments . . . are ten promises. . . . There is not a negative in that law, although it may appear thus" (*SDABC* 1:1105). For further discussion, see Richard M. Davidson, "Ellen White's Insights into Scripture in Light of the Original Biblical Languages," in *The Gift of Prophecy in Scripture and History*, ed. Alberto Timm and Dwain N. Esmond (Silver Spring, MD: Ellen White Estate, 2015), 161–162.

[13] All biblical quotations are from the NASB, unless otherwise indicated.

[14] *HALOT* 2:1407.

[15] Dawn, *Keeping the Sabbath Wholly*, 45, notes that "the necessarily close connection of the sixth and seventh days would imply that human beings, whom God made in his image on the sixth day, will be faithful to that image by resting and ceasing on the seventh day, even as God did."

and many more, exhibit "circaseptan biorhythms, or seven-day cycles."[16] Experiments on the optimum work-rest cycle in Britain during World War II revealed that humans produced most efficiently if they worked six days and had one day to rest.[17]

The work from which we need physical rest includes various kinds of labor. "Whether it is strain of manual labor, the strain of long hours in the office, or the strain of chores at home, work makes physical demands."[18] The need for physical rest is illustrated by the practice of professional athletes, who need recovery time after physical exertion to remain at their peak performance. So, with the physical rest of the Sabbath; it is essential so that we may live life to the full. Physical rest also means getting enough sleep. It is not inappropriate to take a refreshing Sabbath afternoon nap![19]

In various extended stays in Israel, the author's family has had numerous opportunities to celebrate the Shabbat in the homes of observant Jews. One Hebrew scholar in Israel opened his home on a Friday night to welcome the Shabbat. He lived in a modest single-floor flat in downtown Jerusalem. This unassuming man, Dr. Jacob Bazak, was actually a justice on the Israeli Supreme Court! Long before the Shabbat began, Justice Bazak unplugged his phone, and, with a twinkle in his eye, said, "I don't have to answer the phone on the Shabbat!" Whereas Seventh-day Adventists often see the Sabbath commandment in a negative way—"Don't work on Sabbath!"—Jewish Sabbath-keepers regularly viewed it positively: "I don't have to work on the Sabbath!"[20]

---

[16] See the summary of evidence in Richard M. Davidson, "God's Sabbath Stamp," *Adventist Review*, December 2018, 22–25; Kenneth G. Greenaway, "The Biblical Origin of the Seven-day Cycles in Living Organisms" (unpublished manuscript, Spring 2017); and Bernell Baldwin, "Seven-Day Rhythms," *Journal of Health and Healing* 9 (1984): 3, 14. See also the research of Juan-Cardos Lerman at University of Arizona, which shows the biological need of rest for humans every seven days, and examines the energizing value of physical rest, summarized in his lecture at the American Association for the Advancement of Science, Tucson, Arizona, reported by Carla McClain, "Human 'Clock' Orders Day Off," in *The Idaho Statesman*, and cited by Dawn, *Keeping the Sabbath Wholly*, 68–69.

[17] K. Lee, "Hours of Work in Wartime," *Editorial Research Reports 1942*, vol. II (Washington, DC: CQ Press, 1942), http://library.cqpress.com/cqresearcher/cqresrre1942111600 (accessed August 30, 2019). Germany experimented with a five-day week and France with a ten-day week, but with such limited success that the practice had to be discontinued and a seven-day week re-instituted.

[18] Muthiah, *Sabbath Experiment*, 17.

[19] Ibid., 17–19.

[20] Drawing largely from Jewish perspectives and traditions, evangelical Christian writer Rob Muthiah, *Sabbath Experiment*, explores numerous other reasons why the Sabbath gives human beings a better basis for thinking and discerning things and building relationships. See the

According to ancient Near Eastern creation stories outside of the Bible, the gods created humans to be servants/slaves of the gods, to work so the gods could rest.[21] By contrast, only in the biblical creation narrative of the Torah does the deity's rest after creating become the source of human rest as well. God rests after His work of creation and sets apart the Sabbath as a weekly day of rest for humankind. Humans are invited to rest one-seventh of their lives! As Jesus states, "The Sabbath was made for humankind, not humankind for the Sabbath" (Mark 2:27). The Sabbath is a recognition that we are not bound to an uninterrupted, frenzied attempt to control matter by our toil. Every Sabbath we are freed from the potential tyranny of physical toil, to realize the destiny to which we are called, in personal relationship with our Maker. The Creation-rooted Sabbath reminds us not to place ultimate confidence in our work, not to become intoxicated with our own productivity, not to become a slave to toil.

Physical rest on the Sabbath does not imply that labor is inferior or evil. "The Sabbath as a day of abstaining from work is not a depreciation but an affirmation of labor, a divine exaltation of its dignity.... The duty to work for six days is just as much a part of God's covenant with man as the duty to abstain from work on the seventh day."[22] Furthermore, physical rest on Sabbath is not primarily for the purpose of "resting up" so as to be more fit for the coming week of work. Unlike in Greek thought, where relaxation is "for the sake of gaining strength for new efforts," in Hebrew thinking

> labor is the means toward an end, and the Sabbath as a day of rest, as a day of abstaining from toil, is not for the purpose of recovering one's lost strength and becoming fit for the forthcoming labor. The Sabbath is a day for the sake of life.... The Sabbath is not for the sake of the weekdays; the weekdays are for the sake of Sabbath. It is not an interlude but the climax of living.[23]

---

positive review of Muthiah's book by Frank Hasel in the Biblical Research Institute Newsletter 61 (January 2018), 8–9.

[21] See, e.g., Victor P. Hamilton, *Handbook on the Pentateuch* (Grand Rapids, MI: Baker, 1982), 41–42, for further discussion of this point, comparing the biblical creation narrative with the *Enuma Elish* and the Atrahasis Epic.

[22] Heschel, *The Sabbath*, 28, citing Exodus 20:8.

[23] Ibid., 14.

Mental, Attitudinal Rest

The fourth commandment (or better, "Word") of the Decalogue indicates that God also rested in *mental attitude* as well as ceasing His work of creating. Exodus 20:11 reads that "in six days the LORD made the heavens and the earth, the sea, and all that is in them, and rested [*nuakh*] on the seventh day." The verb for "rest" used here is not *shavath*, as in Genesis 2, but *nuakh* (related to the name Noah). This term may encompass physical rest, but also contains within its semantic range the additional nuances of "repose, settle down, be quiet/tranquil."[24] Both the verb *nuakh* and its derivative noun *menukhah* often describe a rest that "is psychic as well as local."[25] After creating in six days, God sat back, as it were, in tranquil repose, mentally/intellectually rejoicing in the world He had created (cf. Prov 8:31). According to the Deuteronomic version of the Sabbath commandment (or "Word"), God invites human beings to join Him in this *nuakh* rest (Deut 5:14). On Sabbath, we may experience a second dimension of Sabbath rest: *mental* (psychic) tranquility, an intellectual attitude of restful repose! One scholar describes the essence of *nuakh/menukhah* rest as follows:

> *Menuha* which we usually render as "rest" means here much more than a withdrawal from labor and exertion, more than freedom from toil, strain or activity of any kind. *Menuha* is not a negative concept but something real and intrinsically positive. . . . "What was created on the seventh day? *Tranquility, serenity, peace* and *repose*."[26]

This mental attitude of tranquil repose is not limited to human beings. In Exodus 23:12 God commands humans to cease from work on the Sabbath "so that your ox and your donkey may rest [*nuakh*]." The divine will is that not only humans experience tranquil repose on the Sabbath, but

---

[24] *HALOT* 1:679.

[25] See H. D. Preuss, "נוח *nuakh*," *TDOT* 9:278, 284: "the opposite [of *nuakh* in the *hiphil*] is not just motion, e.g., wandering, but (psychic) restlessness. . . . As a result, 'rest' (as we have already seen in the case of the verb) can be psychic as well as local." Cf. John N. Oswalt, "נוח *nuakh*," *NIDOTTE* 3:58: "A second meaning of this root is to cease activity. . . . Such cessation of activity should promote both inner and outer tranquility." Even in the *qal* stem, *nuakh* often denotes more than physical rest; it means "repose" (*HALOT* 1:679), which often implies an attitudinal tranquility (peace, calm, restfulness, serenity) as well as physical rest.

[26] Heschel, *The Sabbath*, 22–23. Quotation within the block quote is from *Genesis Rabbah* 10:9.

also the animals! "The Sabbath vision is that *everyone* will be able to rest one day a week, not just those at the top of the food chain."[27]

Evidence from various scientific studies has suggested not only that the pineal gland, at least in some animals, as well as humans, exhibits a circaseptan (seven-day) rhythm, but that this rhythm highlights a specific day of the week—Saturday. In the case of rats, for example, the pineal gland releases its calming and mood-enhancing melatonin maximally on Saturdays.[28] This hypothesis is supported by a mood study of humans, which found a marked enhancement of "positive affect" or "pleasant mood" on Saturday, accompanied by a decrease in "negative affect."[29] Other studies showed comparable results.[30] One scholar points out that the very moods enhanced maximally on Saturday—those conducive to rest, tranquility, and enhanced worship experience—are the same moods connected with the seventh-day Sabbath in Scripture.[31] Research done in the Halberg Chronobiology Center at the University of Minnesota has repeatedly found that seven-day rhythms can be amplified and re-synchronized by a single stimulus—that is, in response to a one-time event.[32] Building upon this research, one intriguing postulate is that perhaps "God's *blessing* and *sanctifying* the seventh day at Creation as recorded in Genesis 2:1–3, acted as a single stimulus which evoked a *literal* physiological, endocrinological and immunological response in the pineal gland with increased melatonin output on that initial seventh day and is amplified at each subsequent seventh day."[33]

---

[27] Muthiah, *Sabbath Experiment*, 23.

[28] L. Vollrath et al. "Mammalian Pineal Gland: 7-day Rhythmic Activity?" *Experientia* 31/4 (1975): 458–460.

[29] G. Cornelissen et al. "Mapping of Circaseptan and Circadian Changes in Mood," *Scripta Medica* 78/2 (2005): 89–98.

[30] C. S. Areni and M. Burger, "Memories of 'Bad' Days Are More Biased than Memories of 'Good' Days: Past Saturdays Vary, but Past Mondays Are Always Blue," *Journal of Applied Social Psychology* 38 (2008): 1395–1415.

[31] Greenaway, "Biblical Origin of the Seven-day Cycles in Living Organisms."

[32] G. Cornelissen and F. Halberg, "The Biological Week and Broader Time Structures (Chronomes): In Memory of Gunther Hildebrandt," *Perceptual and Motor Skills* 90 (2000): 579–586.

[33] Kenneth G. Greenaway, "Understanding the Biblical Concept of Time and Spiritual Rest" (unpublished paper, Jan 2015), 14. The intent of citing such research is not to "prove" the divine legitimacy of the Sabbath. The "proof" of the Sabbath is in Scripture and in the experiential "tasting" of the tranquil repose of the Sabbath. The Sabbath does not follow a "natural theology" of seventh-day rhythms. Rather, all seven-day rhythms in nature follow the Sabbath pattern of God's creation as recorded in Scripture.

Whether or not further research will further support these conclusions—that there is a tendency in humans and animals to reach maximal levels of tranquility-enhancing substances such as melatonin on Saturdays (Sabbath)—it may be affirmed, given the promissory character of the Decalogue as indicated above, that God promises to enhance our Sabbaths with *nuakh/menukhah*—restful mental/attitudinal repose and tranquility. We may cooperate with God in developing practical strategies conducive to mental restfulness on the Sabbath. An evangelical writer who is not a seventh-day Sabbath keeper but who has nevertheless discovered the richness of Sabbath keeping speaks of how she, as an author, teacher, and theologian, practices intellectual/attitudinal Sabbath rest from her professional intellectual life:

> I also think it is important not to *work* at thinking on the Sabbath day. Whenever our creativity begins to be onerous, it destroys our Sabbath resting. . . . I try not to think about whatever writing project I have in the works or about upcoming Bible studies to prepare. If new thoughts come to me, I consider them special Sabbath gifts from God and receive them gladly, but I try not to let myself *work* on them . . . . [F]or me, teaching a class is utter delight and usually the setting for a new experience of the Holy Spirit's empowering. (I feel the same way whenever I play the organ, direct or sing in a choir, or give a sermon on a Sunday morning.) However, I do not do any studying or practicing for those tasks on Sabbath morning! All my studying must be done in the days or weeks beforehand. Then, when it is time for me to teach, the Spirit can bring to my mind what I have learned and also give me new insights as I speak. . . . Then what fun the Sabbath is! I can enjoy it to the hilt the creativity made possible by the intellectual rest of the day and experience the closeness to God that always overwhelms me when I have the privilege of handling the beautiful texts of the Scriptures.[34]

---

[34] This is how Dawn, *Keeping the Sabbath Wholly*, 81, separates her professional intellectual life from her spiritual Sabbath activities. The author of this study seeks to follow the same principle by choosing to refrain from reading professional books used as part of his current academic research, and by mentally shifting gears to enjoy study that is not directly connected with his professional writing projects. This suggestion does not discourage deep Bible study on the Sabbath but allows him to "disconnect" from regular vocational activity on Sabbath so as to experience mental "rest."

Building upon biblical principles of *nuakh/menukhah*, one writer gives various suggestions as to how to enhance one's intellectual rest along with one's emotional and physical rest in our current culture. He writes, "Another aspect of Sabbath rest is resting intellectually. This involves using our minds differently. The mind that is used all week to plan, problem-solve, design, strategize, gather data, and organize is released from these demands on the Sabbath."[35] For example, he points out that in the technological age in which we live, our lives are filled with digital technologies—"tools we use to extend or support our mental powers."[36] He cites scientific studies which have shown how our brains are re-wired by ways we commonly use the Internet, making us "less able to engage in undistracted, deep thinking"[37] and less able to respond with compassion.[38] Part of the Sabbath experience might well be to "disconnect for twenty-four hours" from the Internet and other digital technologies, as part of Sabbath preparation for our brains. The intellectual "rest" from technology could include such activities as reading an inspirational book, allowing time for conversations with family and friends, prayer and meditation, Bible study, etc.[39] Thus we "connect our brains to the rest of the Sabbath."[40]

Emotional, Restorative Rest

In Exodus 31 the Sabbath commandment is repeated, but here God adds a third dimension of Sabbath rest. Verse 17 reads, "For in six days the LORD made heaven and earth, but on the seventh day He ceased *from*

---

[35] Muthiah, *Sabbath Experiment*, 16.

[36] Nicholas G. Carr, *The Shallows: What the Internet Is Doing to Our Brains* (New York: Norton, 2010), 44, cited in Muthiah, *Sabbath Experiment*, 30.

[37] Muthiah, *Sabbath Experiment*, 33, summarizing the research set forth in Carr, *The Shallows*, esp. 121–141.

[38] Muthiah, *Sabbath Experiment*, 37, citing Mary H. Immordino-Yang et al, "Neural Correlates of Admiration and Compassion," *Proceedings of the National Academy of Sciences of the United States of America* 106/19 (2009): 8021–8026; and Helen Y. Weng et al, "Compassionate Training Alters Altruism and Neural Responses to Suffering," *Psychological Science* 24/7 (2013): 1171–1180. Muthiah, *Sabbath Experiment*, 37–38, summarizes that it takes six to twelve seconds for our brains to fully engage the neural pathways related to compassion, and thus in surfing the Internet for news: "While I may retain a snippet of factual data about the story, the research shows that I have not given my brain sufficient time to respond with compassion."

[39] Muthiah, *Sabbath Experiment*, 39. See the rest of Muthiah's book for other practical suggestions for positive Sabbath keeping.

[40] Ibid., 17.

labor, and was refreshed [*nafash* in the *niphal* passive]." The Hebrew verb *nafash* means "breathe freely, recover,"[41] "take breath, refresh oneself,"[42] or more literally, "take on new soul or life (*nefesh*)."[43] On that first Sabbath, although God obviously was not tired (cf. Isa 40:28), the text indicates that He took on new life, new "soul"; He experienced what we may term *emotional* rest. According to Exodus 23:12, God wants human beings, including servants and sojourners, to experience this emotional refreshment on the Sabbath.

On the Sabbath God invites us to recharge our emotional battery, to refresh and restore our souls. In Matthew 11:29, in the immediate context of the Sabbath (see the Sabbath miracle that follows in Matt 12), Jesus promises, "You will find rest *for your souls*." The shepherd's psalm indicates that God "restores my soul" (Ps 23:3). The Greek word for "soul" is *psychē*, and one of the Greek words for "restore" or "heal" is *iatreō* (the noun is *iatreia*, "healing").[44] Repeating these two words together rapidly brings the realization that *psychē iatreia* is the basis for the word "psychiatry!" Psychiatry is "the restoring or healing of the soul." Every Sabbath God offers us, as it were, a free "psychiatric" session, compliments of the great psychiatrist who knows just how to heal our soul. One scholar rejoices in the great gift of the Sabbath to the Jewish people and to the world, using this analogy of psychiatry: "In following God's commandment to observe a day of rest, we Jews gave a great gift to the world. . . . One does not have to pay a psychiatrist to learn that for over thirty centuries Shabbat has been an antidote to boredom, bitterness, stress, anxiety, and depression."[45]

The Jewish tradition (followed at least in traditional observant Jewish homes) has encapsulated this emotionally restorative dimension of the Sabbath. On Friday night at the beginning of the Sabbath, the whole family slows down, and together savors the soul rest that the Sabbath offers. There is time to "breathe freely," to take a breather from the hectic pace

---

[41] *HALOT* 1:711.

[42] *BDB*, s.v. *nafash*.

[43] The verb *nafash* is denominative, i.e., it derives from the noun *nefesh*, "soul, life."

[44] The author does not claim that this is the Greek word used in the LXX to translate "restore" in Psalm 23:3 (it is *epistrephō*), but only that one of the possible nuances of the Heb. *shuv* ("restore") is the idea of repairing, refreshing, or healing (see *HALOT* 2:1429–1434). The Greek noun *iatreia* ("healing") is found in the LXX translation of Exodus 21:19, 2 Chronicles 21:18, and Jeremiah 31:2.

[45] Dov P. Elkins, "Introduction: Shabbat as Universe, as Cosmic, as Joy," in *A Shabbat Reader: Universe of Cosmic Joy*, ed. Dov P. Elkins (New York: UAHC Press, 1998), xxvii.

of the work week, to find refreshment in family fellowship and synagogue worship. A Jewish essayist describes how the Sabbath has functioned to restore the soul of Israel down through history:

> We can affirm without any exaggeration that the Sabbath has preserved the Jews more than the Jews have preserved the Sabbath. If the Sabbath had not restored to them the soul, renewing every week their spiritual life, they would have become so degraded by the depressing experiences of the workdays, that they would have descended to the last step of materialism and of moral and intellectual decadence.[46]

A best-selling playwright tells a story in his autobiography about his celebrating of Shabbat and the wonderful transformation that took place as he left the tense atmosphere of a Broadway production for an emotionally restorative rest of Shabbat in his home:

> Friday afternoon, during these rehearsals, inevitably seems to come when the project is tottering on the edge of ruin. I have sometimes felt guilty of treason, holding to the Sabbath in such a desperate situation. But then, experience has taught me that a theater enterprise almost always is in such a case. Sometimes it does totter to ruin, and sometimes it totters to great prosperity, but tottering is its normal gait, and cries of anguish are its normal tone of voice. So, I have reluctantly taken leave of colleagues on Friday afternoon and rejoined them on Saturday night. . . .
>
> Leaving the gloomy theater, the littered coffee cups, the jumbled scarred-up scripts, the haggard actors, the shouting stagehands, the bedeviled director, the knuckle-gnawing producer, the clattering typewriter, and the dense tobacco smoke and backstage dust, I have come home. It has been a startling change, very like a brief return from the wars. My wife and my boys, whose existence I have almost forgotten in the anxious shoring up of the tottering ruin, are waiting for me, . . . dressed in holiday clothes, and looking to be marvelously attractive. We have sat down to a splendid dinner, at a table graced with flowers and the old Sabbath symbols . . . . I have blessed my boys with the ancient blessing; we have sung the pleasantly syncopated

---

[46] Cited in Dawn, *Keeping the Sabbath Wholly*, 42.

Sabbath table hymns. . . . The boys, knowing that the Sabbath is the occasion for asking questions, have asked them. The Bible, the encyclopedia, the atlas have piled up on the table. We talk of Judaism, and there are the usual impossible boys' queries about God, which my wife and I field clumsily but as well as we can. For me it is a retreat into restorative magic.

Saturday has passed in much the same manner. The boys are at home in the synagogue, and they like it. They like even more the assured presence of their parents. . . . On the Sabbath we are always there, and they know it. They know too that I am not working and that my wife is at her ease. It is their day.

It is my day, too. The telephone is silent. I can think, read, study, walk, or do nothing. It is an oasis of quiet. When night falls, I go back to the wonderful nerve-racking Broadway game. Often I make my best contribution of the week then and there to the grisly literary surgery that goes on and on until opening night. My producer one Saturday night said to me, "I don't envy you your religion, but I envy you your Sabbath."[47]

By celebrating Shabbat, all may find the island of inner peace and tranquility that the Sabbath experience creates in their hearts, and this emotional refreshment will be noted and envied by others.

"Resting on Sabbath involves resting emotionally. Regular weekly life often draws down a person's emotional capacity. In Sabbath rest we press pause to experience refreshment and renewal."[48] One scholar suggests practical strategies to facilitate this emotional rest, such as choosing not to engage in potentially controversial conversations, developing different modes of parent-child relationships besides the usual consultations and interventions, training ourselves to rest even from worry and other emotional struggles on the Sabbath by refocusing on celebratory aspects of Sabbath and giving over the worries and other emotional issues to Christ, laying them at His feet.[49]

This emotional rest provided by the Sabbath may be especially enhanced in connecting with God through His created works. "All of

---

[47] Herman Wouk, *This Is My God*, cited in Elkins, "Introduction," xxiii–xxiv.

[48] Muthiah, *Sabbath Experiment*, 16.

[49] Ibid., 15–16.

creation whispers or shouts in one way or another, 'I'm here! Marvel at what God has made!'"[50] There is also a healing power that comes from contact with nature.[51] We may return from Sabbath excursions into God's "First Book" of nature, emotionally renewed and ready to face a new week. We can celebrate God's works of creation on the day that memorializes His creative work and find emotional tranquility and refreshment in a personal encounter with Him amid the things He has made for human enjoyment. With senses enraptured by such an experience, we cannot help but break forth into songs of love and praise.

This emotional rest, which we can experience especially on the Sabbath, with its healing effects of emotional refreshment, will spill over into all the week. "The Sabbath is a day set apart for deepening our relationship with God, and that necessarily leads to emotional healing. . . . A special day set apart for emotional rest gives us the silence to discover ourselves, to recover our integrity and creativity."[52]

Creative, Celebrative Rest

In Exodus 31:16 God pronounces that "the sons of Israel shall observe the Sabbath, to celebrate [ʿasah] the Sabbath throughout their generations as a perpetual covenant." The Hebrew verb ʿasah has the fundamental meaning "to make," and this is the same word used in the very next verse: "God *made* [ʿasah] the heavens and earth." The juxtaposition of these two occurrences of ʿasah in successive verses implies that we are to "make" the Sabbath, as God "made" the heavens and the earth, with all the creativity and energy and joy that God displayed in His creative process![53] Our

---

[50] Muthiah, Sabbath Experiment, 58. Muthiah continues by highlighting the connection between Sabbath and creation care: "If all that God has created is good, and if God cares about all that God created, and if we are to align ourselves with what God cares about, then we should care about creation. Sabbath helps us to see this" (ibid., 59). Wirzba, *Living the Sabbath*, 145, explains: "There is an inexorable logic at work in the Sabbath that will not allow us to separate ourselves from the rest of creation and the creation from God."

[51] For recent scientific studies affirming the healing power of contact with nature, see, e.g., Quing Li, *Forest Bathing: How Trees Can Help You Find Healing and Happiness* (New York: Viking/Penguin Random House, 2018); Florence Williams, *The Nature Fix: Why Nature Makes Us Happier, Healthier, and More Creative* (New York: Norton, 2017); and Eva M. Selhub and Alan C. Logan, *Your Brain on Nature: The Science of Nature's Influence on Your Health, Happiness, and Vitality* (Toronto: HarperCollins, 2012).

[52] Dawn, *Keeping the Sabbath Wholly*, 74.

[53] For a scriptural window into the joyous celebrative atmosphere of God's creation, see, e.g., Job 38:4–7; and Proverbs 8:22–31, esp. vs. 30–31.

Sabbath rest is not one of slothful inaction. God invites us to experience a *creative, celebratory* rest. The NASB well captures the meaning by translating here "to celebrate the Sabbath."[54] God offers us a chance on the Sabbath to exuberantly celebrate His goodness!

In Leviticus 23:3, the phrase *shabbath shabbathon* is used to describe the weekly Sabbath, which a standard Hebrew lexicon suggests means "a sabbath with special sabbath celebrations."[55] This verse indicates that part of the celebratory aspect of Sabbath is found in partaking in a "holy convocation [*miqra'*]."[56] As Jesus' "custom was" (Luke 4:16), we attend worship services on Sabbath as part of the enriching spiritual discipline of the Sabbath.

The worship services on Sabbath should be characterized by joyous celebration to the Lord! This joyous mode of Sabbath celebration is

---

[54] See also NIV and CSB, which translate '*asah* here as "celebrating."

[55] *HALOT* 2:1412.

[56] Most modern versions translate the Hebrew term *miqra'* as "convocation" or "assembly." All the major Hebrew lexicons give this meaning of the word in its usage in Leviticus 23 (*BDB, HALOT, TDOT, TWOT,* and *CDCH*). However, Jacob Milgrom translates this term as "sacred proclamations" or "sacred occasions" (Jacob Milgrom, *Leviticus 23-27: A New Translation with Introduction and Commentary,* AB [New York: Doubleday, 1991], 1957-1958). Milgrom gives the following reason for this translation: "Since *miqrā'* is the cognate accusative of *qārā'*, the idiom should literally be rendered 'sacred proclamations.' But these proclamations were for the purpose of announcing the arrival of a festival day, so it is only natural that the term *miqrā'* became associated with the designated day itself; hence the rendering 'occasion'" (ibid., 1957). What Milgrom fails to point out is that the verb *qara'* not only means "call, proclaim" but also can mean "summon [to an assembly]" (e.g., Deut 25:8; Exod 2:20; 34:15; Num 25:2; Deut 33:19; see *HALOT* 2:1129 for 24 examples of this usage in the Hebrew Bible). Most probably the verb does mean "proclaim, announce" in Leviticus 23, but to insist that the noun has to have the same meaning as the accompanying verb is an example of the root fallacy. There can be a play on words between the verb and its object without the terms having the same meaning. Instructive is the use of the noun *miqra'* in connection with the silver trumpets in Numbers 10:2, where it clearly has the meaning of the "summons" of the congregation for assembly, in parallel with its opposite, to "break camp." That the noun *miqra'* consistently means "assembly" in the Hebrew Bible is supported by looking at other places where this noun is used, in parallel with synonyms that mean "assembly." See, e.g., Isaiah 1:13, where *miqra'* is in synonymous parallelism with '*atsarah* ("assembly"). Often the context of this latter term explicitly indicates the gathering of the people (e.g., 2 Kgs 10:20; Joel 1:14; 2:15-16). Against this conclusion that *miqra'* was an assembly or a convocation, some insist that this term is used for all the festivals of Leviticus 23, whereas all males were required to attend only for the three pilgrim festivals (Passover, Pentecost, and Tabernacles). But this is not a contradiction. During the pilgrim festivals, there were special days when the congregation was instructed to have a special convocation, and even for the festivals when all Israelite males were not required to be present, there was still special liturgical (worship) events that transpired at the sanctuary, and those who lived near enough to travel were summoned to attend these convocations. Thus, God invited His people, where possible, to assemble on Sabbath, and on the Day of Atonement, as well as on the three pilgrim festivals.

summarized in Psalm 92, the "Song for the Sabbath," where the dominant mood is praise and joy (Ps 92:1–4).[57] It is also summarized in Isaiah 58:13–14, as the gospel prophet calls upon God's people to "call the Sabbath a delight [*'oneg*]." The noun *'oneg* appears only one other time in the Hebrew Bible, referring to the kind of delight that kings and queens experience in their royal palaces—"exquisite delight."[58]

Among observant Jews today, many of the ancient customs of welcoming the Sabbath—some no doubt going back to the time of Jesus—have been preserved. Observant Jews have developed the delicate artistry of Sabbath celebration for three and one-half millennia. As relative "newcomers" to Sabbath keeping, Seventh-day Adventists have much they can learn from Judaism's positive contributions toward experiencing the "exquisite delight" of the Sabbath.[59]

The author's family was introduced to this vigorous, celebrative aspect of Sabbath while living in Israel, joining with Jewish friends in the "Great Sabbath Welcome" on Friday evening in their homes. Every Friday afternoon in Jerusalem there was an air of excitement and expectancy all around—shops closing early; husbands buying Sabbath *challah* bread, a bottle of wine/grape juice, and flowers from sidewalk stands to beautify their table; everyone hastening home to prepare for the arrival of Sabbath.

Here is a brief summary, from the author's own experience, of customs in the traditional observant Jewish homes in Jerusalem on Friday night as family members welcome the Sabbath:[60] The dining room table is covered with a white cloth and set for the Sabbath meal. On the table is placed the two loaves of braided *challah* bread, the wine/juice and a goblet, silver candlesticks and candles, and the Sabbath flowers. The family members are dressed in their best clothes. All are ready to welcome royalty—*shabbat hamalkah*, "Sabbath the Queen."

---

[57] For more on this point, see the author's study on Sabbath theology in Psalm 92 and Wisdom Literature in this volume.

[58] *HALOT* 1:851. Cf. Isaiah 13:22.

[59] As noted earlier, this does not deny the positive contributions of Sabbath-keeping Christians down through the history of Christianity, but in chapter emphasizes the contributions of the Jewish tradition from which the author first encountered this dominant theme of "exquisite delight."

[60] For more details, see Richard M. Davidson, "The Delight of an Exquisite Day," *Adventist Review*, January 2, 1986, 16–18; idem, *Love Song for the Sabbath*, 18–23; cf. Millgram, *Sabbath: Day of Delight*.

Long before the sun actually sets, in their eager expectation the family begins their Sabbath celebration. The mother has the honor of officially receiving the Sabbath by kindling the Sabbath lights. The children watch with wonder as she lights at least two candles. She offers a prayer of blessing upon the family. Then the father tenderly takes his children in his arms or places his hands on their bowed heads and recites a blessing for each. Following this, the husband sings (or reads) a love song to his wife—from Song of Songs or Proverbs 31—extolling her virtues.

Next comes the Sabbath meal. It is begun with the sanctification of the Sabbath over a cup of wine (symbolizing joy and cheer), the blessing over the *challah* bread, and the special Sabbath courses. On Sabbath the choicest food of all the week is eaten.[61] Before each course, someone says, "For the honor of the Sabbath!" During the meal the family heartily sings lively table hymns (*zemirot*) reflecting the joyous mood of the Sabbath. In the singing, eating, and fellowship of the "Great Sabbath Welcome," the family can forget their weekday burdens, worries, and sorrows. What a glorious celebration!

This celebration continues for twenty-four hours, ending with more beautiful customs in a special *Havdalah* ("separation") service held at home to usher out the Sabbath. There is a blessing over the braided *Havdalah* candles, pouring of wine into a goblet until it overflows into the saucer below (symbolizing the overflowing blessings of the Sabbath), passing around of a spice box for everyone to savor the aroma (to symbolize and ensure that all the senses, even that of smell, have been engaged in the Sabbath celebration). There is no hurry. Reluctant to let their "special royal guest" go for another week, the family often prolongs its departure till long after the sun actually sets. The family cherishes Sabbath's exquisite delight as transcending all earthly bliss.

How well have Sabbatarian Christians captured this same sense of Sabbath's "exquisite delight" in harmony with Isaiah 58? Perhaps it would be well to consider adopting/adapting some of the delightful Sabbath-keeping customs of observant and messianic Jews. The author's family has introduced many of the previously mentioned customs into their Sabbath

---

[61] This harmonizes with what Ellen G. White, *Testimonies for the Church*, vol. 6 (Mountain View, CA: Pacific Press, 1901), 357, counsels about Sabbath meals: "Let the meals, though simple, be palatable and attractive. Provide something that will be regarded as a treat, something the family do not have every day." The "choicest food" does not necessarily mean more expensive food, but rather saving and serving something "special" for Sabbath. For example, the author's family did not have desserts during the week, but on Sabbath there was a special "Sabbath bread" (cinnamon rolls) that everyone looked forward to as part of the "exquisite delight" of Sabbath.

celebration, and he is convinced that God longs for the Sabbath to be "made so interesting to our families that its weekly return will be hailed with joy."[62] The "exquisite delight" of the Sabbath need not be limited to—or even include—Jewish customs; families should plan their own creative ways of welcoming and celebrating the Lord of the Sabbath on His holy day.

Another aspect of creatively "making" the Sabbath is to engage in acts of humanitarian service for those in need. This might be called "social rest." Moses' repetition of the fourth commandment (or better, "Word") of the Decalogue in Deuteronomy 5 gives a humanitarian, redemptive reason for Sabbath rest: "Remember that you were a slave in the land of Egypt, and that the LORD God brought you out from there by a mighty hand and by an outstretched arm" (Deut 5:15). As God freed the Israelite slaves at the time of the exodus, so the Sabbath is to be a day for freeing others from various forms of servitude and burden-bearing.[63] Isaiah 58:6–7 describes this creative humanitarian outreach that is appropriate for the Sabbath:

> Is this not the fast which I choose,
> To loosen the bonds of wickedness,
> To undo the bands of the yoke,
> And to let the oppressed go free
> And break every yoke?
> Is it not to divide your bread with the hungry
> And bring the homeless poor into the house;
> When you see the naked, to cover him;
> And not to hide yourself from your own flesh?

Jesus stresses the humanitarian, redemptive function of the Sabbath in each of His seven recorded Sabbath miracles,[64] and by His own commentary: "My Father is always at His work to this very day, and I, too, am working" (John 5:17, NIV). "So then it is lawful to do good on the Sabbath" (Matt 12:11).

---

[62] Ellen G. White, *Testimonies for the Church*, vol. 2 (Mountain View, CA: Pacific Press, 1871), 585.

[63] See Muthiah, *Sabbath Experiment*, 46–74, for a discussion of the ethical implications of Sabbath and how it allows us to view differently various modern forms of servitude, oppression, and burden-bearing beyond the obvious physical ones, such as oppressive economic policies (as in Pharaoh's regime at the time of the exodus), social stratification, and social injustice; and how the Sabbath provides the antidote to consumerism, providing the freedom for grateful contentment, generosity, and Christ-like love.

[64] Luke 4:31–37; 4:38–39; 6:6–11; 13:10–17; 14:1–6; John 5:1–15; 9:1–34.

The author's family and church members often went to a hospital on Sabbath afternoons to visit the pediatric ward and sing to the children too sick to go home on the weekend. Often the sick children's parents were in the hospital room and met the group of Seventh-day Adventist young people who worked and studied hard all week, yet had time on Sabbath to reach out in the community to bring a blessing to others. As the Adventist youth were singing, the pained looks on the sick children gave way to smiles, and the parents rarely failed to express their appreciation. In the eyes of the youth (and in the eyes of the sick children), there was a fulfillment of the promise made by Isaiah to those who engage in such humanitarian service: "Then your light will break out like the dawn, And your recovery will speedily spring forth; And your righteousness will go before you; The glory of the LORD will be your rear guard" (Isa 58:8).

Works of service to those in need includes animals as well as humans. We have already seen how the Sabbath is also a time for beasts of burden to be free to rest (Exod 20:10; 23:12; Deut 5:14; cf. Luke 13:15; 14:5). How do we practically apply the Sabbath rest principle to animals as well as humans? A pastor used to take his daughter to the animal shelter on the Sabbath; he would walk the stray dogs and she would stroke the cats! Our treatment and respect for animals all week long says much about how we value and uphold the principle of Sabbath rest.

The social and ecological and emancipatory dimensions of "creative rest" are captured in the Torah by the extension of the Sabbath principle in the precepts concerning the sabbatical (every seventh) and Jubilee (every fiftieth) years (Lev 25). Every seventh year even the land was to keep a Sabbath (Lev 25:2, 4); it was a "year of rest" (Lev 25:5, NKJV), a "year of release" (Deut 15:9, NKJV), in which debts were released (Deut 15:1–2). The fiftieth year was the Jubilee, "to proclaim liberty throughout all the land to all its inhabitants" (Lev 25:10, NKJV); justice was to be served as everyone "shall return to his possession" and "his family" (Lev 25:10, 13, NKJV). Having failed to follow these injunctions, as OT Israel went into Babylonian captivity God made sure that the land could finally keep its Sabbaths (2 Chron 36:21).

Grace-Filled Gospel Rest

A fifth facet of Sabbath rest, grace-filled gospel rest, is implied from the first reference to the Sabbath in Genesis 2. According to verse 2, it was on the *seventh* day of creation week that God "finished [*kalah*] the work that he had done" (NRSV). This seems to be a puzzle, since the fourth commandment (or "Word") of the Decalogue indicates that God made the heavens and earth in six days and rested on the seventh (Exod 20:11). The LXX translators had difficulty accepting that God finished working on the seventh day, so they arbitrarily changed the text to read "and on the *sixth* day God finished." Some modern translations seek to avoid the difficulty of God finishing His work on the seventh day, rendering the Hebrew preposition *be* as "by," rather than "on": "*By* the seventh day God finished. . . ."[65] However, the clear meaning of *be* as "on" in the exact phrase later in the same verse makes such translations unlikely. The ancient rabbis did not miss the significance of the statement that God finished His work on the seventh and not the sixth day of creation week. They recognized the textual implication that there was indeed an act of creation on the seventh day. According to the rabbinic commentary *Genesis Rabbah*, on the seventh day God created "tranquility, serenity, peace, and repose."[66] In six days God created the heaven and earth in space; on the seventh day He created what Heschel calls "a palace in time."[67]

The Hebrew word *kalah* in the *piel* stem means "finish, complete, bring to an end."[68] God rested by ceasing from His works on the Sabbath, and invited Adam and Eve to rest on that first Sabbath. From what were Adam and Eve resting? From their own works? No, they had just been created only a few hours before. They were resting in God's finished work! Thus even before sin, there is a profound inference of the principle of righteousness by faith. One scholar recognizes this point in his theology of the Sabbath:

> It cannot be emphasized too strongly that this invitation [to observe the Sabbath] comes at a time when creation, and particularly man, had nothing behind it except its creation by God, so that there can be no question whatever of a relationship between this Sabbath observance and any work completed by himself. Before and apart from all work and conflict, irrespective of any merits of his own, he is invited to cease from his own works, to rest, and therefore to enter into the freedom, rest and joy of God Himself. . . .

---

[65] NIV, CSB, NET.

[66] *Genesis Rabbah* 10:9.

[67] Heschel, *The Sabbath*, 12–24.

[68] *HALOT* 1:477.

As far as man is concerned, he has simply to recognize that God has really done all that is necessary, that He has invited him to participate in His rest, and that he may accept this invitation. In other words, he is left wholly and utterly with the grace of God. ... That God rested on the seventh day, and blessed and sanctified it, is the first divine action which man is privileged to witness; and that he himself may keep the Sabbath with God, completely free from work, is the first Word spoken to him, the first obligation laid on him. It is thus decided once and for all that the history of the covenant which begins here is to be the history of the divine covenant of grace.[69]

The book of Hebrews draws the implication for believers (Heb 4:9–10): "So there remains a Sabbath rest [*sabbatismos*] for the people of God. For the one who has entered His rest has himself also rested from his works, as God did from His." Every Sabbath, as we rest from our work, we proclaim to the world our continuing experience of righteousness by faith, that we trust not in our own works, but in the finished work of Christ in our behalf. The Sabbath becomes the outward sign of the "rest of grace"[70] that believers in Christ, the new Joshua, may experience all week long. The gospel rest will not only lead to peace, assurance, and growth in one's spiritual life; it will also prove to be a winning witness to the power of the gospel and the truthfulness of the Sabbath to those who behold our "rest in grace" symbolized by Sabbath rest. The "proof of the pudding is in the eating," and as non-Christians and non-Sabbath keepers observe the spiritual joy and peace of Sabbath rest, they will be led to savor this experience themselves. They will "taste and see that the LORD [of the Sabbath] is good" (Ps 34:8).

Blessed, Empowering Rest

As a sixth dimension of Sabbath rest, we return to Genesis 2:3, where we read that God "blessed [Heb. *barakh* in the intensive *piel*] the seventh day." In Hebrew thought, for God to bless something is to empower it to fulfill the function for which it was designed.[71] The Sabbath is thus filled with

---

[69] Karl Barth, *Church Dogmatics*, vol. 3, *The Doctrine of Creation, Part I* (Edinburgh: T&T Clark, reprint 2004), 218–219.

[70] SDABC 7:928.

[71] See Josef Scharbert, "ברך *barakh*," *TDOT* 2:306–307.

power. We are empowered as we enter into His rest on the Sabbath. And that sabbatic empowerment spills out into all the other days of the week.

In Psalm 92, the psalm for the Sabbath par excellence, the fourth stanza describes the abundant life empowered by the Sabbath blessing:

> But you have exalted my horn like that of the wild ox; you have poured over me fresh oil. My eyes have seen the downfall of my enemies; my ears have heard the doom of my evil assailants. The righteous flourish like the palm tree, and grow like a cedar in Lebanon (Ps 92:10–12, NRSV).

Images of the empowered Christian life come fast and glorious in this stanza. The exalted horn is a symbol of defensive power and victory in the Christian's spiritual life, underscoring that God does the exalting, He takes responsibility for the success. The wild ox (or antelope)[72] calls to mind the poise and gracefulness of the ibex, which still today bound effortlessly from cliff to cliff in the Wilderness of Ein Gedi where David spent many days hiding from King Saul. The one who knows the Lord of the Sabbath experiences the calmness that no amount of trouble or turmoil can dissipate.

The fine oil mixed with the balm of Gilead brings soothing and healing as applied to the wounds of life. The Sabbath experience brings healing from the wounds received during the battles of the week. The Sabbath provides power for joyous victory over spiritual foes, as well as past deliverance and future assurance of spiritual conquest. The date palm is called by the inhabitants of the Near East a "blessed tree, sister of man," with its perennial green foliage symbolic of victory and royalty, its vital force constantly renewing itself from its roots, yielding more than six hundred pounds of succulent fruit in a single season. The Sabbath experience is one of royalty, victory, and fruitful productivity in spiritual graces. The mighty cedar of Lebanon is prince among the trees of the mountains, symbolic of noble power and lofty growth, with fragrance in the evergreen needles, and resin in the bark that renders the tree impervious to decay or infestation with insects. The Sabbath experience offers spiritual strength and nobility, a life of fragrance, impervious to temptation from within or without.[73] In short, the Sabbath experience, says

---

[72] BDB, s.v. re'em; and HALOT 2:1163.

[73] See Muthiah, Sabbath Experiment, 78–88, for practical discussion of how Jesus, through His blessed empowering Sabbath rest, reveals and then calms "the storms that rage within," including

the psalmist, is the embodiment of the abundant and victorious life. Its blessing spills out from the twenty-four golden Sabbath hours into the rest of the week, filling each day with spiritual power!

Holy, Intimate Rest

A seventh dimension of Sabbath rest is captured in Genesis 2:3: "God sanctified [Heb. *qadhash*, "made holy"] it [the seventh day]." How does God make something holy? How did He make the burning bush holy? How did He make the sanctuary holy? By His presence![74] So here is an indication that the gift of Sabbath rest is not just the gift of a day, but the gift of a Person, filling the day with His loving presence! On the Sabbath God invites us into special intimate fellowship with Him, an all-day date with God. As we partake of intimate fellowship with Him on this day, the promise of Exodus 31:13 comes true: "Surely my Sabbaths you shall keep, for it is a sign between Me and you . . . that you may know that I am the Lord who *sanctifies* you [makes you holy]" (NKJV). In fellowship with God on His holy day, *we* ourselves are made holy as well!

This intimate fellowship with God on the Sabbath is the high point of the entire week. "The Sabbath is not for the sake of the weekdays; the weekdays are for the sake of the Sabbath. It is not an interlude but the climax of living."[75] Because the Sabbath is the "climax of living," all the week becomes fraught with meaning in relationship to the Sabbath. Further,

> the more persistently we practice the preparing for the Sabbath in the three days preceding it, and the more thoroughly we enjoy its benefits in the three days following it, the more delightfully restful the Sabbath itself will be for us in its actual practice, as well as in its anticipation and remembrance as these transform the entire week.[76]

One scholar powerfully expresses this point: "All days of the week must be spiritually consistent with the Day of Days. All our life should be a pilgrimage to the seventh day; the thought and appreciation of what this day may bring to us should be ever present in our minds. For the Sabbath

---

the struggle to control various compulsions, boredom, relational voids, and the idols in our lives.

[74] Exodus 3:2–5; 25:8; 40:34–38.

[75] Heschel, *The Sabbath*, 14.

[76] Dawn, *Keeping the Sabbath Wholly*, 54.

is the counterpoint of living."[77] As Christians, we can add that life is a pilgrimage toward the Lord of the Sabbath, who comes to be with us in special intimacy on the Sabbath day.

Conclusion

We have seen how the Torah highlights the spiritual potency of the Sabbath in the life of the individual believer and the corporate faith community. The Sabbath is presented as the crown jewel of spirituality. In the Sabbath one may experience all the facets of divine rest available to humankind—physical/work-free, intellectual/mental, emotional/restorative, creative/celebrative/social, grace-filled/gospel, blessed/empowering, and sacred/intimate rest. All of our spiritual life may find its ultimate expression in the context of this multidimensional experience of the Sabbath.

The various aspects of Sabbath rest discussed here must be seen in relationship to each other: "each kind of resting plays an important part in the working together of the whole. Just as true resting from work is more than ceasing from work, so the complete resting of our whole being is more than mere physical rest without labor. To rest utterly in the grace of God is the foundation for wholistic rest."[78]

The Torah—both the written Torah of Moses and the corroborating living Torah who is the Messiah, giver and embodiment of the Torah—presents the multi-faceted vibrant rest of the Sabbath as the crown jewel of spiritual experience. It remains for God's people in these last days to experientially receive and treasure this divine gift of wholistic Sabbath rest, and share it enthusiastically and unabashedly with a restless, weary world.

---

[77] Heschel, *The Sabbath*, 89.

[78] Dawn, *Keeping the Sabbath Wholly*, 54.

Intertestamental Literature

CHAPTER 13

THE SABBATH AT QUMRAN

Teresa Reeve and Roy Gane[1]

Introduction

The Dead Sea Scrolls form an important link in understanding how the Sabbath was viewed during the period between the writing of the OT and the creation of the formative documents of Christianity and Rabbinic Judaism. Indeed, these scrolls provide the most extensive discussion of Sabbath keeping in a single corpus in the Second Temple period. Copied largely during the first and second centuries BC and found in eleven caves near Qumran on the northwest shore of the Dead Sea, the scrolls are generally thought to have been part of the library of a nearby Jewish sectarian community, and thus to provide some understanding of their thinking.[2]

The scrolls demonstrate both divergence from, and continuity with, other Second Temple literature with regard to the Sabbath. Like other Jewish literature of the time, they are primarily interested in practical matters and give significant attention to the prevalent concern, evidenced in the earliest rabbinic literature and in the Gospels, of wrestling with how to faithfully keep the Sabbath legislation of the Torah. However, they portray the rest of Israel as having failed to appropriately carry out God's commands, making it necessary for an elite few—the sectarians themselves—to be set apart and purified in readiness for the eschatological age. Rather than seeking

---

[1] This study incorporates research by members of Roy Gane's 2009 PhD seminar on Dead Sea Scrolls at Andrews University: Amanda McGuire-Moushon, Alexej Muráň, Christian Vogel, and Chris Chadwick. Reeve and Gane are also grateful to Ingram London and Jonatas Leal, their research assistants, for supplementing and updating resources cited in this chapter.

[2] A sectarian community is here understood as a group of people who have separated themselves from their former societal group, and who proclaim themselves to be the true representatives of the historic values and beliefs of that group.

to explain the reasons for Sabbath keeping to the outside world, as is done in several other Second Temple documents, the scrolls are concerned with community Sabbath observance and with distinguishing themselves from other Jews over points of observance.[3]

This study deals with four primary concerns addressed in the Dead Sea Scrolls with regard to the Sabbath: (1) the place of the Sabbath in the theology and identity formation of those the community understood to be God's chosen ones, (2) calculation of the correct calendar and time allotments related to Sabbath observance, (3) a halakhic exposition of laws for proper Sabbath keeping, and (4) the provision of liturgy and ritual for community Sabbath observance. This study explores these four areas, investigating their main features and some of the ways they agree with, and diverge from, other Second Temple literature on the Sabbath.

The scrolls found at Qumran include many biblical manuscripts and other religious documents, in addition to a number likely written by the sectarians themselves. Primary attention will be given to those texts that scholars have generally accepted as having originated among the sectarian community represented at Qumran or that were especially influential for the Qumran community, as evidenced by the number of manuscripts found, or by quotations and allusions made to these texts by manuscripts established as sectarian.

The Place of the Sabbath in the Theology of the Qumran Community

As with most Jews in the Second Temple period, Sabbath keeping was crucial for the self-understanding of the sectarians associated with the Dead Sea Scrolls.[4] In Qumran literature, the noun "Sabbath" is mentioned

---

[3] See, e.g., *Aristobulus*; Philo (*De vita Mosis* 2.209–216; *De decalogo* 96–164; *De specialibus legibus* 2.41, 56–70). Where the Sabbath is mentioned without qualification in this paper, it will refer to the weekly Sabbath.

[4] Both for Jews of the diaspora as well as in Greek- and Roman-controlled Judea, the Sabbath had become an important boundary marker recognized by Jews and Gentiles alike as separating Jews from the people around them. It was for this reason that Antiochus IV (Epiphanes) abolished the Sabbath as one of his chosen means of forcing the Jews to assimilate with the ruling Seleucid empire (*1 Maccabees* 1:41–49). A helpful summary of Sabbath observance within Judaism of NT times is presented by Christopher Rowland, "A Summary of Sabbath Observance in Judaism at the Beginning of the Christian Era," in *From Sabbath to Lord's Day: A Biblical, Historical, and Theological Investigation*, ed. Donald A. Carson (Eugene, OR: Wipf and Stock, 1982), 46–57.

185 times in non-biblical texts alone.[5] The community's understanding of the Sabbath interacted in distinctive ways with the unique construction of history and eschatology that was foundational to their identity formation.

The book of *Jubilees*, which presents an interpretive narration to Moses on Mount Sinai of Genesis 1 through Exodus 16 by "the angel of the presence," was produced outside Qumran but was of fundamental importance to the sectarians and therefore provides essential background to their thinking.[6] This document gives the Sabbath a central position and places the origins of Sabbath keeping at creation itself, devoting half of the creation account to discussion of the seventh day.[7]

The angel in *Jubilees* states that at creation, God instructed "the angels of the presence" and "the angels of holiness" to observe the Sabbath. God also informed the angels that He had already chosen the descendants of Jacob to be His people, to observe the Sabbath together with Him and the angels, and to be blessed and sanctified just as He had blessed and sanctified the Sabbath day (*Jubilees* 2:17–25).[8] Therefore, the angel tells Moses to command the Israelites to keep the day holy and not do any work, providing him with a brief halakhic exposition on proper Sabbath keeping (*Jubilees* 2:26–30). The creation account ends with the declaration that the Sabbath is to be observed in this way because it is holier than any of the days of Jubilee, having been kept in the heavens before it was made known on earth. The Sabbath is said to be given to the Israelites forever and to them alone, for the Creator did not sanctify any other people to

---

[5] Michael H. Burer, *Divine Sabbath Work* (Winona Lake, IN: Eisenbrauns, 2012), 59.

[6] Written around 160 BC, *Jubilees*' importance at Qumran is evidenced in the fifteen or sixteen fragmentary copies discovered there (more than any other non-biblical work), in allusions to it in manifestly sectarian documents, and in being explicitly cited at least once in an authoritative manner (see *Damascus Document* [CD] 16.2–4). For more details on the relationship between *Jubilees* and the Qumran literature, see Charlotte Hempel, "The Place of the *Book of Jubilees* at Qumran and Beyond," in *The Dead Sea Scrolls in Their Historical Context*, ed. Timothy H. Lim (Edinburgh: T&T Clark, 2000), 188–196.

[7] See Lutz Doering, "The Concept of the Sabbath in the Book of Jubilees," in *Studies in the Book of Jubilees*, ed. Matthias Albani, Jörg Frey, and Armin Lange (Tübingen: Mohr Siebeck, 1997), 179–205.

[8] Not all of *Jubilees* is present among the Qumran fragments, so in-text references are cited from the critical edition based on the ancient Ethiopic version. See James C. VanderKam, trans., *The Book of Jubilees*, vol. 88 of Scriptores Aethiopici, Corpus Scriptorum Christianorum Orientalium 511 (Louvanii: Peeters, 1989); James C. VanderKam, ed., *The Book of Jubilees: A Critical Text*, vol. 87 of Scriptores Aethiopici, Corpus Scriptorum Christianorum Orientalium 510 (Louvanii: Peeters, 1989).

keep it (*Jubilees* 2:30–33).[9] Although the angel goes on, in the main body of the book, to narrate other early biblical events, *Jubilees* closes, as it began, with an exhortation on the importance of the Sabbath (together with the Sabbaths of the land and the Jubilees) and a brief delineation of proper Sabbath keeping (*Jubilees* 50:1–13). Since the book regards the election of Israel as an essential component of creation, it presents Sabbath keeping as something that, like circumcision, "distinguishes between the elect and nonelect."[10]

The Qumran literature echoes these ideas presented in *Jubilees* in several ways. For example, 4Q216 (*Jubilees*[a]) 1 VII, 17, a fragment containing a version of *Jubilees* 2:13–24, places special emphasis on the institution of the Sabbath at creation, stating that "this is the testimony and the first Law."[11] Further, *Songs of the Sabbath Sacrifice*, joined by other sectarian documents from Qumran, builds on the understanding, evidenced in *Jubilees*, of the divinely ordained participation of angels in Sabbath keeping, and seeks to order the Sabbath worship of the community in concert with this angelic worship.[12]

Another Sabbath-related teaching in *Jubilees* is connected to God's prediction of Israel's apostasy, which, though later in biblical history, is placed even before the creation account at the very beginning of the book of *Jubilees*. As God introduces Moses to the divisions of history into distinct periods (*Jubilees* 1:4, 27), a theme central to the purpose of the book, He lists the forsaking of His sabbaths as among the primary reasons for the

---

[9] Although this idea is not further attested at Qumran, it is not incompatible with their separationist views. Later rabbis also echo this idea. In contrast, the apologetic writers of the Second Temple period argued its universal significance (see Philo, *De opificio mundi* 89; *Moses* 11.19–22; Aristobulus frg. 5).

[10] Aharon Shemesh, "Sabbath, Circumcision and Circumcision on Sabbath in Jubilees and the Dead Sea Scrolls," in *Rewriting and Interpreting the Hebrew Bible: The Biblical Patriarchs in the Light of the Dead Sea Scrolls* (Berlin: De Gruyter, 2013), 264.

[11] This is in comparison with the standard critical translation of *Jubilees* 2:24, which has the following: "It was granted to [the descendants of Jacob] that for all times they should be the blessed and holy ones of the testimony and of the first law" (VanderKam, *Jubilees*). For ease of comparison, quotations from the Dead Sea Scrolls will be taken from Martínez and Tigchelaar, *The Dead Sea Scrolls Study Edition*, 2 vols. (Leiden: Brill, 1997). Throughout this chapter, in accordance with SBL style, a superscripted number next to the manuscript name indicates which copy of the manuscript is being referred to, where there is more than one copy. The fragment number (if needed) will be given first in Arabic numerals, followed by the column number in Roman numerals, and the line number in Arabic numerals.

[12] For more on this topic, see below in the section titled "Liturgy and Ritual at Qumran."

exile (*Jubilees* 1:4, 10–11).¹³ A similar revelation is depicted on Mount Nebo, just before Moses' death, by a pseudonymous sectarian document at Qumran (1Q22 [*Words of Moses*]) in which God declares,

> I announce that they will desert [me and ch]oose [the sins of the] peo[ples,] their [abo]minations [and] their [disre]putable acts [and will serve] ido[l]s, who will become a tr[ap and] a snare. They will vio[late all the ho]ly [assemblies], the sabbath of the covenant, [the festivals] which I command you today [to k]eep. [This is why I will stri]ke them with a great [blow] . . . (I, 6–8).¹⁴

The fact that *Jubilees* was produced outside Qumran indicates that ideas such as Sabbath breaking leading to Israel's exile and the participation of angels in Sabbath worship from the time of creation were apparently shared with other segments of Second Temple Judaism. In other respects, however, the Qumran conceptualization of the place of the Sabbath in Jewish history differs significantly from what is known of other Second Temple groups. Most of these differences involve the central role the community saw itself playing in what they understood to be the end of days.

This connection between the Sabbath and the community's place in eschatology is most evident in the *Damascus Document* (CD), an apocalyptic exhortation and law book that was one of the sect's most defining documents.¹⁵ Here, "his holy Sabbaths and his glorious feasts" are placed first in a list of the "hidden matters in which all Israel had gone astray," but which had been revealed to those who had "remained steadfast in God's precepts" (CD 3.13–16). In a later passage, this document describes how God raised up the sectarian community in a period of apostasy, and identifies correct Sabbath keeping as one of its key defining marks.¹⁶ "The exact

---

¹³ This passage is found in fragmentary condition in 4Q216 (*Jubilees*ᵃ) 1 II, 3–17. By contrast, the breaking of the Sabbath as a serious problem in Israel is not noted in the scriptural record until shortly before the exile (see Isa 56:2–6; 58:13; Jer 17:21–27; Ezek 20:12–13, 16, 20–21, 24; 22:8, 38; Amos 8:5; cf. Deut 28).

¹⁴ Here and in the rest of this chapter, brackets are used to indicate areas of text that are illegible or missing in the Qumran scrolls. Israel's violation of the Sabbath is also prominent in the fragmentary 4Q390.

¹⁵ The most complete manuscript of the *Damascus Document* was discovered in 1910 in the Cairo Genizah (a depository for worn-out texts), copied by a medieval copyist. However, its origins are clearly traceable to Qumran, where seven fragmentary copies were found, several of which (4Q266 [4QDᵃ] 3 II; 4Q266 [4QDᵇ] 2; 4Q269 [4QDᵈ] 2; 4 II) reveal portions of these same passages.

¹⁶ This may recall the rampant Hellenization under the Seleucids and especially Antiochus

interpretation of the law for the age of wickedness," which distinguished this community, is here identified as: "to separate themselves from the sons of the pit; to abstain from wicked wealth which defiles . . . ; to separate unclean from clean and differentiate between the holy and the common; to keep the Sabbath day according to the exact interpretation" (CD 6.13-18).

Another characteristic of the sect was the expectation of an imminent eschatological war in which sect members, as the remnant people of God, would achieve victory over the nations by God's power. The *War Scroll* (1QM), which gives the most extensive description and instruction for this battle, is careful to make specific provision for the proper keeping of the weekly Sabbath as well as the sabbath of the land every seventh year. Though the Sabbath itself does not appear to have been used at Qumran to symbolize an age of eternal rest, the idea of a Jubilee of deliverance, based on the sabbatical number seven (cf. Lev 25), was part of the sectarian apocalyptic expectation.[17]

The Sabbath and Calendar

Because the Sabbath, with its heavenly origins, was viewed as the most blessed of all holy days, the exact identification of God's divinely appointed times for the Sabbaths and festivals was a fundamental issue for the sectarians. This is evidenced by the discovery at Qumran of nineteen calendric documents, in addition to a number of other manuscripts featuring calendric themes and segments.[18] The calendar issue appears to have been one of those that divided the group from the main temple cult in Jerusalem. This is attested by the fragmentary inclusion of a calendar at the beginning

---

Epiphanes, as well as the more recent schism between the sectarians and the Temple establishment, likely during the time of John Hyrcanus.

[17] On this, see, e.g., Ben Zion Wacholder, "Chronomessianism: The Timing of Messianic Movements and the Calendar of Sabbatical Cycles," *HUCA* 46 (1975), 201-218. It has been suggested that "one of the reasons the sect also made specific mention of the Sabbath was that in the Second Temple period the Sabbath was considered to be tied in with redemption, as can be seen from the Mishnah (*Tamid* 7:4), which records that the Levites used to sing in the Temple 'a song for the Sabbath day, a song for the future that is to come, for the day that is all Sabbath and repose for life everlasting.' Moore theorizes that the Jews refrained from defending themselves on the Sabbath not only out of loyalty to the Torah, which forbids desecrating the Sabbath but also because they believed that their loyalty would help bring about the redemption" (Baruch Sharvit, "The Sabbath of the Judean Desert Sect," *Immanuel* 9 [1979]: 48).

[18] James C. VanderKam, *Calendars in the Dead Sea Scrolls: Measuring Time* (London: Routledge, 1998), 110; cf. Sacha Stern, "Qumran Calendars: Theory and Practice," in *The Dead Sea Scrolls in Their Historical Context*, ed. Timothy H. Lim (Edinburgh: T&T Clark, 2000), 179-196.

of 4Q394 (4QMMT), a manifesto-type document that seems to put forward arguments regarding some of the main differences the sectarians at Qumran had with the current Jewish leadership.[19]

The calendar used by the late Second Temple establishment appears to have been a 354-day lunar calendar.[20] Thus *Sirach* 43:6–8 looks to the moon for determining the times of festivals, and early rabbinic literature sets the appearance of the new moon at the beginning of each month.[21] The existence of a difference between the temple calendar and the Qumran calendar is further suggested by the sectarian *Habakkuk Pesher* (1QpHab) XI, 4–8, which speaks of a violent attack against the community on the Day of Atonement by a leader designated as "the Wicked Priest." Whatever the specific identity of "the Wicked Priest" might have been, he was apparently a representative of the temple establishment who opposed the Qumran group. Such an individual, being an observant Jew, never would have carried out an attack on the day he recognized as the Day of Atonement, the holiest day of the Jewish year.[22] Sectarian use of a calendar according to which holy days fell on different dates than those of the larger Jewish community would inevitably cause tension.[23]

The primary calendar adopted at Qumran was a 364-day solar calendar that took as its basis the time of one rotation of the sun around the earth, a period they understood as exactly fifty-two weeks.[24] The solar

---

[19] James C. VanderKam, "Calendars in the Dead Sea Scrolls," *Near Eastern Archaeology* 63, no. 3 (2000): 167. It also may be suggested in the eschatological Hosea commentary (4Q166 [*Hosea Pesher*] 1 II, 14–17), which quotes Hosea 2:13, "I will make an end to her joys, her fea[st, her new] moon and her sabbath, and all her celebrations," and asserts that unfaithful Israel determines "[all celebrations] in agreement with the celebrations of the nations, but a[ll joy] will be changed into mourning for them."

[20] The weekly Sabbaths, however, are independent of either the lunar or the solar reckoning. There is no suggestion in any of the literature of a different *day* being kept as Sabbath, a matter that would be certain to provoke comment.

[21] In this system, the sun was not necessarily irrelevant as some groups practiced intercalation, adding a thirteenth month when necessary to bring the dates, including those of festivals, back into alignment with the seasons determined by the sun.

[22] Henry W. Morisada Rietz, "The Qumran Concept of Time," in *The Bible and the Dead Sea Scrolls: The Second Princeton Symposium on Judaism and Christian Origins*, ed. James H. Charlesworth (Waco, TX: Baylor University Press, 2006), 205, 233. See also VanderKam, *Calendars in the Dead Sea Scrolls*, 3–14.

[23] Shemaryahu Talmon, "The Calendar Reckoning of the Sect from the Judaean Desert," in *Aspects of the Dead Sea Scrolls*, ed. C. Rabin and Y. Yadin (Jerusalem: Magnes, 1958), 163–164.

[24] Manuscripts such as the *Songs of the Sabbath Sacrifice* (4Q400 I, 1) evidence that this calendar begins each year with the fourth day, Wednesday, the day on which the sun was created according

calendar is attested in a number of the Dead Sea Scrolls, beginning with the pre-sectarian *Astronomical Book of Enoch* (*1 Enoch* 72–82), written about 200 BC and present at Qumran in four fragmentary copies. This is the earliest Jewish document of any kind to mention the solar calendar. *Jubilees*, which was written later (ca. 160 BC), carries the idea further, presenting the solar calendar as a divine imperative and forbidding the use of a lunar calendar (*Jubilees* 6:35–38).[25]

The precise identification of calendric dates for the Sabbath was an important reason for the use of the solar calendar.[26] With a 364-day calendar, the Sabbath fell on precisely the same dates each year. Use of the solar calendar also helped ensure that the festivals would not fall on the same days as the Sabbaths, which would cause conflict in the correct observance of each.[27] The importance of this is demonstrated in the *Damascus Document* law that only the Sabbath sacrifice could be offered on the Sabbath. Building on the words of Leviticus 23:37–38, it states: "no-one should offer anything upon the altar on the sabbath, except the sacrifice of the sabbath" (CD 11.17–18 = 4Q271 [*Damascus Document*ᶠ] 5 I, 1).[28]

---

to Genesis 1:14–19. See Rietz, "Qumran Concept of Time," 209. Months were still a part of this calendar, but were artificially determined and divided into thirty to thirty-one days.

[25] Rietz, "Qumran Concept of Time," 209–212. For example, *Jubilees* 2:9 states, "The Lord appointed the sun above the earth for days, Sabbaths, months, festivals, years, Sabbaths of years, jubilees, and all the times of the years." See also *1 Enoch* 18:14–16, 80:2–8; *Jubilees* 6:30–38. VanderKam notes that several manuscripts (e.g., 4Q317, 4Q320, 4Q321) evidence interest in intercalating the lunar and solar calendar, suggesting that they may not have totally rejected all uses of the lunar calendar (VanderKam, *Calendars in the Dead Sea Scrolls*, 76–87, 111; idem, "Calendars in the Dead Sea Scrolls," 167). Alternatively, they may simply have found it useful to keep track of the more standard dating system. VanderKam also suggests that the sectarians likely adjusted the calendar periodically to reflect the actual experience of the seasons (making up for the one and one-quarter day shortfall from the 365-day calendar), probably by adding seven days to keep the "sabbatical character" of their calendar (VanderKam, "Calendars in the Dead Sea Scrolls," 167). This is contested by both Beckwith and Rietz, who point out that *Jubilees* insists that the 364-day calendar is divinely ordained (*Jubilees* 6:30–32; cf. *1 Enoch* 72:32; 74:12; 80:2–8) and argue that the sectarian documents speak of the lunar calendar only in a negative sense (Roger T. Beckwith, *Calendar, Chronology, Jewish and Christian: Biblical, Intertestamental and Patristic Studies* (Leiden: Brill, 1996), 125–133; Rietz, *Qumran Concept of Time*, 209–211.

[26] Doering, "Concept of the Sabbath," 19.

[27] Joseph M. Baumgarten, "The Counting of the Sabbath in Ancient Sources," *VT* 16 (1966): 277–278. The *Temple Scroll* makes particular use of the passing of the Sabbaths to calculate the timing of festivals (e.g., 11Q19 *Temple Scroll*ᵃ XVIII, 11–12; XIX, 12–13; XXI, 12). See also Daniel K. Falk, "Liturgical Progression and the Experience of Transformation in Prayers from Qumran," *DSD* 22 (2015): 267–284.

[28] Rietz, "Qumran Concept of Time," 213; E. P. Sanders, "The Dead Sea Sect and Other Jews: Commonalities, Overlaps, and Differences," in *The Dead Sea Scrolls in Their Historical Context*,

Each Sabbath seems to have acquired something of its own distinctive character, as indicated by the organization of the *Songs for the Sabbath Sacrifice* (see below).[29] In several documents, individual Sabbaths were designated according to the priestly courses (divisions of priests) assigned in the organizing of the temple service in 1 Chronicles 24:7–18 (see, for example, 4Q319–321).[30] One small sectarian scroll, 4Q327 (*Calendrical Document E[b]*), is wholly devoted to listing the exact dates on which the Sabbaths, as well as the festivals, would occur on the basis of this calendar.[31]

One scholar points to proper worship as the primary motivating factor for the sectarian focus on the calendar:

> By incorporating the dates of Sabbaths and festivals and the periods of service for the priestly courses into their system for measuring time, the cultic and theological concerns of the authors come to expression. The calendars are, with few exceptions, oriented towards worship.[32]

For the sectarians at Qumran, to violate the divinely designated time of the Sabbath would have entailed "violating the harmony of the universe and mixing the sacred with the profane."[33]

Sabbath Legislation at Qumran

Like other Jews during the late Second Temple period, the sectarians at Qumran viewed the *Torah*—the Pentateuchal law received from God through Moses—as the constitution of their nation and the authoritative

---

ed. Timothy H. Lim (Edinburgh: T&T Clark, 2000), 18–19.

[29] Baumgarten, "Counting of the Sabbath," 116, 118, suggests that this individual character given to each Sabbath made it possible to view the Sabbaths as a yearly sequence of holy days, as could be understood in Leviticus 23:2–3, 37–38 (cf. Num 28:10).

[30] Ibid., 278. VanderKam, *Calendars in the Dead Sea Scrolls*, 74–86. On speculation regarding the addition of two courses to fill out the fifty-two-week solar year, see ibid., 48–50, 72–74. This use of the priestly courses to designate Sabbaths is in spite of the fact that the sect had withdrawn from participating in temple sacrifices because of its negative perception of current temple leadership and practice, and may have been tied to their assurance that they would return to a renewed temple and temple service one day (ibid., 120).

[31] This fragment was originally identified as part of the calendar at the beginning of 4QMMT, but later separated on the basis of penmanship and other features (VanderKam, *Calendars in the Dead Sea Scrolls*, 75, 120n3).

[32] Ibid., 112.

[33] Ibid., 110–111.

guide to personal life. The question that divided Jews was how to apply the biblical laws, for they do not cover all situations; they convey principles in ways that are not always obvious, and they present duplications that apparently cover the same circumstances in somewhat different ways. Various groups during this time answered these challenges with different strategies shaped by their respective attitudes and self-understandings. Inevitably these differing approaches resulted in different practical outcomes.

Having withdrawn from participation in the temple ceremonies in Jerusalem controlled by the religious establishment, which they regarded as having become corrupted, the Qumran community viewed itself as an apocalyptic embodiment of God's true temple system, pending establishment of a glorious new temple in the imminent messianic age.[34] As God's "new covenant" people of divine light in a transitional period, the Qumranites conscientiously sought to follow God in all areas of practical, ethical, and spiritual life in preparation for a climactic eschatological battle with forces of darkness. As the people of God's true temple to come, their community and its table fellowship were protected by regulations for discipline and ritual purity normally applied to priests.[35] This did not mean, however, that they rejected in principle religious leadership by descendants of Aaron and Levi; to the contrary, they accorded special status to the Levites and Aaronic priests who joined them (for example, 1QS [*The Community Rule*] I, 18–20).

The sectarian quest for a holy life in full obedience to God raised the importance of correct interpretation and application of biblical law to a high level.[36] To adapt and expand the *Torah* to meet the needs of their own life situation over a millennium after Moses, they relied on what they regarded as prophetic revelation mediated through the "Teacher of

---

[34] Lawrence H. Schiffman, "The Qumran Scrolls and Rabbinic Judaism," in *The Dead Sea Scrolls After Fifty Years: A Comprehensive Assessment*, ed. Peter W. Flint and James C. Vanderkam, vol. 2 (Leiden: Brill, 1999), 556–557, 562–563; Scott J. Hafemann, "The Spirit of the New Covenant, the Law, and the Temple of God's Presence: Five Theses on Qumran Self-Understanding and the Contours of Paul's Thought," in *Evangelium-Schriftauslegung-Kirche: Festschrift für Peter Stuhlmacher zum 65. Geburtstag*, ed. Jostein Adna, Scott J. Hafemann, and Otfried Hofius (Göttingen: Vandenhoeck & Ruprecht, 1997), 184–185.

[35] Jacobus A. Naudé, "Holiness in the Dead Sea Scrolls," in *The Dead Sea Scrolls After Fifty Years: A Comprehensive Assessment*, ed. Peter W. Flint and James C. Vanderkam, vol. 2 (Leiden: Brill, 1999), 184–185.

[36] Hannah Harrington, "Biblical Law at Qumran," in *The Dead Sea Scroll After Fifty Years: A Comprehensive Assessment*, ed. Peter W. Flint and James C. Vanderkam, vol. 1 (Leiden: Brill, 1998), 160–161.

Righteousness" and his successors.[37] Members of the Qumran community treated as authoritative not only aspects of law keeping known to Jews in general, but also finer points believed to have been hidden to others but made known to them.[38] They regarded their own interpretive tradition as the only valid guide to acceptable observance of Moses' laws.[39]

The literary style of legal documents from Qumran reflects the sectarian approach to divine law. Where they present religious and ethical requirements extending from the Bible, these texts contain many allusions to biblical legal passages but few direct citations. They weave biblical concepts together with their own ideas, harmonizing apparent contradictions, systematizing laws according to their topics, and drawing on passages from the prophets and the writings to supplement their Pentateuchal sources. The Qumran texts thus reflect a kind of underlying exegesis, but do not highlight or explain this factor because their concern was rather to present their interpretations of law as unquestionably correct products of divine inspiration. The Pharisees, by contrast, appear to have made room for the human element in the production of their legal interpretations by citing the traditions of their elders. Furthermore, early rabbinic writings, which are generally believed to have developed from the Pharisaic movement, often explicitly quote biblical laws in order to deduce new legal materials.[40]

---

[37] Alex Jassen, "The Presentation of the Ancient Prophets as Lawgivers at Qumran," *JBL* 127 (2008): 307–310. However, the *Temple Scroll*, preserved at Qumran, presents a rewritten Torah that claims to express God's will as revealed at Sinai in His own words, rather than a later revelation (Schiffman, "The Qumran Scrolls and Rabbinic Judaism," 559, 561; cf. Hans-Aage Mink, "The Use of Scripture in the Temple Scroll and the Status of the Scroll as Law," *SJOT* 1 [1987]: 20–50).

[38] Lawrence H. Schiffman, *Reclaiming the Dead Sea Scrolls: The History of Judaism, the Background of Christianity, and the Lost Library of Qumran* (Philadelphia, PA: Jewish Publication Society, 1994), 247–249; Schiffman, "The Qumran Scrolls and Rabbinic Judaism," 558–559. See, e.g., CD 3.12–17, where the "hidden things" that God reveals to His sectarian "remnant" include aspects of Sabbaths and festivals.

[39] James E. Bowley, "Moses in the Dead Sea Scrolls: Living in the Shadow of God's Annointed," in *The Bible at Qumran: Text, Shape, and Interpretation*, ed. Peter W. Flint (Grand Rapids, MI: Eerdmans, 2001), 164–166.

[40] Schiffman, *Reclaiming the Dead Sea Scrolls*, 218–222; 250–252; Steven D. Fraade, "Looking for Legal Midrash at Qumran," in *Biblical Perspectives: Early Use and Interpretation of the Bible in Light of the Dead Sea Scrolls*, ed. Michael E. Stone and Esther G. Chazon (Leiden: Brill, 1998), 59–79. On the Qumran approach, including that of the *Temple Scroll*, to developing new law in relation to biblical law, cf. Gershon Brin, *Studies in Biblical Law: From the Hebrew Bible to the Dead Sea Scrolls*, ed. David J. A. Clines and Philip R. Davies (Sheffield: JSOT Press, 1994), 104–106; and Moshe J. Bernstein, "Pentateuchal Interpretation at Qumran," in *The Dead Sea Scroll After Fifty Years: A Comprehensive Assessment*, ed. Peter W. Flint and James C. Vanderkam (Leiden: Brill, 1998), 154–158.

The sectarians were strongly opposed to groups such as the Pharisees, with whose legal approaches and conclusions they often disagreed. In general, Qumran law is more stringent than the early rabbinic writings.[41] A sectarian criticism of the Jewish leadership of their own time was that "they sought easy interpretations, chose illusions, scrutinized loopholes" (CD 1.18–19).[42] One example of how the sectarians could have differed from mainstream Judaism concerns the practice of war during the Sabbath. In *1 Maccabees* 2:38–40 Jews are allowed to fight back "if any man comes against [them]." By contrast, in *Jubilees* 50:12–13 war is listed as one of the prohibited undertakings during the Sabbath. This prohibition also appears in the *Habbakuk Pesher* (1QpHab XI, 4–8).[43]

Some scholars have argued that the conflict between the sectarians and other Jewish groups was the primary motivating factor behind the writing of Qumran law.[44] However, although there is certainly evidence of polemics in Qumran law,[45] the clear purpose of the group to seek purity

---

[41] Cf. Sharvit, "The Sabbath of the Judean Desert Sect," 44, who argues the difficulty of determining for certain "whether the strictness with which the sect observed the above-mentioned matters was unique to the members of the sect or whether it was common practice at that time and only later did the sages elaborate a more lenient position."

[42] Although the Qumran connection with the Essenes is not universally accepted, it is worth noting that according to Josephus the Essenes "are stricter than all Jews in abstaining from work on the seventh day." Josephus notes that "not only do they prepare their food on the day before, to avoid kindling a fire on that one, but they do not venture to remove any vessel or even go to stool" (Josephus, *Jewish Wars*, 2.147). Philo suggests a similar idea, stating that on the Sabbath, the Essenes "abstain from all other work and proceed to sacred spots which they call synagogues. There, arranged in rows according to their ages, the younger below the elder, they sit decorously as befits the occasion with attentive ears. Then one takes the books and reads aloud and another of especial proficiency comes forward and expounds what is not understood" (Philo, *That Every Good Person is Free*, 82).

[43] Shemesh, "Sabbath, Circumcision," 267, affirms that the mention of war as prohibited on Sabbath in *Jubilees* is "most probably a polemic against the new law of the Hasmoneans permitting war, at least defensive war, on the Sabbath."

[44] See, e.g., Lawrence H. Schiffman, "The Dead Sea Scrolls and Rabbinic *Halakhah*," in *The Dead Sea Scrolls as Background to Postbiblical Judaism and Early Christianity: Papers from an International Conference at St. Andrews in 2001*, ed. James R. Davila (Leiden: Brill, 2003), 7. Some argue that Qumran law arises out of practice, and then reaches to biblical exegesis as justification (see, e.g., Ephraim E. Urbach, "Ha-Derashah ki-Yesod ha-Halakhah u-Ve' ayat ha-Soferim," *Tarbiz* 27 [1957/8]: 166–182) as opposed to the understanding that exegesis generates halakic statements (e.g., Jacob Z. Lauterbach, "Midrash and Mishnah," *JQR* 5 [1914/15]: 503–527; 6 [1915/16]: 23–95, 303–323). Schiffman, "The Dead Sea Scrolls and Rabbinic *Halakhah*," 15, argues that the Dead Sea Scrolls evidence some of each.

[45] See Alex P. Jassen's comparative historical study, in which he explores the contribution of the Dead Sea Scrolls to Jewish law, focusing particularly on Sabbath keeping as a case study (Alex P.

and holiness in readiness for the apocalyptic end provides plenty of impetus in itself for literary attention to proper law keeping.[46]

The *Damascus Document* contains the bulk of extant Sabbath legislation from Qumran and devotes more space to it than to any other group of laws, thus reflecting its importance to the sect.[47] Sabbath legislation is grouped under the heading, "Concerning the Sabbath, to observe it in accordance with its regulation" (CD 10.14 = 4Q270 [4QD^e] 6 V, 1). From the twenty-two laws that deal with Sabbath keeping, eight are peculiar to the Essenes.[48] The first concern of the *Damascus Document*, following this heading, is to clearly identify the weekly period of time during which the Sabbath laws operate: "No-one should do work on the sixth day, from the moment when the sun's disk is at a distance of its diameter from the gate" (CD 10.15–16). In the 1950s, Shemaryahu Talmon argued that for the sectarians the day began at sunrise and that this passage in the *Damascus Document* was a medieval insertion.[49] His opinion has been largely rejected by scholars on the basis of other documents that speak of the evening and then the morning, and they find no evidence for the medieval insertion theory.[50] In fact, as one scholar states, "in general it may be said that in the second temple period (after c. 520 BCE) almost all cultic texts assume that the day began in the evening."[51]

The text of the *Damascus Document* continues by explicitly citing Deuteronomy 5:12 to identify what might be understood as the underlying principle for the subsequent legislation: "For this is what he said: 'Observe the Sabbath day to keep it holy.'" The laws that follow show some evidence

---

Jassen, *Scripture and Law in the Dead Sea Scrolls* [New York: Cambridge University Press, 2014]).

[46] Hannah Harrington, *The Purity Texts* (London: T&T Clark, 2004), 197.

[47] Two of the *Damascus Document* fragments from Qumran contain portions of the Sabbath legislation: 4Q270 frg. 6 V, 1–21 and 4Q271 5 I, 1–12. A close comparison between the Cairo copy and the Qumran fragments of this document makes it evident that this legislation was not a static product of one individual or period, but evolved over time and, in fact, may never have existed in a single "canonical" edition.

[48] Magen Broshi, "Qumran and the Essenes: Purity and Pollution, Six Categories," *RevQ* 22 (2006): 471.

[49] Talmon, "The Calendar Reckoning," 192–193.

[50] VanderKam, *Calendars in the Dead Sea Scrolls*, 13.

[51] See also Lutz Doering, "Purity Regulations Concerning the Sabbath in the Dead Sea Scrolls and Related Literature," in *The Dead Sea Scrolls Fifty Years after Their Discovery: Proceedings of the Jerusalem Congress, July 20–25, 1997*, ed. Lawrence H. Schiffman, Emanuel Tov, and James C. VanderKam (Jerusalem: Israel Exploration Society in cooperation with The Shrine of the Book, Israel Museum, 2000), 601.

of organizational grouping, although in many places the organization is puzzling. The reasoning behind the sequence of these laws is not fully evident, but in a general sense they deal with the main areas of life for which it would be necessary to give consideration in order to "observe the Sabbath day" with full care. They begin with attention to the human body (laws regarding speech, movement, eating and drinking, cleanliness), followed by a consideration of one's relationship to animals, objects and people, and conclude with the holiest activity of all: the temple sacrifices.[52] Notably, three of the fragments of Sabbath legislation found at Qumran follow the same general order, with the addition of different laws or nuances.[53]

A closer look at a few of the Sabbath laws illustrates some of the general characteristics of the Qumran Sabbath legislation. The first set of laws in the *Damascus Document*, for example, primarily deals with the question of what it means to keep the Sabbath holy in relation to one's speech.

> And on the day of the Sabbath, no-one should say a useless or stupid word. He is not to lend anything to his fellow. He is not to discuss riches or gain. He is not to speak about matters of work or of the task to be carried out on the following day (CD 10:17–19).

This appears to be primarily based on the call of Isaiah 58:13 to "call the Sabbath a delight and the holy day of the LORD honorable; if you honor it, not going your own ways, or seeking your own pleasure, or talking idly" (ESV)."[54] The first law here (the first sentence) may be a general statement of the principle, after which the rest are more specific.[55] The law about

---

[52] Jubilees 50 expresses similar concerns and also adds prohibitions against sex, war, killing an animal, lighting a fire, riding an animal, and traveling by boat. The concern with temple sacrifices suggests the eschatological hope that the community would one day participate in sacrifice.

[53] Other fragments of Sabbath legislation include 4Q251 1.1–7; 4Q264ª 1.1–8; 4Q265 7 I.1–8; II.1–5; and 4Q421 13 + 2 + 8. Vered Noam and Elisha Qimron, "A Qumran Composition of Sabbath Laws and Its Contribution to the Study of Early Halakah," *DSD* 16 (2009): 55–96, propose a composite edition of the Sabbath laws in 4Q264ª and 4Q421 with new reconstructions and readings. Richard Hidary, "Revisiting the Sabbath Laws in 4Q264a and Their Contribution to Early Halakha," *DSD* 22 (2015): 68–92, reviews Noam and Qimron's reconstruction and disagrees with their proposal regarding the place of music, the use of fire, and the requirement to study the Scriptures on the Sabbath.

[54] Cf. Lutz Doering, "New Aspects of Qumran Sabbath Law from Cave 4 Fragments," in *Legal Texts and Legal Issues* (Leiden Brill, 1997), 252. Lawrence Schiffman, "Jewish Law at Qumran," in *The Judaism of Qumran: A Systemic Reading of the Dead Sea Scrolls*, ed. Alan J. Avery-Beck, Jacob Neusner, and Bruce Chilton (Leiden: Brill, 2015), 90, finds that both the rabbis and the sectarians understood verse 13 to prohibit the discussion of business mentioned earlier in the verse.

[55] Schiffman, "Jewish Law at Qumran," 87–88, suggests that the first "passes a value judgment

lending does not, at first, appear to belong in a grouping regarding speech, but it does make sense when read in light of Isaiah 58:13 and in recognition that borrowing and lending generally involve speech. The Mishnah, by contrast, allows certain borrowing, "provided that he does not say to him, 'Lend me them.'"[56] The next two laws in this group in the *Damascus Document*, regarding abstention from dealing with weekday matters, are also found in the writings of Philo (*On the Life of Moses* 2.211) and in later rabbinic literature.[57] This prohibition is stated more specifically in 4Q264ᵃ 1.7-8: "He shall sp[eak no wo]rd apart from speaking holy words as prescribed and from pronouncing blessings of God. He may talk about eating and drink[ing]."[58]

The *Damascus Document* (CD 10.20–21) goes on to state, "No-one is to walk in the field to do the work which he wishes [on] the sabbath [day]. He is not to walk more than one thousand cubits outside his city." This legislation relates to movement on the Sabbath.[59] The influence of Isaiah 58:13 can still be seen here, but one can also see reference to Moses' command to the people in Exodus 16:29 with regard to the collection of manna: "He gives you bread for two days on the sixth day. Remain every man in his place; let no man go out of his place on the seventh day." In order to understand the limits of one's "place," both the sectarians and the rabbis turned to Numbers 35, which describes the extent of the (pasture) lands of the Levitical cities. The sectarian-legislated distance of one thousand cubits is based on verse 4, while the rabbis cite the two thousand cubits in verse 5 as the legitimate extent of a person's "place" in which they are free to move on the Sabbath. Interestingly, in a later section on care of

---

on the three subcategories which follow," communicating, in effect, that "if these exchanges take place on the Sabbath, they become wicked or vain."

[56] *m. Shabbat* 23.1.

[57] Some writings forbid only speaking of work, while others forbid speaking or meditating on work (e.g., *b. Shabbat* 113b; 150a; cf. Doering, "New Aspects of Qumran Sabbath Law from Cave 4 Fragments," 252–254).

[58] Geza Vermes, *The Complete Dead Sea Scrolls in English* (London: Penguin Books, 2011), 234.

[59] More specifically, Alex Jassen, "What Exactly is Prohibited in the Field? A New Suggestion for Understanding the Text and Context of CD 10:20–21," *RevQ* 97 (2011): 61, suggests that "the immediate concern of CD 10:20-21 is not performing labor in one's field on the Sabbath (Schechter) or preparing for work following it (Rabin). Rather, it exploits the twofold appearance and semantic range of עשׂה and חפץ in Isa 58:13 to prohibit the act of traveling through one's field to assess its needs." He continues, "By traveling through one's field to determine its needs, the individual will mentally note what items need to be tended to, how this labor should be performed, and perhaps even a schedule for its future undertaking."

animals, one of the fragmentary copies of the *Damascus Document* gives the two-thousand-cubit distance as the distance that a person may follow after an animal to pasture it on the Sabbath.[60]

As can be seen from these brief examples, biblical teaching (including Deut 5:12; Isa 58:13; Exod 16:23-2; Jer 17:21-22) was central to the decisions the sect made regarding proper Sabbath behavior. The Qumran documents have much in common with the earliest rabbinic writings in regard to Sabbath concerns, yet are in general more stringent. There appears to have been agreement concerning a large core of practice, including biblically mandated abstention from work-related activity and travel on Sabbath, which began on Friday evening. The sectarians also agreed with the rabbis on a number of finer points, such as withholding assistance from an animal that was in trouble through work on the Sabbath (cf. Matt 12:11; Luke 14:5).[61] At the same time, there were exegetical and therefore practical differences over other Sabbath matters, such as the distance one was permitted to walk on Sabbath and whether it was permitted to offer a sacrifice other than the Sabbath burnt offering.[62]

The Sabbath in Liturgy and Ritual

Songs of the Sabbath Sacrifice, made up of thirteen hymns to be recited on thirteen successive Sabbaths, comprises the most extensive group of manuscripts found at Qumran relating to Sabbath liturgy.[63] Fragments of at least eight different manuscripts of this work have been discovered in caves 4 (4Q400–407) and 11 (11Q17), as well as a ninth at Masada.[64] Whether the *Songs* originated at Qumran or were written elsewhere and later brought to Qumran, the multiplicity of copies found attests to their

---

[60] 4Q271 (QD^f) 5 col. I, 2. For a helpful table of congruencies between Qumran Sabbath law, Scripture, and rabbinic writings, see S. T. Kimbrough Jr., "The Concept of Sabbath at Qumran," *RevQ* 5 (1966): 483–502.

[61] See 4Q256 frg. 6 lines 5–8 and CD 11.13–17.

[62] Schiffman, *Reclaiming the Dead Sea Scrolls*, 275–282; cf. Harrington, "Biblical Law at Qumran," 1:167 and Kimbrough, "The Concept of Sabbath at Qumran," 483–502.

[63] On the Songs of the Sabbath sacrifice, see Henry W. L. Rietz, "Collapsing of the Heavens and the Earth: Conceptions of Time in the Sectarian Dead Sea Scrolls" (PhD diss., Princeton, 2000), 103–132 and Falk, "Liturgical Progression," 267–284.

[64] Masada was the site of the last confrontation between Rome and the Jewish rebels in A.D. 73. So it seems that refugees from Qumran may have been present there, bringing with them precious documents.

importance for the Qumran sect.[65] Though the exact purpose of the *Songs* is disputed, it appears that at Qumran their recitation was likely part of a developing cultic practice, meant to stand in place of the ritual of temple sacrifice, and may have acted to draw the community into an experience of the heavenly cult.[66]

The opening of each of the extant songs appears similar to the less fragmentary opening of the eighth: "Of the instructor. Song of the *eighth* sabbath sacrifice on the *t[wenty-]third* of the *second* month. Praise the God of …" (4Q403 1 II, 18).[67] Though the songs are directed to the instructor (*maskil*), they appear to have been meant for group performance at the time of the Sabbath sacrifice and, as songs (*shirim*), were likely set to music.[68] The designations for the dating of the Sabbaths in the introductory formulae provide the only direct mention of the Sabbath preserved in these texts, yet the songs as a whole serve as a witness to the Sabbath offering as a weekly high point of praise, involving participation not only by human beings but also by the heavenly hosts.

Such attention given to the Sabbath sacrifice is evidently built upon Numbers 28:9-10, where Israel is instructed to offer on the Sabbath an extra sacrifice, in addition to the morning and evening burnt offering,

---

[65] Arguments in favor of Qumran origin can be found in Carol Newsom, *Songs of the Sabbath Sacrifice: A Critical Edition* (Atlanta, GA: Scholars Press, 1985), 1–4; Daniel K. Falk, *Daily, Sabbath, and Festival Prayers in the Dead Sea Scrolls* (Leiden: Brill, 1998), 126–129; and Henry W. Morisada Rietz, "Identifying Compositions and Traditions of the Qumran Community: The Songs of the Sabbath Sacrifice as a Test Case," in *Qumran Studies: New Approaches, New Questions*, ed. Michael Thomas Davis and Brent A. Strawn (Grand Rapids, MI: Eerdmans, 2007), 29–52. Arguments to the contrary have been advanced by Carol Newsom, "'Sectually Explicit' Literature from Qumran," in *The Hebrew Bible and Its Interpreters*, ed. W. H. Propp, B. Halpern, and D. N. Freedman (Winona Lake, IN: Eisenbrauns, 1990), 182–185; and idem, "Songs of the Sabbath Sacrifice," in *Encyclopedia of the Dead Sea Scrolls*, ed. Lawrence H. Schiffman and James C. VanderKam (New York: Oxford University Press, 2000), 1:887–889.

[66] A. S. van der Woude, "Fragmente einer Roller der Lieder für das Sabbatopfer aus Hohle XI von Qumran (11QSir Sabb)," in *Von Kanaan bis Kerala: Festschrift für Prof. Mag. Dr. Dr. J. P. M. van der Ploeg O. P.*, ed. W. C. Delsman et al. (Kevelaer: Butzon & Bercker, 1982), 332; and Cecilia Wassén, "Visions of the Temple: Conflicting Images of the Eschaton," *Svensk exegetisk årsbok* 76 (2011): 41–59.

[67] Words in italics vary from song to song.

[68] Esther Chazon, "When Did They Pray? Times for Prayer in the Dead Sea Scrolls and Associated Literature," in *For a Later Generation: The Transformation of Tradition in Israel, Early Judaism, and Early Christianity*, ed. Randal A. Argall, Beverly A. Bow, and Rodney A. Werline (Harrisburg, PA: Trinity Press International, 2000), 49; Falk, *Daily, Sabbath, and Festival Prayers*, 125–126; and Andrea Lieber, "Voice and Vision: Song as a Vehicle for Ecstatic Experience in Songs of the Sabbath Sacrifice," in *Of Scribes and Sages*, ed. Craig A. Evans (London: T&T Clark International, 2004).

equal in size to these two daily offerings.[69] There is precedent for Sabbath songs in Psalm 92, which was designated as a song for the Sabbath, glorifying God for His mighty works and for His justice to the wicked and to the righteous.[70] In the LXX, Psalm 38 is also identified as a Sabbath psalm.

An important Qumran scroll, *Psalms Scroll*ᵃ (11Q5 XXVII, 2–8), asserts that David, whom it calls "wise and a light like the light of the sun,"[71] wrote 4,050 psalms through the spirit of prophecy given him by the Most High. Along with 364 daily songs and thirty festival songs, fifty-two are said to be for the Sabbath offerings—apparently one for each Sabbath of the year. Though this scroll was probably pre-Qumranic, its assertion is in keeping with the importance of song and calendar in the temple cult and reinforces our understanding of the importance of Sabbath worship at Qumran.[72]

The main body of each of the *Songs of the Sabbath Sacrifice* is concerned not with providing words for an earthly liturgy, but with describing a celestial liturgy conducted by the highest princes of the heavenly ranks.[73] Since the actual words of the praises and thanksgivings are not given, this ritualized portrayal can be seen as giving the sense of one standing afar off, seeing and even calling on the angelic hosts to praise, but not fully hearing. As the general pattern of the *Songs* as a whole moves from outer vestibules to innermost sanctum, worshippers could be vicariously drawn into the experience of Sabbath worship going on in heaven, while at the same time a proper distance between the earthly and heavenly is maintained.[74]

In the layered images of the first seven songs, themes of angelic ministry and praise predominate,[75] finding their climax, or pivot point, in

---

[69] Cf. 1 Chronicles 23:31; 2 Chronicles 8:12–13; Nehemiah 10:33; Ezra 45:17.

[70] Maurice Baillet, *Qumrân Grotte 4, III (4Q482–4Q520)* (Oxford: Clarendon, 1982) and Falk, *Daily, Sabbath, and Festival Prayers*, 151.

[71] Translation by Roy Gane.

[72] Chazon, "When Did They Pray?," 48 and Falk, *Daily, Sabbath, and Festival Prayers*, 125–126.

[73] Ra'anan S. Boustan, "Angels in the Architecture: Temple Art and the Poetics of Praise in the Songs of the Sabbath Sacrifice," in *Heavenly Realms and Earthly Realities in Late Antique Religions* (Cambridge: Cambridge University Press, 2004), 199. Cf. the proclamation (*miqra'*) of holiness on the Sabbath in Leviticus 23:3, although the term *miqra'* does not appear in the *Songs*.

[74] Raanan Abusch, "Sevenfold Hymns in the Songs of the Sabbath Sacrifice and the Hekhalot Literature: Formalism, Hierarchy and the Limits of Human Participation," in *Dead Sea Scrolls as Background to Postbiblical Judaism and Early Christianity*, ed. James R. Davila (Leiden: Brill, 2003), 220–247 and Newsom, *Songs of the Sabbath Sacrifice*, 17–20, 59.

[75] Noam Mizrahi, "The *Cycle of Summons*: A Hymn from the Seventh Song of the Sabbath Sacrifice (4Q403 1i 31–40)," *DSD* 22 (2015): 43–67, gives one possible interpretation of why angelic praise is emphasized in the seventh song—namely that God's divine kingship is contingent

song 7.⁷⁶ Around the nucleus of this seventh song, particularly in songs 6 and 8, are many clusters of sevens: for example, seven chief princes of the angels each bring seven praises and seven blessings in song 6; and in song 8, seven princes sound seven mysteries—each seven times louder than the one before. Beginning in the last half of song 7, the final songs depict the structures and furnishings of the heavenly temple also joining in the songs of praise (4Q405 4, 5; 20 II, 13). Song 12 may be seen as opening a final climax in which the divine chariot-throne is described, and the sounds of rejoicing fall silent for a time, possibly portraying the participants of the celestial worship as entering into the fullness of Sabbath rest following celebration of the creative word (4Q405 20 II, 13).⁷⁷ This is followed by the thirteenth song, in which the angelic priests offer their sacrifices. The closest biblical precedent for such scenes is Ezekiel 1, 10, 40–48, with its sublime view of God's divine chariot-throne and ideal temple,⁷⁸ as well as the heavenly temple scene in Isaiah 6:1–4. Here, however, it is all drawn into the context of Sabbath worship.

As one scholar points out, the *Songs* provide an ideology of Sabbath worship particularly highlighting three themes: (1) the heavenly and the earthly realms united in praise to God, (2) God's kingship, and (3) His holiness.⁷⁹ "Through this performance, the community could enact its belief that during the holy moments of the Sabbath, righteous and pure humans have the opportunity to act in a sense as the ministering angels."⁸⁰ Thus, according to one writer, the *Songs* show that "the teaching regarding the

---

on the worship of His subjects, which includes angels.

⁷⁶ Falk, "Liturgical Progression," 267, states, "Thus, the cycle has a pyramid structure, with its focal point in the central song on the seventh Sabbath, with the vision of the inner sanctum, but this in turn anticipates the progression that culminates at the end of the cycle with the vision of the divine throne chariot in the twelfth song." See ibid., 267–284.

⁷⁷ Lieber, "Voice and Vision," 55.

⁷⁸ In addition to the thirteenth, the seventh song describes a chariot-throne scene (Falk, "Liturgical Progression," 267–284).

⁷⁹ Falk, *Daily, Sabbath, and Festival Prayers*, 138–139, 145. Esther Chazon, "On the Special Character of Sabbath Prayer: New Data from Qumran," *Journal of Jewish Music and Liturgy* 15 (1992–1993): 12. See also Anna Maria Schwemer, "Gott Als König Und Seine Königsherrschaft in Den Sabbatliedern Aus Qumran," in *Königsherrschaft Gottes Und Himmlischer Kult Im Judentum, Urchristentum Und in Der Hellenistischen Welt*, ed. Martin Hengel and Anna Maria Schwemer (Tübingen: Mohr, 1991), 50.

⁸⁰ Lieber, "Voice and Vision," 54.

Sabbath was not simply negative, in terms of restrictions on behavior, but positive, in terms of appropriate worship given to God on that day."[81]

Some biblical precedent may be found for this interest in angelic worship in Psalm 103:20–22 and 148:2, which, like the *Songs*, call upon God's angels to praise Him. Such relations to angels are treated with humility by 4Q400 2, 6–7, which asks, "How will it be regarded [amongst] them? And how our priesthood, in their residences? And [...] their holiness? [What] is the offering of our tongue of dust (compared) with the knowledge of the divinit[ies?...]."

Though the concept of the earthly community joining the heavenly praise is not directly found in the OT, it does arise in later apocryphal literature as well as in rabbinic and Christian liturgy (e.g., *1 Enoch* 39:7; 61:12). For example, it was on the Lord's day (Rev 1:10), most likely the Sabbath (cf. Mark 2:28), that John was transported to witness the heavenly temple worship of Revelation 4–5.[82] This concept may also be compared to the early Christian concept of being brothers and sisters in the family of God (e.g., 1 Peter), and having "come to . . . the city of the living God and to myriads of angels" (Heb 12:22). Similarly, the isolated and apocalyptic community of Qumran found hope and comfort in participation in heavenly worship.

The Words of the Luminaries is another composition containing a Sabbath prayer. This early and likely pre-sectarian work is found in two (4Q504, 4Q506) or possibly three manuscripts of widely different dates and consists of prayers to be recited on each day of the week. The fragment with the Sabbath prayer (4Q504 1–2 vii *recto*) includes the clear designation "Praise. /A song/ for the Sabbath day."[83] This song seems to be longer than the other daily prayers in this work, having either multiple stanzas or multiple prayers. While the other prayers recall biblical history in order from Adam to post-exilic times, petitioning God to remember and bestow His mercy and deliverance, the Sabbath prayer is entirely concerned with calling on all creation to glorify God, and with praising Him for His

---

[81] Burer, *Divine Sabbath Work*, 62.

[82] See volume 2 of this series for a discussion of this topic.

[83] Remarkably, the title of this work (also known as 4QDib Ham) is actually found written on the back of 4Q504 frg. 8. The term "luminaries" may possibly refer either to the priests who, like David in 11Q5 Psalms^a carried the light of God (Baillet, *Qumrân Grotte 4, III*, 139), or to the sun and stars, which mark out the times for these prayers (Esther Chazon, "4QDibHam: Liturgy or Literature?," *RevQ* 15 [1992]: 24 and James R. Davila, *Liturgical Works* [Grand Rapids, MI: Eerdmans, 2000], 240–241).

creation. The Sabbath prayer is also distinguished from the daily prayers in that it calls on the angels to join in this praise. Each of these traits of Sabbath prayer—the praise, the avoidance of petition, and the emphasis on the participation of angels[84]—is attested elsewhere at Qumran and also in early rabbinic literature.[85]

One other liturgical work that appears to touch on the Sabbath is 4Q503 (*Daily Prayers*), which contains daily evening and morning prayers for one month of the year.[86] In this work, the days are numbered consecutively but the fragmentary nature of the text makes it impossible to determine which month it is and thus which dates would be Sabbaths. However, scholars have identified the prayers for the evening and morning of the twenty-fifth day (frgs. 37–38) as Sabbath prayers, as well as likely those in fragments 24, 25, and 41. This is based on their themes of "rest and delight," and on their emphasis upon God's holiness and kingship, which are commonly associated with the Sabbath in the OT and Qumran literature.[87] In 4Q503, the Sabbath prayers do not differ from the other prayers in literary form, but simply incorporate the special Sabbath motifs into the same form used for all seven days.[88]

After reviewing these clearly identifiable Sabbath passages in the Qumran liturgical works, one scholar identifies several characteristics of Sabbath prayers as consistent with other Second Temple. Sabbath texts and with early rabbinic Sabbath prayers. Such Sabbath prayers are doxological and incorporate a special element of praise. They tend to exclude petition, and they emphasize themes of rest and delight and joint praise with the

---

[84] Carla Sulzbach, "When Going on a Heavenly Journey, Travel Light and Dress Appropriately," *JSP* 19 (2010): 163–193.

[85] Chazon, "On the Special Character of Sabbath Prayer," 5–6, 12; Davila, *Liturgical Works*, 239–241 and Falk, *Daily, Sabbath, and Festival Prayers*, 149–150. Worship in the company of angels and praise are not themes restricted to Sabbath alone at Qumran, but they are emphasized there.

[86] One other text, 4Q286 (4Q Blessings^a), a liturgy of blessing and cursing, includes a blessing of God for the holy times and festivals including the "Sabbaths of the earth," apparently referring to the sabbatical years, which, according to Leviticus 25:1–4, Israel was to celebrate every seven years (frg. 1a, col. 2b.11).

[87] Esther Chazon, "The Function of the Qumran Prayer Texts: An Analysis of the Daily Prayers (4Q503)," in *The Dead Sea Scrolls Fifty Years after their Discovery: Proceedings of the Jerusalem Congress, July 20–25, 1997*, ed. Lawrence Schiffman et al. (Jerusalem: Israel Exploration Society in collaboration with The Shrine of the Book, Israel Museum, 2000), 219 and Falk, *Daily, Sabbath, and Festival Prayers*, 149. Cf. Isaiah 58:13–14.

[88] Chazon, "The Function of the Qumran Prayer Texts," 224.

angels.[89] One writer points also to themes of holiness and divine kingship, earlier identified as characteristic of Sabbath liturgy, and notes that while a loose tradition can be seen with regard to the Sabbath in this period, these themes are neither invariable nor fully restricted to the Sabbath.[90]

In addition to prayers, several rituals connected with the Sabbath are also mentioned in the Qumran literature. It has been suggested that 4Q493 is a fragment of the *War Scroll*. It contains material not found in the main copy of the *War Scroll* (1QM), expanding on various occasions for the priestly blowing of trumpets spoken of in Numbers 10:1–10. Just before the fragment breaks off, lines 13–14 state, "[…] on the trumpet[s] of the Sabbaths […] and [… over the] perpetual [sacrifice] and the burnt-offerings it is written … […]." One scholar suggests that the Sabbath blowing of trumpets most likely accompanied the Sabbath sacrifice and was likely developed from the instruction in Numbers 10:10 to sound the trumpets "at your appointed feasts … you shall sound the trumpet over your burnt offerings and over your peace offerings."[91]

4Q512 (4Q *Ritual Purity* B) is a text containing instruction for purifications of various kinds, generally in two parts: instructions for the individual undergoing purification, and the words of a confession and blessing he is to say after he is purified. The text includes a fragmentary section referring to purification also "for the feast of the sabbath, on the sa[bbath]s of all the weeks" (33+35 IV, 1), suggesting that it was customary at Qumran to undergo ritual purification before the Sabbath, as well as before other holy days (frgs. 33+35 col. 4).[92] Such a purification is suggested also in *2 Maccabees* 12:38.

11Q19 (*Temple Scroll*ᵃ), the longest scroll from the Qumran caves, gives instruction regarding two additional rituals that were to take place on the Sabbath.[93] Written as a communication directly from God, ostensibly

---

[89] Chazon, "On the Special Character of Sabbath Prayer," 12. Israel's election is another theme mentioned by Chazon, yet it does not seem so much in evidence here.

[90] Falk, *Daily, Sabbath, and Festival Prayers*, 151. See also Schwemer, "Gott Als König Und Seine Königsherrschaft in Den Sabbatliedern Aus Qumran," 49–58.

[91] Joseph M. Baumgarten, "The Sabbath Trumpets in 4Q493 Mc," *RevQ* 12 (1987): 555–559. This is separate from the blowing of Sabbath trumpets to mark the beginning and the ending of the Sabbath, according to some rabbinic texts.

[92] Interestingly, this text is copied on the reverse side of 4Q503 (*Daily Prayers*), which contains the Sabbath prayers described earlier.

[93] Other more fragmentary copies of the *Temple Scroll* are 11Q20, 11Q21, 4Q524 (the earliest copy, made about 150–125 BC, in contrast to 11Q19 at 25 BC–AD 25), and possibly 4Q365ᵃ.

to Moses on Sinai (cf. cols. 44.5; 51.6–7), the *Temple Scroll* has been called a "new Deuteronomy" for the "end of days."[94] It gives plans for an immense new temple, a festival calendar containing festivals and sacrifices unknown outside the scrolls, and purity regulations and other laws. Each of these is presented in the context of covenant and presented in concentric circles of holiness, beginning from the temple out to the surrounding city of Jerusalem and then to the outlying cities and the land as a whole.[95]

The first ritual mention of the Sabbath in the *Temple Scroll* is found in XIII, 17, in a list of regular sacrifices to be offered in the temple. It appears to prescribe the offering of two male lambs as a Sabbath sacrifice, as also called for in Numbers 28:9–10, although the text of the scroll is quite broken here.[96] The second has to do with the eating of a second tithe of the produce. According to Deuteronomy 14:22–26, this was to be done at the place God designated and those who lived far away were to sell their produce and buy what they wished after arriving. *Temple Scroll* XLIII, 1–17 concurs with this, but adds several stipulations: (1) that this second tithe was only to be eaten on the Sabbaths or on the holy days of the festivals in the temple courts, (2) that it was not to be kept longer than one year and any leftovers were to be consecrated and burned, and (3) that it was only those living three days' (or more) journey away who could sell their tithed produce in order to purchase replacements upon arrival at the temple.

Conclusion: The Meaning of the Sabbath at Qumran

The Dead Sea Scrolls make no effort at apologetics to justify Sabbath rest. It was simply accepted as a command from God, instituted at creation and participated in not only by humans but also by God and His holy angels. Worship was the primary focus of weekly Sabbath observance, centered on joyful songs of praise and thanksgiving, magnifying God's righteous sovereignty and holiness. The weekly Sabbath was a high point

---

[94] Cf. Deuteronomy 18:15, 18; CD 1.9–11; 3.12–15. It has been suggested that it is the work of the Teacher of Righteousness, mentioned in other scrolls, here speaking as the "new Moses" (see, e.g., 1QpHab [*Pesher Habakkuk*] 7.5 and Michael O. Wise, *A Critical Study of the Temple Scroll from Qumran Cave 11*, ed. Thomas A. Holland [Chicago, IL: The Oriental Institute of the University of Chicago, 1990], 155–194). However, Sidnie W. Crawford, *The Temple Scroll and Related Texts* (Sheffield: Sheffield Academic Press, 2000), 18, sees a claim to Mosaic authorship.

[95] Wise, *A Critical Study of the Temple Scroll*, 30–33, 200–201. Crawford, *The Temple Scroll and Related Texts*, 17–19, argues that this scroll seeks to invest unwritten halakah with the certainty of Mosaic law.

[96] Remaining are the words, "And on the days of s[abbaths] you shall offer two [...]."

of life in the eschatologically oriented Qumran community, and it would continue in the new age.

Due to the holiness of the Sabbath, as commanded by God, the correct dates and times were considered of utmost importance. The Sabbath was to be observed weekly, beginning on the evening of the sixth day as the sun was nearing the horizon. The 364-day solar calendar observed at Qumran helped ensure that the weekly Sabbath was not to be overshadowed by observance of a festival on the same day. This calendar was an important factor that contributed to their separation from the temple establishment, which followed a 354-day lunar calendar.

Also due to the holiness of the Sabbath, abstinence from work was to be strictly observed. This necessitated precise delineation of activities acceptable on the Sabbath day, with careful attention given to such things as travel, speech, eating and drinking, and dealings with other human beings and with animals. Evidence suggests that the sectarians took part in a ritual purification before the Sabbath began.

The sectarians believed that only they, among all Jews, correctly understood the Sabbath laws and observances desired by God. Violation of the Sabbath was seen to have been a key reason for the exile, and keeping the Sabbath day "according to the exact interpretation" was an important identifying mark of God's true people in the end times. The particular way in which the sectarians sought to keep the Sabbath was based on Scripture, interpreted in accordance with their worldview. Their interpretation shared much in common with that of other Jewish groups of the Second Temple period, though it was often more stringent.

To Christians today, the sectarians tend to appear legalistic, but their texts show them to be deeply spiritual, earnestly desiring God's "new covenant" experience in which His law would be written on their hearts by His Spirit (Jer 31:31–34).[97] The Sabbath was considered central in covenant law for God's remnant who pledge total loyalty to Him as the end-time "Sons of Light" preparing for the messianic age.

---

[97] Hafemann, "The Spirit of the New Covenant," 173–174, 180–183 and Johannes A. Huntjens, "Contrasting Notions of Covenant and Law in the Texts from Qumran," *RevQ* 8 (1974): 361–380.

CHAPTER 14

The Sabbath in the Apocrypha and the Pseudepigrapha

Daegeuk Nam

Introduction

The OT and NT Apocrypha and Pseudepigrapha contain a number of references to the Sabbath, but it is not a prominent concern in these bodies of writings considered deuterocanonical or outright spurious and heretical by Christians. This study explores the concept of the Sabbath to ascertain what significant role it played in Israel during the period covered by these writings.

The Sabbath in the Old Testament Apocrypha

Of the sixteen apocryphal works that Roman Catholics and Orthodox churches in varying degrees have adopted as deuterocanonical books of the OT, only four make at least one direct reference to the Sabbath or the seventh day of the week: *Judith*, *1 Maccabees*, *2 Maccabees*, and *1 Esdras*.

Although the story in the book of Judith begins in the twelfth year of Nebuchadnezzar, many consider this book to have been written in the second half of the second century BC, during the reign of John Hyrcanus, as a "didactic fiction." The book contains two brief references to the Sabbath. In chapter 8, Judith is introduced as a beautiful and devout widow who has mourned the death of her husband for over three years by fasting each day, "except the day before the Sabbath and the Sabbath itself, the day before the new moon and the day of the new moon, and the feasts and days of rejoicing of the house of Israel" (*Judith* 8:6).[1] In chapter 10, Judith goes to "the house where she lived on Sabbaths and on her festal days" (*Judith* 10:2) to remove the sackcloth she had been wearing in mourning and adorn herself, planning to seduce and assassinate the Assyrian general Holofernes. The anonymous author of the book clearly presents Judith as a heroic figure whose unmatched virtue, wisdom, and piety are extolled. Her cessation of fasting on Sabbaths provides an illustration of her religious devotion and inspiration to readers to celebrate the day as sacred even in the midst of deep mourning.

The book of *1 Maccabees* contains one of the most extensive Sabbath references in the OT Apocrypha. This book, which tells the story of the Jewish revolt against the Greeks carried out under the leadership of Mattathias and his five sons and grandsons, opens with a violent scene of the Greek occupation of Jerusalem. Along with the plunder and destruction of the physical structures of the city comes a severe disruption to its religious life. In *1 Maccabees* 1:37–40, the desecration of the Sabbath is given as a clear example of Greek persecution:

> On every side of the sanctuary they shed innocent blood;
> they even defiled the sanctuary.
> Because of them the residents of Jerusalem fled;
> she became a dwelling of strangers;
> she became strange to her offspring,
> and her children forsook her.
> Her sanctuary became desolate as a desert;
> her feasts were turned into mourning,
> her Sabbaths into a reproach,
> her honor into contempt.
> Her dishonor now grew as great as her glory;
> her exaltation was turned into mourning.

As the narrative continues, it quickly becomes clear that the Sabbath is one of the identifying marks of loyalty to the Jewish religion, and ultimately to God, in that time of severe persecution. "Then the king wrote to his whole kingdom that all should be one people" (*1 Maccabees* 1:41), the chapter continues, "and that each should give up his customs" (*1 Maccabees* 1:42). This leads many Jews to sacrifice to idols and give up Sabbath keeping

---

[1] All quotations from OT apocryphal works (*Judith*, *1 Maccabees*, *2 Maccabees*, and *1 Esdras*) are from the RSV, unless otherwise indicated.

(*1 Maccabees* 1:43), among other things. Those who refuse to yield to the imperial policies of religious assimilation go into "hiding in every place of refuge they had" (*1 Maccabees* 1:53).

When the Greek authorities discover that a pocket of Jews are taking refuge in the wilderness away from the pressure to conform religiously, they send troops to fight and subjugate them. When the Sabbath arrives in the midst of their flight from the persecuting army, the Jews choose not to fight back and "so profane the Sabbath day" (*1 Maccabees* 2:34). The Greek army attacks them with all its might, but the Jews chose not to "answer them or hurl a stone at them or block up their hiding places" (*1 Maccabees* 2:36). Instead, they say, "Let us all die in our innocence; heaven and earth testify for us that you are killing us unjustly," resulting in the death of "a thousand persons" (*1 Maccabees* 2:37–38).

While the deaths of the valiant and faithful men, women, and children are mourned, this tragic incident leads the followers of Mattathias to rethink their stance on engaging in battles on the Sabbath. They say to each other, "If we all do as our brethren have done and refuse to fight with the Gentiles for our lives and for our ordinances, they will quickly destroy us from the earth" (*1 Maccabees* 2:40). Thus, they arrive at a different decision than their fallen compatriots: "Let us fight against every man who comes to attack us on the Sabbath day; let us not all die as our brethren died in their hiding places" (*1 Maccabees* 2:41).

This episode illustrates very well the real, painful struggles Jews were facing in this time of foreign occupation and persecution. While the faithful killed as a result of refusing to fight on the Sabbath day were eulogized and mourned for, a more pragmatic and self-protective approach to Sabbath keeping surfaced in response to the massacre of the innocent. At the same time, this account shows that Jews had become stricter in their Sabbath observance from the time of Jehoiada the high priest, when divisions of armed temple guards went on duty on the Sabbath to protect the palace and the temple in Jerusalem (2 Kgs 11:1–8).

The first instance of this "revised policy" is seen in *1 Maccabees* 9. When Bacchides, a Greek general, brings his army to the banks of the Jordan River to attack the Jewish resistance group on the Sabbath day (*1 Maccabees* 9:34, 43), Jonathan, the leader of the Jews, says to those with him, "Let us get up now and fight for our lives, for today things are not as they were before" (*1 Maccabees* 9:44). A battle ensues throughout the Sabbath, though without a clear resolution.

The final Sabbath reference is in *1 Maccabees* 10, where King Demetrius I of the Ptolemaic kingdom beckons Jonathan, now the high priest, to enter into a treaty relationship that would neutralize Seleucid influence in Palestine. Demetrius promises to exempt or lessen a number of tax and tributary requirements, allow Jewish control of Jerusalem, and permit full celebration of all the Jewish religious customs, including all "Sabbaths" (*1 Maccabees* 10:34).

The Sabbath is a very important day in *1 Maccabees*. Though an exceptional provision is made for military self-defense, it clearly remains an honored and distinguished marker of the religion of Israel.

Much like *1 Maccabees*, *2 Maccabees* contains extensive references to the Sabbath in the context of religious oppression by the Greek empire. Chapter 6 tells of the arrival of an Athenian senator sent by Antiochus IV "to compel the Jews to forsake the laws of their fathers and cease to live by the laws of God, and also to pollute the temple in Jerusalem and call it the temple of Olympian Zeus" (*2 Maccabees* 6:1–2). The temple is "filled with debauchery and reveling by the Gentiles" (*2 Maccabees* 6:4), whose orgies fill the sacred grounds. It goes on to report that none can "keep the Sabbath, nor observe the feasts of his fathers, nor so much as confess himself to be a Jew" (*2 Maccabees* 6:6). Anyone who follows Jewish customs and laws is subjected to capital punishment. The chapter describes specifically the fate of those who flee to caves for secret observance of the Sabbath, but are captured and burned together, "because their piety kept them from defending themselves, in view of their regard for that most holy day" (*2 Maccabees* 6:11). Apparently, this group of Israelites does not hold the same view on self-defense on Sabbath that Jonathan the high priest and his men shared.

Chapter 8 provides a glimpse into how Israelites under Judas Maccabeus managed Sabbath keeping in times of war. Judas and his men defeat the Ptolemaic army led by Nicanor, and they do not pursue the fleeing enemies all the way to their complete end because "it was the day before the Sabbath" (*2 Maccabees* 8:26). Thus they stop their pursuit and return to observe the Sabbath properly (*2 Maccabees* 8:25–27). After the Sabbath is over, the men share some of the spoils with the tortured, widowed, and orphaned, and distribute the rest among themselves (*2 Maccabees* 8:28).

Further into the book, another instance of Sabbath keeping is seen in chapter 12. When Judas takes his army to the city of Adullam to retrieve the bodies of those fallen during a previous battle, they encounter the

Sabbath. The soldiers wash and purify themselves through ritual cleansing according to the custom, and keep the Sabbath there (*2 Maccabees* 12:38).

Finally, chapter 15 shows another instance of Jews being attacked by Greeks on Sabbath. Hearing that Judas and his men are in the region of Samaria, Nicanor makes plans to attack them "with complete safety on the day of rest" (*2 Maccabees* 15:1). Nicanor is apparently unaware of the Maccabees' decision to defend themselves on the Sabbath (*1 Maccabees* 2:41). Nicanor's decision to attack on the Sabbath prompts Jews who were forced to fight with him to request that he not "destroy so savagely and barbarously, but show respect for the day which He who sees all things has honored and hallowed above other days" (*2 Maccabees* 15:2). Upon hearing this, Nicanor asks whether there is a God in heaven who has commanded Sabbath keeping. The Jews with him respond, "It is the living Lord himself, the Sovereign in heaven, who ordered us to observe the seventh day" (*2 Maccabees* 15:4). To this, the general replies, "I am a sovereign also, on earth, and I command you to take up arms and finish the king's business." However, the general does not "succeed in carrying out his abominable design" of attacking the Maccabees on the Sabbath (*2 Maccabees* 15:2–5). Ultimately, Nicanor is defeated and the Jews recover control of Jerusalem from the Greeks.

Each part of the narratives involving the Sabbath in *2 Maccabees* shows either directly or indirectly the high value Jews placed on the Sabbath and proper Sabbath keeping throughout the time of Greek occupation of Palestine and Maccabean resistance. Though most continued to allow for the right to defend themselves on the sacred day, some honored the day so much that they offered no resistance when attacked on the Sabbath. Even for those Jews who were compelled to fight on the side of the Greeks, Sabbath keeping was seen as a supreme duty given through a living command of God in heaven—a duty they wanted to fulfill, even while choosing to comply with the imperial pressure to take up arms against their kinsmen.

1 Esdras makes two references to the Sabbath—one metaphorically as a symbol of rest and the other to the weekly (and possibly festival) Sabbaths. Chapter 1, which closely parallels 2 Chronicles 36:1–21, describes the wickedness of Zedekiah and refers to the period of desolation following the destruction of Jerusalem as a period of "Sabbaths" (*1 Esdras* 1:58; see 2 Chr 36:21) that is to continue until the end of seventy years, as prophesied by Jeremiah. Chapter 5, which closely parallels Ezra 3:1–13, depicts the work of Jeshua and Zerubbabel, who restore worship in Jerusalem after those seventy years of "Sabbaths." Among the temple activities restored that are enumerated in this chapter are "the continual offerings and sacrifices on Sabbaths and at new moons and at all the consecrated feasts" (*1 Esdras* 5:52). It is unclear whether the "Sabbaths" refer exclusively to the weekly Sabbaths or to both weekly and festival sabbaths. The inclusion of "all the consecrated feasts" would lead one to surmise that it would be the former. Interestingly, the parallel verse of Ezra 3:5 does not make an explicit mention of the Sabbath, but only of the new moons and sacred festivals. Thus, the inclusion of "Sabbaths" in *1 Esdras* 5:52 seems to betray the author's desire to emphasize the restoration of not only the monthly and annual celebrations, but also of the weekly Sabbath.

The Sabbath in the Old Testament Pseudepigrapha

By far, the most extensive and detailed attention given to the Sabbath in the OT Pseudepigrapha is found in the book of *Jubilees*, which provides an account of the forty days Moses spent on Mount Sinai. The book opens with God's judgment upon Israel, and the breaking of the Sabbath is a prominent reason for the judgment: "Many will be destroyed and seized and will fall into the hand of the enemy because they have forsaken my ordinances and my commandments and the feasts of my covenant and my Sabbaths and my sacred place" (*Jubilees* 1:10).[2] God foretells that more will still forget His laws and judgments and "err concerning new moon, Sabbaths, festivals, jubilees, and ordinances" (*Jubilees* 1:14).

In chapter 2, an angel appears to Moses, commanding him to write "the whole account of creation" (*Jubilees* 2:1). He is to write how God created the world in six days and "observed a Sabbath the seventh day," which "he sanctified ... for all ages," setting it as "a sign for all His works" (*Jubilees* 2:1). After recounting the creation week in the first half, this chapter devotes the second half to the significance of and laws governing the Sabbath. The Sabbath is presented as "a great sign" that has significance both in heaven and on earth (*Jubilees* 2:17–18). It is a day that God and the angels kept in heaven before human beings were commanded to keep it (*Jubilees* 2:30). Thus, it is a holy day that must be guarded with life, for "everyone who pollutes it" will "surely die" (*Jubilees* 2:27). On this day, no one is to work, do "their pleasure," prepare any food or drinks, or carry any items in or out of the house (*Jubilees* 2:29). It is indeed to be guarded as "more holy"

---

[2] The text for the *Book of Jubilees, 2 Enoch, 2 Baruch, Life of Adam and Eve* (*Apocalypse of Moses*), and the Zadokite work (or *Damascus Document*) is taken from R. H. Charles, ed., *The Apocrypha and Pseudepigrapha of the Old Testament* (Oxford: Clarendon, 1913).

and "more blessed than any day of the jubilee of jubilees" (*Jubilees* 2:30), a grand privilege given to Israel alone (*Jubilees* 2:31). The chapter concludes with an unequivocal declaration that the "law and testimony was given to the children of Israel as an eternal law for their generations" (*Jubilees* 2:33).

Throughout the rest of *Jubilees*, God's warning against sin and corruption is frequently accompanied by an exhortation not to forget the Sabbath (*Jubilees* 6:34, 37–38; 23:19). God's injunction against forgetting the Sabbath reaches its climax in the final chapter of the book as He singles out, re-issues, and expands the Sabbath commandment from the Decalogue. Through this, some restrictions not found in the OT are added: "Every man who will profane this day, who will lie with his wife, and whoever will discuss a matter that he will do on it so that he might make on it a journey for any buying or selling . . ., let him die" (*Jubilees* 50:8). God proclaims further: "Any man . . . who travels the sea in a boat, . . . or who fasts or makes war on the day of the Sabbath, let the man . . . die" (*Jubilees* 50:12–13). The only work allowed for Israel was "to offer incense and to bring gifts and sacrifices before the Lord for the days and the Sabbaths" (*Jubilees* 50:10).

Jubilees is categorical in its affirmation of the Sabbath in the OT. Likely due to rabbinic influence, it goes beyond the statements found in the OT in making more explicit demands on proper Sabbath keeping.

Pseudo-Philo includes three references to the Sabbath as part of its imaginative retelling of the history of Israel from Adam to David.[3] The first is found in the portion on the Decalogue. The Sabbath commandment, which is based on the Exodus 20 version, is given thus:

> Take care to sanctify the Sabbath day. Work for six days, but the seventh day is the Sabbath of the Lord. You shall not do any work on it, you and all your help, except to praise the Lord in the assembly of the elders and to glorify the Mighty One in the council of the older men. For in six days the Lord made the heaven and the earth and the sea and all things that are in them and all the world and the uninhabitable wilderness and all things that labor and all the order of heaven. And God rested on the seventh day. Therefore, God sanctified the seventh day, because he rested on it (*Pseudo-Philo* 11:8).

---

[3] The text of *Pseudo-Philo* and *Aristobulus* is taken from James H. Charlesworth, ed., *The Old Testament Pseudepigrapha*, 2 vols. (Garden City, NY: Doubleday, 1983–1985).

In addition to the changes in phraseology, the most significant change that this text makes to the Decalogue of Exodus 20 is the addition of specific instruction on what people ought to do on the Sabbath—"praise the Lord" and "glorify the Mighty One" in the company of the elders of the community. Could this addition be in response to the lack of enthusiasm for Sabbath assemblage that Jews were showing at the time of the writing of this book?

The next is an admission of Sabbath breaking made by some from the tribe of Manasseh to Kenaz, Joshua's successor.[4] The guilty from Manasseh say, "We merely profaned the Sabbaths of the Lord" (*Pseudo-Philo* 25:13), resulting in their execution by fire along with other transgressors of the law from the rest of the tribes of Israel. What is significant about this brief account is that the sinners from the twelve tribes confess to different transgressions of the law—which may be intended as a catalogue of the gravest offenses. Profaning of the Sabbath, for *Pseudo-Philo*, is a serious, even capital offense.

Finally, chapter 44 has God pronouncing judgment upon the people of Israel for having broken each commandment of the Decalogue. Enumerating the Ten Commandments in terse, one-sentence forms, God says, "I commanded them to keep the Sabbath, and they agreed to keep it holy" (*Pseudo-Philo* 44:6). However, the people "have done abominable things" on the Sabbath (*Pseudo-Philo* 44:7). Thus, God pronounces severe judgment and punishment upon the wicked of Israel (*Pseudo-Philo* 44:8–10).

As seen in these three references, *Pseudo-Philo* takes the Sabbath commandment seriously and the breaking of the Sabbath by engaging in profane acts is considered a very serious offense. It portrays God, as does the OT, as having a keen interest in the Sabbath and its proper observance.

The book of *2 Enoch*, an amplification of the story of Enoch and his antediluvian descendants in Genesis 5:21–32, makes one brief reference to the Sabbath. In the recounting of Adam's expulsion from the paradise, God is shown as telling Adam, "I blessed all my creatures, visible and invisible. And Adam was in paradise for 5 hours and a half. And I blessed the seventh day (which is the Sabbath) in which I rested from all my doings" (*2 Enoch* 32:1–2). Though other parts of this narrative do not follow the account in Genesis 1–3, God's blessing of the seventh day, as declared in Genesis 2:2–3, is affirmed here.

---

[4] In Judges 3:9, 11, Kenaz is successor to Othniel, who is the immediate successor to Joshua. Kenaz is mentioned by name only in these two verses, without any accompanying narrative.

The book of *2 Baruch*, which consists of prayers, questions and answers, laments, apocalypses, addresses, and a letter, seems to have been a work written for the Diaspora. The seventh-day Sabbath is referred to twice in this work. The first reference is found in the context of the description of King Josiah's reformation. Expanding beyond the narrative of 2 Kings 23 and 2 Chronicles 34–35, *2 Baruch* points out specifically that Josiah "established the festivals and the Sabbaths with their holy practices" as part of his religious reformation (*2 Baruch* 66:4). The second reference is in chapter 84, where Baruch, upon the bidding of others, is writing a letter to Jews in Babylon. He appeals to them to remember "Zion and the Law, and the holy land and [their] brothers and the covenant and [their] fathers" (*2 Baruch* 84:8). He then adds, "and do not forget the festivals and the Sabbaths" (*2 Baruch* 84:8). In both instances, *2 Baruch* attests to the sanctity and value of the Sabbath as one of the most important markers of Israel's relationship with God.

The *Life of Adam and Eve*, which provides a Midrashic description of the first couple's life after their expulsion from Eden, has been transmitted in two parallel yet distinct versions—one in Latin and the other in Greek. In both versions, Michael the archangel appears to Seth, four days into his mourning for his mother Eve. In the Latin version, Michael says, "Man of God, do not prolong mourning your dead more than six days, because the seventh day is a sign of the resurrection, the rest of the coming age, and on the seventh day the Lord rested from all His works" (*Life of Adam and Eve* 51:2). The last line, of course, comes directly from Genesis 2:2. In the Greek version, which is also known as the *Apocalypse of Moses*, Michael's words are quite different, especially as they relate to the Sabbath reference: "You shall prepare for burial each man who dies until the day of resurrection. And do not mourn more than six days; on the seventh day rest and be glad in it, for on that day both God and we angels rejoice in the migration from the earth of a righteous soul" (*Apocalypse of Moses* 43:2–3). The phrase, "on the seventh day rest and be glad in it," is a clear reference to Psalm 118:24 ("This is the day that the Lord has made; let us rejoice and be glad in it" [NRSV]) and interprets—or, more appropriately, re-appropriates—the verse as a reference to the resurrection of a righteous soul. Neither of the two parallel accounts is really about the Sabbath, but a case of the Sabbath imagery used to theologize on the resurrection and the afterlife.

Aristobulus, apparently an attempt at relating Judaism with Hellenistic culture, is a work that exists in five fragments. The fifth fragment contains a short treatise on the Sabbath. Framing biblical claims in philosophical language, *Aristobulus* states that "God, who established the whole cosmos, also gave us the seventh day as a rest, because life is laborious for all" (*Aristobulus* 5:9). He then makes a connection between the Sabbath rest and wisdom, a supreme Hellenistic ideal: "According to the laws of nature, the seventh day might be called first also, as the genesis of light in which all things are contemplated," which he claims "might be said metaphorically about wisdom also" since "all light has its origin in it" (*Aristobulus* 5:9–10).

Aristobulus goes on to explain that God's rest on the seventh day does not denote cessation of control. Having made the heaven and earth in six days and ordered everything "for all time," he writes, "he maintains and alters them so (in accordance with that order)." This seventh day, he continues, is "legally binding for us as a sign of the sevenfold principle which is established around us, by which we have knowledge of human and divine matters" (*Aristobulus* 5:12).[5] To support these claims, he quotes Greek poets Homer, Hesiod, and Linus, who maintain in different ways that life revolves around in a series of sevens and attributed sacred qualities to the seventh day. He suggests that the Sabbath is a day in which "we receive knowledge of the truth" and all is "made complete" (*Aristobulus* 5:13–16).

This fragmentary reflection on the Sabbath is an early example of an entirely different approach to emphasizing the importance of the seventh day. Rather than finding support for the Sabbath in God's words and acts in the history of Israel, *Aristobulus* appeals to human reason and extra-biblical, pagan authors—that is, those authorities that his intended audience would respect. Essentially, he argues that the seventh-day Sabbath is to be observed because the day represents the wisdom and reason that govern the cosmos and provides a time to contemplate upon and draw closer to *logos*.

Finally, the fragments of a Zadokite work known as the *Damascus Document* (CD) has some significant Sabbath references. It delivers admonitions on Sabbath keeping in keeping with those found in the OT. It calls on those "who have entered into the covenant" with God to "observe the Sabbath according to its true meaning and the feasts and the day of the Fast" (CD 8.15). In addition to the no-work command, it includes some specific injunctions that are more restrictive than those found in the OT, such as "no man shall do work on the sixth day from the time when the sun's orb in its fullness is still without the gate" (CD 13.1); "no man shall utter a word of folly and vanity" (CD 13.2); "none shall dispute on matters of wealth and gain" (CD 13.4); "none shall speak on matters of work and

---

[5] The "sevenfold principle" that Aristobulus refers to is the principle of reason, or *logos*.

labor to be done on the following morning" (CD 13.5); none "shall ... eat or drink unless in the camp" (CD 13.9); "no man shall send the son of a stranger to do his business" (CD 13.11); "no man shall fast of his own will" (CD 13.13); "no man shall provoke his manservant or his maid-servant or his hireling" (CD 13.21); "no man shall help an animal in its delivery on the Sabbath day. And if it falls into a pit or ditch, he shall not raise it" (CD 13.22–23); and "if any person falls into a place of water or into a place of ... he shall not bring him up by a ladder or a cord or instrument" (CD 13.26). While the laws governing Sabbath keeping are made much more rigid here than in the OT, the punishment for "profaning the Sabbath" is more lenient. Though the text does not address directly those who fail to obey the Sabbath regulations in general situations of life, but specifically those who are led "astray into profaning the Sabbath" by the followers of the spirits of Belial, it is interesting to note that these profaners of the Sabbath "shall not be put to death." Instead, "it shall be the duty of the sons of man to watch him; and should he be healed of it, they shall watch him seven years and then he shall come into the congregation" (CD 14.5–6). The Zadokite fragment, which is at once both more restrictive and more lenient, seems to reflect the rabbinic desire for greater specificity and recognition of the possibility that Sabbath breakers may be redeemed and not be subjected to the ultimate punishment of death.

The Sabbath in the New Testament Apocrypha and Pseudepigrapha

The extracanonical books that come from the post-New Testament Christian era show a diversity of understandings of and perspectives on the Sabbath. In this section, major apocryphal and pseudepigraphic Christian gospels, acts, letters, and apocalypses are surveyed for their teachings on the Sabbath and the Lord's Day.

The Sabbath in the Extra-Biblical Gospels

The Sabbath or the Lord's Day receives at least one mention in seven extra-biblical gospels from the early church era. The seven are *Gospel of Peter, Gospel of Thomas, Gospel of Nicodemus, Gospel of the Lord, Infancy Gospel of Thomas, Gospel of Pseudo-Matthew,* and *Narrative of Joseph of Arimathea.*

The *Gospel of Peter* begins with Jesus before Pilate and ends with Jesus' resurrection. This gospel makes several references to the Sabbath in its description of the crucifixion, death, and resurrection. None of these references are unique or significant in that they all simply mention the Sabbath as the day of rest in the Jewish calendar that all disciples kept. What is highly interesting in this gospel, rather, is the usage of the term "Lord's Day" in reference to the first day of the week. The author is quite clear on which day the Lord's Day is—it is the day when Jesus was resurrected (*Gospel of Peter* 9:35–11:49)[6] and when Mary Magdalene and her friends came early in the morning to embalm or, if the stone could be rolled away, at least to mourn the death of Jesus properly (12:50–54). Apparently, by the time this book was written, the distinction between the seventh-day Sabbath and the first day of the week as the Lord's Day had become established among Christians. This pseudepigraphic gospel is generally thought to date from the first half of the second century.

The *Gospel of Thomas*, which the text itself claims to have been written by Judas Thomas, is a collection of purported sayings of Jesus. In the section that bears resemblance to the Sermon on the Mount in Matthew, Jesus says, "If you do not observe the Sabbath as a Sabbath you will not see the Father" (*Gospel of Thomas* 27).[7] As with most other sayings in this gospel, there is no context or explanation provided that helps the reader understand this remark. The second half of the saying parallels a statement from the Beatitudes: "Blessed are the pure in heart, for they will see God" (Matt 5:8). But as to what the connection might be between the purity of heart and proper observation of the Sabbath, no explanation is given. It is assumed that one would understand what a true observation of the Sabbath means. At the very least, the text assumes that the Sabbath remains a requirement to be kept by the followers of Jesus.

The *Gospel of Nicodemus* is written as an account of the trial, crucifixion, and resurrection of Jesus from the perspectives of Ananias, a Roman guard, and Joseph of Arimathea. The first part is called "Acts of Pilate" and the second part "Christ's Descent into Hell." In the first part, Jewish leaders make charges against Jesus before Pilate that "he doth pollute the Sabbaths and He would destroy the law of our fathers" (*Gospel of Nicodemus* I:1). When asked by Pilate as to what Jesus had done to destroy the law, the leaders respond, "We have a law that we should not heal any man on the Sabbath: but this man of his evil deeds hath healed the lame and the bent, the withered and the blind and the paralytic, the dumb and them that were

---

[6] The text of the NT apocryphal and pseudepigraphic works used in this study, unless otherwise noted, comes from M. R. James, ed., *The Apocryphal New Testament* (Oxford: Clarendon, 1924).

[7] The text of the *Gospel of Thomas* comes from Robert J. Miller, ed. *The Complete Gospels: Annotated Scholars Version* (Santa Rosa, CA: Polebridge, 1994).

possessed, on the Sabbath day!" (*Gospel of Nicodemus* I:1). Later, when Pilate asks twelve witnesses who come forward in support of Jesus what cause there is to execute Jesus, the twelve reply that the Jewish leaders "have jealousy, because he healeth on the Sabbath day." To this, Pilate asks, "For a good work do they desire to put him to death?" (*Gospel of Nicodemus* II:6). When the man who was able to walk after thirty-eight years being lame testifies on behalf of Jesus, the Jews are livid about the day on which the healing took place: "Did we not inform thee so, that upon the Sabbath he healeth and casteth out devils?" (*Gospel of Nicodemus* IV:2). In these passages, the author's focus is decidedly on showing the evils and inhumanity of the Jewish leaders. In fact, it is Pilate who comes across as a more reasonable figure in comparison with them. By making the Sabbath breaking charge a prominent one in the Jewish leaders' condemnation of Jesus, it is clear that the author desires to emphasize the enlarged, counter-traditional Sabbath teachings and practices that Jesus modeled through His life and ministry.

The *Gospel of the Lord* is also called the *Gospel of Marcion*, believed to be the work of Marcion from the second century. This gospel is essentially an abridgement of the Gospel of Luke. All the Sabbath passages of Luke are replicated here without any significant change or commentary. In section I, Jesus arrives on the scene in Capernaum and begins teaching "on Sabbath days." One Sabbath, Jesus speaks at a synagogue in Nazareth, which leads the listeners to sit in awe of His teachings only to become angry toward Him at His apparent refusal to perform healings there (*Gospel of Marcion* I; see Luke 4).[8] The Lukan account has Jesus quoting Isaiah 61:1–2 as He proclaims, "the year of the Lord's favor" (Luke 4:19); the author of the *Gospel of Marcion* omits the entire quote. Further in the same section of the gospel, Jesus' disciples are seen plucking ears of corn, resulting in a confrontation between Jesus and the Pharisees. This leads to Jesus' declaration, "the Son of Man is Lord even of the Sabbath" (*Gospel of Marcion* I; see Matt 12:8). This statement is followed immediately by Jesus' healing of the man with a withered hand and another confrontation with the Pharisees (*Gospel of Marcion* I; see Luke 6:1–11).

---

[8] The text and version of the *Gospel of the Lord* used here comes from Gnostic Society Library, http://gnosis.org/library/marcionsection.htm, accessed October 1, 2006. According to this website, the basis of this text is *The Gospel of the Lord* by James Hamlyn Hill (1891), which makes use of the 1823 reconstruction by August Hahn. This version was further revised by Daniel Mahar to reflect the reconstruction done by Theodor Zahn in *Geschichte des neutestamentlichen Kanons*, vol. 2 [Leipzig: Erlangen, 1888]), which places in doubt some of the material Hahn and Hill allowed into their versions.

Section III shows Jesus healing on the Sabbath day in a synagogue a woman who had "a spirit of infirmity" for eighteen years. When the ruler of the synagogue objects to Jesus' work of healing on the Sabbath, Jesus responds, "ought not this woman . . . be loosed from this bond on the day of the Sabbath?" (*Gospel of Marcion* III; see Luke 13:10–17). The following section includes another Sabbath healing by Jesus. This time, the miracle comes to a man with dropsy. After asking the lawyers and Pharisees, "Is it lawful to heal on the Sabbath day?" He rebukes them, as He did in the case of the ill woman in the previous section, for being willing to save livestock on the Sabbath but not a fellow human being from his illness (*Gospel of Marcion* IV; see Luke 14:1–6). The last reference to the Sabbath in this gospel appears in the crucifixion narrative. As the Sabbath was about to begin, women from Galilee who prepare spices and ointments for Jesus' body leave the tomb, and they rest on the Sabbath "according to the commandment." Then, "upon the first [day] of the week, at early dawn, they come to the tomb with the spices but find it empty" (*Gospel of Marcion* VI; see Luke 23:54–24:1). Because of its apparent complete dependency on Luke's gospel, the *Gospel of the Lord* does not present any unique perspective on the Sabbath that is different from its source. Also, in its reference to the day of Jesus' resurrection, it follows Luke in calling it the first day of the week rather than the Lord's Day, as some contemporary writings do.

The *Infancy Gospel of Thomas*, a second-century document that exists in several languages (Greek, Latin, Arabic, and Syriac) with some significant textual variations, has Jesus performing Sabbath miracles at age five. The basic elements of the narrative are the same in all versions. In one instance, Jesus gathers together the waters into pools and makes it clean by His word alone (*Infant Gospel of Thomas*, Greek II:1). On the same day, He fashions twelve sparrows out of clay (*Infant Gospel of Thomas*, Greek II:2). A Jew (a child in the Latin version) sees what Jesus has done and reports to Jesus' father Joseph that his child had "polluted the Sabbath day" (*Infant Gospel of Thomas*, Greek II:3). When Joseph rebukes Jesus, He claps His hands and tells the twelve clay sparrows to go, upon which the sparrows fly away (*Infant Gospel of Thomas*, Greek II:4). One key difference exists in the Arabic version, however, where the story takes a morbid turn. The one who observes and rebukes Jesus of breaking the Sabbath is a Jew, "son of Hanan." This boy not only rebukes Jesus, but also kicks Jesus' fish pond, causing its water to disappear. To this, Jesus responds, "As that water has vanished away, so thy life shall likewise vanish away." Immediately, the boy dries up and dies (*Infant Gospel of Thomas*, Arabic 46). Not only does this account show the miraculous powers of Jesus from His early childhood, but also that the Sabbath was a central point of contention between Jesus and the Jewish tradition. It appears that the author sees the new way of keeping the Sabbath, as a day of creative activity of fashioning and cleansing pools of water as well as giving life to sparrows, as a key feature of Christ's ministry.

The *Gospel of Pseudo-Matthew*, dated as late as the eighth or ninth century, provides another account of Jesus' childhood miracle, in addition to the pool-and-sparrows account. In this gospel, Jesus—on a Sabbath day in the fourth year of His life—makes seven connected pools of clay, filling each with water. One of his playmates, "a son of the devil," shuts the water passage and ruins the pools that Jesus made. Jesus rebukes the boy, saying, "Woe unto thee, thou son of death, thou son of Satan! Dost thou destroy the works which I have wrought?" This curse kills the boy immediately. However, when this act results in an uproar among the people, Jesus' mother Mary begs her Son to undo what He has just done, to which He complies (*Gospel of Pseudo-Matthew*, chap. 26). The gospel then goes on to report the incident of Jesus creating pools of water and twelve sparrows, which is found in the *Infancy Gospel of Thomas*. The basic features of the story are the same, but as the narrative concludes, it includes the following commentary:

> And some praised and admired Him, but others reviled Him. And certain of them went away to the chief priests and the heads of the Pharisees, and reported to them that Jesus the son of Joseph had done great signs and miracles in the sight of all the people of Israel. And this was reported in the twelve tribes of Israel (*Gospel of Pseudo-Matthew*, chap. 27).

This gospel, in its telling of Jesus' childhood, anticipates the conflict that Jesus would have with the religious authorities over the issues of the Sabbath and religious tradition. This again indicates the significance that Christians placed in the new meaning of the Sabbath as a distinctive characteristic of Jesus' mission.

The *Narrative of Joseph of Arimathea* is an interesting gospel written from the first-person perspective of Joseph. In chapter 4, the narrator relates his imprisonment by Jewish leaders after he asked for the body of Jesus for burial. "The Jews, carried away by hatred and rage," he writes, "shut me up in prison." "And this happened to me on the evening of the Sabbath," he continues, "whereby our nation transgressed the law." He then makes a poignant commentary on the plight of the Jewish nation throughout the rest of the first century and beyond: "And, behold, that same nation of ours endured fearful tribulations on the Sabbath" (*Narrative of Joseph of Arimathea*, chap. 4).[9]

The Sabbath in Extra-Biblical Acts of the Apostles

In the second and third centuries, several writings that purport to report on the acts of various apostles arose, out of which five works—*Acts of John*, *Acts of the Holy Apostle and Evangelist John the Theologian* (Apocryphal), *Acts of Peter*, *Acts of Paul*, and *Acts of Thomas*—contain references to the Sabbath and/or the Lord's Day that deserve our attention here.

In the *Acts of John*, considered to be a second-century document, John speaks to his fellow Christians during his last worship with them before his martyrdom. He is seen as "rejoicing in the Lord" with "all the brethren" one day, and then on the next day, which the author calls "the Lord's day," everyone gathers together for John's final worship and farewell sermon (*Acts of John* 106). Based on this single reference, it is impossible to establish whether the Lord's Day here refers to the seventh day or the first day of the week. The problem is further compounded by fact that the book exists only in fragments, with questions regarding what immediately precedes this section.

The *Acts of the Holy Apostle and Evangelist John the Theologian* is another account purporting to describe John's ministry. This work makes an interesting and revealing reference on a possible connection between the Sabbath and the Lord's Day. John, after being captured by the soldiers of Emperor Domitian, fasted for six days, but "on the seventh day, it being the Lord's day," declares himself ready to eat.[10] What is unclear is whether this "seventh day" was meant to denote the same day as the Jewish Sabbath, or that the seventh day of the fast fell on the first day of the week, which the author knew to be the Lord's Day.

The *Acts of Peter*, another second-century writing, contains two significant references to the Lord's Day. First, during his work of healing and preaching in Rome, Peter is said to have had an appointment at the home of one Marcellus "on the Lord's day" to minister to widows. Then the text reads that "on the next day after the Sabbath," the mother of a boy who was resurrected from the dead by Peter came to Marcellus' house with gold as

---

[9] The text of the *Narrative of Joseph of Arimathea* comes from Alexander Roberts and James Donaldson, eds., *The Ante-Nicene Fathers: The Writings of the Fathers Down to A.D. 325*, vol. 8 (Edinburgh: T&T Clark, 1867).

[10] The text of the *Acts of the Holy Apostle and Evangelist John the Theologian* comes from Roberts and Donaldson, *Ante-Nicene Fathers*.

an offering (*Acts of Peter* 29). The second reference is of Peter preaching "on the Lord's day" to Romans, including "many of the senate and many knights and rich women and matrons" (*Acts of Peter* 30). The distinction that the author makes between the Sabbath and the Lord's Day—being the day following the Sabbath—is clear in this document.

In the *Acts of Paul*, as reconstructed by one scholar, Paul is bound as a prisoner in Ephesus and is set to fight with beasts, apparently as part of a gladiatorial contest. The text has Paul praying to God for deliverance "on the Sabbath as the Lord's day drew near, the day on which Paul was to fight with the beasts" (*Acts of Paul* 7).[11]

The *Acts of Thomas*, considered to be a third-century document, has two segments in which the "Lord's day" is mentioned in connection to Thomas' activities. In the first instance, Thomas finishes preaching to King Gundaphorus and his court in India and blesses bread, oil, herbs and salt to the people, while he himself continues his fast, "for the Lord's day was coming on." On the Lord's Day itself, Thomas has prayer, service, and eucharist with believers (*Acts of Thomas* 29). In the second instance the apostle encounters a big serpent who recognizes Thomas as "the twin brother of the Christ." The serpent goes on to say that he killed a young man because the man had sexual intercourse with a young woman whom the serpent fell in love with. "I slew him not at that time," the serpent says, "but waited for him till he passed by in the evening and smote and slew him, and especially because he adventured to do this upon the Lord's day" (*Acts of Thomas* 31). The two references to the Lord's Day in this book are in harmony with the Christian practices of the second century and beyond, which barred fasting and sexual intercourse on Sunday.

The Sabbath in Extra-Biblical Apocalypses

It is only in two apocalyptic works that the Sabbath or the Lord's Day receives a meaningful mention. The two are the *Book of Elchasai* and the *Apocalypse of Paul*.

The *Book of Elchasai*, an apocalyptic work from the second century, is a work that represents the syncretism of Judaism and Gnostic Christianity.[12] In this work, certain Jewish practices such as circumcision and prayer

---

[11] The text of the reconstructed *Acts of Paul* comes from Wilhelm Schneemelcher, ed., *New Testament Apocrypha*, vol. 2 (Philadelphia, PA: Westminster, 1965). In this edition, Schneemelcher reconstructs the *Acts of Paul* based on various related manuscripts. This particular section is from page 3 of the Greek Papyrus of the Hamburgs Staats-und Universitäts-bibliothek.

[12] The text of the *Book of Elchasai* comes from Schneemelcher, ed., *New Testament Apocrypha*.

toward Jerusalem are required, while others such as sacrifice and complete acceptance of the OT as Scripture are rejected. In chapter 7, readers are exhorted to Sabbath keeping: "Honour the day of the Sabbath," for it is a day on which the powers of godlessness have departed.

In the *Apocalypse of Paul*, which is a later work that takes the readers on a fantastic journey to heaven, a brief mention is made of the Lord's Day. The unrepentant sinners who crucified Jesus are punished with great anguish and torment. Paul asks Jesus to have mercy upon these sinners. And Jesus says, "On the very day on which I rose from the dead I grant to you all who are being punished a day and a night of ease for ever." Later, the evil angels in charge of the wicked echo the words of Jesus as they speak to the tormented souls: "You have received this great grace—ease for the day and night of the Lord's day for the sake of Paul, the dearly beloved of God, who has come down to you" (*Apocalypse of Paul* 44). Though the precise meaning of the "ease," or rest, is unclear, what is clear is that the idea of rest that was once associated with the seventh-day Sabbath is being attributed to the Lord's Day, which is the day of resurrection, or Sunday, in the mind of the author.

The Sabbath in the Extra-Biblical Epistles

Of the few letters that are associated with the apostles and their first-century contemporaries, two works—the *Epistles of the Apostles* and the *Epistle of Barnabas*—make significant references to the Sabbath and the Lord's Day. Both works, coming from the early second century, show important developments in Christian thinking on the interrelationship between the Sabbath and the "eighth day," the day of Jesus' resurrection.

The *Epistles of the Apostles*, composed as a letter to Christians everywhere and written in the form of a conversation between Jesus and the eleven disciples after His resurrection, is dated to the early second century during the time of controversy over Gnosticism. Two versions of this work exist—Ethiopic and Coptic. The Coptic version contains one relevant reference to the "Lord's day." Referring to His resurrection, Jesus says to the disciples, "I have come into being on the eight[h day] which is the day of the Lord" (*Epistles of the Apostles* 17).

The *Epistle of Barnabas* is another work considered to have been composed in the first half of the second century. Though this book was once widely believed to be the work of Barnabas, a companion to Paul on his first missionary journey, that theory seems now to be just as widely discredited. It seems that this work intends to provide a theological rationale for the shift from seventh-day Sabbath observance to first-day Lord's Day observance. In chapter 2, the author quotes Isaiah 1:1–13, where God says, "Tread no more My courts . . . your new moons and Sabbaths I cannot endure." The author goes on to say that God "has therefore abolished these things, that the new law of our Lord Jesus Christ, which is without the yoke of necessity, might have a human oblation" (*Epistle of Barnabas* 2:5–6).[13] Then, in chapter 15, the author takes one more step to tackle the issue of the Sabbath. After quoting key OT passages commanding Sabbath keeping (e.g., Exod 20:8; Jer 17:24–25; Gen 2:2–3), he describes the reasons why Christians now "keep the eighth day with joyfulness, the day also on which Jesus rose again from the dead" and, after few weeks, ascended to heaven (*Epistle of Barnabas* 15:9). The author argues for the keeping of the eighth day in the typological equating of the six days of the creation week to six thousand years of earth's history, after which Jesus will come. After this, Jesus "shall make a beginning of the eighth day, that is, a beginning of another world" (*Epistle of Barnabas* 15:4–8). Thus, according to the author, it is to celebrate the connection between the new world that will be established in the future and Jesus' resurrection that Christians are to keep the "eighth day," rather than the Sabbath of the present age (*Epistle of Barnabas* 15:8–9). However, it seems that the author of this epistle was strongly influenced by a dispensational viewpoint of history that cannot be supported by the Bible.

Summary and Conclusion

This study has surveyed four OT apocryphal books (*Judith, 1 Maccabees, 2 Maccabees,* and *1 Esdras*) and seven OT pseudepigraphic books (*Book of Jubilee, Pseudo-Philo, 2 Enoch, 2 Baruch, Life of Adam and Eve, Aristobulus,* and *Damascus Document*) to ascertain how the Israelites kept the Sabbath and what value or significance they placed on it.

With the same purpose, this study has reviewed the following NT apocryphal and pseudepigraphic documents: seven extra-biblical gospels (*Gospel of Peter, Gospel of Thomas, Gospel of Nicodemus, Gospel of the Lord/Gospel of Marcion, Infancy Gospel of Thomas, Gospel of Pseudo-Matthew,* and *Narrative of Joseph of Arimathea*), five extra-biblical acts of the apostles (*Acts of John, Acts of the Holy Apostle and Evangelist John, Acts of Peter, Acts of Paul,* and *Acts of Thomas*), two apocalyptic books (*Book of Elchasai* and

---

[13] The text of the *Epistle of Barnabas* comes from Roberts and Donaldson, *Ante-Nicene Fathers*.

Apocalypse of Paul), and two epistles (*Epistles of the Apostles* and *Epistle of Barnabas*).

Based on this study, the following conclusions have been reached:

1. Sabbath observance was maintained throughout the OT era, and the Sabbath was the marker of identity for the chosen people of God and the sign of their allegiance to Him.

2. The faithful ones did not reject the keeping of the Sabbath as a people, even when they were faced with severe persecutions and oppressions.

3. Many faithful Israelites laid down their lives instead of breaking the Sabbath.

4. Although, in one extreme case, the Maccabees changed the way they kept the Sabbath, they did not give up Sabbath keeping.

5. Some post-New Testament Christians made efforts to transfer the keeping of the Sabbath from the seventh day to the first day of the week.

Epilogue

Lately, the topic of the Sabbath has seen renewed interest in Christianity. Reasons for this interest are threefold:

On the personal level, the Sabbath is understood as an antidote to the rat race of life—especially in Western societies, with the optimization of material and financial profits and the accompanying detrimental effects of human restlessness, anxiety, burnout, meaningless of life, and the breakdown of families.

On the societal level, the Sabbath can be an antidote against "the gods of market ideology"[1] and acquisitiveness—that is, the excessive interest in and unending pursuit of material possessions and wealth. This extremely materialistic attitude artificially creates desires, covetousness, economic abuse, control, oppression, and defines human worth in terms of production, consumption, and financial wealth.

On the level of ecology, the Sabbath points to the importance of creation care and the preservation of the earth and its flora and fauna, as indicated in the Sabbath commandment and the regulation of the Sabbath year. Humanity is to live in harmony with its environment—not as abusers of it. This is not only necessary because exploitation of creation will, at the end, destroy people's own livelihoods, but also because humans have the mandate to live as stewards of what God has entrusted to them.

While these are very important concerns, the Sabbath involves even more than these legitimate issues. This volume, *The Sabbath in the Old Testament and the Intertestamental Period with Implications for Christianity*, has dealt with the Sabbath in larger parts of the Old Testament with

---

[1] Walter Brueggemann, *Sabbath as Resistance: Saying No to the Culture of Now* (Louisville, KY: Westminster, 2014), 39. Brueggemann speaks even about the "lethal cycle of acquisitiveness" (ibid., 84) and a "commodity-propelled society that specializes in control and entertainment, bread and circuses . . . along with anxiety and violence" (ibid., xiv).

thematic and theological perspectives, and some historical studies. But it has also addressed the issue of how to keep and celebrate the Sabbath.

The seventh-day Sabbath in the Old Testament is not much of a disputed study today. It is evident that the Jews of the first century A.D. inherited the Sabbath from former generations. The Old Testament claims that the Sabbath goes back to creation and has a strong Sabbath theology. However, the replacement of Sabbath observance with Sunday observance in early Christian centuries may have influenced biblical scholars and theologians to approach with a certain agenda not only Sabbath texts and Sabbath theology in the New Testament, but also those in the Old Testament.

Among other things, this volume has attempted to establish that the Sabbath is a wonderful divine gift, given to all of humanity and therefore also to all Christians. It was not and is not only a Hebrew and Jewish institution. While in the history of Israel it became a sign of the covenant God established with Israel, non-Israelites were welcome to enjoy its blessings, and the Old Testament looked to a future when on the Sabbath all people would worship the Lord.

The Sabbath allows all humans to experience a special encounter with God. The Sabbath is a day of rest and is blessed and sanctified in a special way. It is neither superfluous nor outdated. This special day, with its distinctive benefits, is indispensable not only for the survival of the planet and the human race, but also for the individual's conscious or unconscious needs to experience a transcendent reality, a reality beyond that which is perceivable to the natural senses. Life is more than what we encounter here and now.

While the Sabbath is a reminder of God's creation, it is also a reminder of divine liberation and salvation. Although God wants it to be observed, it is not a means to gain redemption. Salvation precedes the giving of the Decalogue at Mount Sinai. God's grace precedes the gift of His law. The Sabbath is not ceremonial, but moral in nature. It forms the bridge or hinge between the first table of the Ten Commandments and the second. It is not to be understood and practiced as a burden, but as a tremendous opportunity to connect with God, fellow humans, and one's own self.

The Sabbath passage in Exodus 31:12–17 is rich in theological insights and addresses some of the preceding points, which could be further developed: (1) keeping the Sabbath is a divine commandment (Exod 31:13, 16), (2) the orientation of the Sabbath is theocentric (Exod 31:13, 15), (3) the Sabbath is a sign of the special relationship between God and humans (Exod 31:13, 17), (4) the holiness of the Sabbath consists of the sanctifying presence of God with His people (Exod 31:13–15), (5) God is serious about Sabbath observance (Exod 31:14–15), (6) keeping the Sabbath has to do with both the rest of humans and the rest of God (Exod 31:15, 17), (7) the Sabbath is a sign of the eternal covenant between God and His people (Exod 31:16), (8) it points back to creation and the Creator (Exod 31:17), and (9) it has a future dimension (Exod 31:16–17).

There are four aspects we would like to emphasize, which may be particularly relevant for us today:

- Because the Sabbath reminds us of the origin of the world and of humankind, enabling us to find an answer to the quest for the meaning of life, it is *a feast of joy*.
- Because the Sabbath raises our awareness of the constant presence and closeness of God, it is *a feast of communion* with God, the community of believers, family, and others.
- Because the Sabbath bears witness to the liberation of humankind, it is *a celebration of freedom*, freeing us for physical, mental, and spiritual recovery, the liberation from the slavery of work, from self-centeredness, and from the worries of everyday life.
- Because the Sabbath points to final consummation and rest, it is *a feast of hope*. While each Sabbath is a piece of a paradise lost, it is also a foretaste of the paradise to come. This principle of hope includes reflecting on the true goals of life and arranging our priorities. Hope denies despair and nihilism, and it allows for new perspectives to be gained.

We need the Sabbath. May our experience of keeping the Sabbath be rich and meaningful!

Ekkehardt Mueller

Scripture Index

Genesis
1   11, 30, 83, 138, 139, 142, 143, 145, 182, 199, 221, 223, 224, 225, 226, 228, 229, 237, 355
1–3   30, 384
1:26–29   39
1:1   7, 145, 224, 241, 242
1:1–2:3   vii, 5, 9, 15, 28, 40, 44, 83, 190, 192, 203, 214, 215, 218, 219, 227, 228, 231, 242
1:1–2:4   5, 6, 7, 141, 142, 188, 190, 194
1:1; 2:4   223
1:1–8   220
1:1–31   220, 227
1–2   39, 63, 64, 142, 236, 255, 261, 329
1:2   191
1:3   8, 191, 221, 224, 226
1:3–2:3   177
1:3–5   76, 83, 139, 254
1:4   8, 10, 191, 220, 221
1:4–5   191
1:5   8, 15, 130, 187, 189, 190, 220, 231, 233
1:5, 8, 13   83
1:5, 8, 13, 19, 23, 31   8, 15, 130
1:6   8, 191, 221
1:6–7   224
1:6–8   139
1:7   191, 226, 242
1:8   8, 231, 233
1:9   8, 191, 221, 224
1:9–10   139
1:10   8, 10, 191, 220, 221
1–11   5, 12, 195, 199, 203, 221, 253, 284
1:11   8, 191, 221, 224
1:11–13   139
1:12   8, 10, 191, 220
1:13   8, 189, 231, 233
1:14   8, 83, 191, 221, 254, 274, 275
1:14–15   191, 224
1:14–16   83, 188
1:14–19   139, 300, 360
1:15   8
1:16   227, 242
1:17–18   221
1:18   8, 10, 189, 191, 220
1:19   8, 189, 231, 233
1:20   8, 191, 221
1:20–23   139
1:21   8, 10, 191, 220, 221, 222, 223, 224, 227, 236, 242
1:21–22   235
1:22   194, 236
1:22, 28   253
1:23   8, 189, 231, 233
1:24   8, 191, 221, 224
1:24–28   139
1:25   8, 10, 191, 220, 221, 227, 242
1:26   62, 191, 221, 242
1:26–27   25, 62, 254, 256
1:26–28   199, 203, 254, 298
1:27   8, 65, 223, 224, 227, 229, 236, 242
1:27–30   235
1:28   191, 194, 199, 202, 211, 253
1:28–30   236
1:29   17, 37, 191, 226
1:29–31   139
1:30   8, 191
1:31   8, 10, 185, 186, 189, 190, 191, 217, 218, 220, 231, 242
2   7, 9, 10, 11, 17, 24, 40, 57, 60, 62, 64, 107, 130, 141, 142, 143, 145, 167, 168, 181, 182, 183, 184, 185, 186, 187, 188, 189, 190, 194, 195, 196, 197, 198, 199, 205, 209, 211, 215, 216, 217, 218, 219, 220, 228, 229, 232, 237, 238, 242, 245, 247, 250, 253, 254, 256, 257, 261,

	265, 279, 285,	2:18–24	203	18:19	157
	305, 329, 332,	2:21–22	256	19:1–25	193
	333, 344, 346,	2:22	236	20:1	195
	348, 384, 385	2:24	8, 63, 203, 204,	20:3–6	193
2:1	142, 217, 218,		205, 211	20:17	206
	228, 233	3	17, 255	21:2	206
2:1–2	232	3:6	255	21:3	206
2:1–3	6, 7, 8, 9, 11, 15,	3:16	203	21:3–10	206
	24, 40, 107, 109,	3:16–19	255	21:10, 13	27
	142, 143, 145,	3:17–19	194	21:11	157
	167, 168, 182,	3:18–20	203	21:12	206
	183, 184, 187,	3:19	84	21:14	206
	188, 189, 190,	3:23	203	21:33	206
	195, 196, 198,	4:6–11	193	22:9	206
	199, 211, 214,	4:9–15	255	22:14	206
	215, 216, 217,	4:19–24	193	22:17–18	206
	220, 228, 232,	5:1–2	223	22:18	206
	237, 238, 242,	5:21–32	384	23:4	28
	247, 250, 253,	6–8	14	26:3	205
	254, 278, 279,	6:11–13	193	26:5	14, 205, 206,
	291, 300, 305,	7:1–8:19	270		207, 208, 211
	321, 322, 333	7:4	184, 205	29:27–28	184, 205
2:2	186, 217, 218,	7:10	184, 205	31:23	184, 205
	228, 229, 233,	8:4	250	31:54	84
	260, 307	8:10	184, 205	38:21–22	195
2:2–3	9, 10, 15, 17, 24,	8:12	184, 205	39:9	193
	35, 60, 62, 72,	8:21–22	270	40:3–4	103
	76, 86, 111, 130,	9:1–7	270	41:10	103
	141, 142, 153,	9:4	252	42:17,19	103
	169, 183, 185,	9:5–6	192	43:32	84
	186, 188, 189,	9:8–17	270	49:28	72
	190, 192, 193,	11:27–25:11	206	50:3	205
	194, 196, 203,	12:1	206	50:10	60, 184, 205
	205, 209, 215,	12:1–3	39, 68, 236	Gen 6:5	193
	217, 229, 245,	12:3	298		
	250, 256, 258,	12:4	206	Exodus	
	261, 265, 269,	12:7–8	206	1:1–5	47
	273, 275, 384,	12:17–19	193	1:1–7	47
	395	12–36	206	1–18	174
2:2, 3	204	13:4	206	2	47
2:3	7, 10, 11, 33, 60,	13:17	206	2:23–25	47
	145, 185, 186,	13:18	206	3	47
	194, 195, 196,	14	207, 270	5:7, 12	19
	197, 198, 217,	14:7	195	15:22	48, 98
	219, 229, 232,	15:6	206	20	22
	233, 234, 244,	15:9	206	20:2–6	51
	253, 254, 285,	15:10	206	22:21–27	27
	346, 348	15, 17	270	25:22	32
2:4	5	16:7	157	25–31	33
2:4–25	142, 203	16:14	195	29:44	33
2:5	203	17:10–14	207	30:6	32
2:7	236	17:12	206	31:12–13	32
2:15	194, 199, 202,	17:13	79	31:13	31, 32, 33, 42,
	203, 211, 254	17:19	206		79, 84, 151, 169,

	183, 186, 269,	12:16	24, 60, 288	16:23–25, 29–30	93
	272, 398	12:17	207	16:23–29	211
35:20–29	42	12:19	184, 205	16:23–30	183, 192, 256
39:26	56	12:29	47	16:25	16, 17, 197
40:21	56	12:29–32	224	16:26, 29–30	40, 202
40:23	56	12:31–36	47	16:27	168, 186
40:25	56	12:43	207	16:28	207, 208, 210,
2:2–4	104	12:48	25		211, 238
2:11–15	47	12:49	207	16:29	15, 16, 186, 216
2:15–16	50	13:3	22, 23, 38, 309	16:29–30	202
2:20	84, 340	13:4–8	309	16,30	173
2:23	47	13:6	60	16:30	15, 169, 209
2:24	23	13:6–7	184, 205, 309	16:31, 35	40
3	47	13:9	207	16:31–36	282
3:2–5	348	13:9–10	309	16:32	283
3:5	12, 197, 238	13:10	207	16:32–34	84, 207
3:7	27	13:17–22	47	16:33–34	74
3:7–8	294	13:22	223	16:34	283
3:15	23	14	47	16:35	17, 103
3:20	223	14:8	99	17:1–7	14
4	225, 226	14:9–12	210	17:2–7	260
4:2	225	15:2	131, 294	18:5	98
4:2–7	226, 227	15:6	294	18:16	207
4:3	225, 226	15:11	11, 86	18:20	207
4–5	15	15:22–19:2	48	19	12, 21, 23, 29,
5	14, 102, 104,	15:22–27	14		31, 48, 49, 50,
	208, 209	15:23	48		51, 55, 56, 58,
5:1	98	15:24	210		59, 80, 84, 89,
5:4	209	15:25	210		174, 181, 190,
5:4–5	210, 211	15:26	207, 210		283, 284
5:5	14, 208, 209,	15:27	48	19:1	48
	257	16	13, 14, 15, 16,	19:3–5	25
5:7, 12	102		17, 40, 60, 84,	19:3–6	72
5:7–19	107		98, 100, 103,	19:4	21
5:8	208		104, 182, 194,	19:5	49
5:13	208, 209		204, 208, 209,	19:5–6	84
5:18	208		210, 216, 237,	19:6	39, 68, 85, 86
6:5	23		238, 355, 367	19:10	12
7:14–8:31	223	16:1–36	6, 13, 14	19:10, 14–15	49
7:25	184, 205	16:2	98	19:11	49, 186
8:12–14	223	16:4	17, 207, 210	19:11–20:17	12
9:1	287	16:4–5	17	19:12	106
9:22	225	16:5	186	19:12–13, 17	49
9:31–32	310	16:15	15, 74	19:13	108
10:3	210	16:18	16	19:14	12
10:7	210	16:22	186	19:22	12
10:21	225	16:22–23	102	19–24	93, 111
12	47	16:22, 26–27	93	20	51, 65, 104, 209,
12:2	307, 310	16:22–30	76, 103		229, 232, 243,
12:6	207	16:23	15, 16, 169, 193,		244, 255, 270,
12:8	310		207, 208, 307		299, 328, 383,
12:14	207, 307	16:23–2	368		384
12:15	184, 186, 205	16:23–24	20	20:1	49
12:15–20	309	16:23, 25–26	15	20:1–8	256

20:1–17	49, 176		345	24:16	283
20:1–21	80	20:12–13	322	24:16–17	142
20:2	25, 33, 38, 41, 50, 270, 329	20:12–17	22	24:17	283
		20:13	22, 58	24:18, 21	172
20:2–3	50	20:14	22, 58	25:1	28, 32, 186, 285
20:2, 9	25	20:15	22, 58	25:1–9	81
20:3	22, 50, 58	20:16	22, 58	25:1–31:11	31, 84, 86
20:3–6	50, 90	20:17	22, 50, 51, 58	25:1–31:17	31
20:3–7	22	20:18–21	49	25:8	32, 72, 112, 241, 248, 284, 314, 348
20:3–17	255, 270	20:22–23:33	49, 176		
20:4	22	20:22–26	80		
20:4-5	58	20:23–23:19	49	25:8–10	280
20:4–6	50, 58	20; 31; 35	107	25:9	264
20:5	22	21:1–6	132	25:10–31:11	81
20:6	207, 208	21:12	106	25:16, 21	50
20:7	22, 58, 256	21:12–14	108	25:21–22	87
20:8	21, 22, 23, 59, 64, 66, 68, 111, 151, 158, 185, 195, 196, 244, 320, 331, 395	21:16	108, 109	25:22	32, 42, 76, 267
		21:17–17	109	25–26, 27	15
		21:19	336	25:30	35
		21:22–27	113	25–31	28, 31, 42, 284, 287
		21–23	21, 80		
20:8–1	41	21:28–29	109	25:33–34	87
20:8–9	184	21:28–32	107	25:37	83
20:8–10	22	22	15	25–40	28, 30, 31, 41, 57
20:8–11	6, 15, 22, 23, 24, 26, 38, 39, 41, 45, 51, 56, 57, 59, 61, 62, 64, 65, 67, 72, 76, 93, 103, 109, 130, 151, 182, 183, 185, 186, 187, 192, 202, 237, 238, 239, 250, 251, 257, 258, 275, 294, 322	22:18	108		
		22:19	108, 109	25:40	314
		22:29	184	26–27	15
		22:31	12	26:33–34	87
		23:6–11	27	27:20–21	75
		23:9	26	27:21	83, 207
		23:10–12	60, 80, 88, 132	28:2	12
		23:11	150	28:9–12	78
		23:12	6, 20, 21, 25, 26, 27, 28, 38, 41, 57, 66, 88, 134, 169, 172, 173, 176, 185, 188, 198, 202, 209, 216, 251, 332, 336, 344	28:21	72
				28–29	84
				28:36	12, 86
				28:43	207
				29	15
20:8, 24	23			29:9	207
20:9	59, 60, 62, 244			29:29, 37	12
20:10	21, 25, 27, 40, 41, 59, 62, 63, 69, 102, 154, 158, 168, 181, 186, 197, 238, 329, 344			29–30	15
		23:13	23	29:30	184
		23:14–17	80, 88, 266	29:35–37	60, 86
		23:15	184	29:37	184
		23–29	16	29:39	83
		23:32	49	29:40	133
20:10–11	216	23:34	230	29:42–43	32
20:11	20, 21, 22, 23, 25, 27, 38, 57, 60, 63, 65, 68, 74, 88, 102, 185, 186, 196, 208, 215, 216, 234, 237, 239, 242, 250, 257, 332,	24	80, 88	29:43	197
		24:1–18	280	29:44	12
		24:3–8	72	30:7–8	83
		24:4	72	30:11	28, 186, 285
		24:7	107	30:17	28, 186, 285
		24:7–8	49	30:22	28, 285
		24:12	50, 207, 208	30:27	12
		24:15–16	184	30:34	28, 186, 285

Scripture Index

30:35	12	32:15–16	88	40:16	286		
30:37	12	32:15–19	50	40:17	48		
31	101, 104, 116, 117, 335	32:19	88	40:19	56		
		32:26–28	79	40:20	50		
31:1	28, 186, 285	32:28–29	72	40:21	286		
31:8	36	32–34	33	40:23	71, 286		
31:10	12	32:35	79	40:25	286		
31:12	285	33:12, 17	33	40:27	56, 286		
31:12–13	127	33–34	20	40:29	57, 286		
31:12–15	286	34	88	40:32	57, 286		
31,12–17	182	34:1, 28	50	40:34	33		
31:12–17	6, 12, 19, 28, 30, 31, 32, 33, 42, 72, 73, 74, 79, 81, 82, 83, 84, 85, 86, 87, 90, 110, 182, 186, 197, 251, 280, 398	34:10	88, 223	40:34–35	72, 286		
		34:10–28	81	40:34–38	12, 42, 89, 348		
		34:11–26	176	40–42	179		
		34:15	340	229:35	184		
		34:18	184, 310				
		34:21	6, 169, 172, 173, 176, 180, 181, 185, 188, 202, 216	Leviticus			
				1:1	89		
				1:5	251		
31:12–18	82, 84, 87			1–7	80		
31:13	24, 85, 134, 150, 187, 197, 209, 269, 348	34:22–24	266	1:9	252		
		34:28	49	1:13	74		
		34:29–35:1	82	1:14–18	254		
		35	87, 103, 104	1–16	12, 85, 252		
31:13–15	399	35:1–3	31, 33, 127, 197, 280	2:4–5	133		
31:13–17	202			2:7	256		
31:14	99, 105			19:2	85		
31:14–15	31, 93, 108, 187, 399	35:1–40:38	31	21:8	11		
		35:2	87, 108, 168, 169, 186, 197, 216	21:22	36		
31:15	168, 169, 186, 187, 216, 398, 399			23	34, 36, 76, 82, 305, 340		
		35:2–3	6, 82, 88, 93, 102, 183, 202	23:15–16	35, 168, 172		
31:16	34, 36, 37, 42, 79, 80, 83, 130, 133, 150, 151, 169, 258, 285, 339, 398, 399			23:21	82		
		35:3	103, 178	23:25	82		
		35:4–19	82, 89, 90	3:17	72		
		35:4–40:38	31	4–5	89, 95		
		35:13	71, 87	4:6–7	251		
31:17	26, 41, 57, 83, 130, 134, 151, 169, 186, 187, 198, 215, 216, 237, 239, 242, 251, 269, 335, 398, 399	35:14–15	87	4:7	252		
		35:20–40:33	89	4:25	251		
		35–40	33	4:26	313		
		36–40	151	4:31	313		
		37:23	83	4:35	313		
		39	87	5:1, 5–6	98		
		39:1	56	6:1–7	96, 98		
31:18	50, 79, 81	39:5	56	6:20	83		
32	90	39:7	56	7:10, 12	133		
32:1–6	81, 88	39:14	72	7:22–27	72		
32:1–8	90	39:21	56	8	60, 72, 86		
32:1–34:9	79	39:22	186	8–10	80		
32:7–34:9	81	39:29	56	8:10–12	253		
32:7–35:1	88	39:31	56	8:33–35	60, 86, 184		
32:10	88	39:34–40	292	9:23–24	72		
32:11–13	88	39:36	71, 87	10	77		
32:13	23	39:37–38	87	10:1–5	77		
32:14	88	40:10	12				

10:3	77	20:11–12	109	23:6–8	184, 304, 309
10:6–11	72	20:13	108, 109	23:7–8	82, 230, 288
11–15	80	20:14	108, 109	23:10–11	85, 310
11:44–45	72, 86	20:16	109	23:10–14	304
12:2	60, 184	20:17	99, 109	23:11	266, 310
13:4–5	184	20:19–21	109	23:13	133
13:21	184	20:26	85	23:15	310
13:26	184	20:27	107, 108	23:15–21	304
13:31	184	21:1–22:16	76	23:16–17	85
13:33	184	21:6	36	23:21	230, 288
13:50	184	21:8	36, 72, 85, 86	23:24	169, 277, 288,
13:54	184	21:16–23	88		305, 312
14:8	184	21:21–22	36	23:25	76, 230
14:8, 38	60	21:22	12	23:27	288
14:10, 21	133	22:4, 6–8	36	23:27–32	305
15:13	60, 184	22:10–14	36	23:28	231, 313
15:19	60, 184	22:16	36	23:29	313
15:24	60, 184	22:17–25	88	23:30–31	231
15:28	60, 184	22:17–33	76	23:32	35, 82, 169, 254
15:30–36	78	22:25	36	23:33–43	266
16	80, 313, 314	22:27	184, 186	23:34–36	305
16:3–4	314	22:30	36	23:34–42	184
16:16	313	23	34, 35, 36, 37,	23:35–36	82, 230, 288
16:19	313		75, 76, 77, 81,	23:37	323
16:29–34	72		82, 83, 84, 85,	23:37–38	361
16:31	35, 169, 277		87, 88, 89, 90,	23:38	323
16:33	313		150, 168, 179,	23:39	85, 169, 254,
17:10–12	252		197, 201, 216,		277
17–20	108		266, 275, 288,	23:39–43	305
17–22	81, 85, 86		303, 304, 305,	23:42–43	85
17–26	72, 95		310, 311, 315,	23:43	315
18:3	230		317, 322, 340,	24	35, 71, 72, 73,
18:6–18	109		360, 361, 370		74, 75, 76, 77,
18:24–30	112	23:1–2	305		78, 79, 80, 83,
19	34, 89, 265	23:1–3	76		85, 86, 87, 88,
19:2	72, 86, 197, 254,	23:1–4	317		90, 103, 104,
	265, 272	23:1–24:9	76, 82		106, 108
19:3	6, 28, 34, 169,	23:2	201, 322	24:1–4	35, 75, 76, 81,
	197	23:2–3	305		83
19:3–4	89	23:3	6, 28, 34, 35, 76,	24:1–9	35, 75, 76, 77,
19:6	186		82, 154, 168,		78
19:18	271		169, 185, 186,	24:2, 8	78
19–20	76		197, 201, 202,	24:3	83
19–24	76		216, 238, 275,	24:3–4, 8	75
19:30	6, 28, 31, 33, 34,		288, 304, 305,	24:4	83
	36, 169, 280,		322, 340, 370	24:5–6	78
	285	23:4	201, 305, 322	24:5–9	6, 28, 35, 71, 72,
20:2	106, 108	23:4–11	310		73, 74, 75, 79,
20:2–3	99	23:4, 37	305		81, 85, 87, 90,
20:2–5	107, 108, 109	23:4–43	275		290
20:3	313	23:4–44	76	24:7	76
20:7–8	84	23:5	304	24:8	35, 79, 83, 258,
20:7, 26	86	23:5–6	85		280, 290
20:10	108, 109, 114	23:5–16	310	24:10–11	79

Scripture Index

24:10–12	81, 90	26:34	168	14:1–45	14
24:10–23	75, 76, 78, 79	26:34–35	169	14:2–4	88, 97
24:11–16	256	26:35	169	14:4	97, 106
24:12	102, 103, 104	26:43	168	14:9–11	97
24:13–14	81	26:46	89	14:10	105
24:13–23	88	27	82, 89	14:11	210
24:14–16	108	27:34	89	14:20–23	105
24:15–16	107			14:20, 40–43	95
24:15–22	79, 81	Numbers		14:22–29	97
24:16	106, 108, 109	1	94	14:23	95
24:17, 21	108	1:1; 10:11	94	14:27	210
24:23	80, 82, 256	1–25	95	14:31	96
25	75, 88, 194, 230, 317, 318, 344, 373	1:31	98	14:33	98
		1:47–53	72	14:33–35	55
		2:33	72	14:36–38	93
25:1–7	82, 88, 317	3:1–4:49	72	14:44	87
25:1–55	132	3:7	103	15	13, 93, 94, 95, 96, 97, 99, 100, 101, 102, 103, 104, 105, 116
25:2	169, 197	3–31	98		
25:2, 4	344	4:7	87		
25:2, 4, 6	168	5:5–8	98		
25:2, 4, 6, 8	76	5:9	12	15:1–21	96, 98, 100
25:3–4	317	6:9	184	15:1–31	14, 95
25:4	169	6–17	97	15:2	96
25:5	169, 344	6:23–27	265	15:2–3	96
25:6	317	7	133	15:2, 18	100
25:8	317	7:2–3	78	15:3–29	111
25:8–9	317	7:84	78	15:16	100
25:8–13	317, 318	7:86–87	78	15–17	97
25:8–26:2	60	7:89	76	15:17	100
25:8–55	82, 88, 318	9:13	106	15:17–21,	98
25:9	317	10:2	340	15:17–31	110
25:10	344	10:10	316	15:18–19	96
25:13	344	10:12	98	15:22–24	18, 19
25:14, 17	317	10:33	87	15:22–29	77, 100
25:18–22	318	10:35	125, 131	15:22–31	18, 19, 96, 98, 99, 116
25:23	112	11:1–14:45	94		
25:23–24	318	11:4–6	93	15:22–36	18, 100, 116
25:23–55	318	11:5, 18, 20	88	15:25	18
25:25–28	318	11–25	95	15:26	18
25:25–55	318	11:25–26	25, 250	15:27–29	18
25:29–34	318	11:31–33	93	15:29–31	97, 104
25:35–38	318	12:14–15	184	15:30	19, 98
25:39–43	318	13:2	96	15:30–31	14, 18, 98, 99, 104, 106, 111, 116
25:39–46	318	13:3, 26	97, 98		
25:44–46	318	13–14	95, 96, 97, 99, 100, 104, 111, 116	15:30–36	100
25:47–55	318			15:31	99
26	82, 88, 89, 110, 134, 205	13–15	97	15:32	97, 98, 102, 110, 178
		13–17	95, 96, 97, 100, 104, 109, 111		
26:1–2	89			15:32–33	19
26:2	36, 169, 285	13:27; 14:8	96	15:32–34	18
26:2, 34–35, 43	76	13:31	97	15:32–36	6, 13, 14, 18, 20, 79, 93, 94, 96, 97, 98, 99, 100,
26:3–14	134	13:32–33	93		
26:33–35, 43	89	14	18, 96, 97, 104		
26:33, 38	78				

	101, 102, 104,		258, 263, 290,	5:1–33	37
	106, 107, 108,		291, 306, 307,	5:3	38, 54, 55
	109, 110, 111,		320, 369, 375	5:6	329
	112, 116, 117	28:10	361	5:6–21	37
15:34	94, 101, 102,	28:11–15	263, 264, 274,	5:6–22	300
	103, 104, 105,		275, 306, 316	5–11	54
	106	28:16	306	5:12	21, 22, 23, 37,
15:35	18, 106, 107,	28:16–29:40	263		38, 39, 46, 51,
	115	28:17	184		56, 57, 59, 64,
15:36	18, 19, 107, 108,	28:17–25	306, 309		65, 66, 132, 185,
	109	28:18	230, 288		195, 258, 293,
15:37–41	95, 96, 99, 111,	28:24	184		320, 365, 368
	116	28:25	230, 288	5:12–14	37
15:39	100, 111	28:25–26	230	5:12–15	6, 26, 41, 45, 46,
15:40	84	28:26	230, 288		51, 56, 57, 59,
16	18, 97	28:26–31	306		64, 65, 66, 132,
16:1–17:13	94	28–29	36, 263, 266,		151, 161, 185,
16:1–50	14		277, 303, 305,		202, 258, 294
16:2–3	106		306, 315	5:13	64
16:9	230	29	266	5:14	20, 25, 27, 39,
16–17	95, 96, 116	29:0	98		40, 56, 57, 65,
17:2, 6	78	29:1	230, 288, 312		69, 168, 186,
18:1–32	72	29:1–6	306, 312		197, 216, 251,
18:6	230	29:7	231, 288		257, 332, 344
19:11	184	29:7–11	306	5:15	20, 21, 38, 57,
19:13	313	29:12	184, 230, 288		65, 66, 67, 68,
19:13, 20	106	29:12–38	266, 306		99, 110, 132,
19:14	184	29:35	230		257, 287, 343
19:16	184	30:31	98	5:16	56
19:20	313	31:19	184	5:22	50
20:1	97, 98	32:13	55	6	271
20:5	88	32–36	98	6:5	39
21:1–3	95	35	367	6:5–6	271
21:4–9	94	35:4	367	7:7–8	156
21:5	88	35:5	367	7:18	22
21:21–35	95	35:16–18	106	7:23	125, 132
22:26	98	35:33–34	112	9:9	50
22:29	98	37:41	99	10:4	50
22:31	98			11:1	205
23:22	133	Deuteronomy		13	115
24:8	133	1:2	54	13:3	33
24:22	210	1:3	94	13:6–10	108
25	95	1:33	223	13:7–11	107
25:1–18	93	5:12	56	13:15	108
25:2	340	4	54	14:22–26	375
25:28	98	4:14; 10:4	49	15:1–2	344
26–35	95	4:34	99	15:1–3	60
27:29	98	4:13	50	15:1–18	132
28	133, 275, 305,	5	51, 54, 65, 127,	15:9	344
	323		132, 229, 232,	15:15	38
28:2	74, 252		294, 299, 328,	16	315
28:2, 6, 8	74		343	16:3–4	184, 309
28:4	83	5:1	300	16:5	308
28:9–10	28, 36, 154, 201,	5:1–5	53	16:12	38

16:13	184	7:25	107	8:56	287
16:15	184, 315	18:3	210	8:65–66	184
16:16	308	23:1	261	10:5	292
17	111			10:6	157
17:2–5	108	Judges		17:10–12	102
17:7–12	114	1–3	261	17	102
17:12	109	2:22	157	18:21	210
18:1	252	5:31	125, 132	21:10	108
18:15	375	14:12	184		
18:18	375	14:17–18	184	2 Kings	
18:20	108			2:23–24	113
19:16–19	109	1 Samuel		3:9	184
19:19–20	114	1:10–11	265	4:22–23	173
20	207	1:14	210	4:23	175, 201, 289, 316
21:1–9	112	2:1–10	265		
21:18–21	107, 108, 109	2:1, 10	133	10:20	340
21:21	115	2:2	253	11:1–8	379
21:22–23	108	4:4	76, 267	11:4–12	175
22:13–21	109	10:8	184	11:5	103
22:20–24	108	13:8	184	11:4–9	36
22:21–24	114	15:22	157	16:17–18	291, 292
22:23–24	107, 109	16:1	210	16:18	175, 292
23:1	160	16:18	157	17:13	205
23:1–6	159	17:26	104	17:34	205
24:9	22	18:25	157	19:15	267
24:18, 22	38	20:18	316	21:22	157
25:8	340	21:8	157	23	385
25:17	22	28:9	108, 109	23:20	109
26:8	99	31:13	60, 184	25:4	157
27:12–13	78			25:8–9	153
27:15	230	2 Samuel			
28	134, 357	2:26	210	1 Chronicles	
28:1–14	161, 162	6:2	76, 267	6:31–46	265
28:9	134	7:1	261	9:25	184
31:8	248	16:14	251	10:12	184
32	65	12:9–10	111	13:8	128
32:4	136	12:13–14	111	15:16, 20–21, 28	128
33:17	133	12:18	184	15:41–42	265
33:19	340	16:14	26, 251	16:4–37	265
Hosea 2:13	359	21:10	250	22:9–10	287
				22:18–19	287
Joshua		1 Kings		23:3	154
1:13	22	2:3	157, 205	23:25	287
1 Kgs 20:29	184	2:29–32	109	23:30–31	291
2:6	310	3:10	157	23:31	175, 316
2:7	157	5:4	287	24:7–18	361
3:15	310	5:22–24	157	25:1, 6	128
4:19	310	6:19; 8:6	87	25:1–31	265
5:12	17	7:40	30	28:2	287
6:1–20	184	8	30		
7	19	8:4	12	2 Chronicles	
7:1, 10–26	111	8:10–11	12	2:3	175
7:13	114	8:22–54	265	2:4	154, 289
7:24–25	108	8:27	267	2:4; cf. 8:13	291
		8:30	268		

5:12	128	38:41	144	33:6	224, 229, 237		
7:8–9	184	38–42	143, 144, 147	33:6, 9	221		
8:13	175	39:13–18	144	33:9	224, 225, 226, 227, 229		
9:5	157	39:26–30	144				
13:22	157	40:1–5	144	34:8	346		
16:5	209	40:6–14	144	35:23	250		
21:18	336	40:9–10	144	37	65		
23:4–6	36	40:15	144	38	370		
30:21–23	184	40:24	144	39	65		
31:3	175	40:33–34	144	44:23	250		
34–35	385	41:1–10	144	48	120, 295		
36:1–21	381	41:4	144	50:12–13	73		
36:21	155, 168, 169, 344, 381	42:1–3	144	50:23	280		
		42:5	145	51:10	84		
		42:5–6	144	52:8–9	135		
Ezra				54:7	134		
3:5	382	Psalms		59:4	250		
6:11	108	1:2	157	59:10	134		
6:22	184	2	128	59:11	134		
		2–5	122	62:4	210		
Nehemiah		2:194–195	136	73:24	135		
2:6	210	3:39	141	74:9	210		
4:5	209	3:66–67	137	74:10	210		
6:3	209	3:69	132	78:24–25	40		
8:18	184	3:71	134	79:5	210		
9:13	205	3:125	139	80:5	210		
9:16–21	95	4	130	81	120, 295		
9:20	271	4:3	210	82	120, 295		
10:34	175	6:4	210	82:2	210		
13:15	158	7:6	250	86:12	280		
13:15–22	153	7–8	122	89:47	210		
13:17–18	151	7,9	124	90:13	210		
13:22	195	8:3, 6	130	92	119, 121, 123, 126, 127, 129, 134, 147, 201, 202, 295, 296, 301, 327, 341, 347, 370
		10–12	122, 133				
Esther		11:4	264, 267				
1:5, 10	184	12,13	134				
		13:2	210				
Job		13:3	210				
2:13	184	13,14	134	92:1–3	128		
12:10	74, 270	13–15	122	92:1–4	341		
18:2	210	19	11, 121	92:2	121, 128, 129		
19:2	210	92:9	132	92:2–4	137		
26:9	175	19:1	130	92:2–4	128		
38:2–3	144, 145	19:2	141	92:3	123, 128, 129		
38:4–7	144, 339	19:8–10	205	92:4	123		
38:6	146	22:23	280	92:4–6	130		
38:7	241	22:30	135	92:5	123, 130, 296		
38:8–11	144	23	120	92:5–7	137		
38:12	144	23:3	336	92:5–7	130		
38:15	99	24	120, 295	92:6	122, 123, 130		
38:24	144	24:1	244	92:7	121, 123, 124, 130, 131, 132		
38:31–32	144	29:2–3	141				
38:33–38	144	33	221, 224, 225, 226	92:7–9	131		
38:39–39:30	144			92:7, 9	122		
38–41	143, 145						

92:7,9	122	104:21–24	139	104:35	143
92:8	121, 122, 124,	104:25–26	139		
	125, 131, 132,	104:27–28	139	Ecclesiastes	
	133, 137	104:30	223	3:1	157
92:8–10	131	104:31	140, 142	5:8	157
92:8, 10	122	104:31–32	141, 142	8:6	157
92:8,10	122, 124	104:31, 34	145		
92:8–12	121	104:31–35	139	Isaiah	
92:9	121, 122, 125,	104:31–35	139, 140, 141,	1	316
	131, 132, 133,		143	1:1–13	395
	137	104:32	142	1:13	149, 153, 173,
92:9–10	131	104:33	143		175, 201, 254,
92:10	121, 122, 123,	104:34	140, 143		289, 340
	124, 131, 132,	105:10	36	1:13–14	152, 316
	133, 137	112:8	134	2:1–4	160
92:10–12	347	114:14–15	270	4:5	223
92:11	121, 123, 133,	118	294	6:1	268
	134	118:14	294	6:1–4	238, 371
92:11-13	137	118:15–16	294	6:3	154
92:11-13	133	118:24	293, 385	6:11	210
92:12	121, 123, 133,	118:28	294	13	238
	134	119	205, 299	13:22	129, 341
92:13	121, 122, 123,	119:89–90	299	14:3	250
	133, 134, 135	119:160	299	21–24	65
92:13–14	135	120–134	293	24:5	112
92:13–15	134	121:3–4	250, 273	28:9–13	238
92:13–16	121, 136	132:7–8	286	28:10	238
92:14	122, 135	132:8	86	28:12	250
92:14–15	135	138:8	130	28:13	238
92:14–16	137	139:14	230	30:23	135
92:14–16	134	139:23	33	30:26	184
92:15	122, 123, 135	145:4	230	39:6	159
92:16	122, 123	145:11	141	40:26	39, 68, 223
93	295	145:15–16	74, 84, 270	40:28	250, 336
94	120, 295	148:2	372	40–55	159
94:3	210			41	159
95:7–8	261	Proverbs		41:1	159
95:11	260, 293	1:22	210	41:18–20	223
102:18	223	3:15	157	42:5	39
102:25	130	6:9	210	43:1, 7, 15	39
103:20–22	372	7:20	175	43:23	280
104	138, 142, 145,	8–9	147	44	159
	147	8,9	145	44:8	151
104:1–30	139, 140	8:21–31	145	44:16	103
104:1,33	142	8:22	130, 145	47:14	103
104:2	139	8:22–31	145, 146, 339	48	159
104:2–4	139	8:29	146	51:11	159
104:2–30	139	8:30–31	145, 146, 339	52	159
104:5	146	8:31	145	53:5	156
104:5–9	139	8:32–34	145	53:10	159
104:14–15	74	9:1	145	55:1–3	271
104:14–17	139	10:29	157	56	159
104:16	134	11:28	134	56:1–2	133
104:19–23	139	31	342	56:1–7	280

56:1–8	160	12:4	210	20:20, 21	149		
56:2, 4, 6	149, 154, 169	17	110, 153	20:21	153		
56:2–6	357	17:19–27	175	20:21–24	155		
56:2–7	159	17:21–22	368	20:24	149, 150, 153, 197, 357		
56:2–8	160	17:21, 22	149				
56:4	197	17:21–22, 27	153	20:25	239		
56:4–7	159	17:21–23	162	20:26	149		
56:5	135	17:21–27	357	22:8	149, 153, 197, 357		
56–66	160	17:22	195				
58	117, 156, 159, 272, 327, 342	17:24	149, 195	22:26	155, 197		
		17:24–25	395	22:38	357		
58:2–3	326	17:27	149, 153, 155, 162, 195	23:38	149, 150, 153, 197		
58:5–12	164						
58:6–7	343	23:24	154	48:35	12		
58:6–12	132	23:26	210	27:5	134		
58:8	344	2:7	112	36:17	112		
58:11	156	25:6	230	37:28	151		
58:12–14	159	31:2	336	40:1	297		
58:13	129, 149, 154, 156, 157, 158, 280, 326, 341, 357, 366, 367, 368, 373	31:2–6	162	40:24	195		
		31:22	210	40–45	163		
		31:23	162	40–48	296, 297, 371		
		31:30–34	299	43:25–26	184		
		31:31–34	162, 271, 376	44:24	149, 150, 163, 169, 197		
58:13–14	156	31:33	299				
58:13–14	15, 109, 129, 158	31:35–37	299	44:26	184		
		31:36	300	45	163		
60–62	160	47:5	210	45:17	149, 163, 173, 175		
61	319	47:6	210				
61:1	28	51:12	103	45:23	184		
61:1–2	389			45:25	184		
63:8	224	Lamentations		45–46	277		
65:17	296	1:7	169	46	95		
65:17–25	162	2:6	149, 155, 173, 175	46:1–2	292		
65:17–66:24	163			46:1–3	173		
65:20	163			46:1, 3	175		
65:22	135	Ezekiel		46:1, 3, 4	149		
65:25	163	1	371	46:1, 3–4, 12	163		
65–66	162	3:15–16	184	46:3–4	297		
66	296	8:16	297	46:12	149		
66:5	280	10	371				
66:10–11	296	16	272	Daniel			
66:18–21	274	17:22–23	134	1:14	157		
66:18–24	159	20:10	150	5:23	74, 258, 270		
66:22	296	20:11	150	6:10	268		
66:22–23	135, 274	20:12	150, 151, 152, 248, 269	7:5–27	314		
66:23	136, 149, 161, 163, 173, 175, 202, 248, 274, 275, 296, 316			8:9–14	52		
		20:12–13	197, 357	8:11–12	314		
		20:12, 13	149, 150	8:13	210		
		20:12, 20	133	8:13–14	314		
66:24	163	20:13	153	8:14	231, 313		
		20:16	149, 150, 151, 153, 197, 357	9:14	230		
Jeremiah				10:2	184		
4:14	210	20:20	150, 169, 195	12:6	210		
4:21	210	20:20–21	197, 357				

Scripture Index

Hosea		12:1–8	320	John			
2:11	149, 153, 201, 289, 316	12:8	389	0:32–33	108		
		12:11	343, 368	1:3	242		
2:13	173, 175, 316	13:33	309	1:14	248		
8:5	210	13:41	116	1:29	309		
9:5	308	13:41–42	115	3:16	272		
14:8	135	13:49–50	115	3:16–18	113		
14:9	135	18:17	114	5:1–15	343		
		18:21–35	319	5:2–18	273		
Joel		22:21	112	5:17	260, 261, 273, 343		
1:14	340	22:36–40	271				
2:15–16	340	24:20	91, 114	7:2	315		
		26:17–30	319	7:2, 10	319		
Amos		26:26	90	7:37	319		
5:26	178	26:26–29	267	8:3–11	108		
6:3	173	28:20	248	8:3–12	113		
8:2–6	162			9:1–34	343		
8:4	173	Mark		9:1–41	273		
8:4–6	155	2:23	2	11:26	309		
8:5	149, 174, 175, 357	2:27	13, 200, 211, 252, 257, 273, 331	12:31	272		
				14:3	248		
8:5–6	155	2:28	240, 248, 372	14:15	114		
		3:1–6	273	18:36	112		
Nahum		4:35–41	250	19:14	260, 265		
1:7	34	9:5	315	20:1	266		
		14:12–26	319	8:59	108		
Habakkuk		15:42	103				
1:2	210	10:45	113	Acts			
2:6	210			2	266, 311		
				2:41	311		
Haggai		Luke		2:47	311		
2:7, 9	12	2:21	273	5:1–11	109, 113		
		4:16	340	6:11–14	108		
Zechariah		4:16–17	114	7:38	239		
1:12	210	4:16–30	319	7:59–60	108		
2:16	112	4:18	28	13:14–15	114		
9:17	135	4:18–19	319	13:42–45	114		
		4:19	389	15	264		
Malachi		4:31–37	343	16:11–15	114		
2:10	39, 68	4:38–39	343	17:2	114		
3:12	161	6:1–11	389	17:27	221		
		6:5	240	17:28	247		
Matthew		6:6–11	343	18:4	114		
3:13–14	252	8:23–27	250	25:10–11	113		
3:15	252	13:10–17	343, 390				
5–7, 18	112	13:15	344	Romans			
5:8	388	14:1–6	343, 390	3:31	113, 116		
5:17–20	113	14:5	344, 368	5:5	271		
5:17–48	271	14:12–24	319	6:1–5	252		
5:19	114	22:1–23	319	6:14	309		
5:38–48	113	23:54–24:1	390	7:7	256		
8:23–27	250	23:56–24:1	237	8:24	314		
11:2–6	319			13:1	112		
11:29	336			13:1–7	114		
12	320, 336						

14:5–6	321	Colossians		10	116
13:1–4	113	1:16	224, 236	10:1	307, 321, 322
		2	320	10:24–31	116
1 Corinthians		2:16	263, 321	10:25–31	116
3:16–17	86, 114, 115	2:16–17	263, 264, 307,	10:26–31	113, 115
5	114, 115, 116,		321, 322	10:27	113
	309, 310	2:17	263, 321	12:22	372
5:1–2	115			13	149
5:1–5	114	2 Thessalonians		13:5	248
5:1–8	115	1:9–10	115		
5:4–5	115			James	
5:5	114, 115	1 Timothy		2:26	271
5:5–8	114	1:8–11	114, 116		
5:6–7	309	1:20	114	1 Peter	
5:6–8	309			1:16	265
5:7	115, 267, 308	Hebrews		1:19	309
5:8	309, 319	2:15	309	2:13–14	114
5:13	115	3:7–11	293		
6:9–11	114, 115	4	259, 260, 261,	2 Peter	
6:19	86		262, 263	3:3–7	115
11:23–26	267, 319	4:1–11	262		
12:12–27	114	4:3	242, 260, 262	Revelation	
15:20	265, 311	4:4	215	1:10	372
15:20–23	311, 319	4:4–9	114, 262, 307	4–5	372
16	320	4:5	260	7:9–10	274
11:23–24, 26	90	4:7	261	7:14	309
		4:8	261	11:1–2	314
2 Corinthians		4:9–10	346	11:18	313
2:5–11	115	4:9–11	242	11:18–19	314
3	271	4:15	252	12:11	309
3:4–6	114	4:16	268	12:17	133
6:16	86	7–10	258, 260, 265,	14	161
			266, 268	14:4–12	116
Galatians		7:25	314	14:7	133
3:28	161	8:1	314	14:9–11	115
4:10	321	8:3	314	19:19–21	115
5:6	271	8:5	264, 314	20–22	261
5:9	309	9:4	84	21	163
5:19–21	115	9:6	314	21:1	163
		9:9–10	314	21:2	163
Ephesians		9:11	314	21:4	163
2:8	270, 271	9:14	113	21–22	274, 297
2:8–9	262	9:22–23	314	22:14–15	115
2:19–22	86	9:23–28	314	14:9–12	113
		9:28	113		

Index of Extrabiblical Writings

1Q22 I, 6-8 (Words of Moses)	357	5 I, 1	360
		5 I, 1–12	365
4Q216 (Jubilees a)		4Q286 (4Q Blessings a)	
1 II, 3–17	357	frg. 1a, col. 2b.11	373
1 VII, 17	356		
		4Q317	360
4Q251			
1.1–7	366	4Q319–321	361
4Q256		4Q320	360
frg. 6 lines 5–8	368		
		4Q321	360
4Q264a	366		
1.1–8	366	4Q327 (Calendrical Document Eb)	361
1.7–8	367		
4Q265		4Q365	374
7 I.1–8; II.1–5	366	4Q390	357
4Q266 [4QDa]			
3 II	357	4Q394 (4QMMT)	359
4Q266 [4QDb]		4Q400-407 (Songs of the Sabbath Sacrifice)	368, 370
2	357		
4Q269 [4QDd]		4Q400 (Songs of the Sabbath Sacrifice)	
2; 4 II	357	I, 1	359
4Q270		2, 6–7	372
frg. 6 V, 1–21	365	4Q403	
4Q270 [4QDe]		1 II, 18	369
6 V, 1	365	4Q405	
4Q271		4, 5	371
5 col. I, 2 (QDf)	368	20 II, 13	371

4Q421	
13 + 2 + 8	366
4Q493 (fragment of the War Scroll)	
13–14	374
4Q504	372
1–2 vii recto	372
frg. 8	372
4Q506	372
4Q512 (4Q Ritual Purity B)	
33+35 col. 4	374
33+35 IV, 1	374
4Q524 (copy of the Temple Scroll)	374
11Q5 Psalms a	372
11Q17	368
11Q20 (copy of the Temple Scroll)	374
11Q21 (copy of the Temple Scroll)	374
Acts of John	392, 395
106	392
Acts of Paul	392, 393, 395
7	393
Acts of Peter	392, 395

29	393	13.5	387	Gospel of Thomas	387, 395
30	393	13.9	387	27	388
		13.11	387		
Acts of the Holy Apostle		13.13	387	Gospel of Thomas, Greek	
and Evangelist John the		13.21	387	II:3	390
Theologian	392, 395	13.22–23	387		
		13.26	387	Habakkuk Pescher (1QpHab)	
Acts of Thomas	392, 393, 395	14.5–6	387	XI, 4–8	359, 364
29	393	16.2–4	355	7.5	375
31	393				
		1 Enoch		Hosea Pescher (4Q166)	
Apocalypse of Moses		18:14–16	360	1 II, 14–17	359
43:2–3	385	39:7	372		
		61:12	372	Infant Gospel of	
Apocalypse of Paul	393, 396	72:32	360	Thomas, Arabic	
44	394	72–82	360	46	390
		74:12	360		
Aristobulus	354, 385, 395	80:2–8	360	Infant Gospel of	
5:9	386			Thomas, Greek	
5:9–10	386	2 Enoch	384, 395	II:1	390
5:12	386	32:1–2	384	II:2	390
5:13–16	386			II:4	390
frg. 5	356	1 Esdras			
		1:58	381	Josephus, Jewish Wars	
2 Baruch		5:52	382	2.147	364
66:4	385				
84:8	385	Epistle of Barnabas	394, 396	Jubilees	382, 395
		2:5–6	395	1:4, 10–11	357
Book of Elchasai	393, 395	15:4–8	395	1:4, 27	356
		15:8–9	395	1:10	382
Daily Prayers (4Q503)	373, 374	15:9	395	1:14	382
24, 25, and 41	373			2:1	382
frgs. 37–38	373	Epistles of the Apostles	394, 396	2:9	360
		17	394	2:13–24	356
Damascus Document				2:17–18	382
(CD)	386, 395	Gospel of Marcion*	387, 389, 395	2:17–25	355
1.9–11	375	I	389	2:24	356
1.18–19	364	III	390	2:26–30	355
3.12–15	375	IV	390	2:27	382
3.12–17	363	VI	390	2:29	382
3.13–16	357			2:30	382, 383
6.13–18	358	Gospel of Nicodemus	387, 395	2:30–33	356
8.15	386	I:1	388, 389	2:31	383
10.14	365	II:6	389	2:33	383
10.15–16	365	IV:2	389	6:30–32	360
10.17–19	366			6:30–38	360
10.20–21	367	Gospel of Peter	387, 395	6:34, 37–38	383
11.13–17	368	9:35–11:49	388	6:35–38	360
11.17–18	360			21:5	207
13.1	386	Gospel of Pseudo-Matthew		21:10–11	207
13.2	386	26	391	23:19	383
13.4	386	27	391	37–38	383

* (= Gospel of the Lord)

50, 52	366	6:6	380	Psalms Scroll (11Q5)	
50:1–13	356	6:11	380	XXVII, 2–8	370
50:8	383	8:25–27	380		
50:10	383	8:26	380	Pseudo-Philo	383, 395
50:12–13	364, 383	8:28	380	11:8	383
		12:38	374, 381	25:13	384
Judith	377, 395	15:1	381	44:6	384
8:6	378	15:2	381	44:7	384
10:2	378	15:2–5	381	44:8–10	384
		15:4	381		
Life of Adam and Eve	385, 395			Sirach	
51:2	385	Narrative of Joseph of Arimathea	387, 391, 392, 395	29:21	83
		4	392	38:8	209
1 Maccabees	377, 395			43:6–8	359
1:37–40	378	Philo, De decalogo			
1:41	378	96–164	354	Temple Scroll (11Q19)	374
1:41–49	354			cols. 44.5; 51.6–7	374
1:42	378	Philo, De opificio mundi		XIII, 17	375
1:43	379	89	356	XVIII, 11–12	360
1:53	379			XIX, 12–13	360
2:34	379	Philo, De specialibus legibus		XXI, 12	360
2:36	379	2.41, 56–70	354	XLIII, 1–17	375
2:37–38	379				
2:38–40	364	Philo, De vita Mosis (On the Life of Moses)		The Community Rule (1QS)	
2:40	379	2.209–216	354	I, 18–20	362
2:41	379, 381	2.211	367		
9	379	11.19–22	356	War Scroll (1QM)	358
9:34, 43	379				
9:44	379	Philo, That Every Good Person is Free			
10	380	82	364		
10:34	380				
2 Maccabees					
6:1–2	380				
6:4	380				

www.ingramcontent.com/pod-product-compliance
Lightning Source LLC
Chambersburg PA
CBHW051031160426
43193CB00010B/906